Table of Contents

Preface iii

Acknowledgments v

Table of Contents vii

Chapter 1
Introduction To Weight-Shift Control 1-1
Introduction 1-1
History 1-2
    Hang Glider 1-4
    Motorized Hang Gliders 1-4
    New Challenges 1-5
Light Sport Aircraft (LSA) 1-6
    Weight-Shift Control Aircraft 1-7
    Weight-Shift Control LSA Requirements 1-8
Flight Operations and Pilot Certificates 1-8
    Basic Pilot Eligibility 1-9
Flight Safety Practices 1-9
    Collision Avoidance 1-9
    Runway Incursion Avoidance 1-10
    Positive Transfer of Controls 1-10
Aeronautical Decision-Making (ADM) 1-10
    Avoiding Pilot Errors 1-11
    Scenario-Based Training 1-12
    Resource Management 1-12
    Use of Checklists 1-12
Medical Factors 1-13
    Fatigue 1-13
    Hypothermia 1-13
    Medical Summary 1-14
Chapter Summary 1-14

Chapter 2
Aerodynamics 2-1
Introduction 2-1
    Aerodynamic Terms 2-1
WSC Wing Flexibility 2-6
Forces in Flight 2-7
    Dynamic Pressure (q) 2-7
    Lift 2-7
    Drag 2-8
    Thrust 2-10
    Ground Effect 2-11
    Center of Gravity (CG) 2-11
Axes of Rotation 2-12
    Lateral Axis—Pitch 2-12
    Longitudinal Axis—Roll 2-13
    Vertical Axis—Yaw 2-13
Stability and Moments 2-13
    WSC Unique Airfoil and Wing Design 2-13
    Trim—Normal Stabilized Flight 2-13
    High Angles of Attack 2-13
    Low Angles of Attack 2-14
    Pitch Pressures 2-14
    Roll Stability and Moments 2-16
    Yaw Stability and Moments 2-17
    Thrust Moments 2-18
Stalls: Exceeding the Critical AOA 2-18
    Whip Stall–Tuck–Tumble 2-19
Weight, Load, and Speed 2-20
Basic Propeller Principles 2-20
Chapter Summary 2-20

Chapter 3
Components and Systems 3-1
Introduction 3-1
Wing 3-2
    Wing Frame Components 3-2
        Keel 3-3
        Crossbar 3-4
        Control Frame 3-4
        King Post With Wires-on-Top Wing Design ... 3-5
        Topless Wings With Struts 3-5
        Battens and Leading Edge Stiffener 3-7
        Sail Material and Panels 3-7
        Pockets and Hardware 3-7
        Sail Attachment to Wing Frame 3-7
    Cables and Hardware 3-7
    Wing Systems 3-8
        Reflex Systems 3-8

Roll Control System 3-9
Trim Systems 3-9
   Ground Adjustable Trim Systems 3-9
   Inflight Adjustable Trim Systems 3-10
Structure 3-11
Landing Gear 3-11
   Landing Gear for Water and Snow 3-14
Electrical Systems 3-15
Ballistic Parachute 3-15
Flight Deck 3-16
   Dashboards and Instrument Panels 3-16
     Flight Instruments 3-17
     Navigation Instruments 3-17
     Engine Instruments 3-17
   Instrument Panel Arrangements 3-17
     Communications 3-19
   Powerplant System 3-19
     Fuel System Components 3-20
     Engine and Gearbox 3-20
     The Propeller 3-20
Chapter Summary 3-22

Chapter 4
Powerplants 4-1
Introduction 4-1
Reciprocating Engines 4-2
   Two-Stroke Engines 4-2
   Two-Stroke Process 4-4
   Four-Stroke Engines 4-6
Exhaust Systems 4-6
   Two-Stroke Tuned Exhaust Systems 4-6
   Four-Stroke Engine Exhaust Systems 4-7
Engine Warming 4-7
   Two-Stroke Engine Warming 4-7
   Four-Stroke Engine Warming 4-8
Gearboxes 4-8
Propeller 4-8
   Fixed-Pitch Propeller 4-8
   Ground Adjustable-Pitch Propeller 4-9
Induction Systems 4-9
Carburetor Systems 4-9
   Two-Stroke Carburetor Jetting for Proper Mixture .. 4-10
   Four-Stroke Mixture Settings 4-10
   Carburetor Icing 4-10
Fuel Injection Induction Systems 4-11
Ignition System 4-12
Combustion 4-12
Fuel Systems 4-13
   Fuel Pumps 4-13
   Fuel Plunger Primer 4-14

Choke 4-14
Fuel Bulb Primer 4-14
Fuel Gauges 4-14
Fuel Filter 4-14
Fuel 4-14
Fuel Contamination 4-15
Refueling Procedures 4-15
   Mixing Two-Stroke Oil and Fuel 4-16
Starting System 4-16
Oil Systems 4-17
Engine Cooling Systems 4-17
Chapter Summary 4-18

Chapter 5
Preflight and Ground Operations 5-1
Introduction 5-1
Where To Fly 5-2
Preflight Actions 5-3
Weather 5-3
   Regional Weather 5-3
   Local Conditions 5-4
Weight and Loading 5-7
Transporting 5-7
   Setting Up the WSC Aircraft 5-8
   Taking Down the WSC Aircraft 5-12
Wing Tuning 5-14
   Tuning the Wing To Fly Straight 5-14
Preflight Inspection 5-15
   Certificates and Documents 5-15
   Routine Preflight Inspection 5-16
     Wing Inspection 5-17
     Carriage Inspection 5-18
     Powerplant Inspection 5-19
     Cooling Systems 5-20
     Exhaust Systems 5-20
     Propeller Gearbox 5-20
     Throttle System 5-20
Flight Deck Inspection 5-20
Fuel 5-20
Oil 5-21
Ready Aircraft To Enter Flight Deck 5-22
Occupant Preflight Brief 5-22
Flight Deck Management 5-23
   Checklist After Entering Flight Deck 5-23
Engine Start 5-23
Taxiing 5-24
   Checklist for Taxi 5-25
   Before Takeoff Check 5-26
   After Landing 5-26
Chapter Summary 5-28

Chapter 6
Flight Manuevers 6-1
Introduction 6-1
Effects and the Use of the Controls 6-2
Attitude Flying 6-4
Straight-and-Level Flying 6-4
Trim Control 6-7
Level Turns 6-7
   Coordinating the Controls 6-8
Climbs and Climbing Turns 6-12
Descents and Descending Turns 6-14
   Gliding Turns 6-16
Pitch and Power 6-16
Steep Turn Performance Maneuver 6-16
Energy Management 6-19
Slow Flight and Stalls 6-20
   Slow Flight 6-20
   Stalls 6-21
   Power-Off Stall Manuever 6-23
Whip Stall and Tumble Awareness 6-24
   A Scenario 6-24
Chapter Summary 6-26

Chapter 7
Takeoff and Departure Climbs 7-1
Introduction 7-1
   Terms and Definitions 7-2
Prior to Takeoff 7-2
Normal Takeoff 7-2
   Takeoff Roll 7-3
   Lift-Off 7-3
   Initial Climb 7-4
Crosswind Takeoff 7-6
   Takeoff Roll 7-6
   Rotation and Lift-Off 7-6
   Initial Climb 7-6
Ground Effect on Takeoff 7-7
Short Field Takeoff and Steepest Angle Climb 7-8
   Takeoff Roll 7-9
   Lift-Off and Climb Out 7-9
Soft/Rough Field Takeoff and Climb 7-10
   Takeoff Roll 7-12
   Lift-Off and Initial Climb 7-12
Rejected Takeoff/Engine Failure 7-12
Noise Abatement 7-13
Chapter Summary 7-13

Chapter 8
The National Airspace System 8-1
Introduction 8-1
Uncontrolled Airspace 8-2
   Class G Airspace 8-2
Controlled Airspace 8-4
   Class E Airspace 8-4
   Towered Airport Operations 8-6
   Class D Airspace 8-6
   Class C Airspace 8-6
   Class B Airspace 8-7
   Airspace Above 10,000' MSL and Below 18,000' 8-8
   Class A Airspace 8-8
Special Use Airspace 8-8
   Prohibited Areas 8-8
   Restricted Areas 8-9
   Warning Areas 8-9
   Military Operations Areas (MOAs) 8-9
   Alert Areas 8-10
   Controlled Firing Areas 8-10
   Parachute Jump Areas 8-11
Other Airspace Areas 8-11
   Local Airport Advisory 8-11
   Military Training Routes (MTRs) 8-11
   Temporary Flight Restrictions (TFRs) 8-11
   Terminal Radar Service Areas (TRSA) 8-12
   National Security Areas (NSAs) 8-12
Published VFR Routes 8-12
Flight Over Charted U.S. Wildlife Refuges,
Parks, and Forest Service Areas 8-12
WSC Operations 8-12
   WSC and Air Traffic Control 8-12
   Navigating the Airspace 8-13
Chapter Summary 8-13

Chapter 9
Ground Reference Maneuvers 9-1
Introduction 9-1
Maneuvering by Reference to Ground Objects 9-2
Drift and Ground Track Control 9-2
Rectangular Course 9-4
S-Turns Across a Road 9-7
Turns Around a Point 9-9
Chapter Summary 9-12

Chapter 10
Airport Traffic Patterns 10-1
Introduction 10-1
Airport Operations 10-2
Standard Airport Traffic Patterns................................10-2
Chapter Summary 10-8

Chapter 11
Approaches and Landings 11-1
Introduction..11-1
Normal (Calm Wind) Approaches and Landings 11-2
    Throttle Use..11-2
    Base Leg...11-2
    Estimating Height and Movement..........................11-5
    Roundout (Flare) 11-6
    Touchdown 11-7
    After-Landing Roll 11-7
Effect of Headwinds During Final Approach 11-8
Stabilized Approach Concept 11-10
Go-Around (Rejected Landings)...............................11-13
    Power..11-13
Short and Soft Field Landing Techniques 11-14
    Short-Field Approaches and Landings..................11-14
    Soft and Rough Field Approaches and Landings...11-15

Power-on Approach and Landing for Turbulant Air 11-16
Crosswind Approaches and Landings.......................11-17
    Crosswind Pattern Procedures 11-17
    Effects and Hazards of High Crosswinds
    for Approaches and Landings 11-17
    Crosswind Landings 11-19
    Maximum Crosswind Velocities 11-19
Steep Approaches..11-20
    Steep Angle 11-21
    Alternating Turns 11-21
Power-Off Accuracy Approaches 11-21
    90° Power-Off Approach 11-22
    180° Power-Off Approach 11-23
    360° Power-Off Approach 11-25
Emergency Approaches and Landings
(Simulated Engine Out) 11-26
Faulty Approaches and Landings..............................11-27
    Low Final Approach...11-27
    High Final Approach 11-27
    Slow Final Approach..11-27
    Use of Power..11-28
    High Roundout 11-28
    Late or Rapid Roundout 11-28
    Floating During Roundout 11-28
    Ballooning During Roundout 11-29
    Bouncing During Touchdown 11-29
    Porpoising...11-29
    Wing Rising After Touchdown 11-30
    Hard Landing 11-30
Chapter Summary 11-30

Chapter 12
Night Operations 12-1
Introduction..12-1
Pilot Requirements 12-2
Equipment and Lighting 12-2
    Pilot Equipment...12-3
    Airport and Navigation Lighting Aids 12-4
Night Vision 12-5
Unique WSC Flight Characteristics 12-7
Night Illusions 12-7
Preparation and Preflight..12-8
Starting, Taxiing, and Runup 12-8
Takeoff and Climb 12-9
Orientation and Navigation 12-10
Approaches and Landings 12-11
Night Emergencies 12-12
Chapter Summary 12-13

Chapter 13
Abnormal and Emergency Procedures 13-1
Introduction..13-1
Ballistic Parachute System (BPS)...............................13-2
    Procedures for Using a BPS 13-3
Emergency Landings 13-3
    Types of Emergency Landings...............................13-3
    Psychological Hazards 13-3
    Basic Safety Concepts 13-4
    Attitude and Sink Rate Control 13-5
    Terrain Selection 13-6
    Approach 13-6
    Terrain Types 13-7
    Water Landings (Ditching)....................................13-8
    Emergency Equipment and Survival Gear.............13-8
    Engine Failure After Takeoff 13-9
Emergency Descents 13-10
Inflight Fire 13-10
    Engine Fire 13-10
    Electrical Fires...13-12
System Malfunctions 13-12
    Electrical System..13-12
    Pitot-Static System 13-12
    Landing Gear Malfunction 13-13
    Inadvertant Propeller Strike 13-13
    Stuck or Runaway Throttle 13-13
    Abnormal Engine Instrument Indications 13-13
Weather Related Emergencies 13-15

    High Winds and Strong Turbulence 13-15
        High Winds and Turbulence During
        Cruise Flight 13-15
        High Winds and Turbulence During Takeoffs
        and Landings 13-15
        High Winds During Taxi 13-15
    Inadvertent Flight into Instrument Meteorological
    Conditions (IMC) 13-16
        Recognition 13-17
        Maintaining Aircraft Control 13-17
        Attitude Control 13-18
        Turns 13-18
Chapter Summary 13-19

Glossary G-1

Index I-1

Chapter 1
Introduction To Weight-Shift Control

Introduction

Weight-shift control (WSC) aircraft means a powered aircraft with a framed pivoting wing and a fuselage controllable only in pitch and roll by the pilot's ability to change the aircraft's center of gravity (CG) with respect to the wing. Flight control of the aircraft depends on the wing's ability to deform flexibly rather than on the use of control surfaces.

This chapter provides background on the development of the WSC aircraft, its unique characteristics, the requirements for obtaining a WSC license (airman certificate), aeronautical decision-making (ADM), and the unique medical factors required to operate WSC aircraft safely. Further, it is highly recommended that all pilots develop a general understanding of aviation by becoming familiar with the Pilot's Handbook of Aeronautical Knowledge and the Aeronautical Information Manual (AIM). Listings of other available handbooks can be found on the Federal Aviation Administration (FAA) website at www.faa.gov.

History

From the beginning of mankind, we have looked to the skies where legends and myths have entertained and provided us the dream to fly. Through the middle ages, the idea of flight evolved across Europe, with Leonardo Da Vinci well known for designing flying machines to carry humans. In 1874, Otto Lilienthal, a German mechanical engineer, started designing, building, and flying bird-like wings. *[Figure 1-1]* He published his work in 1889, and by 1891 made flights of over 100 feet in distance. Otto was the first successful hang glider pilot to design, build, and fly a number of wing designs. *[Figure 1-2]*

In 1903, the Wright brothers' gliders became powered and the airplane was born as the Wright Flyer. In the early 1900s, aircraft configurations evolved as faster speeds and heavier loads were placed on aircraft in flight. As a result of the new demands, the simple flexible wing was no longer sufficient and aircraft designers began to incorporate rigid wings with mechanical aerodynamic controls. These new ideas in wing design eventually resulted in the familiar aileron and rudder configurations found on the modern airplane.

Commercial applications were driving the need for faster and heavier aircraft; however, the dream of achieving manned powered flight in its most bird-like form was evolving along a different path. As rigid wing design enjoyed development for military and commercial applications, the flexible wing concept lay largely dormant for decades. In 1948, a flexible wing design was created by Francis Melvin Rogallo as a flying toy kit for which he obtained a patent in 1951. *[Figure 1-3]*

Rogallo's design concept evolved down two parallel paths in the early 1960s, military and sport flight. The military application was the National Aeronautics and Space Administration (NASA) development of the Rogallo wing into the Paresev (Paraglider Research Vehicle) later renamed the Parawing. That aircraft had rigid leading edges shown in *Figure 1-4*. NASA had the cart attached to the keel hanging below the wing and using weight shift to control the wing in the same fashion as modern WSC aircraft today.

Figure 1-1. *Otto Lilienthal, the German "Glider King."*

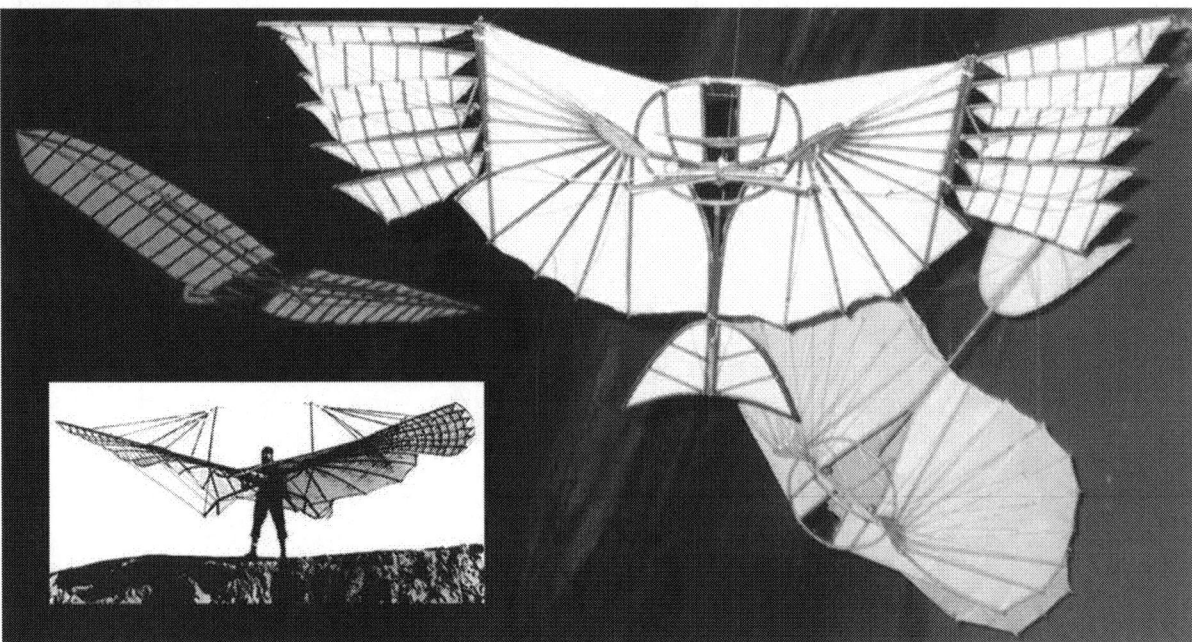

Figure 1-2. *Various models of Otto Lilienthal's glider, the forerunner of weight-shift control aircraft today.*

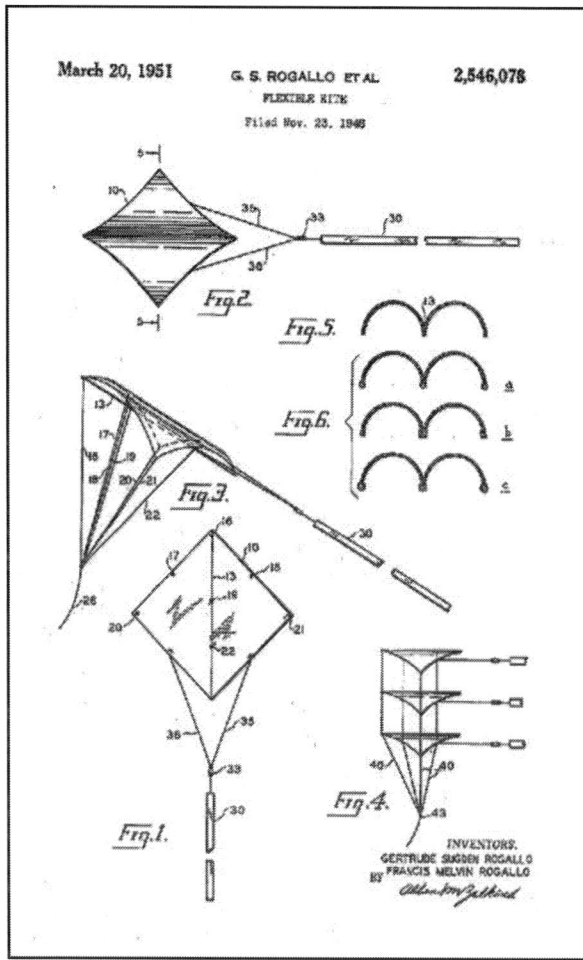

Figure 1-3. *Rogallo's flexible wing for a kite, submitted for patent in 1948.*

During this same period, other pioneering engineers and enthusiasts started developing the Rogallo wing for sport. One was aeronautical engineer, Barry Palmer, who saw pictures of the NASA wings and, in 1961, constructed and flew a number of hang gliders based on the Rogallo design. *[Figure 1-5]* His efforts and others evolved to the WSC aircraft in the late 1960s. Another pioneer was John Dickenson of Australia who used the NASA Rogallo wing design but incorporated a triangular control bar that provided structure for the wing during flight with flying wires. *[Figure 1-6]*

Figure 1-5. *Barry Palmer flying a foot-launched hang glider in 1961.*

Figure 1-4. *NASA testing the Rogallo wing, which led to the modern hang glider and WSC aircraft.*

1-3

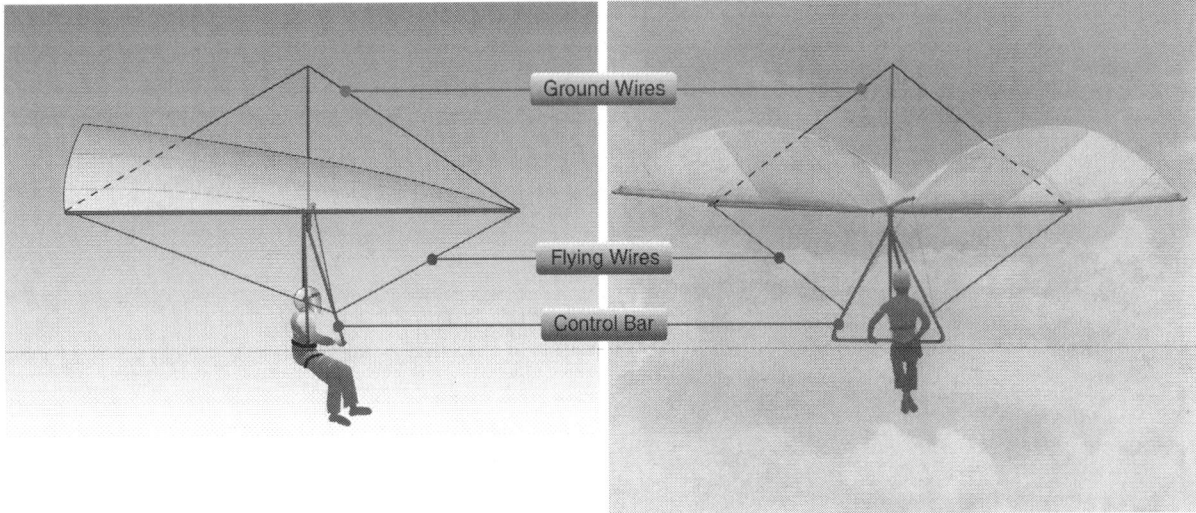

Figure 1-6. *Simple structure added to the Rogallo wing allows wires to hold up the wings on the ground and support the wing in flight.*

Hang Glider

The WSC system and the good flying qualities of the Rogallo wing and Dickenson wing, combined with its easy set-up and portability, started the hang gliding craze in the early 1970s. *[Figure 1-7]* In 1967, the first powered aircraft based on the flexible wing concept of Dr. Rogallo was registered as amateur-built experimental. Flexible wing development continued, and by the early 1970s several adventurous entrepreneurs were manufacturing Rogallo wings for sport use.

Figure 1-7. *An original Rogallo wing, 1975.*

Another significant step in wing design was an airfoil that would change shape for optimum performance at slow and fast speeds. It was the first Rogallo wing with a lower surface that could enclose the structure that holds the wings out. Enclosing this cross bar tube and providing a thicker airfoil similar to the airplane wing provided a jump in high speed performance. This double-surface wing was quickly adopted by manufacturers as the high performance standard and is used on faster WSC aircraft today. *[Figure 1-8]*

Activity in the hang gliding community increased throughout the 1970s, which resulted in the proliferation and development of stable, high-quality modern hang gliders like the one shown in *Figure 1-9*.

Motorized Hang Gliders

In the late 1970s, performance had increased enough to allow motors to be added to hang gliders and flown practically. It was not until the wings had become efficient and the engines and propeller systems evolved that the first commercial motor for a hang glider was introduced in 1977, the Soarmaster. It used a two-stroke engine with a reduction system, clutch, and long drive-shaft that bolted to the wing frame. It had a climb rate as high as 200 feet per minute (fpm) which was acceptable for practical flight. However, during takeoff the wing would overtake the running pilot, and launching was very difficult. Also while flying, if the pilot went weightless or stalled under power, the glider would shoot forward and nose down into a dive. Overall, with the propeller pushing the wing forward during takeoffs and in some situations while flying, this was unsafe for a wide application. *[Figure 1-10]*

A Maturing Industry

Engines and airframe technology had made great advances because the ultralight fixed wing evolution was providing lighter weight, higher power, and more reliable propulsion systems.

The propeller was moved lower for better takeoff and flight characteristics, wheels were added, and the trike was born at the end of the 1970s. A trike describes a Rogallo type wing with a three wheeled carriage underneath (much like a tricycle arrangement with one wheel in front and two in back). Trike is the industry term to describe both ultralight vehicles and

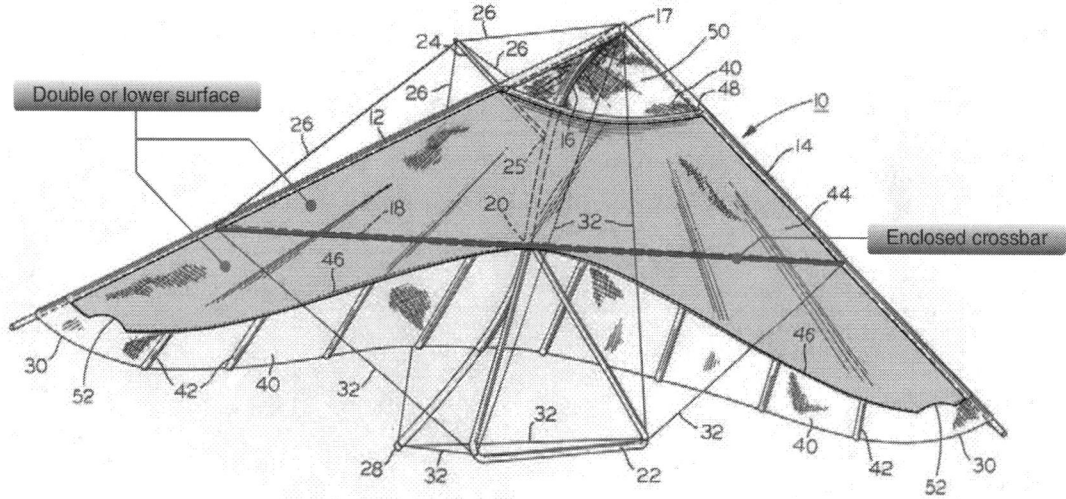

Figure 1-8. *The double-surface patented wing, 1978.*

Figure 1-9. *A modern high-performance hang glider soaring high over the mountains from which it was launched.*

Light-Sport Aircraft (LSA) WSC aircraft. *[Figure 1-11]* The major trike manufacturers were formed in the early 1980s and continue to deliver trikes worldwide today.

New Challenges

By the 1980s, individuals were rapidly developing and operating small powered trikes. This development failed to address the sport nature and unique challenges these new aircraft presented to the aviation community. In an attempt to include these flying machines in its regulatory framework, the FAA issued Title 14 of the Code of Federal Regulations (14 CFR) part 103, Ultralight Vehicles, in 1982. Aircraft falling within the ultralight vehicle specifications are lightweight (less than 254 pounds if powered, or 155 pounds if unpowered), are intended for manned operation

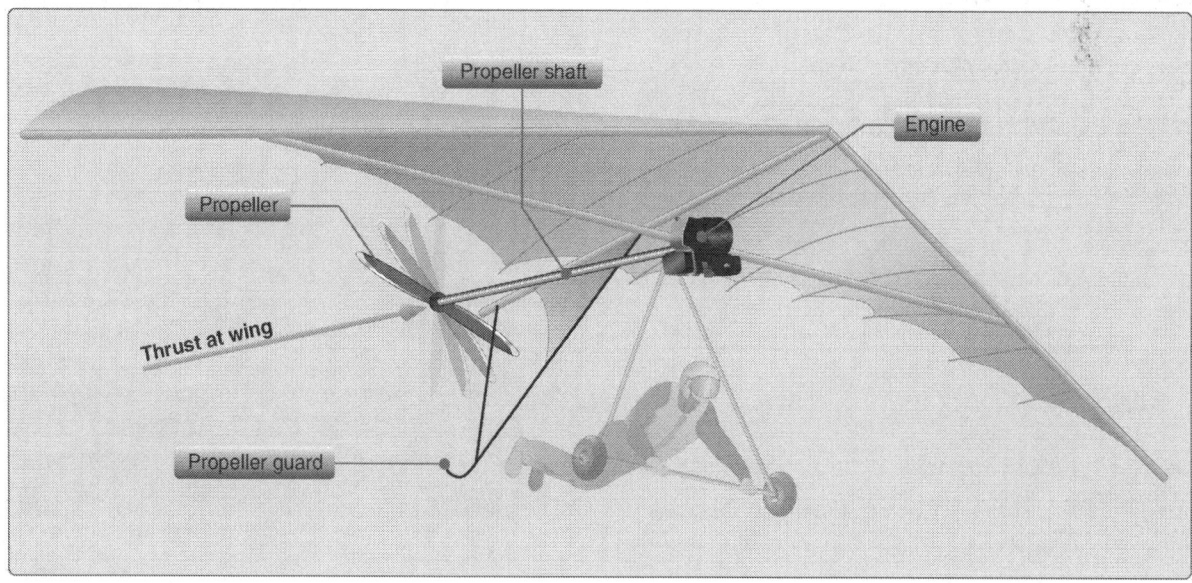

Figure 1-10. *First motorized system design sold as an add-on kit for a hang glider.*

Figure 1-11. *An ultralight vehicle trike: a Rogallo wing on a modified undercarriage.*

by a single occupant, have a fuel capacity of five gallons or less, a maximum calibrated airspeed of not more than 55 knots, and a maximum stall speed of not more than 24 knots. Ultralight vehicles do not require pilot licensing, medical certification, or aircraft registration. Ultralight vehicles are defined in more detail with their operating limitations in 14 CFR part 103.

Because training was so important for the single-place ultralight vehicle pilots, the FAA granted an exemption that allowed the use of two-seat ultralight vehicles for training, and the sport of two-seat ultralight training vehicles grew. Throughout the 1990s, worldwide sales of both single-seat and two-seat ultralight vehicles soared, but it was the proliferation of two-seat trainers that took the industry and the regulators by surprise. Worldwide sales of two-seat ultralight vehicle trainers vastly outnumbered the sales of single-seat ultralight vehicles; and it became clear that the two-seat trainers, which were intended to be operated as trainers only, were being used for sport and recreational purposes. This created a demand for increased comfort and reliability, which resulted in heavier, more sophisticated machines.

Light Sport Aircraft (LSA)

To address the evolution of the ultralight vehicle and its community of sport users, the FAA issued new rules on September 1, 2004. These rules created a new category of LSA and a new classification of FAA pilot certification to fly LSA, called Sport Pilot. Additional guidelines established by the FAA can be found in 14 CFR part 61. *[Figure 1-12]* This handbook focuses on the WSC aircraft.

Aircraft certificated as LSA exceed the limitations defined for ultralight vehicles and require that the pilot possess, at a minimum, a Sport Pilot certificate. The sport pilot rule defines the limitations and privileges for both the sport pilot and the

Figure 1-12. *Examples of LSA, from top to bottom: gyroplane, airplane, powered parachute, and weight-shift control aircraft.*

1-6

LSA. In addition, the regulations governing the sport pilot rule define the training requirements of prospective sport pilots and the airworthiness requirements for their machines. For instance, an ultralight vehicle must not exceed 254 pounds or carry more than one person. Aircraft that carry more than one person and weigh over 254 pounds but less than 1,320 pounds may be certified as LSA provided they meet specific certification requirements. Therefore, many WSC ultralight vehicles became LSA (provided they were properly inspected and issued an airworthiness certificate by the FAA).

Weight-Shift Control Aircraft
WSC aircraft are single- and two-place trikes that do not meet the criteria of an ultralight vehicle but do meet the criteria of LSA. The definition for WSC can be found in 14 CFR part 1. Flight control of the aircraft depends on the wing's ability to flexibly deform rather than on the use of control surfaces.

The common acronyms for this LSA are WSC (weight-shift control); WSCL (WSC land), which can be wheels or ski equipped; and WSCS (WSC Sea) for water operations. A LSA WSC used for sport and private pilot flying must be registered with a FAA N-number, have an airworthiness certificate, a pilot's operating handbook (POH), and/or limitations with a weight and loading document aboard. The aircraft must be maintained properly by the aircraft owner or other qualified personnel and have the aircraft logbooks available for inspection. Dual flight controls are required in two-seat aircraft used for training.

The carriage is comprised of the engine and flight deck attached by a structure to wheels, floats, or skis; it may also be referred to as the fuselage. The wing is the sail, structure that supports the sail, battens (ribs) that form the airfoil, and associated hardware. *[Figure 1-13]*

Figure 1-13. *Carriage and wing of a WSC aircraft.*

There are several unique features of the WSC aircraft:

- The wing structure is in the pilot's hands and is used to control the aircraft. There are no mechanical devices between the pilot and the wing. The pilot can directly feel the atmosphere while flying through it because the pilot is holding the wing. This is a direct connection between the wing and the pilot like no other aircraft.

- The pilot can feel the wing as the wingtips or nose moves up and down, but the carriage and passenger are more stable. Turbulence is not felt as much as in a fixed-wing aircraft.

- Different wings can be put on a single carriage. This allows the pilot to have a large wing that can take off in short distances, which would be good for low and slow flying. A large wing with a lightweight carriage can also be used for soaring and is capable of flying at speeds below 30 miles per hour (mph). At the other extreme, a smaller high performance wing can be used for flying long distances at high speeds. With a small wing and a larger motor, WSC aircraft can fly at speeds up to 100 mph.

- The wing can be taken off the carriage and folded up into a tube that can be easily transported and stored. This allows owners to store the WSC aircraft in a trailer or garage, transport the WSC aircraft to a local site, and set it up anywhere. *[Figure 1-14]*

Figure 1-14. *Wing folded and on top of a recreational vehicle with the carriage in a trailer.*

- Since the WSC aircraft is designed without the weight and drag of a tail, the performance is significantly increased. The aircraft can take off and land in short fields, has good climb rates, can handle a large payload, has a good glide ratio, and is fuel efficient. The WSC LSA typically can carry 600 pounds of people, fuel, and baggage.

Besides having large and small wings for different speeds, the WSC aircraft wings can have wires for bracing, struts, or a combination of both. Throughout this handbook, both are used in diagrams and pictures. WSC aircraft are typically on wheels, but there are models that can land and take off on water and snow. *[Figure 1-15]*

Figure 1-15. *WSC aircraft with struts similar to those on an airplane (top) and WSC aircraft operating on water (bottom).*

Weight-Shift Control LSA Requirements
A WSC LSA must meet the following requirements:
1. A maximum takeoff weight of not more than—
    - 1,320 pounds (600 kilograms) for aircraft not intended for operation on water; or
    - 1,430 pounds (650 kilograms) for an aircraft intended for operation on water
2. A maximum airspeed in level flight with maximum continuous power (V_H) of not more than 120 knots calibrated (computed) air speed (CAS) under standard atmospheric conditions at sea level.
3. A maximum stalling speed or minimum steady flight speed without the use of lift-enhancing devices (V_{S1}) of not more than 45 knots CAS at the aircraft's maximum certificated takeoff weight and most critical center of gravity.
4. A maximum seating capacity of no more than two persons, including the pilot.
5. A single reciprocating engine.
6. A fixed or ground-adjustable propeller.
7. Fixed landing gear, except for an aircraft intended for operation on water.
8. Fixed or retractable landing gear, or a hull, for an aircraft intended for operation on water.

Flight Operations and Pilot Certificates
The FAA is empowered by the United States Congress to promote aviation safety by prescribing safety standards for civil aviation programs and pilots. Title 14 of the Code of Federal Regulations (14 CFR), formerly referred to as Federal Aviation Regulations (FAR), is one of the primary means of conveying these safety standards. *[Figure 1-16]* 14 CFR part 61 specifies the requirements to earn a pilot certificate and obtain additional WSC privileges if already a pilot. 14 CFR part 91 is General Operating and Flight Rules for pilots. The Aeronautical Information Manual (AIM) provides basic flight information and operation procedures for pilots to operate in the National Airspace System (NAS).

Figure 1-16. *Federal Aviation Regulations (FAR) and Aeronautical Information Manual (AIM).*

Basic Pilot Eligibility

Title 14 CFR, part 61 specifies the requirements to earn a pilot certificate. This regulation also states the pilot applicant must be able to read, speak, write, and understand the English language. The FAA Practical Test Standards (PTS) establish the standards for the knowledge and skills necessary for the issuance of a pilot certificate. It is important to reference both of these documents to understand the knowledge, skills, and experience required to obtain a pilot certificate to fly a WSC aircraft. *[Figure 1-17]*

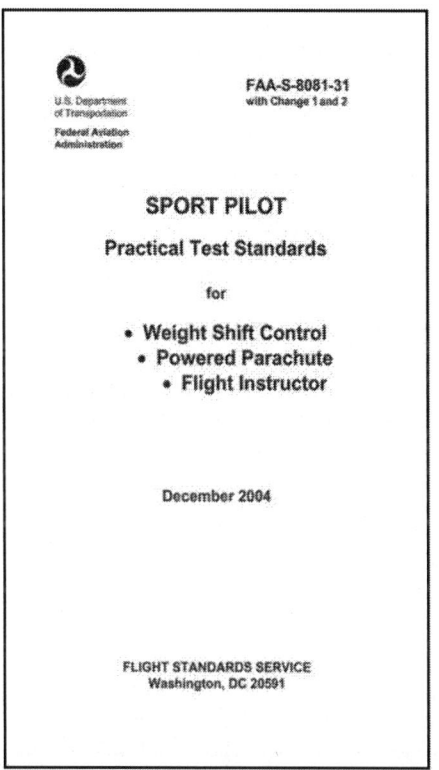

Figure 1-17. *Sport Pilot Practical Test Standards for Weight Shift Control, Powered Parachute, and Flight Instructor.*

Pilot applicants and students flying solo must have a valid driver's license or a current third-class medical certificate issued under 14 CFR part 67. In addition to a valid driver's license or a medical certificate, each pilot must determine before each flight that he or she is medically fit to operate the aircraft in a safe manner. If using a valid driver's license to exercise the privileges of a sport pilot certificate, then all restrictions on that driver's license are also upheld. A current FAA third-class medical certificate must be obtained to exercise the privileges of a WSC private pilot certificate. Existing pilots, including previous student pilots, who have had their FAA medical certificate or most recent application denied, revoked, withdrawn, or suspended by the FAA, are not allowed to operate using a driver's license until the denial on the airman record is cleared by having a valid third class medical certificate issued.

Flight Safety Practices

In the interest of safety and good habit pattern formation, there are certain basic flight safety practices and procedures that must be emphasized by the flight instructor and adhered to by both instructor and student, beginning with the very first dual instruction flight. These include, but are not limited to, collision avoidance procedures including proper scanning techniques and clearing procedures, runway incursion avoidance, and positive transfer of controls.

Collision Avoidance

All pilots must be alert to the potential for midair collision and near midair collisions. The general operating and flight rules in 14 CFR part 91 set forth the concept of "see and avoid." This concept requires that vigilance shall be maintained at all times by each person operating an aircraft. Most midair collision accidents and reported near midair collision incidents occur in good visual flight rules (VFR) weather conditions and during the hours of daylight. Most of these accident/incidents occur within five miles of an airport and/or near navigation aids.

The "see and avoid" concept relies on knowledge of the limitations of the human eye, and the use of proper visual scanning techniques to help compensate for these limitations. The importance of, and the proper techniques for, visual scanning should be taught to a student pilot at the very beginning of flight training. The competent flight instructor should be familiar with the visual scanning and collision avoidance information contained in Advisory Circular (AC) 90-48, Pilot's Role in Collision Avoidance, and the Aeronautical Information Manual (AIM).

It should be noted that any turn or maneuver must be cleared before initiating. This is a most important concept in flying any aircraft. Look and clear the area of any aircraft or obstructions before any maneuver is performed. As an example, if a right hand turn is to be performed, the pilot must look right and clear the area before initiating any turn to the right. This "clearing procedure" must be done before performing any maneuver.

This is an important habit for any student for safety purposes and is incorporated into the pilot certification process. The pilot must be trained by a CFI in effectively clearing the area before any maneuver is performed.

There are many different types of clearing procedures. Most are centered around the use of clearing turns. Some pilot training programs have hard-and-fast rules, such as requiring two 90° turns in opposite directions before executing any training maneuver. Other types of clearing procedures may be developed by individual flight instructors. Whatever the preferred method, the flight instructor should teach the beginning student an effective clearing procedure and require its use. The student pilot should execute the appropriate clearing procedure before all turns and before executing any training maneuver. Proper clearing procedures, combined with proper visual scanning techniques, are the most effective strategy for collision avoidance.

Runway Incursion Avoidance

A runway incursion is any occurrence at an airport involving an aircraft, vehicle, person, or object on the ground that creates a collision hazard or results in a loss of separation with an aircraft taking off, landing, or intending to land. The three major areas contributing to runway incursions are:

- Communications,
- Airport knowledge, and
- Flight deck procedures for maintaining orientation.

Taxi operations require constant vigilance by the pilot and can be assisted by the passenger. This is especially true during flight training operations. Both the student pilot and the flight instructor need to be continually aware of the movement and location of other aircraft and ground vehicles on the airport movement area. Many flight training activities are conducted at nontowered airports. The absence of an operating airport control tower creates a need for increased vigilance on the part of pilots operating at those airports.

Planning, clear communications, and enhanced situational awareness during airport surface operations will reduce the potential for surface incidents. Safe aircraft operations can be accomplished and incidents eliminated if the pilot is properly trained from the outset and, throughout his or her flying career, accomplishes standard taxi operating procedures and practices. This requires the development of the formalized teaching of safe operating practices during taxi operations.

Positive Transfer of Controls

During flight training, there must always be a clear understanding between the student and flight instructor of who has control of the aircraft. Prior to any dual training flight, the instructor should conduct a briefing that includes the procedure for the exchange of flight controls. The following three-step process for the exchange of flight controls is highly recommended.

When a flight instructor wishes the student to take control of the aircraft, he or she should say to the student, "You have the flight controls." The student should acknowledge immediately by saying, "I have the flight controls." The flight instructor confirms by again saying, "You have the flight controls." Part of the procedure should be a visual check to ensure that the other person actually has the flight controls. When returning the controls to the flight instructor, the student should follow the same procedure the instructor used when giving control to the student. The student should stay on the controls until the instructor says: "I have the flight controls." There should never be any doubt regarding who is flying the WSC aircraft. Numerous accidents have occurred due to a lack of communication or misunderstanding regarding who actually had control of the aircraft, particularly between student and flight instructor. Establishing the positive transfer of controls procedure during initial training will ensure the formation of a very beneficial habit pattern.

Aeronautical Decision-Making (ADM)

A PIC's attitude or mindset must always be alert in order to maintain the safety of the aircraft, passengers, and the general public on the ground. To accomplish sound aeronautical decision-making (ADM), a pilot must be aware of his or her limitations and well-being (physical and psychological health), even before beginning the first preflight routine. While technology is constantly improving equipment and strengthening materials, safe flight comes down to the decisions made by the human pilot prior to and during flight.

The well-being of the pilot is the starting point for the decision-making process that occurs while in control of the aircraft. Just as physical fatigue and illness directly affects a pilot's judgment, so too will attitude management, stress management, risk management, personality tendencies, and situational awareness. Hence, it is the awareness of human factors and the knowledge of the related corrective action that not only improves the safety of operating a WSC aircraft, but also enhances the joy of flying. *[Figure 1-18]*

A good starting point is the Pilot's Handbook of Aeronautical Knowledge (FAA-H-8083-25), which explains the decision-making process, resource management, situational awareness, pilot error, stress management, risk management techniques, and hazardous attitude antidotes. After reading and understanding those subjects, it should be understood that the scenarios presented are generally for more complex airplanes, but the thought process and results are the same for all aircraft. The information is not duplicated but the

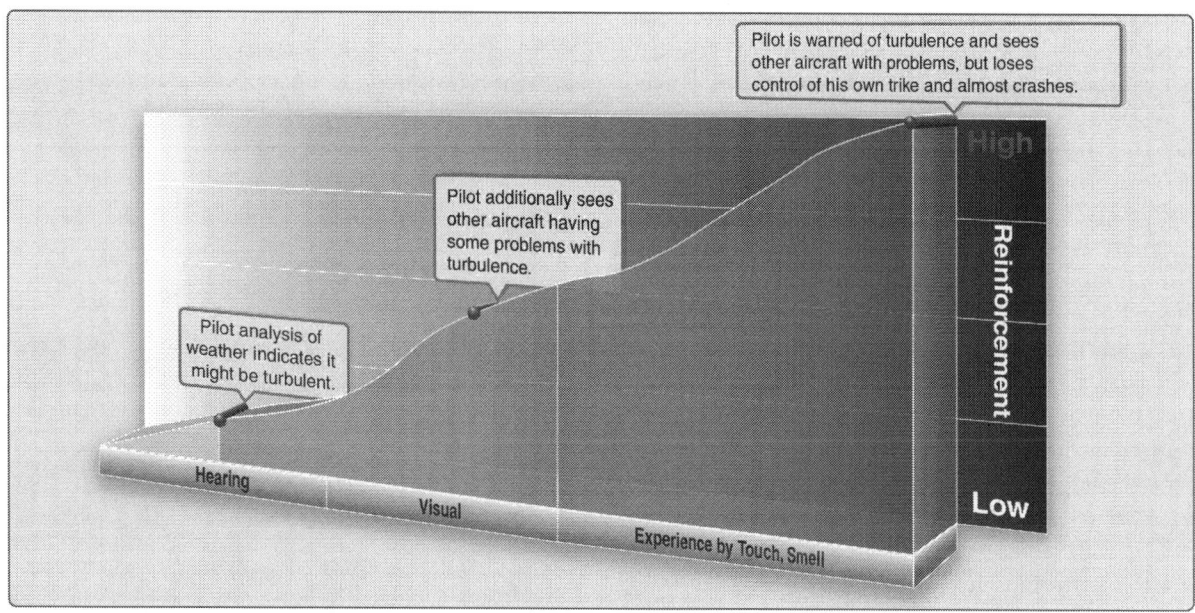

Figure 1-18. *Awareness of human factors and how it affects the decision-making process.*

differences and additional information specific to WSC is provided in subsequent sections.

The differences in the more complex airplane requirement scenarios presented in the Pilot's Handbook of Aeronautical Knowledge versus WSC aircraft characteristics can easily be compared. Overall, the advantage of an LSA is the simpler design requiring less pilot attention than the complex requirements of more complicated designs that add to the pilot's workload, such as:

- Constant speed propellers
- Multiple engines
- Retractable landing gears
- Faster airspeeds

The unique characteristics on the WSC aircraft that increase ADM tasks are:

- Open flight deck where maps or other materials cannot be opened, shown, and discussed with passenger.
- Pusher propeller in the back, through which any loose item on the flight deck can be pulled, possibly producing severe damage, depending on the size of the object.
- More physical strength and endurance required to fly in turbulent conditions, which adds an additional risk element.

Avoiding Pilot Errors

Overall, WSC aircraft are flown for fun and not for transportation. Generally, it is determined that the pilot will not fly in instrument meteorological conditions (IMC) without the assistance and training of the attitude indicator. Pilots must make the decision to stay out of IMC conditions and turn back immediately if the situation occurs. This is what most pilots should do, but the information provided by the attitude indicator allows pilots to start the "error chain" that can lead to catastrophic consequences. The best immediate decision is always to turn back and not go into IMC conditions in a WSC aircraft.

With an open flight deck, the problem of items getting loose and hitting the propeller requires extra caution. Being in a hurry, not making sure everything is secured, and forgetting to brief the passenger can trigger one event that leads to another. Exercising caution in the open flight deck is an important step for WSC pilots.

If flying a WSC aircraft in turbulence, the pilot must have both hands on the bar to maintain control of the aircraft. Therefore, changing radio frequencies, measuring courses on the map, or operating any of the flight deck controls becomes difficult and secondary to maintaining control of the aircraft. This is different from flying an airplane or a powered parachute, which requires less physical effort to maintain control of the aircraft and at least one hand is available to tend to flight deck duties. It must be noted that the first priority always is maintaining control of the aircraft, and all other duties are secondary. Generally, preflight planning and good pilot judgment would prevent a situation of flying in moderate to extreme turbulence. However, when you do find yourself flying in this situation, fly the aircraft first, and attend to flight deck duties second.

Scenario-Based Training

A good instructor immediately begins teaching ADM when the student has the ability to control the WSC aircraft confidently during the most basic maneuvers. The instructor incorporates "scenario-based training" in which the instructor provides pilot, aircraft, environment, and operational risk elements to train the student to utilize ADM in making the best decision for a given set of circumstances. During a proficiency or practical test, the instructor or examiner evaluates the applicant's ability to use satisfactory ADM practices as the pilot determines risks and coordinates safe procedures.

Resource Management

Resource management is similar to that described in the Pilot's Handbook of Aeronautical Knowledge (FAA-H-8083-25) except the passenger cannot help in the same ways as in an airplane. The passenger cannot hold or help read the map unless the pilot has provided a knee board or other means for the passenger to assist. *[Figure 1-19]*

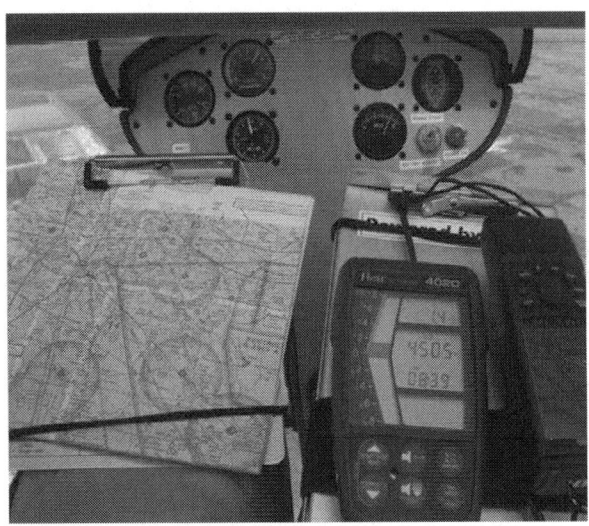

Figure 1-19. *Kneeboards help secure items in the flight deck.*

In addition to having the passenger scan the skies for other aircraft, the passenger can maintain control of the aircraft for short periods as the WSC is relatively easy to fly straight. This permits the pilot to perform unanticipated flight deck functions during flight. Overall, preflight planning and passenger briefings are additional tasks of resource management for the WSC aircraft.

Use of Checklists

Checklists have been the foundation of pilot standardization and flight deck safety for many years and the first defense against the error chain that leads to accidents. *[Figure 1-20]* The checklist is an aid to the fallible human memory and helps to ensure that critical safety items are not overlooked or forgotten. However, checklists are of no value if the pilot is not committed to their use. Without discipline and dedication in using a checklist, the odds favor the possibility of an error.

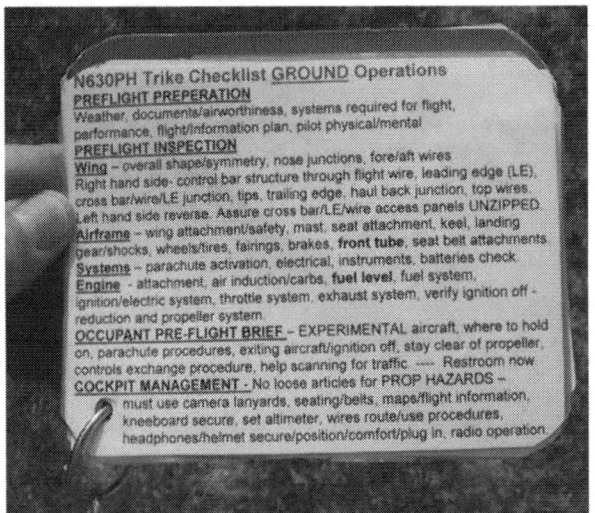

Figure 1-20. *Example of a checklist.*

The importance of consistent use of checklists cannot be overstated in pilot training. A major objective in primary flight training is to establish habitual patterns that will serve pilots well throughout their flying careers. The flight instructor must promote a positive attitude toward the use of checklists, and the student pilot must recognize their importance.

Because of the evolution of WSC aircraft and their simplicity, it could be thought that written checklists are not required. Nothing is further from the truth. Following good written checklists provides significant safety for human factors, which is the greatest cause of accidents in aviation.

Five important written checklists must be used before flight. These specific checklists are emphasized because of their importance in avoiding pilot errors that can occur before or during flight:

1. Preflight preparation
2. Routine preflight inspection
3. Passenger preflight brief
4. Engine start/taxi
5. Preflight check

Because checklists may not be practical in the open flight deck during flight, and depending on the manufacturer and make/model of the WSC aircraft, checklists used for climb, en route, and landing may be placards in the flight deck that can be read by the pilot in flight or used on kneeboards as appropriate. Checklists must be secured to prevent their flying through the propeller during taxi or flight.

An additional written checklist that can be used on the ground after landing is taxi, engine shutdown, postflight inspection, and securing aircraft.

Medical Factors

A number of physiological effects can be linked to flying. Some are minor, while others are important enough to require special attention to ensure safety of flight. In some cases, physiological factors can lead to inflight emergencies. Some important medical factors that a WSC pilot should be aware of include hypoxia, hyperventilation, middle ear and sinus problems, spatial disorientation, motion sickness, carbon monoxide poisoning, stress and fatigue, dehydration, heatstroke, and hypothermia. Other factors include the effects of alcohol and drugs, and excess nitrogen in the blood after scuba diving.

A prerequisite to this chapter is the aeromedical factors portion of the Pilot's Handbook of Aeronautical Knowledge (FAA-H-8083-25) which provides detailed information a pilot must consider in all flight operations. All of the aeromedical factors described in that book are applicable to WSC. However, the following are additional topics applicable to WSC not specifically covered.

Fatigue

Because the WSC aircraft moves weight through pilot input, there is significant arm and upper body strength required to fly a WSC aircraft, especially in turbulence. If flying a cross-country flight midday in moderate turbulence for more than an hour, a pilot would require significant strength and endurance. This significantly adds to fatigue, as discussed in the Pilot's Handbook of Aeronautical Knowledge. This is accomplished all the time by experienced pilots, but it is a workout. If this type of workout is combined with dehydration in a desert environment, a greater than anticipated headwind, or flying an unfamiliar cross-country route, the added aeromedical risk factors could lead to a fatal error chain.

Hypothermia

Hypothermia is an important factor and knowledge requirement in the WSC Practical Test Standards. Cold temperatures for long periods reduce the inner body core temperature when the heat produced by the body is less than the amount of heat being lost to the body's surroundings. This loss of heat is highly accelerated in WSC open flight decks with wind chill. The first symptom of flying a WSC aircraft is cold hands because of exposure to wind chill. Symptoms continue with other parts of the body becoming cold until the entire body feels cold. Hypothermia results in weakness, shivering, lack of physical control, and slurred speech followed by unconsciousness and death. Dressing warm and/or aircraft heating systems to help the pilot remain warm during flight prevents hypothermia. Motorcycle gloves and socks that run off the aircraft electric system are commonly used and can keep a pilot from getting cold. *[Figure 1-21]* Also, carrying an appropriate survival kit

Figure 1-21. *Motorcycle gloves and socks hooked to the 12-volt WSC electrical system keep the pilot and passenger warm.*

1-13

prepares a pilot against hypothermia if forced down in cold temperatures.

Medical Summary

Before approaching the WSC aircraft, a pilot must take a moment to reflect upon current medical, physical, and psychological conditions. During this time, a pilot should evaluate his or her ability to conduct the flight considering self, passenger, and people and property on the ground. Using the "I'M SAFE" checklist is a smart way to start a preflight before getting to the WSC aircraft. Prior to flight, assess overall fitness as well as the aircraft's airworthiness. *[Figure 1-22]*

Chapter Summary

This chapter provides basic knowledge that is essential for WSC pilots and should serve as a starting point for them. However, there are many other handbooks, advisories, and regulations with which all WSC pilots should become familiar as their maturity within the aeronautical realm increases and/or the need for greater depth of understanding becomes necessary due to location, temperature, altitude, etc.

Figure 1-22. *Prior to flight, a pilot should assess overall fitness.*

Chapter 2
Aerodynamics

Introduction

This chapter focuses on the aerodynamic fundamentals unique to weight-shift control (WSC) operations. The portions of the Pilot's Handbook of Aeronautical Knowledge (FAA-H-8083-25) on principles of flight and aerodynamics apply to WSC and are a prerequisite to reading this chapter.

Aerodynamic Terms

Airfoil is the term used for a surface on an aircraft that produces lift, typically the wing itself. Although many different airfoil designs exist, all airfoils produce lift in a similar manner. Camber refers to the curvature of a wing

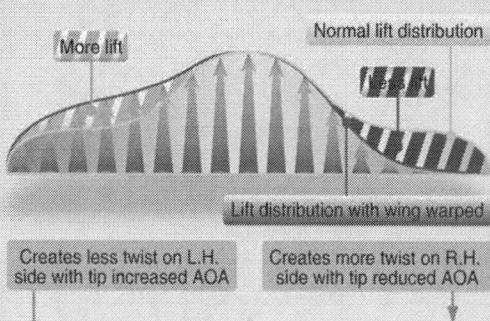

when looking at a cross-section. A wing possesses upper camber on its top surface and lower camber on its bottom surface. WSC airfoils can be single surface, with one piece of fabric for most of the airfoil, for slower wings. Faster airfoils have two surfaces and are called double surface wings, which are more like an airplane wing. *[Figure 2-1]* This double

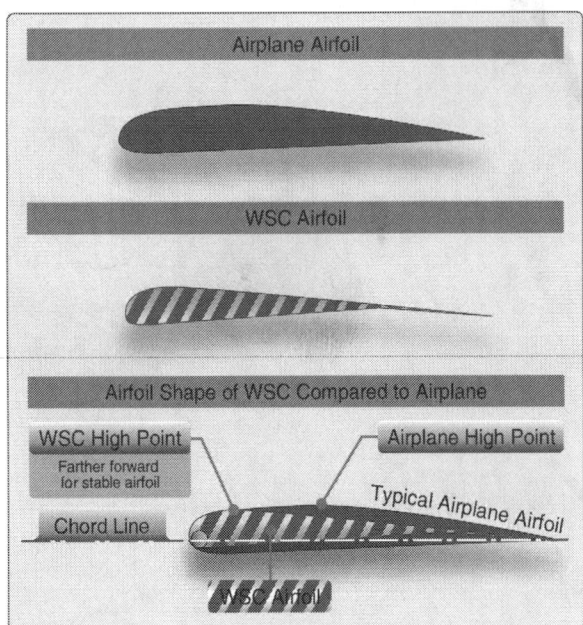

Figure 2-2. *Airplane airfoil compared to WSC airfoil.*

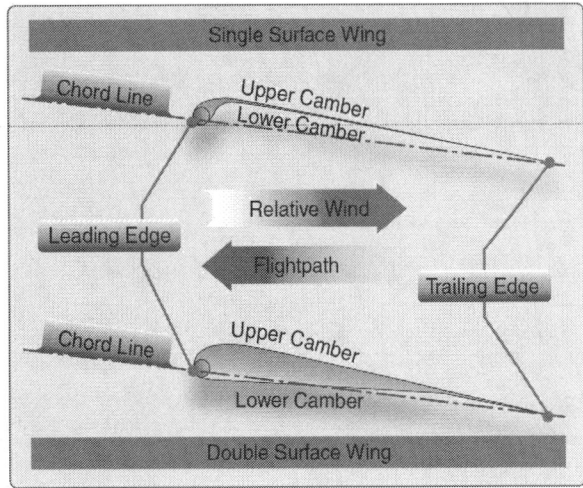

Figure 2-1. *WSC airfoil terms showing a single surface and a double surface wing.*

surface allows the wing structure to be enclosed inside the wing, similar to an airplane wing, reducing drag and allowing for faster speeds for the same thrust. The leading edge is the forward edge of the airfoil, and the rear edge of the airfoil is called the trailing edge. The chord line is an imaginary straight line drawn from the leading edge to the trailing edge. The WSC airfoil typically uses a different camber with the airfoil high point farther forward than the airplane airfoil, creating a more stable airfoil. *[Figure 2-2]*

The WSC wing is a unique design of airfoils that differ throughout the wing span. Looking at a top view of the wing, in the center is the wing root and on each end is the wingtip. Wing chord is any section of the wing parallel to the wing root. *[Figures 2-3 and 2-4]* The wingtip chord is the chord where the trailing edge is furthest to the rear of the wing. This can be inboard of the tip (as shown) and can vary depending on the specific wing design. The nose angle is the angle made by the leading edges, typically ranging from 120° to 130°. Sweep is the angle measured between the quarter chord line (line of 25 percent chords) and a line perpendicular to the root chord. *[Figure 2-3]*

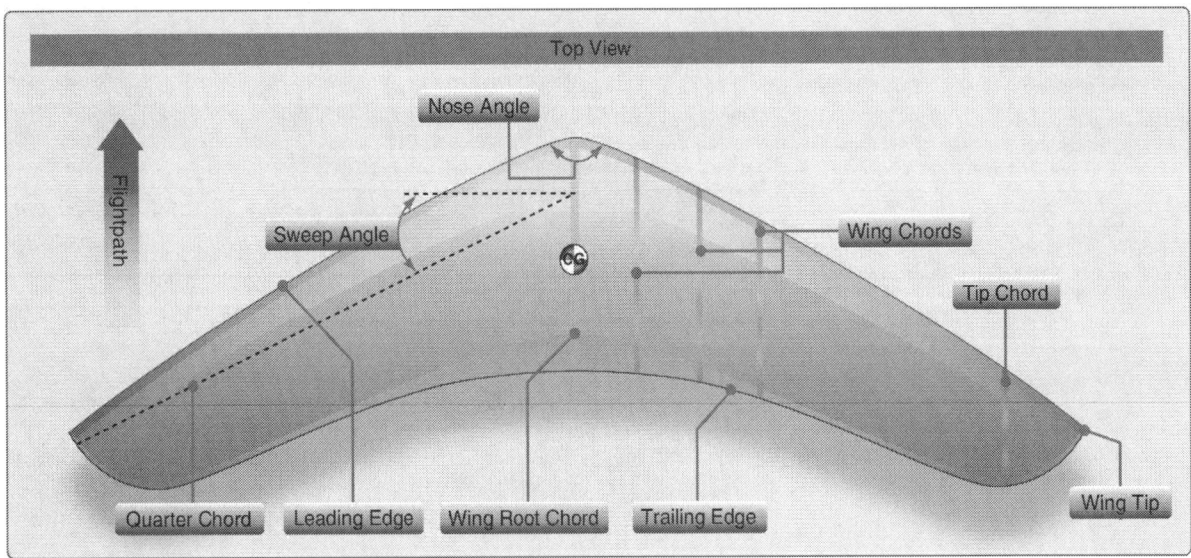

Figure 2-3. *Top view of a WSC wing and aerodynamic terms.*

2-2

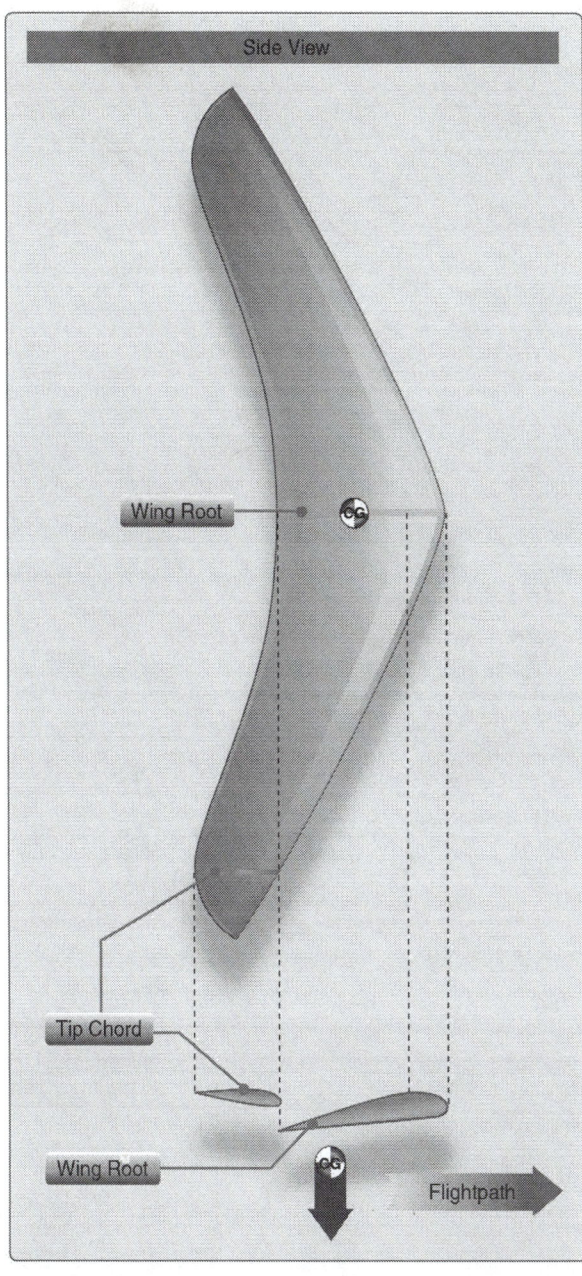

Looking at the rear view of the wing, anhedral is the angle the wings make angling down and dihedral is the angle the wings make angling up. *[Figure 2-5]* Dihedral is the positive angle formed between the lateral axis of an airplane and a line which passes through the center of the wing. Anhedral is the similar negative angle. Wings with sweep have an "effective dihedral" characteristic that counteracts the physical anhedral to develop the required roll stability for the particular make/model design objective. This is explained in the Pilot's Handbook of Aeronautical Knowledge in much greater detail for further reference. Unlike airplanes which typically have significant dihedral as viewed from the front or back for roll stability, WSC wings typically have a slight amount of anhedral as shown in *Figure 2-5* and effective dihedral which is a characteristic of the swept wing design.

Wing twist is the decrease in chord angle from the root to the tip chord, common to all WSC wings and ranging from 5° to 15°. This wing twist is also called washout as the wing decreases its angle of attack from root to tip. The term billow was originally used for the early Rogallo wings as the additional material in degrees that was added to the airframe to create the airfoil. It is still used today to define the amount of twist or washout in the wing. The WSC may not have twist/washout when sitting on the ground, and must be flying and developing lift to display the proper aerodynamic twist characteristic of WSC wings. *[Figure 2-6]*

The longitudinal axis is an imaginary line about which the aircraft rolls around its center of gravity (CG); it is also called the roll axis. The longitudinal axis is not necessarily a fixed line through the carriage because the roll axis changes for different flight configurations, but can be approximated by the middle of the propeller shaft for a properly designed WSC aircraft and is typically parallel with the flightpath of the aircraft as shown in *Figure 2-7*. Angle of incidence is the angle formed by the root chord line of the wing and the longitudinal axis of the WSC aircraft.

Figure 2-4. *Side view of a WSC wing and aerodynamic terms.*

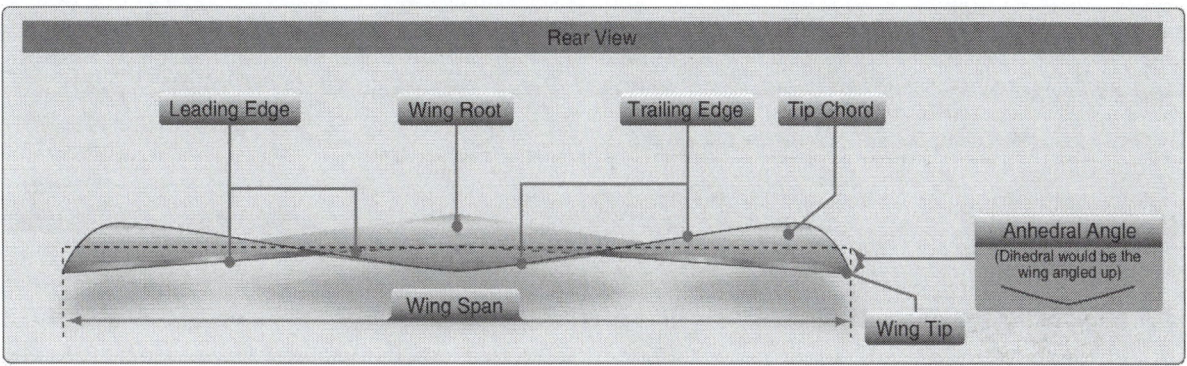

Figure 2-5. *Rear view of a WSC wing and aerodynamic terms.*

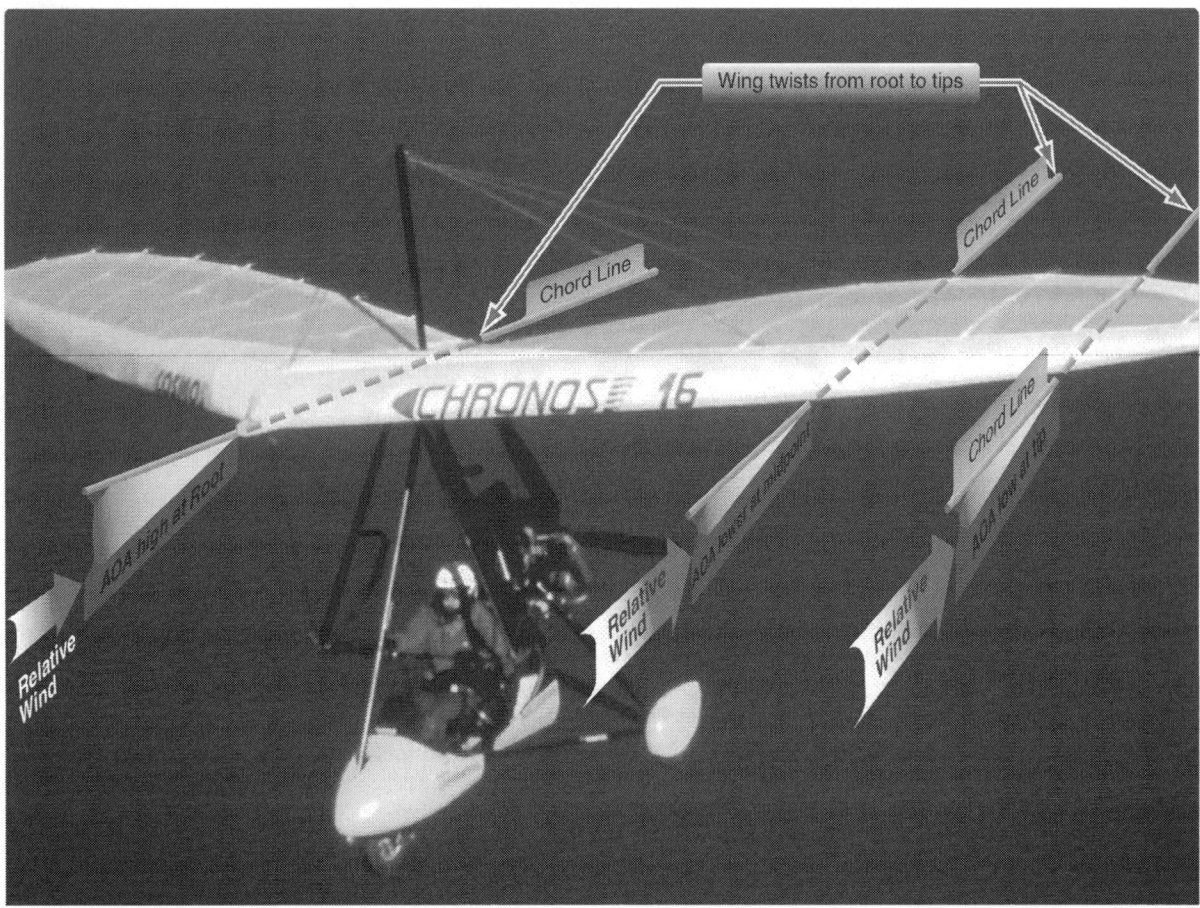

Figure 2-6. *Wing twist shown for a WSC wing in flight.*

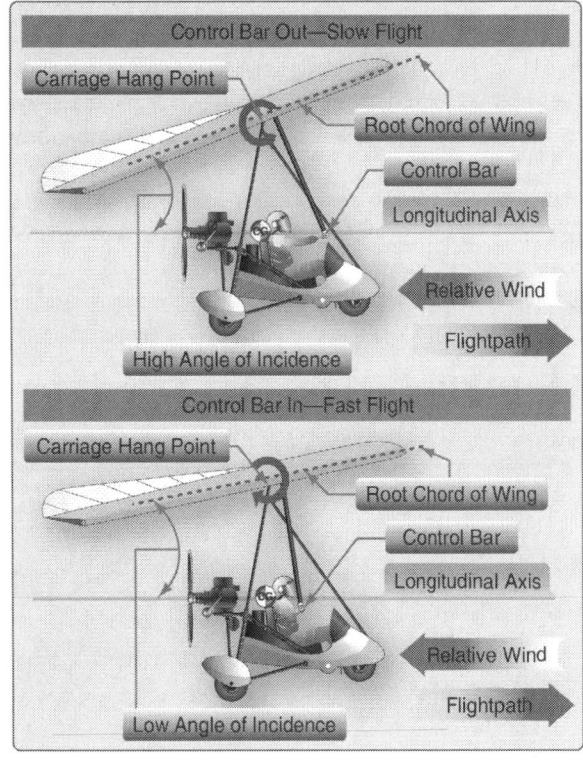

Figure 2-7. *Angle of incidence.*

Unlike that of an airplane, the WSC angle of incidence has a significant change in flight because the carriage is attached to the wing, which allows the wing to rotate around the carriage hang point on the wing and is controlled by the pilot as shown in *Figure 2-7*.

Pitch angle is the angle the WSC wing root chord (center of wing) makes with the Earth's horizontal plane. Many pilots confuse the pitch angle, which is easily seen and felt, with the angle of attack (AOA) which is not as perceptible. For example, if flying in a glide with the engine idle and the nose lowered, the pitch angle can be below the horizon. Another example would be flying at full power climb with the nose raised, resulting in the pitch angle being well above the horizon. *[Figure 2-8]* Pitch angles are covered in greater detail in chapter 6.

Deck angle is the angle of the cart's wheel axles to the landing surfaces, as in the powered parachute (PPC) deck angle. Relative wind is the direction of the airflow with respect to the wing; it is parallel to and opposite the WSC flightpath. Relative wind may be affected by movement of the WSC through the air, as well as by all forms of unstable, disturbed air such as wind shear, thermals, and turbulence. When a

WSC is flying through undisturbed air, the relative wind is parallel to and opposite the flightpath. *[Figure 2-7]*

AOA is the angle between the relative wind and the wing chord line. Because of the wing twist, the AOA is greatest at the wing root and decreases along the wing span to the tips. This is an important concept covered in the stability section of this chapter. For changing speeds during gliding, level flight, and climbs, AOA is the primary control for speed changes. Lower angles of attack produce higher speeds, and higher angles of attack result in slower speeds.

The pilot changes the AOA by moving the control bar forward for high angles of attack and slow speeds as shown in *Figure 2-7* (top) for high angle of incidence and *Figure 2-8* (top) for high pitch angle. Low angles of attack for fast speeds are shown in *Figure 2-7* (bottom) for low angle of incidence and *Figure 2-8* (bottom) for low pitch angle.

Most of the time, the pilot is flying at the cruise AOA, which is the trim position of the control bar, and the pilot is neither pushing out nor pulling in on the control bar. This trim position is the AOA and speed the aircraft flies if the pilot is flying straight and releases the control bar in calm air. *[Figure 2-9, middle]*

Planform is the shape or form of a wing as viewed from above. The WSC wing comes in a number of planforms ranging from the larger and slower wings to the smaller and faster wings.

Aspect ratio is the wingspan divided by the average chord line. A WSC aircraft with a common 200 square foot training wing (about a 35 foot wingspan), and with a typical mean chord line of 7 feet, would have an average aspect ratio of 5. This relatively low aspect ratio is less efficient at producing lift. A higher performance wing with 140 square feet, a 35 foot wing span, and an average 5 foot average chord would have an aspect ratio of 7. The WSC wing is similar to airplane wings in that the aspect ratio differs with the specific design

Figure 2-8. *Pitch angle examples of nose high (top) and nose low (bottom).*

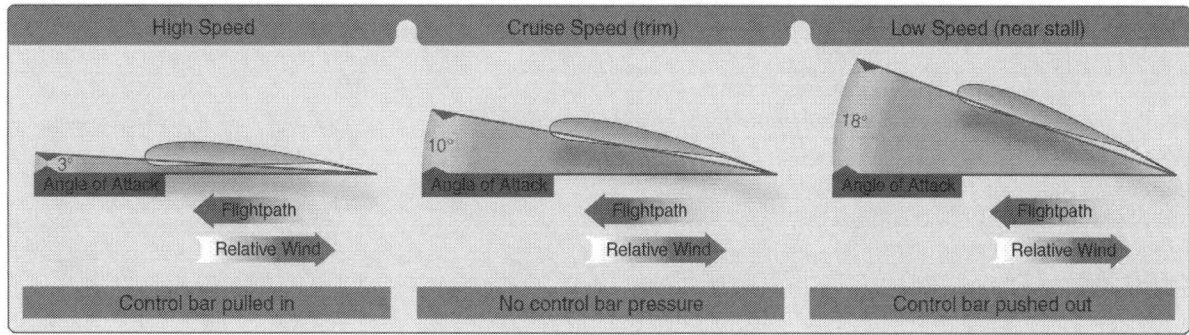

Figure 2-9. *Angle of attack effect on speeds, relative wind, and flightpath for level flight.*

mission for the aircraft. For the same wing area and similar design, the lower aspect ratio wings produce less lift and more drag; higher aspect ratio wings produce more lift, less drag, and may require more pilot effort to fly, depending on the design. *[Figure 2-10]*

root to the tip along the span of the wing (similar to ribs for an airplane wing) and a piece of foam or mylar running along the top side of the leading edge to the high point, which maintains its front part of the airfoil shape in between the battens. *[Figure 2-11]*

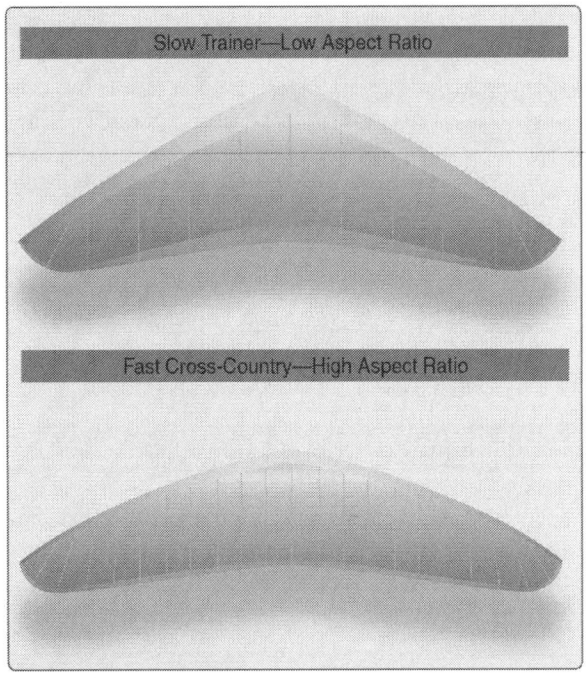

Figure 2-10. *Wing planforms showing the slow trainer with a low aspect ratio and the fast cross-country with a high aspect ratio.*

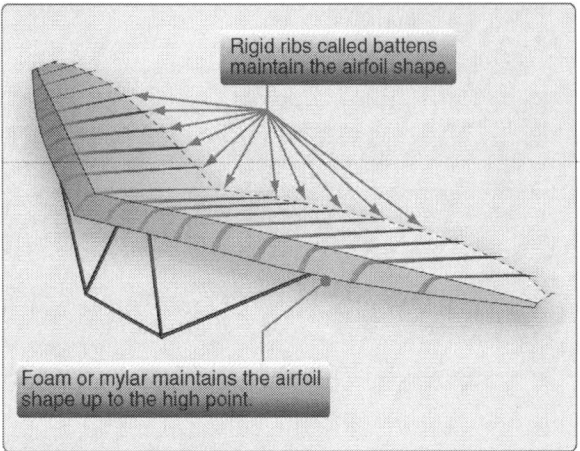

Figure 2-11. *Rigid airfoil preformed ribs called battens and leading edge stiffener maintain the rigid airfoil shape.*

Some WSC double surface wing designs use a rib similar to a PPC wing that attaches to the lower surface and the upper surface to maintain the wing camber in addition to the battens.

Even though the airfoil sections are rigid, the WSC aircraft is called a "flex wing" for two reasons. First, it is designed so the outboard leading edges flex up and back when loaded. The flexing of the outboard section of the wing also allows load relief because the tips increase twist and decrease AOA—the greater the weight, the greater the flex and wing twist. This flexing allows the WSC aircraft to automatically reduce loads in unstable air, providing a smoother ride than a rigid wing. Since the wing flexes and reduces the load for a given angle of attack at the root chord, WSC aircraft cannot obtain loads as high as those obtained by a rigid wing. This flexing of the outboard leading edges also assists in initiating a turn.

Second, the wing is designed to flex as it changes twist from side to side for turning, historically known as wing warping. WSC wing warping is similar to what the Wright Brothers did on their early aircraft, but they did it with wires warping the wing. The WSC aircraft uses no wires and warps the wing by shifting the weight, which is covered in Chapter 3, Components and Systems.

This flexibility is designed into the wing primarily for turning the aircraft without any movable control surfaces like the ailerons and rudder on an airplane.

Wing loading is a term associated with total weight being carried by the wing in relation to the size of the wing. It is the amount of load each square foot of the wing must support. Wing loading is found by dividing the total weight of the aircraft, in pounds, by the total area of the wing, in square feet. For example, the wing loading would be 5.0 pounds per square foot when 1,000 pounds total weight for a two-seat WSC aircraft with two people is supported by a 200 square foot wing. If flying the same wing with one person and a lighter total weight of 500 pounds, the wing loading would be 2.5 pounds per square foot. In the small, high performance wing of 140 square feet loaded at 1,000 pounds, wing loading would be 7.1 pounds per square foot.

Gliding flight is flying in a descent with the engine at idle or shut off. For example, use a glide ratio of 5, which is five feet traveled horizontally for every foot descended vertically. Glide ratios vary significantly between models.

WSC Wing Flexibility

The WSC wing retains its rigid airfoil shape due to rigid preformed ribs called battens, which are inserted from the

Forces in Flight

The four forces that affect WSC flight are thrust, drag, lift, and weight. *[Figure 2-12]* In level, steady WSC flight:

1. The sum of all upward forces equals the sum of all downward forces.
2. The sum of all forward forces equals the sum of all backward forces.
3. The sum of all moments equals zero.

Note that the lift and weight forces are much greater than the thrust and drag forces. A typical example for many WSC aircraft is that the lift/weight forces are five times the thrust/drag forces.

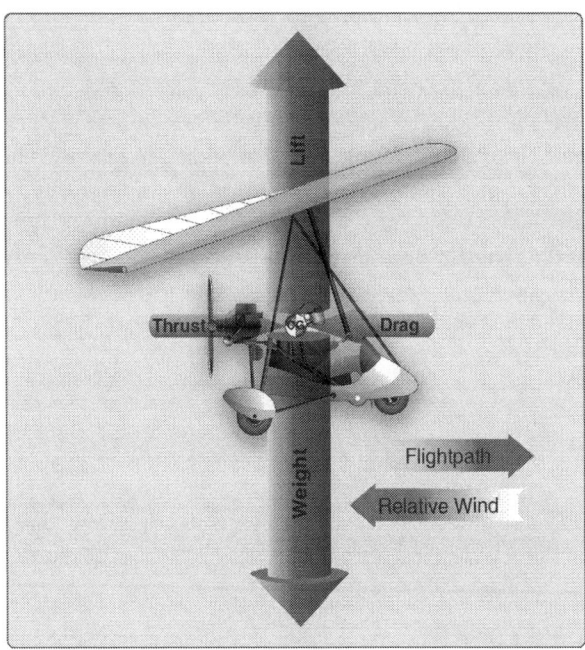

Figure 2-12. *The four basic forces in level flight.*

Thrust—the forward force produced by a powerplant/propeller as it forces a mass of air to the rear (usually acts parallel to the longitudinal axis, relative wind, and flightpath).

Drag—the aerodynamic force acting on the wing and carriage in the same plane and in the same direction as the relative wind.

Lift—the aerodynamic force caused by air flowing over the wing that is perpendicular to the relative wind.

Weight—the force of gravity acting upon a body straight down and perpendicular to the Earth.

During level flight, these forces are all horizontal and vertical. During descents or climbing, these forces must be broken down into components for analysis.

Dynamic Pressure (q)

Both lift and drag are a direct result of the dynamic pressure of the air. Dynamic pressure (q) is created from the velocity of the air and the air density. An increase in velocity has a dramatic effect on dynamic pressure (q) because it increases with the square of the velocity. Doubling the velocity means "q" increases by four times. Increasing the velocity by a factor of three means that the dynamic pressure (q) increases by a factor of nine. This is a very important concept in understanding the aerodynamics of WSC.

Formula for dynamic pressure: $q = V^2 \times \rho/2$

V = velocity

ρ = density factor

Lift

Lift opposes the downward force of weight and is produced by the dynamic effects of the surrounding airstream acting on the wing. Lift acts perpendicular to the flightpath through the wing's center of lift. There is a mathematical relationship for lift which varies with dynamic pressure (q), AOA, and the size of the wing. In the lift equation, these factors correspond to the terms q, coefficient of lift (C_L), and wing surface area. The relationship is expressed in *Figure 2-13*.

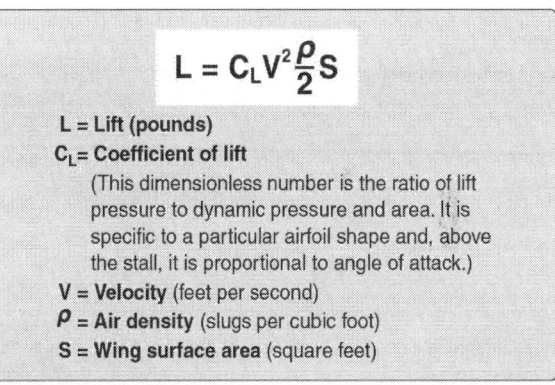

Figure 2-13. *The lift equation.*

Figure 2-13 shows that for lift to increase, one or more of the factors on the other side of the equation must increase. Generally, the lift needed is about the same for most flight situations. A slower speed requires a higher AOA to produce the same amount of lift. A faster speed requires a lower AOA to produce the same amount of lift.

Because lift is a function of dynamic pressure (q), it is proportional to the square of the airspeed; therefore, small changes in airspeed create larger changes in lift. Likewise, if other factors remain the same while the C_L increases, lift also increases. The C_L goes up as the AOA is increased. As air density increases, lift increases. However, a pilot is usually more concerned with how lift is diminished by reductions in air density on a hot day, or if operating at higher altitudes.

All wings produce lift in two ways:

1. Airfoil shape creates a higher velocity over the top of the wing and a lower velocity over the bottom of the wing with Bernoulli's venturi effect.
2. Downward deflection of airflow because of the curvature of the wing with the principle of Newton's Third Law of Motion: for every action, there is an equal and opposite reaction.

Both principles determine the lifting force. Review the Pilot's Handbook of Aeronautical Knowledge to understand Newton's laws of motion and Bernoulli's venturi effect.

Figure 2-14 (top) shows the amount of lift produced along the wing for an airplane wing with an elliptical planform. Notice how the amount of lift generated is smallest at the tips and increases slightly towards the root of the wing. This is known as the "elliptical lift distribution."

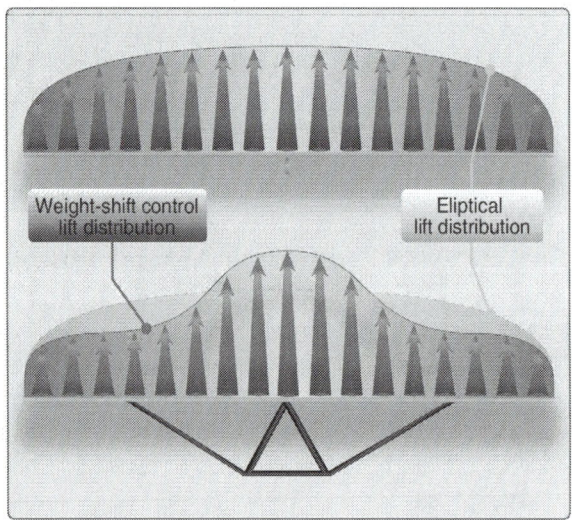

Figure 2-14. *Elliptical lift distribution compared to lift distribution of a WSC wing.*

The WSC wing lift distribution is different because the wing twist at the root is at a higher AOA than the tips. Most of the lift is produced at the center of the wing with less lift produced at the tips. The WSC lift distribution is compared to the lift distribution for an optimum design elliptical wing in *Figure 2-14*.

Drag

Drag is the resistance to forward motion through the air and is parallel to the relative wind. Aerodynamic drag comes in two forms:

1. Induced drag—a result of the wing producing lift.
2. Parasite drag—resistance to the airflow from the carriage, its occupants, wires, the wing, interference drag from objects in the airstream, and skin friction drag of the wing.

Induced drag is the result of lift, and its amount varies as discussed above for lift. Induced drag creates organized circular vortices off the wingtips that generally track down and out from each wingtip. Refer to the Pilot's Handbook of Aeronautical Knowledge for additional discussion on wingtip vortices formation.

These wingtip vortex formations are typical for all aircraft that use wings including WSC, PPC, helicopters, sailplanes, and all fixed-wing airplanes. The bigger and heavier the aircraft, the greater and more powerful the wingtip vortices are. This organized swirling turbulence is an important factor to understand and avoid for flight safety. Refer to the Aeronautical Information Manual (AIM) or the Pilot's Handbook of Aeronautical Knowledge (FAA-H-8083-25) for additional discussion.

Parasite drag is caused by the friction of air moving over all the components of the aircraft. Just as with lift, parasite drag increases as the surface area of the aircraft increases, and dramatically increases as airspeed increases (the square of the velocity). Therefore, doubling the airspeed quadruples parasite drag. *[Figure 2-15]*

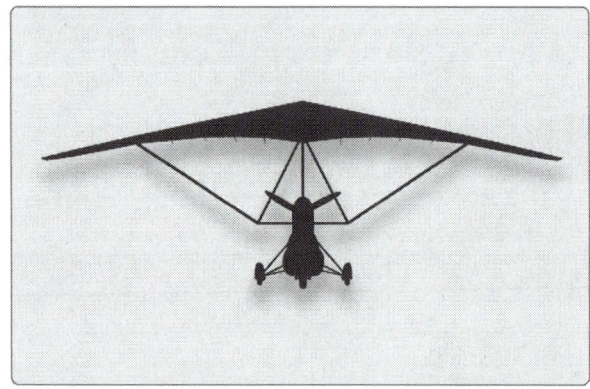

Figure 2-15. *Front view with projected area shown that produces drag.*

The WSC aircraft can be designed for the purpose of being a slow flying aircraft with a large wing where drag is not a major concern, or can be designed to be a fast flying aircraft with a small wing where drag is more of a concern.

2-8

The aircraft has plenty of items (area) for the wind to strike including wing, wires, struts, pilot, carriage, engine, wheels, tubes, fuel tanks, etc. Parasitic drag can be reduced by streamlining the items. Round tubes can be streamlined reducing the drag to one-third, and cowlings can be used to streamline the pilot and the carriage completely, but not without the additional expense and additional weight of the streamlining. Streamlining does make a noticeable difference in the speed and gas mileage of the WSC, especially for the faster aircraft. *[Figure 2-16]*

With the large speed range of WSC aircraft, weight, complexity, amount and expense of streamlining, and resultant drag reduction are determined by the specific mission for the aircraft and the manufacturers' make and model. *[Figure 2-17]*

Total drag is the combination of parasite and induced drag.
Total drag = parasitic drag + induced drag

To help explain the force of drag, the mathematical equation $D = C_D \times q \times S$ is used. The formula for drag is the same as the formula for lift, except the C_D is used instead of the C_L. In this equation, drag (D) is the product of the coefficient of drag (C_D), dynamic pressure (q) determined by the velocity squared times the air density factor, and surface area (S) of the carriage and wing. The overall drag coefficient is the ratio of drag pressure to dynamic pressure.

Induced and parasitic drag have opposite effects as AOA decreases and speed increases. Note the total drag in *Figure 2-18*. It is high at the slowest air speeds at high angles of attack near the stall, decreases to the lowest at the most efficient airspeed, and then progressively increases as the speed increases. The WSC wing can fly with a large range of airspeeds.

Generally, the most efficient speed is at the lowest total drag providing the best rate of climb, glide ratio, and cruise economy. However, slower speeds provide higher angles of climb, and faster speeds provide quicker transportation. *[Figure 2-18]*

Figure 2-17. *Fast WSC aircraft with complete streamlining (top) and slow WSC aircraft with minimum streamlining (bottom).*

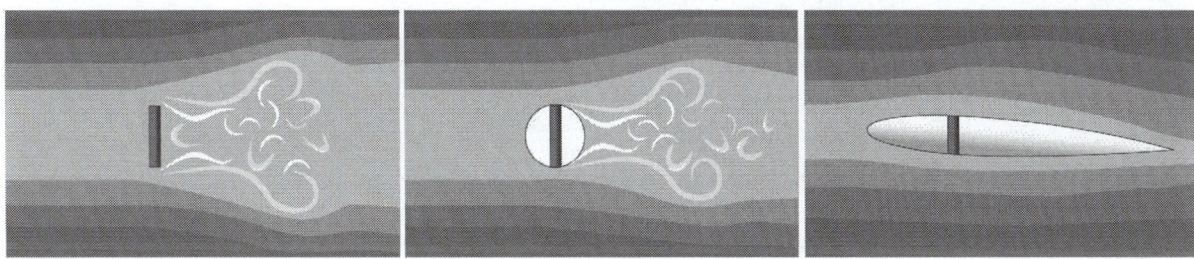

Figure 2-16. *Air flow around objects.*

2-9

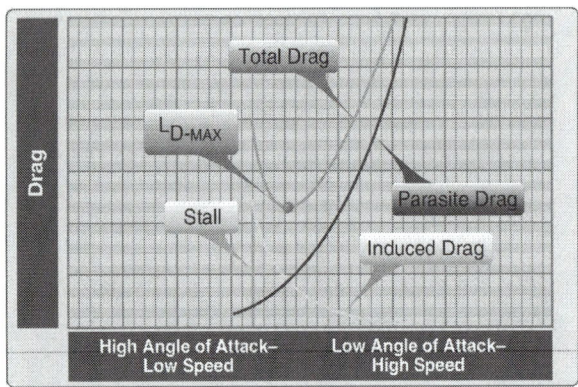

Figure 2-18. *Airspeed versus drag.*

Weight

Weight is a measure of the force of gravity acting upon the mass of the WSC aircraft. Weight consists of everything directly associated with the WSC aircraft in flight: the combined load of the total WSC aircraft (wing, wires, engine, carriage, fuel, oil, people, clothing, helmets, baggage, charts, books, checklists, pencils, handheld global positioning system (GPS), spare clothes, suitcase, etc.).

During gliding flight, weight is broken down into two components. The component that opposes the lift, acting perpendicular to flight/glide path, and the component that opposes the drag and acts in the direction of the flight/glide path. During gliding flight, this component of weight is the weight component providing the forward force which some call thrust for gliding flight.

During gliding, straight, and descending in unaccelerated flight:

Lift (L) and Drag (D) components = Resultant force (RF) = Weight (W)

Total Drag (D_T) = Weight component (W_D) in the direction of flight

Lift (L) = Weight component (W_L) that opposes lift

Similar to airplanes, gliders, and PPC during gliding flight, less lift is required because the resultant force composed of lift and drag provides the force to lift the weight. In other words, in gliding flight, drag helps support the weight. *[Figure 2-19]*

Thrust

At a constant air speed, the amount of thrust determines whether an aircraft climbs, flies level, or descends. With the engine idle or shut off, a pilot is descending or gliding down. Maintaining a constant airspeed, when enough thrust is added

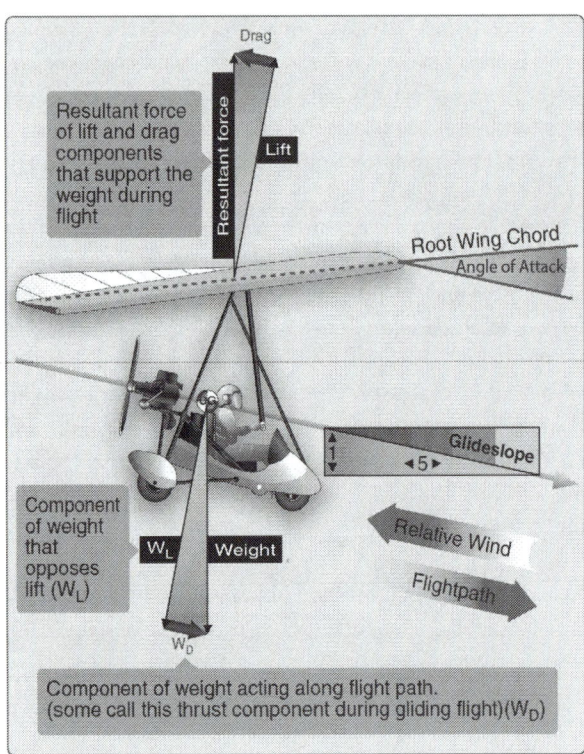

Figure 2-19. *Typical forces in gliding flight with no engine thrust.*

to produce level flight, the relative wind stream becomes horizontal with the Earth and the AOA remains about the same. As described for the airplane in the Pilot's Handbook of Aeronautical Knowledge, thrust equals total drag for level flight. *[Figure 2-20]*

When in straight and level, unaccelerated flight:

Lift (L) = Weight (W)

Thrust = Total Drag (D_T)

At a constant airspeed, when excess thrust is added to produce climbing flight, the relative air stream becomes an inclined plane leading upward while AOA remains about the same. The excess thrust determines the climb rate and climb angle of the flightpath. *[Figure 2-21]*

When in straight and climbing, unaccelerated flight:

Lift (L) = Component of weight that opposes lift
Weight (W) = Resultant force (F_R) of lift (L) and excess thrust to climb (T_E)
Thrust = Total drag (D_T) plus rearward component of weight

2-10

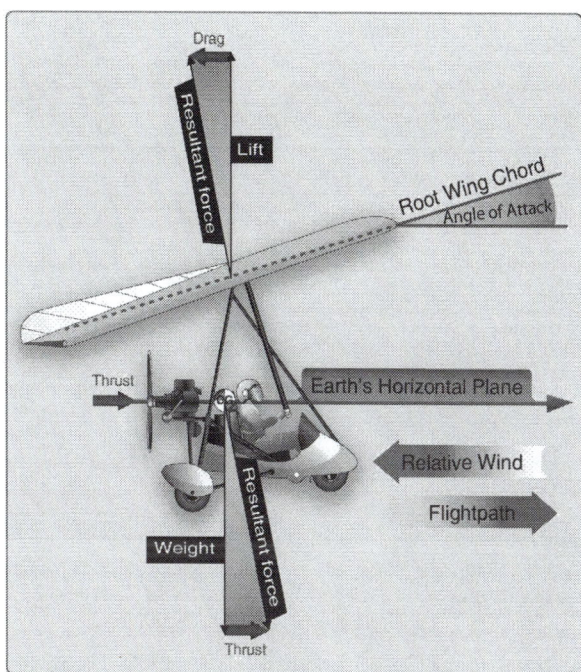

Figure 2-20. *Typical forces in level flight.*

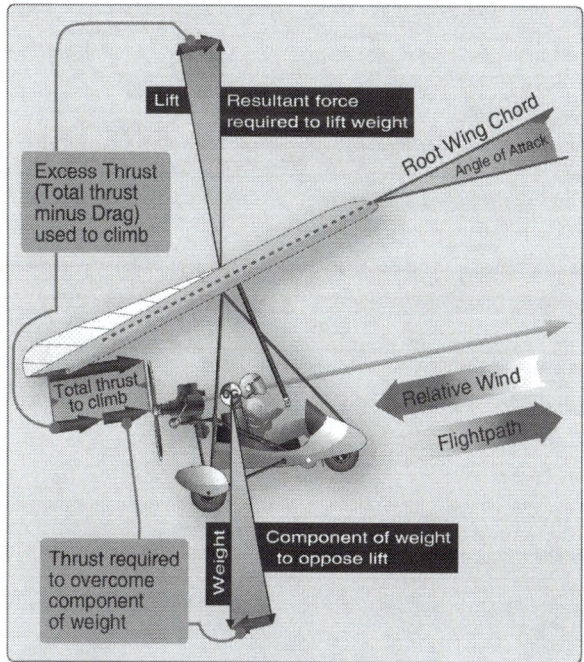

Figure 2-21. *Typical forces in climbing flight.*

Thrust Required for Increases in Speed

Above the lowest total drag airspeed *[Figure 2-18]*, faster speeds (lower angles of attack) for level and climbing flight requires greater thrust because of the increased drag created from the faster speeds.

AOA is the primary control of increasing and decreasing speeds, and increasing thrust generally does not produce higher speeds, but additional thrust is required to maintain level flight at higher speeds.

Ground Effect

Ground effect is when the wing is flying close to the ground and there is interference of the ground with the airflow patterns created by the wing. At the same angle of attack, lift increases slightly and the drag decreases significantly. The most apparent indication from ground effect is the unexpected lift given to an aircraft as it flies close to the ground—normally during takeoffs and landings. More details for ground effect aerodynamics are found in the Pilot's Handbook of Aeronautical Knowledge. Flight characteristics for ground effect are covered in the takeoff and landing chapters.

Center of Gravity (CG)

The CG is the theoretical point of concentrated weight of the aircraft. It is the point within the WSC aircraft about which all the moments trying to rotate it during flight are balanced. The most obvious difference in the CG for a WSC aircraft is the vertical position compared to an airplane, as it is always lower than the wing. The Pilot's Handbook of Aeronautical Knowledge accurately states the CG is generally in the vertical center of the fuselage. The same is true for the WSC aircraft. However, the WSC wing is higher above the fuselage/carriage and, since most of the weight is centered in the carriage, the CG is well below the wing.

In a two-seat WSC aircraft, the second seat is typically behind the pilot's seat and the CG is usually located close to the rear passenger seat. Therefore, the CG location does not change significantly with a passenger. Fuel tanks are typically located near the vertical CG so any difference in fuel quantity does not significantly change the CG fore and aft with different fuel quantities.

For level flight, the CG is directly below the wing/carriage attachment point known as the hang point, and the propeller thrust line is typically designed to be near the vertical position of the CG. *[Figure 2-22]*

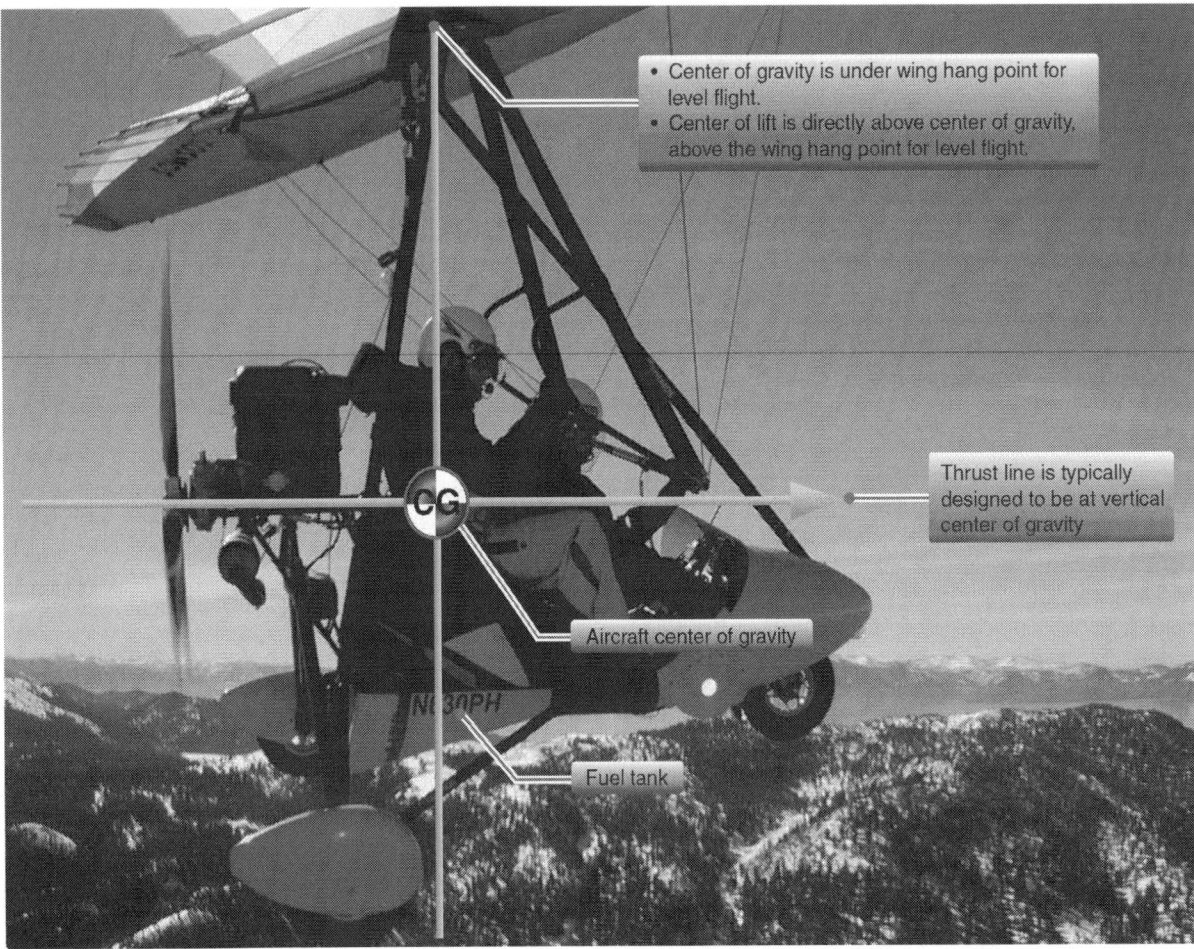

Figure 2-22. *CG location with passenger shown for level flight.*

Axes of Rotation

The three axes of rotation intersect at the CG. *[Figure 2-23]*

Lateral Axis—Pitch

Motion about the lateral axis, or pitch, is controlled by AOA/speed and the throttle. Lowering the AOA (increasing speed) rotates the nose down while increasing the AOA (decreasing speed) rotates the nose up.

Increasing the thrust of the propeller rotates the WSC aircraft pitch up (nose up) to climb and pitch down (nose down) at reduced throttle.

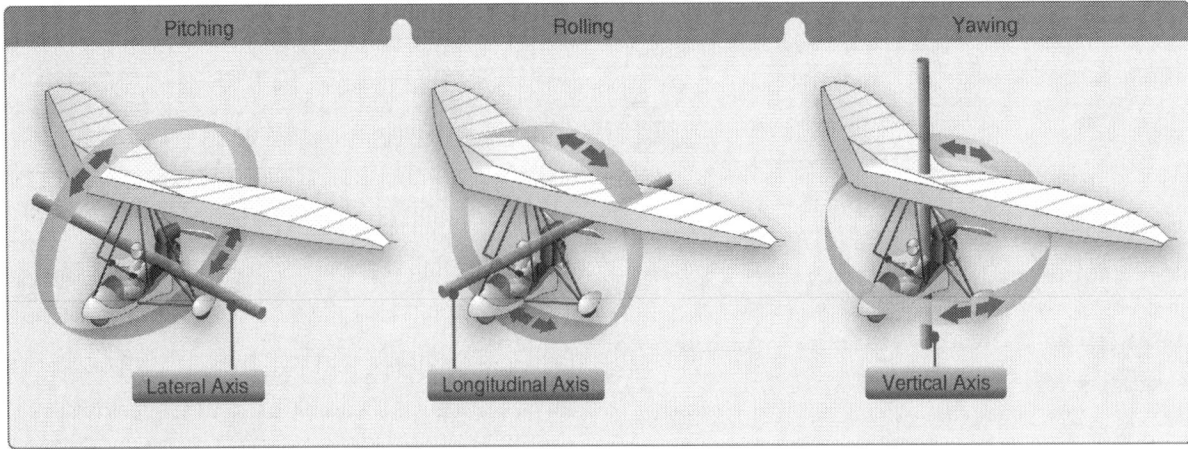

Figure 2-23. *Axes of rotation.*

Longitudinal Axis—Roll

Turning is initiated by rolling about the longitudinal axis, into a bank similar to an airplane using aileron and rudder control. To turn, shift the weight to the side in the direction of the turn, increasing the weight on that side. This increases the twist on that side while decreasing the twist on the other side, similar to actuating the ailerons on an airplane. The increased twist on the side with the increased weight reduces the AOA on the tip, reducing the lift on that side and dropping the wing into a bank. The other wing, away from which the weight has been shifted, decreases twist. The AOA increases, increasing the lift on that wing and thereby raising it.

Thus, shifting the weight to one side warps the wing (changes the twist) to drop one wing and raise the other, rolling the WSC aircraft about the longitudinal axis. *[Figure 2-24]* More details on the controls that assist wing warping are covered in chapter 3, which should be considered with use of the controls in the takeoff, landing, and flight maneuvers sections of this handbook.

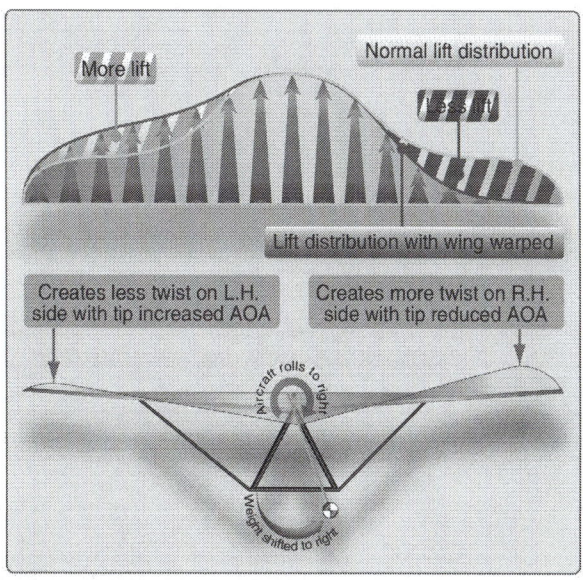

Figure 2-24. *Shifting weight to one side warps the wing by increasing the twist on the loaded side and decreasing the twist on the unloaded side.*

Vertical Axis—Yaw

The WSC wing is designed to fly directly into the relative wind because it does not provide for direct control of rotation about the vertical axis.

Stability and Moments

A body that rotates freely turns about its CG. In aerodynamic terms for a WSC aircraft, the mathematical value of a moment is the product of the force times the distance from the CG (moment arm) at which the force is applied.

Typical airplane wings generally pitch nose down or roll forward and follow the curvature of the upper airfoil camber creating a negative pitching moment. One of the reasons airplanes have tails is to create a downward force at the rear of the aircraft to maintain stabilized flight, as explained in greater detail in the Pilot's Handbook of Aeronautical Knowledge.

The WSC wing is completely different and does not need a tail because of two specific design differences—a completely different airfoil design creating a more stable airfoil and lifting surfaces fore and aft of the CG, similar to the airplane canard design.

WSC Unique Airfoil and Wing Design

As shown in *Figure 2-2*, the WSC airfoil has the high point significantly farther forward than does the typical airplane airfoil. This makes the center of lift for the airfoil farther forward and creates a neutral or positive pitching moment for the airfoil. Most WSC airfoils have this unique design to minimize negative moments or pitch down during flight.

Additionally, the design of the complete wing is a unique feature that provides stability without a tail. To understand the WSC aircraft pitch stability and moments, examine the wing as two separate components—root chord and tip chord.

Trim—Normal Stabilized Flight

In *Figure 2-25A*, during normal unaccelerated flight at trim speed, the lift at the root (L_R) times the arm to the root (A_R) equals the lift of the tip (L_T) times the arm to the tip (A_T).

$$(L_R \times A_R) + (L_T \times A_T) = 0$$
$$L_R + L_T = \text{Total Lift of the Wing } (L_W)$$

Adding all the lift from the wing puts the center of lift of the wing (CLW) directly over the CG for stabilized flight. *[Figure 2-25A]* If the pilot wishes to increase the trim speed, the CG is moved forward. This is done by moving the hang point forward on the wing. Similarly, to reduce the trim speed, the hang point/CG is moved rearward on the wing.

High Angles of Attack

In *Figure 2-25B*, if the wing AOA is raised to the point of minimum controlled airspeed at which the wing begins to stall towards the center of the wing (root area), the lift in this area decreases dramatically. The CLW moves back a distance "b" creating a moment to lower the nose. Therefore, the center of lift moves behind the CG at higher angles of attack, creating a nose-down stabilizing moment. The average lift coefficient verses AOA is shown for this minimum controlled airspeed in *Figure 2-26*. The root area is partially stalled and

2-13

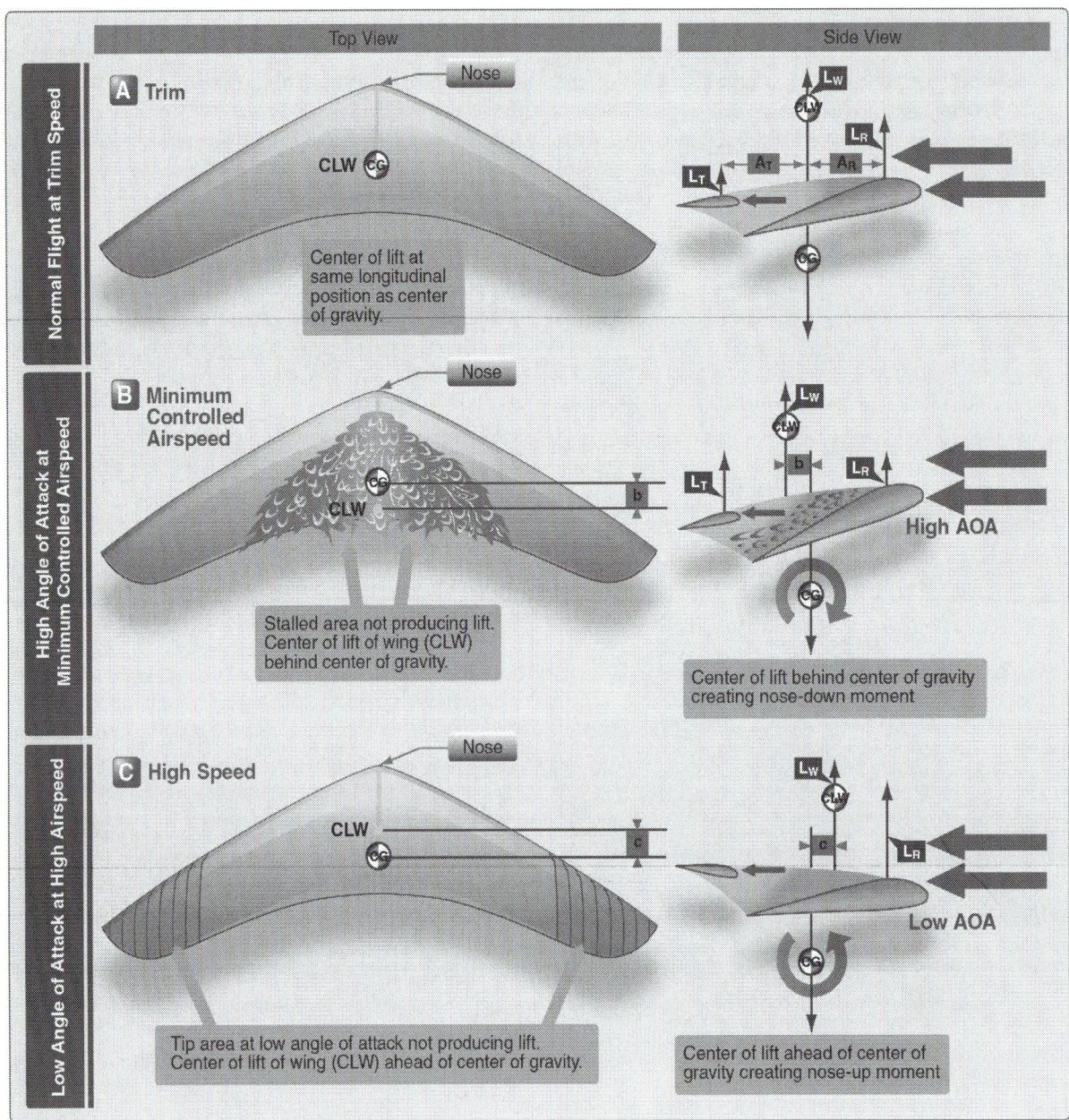

Figure 2-25. *Trim, minimum controlled airspeed, and high speed pitching moments.*

the tips are still flying. The specific stall characteristics of each wing are different and this stall pattern shown here is used for example.

Low Angles of Attack

At very low AOA, the tip chords are near zero AOA or below, not producing any lift, as shown in *Figure 2-25C.* At this point, the nose area is producing all of the lift for the wing. The CLW moves forward a distance "c," creating a positive stabilizing moment to raise the nose.

Pitch Pressures

As the pilot pushes out on the control bar, this creates a pilot input force that has a moment arm from the control bar up to the wing hang point. *[Figure 2-27]*

From this pilot-induced pitch moment, the control bar is pushed out, the nose raised, and the AOA increases an equal amount for both the root and the tip chords. However, as shown in *Figures 2-26* and *2-28,* the average C_L change is greater at the low AOA at the tip chords, while the amount

2-14

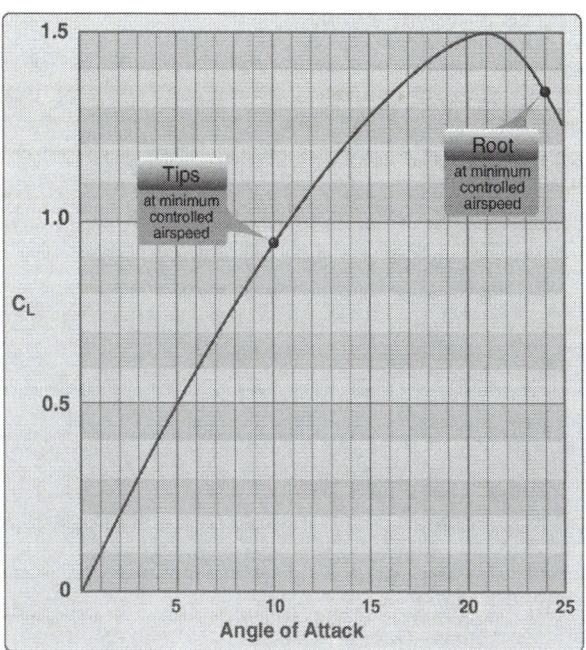

Figure 2-26. *Example of AOA versus C_L for wing at minimum controlled airspeed.*

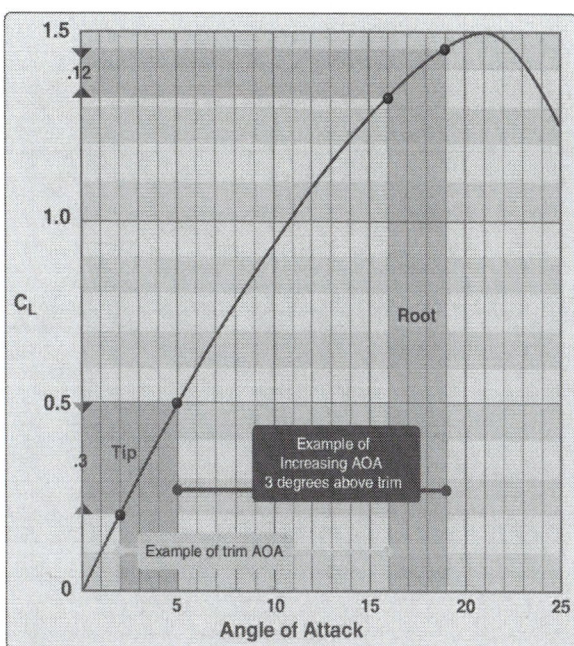

Figure 2-28. *Example AOA versus C_L showing the wing increasing AOA three degrees with the tip C_L increasing more than the root.*

Based on the same principle, when the wing AOA is lowered below the trim position, the tip chords' C_L decreases more than the root chord and the center of lift for the wing moves forward creating a positive moment to raise the nose at lower AOA.

In situations where the pilot is flying in severe/extreme turbulence, wind sheer, or the pilot is exceeding the limitations of the aircraft, the WSC aircraft can get into a situation where the root chord is at a negative AOA and not producing lift. This could result in an emergency vertical dive situation, as discussed later in the Whip Stall-Tuck-Tumble section. When at very low angles or negative angles of attack, the WSC wing is designed so that the wing has positive stability or a nose-up aerodynamic moment. This is accomplished by a number of different systems (washout struts, sprogs and reflex lines) further explained in chapter 3 that simply keep the trailing edge of the wing up in an emergency low/negative AOA dive situation. As shown in *Figure 2-29*, the root area of the wing has reflex which creates a positive pitching moment for the root chord to rotate the nose up towards a level flying attitude. At the same time, the tips are at a negative AOA producing lift in the opposite direction as usual, creating a moment to bring the nose/root chord up to a positive AOA to start producing lift and raising the nose to a normal flight condition. The negative lift or downward force as produced at the tips and root as shown provide a positive moment to raise the nose back to a normal flying attitude.

Figure 2-27. *Pilot actuated pitching moment.*

of change of the C_L is much less at higher AOA at the root chord. Therefore, an increase in AOA for the wing results in the tips creating a greater proportion of the lift and moving the center of lift behind the CG, creating a negative pitching moment to lower the nose at high AOA.

2-15

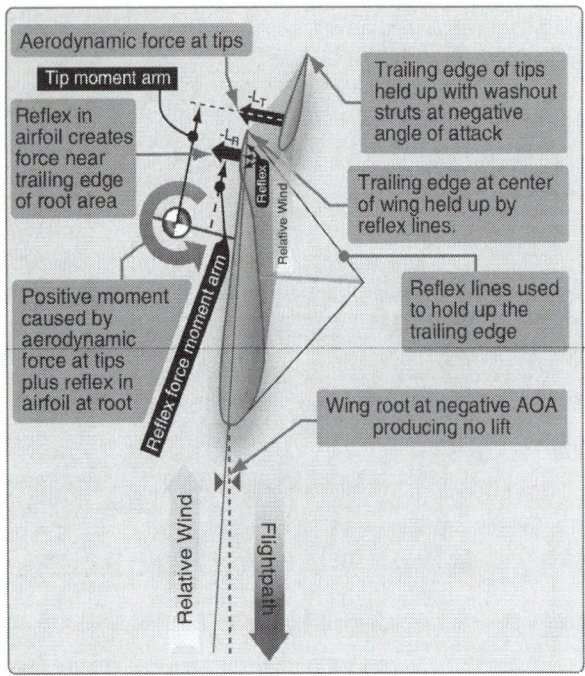

Figure 2-29. *Emergency vertical dive recovery for a WSC wing.*

Reflex also provides a stable pitch up moment for an airfoil when it is flying at normal flight angles of attack. The greater the reflex, the greater the nose up moment of the airfoil. This is used in some WSC airfoil designs and also for trim control as discussed in Chapter 3.

Carriage Moments

The wing design is the main contributing factor for pitch stability and moments, but the carriage design can also influence the pitching moment of the WSC aircraft. For example, at very high speeds in a dive, a streamlined carriage would have less drag and, therefore, a greater nose-up moment because of less drag. The design of the carriage parts can have an effect on aerodynamic forces on the carriage, resulting in different moments for different carriage designs.

The drag of the wing in combination with the drag of the carriage at various airspeeds provides a number of pitching moments, which are tested by the manufacturer—a reason the carriage is matched to the wing for compatibility. Each manufacturer designs the carriage to match the wing and takes into account these unique factors.

Pitch Moments Summary

Overall, the amount of sweep, twist, specific airfoil design from root to the tip, and the carriage design determine the pitching moments of the WSC aircraft. Some have small pitching moments, some have greater pitching moments. Each WSC model is different with a balance of these aerodynamic parameters to accomplish the specific mission for each unique carriage and wing combination.

Roll Stability and Moments

As described in the Pilot's Handbook of Aeronautical Knowledge, more dihedral or less anhedral in a WSC wing creates more roll stability. More roll stability might be helpful for a training wing or a fast wing made for long cross-country straight flight, but most pilots want a balance between roll stability and the ability to make quicker turns and a sport car feel for banking/turning. Therefore, a balance between the stability and the instability is achieved through anhedral plus other important wing design features such as nose angle, twist, and airfoil shape from root to tip.

An aerodynamic characteristic of swept wings is an "effective dihedral" based on the sweep of the wing and angle of attack. The combination of the physical anhedral in the wing and the effective dihedral due to wing sweep provides the balance of stability and rolling moments for a particular wing design.

The design of the wing can have actual dihedral or anhedral in the wing. Even with anhedral designed in the inboard section of the wing, the outboard sections of the wing could have some dihedral because of the flex in the outboard leading edges. As the wing is loaded up from additional weight or during a turn, the tips flex up more creating more dihedral and a roll stabilizing effect when loaded. *[Figure 2-30]*

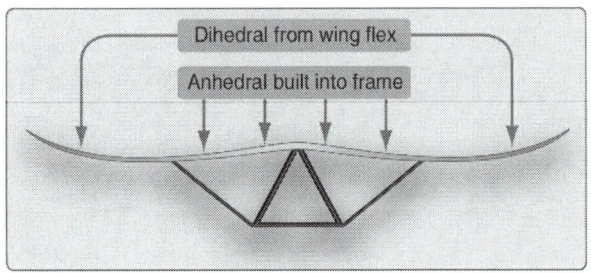

Figure 2-30. *Wing front view example showing anhedral in the middle of the wing and dihedral at the outboard section of the wing because of leading edge flex.*

Generally, it is thought that the wing remains level and the weight shifts to the side to initiate a turn. Another way to look at how the WSC wing rolls is to examine the carriage and the wing moment from the carriage point of view. For example, the CG hangs far below a wing weighing ⅛ of the carriage weight. When the control bar is moved to the side, creating a moment about the carriage/wing hang point, the carriage stays vertical and the wing rotates around the carriage. Therefore, there are two rolling moments that both contribute to the WSC rolling into a bank:

- The pilot creating the force on the control bar rotating the wing about the wing/carriage hang point.

- Shifting weight to one side of the wing, thus warping the wing to aerodynamically change the lift on each side, as in airplane roll control. *[Figure 2-31]*

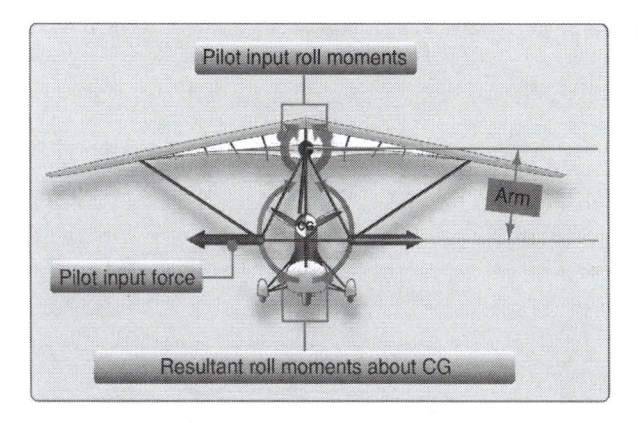

Figure 2-31. *Pilot induced moments about wing/carriage hang point and resultant CG rolling moment.*

Carriage Moments

Carriage weight and resultant CG are the main factors that contribute toward increasing the roll moment for the carriage. Carriage aerodynamic forces are not typically a factor for rolling moments.

Roll Stability Summary

Overall, roll stability and moments are a manufacturer/make/model balance between dihedral/anhedral, wing twist, nose angle, airfoil shape from root to tip, and leading edge stiffness. Some designs are stable, others neutral, and others can be designed to be slightly unstable for quick side-to-side rolling.

Yaw Stability and Moments

There is no significant turning about the vertical axis because the WSC wing is designed to fly directly into the relative wind. Any sideways skidding or yaw is automatically corrected to fly straight with the swept wing design. An airplane uses the vertical tail to stabilize it to fly directly into the relative wind like a dart. The unique design of the WSC aircraft performs the same function through the swept wing design, but also the wing twist and airfoil shape from root to tip assists in the correction about the vertical axis. A simple way to understand the yaw stability is to see that any yawing motion is reduced simply through the increased area of the wing as it rotates about its vertical axis. *[Figure 2-32]*

There is a slight amount of adverse yaw similar to an airplane that can be noticed when a roll is first initiated. The amount varies with the specific manufacturer's design and make/model. In addition, the wing can yaw side to side to some degree, with some different manufacturer's make/model more than others. The higher performance wings with less twist and a greater nose angle are noted for less yaw stability to gain performance. These wings also require more pilot input and skill to minimize yaw instability through pitch input. An addition to the wing planform, twist, and airfoil shapes to minimize yaw, some wings utilize vertical stabilizers similar to these in airplanes and others use tip fins. *[Figure 2-33]* Generally, the WSC wing is yaw stable with minor variations that are different for each wing and can be controlled by pilot input, if needed.

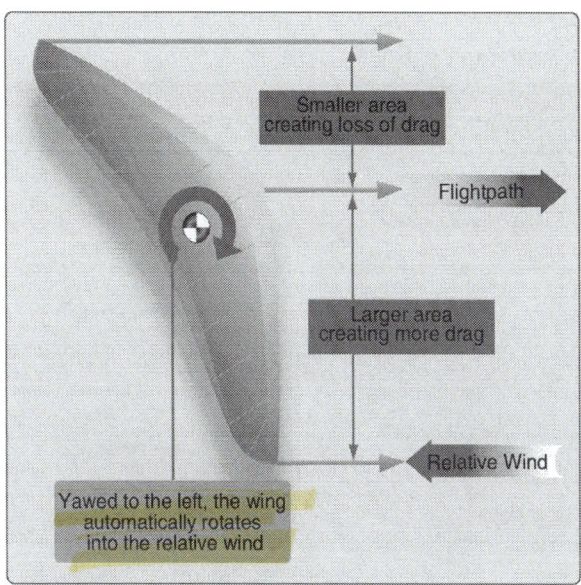

Figure 2-32. *Yaw correction about the vertical axis.*

Figure 2-33. *Keel pockets and vertical stabilizers are additional tools designers use for yaw stability on the wing.*

Carriage Moments

The wing is a significant factor in the design of yaw stability, but the carriage can be a large factor also. If the area in front of the CG is greater than the area in back of the CG, and the wing yaws to the side, then the front would have more drag and create a moment to yaw the WSC aircraft further from the straight flight. Therefore, fins are sometimes put on the carriage as needed so the carriage also has a yawing aerodynamic force to track the WSC aircraft directly into the wind. *[Figure 2-34]*

Figure 2-34. *Wheel fins for carriage yaw stability.*

Since the carriage has such a large effect on yaw stability, the carriage is matched to the wing for overall compatibility. Each manufacturer designs the carriage to match the wing and takes into account these unique factors of each design.

Yaw Stability Summary

These factors make the WSC aircraft track directly into the relative wind and eliminate the need for a rudder to make coordinated turns. Designs and methods vary with manufacturer and wing type, but all WSC wings are designed to track directly into the relative wind.

Thrust Moments

WSC aircraft designs can have different moments caused by thrust based on where the thrust line is compared to the CG. This is similar to an airplane except the WSC aircraft has no horizontal stabilizer that is affected by propeller blast.

If the propeller thrust is below the CG *[Figure 2-35, top]*, this creates a pitch-up moment about the CG when thrust is applied and a resultant decrease in speed. When reducing the throttle, it reduces this moment and a nose pitch down results with an increase in speed.

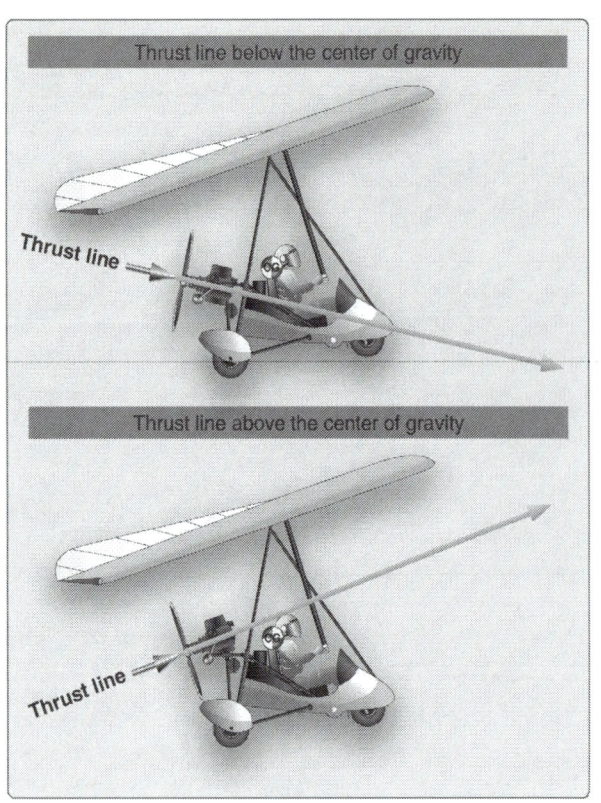

Figure 2-35. *Thrust line moments.*

If the propeller thrust is above the CG *[Figure 2-35, bottom]*, this creates a pitch-down moment about the CG when thrust is applied and a resultant increase in speed. When reducing the throttle, it reduces this moment and a nose pitch up results with a decrease in speed.

With the thrust line above or below the CG producing these minor pitch and speed changes, they are usually minor for most popular designs. Larger thrust moments about the CG may require pilot input to minimize the pitch and speed effects. Most manufacturers strive to keep the thrust as close as possible to the vertical CG while also balancing the drag of the carriage and the wing for its speed range. This is why the carriage must be matched to the wing so these characteristics provide a safe and easy to fly WSC aircraft.

Stalls: Exceeding the Critical AOA

As the AOA increases to large values on the wing chord, the air separates starting at the back of the airfoil. As the AOA increases, the separated air moves forward towards the leading edge. The critical AOA is the point at which the wing is totally stalled, producing no lift—regardless of airspeed, flight attitude, or weight. *[Figure 2-36]*

2-18

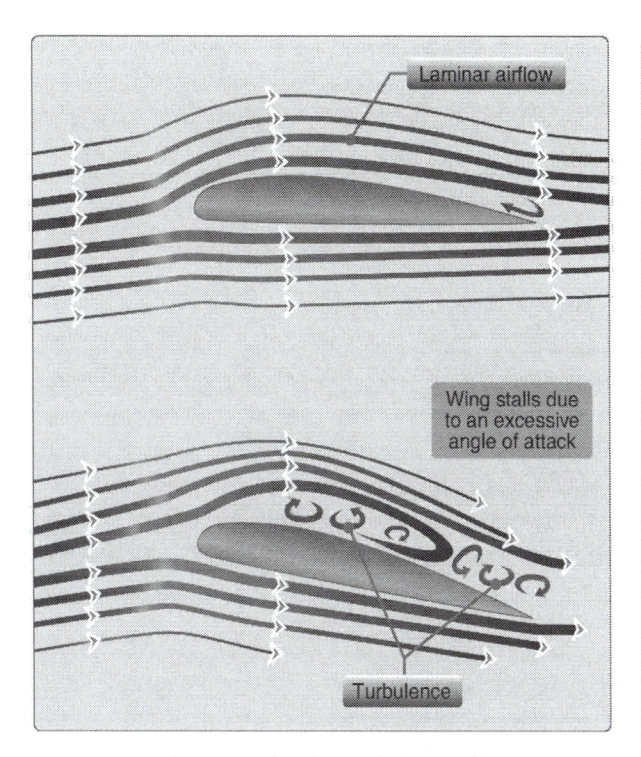

Figure 2-36. *Stall progression for an airfoil chord as the angle of attack is increased.*

Because the AOA of the WSC wing root chord/nose is so much higher than the AOA of the tips, the nose stalls before the tips. It is similar to stalling with the airplane canard in which the nose stalls first, the main wing (or tips for the WSC aircraft) continues to fly, and the nose drops due to lack of lift.

In most normal situations, the root chord/nose stalls first because it is at a much higher AOA. The tips continue to fly, making the WSC wing resistant to a complete wing stall. A pilot can even bring the aircraft into a high pitch angle stall attitude and keep the nose high. The nose stalls and rotates down because of the loss of lift, while the tips keep flying and maintain control of the aircraft.

If flying within the operating limitations of the aircraft and the WSC reaches a high AOA, the nose stalls, but the tips continue flying. However, it must be understood that there are many wing designs with many types of stall characteristics for each unique design. For example, high-performance wings could have less twist to gain performance, which could cause the wing to stall more abruptly than a training wing with more twist.

Whip Stall–Tuck–Tumble

A WSC aircraft can get to a high pitch attitude by flying outside the its limitations or flying in extreme/severe turbulence. If the wing gets to such a high pitch attitude and the AOA is high enough that the tips stall, a whip stall occurs. *[Figure 2-37]*

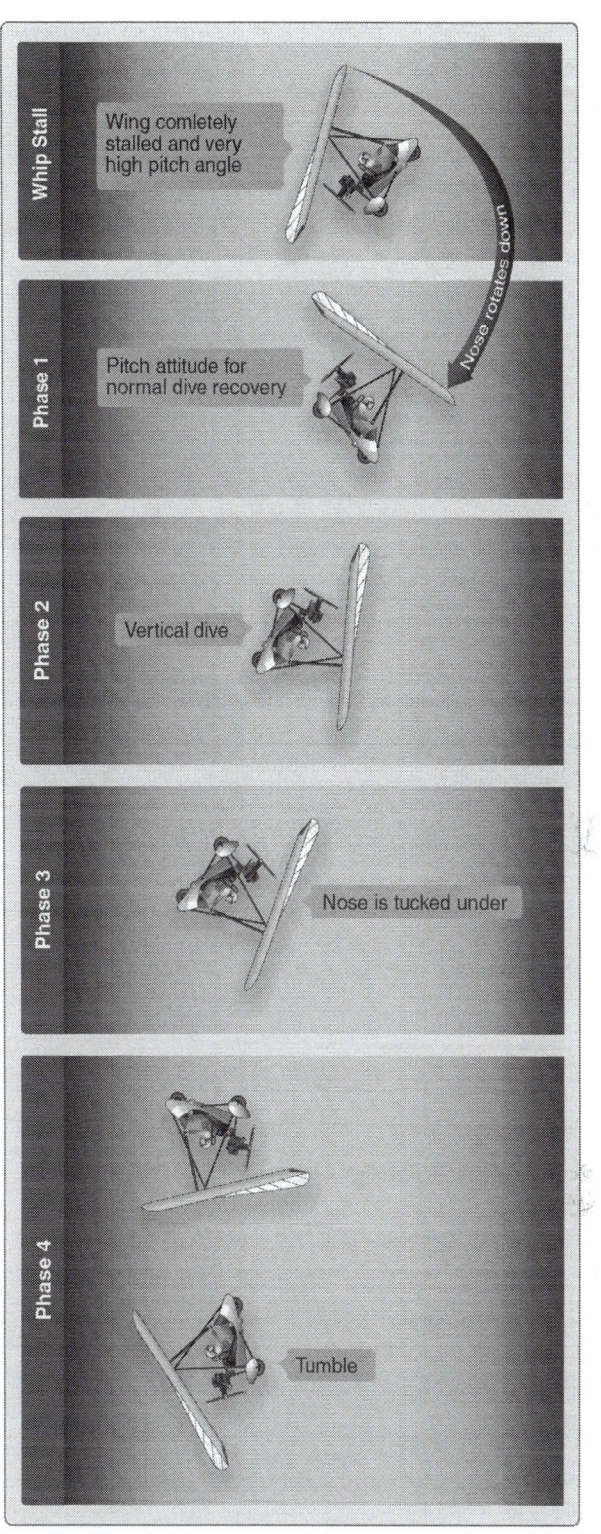

Figure 2-37. *Whip stall to tumble phases and sequence.*

In a WSC wing, most of the area of the wing is behind the CG (about three-quarters). With the tips and aft part of the wing having the greatest drag, and the weight being forward, an immediate and strong nose-down moment is created and the WSC nose starts to drop. Since both the relative wind and the wing are rapidly changing direction, there is no opportunity to reestablish laminar airflow across the wing.

This rotational momentum can pull the nose down into a number of increasingly worse situations, depending on the severity of the whip stall. *Figure 2-37* shows a whip stall and the phases that can result, depending on the severity.

> Phase 1—Minor whip stall results in a nose-down pitch attitude at which the nose is at a positive AOA and the positive stability raises the nose to normal flight, as described in *Figure 2-25C*.
>
> Phase 2—If the rotational movement is enough to produce a vertical dive, as illustrated in *Figure 2-29*, the aerodynamic dive recovery might raise the nose to an attitude to recover from the dive and resume normal flight condition.
>
> Phase 3—The rotational momentum is enough to bring the nose significantly past vertical (the nose has tucked under vertical), but could still recover to a vertical dive and eventually resume a normal flight condition.
>
> Phase 4—The rotational momentum is severe enough to continue rotation, bringing the WSC wing into a tumble from which there is no recovery to normal flight, and structural damage is probable.

Avoidance and emergency procedures are covered in Chapter 6, Basic Flight Maneuverers, and Chapter 13, Abnormal and Emergency Procedures.

Weight, Load, and Speed

Similar to airplanes, sailplanes, and PPCs, increasing weight creates increases in speed and descent rate. However, the WSC aircraft has a unique characteristic. Adding weight to a WSC aircraft creates more twist in the wing because the outboard leading edges flex more. With less lift at the tips, a nose-up effect is created and the trim speed lowers.

Therefore, adding weight can increase speed similar to other aircraft, but reduce the trim speed because of the increased twist unique to the WSC aircraft. Each manufacturer's make/model has different effects depending on the specific design. As described in the Pilot's Handbook of Aeronautical Knowledge, the stall speed increases as the weight or loading increases so some manufacturers may have specific carriage/wing hang point locations for different weights. Some require CG locations to be forward for greater weights so the trim speed is well above the stall speed for the wing.

WSC aircraft have the same forces as airplanes during normal coordinated turns. Greater bank angles result in greater resultant loads. The flight operating strength of an aircraft is presented on a graph whose horizontal scale is based on load factor. The diagram is called a VG diagram—velocity versus "G" loads or load factor. Each aircraft has its own VG diagram which is valid at a certain weight and altitude. See the Pilot's Handbook of Aeronautical Knowledge for more details on the VG diagram. Load factors are also similar to the VG diagram applicable to WSC.

Basic Propeller Principles

The WSC aircraft propeller principles are similar to those found in the Pilot's Handbook of Aeronautical Knowledge, except there is no "corkscrewing effect of the slipstream" and there is less P-factor because the carriage is generally flying with the thrust line parallel to the relative wind. The wing acts independently, raising and lowering the AOA and speed. This was introduced at the beginning of this chapter when angle of incidence was defined.

The torque reaction does have a noticeable effect on the WSC aircraft. With the typical left hand turn tendency (for right hand turning propellers), turns are not typically built into the wing. As in airplanes, some cart designs point the engine down and to the right. Others do not make any adjustment, and the pilot accounts for the turning effect through pilot input.

It should be noted that many of the two-stroke propellers turn to the right, as do conventional airplanes. However, many four-stroke engine propellers turn to the left, creating a right hand turn. Consult the POH for the torque characteristics of your specific aircraft.

Chapter Summary

Basic principles of aerodynamics apply to all aircraft; however, the unique design of the wing and the separate fuselage/carriage provide a simplistic and efficient aircraft. The following provide a summary of the unique aerodynamics for the WSC wing:

- The WSC wing is pitch stable without a tail because of the combination of airfoil design from root to tip, sweep, twist, and planform.

- WSC wing flexibility allows the wing to twist from side to side by shifting the weight providing the control to roll the aircraft without control surfaces.

- The WSC wing only has two axes of control, pitch and roll, while no yaw control is needed because it is yaw stable.

- The WSC wing is stall resistant because under normal flight conditions the tip chord is still flying while the rest of the wing is stalled—similar to the airplane canard system.

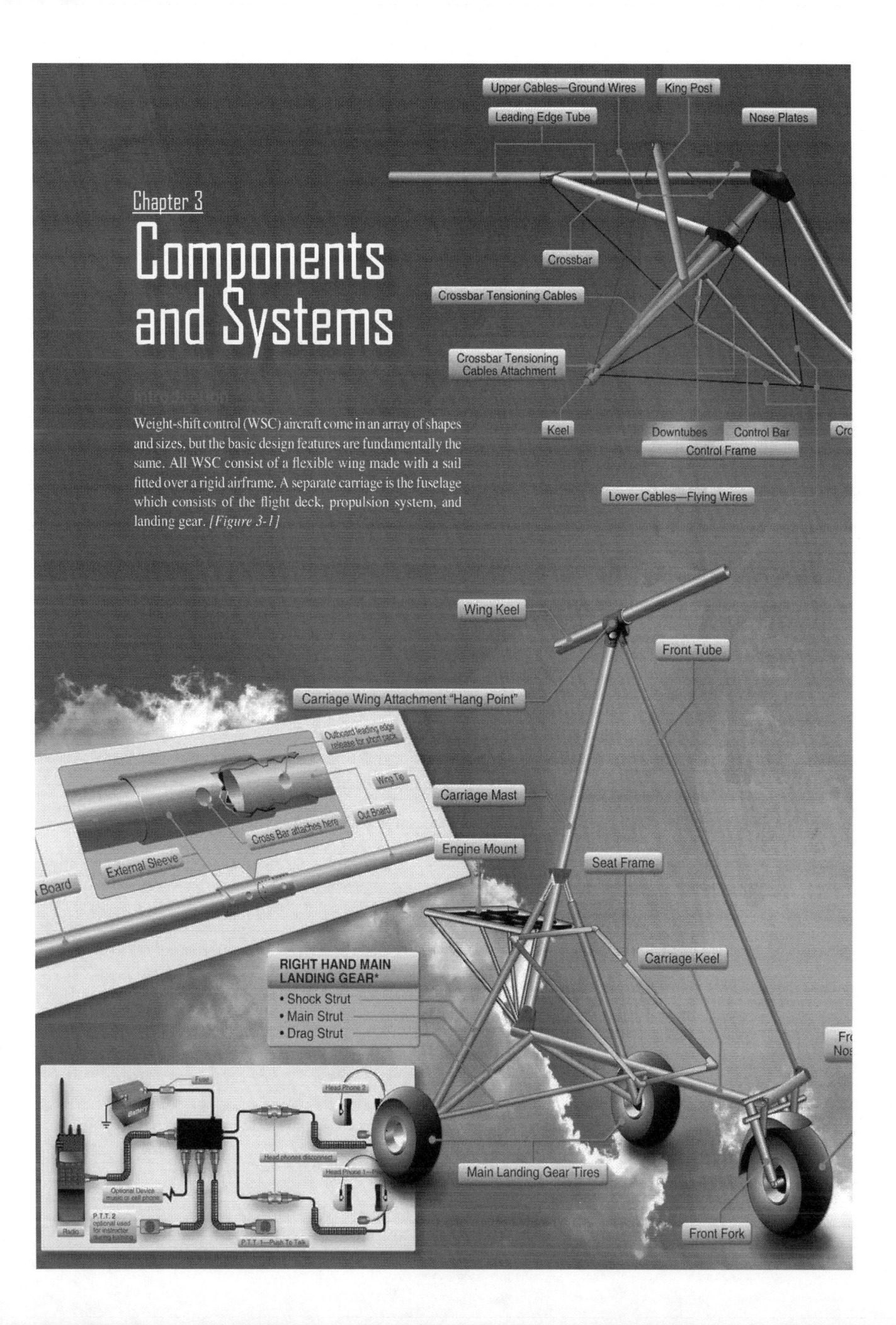

Chapter 3
Components and Systems

Introduction

Weight-shift control (WSC) aircraft come in an array of shapes and sizes, but the basic design features are fundamentally the same. All WSC consist of a flexible wing made with a sail fitted over a rigid airframe. A separate carriage is the fuselage which consists of the flight deck, propulsion system, and landing gear. *[Figure 3-1]*

Figure 3-1. *Wing and carriage of WSC aircraft.*

Wing

The wing has a structural frame that the sail fits over. Although the wing structure is rigid, it is designed to move and allow the sail to flex and the wing to deform or "warp," to provide a simple control system with no pulleys, push rods, hinges, control cables, or separate control surfaces. This simplifies maintenance and reduces the cost and weight of the wing. Each wing is built from high quality aircraft parts including alloyed aluminum tubes, stainless steel cables, hardware, and specially designed sail cloth.

Wing Frame Components

The structural frame of the wing is composed of the leading edges, keel, crossbar, pilot control frame, king post and wires/struts. The wing frame is a number of structural triangles formed by the wing components. These triangles, braced by wires and struts, provide a strong and lightweight frame to support the flexible sail. *[Figure 3-2]*

Leading Edges

Leading edges are tube assemblies that are at the front of the wing, the leading edges of the wing airfoil. These are swept back to form the front shape of the wing and attached to each other with nose plates. The leading edges support the airfoil and are designed to flex as part of the wing structure.

The leading edges are each made up of two main sections, an inboard and an outboard section, as shown in *Figures 3-2* and *3-3*. Additional tubing "sleeves" are typically used for added strength where the leading edge attaches to the nose plates, and where the inboard and outboard tubes join at the crossbar attachment. This sleeving can be internal or external depending on the specific manufacturer's design. Typically, additional sleeving is used throughout the leading edges at various locations to strengthen and vary the flex for the particular design of the wing. Each manufacturer and make/model uses different internal and external sleeving to accomplish specific strength and flex characteristics. Generally, the inboard sections are stiffer and the outboard leading edge section flexes as part of the flexible wing design. Sleeving is commonly added throughout the aircraft where bolt holes are drilled through the tubing to reinforce it around the bolt hole.

The outboard leading edge sections can be removed to pack up the wing into a "short pack" which is commonly used for shipping. *[Figure 3-3]*

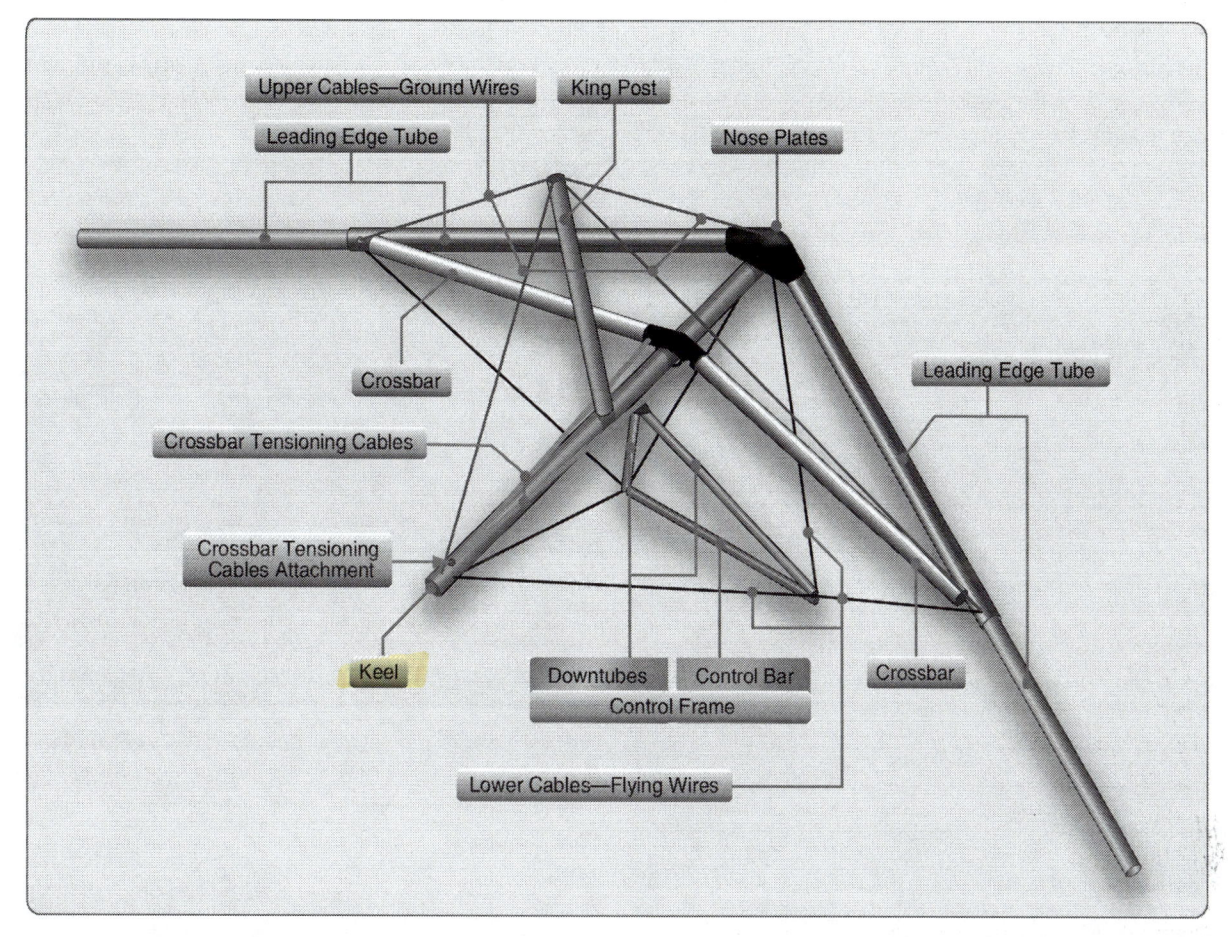

Figure 3-2. *Wing frame components.*

Keel

The wing keel is like that of a boat keel, the center of the wing, fore and aft. It attaches to the leading edges at the nose plate and performs a number of important functions. It is the structure where the carriage attaches to the wing, and it is the wing structure that connects the center section of the sail at the "keel pocket" (discussed later in this chapter in the sail section). The control frame and king post (if so equipped) also attaches to the keel. It also provides structure for the upper and lower wires (if so equipped) and a reference or anchor for the crossbar which needs some movement in relation to the keel for roll control.

The keel is rigid and is not designed to flex nor is it highly stressed like the leading edges except where the under carriage attaches to the wing. Sleeving is normally added to strengthen this middle area as well at the nose attachment and rear cable attachments.

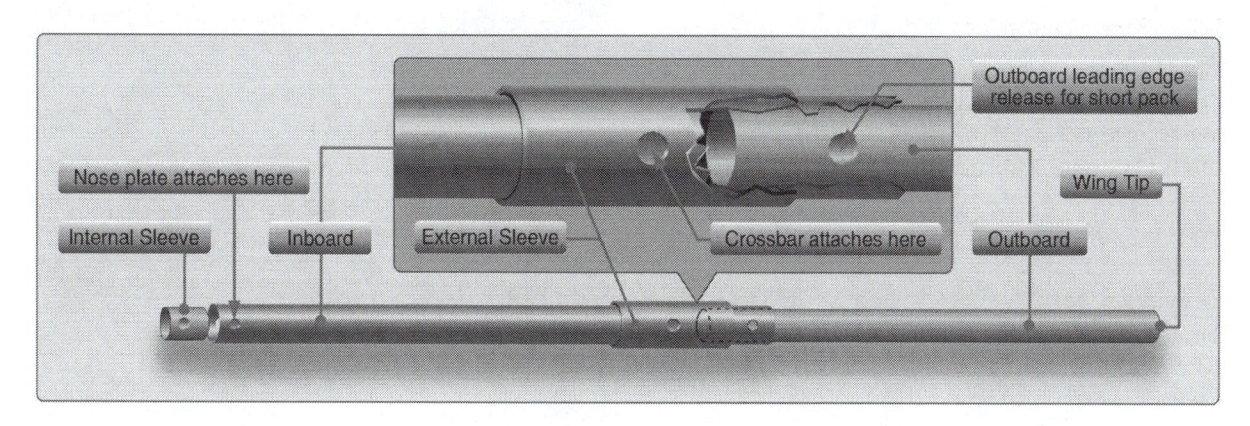

Figure 3-3. *Leading edge assembly.*

Crossbar

The crossbar is two aluminum tube sections hinged above the keel that attach to the leading edges. The crossbar is tensioned back with the crossbar tensioning cables, which pushes the leading edges forward to conform to the sail. These crossbar tensioning cables are attached at the rear of the keel when the wing is tensioned into flying position. *[Figure 3-4]*

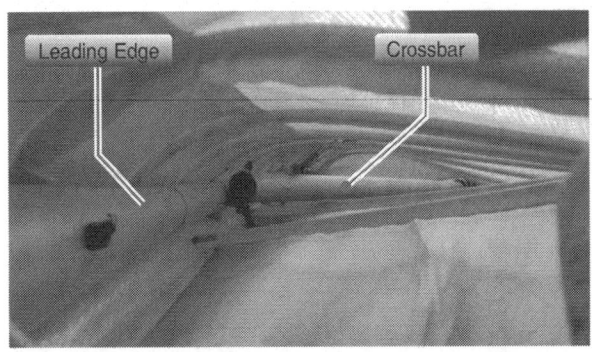

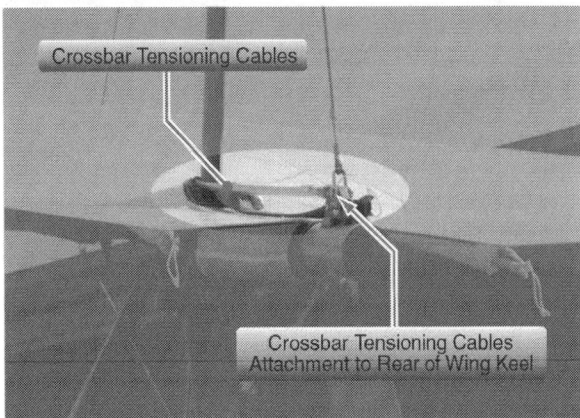

Figure 3-4. *View looking inside left hand wing from the tip showing crossbar tensioned and pushing the leading edges into the sail. Notice the slight bending of the leading edges to fit into the sail (top). Crossbar tensioning cables attached to rear of keel in flying position detail. See specific location on airframe with figure 3-2. (bottom).*

These crossbar sections are under a compression load and designed to be stiff with no bending. A larger diameter tube is typically used to avoid any bending when the wing is flying. A ding, dent, or bend in the crossbar could spell disaster during flight because it is one of the main structural members that holds leading edges into position during flight.

For wing take down and packing, the crossbar haul back cables are released, the crossbar hinged center moves forward, and the leading edges rotate in toward the keel about the nose plates and come together, allowing the wing to fold down into a long tube for transport and/or storage.

Control Frame

The triangle-shaped control frame serves two main purposes. It provides the lower structure for the wing and is the control bar for the pilot. The control frame is bolted to the keel with two downtubes extending from the keel attachment to the horizontal base tube, which is the pilot's control bar. *[Figures 3-2, 3-5, and 3-6]*

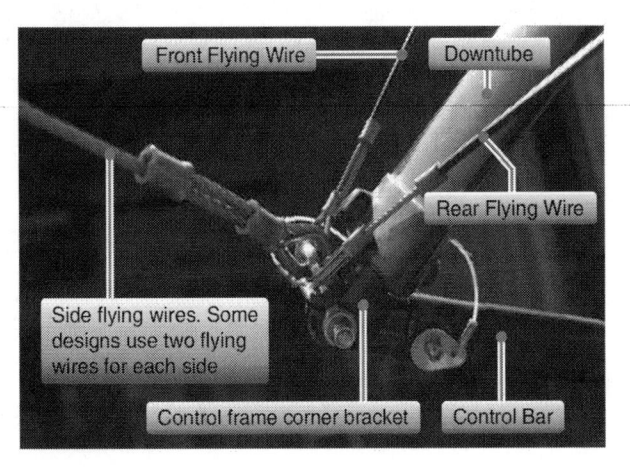

Figure 3-5. *Control frame corner bracket with wire attachments. Notice the thick structural ⅛-inch flying wires that support the wing and smaller ³⁄₃₂-inch cables holding the control frame in place fore and aft.*

Figure 3-6. *Control frame with downtubes, control bar, and corner bracket with flying wing wires, and control frame fore and aft wires.*

Control frame corner brackets at the bottom of the downtubes provide the wing structural attachments for the flying cables or struts that attach to each leading edge/crossbar junction, and secure the control bar fore and aft to the wing with the front and back wires attached to nose plates and the aft section of the keel. *[Figures 3-5 and 3-6]*

During flight, the downtubes are similar in compression to the crossbar and must be stiff and straight to maintain structural integrity. The base tube/control bar is under tension during flight.

Front and rear flying wires hold the control frame in place fore and aft. Side flying wires hold the control frame in place side to side and provide structure to hold the wings in place while flying. *[Figures 3-2, 3-5, and 3-6]* Strutted wings use struts in place of the side flying wires, which is discussed later in this chapter.

Training bars are added for dual controls so the person in back can fly the aircraft. These are typically used by an instructor for training but can be used by a passenger in the back also. *[Figure 3-7]*

King Post With Wires-on-Top Wing Design
Similar to the lower control frame holding the wing in position during flight, the king post is attached to the keel and supports the upper ground wires which hold the wing in position on the ground and negative loads during flight. *[Figure 3-2]* It also provides a structure for reflex lines which is discussed later in wing systems.

Topless Wings With Struts
Similar to airplanes with struts to support the wings, some WSC aircraft replace side flying wires with struts, eliminating the king post and ground wires on top of the wing. This provides a number of benefits, but primarily, no king post is needed because the struts can take a compression load and hold the wings up on the ground and also take the negative loads during flight. With struts, a WSC aircraft is much shorter in height allowing it to fit into hangars with lower doors and ceilings. This can make a big difference in finding a suitable storage for the aircraft if leaving it set up. *[Figure 3-8]*

Figure 3-8. *Strutted wing on WSC aircraft carriage.*

Figure 3-7. *Passenger using training bars which are also used by the instructor during training.*

3-5

Some strutted designs allow the wings to be folded back while still on the carriage. This can also be helpful when using a smaller space for storage by folding the wing up without taking it off the carriage. *[Figure 3-9]* It is also convenient for sea trikes since the aircraft does not have to be taken out of the water to fold up the wing.

Figure 3-9. *A strutted wing folded back so it can fit into a trailer for storage and easy transport (top). Strutted wing with wings folded back for easy storage (bottom).*

Strutted wings have a clean upper surface with no holes required for the king post or wires to go through the top of the sail. This reduces interference drag on the top of the wing. Increasing overall efficiency, no holes in the sail also eliminates any high pressure leakage from underneath the wing getting sucked up to the lower pressure on top of the wing. *[Figure 3-10]*

Sail Components
The sail is a highly refined design that integrates with its wing frame. Each sail and wing frame are designed for each other and are not interchangeable with other sails or wings.

Figure 3-10. *Clean upper surface of strutted wing.*

Modern sails are designed with complex geometry and sewn to precision to achieve a highly efficient design. Because of the flexibility of the wing frame and the modern techniques in sail design, the leading edge can have a curved shape which adds to the efficiency and stability of the wing. *[Figure 3-11]*

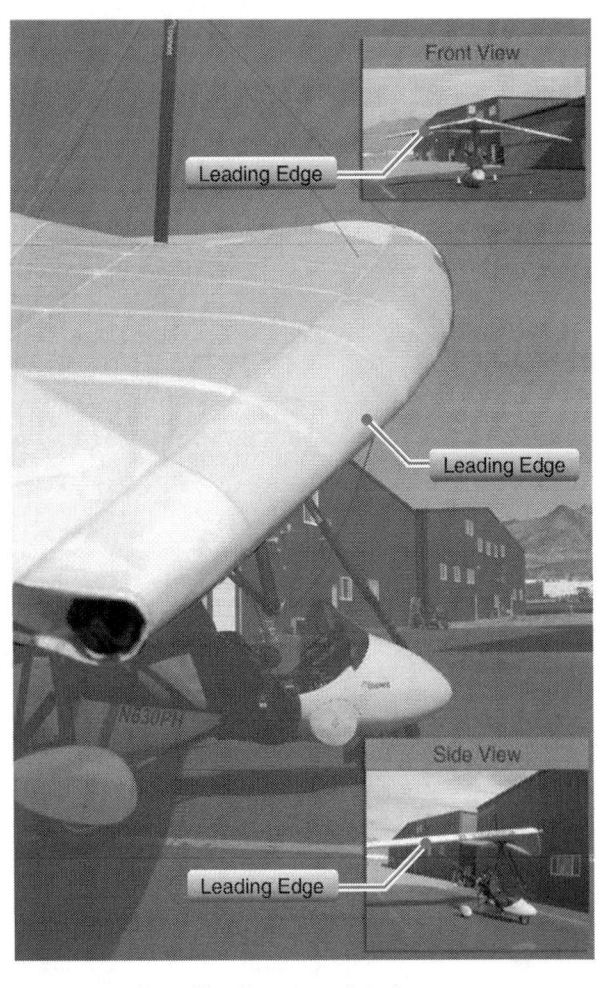

Figure 3-11. *Curved leading edge sail design.*

Battens and Leading Edge Stiffener

As discussed in the aerodynamics section, stiff preformed battens are the airfoil ribs that maintain the airfoil shape from the root to the tips. Additionally, a foam or mylar stiffener is inserted in a pocket at the leading edge to keep a rigid airfoil shape between the battens from the leading edge up to the airfoil high point. Double surface wings have additional ribs on the bottom surface that are straight or formed to maintain the bottom surface camber.

Sail Material and Panels

Sail material is a combination of polyester materials designed with different weaves, thickness, and orientation to fit the design mission of the wing. Panels are cut to different shapes and laid down at different angles to provide the stiffness and flexibility where needed for the specific wing design. Automated machines typically cut the fabric to precision tolerances and the panels are sewn together with high strength thread.

Pockets and Hardware

Pockets are added for battens and hardware is installed for the wing frame and wire attachments. Trailing edge line or wires are sometimes added for reinforcement and can be used for tuning. Battens are held in with a variety of batten ties or other methods unique to the manufacturer. *[Figure 3-12]*

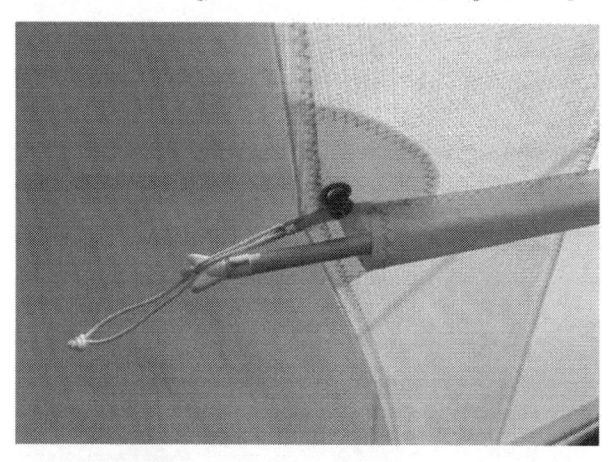

Figure 3-12. *Trailing edge of the sail showing reinforcement panels, trailing edge line, and batten ties with attachment hardware.*

Sail Attachment to Wing Frame

The sail is attached to the wing frame at the nose and the tips. A keel pocket towards the back of the sail secures the sail to the wing keel. *[Figure 3-13]*

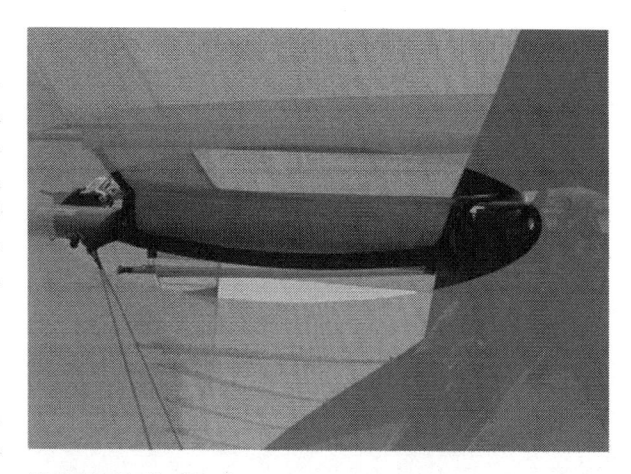

Figure 3-13. *Keel pocket.*

Cables and Hardware

Cables are used throughout the wing frame and sail to hold components in place and act as structure to carry loads. Flight and ground cables are stainless steel and attach to components with tangs or other hardware depending on the application. Cables are secured at each end with thimbles and swaged fittings. *Figure 3-5* shows detail of typical swaged fittings. A variety of hardware is used for attaching these swaged cable fittings to the airframe. Each manufacturer has different hardware for wing components. *[Figures 3-14 and 3-15]*

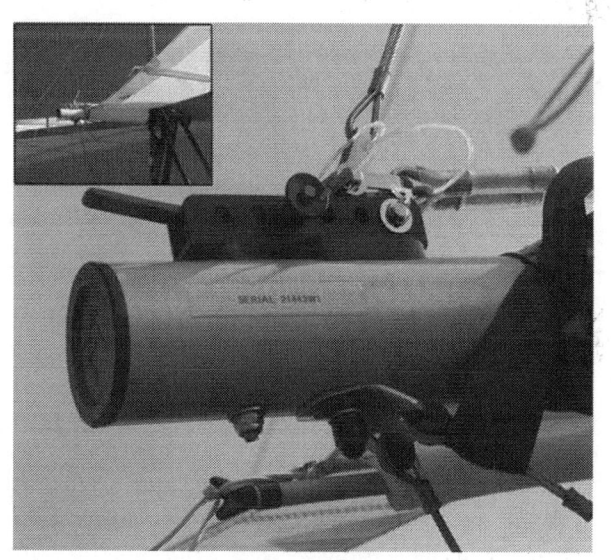

Figure 3-14. *Crossbar tensioning junction attachment example.*

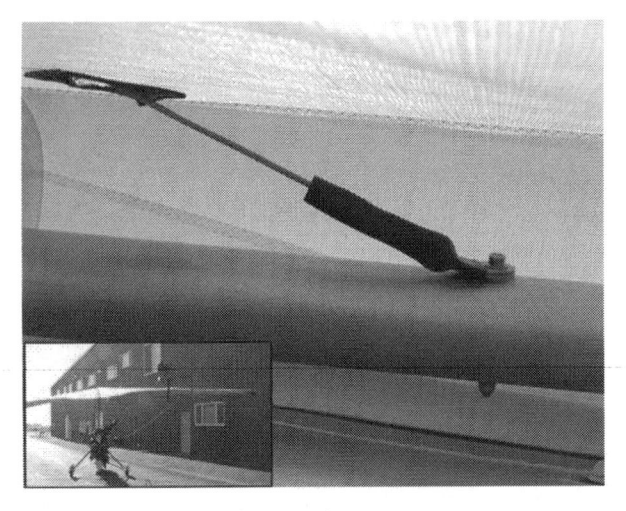

Figure 3-15. *View inside wing showing top wire coming though sail that is reinforced, being attached to the crossbar by a tang, an aircraft bolt, washers, and lock nut.*

Wing Systems
Reflex Systems

As discussed in the aerodynamics section, the trailing edge near the root and the tips must stay up during unusually low or negative angles of attack *[Figure 2-29]* to maintain a positive pitch stability for the aircraft. There are a number of reflex systems used to accomplish this in emergency situations.

Reflex cables—most wings with a king post use cables to hold the trailing edge up at unusually low or negative angles of attack. These reflex cables are secured to the top of the king post and attach to several positions on the trailing edge where the battens are located. Different manufacturers have different positions where these are attached, depending on the design of the wing. Reflex cables also provide additional reflex at high speeds because the drag of the wires pulls up the trailing edge, creating more reflex at these higher speeds. *[Figure 3-16]*

Washout struts—tubes near the tips that keep the tip trailing edge up during very low or negative angles of attack. They can be inside or outside the double surface of a wing. The reflex cables may not go to the wingtip, so washout struts are used to hold up the trailing edge at the tip at very low and negative angles of attack. *[Figure 3-17]*

Sprogs—for wings using struts with no king post, sprogs are used to keep the inboard trailing edge up in place of the reflex cables. A wire attached to the top of the leading edge holds the sprog up in place. *[Figure 3-18]*

Pitch Control System

The pitch control system is a simple hinge on the keel at the hang point that allows the pilot to push the control bar out and

Figure 3-16. *Reflex cables.*

Figure 3-17. *Washout struts.*

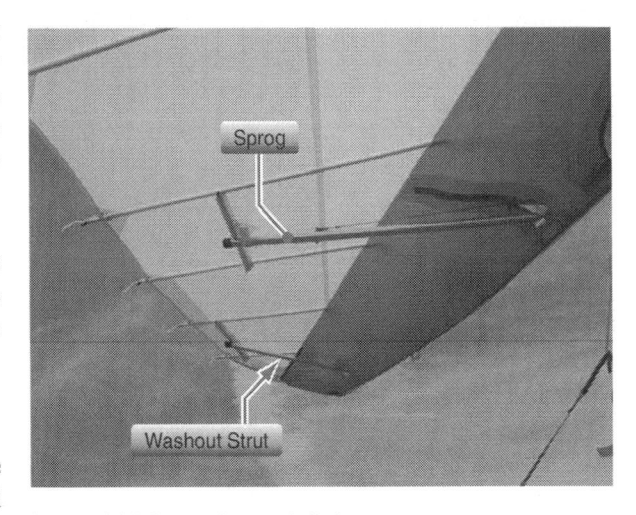

Figure 3-18. *Sprogs for strutted wing.*

pull the control bar in to control pitch. This wing attachment is different for each manufacturer, but all designs have this hang point wing attachment so the control bar is always perpendicular to the longitudinal axis of the aircraft. This raising and lowering of the nose is the pitch control system for the WSC aircraft. *[Figures 2-7 and 3-19]*

Figure 3-19. *Hang point wing attachment.*

Roll Control System

Control bar movement from side to side controls the roll about the longitudinal axis. The wing attachment hang point allows the carriage to roll around the wing keel. Thus, it can also be looked at from the carriage point of view, when the control bar is moved side to side, the wing rotates around the wing keel relative to the carriage. *[Figures 2-31 and 3-19]*

It would first appear that moving the control bar to one side, thus shifting weight to the opposite side, could alone bank the aircraft. It is true that shifting weight to the right would naturally bank the aircraft to the right and put it into a right hand turn. However, the weight alone is not enough to provide adequate roll control for practical flight.

As weight is moved to one side, the keel is pulled closer to that side's leading edge. The actual keel movement is limited to only 1 to 2 inches each side of center. However, this limited keel movement is sufficient to warp the wing, changing the twist side to side (as discussed earlier in the aerodynamics section) to roll the aircraft *[Figure 2-24]* by changing the lift side to side. Simply, the shifting of weight from side to side pulls the keel toward the leading edge on that side and warps the wing to roll the aircraft.

Besides the keel shifting relative to the leading edges and crossbar, overall roll control is adjusted by the designers to fit the mission of the wing through sail material/stiffness, leading edge stiffness/flexibility, amount of twist, amount of travel the keel is allowed, airfoil shape, and the planform of the wing. *[Figures 3-20 and 3-21]*

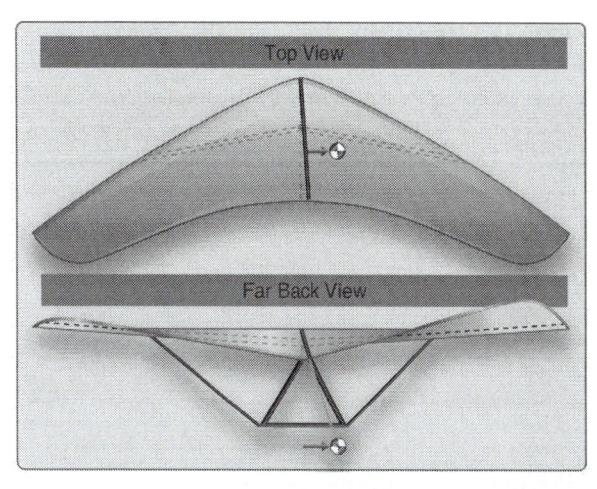

Figure 3-20. *Shifting weight to the right pulls the keel to the right (or lets the crossbar shift to the left) and increases twist on the right side for roll control.*

Figure 3-21. *Crossbar travel limiter.*

Trim Systems

There are a number of trim systems to relieve the control pressures for pilots to fly at different "hands off" trim speeds. Ground adjustable trim allows the pilot to adjust the trim speed of the wing on the ground and remain at one speed during flight, while flight adjustable trim systems can change the trim speed in flight.

Ground Adjustable Trim Systems

The most common ground adjustable trim system, and typical of most aircraft, is moving the wing attachment hang point forward for faster trim speeds and aft for slower trim speeds. Each manufacturer has different hardware, but the basics of sliding the carriage wing hang point forward and backward on the keel is similar for all. As an example, moving the hang point at the furthest aft position to the furthest forward position could speed the wing up 20 knots. This in turn moves the control bar position back to a new "hands off" trim speed.

3-9

Another less commonly used method of increasing trim speed is to increase tension on the crossbar by pulling it back further, slightly increasing the nose angle and reducing twist. This increases the angle of attack (AOA) of the tips producing more lift, and it lowers the nose to a higher trim speed. This is a typical in-flight trim adjustment for high performance hang gliders. The roll control is diminished with this faster and stiffer wing.

Ground adjustable trim systems are described in the Pilot's Operating Handbook (POH) for each aircraft. Different loads may require different pitch settings.

Inflight Adjustable Trim Systems

Being able to adjust the trim systems in flight has a number of advantages as discussed later in the flight sections. A number of inflight adjustable systems are available with different manufacturers. A common in-flight adjustable trim system is raising and lowering the trailing edge. Raising the trailing edge increases airfoil reflex and slows the wing. Lowering the trailing edge decreases airfoil reflex and speeds up the wing. Typically, a crank on a downtube controls a wire that runs up the downtube to the top of the wing. As a result of moving the crank, the trailing edge wires are raised and lowered and the trim speed changed. *[Figure 3-22]* Hydraulic or electrical systems can move the hang point on the wing for other inflight trim systems. *[Figure 3-23]*

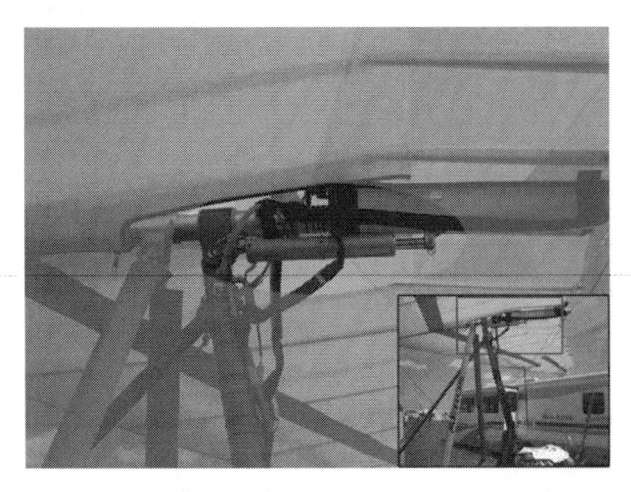

Figure 3-23. *Hydraulic inflight trim systems that move the hang point in flight controlled by the pilot.*

Another pilot-actuated trim system in flight is an elastic system in which the pilot increases tension on the elastic system which raises the nose for climb and slower flight. *[Figure 3-24]*

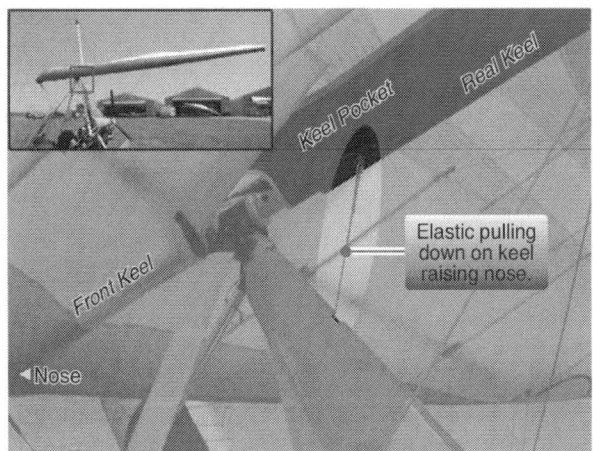

Figure 3-24. *More tension on elastic pulling down on the rear of the wing keel reduces the trim speed and is controlled by the pilot in flight.*

Carriage

The carriage is a completely separate structure from the wing. Without the wing, the carriage can be driven around if needed. Most of the weight and cost of the WSC aircraft is in the carriage. There is a wide range of carriage designs from the most simple and basic open trikes to the more sophisticated and complex trikes that integrate cowlings and offer a number of adjustments for the pilot and passenger, resulting in comfort and less fatigue during flying. Generally,

Figure 3-22. *A crank on the downtube of the control bar that adjusts the trailing edge reflex during flight.*

Figure 3-25. *Simple basic trike (left) and sophisticated trike with adjustments for pilot and passenger (right).*

the more complex the trike, the more it costs, weighs, and the more power it requires for similar wings. *[Figure 3-25]*

Structure

Similar to the wing, the carriage is designed with a number of structural triangles for optimum strength and minimum weight. Each manufacturer and model have specific details that vary, but the carriage structure is typically a mast, keel, and front tube that form the main triangle components of the carriage structure with the wing attachment at the top of the mast. A seat frame attached to the mast and keel provides rigidity to the main components while providing structure for the pilot and passenger. *[Figure 3-26]*

Landing struts attached to the rear wheels provide structure for the main landing gear, and a front fork provides the landing gear structure for the front wheel. An engine mount attaches to the mast, providing structure for the propulsion system to attach to the carriage. *[Figure 3-26]*

Landing Gear

The landing gear provides support to the WSC aircraft on the ground and absorbs the shock to reduce the stresses on the pilot and the aircraft during landings.

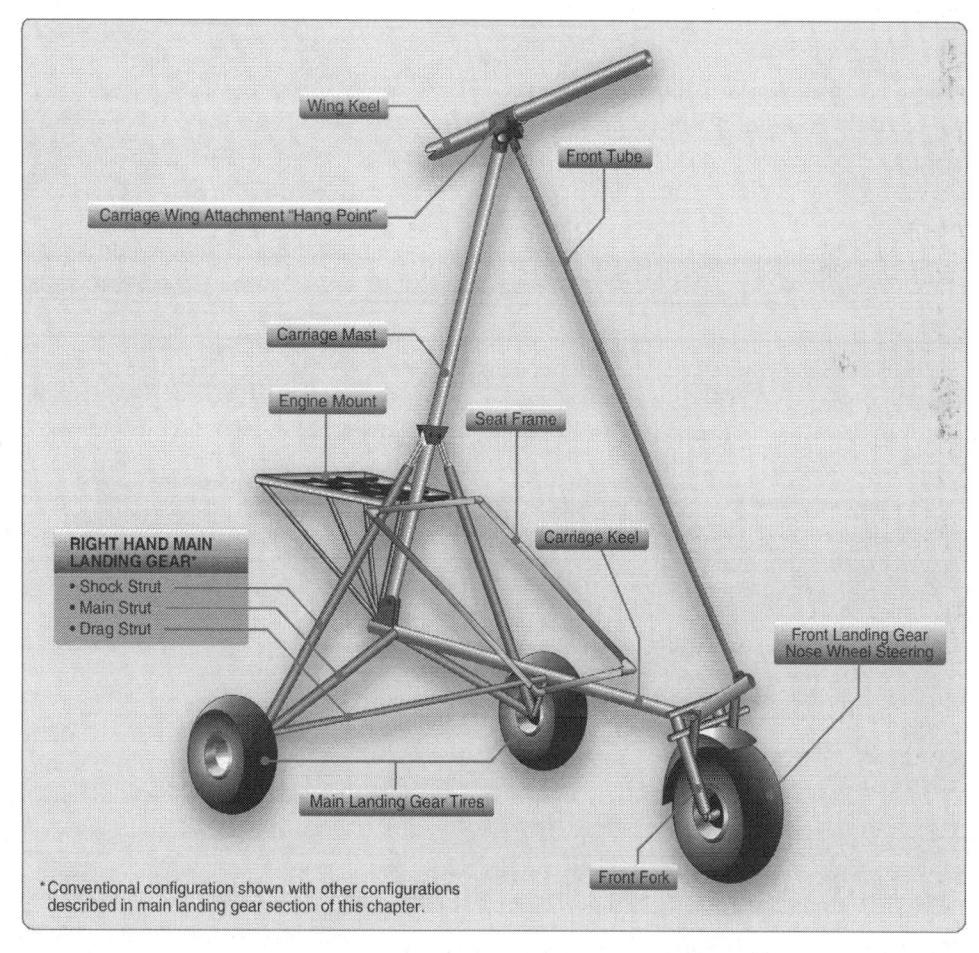

Figure 3-26. *Basic components of the carriage structure.*

3-11

The landing gear is made up of the front wheel, which has a lighter load and is used for steering, and the main or rear landing gear, which takes most of the load for the aircraft. *[Figure 3-26]* The front steering fork for the nosewheel has foot rests attached that the pilot uses for steering the WSC aircraft on the ground. Besides ground steering, the foot controls are similar to driving a car, left foot pedal is brakes on the ground only, and right foot is throttle and power on the ground and in flight. *[Figure 3-27]* The front fork typically has camber so it naturally tracks in the direction of travel similar to a motorcycle front fork.

Figure 3-27. *Large foot rests used for steering the aircraft on the ground (left hand ground brake shown).*

For training, a second steering control is installed with a connecting rod so the instructor can sit in back and steer the carriage on the ground using the nosewheel. *[Figure 3-28]* Steering dampers are sometimes used to stabilize the front wheel from shimmying at higher speeds during takeoff and landing. *[Figure 3-29]* The front wheel sometimes has shock absorbers or the tire itself can act as the shock absorber. The

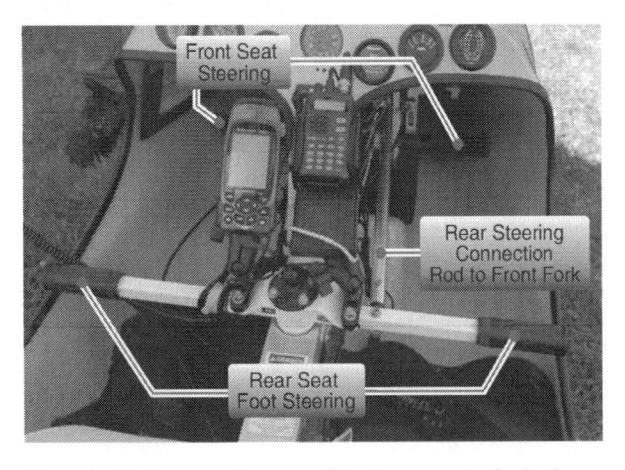

Figure 3-28. *Foot steering control for instructor in the back seat and connecting rod to front fork.*

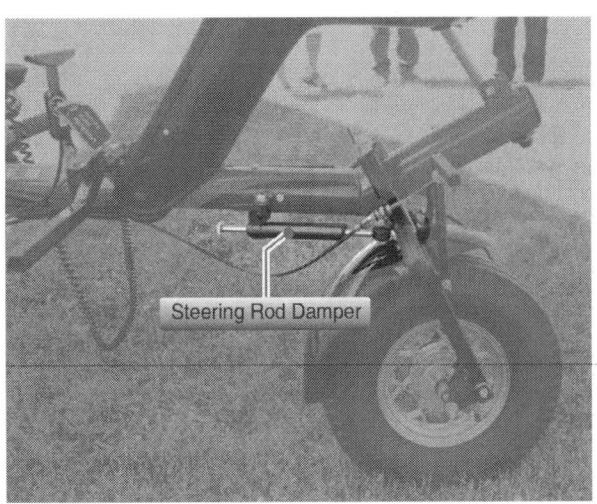

Figure 3-29. *Steering rod damper.*

front wheel typically has a disk or a drum brake, mechanical or hydraulic. *[Figures 3-30 and 3-31]* A front brake is lighter and simpler than rear brakes, but some carriage brake systems utilize the rear brakes.

Figure 3-30. *Mechanical drum brake system.*

A parking brake is extremely useful for securing the aircraft on the ground without needing chocks for securing the aircraft before takeoff and after landing. A number of parking brake systems are utilized by different manufacturers. *[Figure 3-32]*

The main landing gear is the two rear wheels of the WSC aircraft. Since the center of gravity (CG) is much closer to the rear wheels, most of the weight for the aircraft is carried on the rear wheels for taxi, takeoff, and landings.

There are a number of different configurations for the main gear. A conventional configuration has two separate systems for each rear wheel. Each side is two structural triangles, one

Figure 3-31. *Hydraulic disk brake system.*

Figure 3-32. *Mechanical parking brake system.*

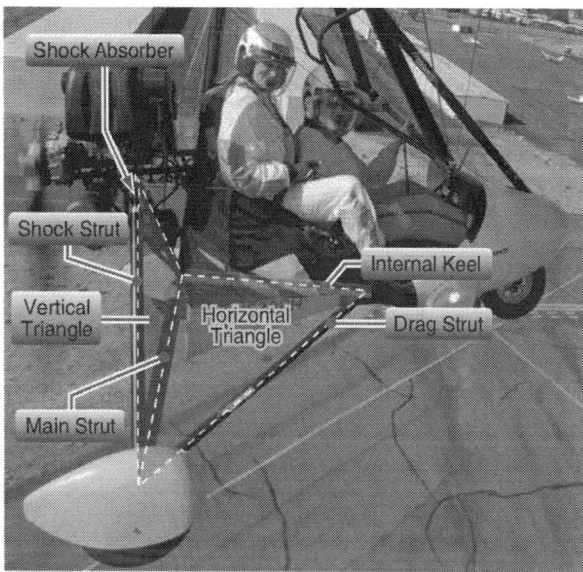

Figure 3-33. *Conventional landing gear configuration.*

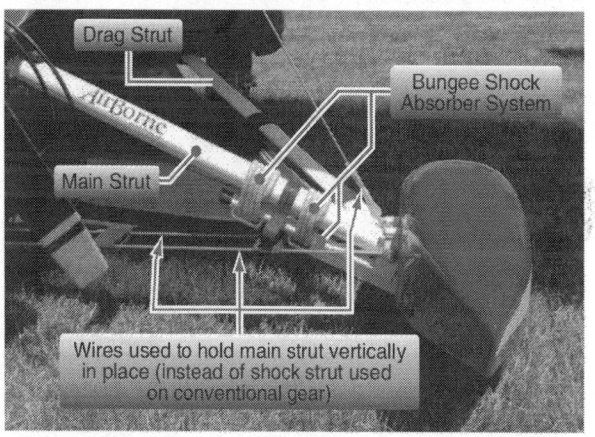

Figure 3-34. *Alternate vertical system utilizing streamlined wires and bungee cords.*

Figure 3-35. *Solid flexible main gear.*

horizontal and one vertical. The horizontal triangle consists of a drag strut from the wheel forward to the keel or forward structure to maintain the wheel's fore and aft position, and the main landing gear strut. Both the main and the drag struts can pivot about the attachment to the keel as part of the shock system.

The vertical triangle consists of the main landing strut and the shock strut attached to the wheel and up to the keel structure *[Figure 3-36]* or other structure such as the engine mount shown in *Figure 3-33*, which houses the compressed nitrogen and oil "oleo" shock absorber.

There are a number of other main landing gear configurations and shock absorbing systems such as wire bracing with bungee cord shocks *[Figure 3-34]*, fiberglass or flexible (fiberglass or steel) main gears with no struts *[Figure 3-35]*, and any variation of these. Carriages designed for faster speeds may have streamlined landing gear systems. *[Figures 3-36 and 3-37]*

3-13

Figure 3-36. *Conventional landing gear with streamlined drag and main struts.*

Figure 3-37. *Solid flexible main landing gear that is streamlined.*

As discussed in the nosewheel section, the carriage can have main landing gear brakes on both main landing gear wheels that can be drum or disk and controlled by mechanical or hydraulic actuation. Each manufacturer has different designs and options.

Tires can also assist as shock absorbers for landings. Large tundra tires add significant shock absorbing capability and are used for operations on soft fields, rough fields, and sand. *[Figure 3-38]* Generally, the faster WSC aircraft used for airport operations have narrower tires to eliminate drag.

Landing Gear for Water and Snow

Besides landing gear for land, there are landing gear systems for water (Weight-Shift Control Sea) and snow (ski-equipped). If ski-equipped, skis are added to the bottom of the wheels or replace the wheels. If sea-equipped, a complete system provides aircraft flotation and steering using rudders similar to a boat. The water rudders are foot controlled, similar to WSCL steering on the ground. Two types of sea-equipped systems are the flying boat and pontoon.

Figure 3-38. *WSC aircraft with large tundra tires for soft or rough field operations.*

The flying boat is a solid or inflatable boat that the WSC aircraft fits into, and its fuselage is secured to as well. *[Figure 3-39]* This is generally used for rougher seas in the ocean and, with the extra drag of the boat itself, this typically uses a larger wing and is therefore a slower flying WSC aircraft. The boat design is known to be more stable in rough seas and assists in keeping less water from splashing up so pilot and passenger stay dryer.

Figure 3-39. *Flying boat.*

The pontoon system is used for calmer water, has less drag while flying, and therefore can accommodate faster, smaller wings. *[Figure 3-40]* Both the flying boat and the pontoon system need more horsepower than land operations for two reasons: first, to provide enough thrust to accelerate to takeoff speed with the extra drag of the boat or pontoons on the water,

Figure 3-40. *Pontoon system.*

and second, to provide enough extra thrust to overcome the additional drag of the boat or pontoons in the air for flight.

Electrical Systems

WSC aircraft are typically equipped with a 12-volt direct current (DC) electrical system. A basic WSC aircraft electrical system consists of a magneto/generator, voltage regulator, battery, master/battery switch, and associated electrical wiring. Electrical energy stored in a battery provides a source of electrical power for starting the engine and other electrical loads for the WSC aircraft.

The electrical system is typically turned on or off with a master switch. Turning the master switch to the on position provides electrical energy from the battery to all the electrical equipment circuits with the exception of the ignition system. Equipment that commonly uses the electrical system energy includes:

- Position lights
- Anticollision lights
- Instrument lights
- Radio equipment
- Navigation equipment
- Electronic instrumentation
- Electric fuel pump
- Starting motor
- Electric heating systems (gloves, socks, pants, vests, jackets, etc.)

Fuses or circuit breakers are used in the electrical system to protect the circuits and equipment from electrical overload.

Spare fuses of the proper amperage should be carried in the WSC aircraft to replace defective or blown fuses. Circuit breakers have the same function as a fuse but can be manually reset, rather than replaced, if an overload condition occurs in the electrical system. Placards at the fuse or circuit breaker panel identify the circuit by name and show the amperage limit.

An ammeter may be used to monitor the performance of the electrical system. The ammeter shows if the magneto/generator is producing an adequate supply of electrical power. It also indicates whether or not the battery is receiving an electrical charge. A voltage meter also provides electrical information about battery voltage, an additional status of the electrical system.

Ballistic Parachute

An additional safety system available is a ballistic parachute system. In the case of a structural failure because of a mid-air collision or an engine out over hostile terrain such as a forest, the ballistic parachute provides an added safety system. The parachute is sized so that when used, the complete aircraft comes down under canopy. Details of ballistic parachute system use are covered in more detail in Chapter 13, Abnormal and Emergency Operations.

When the system is activated, a rocket shoots out, pulling the parachute system to full line stretch, and forcing the parachute out and away from the carriage and wing.

The preferred point of attachment for the parachute is on top of the wing at the hang point. This allows the WSC aircraft to descend level and land on the wheels, helping to absorb the shock. This requires routing from the chute to the top of the wing with "O" rings to be able to remove this routing to easily take the wing off the carriage. Alternate attach points where there is no routing to the top of the wing are the mast and engine attachment points; however, this has the WSC aircraft descending nose down when activated.

The ballistic parachute canister can be mounted in a number of locations on the WSC, typically on the carriage pointed sideways to avoid entanglement with the propeller. The actuation handle is mounted in the flight deck for pilot use when needed. *[Figures 3-41 and 3-42]*

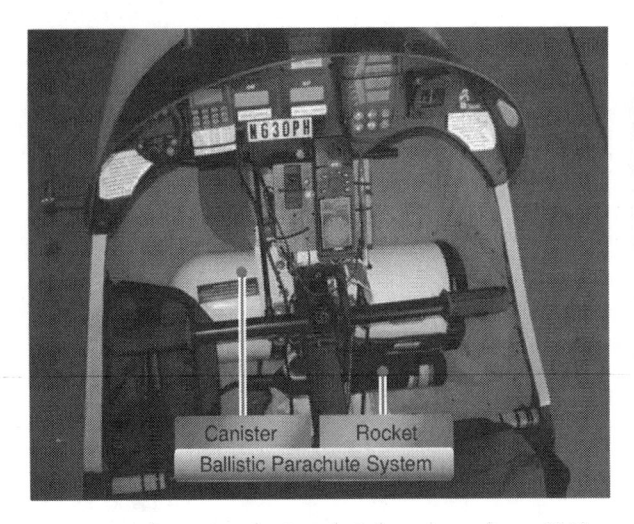

Figure 3-41. *Located under the pilot's legs, the canister will blow through the break-away panel in the cowling.*

Figure 3-42. *Canister mounted under engine.*

Flight Deck

The flight deck is where the pilot and passenger sit. It is typically a tandem seating with the pilot in front and the passenger in back. When the WSC aircraft is used for instruction, the instructor typically sits in back and must have access to the flight controls.

The pilot in the front has ground and flight controls. The right foot controls a foot throttle and the left foot controls the brake. This is similar to throttle and brake controls on an automobile. The feet also control ground steering by moving the front fork with the foot pedals. A foot throttle and foot brake can be added to optional ground steering control for use by an instructor sitting in back.

A hand cruise throttle is typically used when the pilot can set it and it stays set. This cruise throttle is usually in a position where the instructor in the back seat can also operate it. *[Figures 3-43]*

The wing flight control bar is in a position at chest height for the pilot in the front seat. Additional extensions are added for a passenger or instructor to use if seated in the back seat. *[Figure 3-7]*

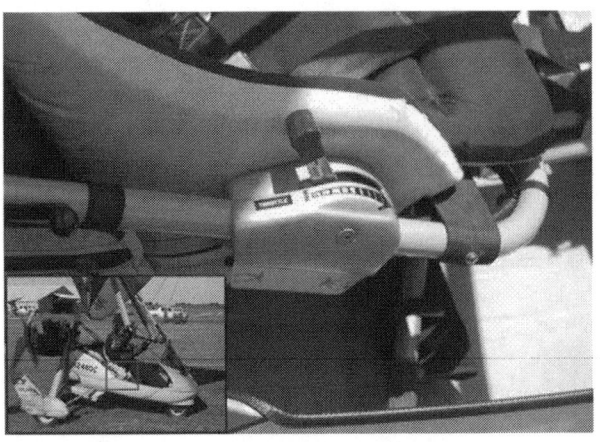

Figure 3-43. *Cruise throttle control and ignition switches.*

Ignition switches are sometimes included in the cruise control throttle housing or as a separate set of switches. If a WSC is used for instruction, the ignition switches should be within reach of the instructor sitting in the back seat. *[Figures 3-43]*

The ballistic parachute handle must be accessible for use when needed but not put in a position where it could be accidentally deployed. Some WSC aircraft have two handles, one for the front and one for the back. Additional controls for starting, such as the choke or enricher, must be accessible to the pilot.

Dashboards and Instrument Panels

The instrument panel is in front of the pilot and provides engine, flight, navigation, and communications information. The pilot is responsible for maintaining collision avoidance with a proper and continuous visual scan around the aircraft, as well as monitoring the information available from the instrument panel. The pilot must process the outside cues along with the instrumentation throughout the flight for a sound decision-making process.

The ignition switches, which may be located on the instrument panel or within the instructors reach for WSC used for instruction, has two positions: ON, which allows power to make contact with the spark plugs, or OFF, which is a closed switch to GROUND and removes the power source from the spark plugs. Typically, WSC engines have two spark plugs per cylinder, two switches, and two completely separate ignition systems. Some single-place WSCs with smaller engines have only one spark plug per cylinder, one ignition switch, and a single ignition system.

For example, for a two-stroke liquid-cooled engine, the manufacturer may require instrumentation to monitor engine exhaust gas temperatures (EGT), water temperatures, and revolutions per minute (rpm). Additionally, for a four-stroke engine, the manufacturer may additionally require oil temperature and pressure gauges. For a simple two-stroke air-cooled engine, the manufacturer's requirement may be EGT, cylinder head temperature (CHT) and rpm instrumentation. Generally, most electrical or engine controls are located on the dashboard unless required to be reached by the instructor for flight instruction.

Dashboards are as varied as the manufacturers and the purpose of the aircraft, from simple to complex. Classical analog gauges are common, but digital instruments are becoming more popular with light-sport aircraft (LSA).

Overall, no instrumentation is required for E-LSA, but for S-LSA an airspeed indicator is usually required, and engine manufacturers require certain instruments be installed on the aircraft to monitor the performance of the particular engine.

Flight Instruments

The specific theory of operation and details of instruments is covered in the Pilot's Handbook of Aeronautical Knowledge, and is a prerequisite to this section on flight instruments. The altimeter is the most important flight instrument and should be on every WSC aircraft. It is used to maintain the proper altitude at airports, during cruise, and provides other aircraft position information for the safety of all.

The vertical speed indicator (VSI) is one tool to assist the pilot with the performance of the aircraft. The airspeed indicator (ASI) is used to optimize performance of the aircraft, compare predicted to actual performance, and to operate within the limitations of the aircraft.

Navigation Instruments

A global positioning system (GPS) is typically used as a navigation and flight aid for most WSC aircraft. A magnetic compass is commonly used as a primary navigation system or as a backup when a GPS system is used.

Engine Instruments

There is a variety of engine instruments that are used. The most basic is the engine rpm, which determines the power of the engine. Specific engine instruments are discussed in the powerplant section.

Instrument Panel Arrangements

Instrument panels vary greatly from the basic to the complex. *Figure 3-44* depicts a standard instrument panel supplied by the manufacturer with a portable GPS added in the middle. Electrical components are neatly arranged along the top. Large analog airspeed (left) and altitude (right) flight instruments are installed in the middle with the portable GPS installed between the two. The bottom stack consists of the basic engine instruments for a simple two-stroke air-cooled engine: RPM for power (top), CHT (middle) and EGT (bottom).

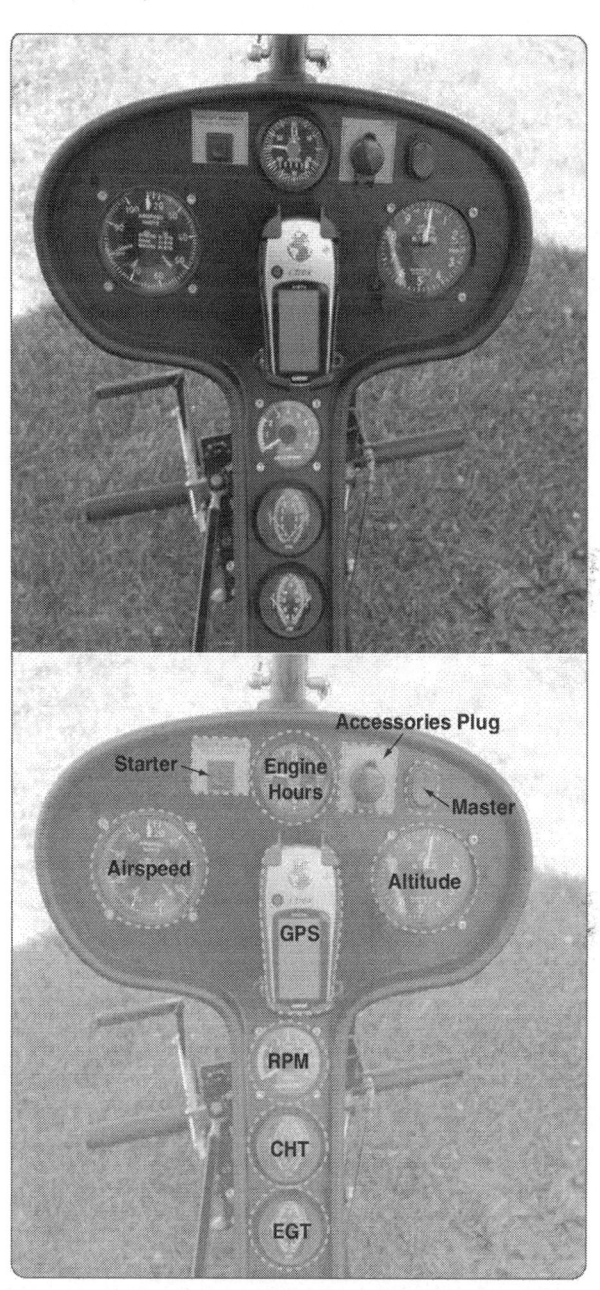

Figure 3-44. *Basic analog flight and engine instruments.*

A more advanced analog panel with a user radio and GPS added is shown in *Figure 3-45*. Airspeed, vertical speed indicator, and altitude large flight instruments are along

3-17

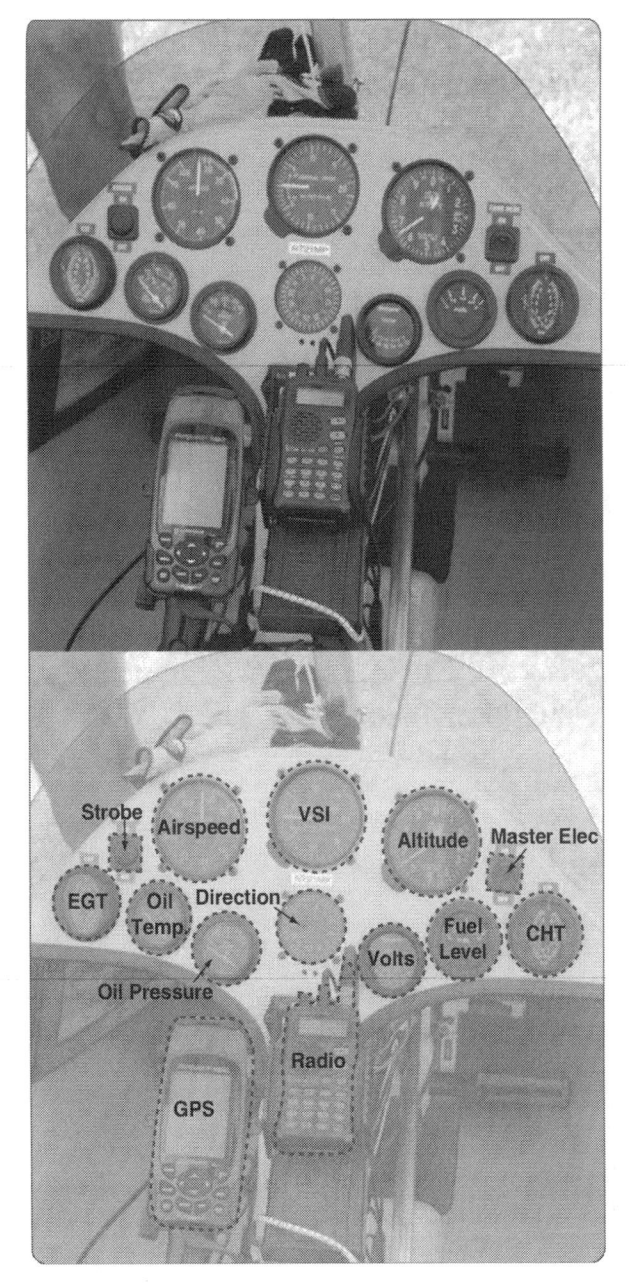

Figure 3-45. *Full analog instruments.*

the top. A navigational gyro is in the middle of the panel. The bottom row consists of four-stroke engine instruments, electrical and remote fuel gauge. The user installed radio and GPS complete a well equipped instrument panel. A hybrid panel of analog, digital, and portable instruments is shown in *Figure 3-46.*

The integrated digital panel does provide more options in a smaller space. One panel can now have aircraft performance screens, engine systems screens, navigation screens, communications screens, attitude indicator, and any combination of these. *[Figure 3-47]*

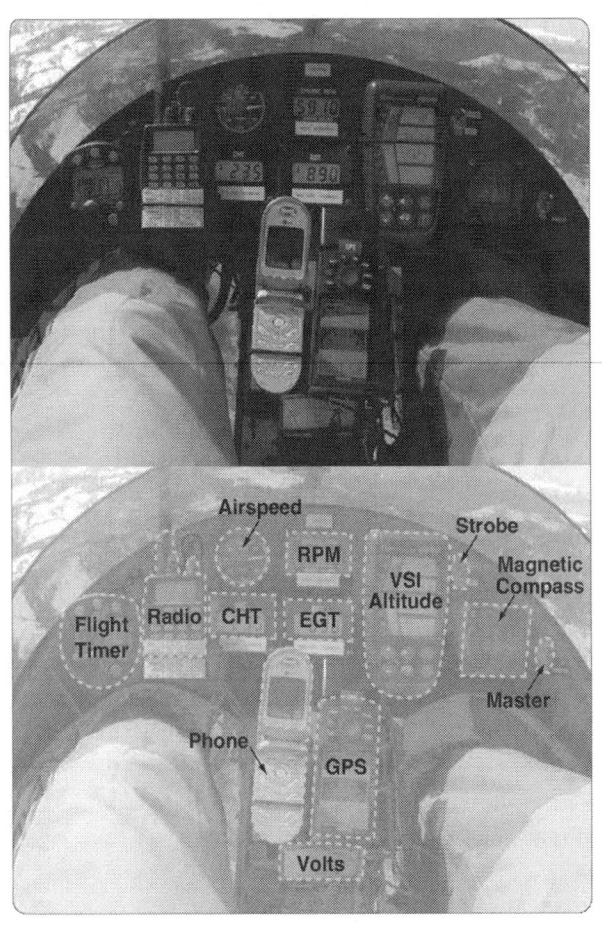

Figure 3-46. *Instrument hybrid—analog airspeed and compass indicator with separate digital instruments.*

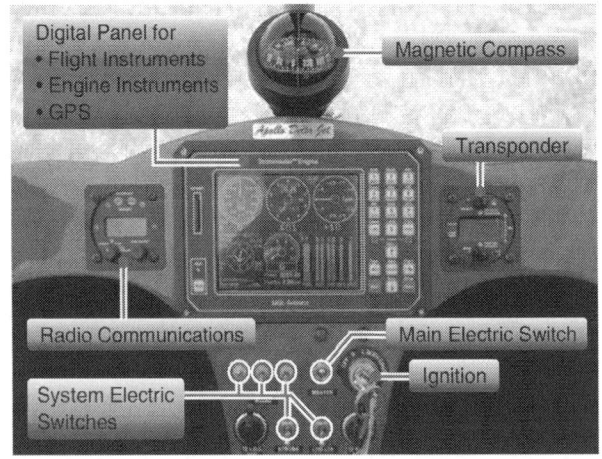

Figure 3-47. *Digital instrument panel.*

3-18

Communications

There are three types of communications systems used in WSC aircraft:

1. Communications between the pilot and passenger while inside the aircraft.
2. Aircraft radio communications with other aircraft and control towers.
3. Radar position indicator communications from the WSC aircraft to control towers (transponder).

Easy and clear communications between the pilot and passenger, or between the instructor and student inside the flight deck is important for the safety and enjoyment of both. Modern communications systems have advanced noise canceling systems in headphones and microphones to reduce engine noise and blast of air. Each system is unique, and the quality of the sound and noise canceling capability of the system varies. Some use voice-activated systems in which headphones activate only when someone is speaking into the microphone; others have a steady state in which there is no additional control of the voice activation. Since there is a large difference in systems available, it is best to test systems to determine what is best for the WSC aircraft being flown. *[Figure 3-48]*

An aircraft radio is required for flying in any tower controlled airspace. Using a radio is not required at airports without a control tower but it is recommended for the safety of self, passengers, pilots in the air, and people/property on the ground. To broadcast to a tower or other aircraft, press a Push To Talk (PTT) button. A complete flight deck radio and accessory system schematic is shown in *Figure 3-49*.

Figure 3-48. *Basic pilot-to-passenger communication system.*

A radar signal receiver/transmitter system is required at busy commercial airports (Classes C and B) and at altitudes above 10,000 feet mean sea level (MSL) (unless the aircraft was certified without an electrical system to power the unit). This is known as a Mode C transponder that sends a signal giving the control tower an exact location and altitude of aircraft. *[Figure 3-47]*

Powerplant System

The powerplant system is composed of the fuel system, engine, gearbox, and propeller. Here we will point out the basic components of these systems with their function and details covered in Chapter 4, Powerplant System.

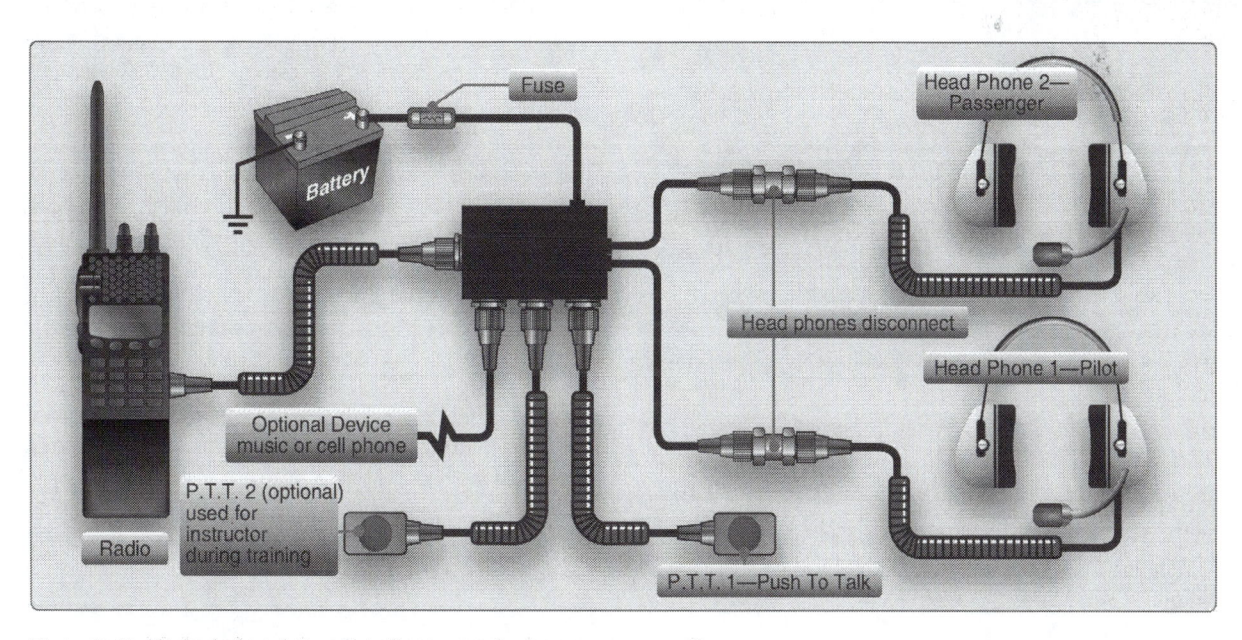

Figure 3-49. *Flight deck and aircraft radio communications system example.*

Fuel System Components

The WSC aircraft is equipped with fuel tanks usually ranging in capacity from 5 to 20 gallons. As with any aircraft, knowing how much fuel the tank holds is crucial to flight operations. The LSA definition has no limitations on the size of the fuel tank, unlike its ultralight vehicle predecessor.

Generally, the fuel tank is located close to the CG, so fuel burn does not affect the balance of the carriage. Some fuel tanks are clear for visual inspection of the amount of fuel on board *[Figure 3-50]*, while others have tanks that are not visible and require fuel level probes for instrument panel indication of fuel. *[Figure 3-51]*

Figure 3-50. *Fuel tank with visible fuel quantity.*

Figure 3-51. *Fuel fill to fuel tank under passengers seat.*

Fuel lines exit the fuel tank, and may incorporate a primer bulb, fuel filters, fuel pump, and/or a primer system, all of which must be integrated into the carriage. A fuel venting system is also required, which can be a hole in the fuel filler or lines running to vent at an appropriate location.

A fuel shut-off valve may be installed and can be located anywhere in the fuel line. Some designs have a fuel tank sump drain valve to remove water and solid contaminants.

Engine and Gearbox

The typical WSC aircraft engine can be two or four stroke, liquid or air cooled, and normally ranges from 50 to 100 horsepower. Some engines have electric starters and some have pull starters. Most WSC aircraft engines have reduction drives that, when attached, reduce the propeller rpm from ½ to ¼ the engine rpm. *[Figure 3-52]*

Figure 3-52. *Engine gearbox.*

A significant amount of the total aircraft empty weight is determined by the powerplant (engine, gearbox, and propeller) and mounting configuration. When trailering the WSC aircraft over bumpy terrain or over long trips, the bouncing of the carriage in the trailer can put extreme stress on this mounting system. In addition, repeated hard landings of the carriage can also stress the welds of the engine mount. Consistent detailed inspections of the engine mount should be an important part of every preflight and postflight inspection.

The powerplant systems are as varied as the WSC aircraft they power. Modern technology has allowed these systems to become lighter, quieter, more efficient, and, most importantly, dependable.

The Propeller

Propellers are "power converters" that change the engine horsepower into thrust. Thrust is the force that propels the aircraft through the air by pushing the WSC aircraft forward. Aerodynamically speaking, a propeller is a rotating airfoil and the same principles that apply to the wing applies to the propeller, except the propeller provides a horizontal force of thrust.

Figure 3-53. *Four-blade propeller.*

Propellers typically consist of two, three, or four blades. *[Figures 3-53 and 3-54]* Propellers can be ground adjustable or fixed pitch. Variable pitch flight propellers are not allowed on LSA. The pitch should be properly set for your WSC aircraft to provide the recommended rpm of the engine at full power. The POH should be consulted if there is any question about the propeller rpm and adjusting or replacing the propeller. Propellers are specifically matched to the engine power, gear reduction and speed range of the aircraft. Therefore, not just any propeller may be put on any engine. The POH requires specific propellers that are matched for each aircraft.

As with an airplane propeller, the WSC aircraft propeller turns at such high speeds that it becomes invisible when in motion. The dangers of a turning propeller require every pilot to maintain the highest level of safety and respect for the consequences of body parts, pets, and debris coming

Figure 3-54. *Three-blade propeller.*

in contact with a rotating propeller. Debris on the takeoff/landing field is a danger to the propeller, as well as to the people who may be in the prop-wash area behind or on the side of the propeller. Stones, small pieces of metal, and sticks can become dangerous projectiles if kicked into the propeller during start-up, taxi, takeoff, and landing. Just as with any airframe or wing component of a WSC aircraft, if the propeller becomes damaged, nicked, or dinged, the aircraft's performance can be greatly affected. Some pilots elect to use tape or rock deflector guards to protect the leading edge from rock/debris damage. Regardless, taking proper care of the propeller is as critical as proper engine and wing care.

Chapter Summary

Components and systems consist of two primary subassemblies: wing and carriage. The main wing component is the frame, which is composed of the leading edges, keel, crossbar, and control frame. The typical wing frame has lower wires and upper wires with a king post. The strutted version has wing struts and no upper rigging. The frame is designed so the outboard leading edges flex, and it also has a control system that allows the keel to move side to side relative to the leading edges for roll control. The sail is designed specifically for the frame with battens and leading edge stiffner provide the rigid airfoil shape of the sail.

The carriage is separate from the wing. Different wings can be put on the same carriage at separate times for different types of flying (example: large wing is used for flying low and slow where a small wing can be used for flying fast and long cross-country missions). As discussed in Chapter 2, Aerodynamics, each wing must be approved by the manufacturer to go on a specific carriage.

Main carriage components are the mast, carriage keel, front tube, and engine mount. This structure houses the flight deck, powerplant, and landing gear. The carriage structure also houses system components such as the electrical system, ballistic parachute, and fuel tank. The flight deck is the heart of the carriage providing pilot systems for communications, navigation, engine/flight/navigation instruments, and electrical controls.

Chapter 4
Powerplants

Introduction

This chapter covers the engines found on most weight-shift control (WSC) aircraft and includes the exhaust, ignition, lubrication, cooling, propeller, gearbox, induction, charging, and fuel systems. Reciprocating engine operating theory is covered for both two-stroke and four-stroke engines. The WSC engine and propeller, often referred to as a powerplant, work in combination to produce thrust. The powerplant propels the aircraft and charges the electrical system that supports WSC operation.

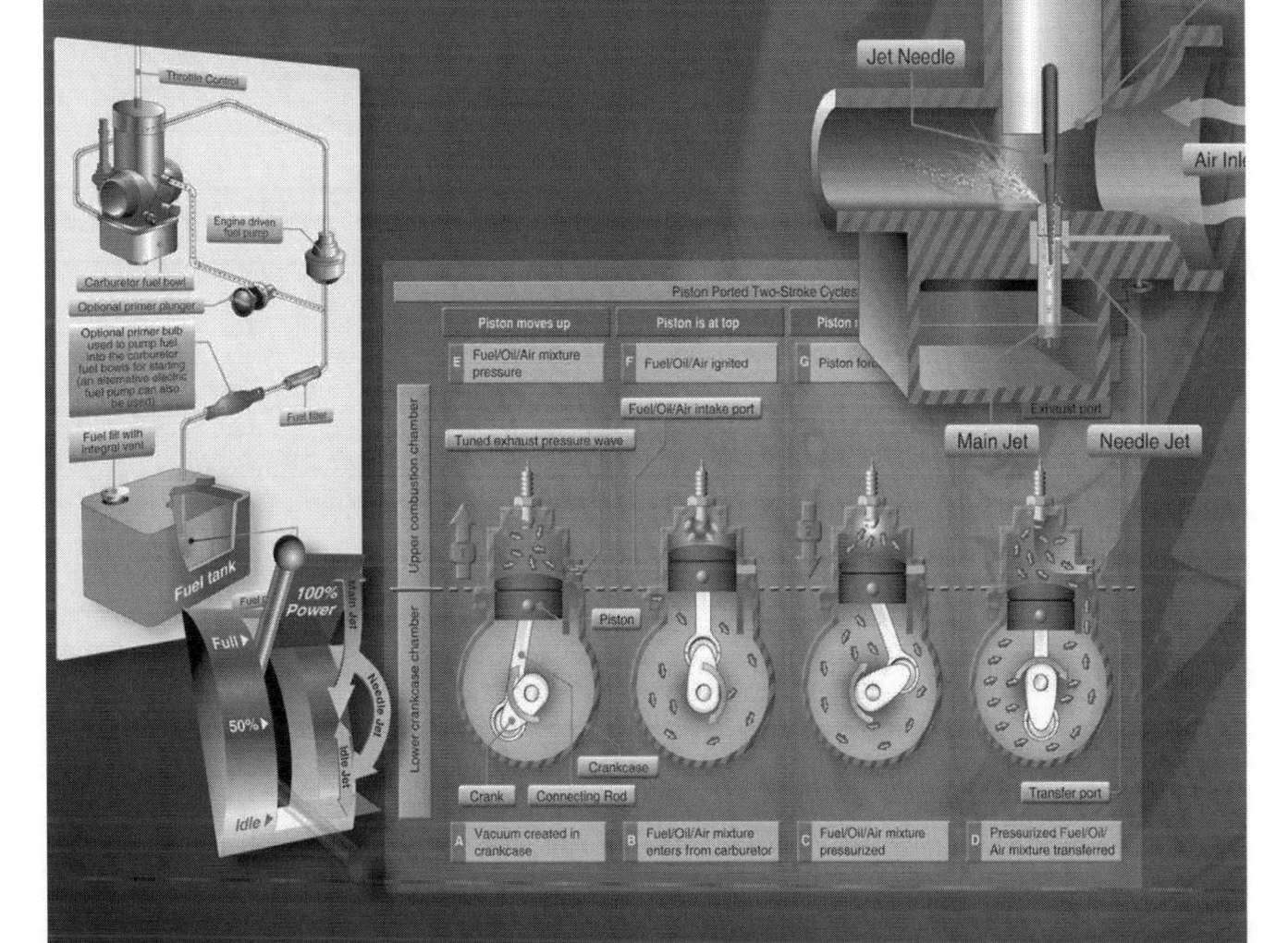

The powerplant system is composed of the engine, gearbox, and propeller. It is a key component of a WSC aircraft and should be maintained according to both the engine and airframe manufacturer recommendations.

Preflight information, along with maintenance schedules and procedures, can be found in the pilot's operating handbook (POH) for Special Light-Sport Aircraft (S-LSA), and/or maintenance references from the manufacturers. Engine inspections and maintenance must be performed and documented in a logbook. A pilot should review this logbook before flying an unfamiliar aircraft.

Reciprocating Engines

WSC aircraft are designed with reciprocating engines. *[Figures 4-1* through *4-3]* Two common means of classifying reciprocating engines are the:

1. Number of piston strokes needed to complete a cycle—two or four.
2. Method of cooling—liquid or air.

Refer to the Pilot's Handbook of Aeronautical Knowledge for a comprehensive review of how reciprocating four-stroke engines operate.

Two-Stroke Engines

Two-stroke engines are commonly used in WSC aircraft. Two-stroke aviation engines evolved from two-stroke snowmobile and watercraft engines, the difference being that an aircraft engine is optimized for reliability with dual ignition often installed for each cylinder. Two-stroke engines are popular because they have fewer components than four-stroke engines which makes them less expensive to manufacture and lighter, thus increasing the power-to-weight ratio.

Two-stroke engines require that oil be mixed into the fuel to lubricate the engine, instead of being held in a sump and requiring a separate pressurized recirculating system like that of a four-stroke engine. Details on two-stroke oil mixing are covered in the lubrication section. One stroke as the piston moves up is intake and compression, while the second stroke as the piston moves down is power and exhaust. The two-

Figure 4-1. *Two-stroke air-cooled engine.*

Figure 4-2. *Two-stroke water-cooled engine.*

Figure 4-3. *Four-stroke water- and oil-cooled engine.*

4-3

stroke engine performs the same functions as a four-stroke engine in half the number of strokes.

A wide range of valve systems are found on two-stroke engines for the purpose of opening and closing ports in the cylinder to let fuel in and exhaust out at the proper time. This is similar to the intake and exhaust valves on a four-stroke engine. One-way pressure valves, called spring, reed, or poppet valves, open when the pressure drops within the crankcase, pulling the fuel from the carburetor into the crankcase. *[Figure 4-4]*

Mechanical rotary valves are driven off the engine, rotate to provide an opening at the precise time, and can be on the intake and exhaust ports. *[Figure 4-5]*

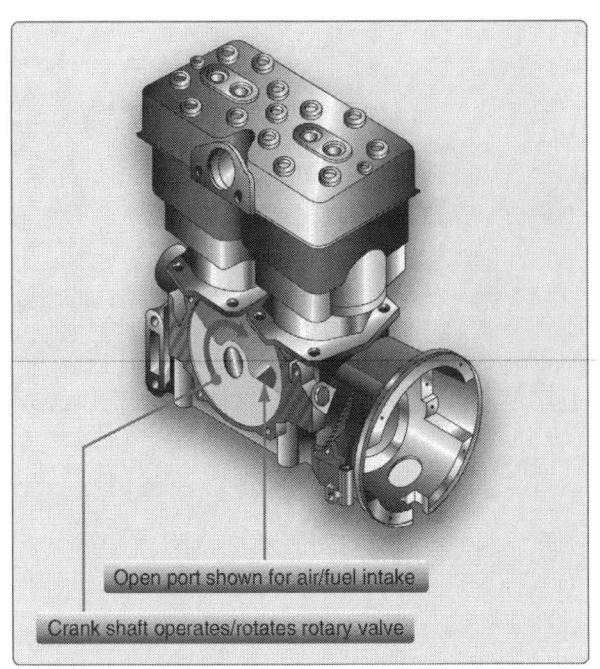

Figure 4-5. *Intake rotary valve for a two-stroke engine.*

Piston porting does not use any valves. The fuel inlet port is opened and closed by the piston position as it moves up and down in the cylinder. This is called a "piston ported inlet" and is used in the two-stroke process description that follows.

Two-Stroke Process

The two-stroke process begins with the fuel entering the engine and concludes as it exits as exhaust.

Crankcase Vacuum Intake Stroke—Piston Moving Up

The upward stroke of the piston *[Figure 4-6A]* creates a vacuum in the crankcase and pulls the fuel/air/oil mixture into the crankcase through the intake valve system from the carburetor. *[Figure 4-6B]* This can be a pressure-actuated reed valve, a rotary valve, or a ported inlet system where the lower piston skirt provides an opening for the fuel/air/oil mixture to flow in when the piston is reaching its highest point of top dead center (TDC). At this point, the greatest portion of the fuel/oil/air mixture has filled the crankcase. *[Figure 4-6B]*

Crankcase Compression Stroke—Piston Moving Down

During the downward stroke, the pressure valve is forcibly closed by the increased crankcase pressure, the mechanical rotary valve closes, or the piston closes off the fuel/air oil mixture intake port as shown. The fuel/oil/air mixture is then compressed in the crankcase during the downward stroke of the piston. *[Figures 4-6B to 4-6D]*

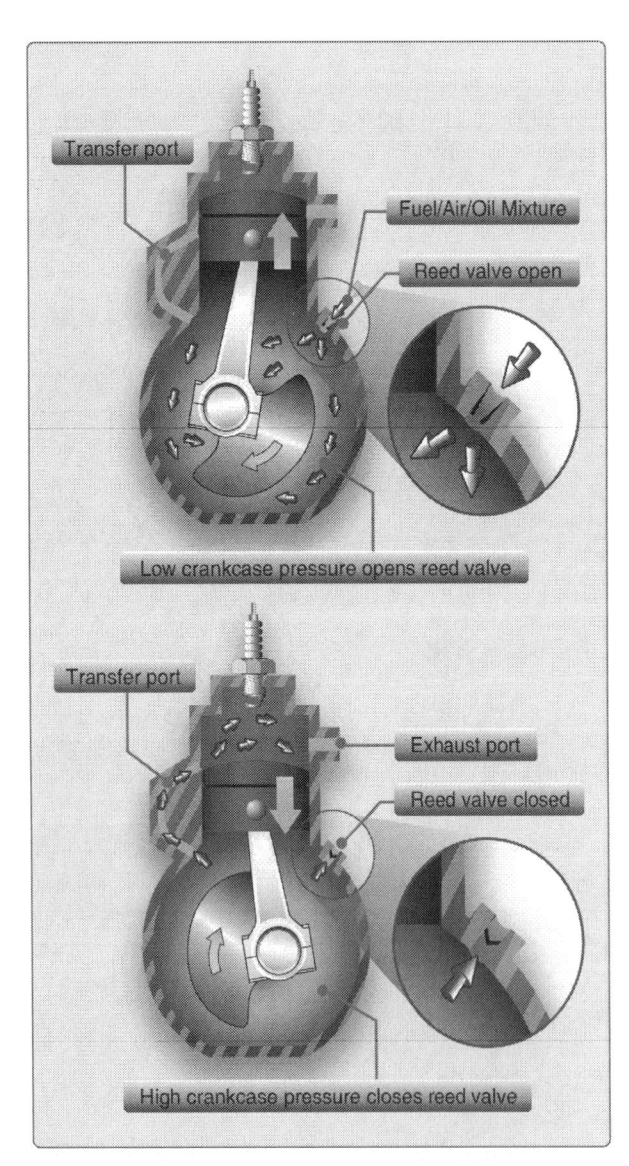

Figure 4-4. *Reed valve is open with low pressure and closes when the pressure increases in a two-stroke engine.*

4-4

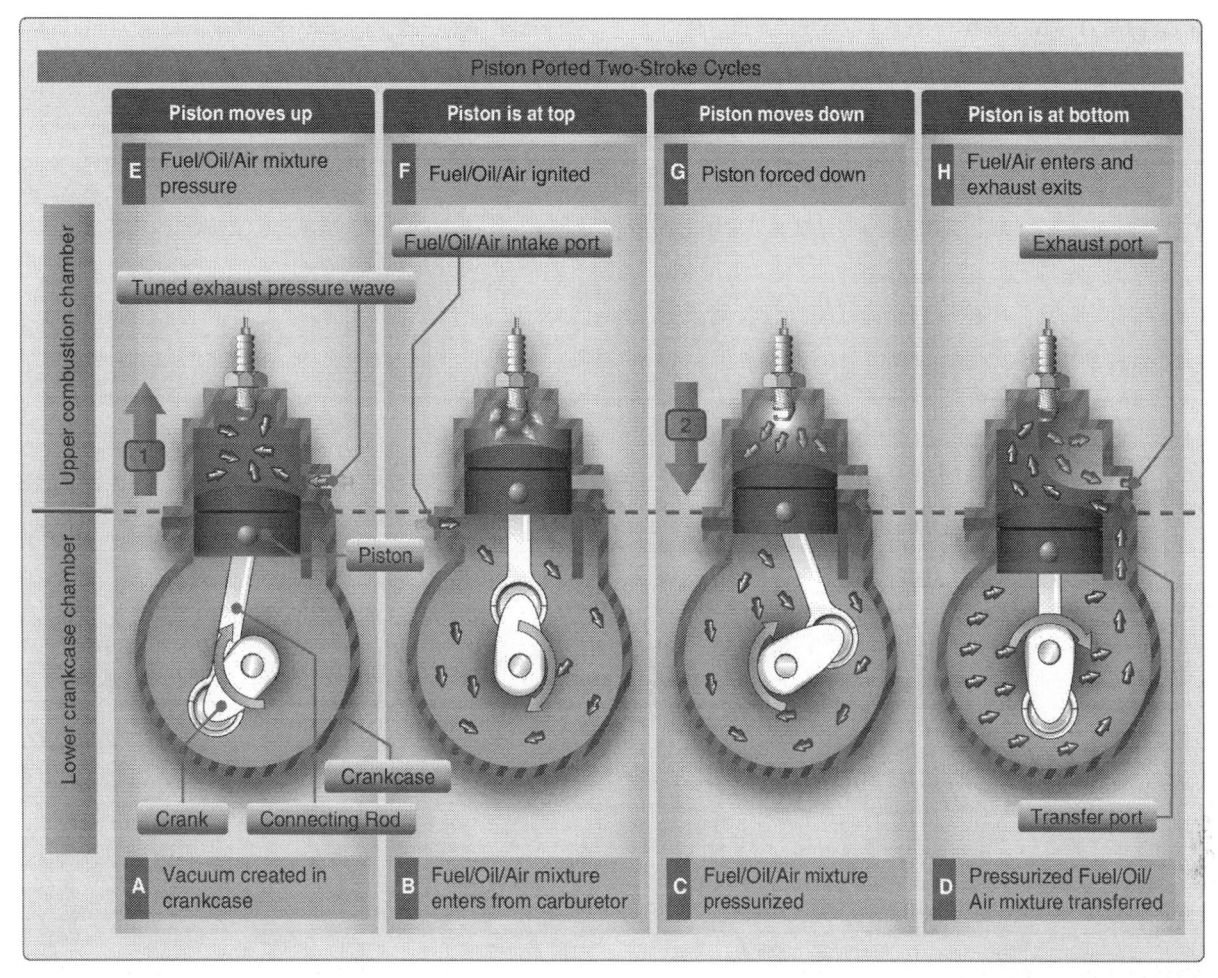

Figure 4-6. *Piston ported inlet cycles for a two-stroke engine.*

Crankcase Transfer/Exhaust—Piston at Lowest

When the piston is near the bottom of its stroke, the transfer port opening from the crankcase to the combustion chamber is exposed, and the high pressure fuel/air mixture in the crankcase transfers around the piston into the main cylinder. This fresh fuel/oil/air mixture pushes out the exhaust (called scavenging) as the piston is at its lowest point and the exhaust port is open. Some of the fresh fuel/oil/air mixture can escape through the exhaust port, resulting in the higher fuel use of the two-stroke engine. *[Figure 4-6D]*

Cylinder Start of Compression Stroke—Piston Initially Moving Up

As the piston starts to move up, covering the transfer port, the tuned exhaust bounces a pressure wave at the precise time across the exhaust port to minimize the fuel/air/oil mixture escaping through the exhaust port. *[Figure 4-6E]*

Cylinder Compression Stroke—Piston Moving Up

The piston then rises and compresses the fuel mixture in the combustion chamber. *[Figure 4-6E to 4-6F]* During this piston compression process, the crankcase vacuum intake process is happening simultaneously, as described earlier. This is why four processes can happen in two strokes. *[Figures 4-6B and 4-6C]*

Cylinder Power Stroke—Initial Piston Moving Down

At the top of the stroke, the spark plug ignites the fuel/oil/air mixture and drives the piston down as the power stroke of the engine. *[Figures 4-6F and 4-6G]*

Cylinder Power Stroke—Final Piston Moving Down

As the piston passes the exhaust port, the exhaust exits the combustion chamber. As the piston continues down, the transfer port opens and the swirling motion of the fuel/oil/air mixture pushes the exhaust out of the exhaust port. *[Figures 4-6H]*

Piston Reverses Direction From Down Stroke to Up Stroke

As the piston reverses direction from the down stroke to the up stroke, the process is complete. *[Figures 4-6H and 4-6A]*

Four-Stroke Engines

Four-stroke engines are very common in most aircraft categories and are becoming more common in WSC aircraft. *[Figure 4-7]* Four-stroke engines have a number of advantages, including reliability, fuel economy, longer engine life, and higher horsepower ranges.

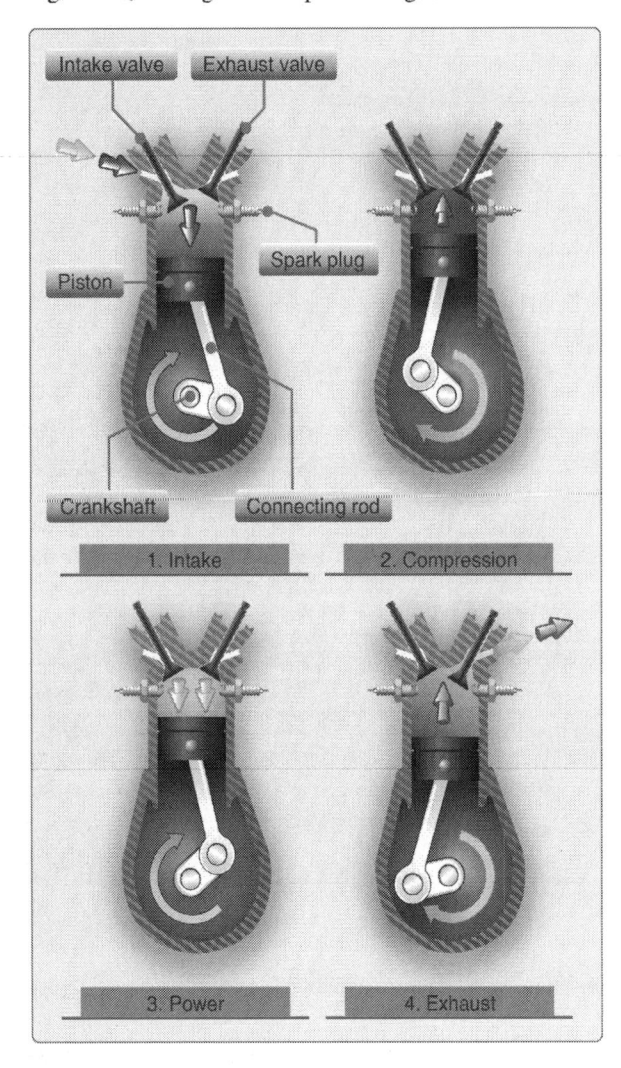

Figure 4-7. *The cycles in a four-stroke engine.*

These advantages are countered by a higher acquisition cost, lower power-to-weight ratios, and a higher overall weight. The increased weight and cost are the result of additional components (e.g., camshaft, valves, complex head to house the valve train) incorporated in a four-stoke engine.

Exhaust Systems

Engine exhaust systems vent the burned combustion gases overboard, reduce engine noise, and (in the case of two-stroke engines) help keep the fresh fuel/oil/air mixture in the cylinders. An exhaust system has exhaust piping attached to the cylinders, as well as a muffler. The exhaust gases are pushed out of the cylinder and through the exhaust pipe system to the atmosphere.

Some exhaust systems have an exhaust gas temperature probe. This probe transmits an electric signal to an instrument in front of the pilot. This instrument reads the signal and provides the exhaust gas temperature (EGT) of the gases at the exhaust manifold. This temperature varies with power and with the mixture (ratio of fuel to air entering the cylinders), and is used to make sure the fuel/air mixture is within specifications. When there is a problem with carburetion, the EGT gauge will normally be the first notification for a pilot. *[Figure 4-8]*

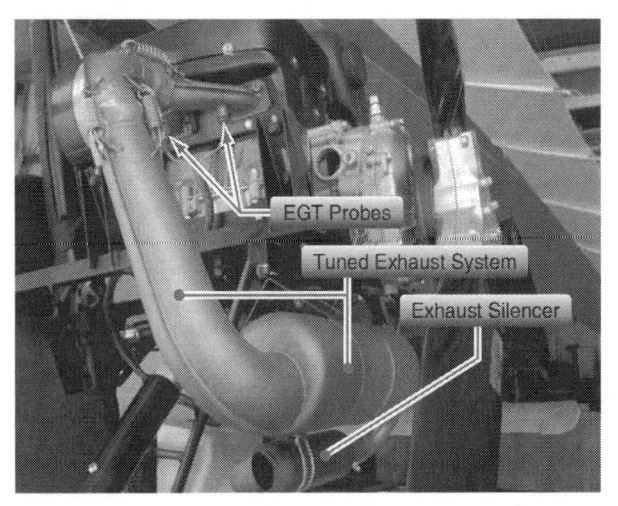

Figure 4-8. *Two-stroke tuned exhaust system with EGT probes installed where the exhaust enters the exhaust system.*

Two-Stroke Tuned Exhaust Systems

In two-stroke engines, the exhaust system increases the fuel economy and power of the engine. The two-stroke exhaust system is an integral part of any two-stroke engine design, often controlling peak power output, the torque curve, and even the revolutions per minute (RPM) limit of the engine.

The exhaust system must be tuned to produce a back pressure wave at the exhaust port to act as an exhaust valve as shown in *Figure 4-6E*. When hot spent gases are vented out of the exhaust port, they are moving fast enough to set up a high pressure wave. The momentum of that wave down the exhaust pipe diffuser lowers the pressure behind it. That low pressure is used to help suck out all of the residual, hot, burnt gas from the power stroke and at the same time help pull a fresh fuel/air charge into the cylinder. This is called scavenging and is an important function of a tuned two-stroke exhaust system. *[Figure 4-6H]*

The design of the exhaust converging section causes a returning pressure wave to push the fresh fuel/air charge back into the exhaust port before the cylinder closes off that port. Called pulse charging, it is another important function of the exhaust system. *[Figure 4-6E]*

Tuned exhaust systems are typically tuned to a particular rpm range. The more a certain rpm range is emphasized, the less effective the engine will operate at other rpm. Vehicles like motorcycles take advantage of this with the use of transmissions. Motorcycle exhaust pipe builders can optimize a certain rpm range and then the driver shifts gears to stay in that range. Aircraft, with no transmission, do not have this ability. On an aircraft, an exhaust pipe has to be designed to operate over a broad range of rpm from idle to full speed, a reason that simply putting a snowmobile engine on a WSC does not work well.

Overall, the two-stroke exhaust system for a WSC aircraft is a specific design and must be matched to the engine to operate properly and obtain the rated power. It also reduces noise and directs the exhaust to an appropriate location. Exhaust silencers can be added to reduce noise, but additional weight, cost, and slight power reduction are the byproducts.

Four-Stroke Engine Exhaust Systems
Four-stroke engines are not as sensitive as two-stroke engines because they have exhaust valves and, therefore, do not need the precision pulse tuned exhaust system. However, directing the exhaust out appropriately and reducing the noise are important considerations. Again, using the manufacturer's recommended configurations is required for S-LSA and recommended for Experimental Light-Sport Aircraft (E-LSA).

Engine Warming
Two-Stroke Engine Warming
Two-stroke engines must be warmed because different metals expand at different rates as they are heated. When heating steel and aluminum, the aluminum parts expand faster than the steel parts. This becomes a problem in two different areas of many two-stroke engines. The first place is in the cylinders of the engine.

The cylinders have steel walls that expand slowly, compared to aluminum pistons that expand quickly. If an engine is revved too quickly during takeoff before warming up, a lot of heat is generated on top of the piston. This quickly expands the piston, which can then seize in the cylinder. A piston seizure will stop the engine abruptly.

The second area of concern is lower in the engine around the crankshaft. This is an area where parts may get too loose with heat, rather than seizing up. Additionally, the crankcase has steel bearings set into the aluminum which need to expand together or the bearings could slip. Many two-stroke engines have steel bearings that normally hug the walls of the aluminum engine case. The crank spins within the donuts of those steel bearings.

If the engine heats too quickly, the aluminum case out-expands those steel bearings and the crank causes the bearings to start spinning along with it. If those steel bearings start spinning, it can ruin the soft aluminum walls of the case, which is very expensive. If heat is slowly added to an engine, all parts will expand more evenly. This is done through a proper warm-up procedure. Many two-stroke engines are best warmed up by running the engine at a set rpm for a set amount of time. Follow the instructions in the POH; however, a good rule of thumb is to start the engine initially at idle rpm, get it operating smoothly at 2,500 rpm for 2 minutes for initial warm up, and then warm the engine at 3,000 rpm for 5 minutes. The cylinder head temperature or coolant temperature must be up to the manufacturer's recommended temperatures before takeoff. This may require running the engine at higher rpm to reach required temperatures on some engines.

Once the engine is warmed up and the aircraft is flying, it is still possible to cool down the engine too much. This happens when the engine is idled back for an extended period of time. Even though the engine is running, it is not generating as much heat as the cooling system is efficiently dumping engine heat into the atmosphere. An immediate power application with a cooled engine can seize the engine just as if the engine had not been warmed in the first place.

In water-cooled engines, on a long descent at idle, the coolant cools until the thermostat closes and the engine is not circulating the radiator fluid through the engine. The engine temperature remains at this thermostat closed temperature while the radiator coolant continues to cool further. If full throttle is applied, the thermostat can open, allowing a blast of coolant into the warm engine. The piston is expanding due to the added heat, and the cylinder is cooling with the cold radiator water, resulting in piston seizure. To prevent this, slowly add power well before getting close to the ground where power is needed. This gives the system a chance to open the thermostat gradually and warm up the radiator water.

Just as it takes time for the engine crankcase and bearings to warm up, it also takes those steel parts a long time to cool down. If a pilot lands, refuels, and wants to take off again quickly, there is no need to warm up again for 5 minutes. The lower end of the engine stays warmed up after being shut down for short periods.

Any engine restart is an example in which it would be appropriate to warm the engine up until the gauges reach operating temperatures. The lower end of the engine is warm and now a pilot needs to be concerned only with preventing the pistons from seizing.

Four-Stroke Engine Warming

A four-stroke engine must also be warmed up. The four-stroke engine has a pressurized oil system that provides more uniform engine temperatures to all of its components. Takeoff power can be applied as soon as the water, cylinder head temperature (CHT), oil temperatures, and oil pressure are within the manufacturer's recommended tolerances for takeoff power applications.

Gearboxes

Gearboxes are used on most WSC reciprocating engines to take the rotational output of an internal combustion engine which is turning at a high rpm and convert it to a slower (and more useful) rpm to turn the propeller. Gearboxes come in different gear ratios depending on the output speed of the engine and the needed propeller turning speeds.

Some examples are a two-stroke rpm reduction from 6,500 engine rpm with a 3.47 to 1 reduction, resulting in 1,873 propeller rpm. A four-stroke rpm reduction could be from 5,500 engine rpm with a 2.43 to 1 reduction, resulting in 2,263 propeller rpm. A gearbox is a simple device that bolts directly to the engine and, in turn, has the propeller bolted directly to it.

A two-cycle engine gearbox is kept lubricated with its own built-in reservoir of heavy gearbox oil. The reservoir is actually part of the gearbox case itself. The gearbox oil has to be changed periodically since the meshing of the gears will cause them to wear and will deposit steel filings into the oil. If the oil is not changed, the abrasive filings cause even more wear.

Some gearboxes have a built-in electric starter motor. When activated, the motor turns the gearing which cranks the engine.

Four-stroke propeller reduction gearboxes use oil from the engine oil system for lubrication.

Some gearboxes come with a built-in centrifugal clutch and others have allowances for installation. A centrifugal clutch is very useful in a two-stroke engine because it allows the engine to idle at a lower speed without the load of the propeller. Otherwise, two-stroke engines can generate a great deal of vibration at low rpm when loaded. As the engine speeds up, the centrifugal clutch engages and smoothly starts the propeller spinning. When the engine is brought back to idle, the clutch disengages and allows the engine to idle smoothly again; the propeller stops when on the ground and windmills when flying.

Propeller

The propeller provides the necessary thrust to push the WSC aircraft through the air. The engine power is used to rotate the propeller, which generates thrust very similar to the manner in which a wing produces lift. The amount of thrust produced depends on the airfoil shape, the propeller blade angle of attack (AOA), and the engine rpm. *[Figure 4-9]* Light-sport aircraft (LSA) are equipped with either a fixed-pitch or a ground adjustable-pitch propeller.

Figure 4-9. *Engine rpm is indicated on the analog gauge (top) and the digital gauge (bottom).*

Fixed-Pitch Propeller

The pitch of the fixed-pitch propeller is set by the manufacturer and cannot be changed. Refer to the Pilot's Handbook of Aeronautical Knowledge for basic propeller principles.

Ground Adjustable-Pitch Propeller

Adjustable-pitch propellers for WSC aircraft can be adjusted only on the ground with hand tools. If an engine is over-revving, more pitch can be added to the propeller. If the engine is not developing the full recommended rpm during flight, then some pitch can be taken out of the blades. This should be done according to the WSC aircraft's POH and by a qualified technician.

Induction Systems

The induction system brings air in from the atmosphere, mixes it with fuel, and delivers the fuel/air mixture (fuel/oil/air mixture for two stroke engines) to the engine intake and to the cylinders where combustion occurs. Outside air enters the induction system through an air filter on the engine. The air filter inhibits the entry of dust and other foreign objects. Two types of induction systems are used in WSC engines:

1. The carburetor system is most common. It mixes the fuel and air in the carburetor before this mixture enters the engine intake.

2. The fuel injection system injects the fuel into the air just before entry into each cylinder.

Carburetor Systems

WSC aircraft use float-type carburetors. The "float-type carburetor" acquires its name from a float that rests on fuel within the carburetor float chamber, commonly known as the fuel bowls. The float maintains the fuel level in the fuel bowls. As fuel is used by the engine, the fuel and float levels drop, opening the valve letting more fuel into the fuel bowls until the proper level of fuel in the fuel bowls is achieved and the valve is closed. Reference the Pilot's Handbook of Aeronautical Knowledge for basic information on float carburetor operation. Modern two- and four-stroke carburetors operate with three separate jetting systems depending on engine power. *[Figure 4-10]*

When the throttle is closed for engine idling, the throttle valve is closed and the fuel/air mixture is supplied through the idle (pilot) jet and idle (pilot) air passage. The fuel/air mixture is supplied to the cylinders through the bypass hole. *[Figure 4-11]*

As the throttle is advanced and the throttle valve is raised, the fuel is sucked up through the main jet but is controlled by the opening and taper of the jet needle and needle jet. This is effective throughout most of the midrange operation. About half throttle, the main jet size starts to influence the amount of fuel mixed with the air and this effect continues until it is the main influence at the highest throttle settings. *[Figures 4-10 and 4-12]*

Figure 4-10. *Throttle position and jetting system used.*

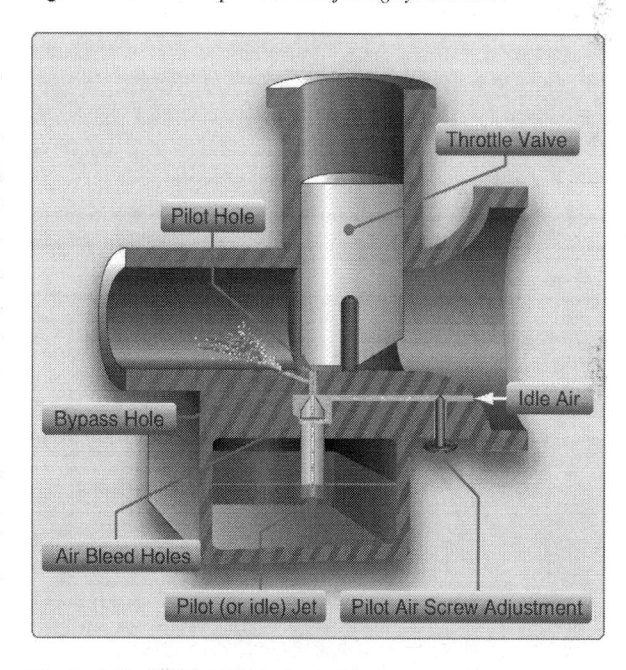

Figure 4-11. *Pilot or idle jet system.*

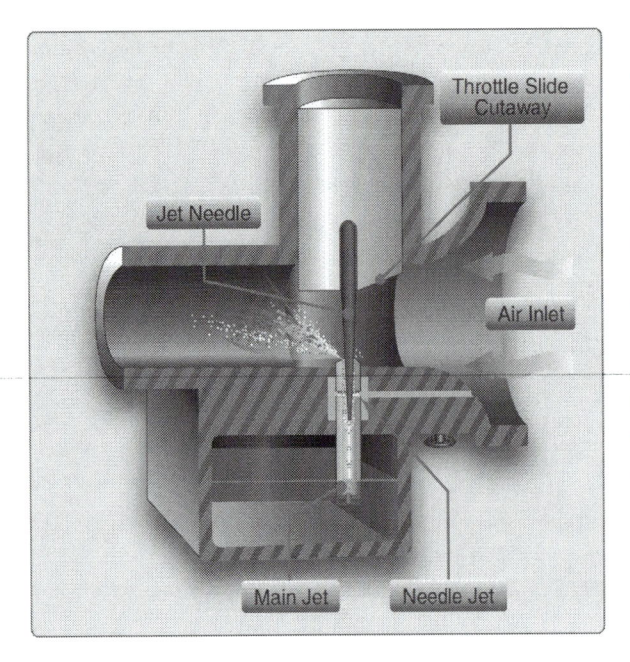

Figure 4-12. *Jet needle/needle jet and main jet system.*

Two-Stroke Carburetor Jetting for Proper Mixture

Carburetors are normally set at sea level pressure with the jets and settings determined by the manufacturer. *[Figure 4-13]* However, as altitude increases, the density of air entering the carburetor decreases, while the density of the fuel remains the same. This creates a progressively richer mixture, same fuel but less air, which can result in engine roughness and an appreciable loss of power. The roughness is usually due to spark plug fouling from excessive carbon buildup on the plugs. Carbon buildup occurs because the excessively rich mixture lowers the temperature inside the cylinder, inhibiting complete combustion of the fuel.

Figure 4-13. *Typical two-stroke carburetor.*

This condition may occur at high elevation airports and during climbs or cruise flight at high altitudes. To maintain the correct fuel/oil/air mixture, the main jets are usually changed for smaller jets based on the density altitude of the base airport. Operating from low altitude airports and climbing to altitude where the mixture becomes rich for short periods is acceptable.

Operating an aircraft at a lower altitude airport with the jets set for higher altitudes will create too lean of a mixture, heat up the engine, and cause the engine to seize. The pilot must be aware of the jetting for the machine to adjust the mixture. Consult your POH for specific procedures for setting jets at different density altitudes.

Four-Stroke Mixture Settings

Four-stroke engines typically have automatic mixture control for higher altitudes or a mixture control that can be operated by the pilot.

Carburetor Icing

One disadvantage of the carburetor system versus the fuel injected system is its icing tendency. Carburetor ice occurs due to the effect of fuel vaporization and the decrease in air pressure in the venturi, which causes a sharp temperature drop in the carburetor. If water vapor in the air condenses when the carburetor temperature is at or below freezing, ice may form on internal surfaces of the carburetor, including the throttle valve.

Ice generally forms in the vicinity of the venturi throat. This restricts the flow of the fuel/air mixture (fuel/oil/air mixture for two stroke) and reduces power. If enough ice builds up, the engine may cease to operate. Carburetor ice is most likely to occur when temperatures are below 70 °F (21 °C) and the relative humidity is above 80 percent. However, due to the sudden cooling that takes place in the carburetor, icing can occur even with temperatures as high as 100 °F (38 °C) and humidity as low as 50 percent. This temperature drop can be as much as 60 to 70 °F. Therefore, at an outside air temperature of 100 °F, a temperature drop of 70 °F results in an air temperature in the carburetor of 30 °F. *[Figure 4-14]*

The first indication of carburetor icing is a decrease in engine rpm, which may be followed by engine roughness. Although carburetor ice can occur during any phase of flight, it is particularly dangerous when using reduced power during a descent. Under certain conditions, carburetor ice could build unnoticed until trying to add power. To combat the effects of carburetor ice, some engines have a carburetor heat option. Some of the newer four-stroke engines have carburetor heat turned on all the time to combat icing. Two-stroke engines are typically less susceptible to icing but specific installations

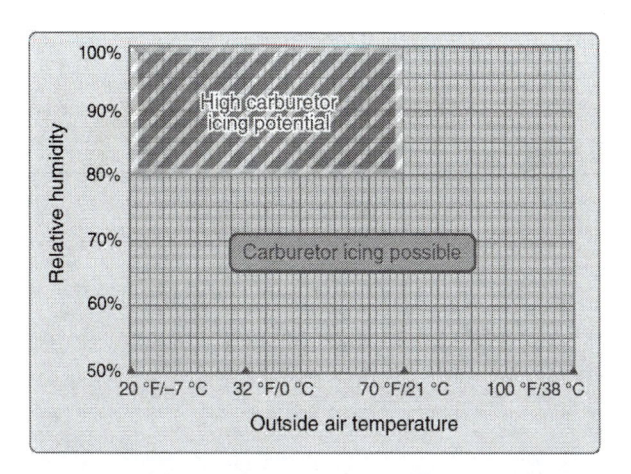

Figure 4-14. *Although carburetor ice is most likely to form when temperature and humidity are in ranges indicated by this chart, carburetor ice is also possible under conditions not depicted.*

dictate how susceptible the carburetor is to icing. Consult the aircraft POH for the probability of carburetor ice for the specific installation and for carburetor ice procedures.

Fuel Injection Induction Systems

In a fuel injection system, the fuel is injected either directly into the cylinders or just ahead of the intake valve. A fuel injection system usually incorporates these basic components: engine-driven fuel pump, fuel/air control unit, fuel manifold (fuel distributor), discharge nozzles, auxiliary fuel pump, and fuel pressure/flow indicators. *[Figure 4-15]*

The engine-driven fuel pump provides fuel under pressure from the fuel tank to the fuel/air control unit. This control unit, which essentially replaces the carburetor, meters the fuel and sends it to the fuel manifold valve at a rate controlled by the throttle. After reaching the fuel manifold valve, the fuel is distributed to the individual fuel discharge nozzles. The discharge nozzles, which are located in each cylinder head, inject the fuel/air mixture at the precise time for each cylinder directly into each cylinder intake port.

Some of the advantages of fuel injection are:

- No carburetor icing.
- Better fuel flow.
- Faster throttle response.
- Precise control of mixture.
- Better fuel distribution.
- Easier cold weather starts.

Disadvantages include:

- Difficulty in starting a hot engine.
- Vapor locks during ground operations on hot days.
- Problems associated with restarting an engine that quits because of fuel starvation.

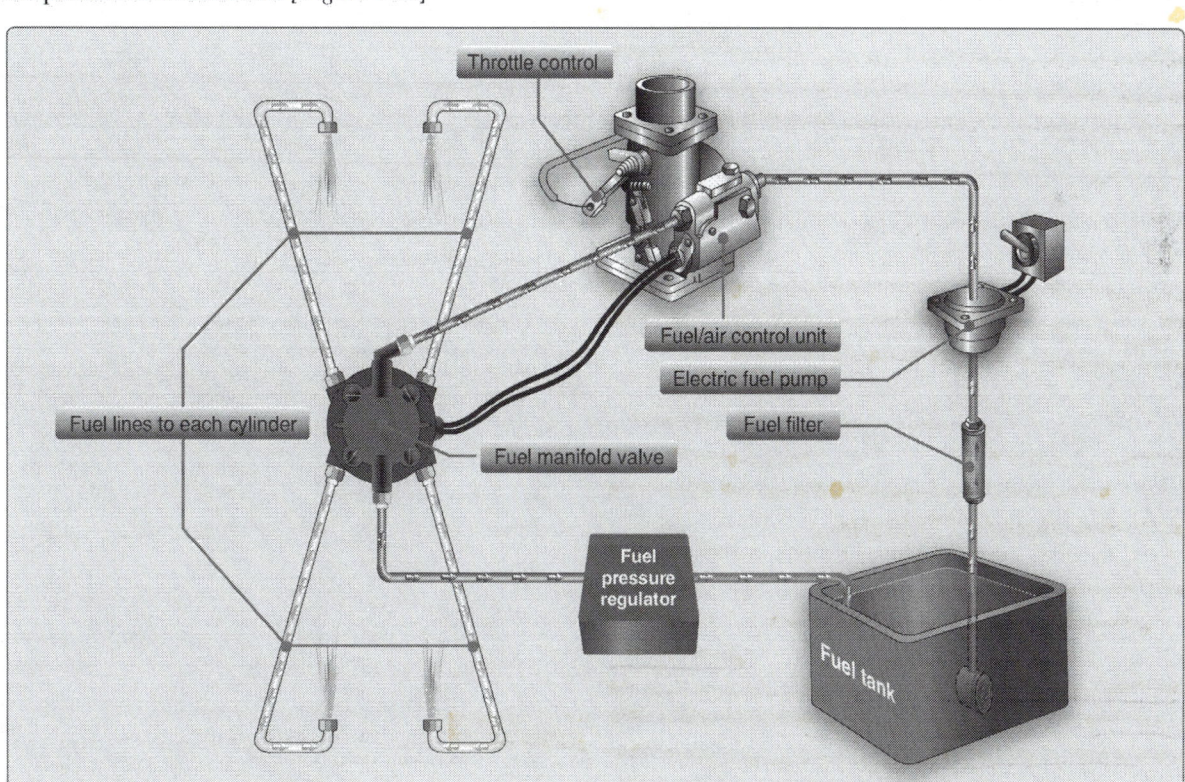

Figure 4-15. *Fuel injection system.*

Ignition System

The typical ignition system on WSC aircraft provides the spark that ignites the fuel/air mixture in the cylinders and is made up of magneto/generators, control boxes, spark plugs, high-voltage leads, and the ignition switch. For most LSA engines designed specifically for aircraft, a magneto/generator uses a permanent magnet to generate an electric current independent of the aircraft's electrical system, which might include a battery. The aircraft electrical system can fail—the battery can go dead. However, this has no effect on the ignition system.

The electricity from the ignition magneto/generator goes into the ignition control box where the correct voltage is produced and timed to fire the spark plugs at the proper time. Modern WSC aircraft use an electronic capacitance discharge system that operates without any moving parts to increase reliability and efficiency. Capacitance Digital Systems (CDI) operate similarly but they have the ability to change the timing of the spark for different rpm. Consult the POH for the particular system for each engine.

The system begins to fire when the starter is engaged and the crankshaft begins to turn. It continues to operate whenever the crankshaft is rotating. Most WSC aircraft incorporate a dual ignition system with two individual magneto/generators, separate sets of wires, separate sets of control boxes, and separate sets of spark plugs to increase reliability of the ignition system. Each magneto/generator operates independently to fire one of the two spark plugs in each cylinder. If one of the systems fails, the other is unaffected. The engine will continue to operate normally, although a slight decrease in engine power can be expected.

The operation of the magneto/generator output to the ignition system is controlled in the flight deck by the ignition switch. Since there are two individual ignition systems, there are normally two separate ignition toggle switches or separate positions on the ignition control, as shown in *Figure 4-16*.

Identification of a malfunctioning ignition system during the pretakeoff check is observed by the decrease in rpm that occurs when first turning off one ignition switch, turning it back on, and then turning off the other. A noticeable decrease in engine rpm is normal during this check. If the engine stops running when switching to one ignition system or if the rpm drop exceeds the allowable limit, do not fly until the problem is corrected. The cause could be fouled plugs, broken or shorted wires between the magneto/generator and spark plugs, or improperly timed firing of the plugs because of a defective control box. It should be noted that "no drop" in rpm is not normal, and in that instance, the aircraft should not be flown. Following engine shutdown, keep the ignition

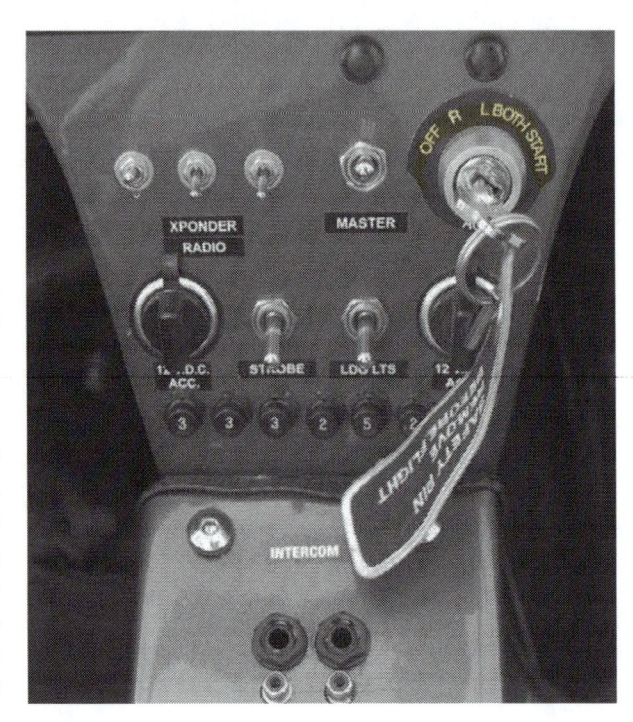

Figure 4-16. *Keyed ignition system with integral starter.*

switches in the OFF position. Even with the battery and master switches OFF, the engine can fire and turn over if an ignition switch is left ON and the propeller is moved because the magneto/generator requires no outside source of electrical power. The potential for serious injury in this situation is obvious.

Standard category aircraft engine systems are described in the Pilots Handbook of Aeronautical Knowledge; however, these engines are not typically used on WSC. Automobile engines or other non aircraft engines may be used on WSC where the ignition system runs off the battery rather than a magneto/generator system. In this case if the battery system fails, the engine ignition system will fail and the engine will stop.

Combustion

During normal combustion, the fuel/air mixture burns in a very controlled and predictable manner. Although the process occurs in a fraction of a second, the mixture actually begins to burn at the point where it is ignited by the spark plugs, then burns away from the plugs until it is consumed completely. This type of combustion causes a smooth buildup of temperature and pressure and ensures that the expanding gases deliver the maximum force to the piston at exactly the right time in the power stroke.

Detonation is an uncontrolled, explosive ignition of the fuel/air mixture within the cylinder's combustion chamber. It causes excessive temperatures and pressures which, if not

4-12

corrected, can quickly lead to failure of the piston, cylinder, or valves. In less severe cases, detonation causes engine overheating, roughness, or loss of power.

Detonation is characterized by high cylinder head temperatures and is most likely to occur when operating at high power settings. Some common operational causes of detonation include:

- Using a lower fuel grade than that specified by the aircraft manufacturer or operating the engine after it has been sitting for an extended period; after 3 weeks or as indicated by the POH, drain old fuel and replenish with fresh fuel.
- Operating the engine at high power settings with an excessively lean mixture.
- Extended ground operations.

Detonation may be avoided by following these basic guidelines during the various phases of ground and flight operations:

- Make sure the proper grade of fuel is being used. Drain and refuel if the fuel is old.
- Develop a habit of monitoring the engine instruments to verify proper operation according to procedures established by the manufacturer.

Preignition occurs when the fuel/air mixture ignites prior to the engine's normal ignition event. Premature burning is usually caused by a residual hot spot in the combustion chamber, often created by a small carbon deposit on a spark plug, a cracked spark plug insulator, or other damage in the cylinder that causes a part to heat sufficiently to ignite the fuel/air charge. Preignition causes the engine to lose power and produces high operating temperature. As with detonation, preignition may also cause severe engine damage because the expanding gases exert excessive pressure on the piston while still on its compression stroke.

Detonation and preignition often occur simultaneously and one may cause the other. Since either condition causes high engine temperature accompanied by a decrease in engine performance, it is often difficult to distinguish between the two. Using the recommended grade of fuel and operating the engine within its proper temperature and RPM ranges reduce the chance of detonation or preignition.

Fuel Systems

The fuel system is designed to provide an uninterrupted flow of clean fuel from the fuel tank to the engine. See Chapter 3, Components and Systems, for more information on fuel tanks. See earlier section in this chapter for specifics on fuel injection systems. The fuel must be available to the engine under all conditions of engine power, altitude, attitude, and during all approved flight maneuvers. *[Figure 4-17]*

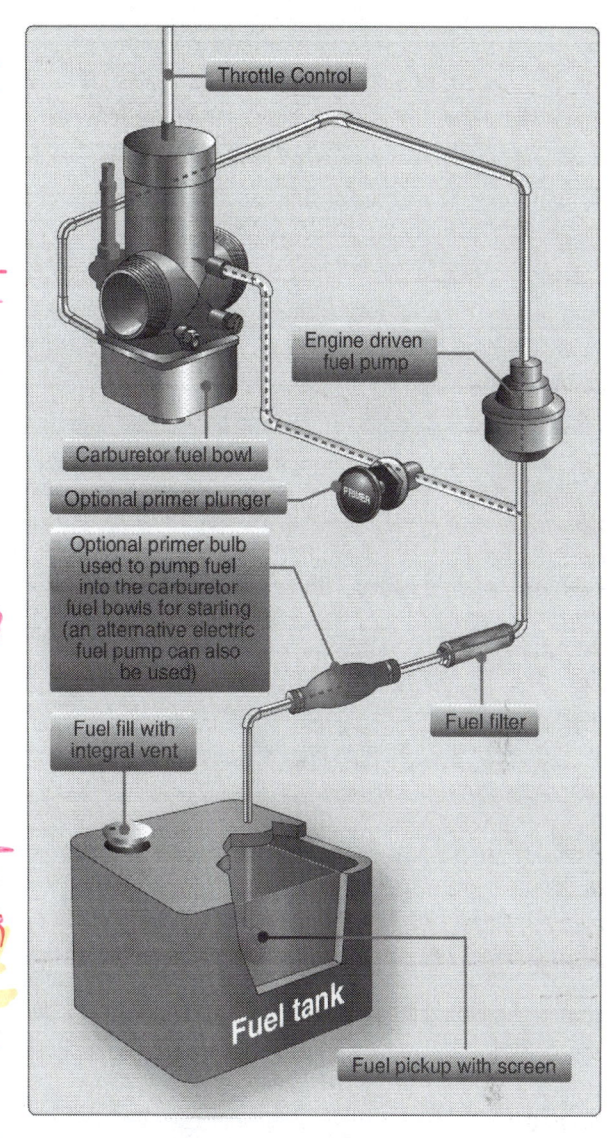

Figure 4-17. *Typical Carburetor Fuel System.*

Fuel Pumps

WSC aircraft with carburetors have engine-driven fuel pump systems. A diaphragm pump is the primary pump in the fuel system for two-stroke engines. Air pulses in the crankcase actuate a diaphragm and provide fuel under pressure to the carburetor. Four-stroke engines have a mechanical pump driven directly off the engine.

Sometimes an electric auxiliary pump is provided for use in engine starting and in the event the engine pump fails. The auxiliary pump, also known as a boost pump, provides added reliability to the fuel system. The electric auxiliary pump is controlled by a switch in the flight deck.

4-13

Fuel Plunger Primer

The optional fuel plunger primer is used to draw fuel from the tanks to supply it directly into the engine prior to starting. This is particularly helpful during cold weather when engines are hard to start because there is not enough heat available to vaporize the fuel in the carburetor. For some aircraft, it is the only way to deliver fuel to the engine when first starting. After the engine starts and is running, the fuel pump pushes fuel to the carburetors and begins normal fuel delivery. To avoid overpriming, read the priming instructions in the POH.

Choke

A choke or fuel enriching system is an alternate method to provide additional fuel to the engine for initial cold starting. Actuating the choke control allows more fuel to flow into the carburetor.

Fuel Bulb Primer

The fuel bulb primer is manually actuated by squeezing the bulb to draw fuel from the fuel tanks. This charges the fuel lines and carburetor float bowls before starting the engine the first time on a given day. After the engine starts, the fuel pump is able to deliver the fuel to the fuel bowls. An electric auxiliary fuel pump can also be used to charge the fuel lines and carburetor fuel bowls before starting. This auxiliary fuel pump is also used as a backup pump of the engine driven fuel pump fails.

Fuel Gauges

The fuel quantity gauge indicates the amount of fuel measured by a sensing unit in each fuel tank and is displayed in gallons. Do not depend solely on the accuracy of the fuel quantity gauge. Always visually check the fuel level in the tank during the preflight inspection, and then compare it with the corresponding fuel quantity indication. It is also important to track inflight fuel consumption. Be sure to consult the POH and know the approximate consumption rate to ensure sufficient fuel for flight. If an auxiliary electric fuel pump is installed in the fuel system, a fuel pressure gauge is sometimes included. This gauge indicates the pressure in the fuel lines. The normal operating pressure can be found in the POH.

Fuel Filter

After leaving the fuel tank, the fuel passes through a filter before it enters the fuel pump or carburetor. This filter removes sediments that might be in the fuel. *[Figure 4-18]*

Fuel

Aviation gasoline (AVGAS) is identified by an octane or performance number (grade) which designates the antiknock value or knock resistance of the fuel mixture in the engine

Figure 4-18. *Fuel system showing fuel filter to fuel pump to carburetor float bowls.*

cylinder. The higher the grade of gasoline, the more pressure the fuel can withstand without detonating. Lower grades of fuel are used in lower compression engines because these fuels ignite at a lower temperature. Higher grades are used in higher compression engines, because they must ignite at higher temperatures but not prematurely. If the proper grade of fuel is not available, use the next higher grade as a substitute. Never use a lower grade. This can cause the cylinder head temperature to exceed its normal operating range, which may result in detonation. Unfortunately, AVGAS 100 Low Lead (LL) may not be recommended by two-stroke engine manufacturers and may not be preferred by the four-stroke manufactures. Even though the "LL" stands for low lead, 100LL contains more lead than the old leaded gas dispensed at automotive filling stations. The lead in the fuel leaves deposits in the piston ring grooves, freezing the rings in position and reducing engine performance. Spark plugs are also very susceptible to lead fouling. This is especially true in two-stroke engines that use cooler ignition temperatures than standard aircraft engines.

AVGAS does have some advantages. It degrades slower than auto gas, maintaining its efficiency for a full 3 months. AVGAS 100LL has no seasonal or regional variations and is manufactured according to a standardized "recipe" worldwide. If the airport has only 100LL available, it is permissible, absent any limitations of the engine manufacturer, to mix 100LL and auto gasoline for use in two-stroke engines. A 50–50 ratio will boost the octane rating and limit the amount of lead available for fouling. Generally speaking, this is a reasonable compromise when the proper auto gas octane is not available.

Manufacturers of two-stroke engines and four-stroke engines used on WSC aircraft typically recommend the use of 89 octane minimum auto fuel for their engines. Additives are put into auto gas primarily to reduce harmful emissions rather than boost performance. The additives are supposed to be listed at the pump, but the accuracy of this posting should be questioned.

Methanol alcohol has corrosive properties and can damage engines. Engine manufacturers do not recommend more than five percent methanol in fuel. Consult the POH for specifics on an engine.

Ethanol alcohol is less corrosive than methanol. However, it attracts water and is not as economical as gasoline. Ethanol does not get very good fuel economy. Avoid fuels with any more than 10 percent of ethanol.

Consult the POH for specifics on an engine. Manufacturers provide specific recommendations for the percentage of alcohol in fuel. The posting on the pump may not be accurate and alcohol content can vary greatly between fuel brands and stations. Additionally, higher percentages of alcohol will be added to auto gas in the future.

A simple test can be conducted to measure the fuel's alcohol content to ensure the fuel used stays within the manufacturer's recommendations. Use a general aviation sump collector which includes graduation marks. Add water to a specific mark. Then add fuel to fill the collector up to the line for gas. Cover the top and shake it vigorously. After it settles, the water and alcohol will combine and it will look like there is now more water in the sump collector. The difference between the initial amount of water first put into the collector and the new level of combined water and alcohol equals the amount of alcohol in the fuel. Compare this amount of alcohol and the amount of fuel to determine the percentage of alcohol content in the fuel.

Methyl tertiary–butyl ether (MTBE) does not have the corrosive or water attractive properties of the previously mentioned additives and is added to fuel to improve air quality. It has been banned in several states because it is carcinogenic and has been found in ground water. It does not attract water, but it is expensive, and found only in some of the better grade fuels.

Fuel Contamination

Clean fuel is imperative for the safe operation of a WSC aircraft. Of the accidents attributed to powerplant failure from fuel contamination, most have been traced to:

- Failure to remove contamination from the fuel system during preflight.
- Servicing aircraft with improperly filtered fuel from small tanks or drums.
- Storing aircraft with partially filled fuel tanks.
- Lack of proper maintenance.

Rust is common in metal fuel containers and is a common fuel contaminant. Metal fuel tanks should be filled after each flight, or at least after the last flight of the day to prevent moisture condensation within the tank.

Another way to prevent fuel contamination is to avoid refueling from cans and drums. Use a water filtering funnel or a funnel with a chamois skin when refueling from cans or drums. However, the use of a chamois will not always ensure decontaminated fuel. Worn out chamois will not filter water; neither will a new, clean chamois that is already water-wet or damp. Most imitation chamois skins will not filter water.

Bad Gasoline

Letting fuel sit for weeks without using it will cause it to go bad. Even if gas does not go bad, it will often lose octane with time. For premixed gasoline and two-stroke oil, there is another set of problems. Fuel and oil are normally mixed at a 50:1 ratio. If premixed gas sits in a plastic container for a while, the gas will evaporate leaving a richer oil mixture in the container. In any case, fresh gas should be used when possible.

Refueling Procedures

Never mix oil and fuel in an enclosed area. Not only are the fumes irritating, but with the right fuel/air mixture can cause an explosion. Do all oil and gas mixing outside. Refueling from fuel cans should also be done outside. Never smoke while refueling. Be careful when refueling an aircraft that has just landed. There is danger of spilling fuel on a hot engine component, particularly an exhaust system component. Refueling should be done using only safety-approved fuel containers marked with the type of fuel stored in them. Confusing premixed fuel and fuel that has no oil in it can be disastrous.

Metal Versus Plastic Fuel Containers

There are advantages to using both metal and plastic containers. Metal cans will not allow the sun's ultraviolet rays in to harm the fuel. It also will not develop static charges that a plastic container develops. However, a metal can is more prone to sweating when going from cool to warm temperatures on humid days. Metal cans and gas tanks are best kept either empty or full of fuel to leave no room for moist air.

Plastic fuel containers are easy to handle, inexpensive, available at discount stores, and do not scratch the finish on airframes. Plastic cans also do not sweat, and do not need to be stored topped off. However, fuel does deteriorate a little faster in plastic. Also, plastic containers can get charged with static electricity while sliding around in the bed of a pickup truck, especially if the truck has a plastic bed liner. [Figure 4-19]

Figure 4-19. *With these translucent containers, it can be noted that the left hand container is just auto fuel and the right hand container shows the auto fuel is premixed with oil for a two-stroke engine.*

Many states now have laws prohibiting people from filling plastic containers unless first placed on the ground. Static electricity can also be formed by the friction of air passing over the surfaces of a WSC aircraft in flight and by the flow of fuel through the hose and nozzle during refueling, if fueling at a pump. Nylon, Dacron, and wool clothing are especially prone to accumulate and discharge static electricity from the person to the funnel or nozzle. To guard against the possibility of static electricity igniting fuel fumes, a ground wire should be attached to the aircraft before the fuel cap is removed from the tank. The refueling nozzle should then be grounded to the aircraft before refueling is begun and should remain grounded throughout the refueling process.

The passage of fuel through a chamois increases the charge of static electricity and the danger of sparks.

The aircraft must be properly grounded and the nozzle, chamois filter, and funnel bonded to the aircraft. If a can is used, it should be connected to either the grounding post or the funnel. Cell phones should not be used while refueling due to possible fire risks.

Mixing Two-Stroke Oil and Fuel

Two-stroke engines require special two-stroke oil to be mixed into the fuel before entering the engine to provide lubrication. In some engines, an oil injection pump is used to deliver the exact amount of oil into the intake of the engine depending on the throttle setting. An advantage of an oil injection system is that pilots do not need to premix any oil into the fuel. However, an important preflight check is to ensure the two-stroke oil reservoir is properly filled.

If a two-stroke engine does not have an oil injection system, it is critical to mix the oil with the fuel before it is put into the tank. Just pouring oil into the fuel tank does not allow the oil to mix with the gas, and makes it difficult to measure the proper amount of oil for mixing.

To mix two-stroke oil:

- Find a clean, approved container. Pour some gas into it to help pre-dilute the two-stroke oil.

- Pour in a known amount of two-stroke oil into the container. Oil should be approved for air-cooled engines at 50:1 mixing ratio (check the engine manufacturer for proper fuel to oil ratio for the WSC aircraft). Use a measuring cup if necessary. Shake the oil-gas mixture to dilute the oil with gasoline.

- Add gasoline until the 50:1 ratio is reached. If using a water separating funnel, ensure the funnel is grounded or at least in contact with the fuel container.

- Put the cap on the fuel can and shake the gasoline and oil mixture thoroughly.

Starting System

Most small aircraft use a direct-cranking electric starter system. This system consists of a source of electricity, wiring, switches, and solenoids to operate the starter and a starter motor. The starter engages the aircraft flywheel or gearbox, rotating the engine at a speed that allows the engine to start and maintain operation.

Electrical power for starting is usually supplied by an on-board battery. When the battery switch is turned ON, electricity is supplied to the main power bus through the battery solenoid. Both the starter and the starter switch draw current from the main bus, but the starter will not operate until the starting solenoid is energized by the starter switch being turned to the "start" position. When the starter switch is released from the "start" position, the solenoid removes power from the starter motor. The starter motor is protected from being driven by the engine through a clutch in the starter drive that allows the engine to run faster than the starter motor.

Oil Systems

In a four-stroke engine, the engine oil system performs several important functions, including:

- Lubricating the engine's moving parts.
- Cooling the engine by reducing friction.
- Removing heat from the cylinders.
- Providing a seal between the cylinder walls and pistons.
- Carrying away contaminants.

Four-stroke engines use either a wet sump or dry sump oil system. Refer to the Pilot's Handbook of Aeronautical Knowledge for more information on four-stroke oil systems.

Engine Cooling Systems

The burning fuel within the cylinders produces intense heat, most of which is expelled through the exhaust system. Much of the remaining heat, however, must be removed, or at least dissipated, to prevent the engine from overheating.

While the oil system in a four-stroke engine and the fuel-oil mix in a two-stroke engine is vital to the internal cooling of the engine, an additional method of cooling is necessary for the engine's external surface. WSC engines operate with either air-cooled or liquid-cooled systems.

Many WSC aircraft are equipped with a cylinder head temperature (CHT) gauge. This instrument indicates a direct and immediate cylinder temperature change. This instrument is calibrated in degrees Celsius or Fahrenheit. Proper CHT ranges can be found in the POH/AFM/AOI for that machine. *[Figure 4-20]*

Air cooling is accomplished by air being pulled into the engine shroud by a cooling fan. Baffles route this air over fins attached to the engine cylinders where the air absorbs the engine heat. Expulsion of the hot air takes place through one or more openings in the shroud. If cylinder head temperatures rise too much in an air-cooled engine, it is because of lubrication problems, cooling fan drive belt damage or wear,

Figure 4-20. *Cylinder head temperature probe (yellow wire) is under spark plug.*

or air blockage in the cooling fins by a bird or insect nest. *[Figure 4-1]*

Figure 4-21. *Cooling radiators—oil cooler is on top and water cooler is on bottom.*

Liquid cooling systems pump coolant through jackets in the cylinders and head. The heated liquid is then routed to a radiator where the heat is radiated to the atmosphere. The cooled liquid is then returned to the engine. If the radiator is mounted close to the propeller, the propeller can constantly move air across the radiator and keep the engine cool even when the WSC is not moving. *[Figure 4-21]* Radiators mounted away from the propeller make it more difficult for the radiator to cool the engine unless the WSC is moving. *[Figure 4-22]*

Breaking in an engine through ground runs on a hot day is when radiator placement is most critical. Liquid-cooled engines can overheat for a number of reasons, such as coolant

4-17

Figure 4-22. *Side mounted water cooler radiators integral with cowl.*

not at proper levels, a leak, failed water pump, or a blockage of the radiator.

Operating an engine above its maximum design temperature can cause a loss of power and detonation. It will also lead to serious permanent damage, such as scoring the cylinder walls and damaging the pistons and rings. Monitor the engine temperature instruments to avoid high operating temperature. Operating the engine lower than its designed temperature range can cause piston seizure and scarring on the cylinder walls. This happens most often in liquid-cooled WSC aircraft in cold weather where large radiators designed for summer flying may need to be partially blocked off.

Chapter Summary

Powerplants are generally classified by:

1. Number of piston strokes needed to complete a cycle—two strokes or four strokes.
2. Method of cooling—liquid or air.

Exhaust systems route the exhaust gases from the cylinders out to the atmosphere. Two-stroke engines require tuned exhaust systems matched to the specific engine for proper operation.

Engines must be warmed up properly or engine damage and seizure can result. Gearboxes reduce the engine rpm to a usable propeller rpm. Induction systems mix gas and air for cylinders and must be properly adjusted for different altitudes.

Typical aircraft ignition systems are separate from the electrical systems and typically have two separate ignition systems. Aircraft ignition systems are composed of a magneto/generator, control box, high voltage wires, spark plugs, and ignition switches. Automotive engines typically run the ignition system off the battery.

Proper combustion is a result of proper mixture and good fuel. Good fuel management and proper engine cooling are important considerations for reliable engine operation.

Chapter 5
Preflight and Ground Operations

Introduction

Preflight preparations should include the overall evaluation of the:

- **P**ilot: experience, sleep, food and water, drugs or medications, stress, illness
- **A**ircraft: certificates/documents, airworthiness, fuel, weight (does not exceed maximum), performance requirements, equipment
- En**V**ironment: weather conditions, density altitude, forecast for departure and destination airfields, route of flight, runway lengths
- **E**xternal pressures: schedules, available alternatives, purpose of flight

Often remembered as PAVE, it is important to consider each of these factors and establish personal minimums for flying.

Where To Fly

The weight-shift control (WSC) aircraft can be transported by trailer from one flying field to the next. For as many benefits as this provides, transporting the aircraft into unfamiliar territory also includes some safety and operational issues.

Contact airport management to inquire about any special arrangements to be made prior to arriving by trailer *[Figure 5-1]* and there may be special considerations for flying WSC aircraft with other aircraft. With smaller patterns typically used by WSC aircraft, as covered in Chapter 10, Airport Traffic Patterns, airport management may want a pilot to operate over sparsely populated areas rather than the normal airplane patterns over congested areas because of the unique noise of the WSC aircraft. *[Figure 5-2]* Check the Airport/Facility Directory (A/FD) all required airport information per Title 14 of the Code of federal Regulations (14 CFR) part 91 section 103, Preflight information. Some operation examples are traffic pattern information, noise abatement procedures, no fly zones surrounding the airport, and special accommodations that may need to be arranged for WSC aircraft..

Because of the wide range of flying characteristics of the WSC aircraft, inform local pilots about some of the incidentals of the specific WSC aircraft (e.g., flying low and slow for certain configurations). The more non-WSC aircraft pilots know about WSC flight characteristics and intentions, the better they understand how to cooperate in flight. Sharing the same airspace with various aircraft categories requires pilots to know and understand the rules and understand the flight characteristics and performance limitations of the different aircraft.

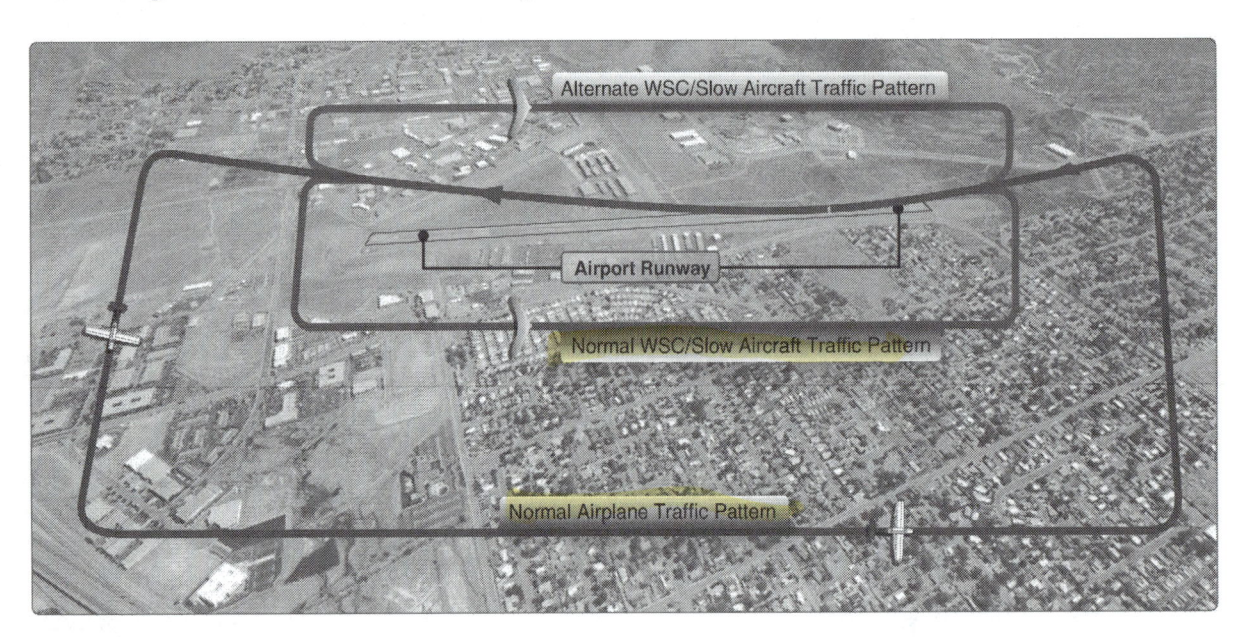

Figure 5-2. *Contact local airport management to determine best operation for the aircraft and its type of operation.*

Figure 5-1. *Contact the local airport management to find an acceptable location to stay at the airport.*

For operations at nonaircraft fields, special considerations must be evaluated. Permission is necessary to use private property as an airstrip. Locate the area on an aeronautical sectional chart to check for possible airspace violations or unusual hazards that could arise by not knowing the terrain or location. Avoid loitering around residential structures and animal enclosures because of the slow flight characteristics of WSC aircraft and distinct engine noise.

While selecting a takeoff position, make certain the approach and takeoff paths are clear of other aircraft. Fences, power lines, trees, buildings, and other obstacles should not be in the immediate flightpath unless the pilot is certain he or she is able to safely clear them during takeoff and landing operations.

Walk the entire length of the intended takeoff and landing area prior to departure. *[Figure 5-3]* Look for holes, muddy spots, rocks, dips in the terrain, high grass, and other objects that can cause problems during takeoff and landing. Physically mark areas of concern with paint, flags, or cones. Uneven ground, mud, potholes, or items in fields such as rocks might not be visible from the air. Plowed rows and vegetation are larger than they appear from the air. Unfamiliar fields can make suitable landing areas for emergencies, but should not be used as intended landing areas. Extreme caution must be exercised when operating from a new field or area for the first time.

Figure 5-3. *Fields that look like good landing areas from the air may actually be hazardous.*

Preflight Actions

A pilot must become familiar with all available information concerning the flight, including runway lengths at airport of intended use, takeoff and landing distance accounting for airport elevation and runway slope, aircraft gross weight, wind, and temperature. For a cross-country flight not in the vicinity of the takeoff/departure airport, information must include weather reports and forecasts, fuel requirements, and alternatives available if the planned flight cannot be completed.

Weather

Weather is a determining factor for all flight operations. Before any flight is considered, pilots should obtain regional and local information to first determine if the predicted weather for the planned flight is safe.

Regional Weather

Understanding the overall weather in the region being flown provides an overview of conditions and how they can change during flight. Fronts, pressure systems, isobars, and the jet stream determine the weather. There are a number of information resources from which to find the regional view of weather systems, observed and predicted. Surface analysis charts show these regional systems, which are common on weather internet sites and TV broadcasts. *[Figure 5-4]* Review the Pilot's Handbook of Aeronautical Knowledge for a comprehensive understanding of weather theory, reports, forecasts, and charts for weather concepts covered throughout this weather section.

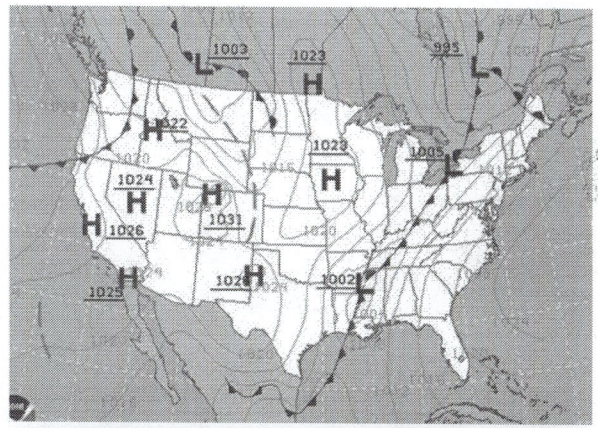

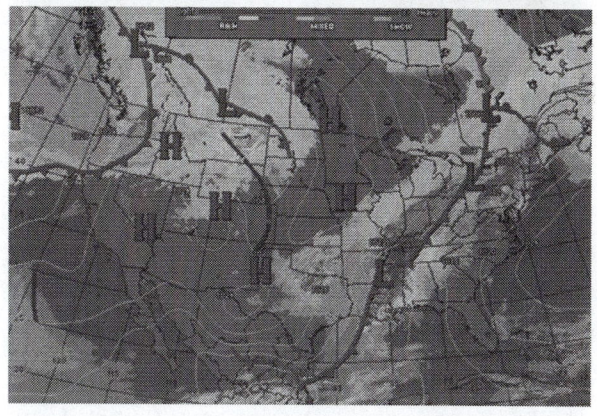

Figure 5-4. *Standard surface analysis showing fronts, pressure systems, and isobars (top) and composite surface analysis which adds radar and infrared satellite to show cloud cover (bottom).*

There are many sources for obtaining a weather briefing, such as www.aviationweather.gov, www.nws.noaa.gov, 1-800-WX-BRIEF, and a variety of internet sites that specialize in local and regional weather.

Local Conditions

In gathering weather information for a flight, obtain current and forecast conditions where flying, as well as alternate airports in case landing at the intended destination is not possible. These conditions should include wind (surface and winds aloft), moisture, stability, and pressure.

Surface wind predictions and observations can be looked at with a number of internet resources. The National Weather Aviation service provides observations (METAR) and forecasts (TAF) for areas with weather reporting capabilities.

Winds aloft are forecast winds at higher altitudes than the surface for locations throughout the United States. Refer to the Pilot's Handbook of Aeronautical Knowledge for an understanding of the winds and temperatures aloft tables. Winds aloft, too, are important for flight planning and safety.

A typical situation during morning hours is cold air from the night settling, creating calm winds at the surface with the winds aloft (300 to 3,000 feet) at 30 knots. As the surface begins to warm from the sun, the cold surface air starts to warm and rise, allowing the high winds from above to mix and lower to the surface. The wind sheer area in between the high winds above and calm winds below is usually turbulent and can overwhelm aircraft or pilot capabilities. Therefore, it is a dangerous practice to look only at the wind sock for surface winds when there could be strong winds above. Winds aloft must be evaluated for safe flight. *[Figure 5-5]*

During initial solo flights, the wind should be relatively calm to fly safely. As experience is gained, pilot wind limitations can be increased. It is not until the pilot has had dual training in crosswinds, bumpy conditions, and significant pilot in command (PIC) time soloing in mild conditions that pilot wind conditions should approach the aircraft limitations. A safe pilot understands aircraft and personal limitations.

Moisture in the air has a significant effect on weather. If the relative humidity is high, the chance of clouds forming at lower altitudes is more likely. Clouds forming at lower altitudes create visibility problems that can create Instrument Meteorological Conditions (IMC) in which the visibility is below that required for safe flight. The temperature-dew point spread is the basis for determining at what altitude moisture condenses and clouds form. It is important to be particularly watchful for low visibilities when the air and dew point temperatures are within a spread of three to four degrees.

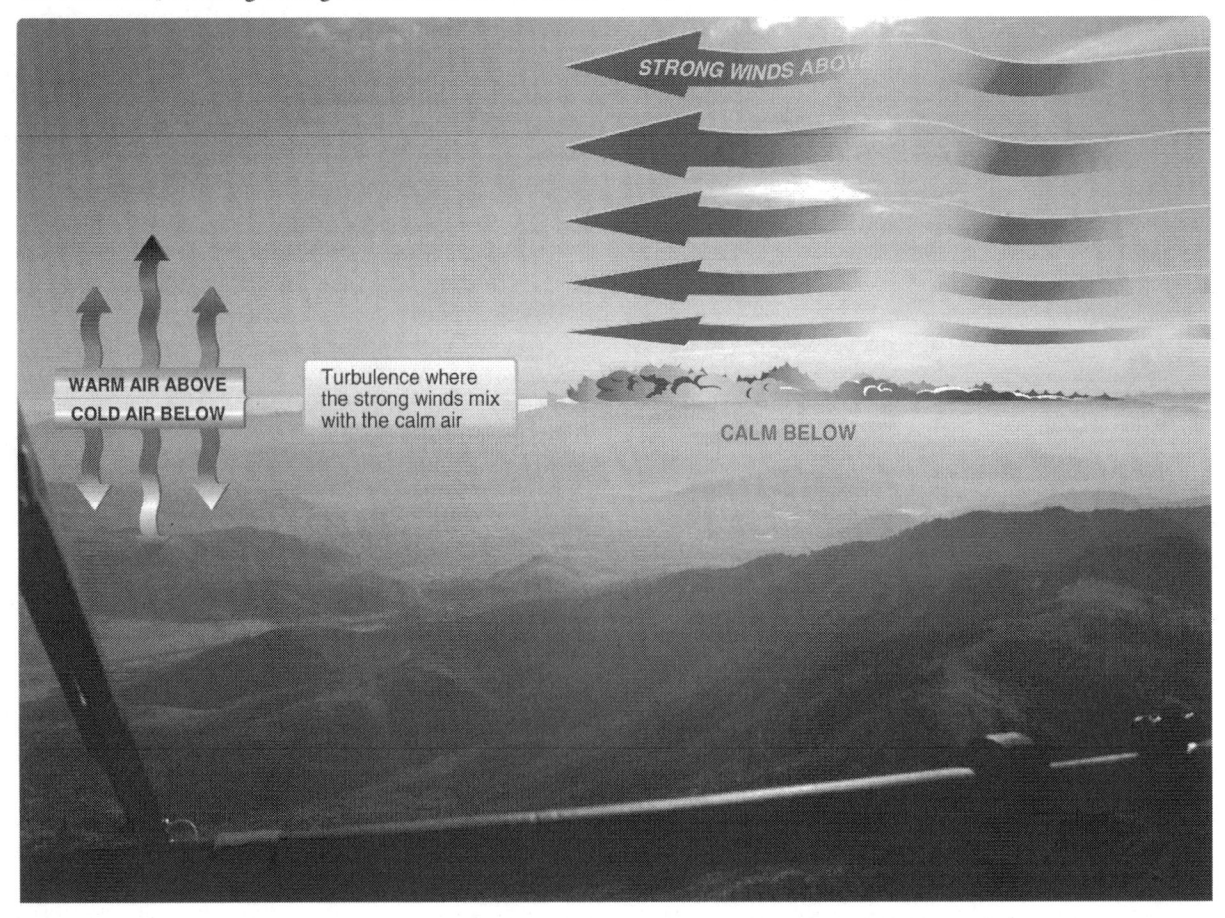

Figure 5-5. *Typical morning inversion layer—calm cold air is below; high winds are above.*

The closer these temperatures are to each other, the greater the chance for fog or clouds forming with reduced visibility conditions. Consider a scenario where the destination airport currently has a temperature-dew point spread of 4 °F, and it is evening when the atmosphere is cooling down. Since the temperature-dew point convergence rate is 4.4° for every thousand feet, the clouds/ceiling would be about 1,000 feet above ground level (AGL). Since it is cooling down, the temperature-dew point spread is decreasing, lowering the cloud level. Therefore, the 1,000 foot AGL ceiling is lowering, creating IMC conditions that are not safe. For this scenario, the flight should not be attempted.

Air temperature and humidity directly affect the performance of the WSC wing and engine. The higher the temperature, humidity, and actual altitude of the operating field, the greater role density altitude plays in determining how much runway the WSC aircraft needs to get off the ground with the load on board, and how much climb performance is required once airborne. The WSC aircraft may have cleared the obstacle at 8 a.m. when the weather conditions were cooler with less humidity; at 1 p.m. with increased air temperature and higher humidity levels, the pilot must reevaluate the performance of that same aircraft. A full understanding of density altitude is necessary to be a safe WSC pilot; refer to the Pilot's Handbook of Aeronautical Knowledge for density altitude and weight effects on performance.

The rate of temperature decrease with increased altitude determines the stability of the air. The stability of the air determines the vertical air currents that develop during the day as the area is heated by the sun. These rising vertical air currents are commonly known as thermals. Generally, stable air has mild thermals and therefore less turbulence than unstable air. Unstable air rises faster, creating greater turbulence. Highly unstable air rises rapidly and, with enough moisture, can build into thunderstorms.

Air stability is easily determined by the rate at which the temperature drops with increased altitude. A standard atmosphere is where the temperature drops 2 °C for every 1,000 foot increase. If the temperature drops less than 2 °C per thousand feet, the air is more stable with less vertical wind (thermals) developed during the day. If the temperature drops more than 2 °C per thousand feet, the air is more unstable with more powerful vertical air currents developed during the day, creating greater turbulence.

In addition to air stability, barometric pressure has a large effect on weather. Low pressure in the area, below the standard atmosphere of 29.92 "Hg, is generally rising air with dynamic and unsettled weather. High pressure above the standard atmosphere in the area is generally sinking air resulting in good weather for flying.

Many airports have automated weather systems in which pilots can call the automated weather sensor platforms that collect weather data at airports and listen to this information via radio and/or land line. Radio frequencies are on the sectional chart and the A/FD has the telephone numbers for these stations. The systems currently available are the Automated Surface Observing System (ASOS), Automated Weather Sensor System (AWSS), and Automated Weather Observation System (AWOS).

Local conditions of wind, moisture, stability, and barometric pressure are factors that should be researched before flight to make a competent decision of go or no go to fly. High winds and moist unstable air with a low barometric pressure indicate undesirable flying conditions. Light winds and dry stable air with high pressure indicate favorable flying conditions.

Pilots should research and document these local conditions before flight to predict the flying conditions and compare the actual flying conditions to the predictions to learn and develop knowledge from the information resources available for flight.

In addition to weather, the National Airspace needs to be checked to ensure there are no temporary flight restrictions (TFR) for the locations planned to fly. TFRs may be found at www.tfr.faa.gov/. For a complete preflight briefing of weather and TFRs, call 1-800-WX-BRIEF.

Clouds visually tell what the air is doing, which provides valuable information for any flight. To understand the different cloud formations and the ground/air effects produced, refer to weather theory in the Pilot's Handbook of Aeronautical Knowledge. *[Figure 5-6]* Cloud clearance and visibility should be maintained for the operations intended to be conducted. The chapter covering the National Airspace System (NAS) provides cloud clearance requirements in each class of airspace. A pilot should not fly when ground and flight visibility are below minimums for his or her pilot certificate and the class of airspace where operating.

Knowledge of mechanical turbulence and how to determine where it can occur is also important. The lee side of objects can feel turbulence from the wind up to ten times the height of the object. The stronger the wind is, the stronger the turbulence is. *[Figures 5-7 and 5-8]*

In addition to adhering to the regulations and manufacturer recommendations for weather conditions, it is important to develop a set of personal minimums such as wind limitations, time of day, and temperature-dew point spread. These minimums will evolve as a pilot gains experience and are also dependent on recency and currency in the make/model of aircraft being flown.

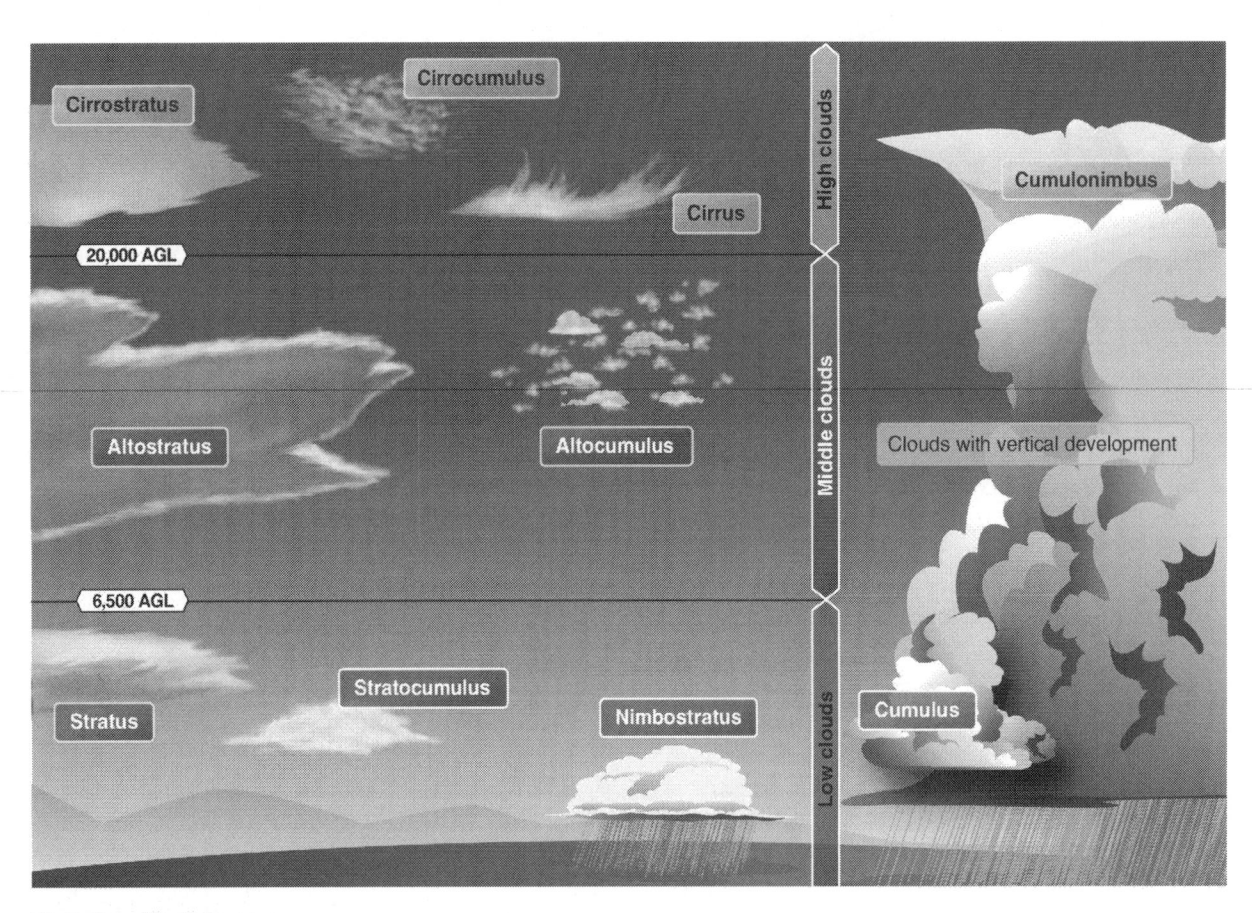

Figure 5-6. *Cloud diagram.*

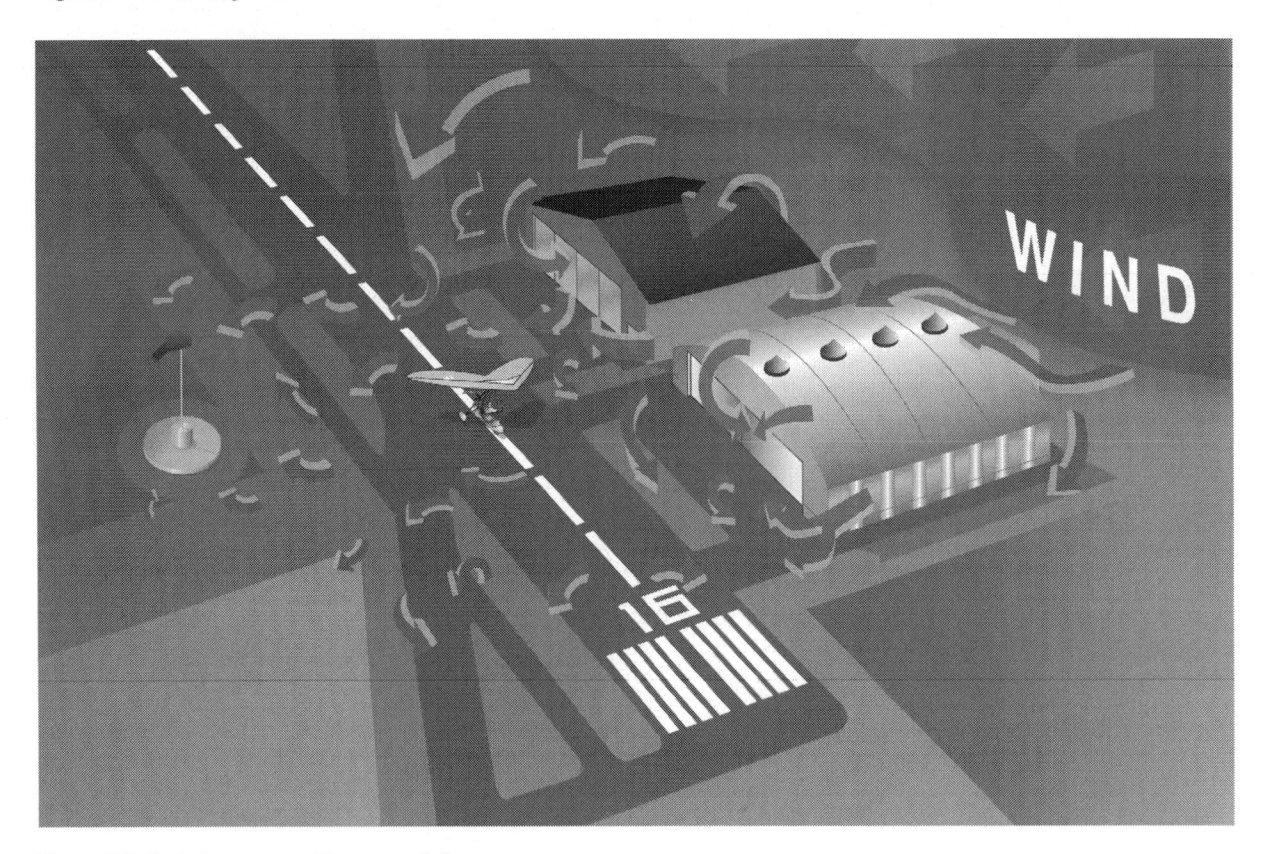

Figure 5-7. *Turbulence created by manmade items.*

5-6

Figure 5-8. *Turbulence created by natural land formations.*

Weight and Loading

Weight and loading must be considered before each flight. Do not exceed the maximum gross weight as specified in the pilot's operating handbook (POH). The balance of the pilot, passenger, fuel, and baggage is usually not an issue, but must be reviewed in the POH for the specific make/model since some may have balance limitations. The fore and aft carriage attachment to the wing hang point must be within the limits as specified in the POH for weight and loading of the carriage. Always follow the POH performance limitations.

Transporting

It is best to keep the WSC aircraft in an enclosed hangar, but trailers may be used to transport, store, and retrieve the WSC carriage. If the trailer is large enough, the wing can also fit inside the trailer. If not, then it must fit on top of a trailer, truck, or recreational vehicle (RV). *[Figure 5-9]*

Figure 5-9. *Enclosed trailer containing carriage and wing on top of RV.*

Enclosed trailers are preferred so the carriage is protected from the outside elements such as dust, rain, mud, road debris, and the interested person who may want to tinker with the carriage. The WSC carriage should fit snuggly without being forced, be guarded against chafing, and well secured within any trailer. It is best to utilize hard points on the carriage frame and secure each wheel so the carriage cannot move fore and aft during transport. This is best accomplished by first tying the front wheel from the axles, the fork, or a hard point on the frame with a slight forward pull. Then, secure the rear wheels from the axles or a hard point on the frame with a slight rearward pull. Guides on the side of the wheels and wheel chocks in front and back of each wheel are additionally helpful to secure the carriage on any trailer.

The wing must have ample padding and should have at least three support points where it rests for transport. Transporting the wing properly is of critical importance because the wing resting on any hard surface can wear a hole in the sail and cause structural damage to the tubing. The greatest wear and tear on a wing can occur during transportation. Each support point should have equal pressure—no single point taking most of the load. The wing should be tied down at each attachment point to secure it, but not tight enough to damage the wing. Wide straps are better than thin ropes because the greater width creates less concentrated pressure on the wing at each tie-down point.

Once the loading of the carriage and wing is complete *[Figure 5-9]*, take a short drive, stop, and check for rubbing or chafing of components.

Prior to taking the tow vehicle and trailer on the road, inspect the tires for proper inflation and adequate tread. Ensure all lights are operable, the hitch is free moving and well lubricated, the tow vehicle attachment is rated for the weight of the trailer, and the vehicle and trailer brakes are operable. Avoid towing with too much or too little tongue weight, which causes the trailer to fishtail at certain speeds, possibly rendering it uncontrollable.

Be extremely cautious when unloading the wing and carriage. This is best done with two people since the wing usually weighs more than 100 pounds *[Figure 5-10]* and the carriage

Figure 5-10. *Crane used for one person to lift 110-pound wing on top of RV for transport.*

usually must roll down some incline to get from the trailer to the ground. Some carriages may be tail heavy without the wing, and caution must be exercised, especially moving up and down ramps. Check propeller clearance on the ground when transitioning onto or off of a ramp and propeller clearance going into and out of an enclosed trailer. If the carriage is transported in an open trailer, it should be covered and the propeller secured so it does not rotate/windmill during transport.

Setting Up the WSC Aircraft

Find a suitable area to set up the wing, such as grass, cement, or pavement out of the wind. Inside a large hangar is preferable since wind gusts are not a problem. If setting up outside, align the wing perpendicular to the wind. Most wings set up with the same basic procedure shown in *Figures 5-11* through *5-33*, but the POH should be referenced for the specific WSC aircraft.

Rotate the wing bag so the zipper is facing up. *[Figure 5-11]* Unzip the bag. When setting up the wing, pay close attention to the specific pads, where they are located, and how they are attached for each component of the wing. As shown in *Figure 5-12*, the padding is made specifically for the control frame between the downtubes and the control bar. If every pad is not utilized when taking it down and transporting, there

Figure 5-11. *Wing positioned for setup.*

Figure 5-12. *Wing cover bag unzipped, showing unique padding around control frame corner brackets.*

Figure 5-13. *Assembling control frame.*

will be wear on components with cosmetic and/or structural damage to the wing. The POH may specify where pads go during the setup and takedown. However, when setting up any wing it is a good idea to take pictures, draw sketches, or take notes regarding protective pad location so they can be put back in the proper location during take down.

Assemble the triangular control frame without attaching the wires to the nose. *[Figure 5-13]* Rotate the wing up onto its control frame. *[Figure 5-14]* Place the front wires near the control bar so no one walks on them, remove, and roll up the cover bag. *[Figure 5-15]* Release the wing tie straps that are holding the leading edges together. *[Figure 5-16]* Spread the wing slightly. Remove the pads from the wing keel and kingpost. Note the protective pads still on the wing tips protecting them from the ground during most of the wing set up procedure. *[Figure 5-17]* Continually manage the wing pads and wing tie straps by rolling the pads into the cover bag so they do not blow away. *[Figure 5-18]* If the kingpost is loose, insert it onto the keel to stand upright. If the kingpost is attached, swing it upright. Topless wings have no kingpost. Spread the wings as necessary to keep the kingpost straight up, *[Figure 5-19]* spreading them out carefully and evenly. Do not force anything. Ensure the wires are not wrapped around anything. Separate the right and left battens. Separate the straight battens (for a double surface wing) and set them to the side. Lay out the battens, longest to shortest from the root to the tip next to the pocket they

Figure 5-16. *Removing the straps holding the two wings together.*

Figure 5-14. *Rotating the wing onto its control frame.*

Figure 5-17. *Wings spread slightly to raise the kingpost.*

Figure 5-15. *Placing the front wires at the control frame.*

Figure 5-18. *Pads and wing tie straps neatly rolled into wing cover bag.*

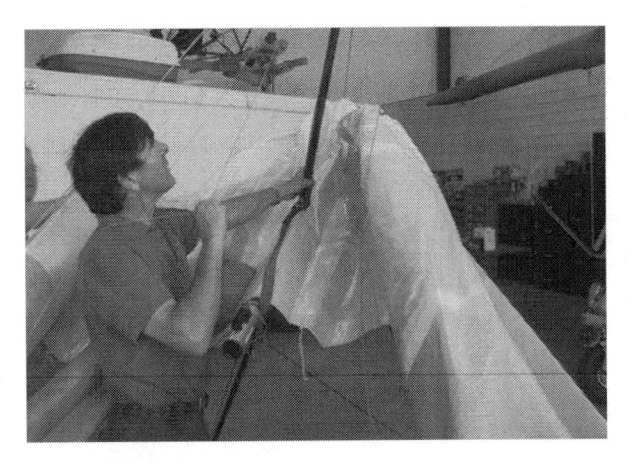

Figure 5-19. *Raising the kingpost and spreading the wings as needed to keep the kingpost upright.*

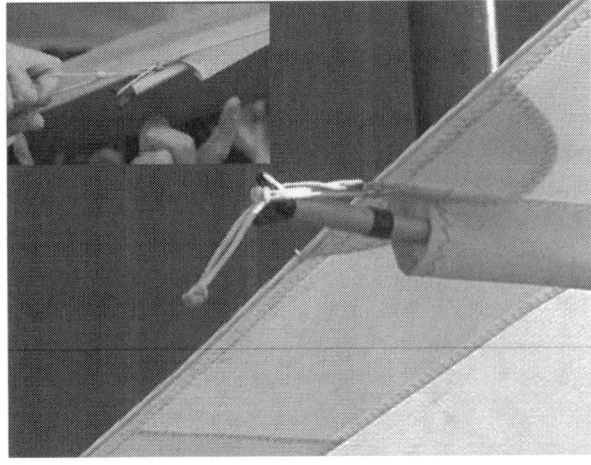

Figure 5-22. *Attaching double pull batten (inset). Batten secured into batten pocket.*

go into on both sides. Note the protective pads are still on the wing tips so they are protected. *[Figure 5-20]* Insert the battens into the batten pockets, starting at the root and work out to the tip. *[Figure 5-21]* Most batten attachments are double pull. *[Figure 5-22]* Some manufacturers use cord or elastic, and others use a system that slips into the sail itself. See the POH for wing details. Insert battens from the root towards the tip about ¾ the way out on each side. Leave the tip battens for later. Spread the wings as far as possible. *[Figure 5-23]* Check to ensure all the wires are straight, not wrapped around, and clear to tension the wing. Tension the wing by pulling back on the crossbar tensioning cable and

Figure 5-20. *Wings spread and battens organized to insert into wings. Note small stepladder holding up keel.*

Figure 5-23. *Wing ready to tension.*

pulling the crossbar back into position. This may require significant effort for some wings. Secure the tensioning cable to the back of the keel. *[Figure 5-24]* If the keel does not extend out, then support the aft end of the keel to lift the tips off of the ground. *[Figure 5-25]* Move to the front and secure the front control frame flying wires to the underside nose attachment. *[Figure 5-26]* Remove the tip bag protectors and install the tip battens, continuing to move from the root to the tips on each side. Insert the washout strut into the leading edge. Each manufacturer has its own washout strut systems and tip battens. Some manufacturers have no washout struts. Refer to the POH for wing specifics. *[Figure 5-27]*

Figure 5-21. *Inserting batten into batten pocket.*

5-10

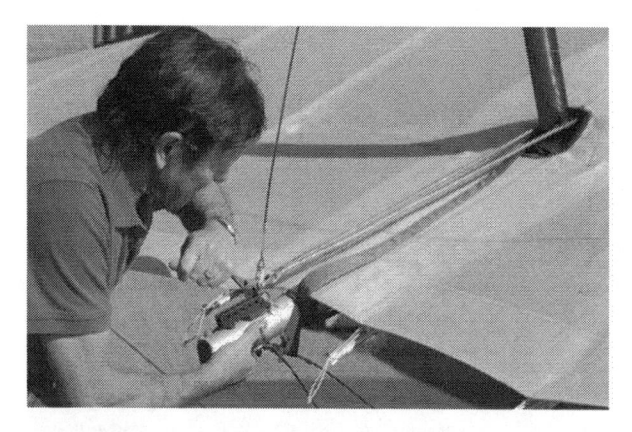

Figure 5-24. *Attaching the tensioning cables to the back of the wing to complete the wing tensioning step.*

Figure 5-27. *Installing the wing tip battens.*

Figure 5-25. *The wing tensioned.*

Figure 5-28. *Installing the lower surface battens.*

Figure 5-26. *Attaching the front flying wires to the nose attachment.*

Insert bottom battens for a double surface. If inside a hangar where there is no wind, this can be done by putting the nose down, making it easier to install the lower battens. *[Figure 5-28]* If not already accomplished, lift up on the back of the keel and put the wing on its nose. Lower the undercarriage mast and line up the undercarriage behind the wing exactly in the middle. Move the undercarriage forward and attach the mast to the proper hang point location on the wing keel. Consult the POH for the proper hang point for desired trim, speed, and loading at this time. Attach the backup cable at this time also. *[Figure 5-29]*

Figure 5-29. *Attaching the mast to the wing after checking the POH for the proper hang point location.*

5-11

Lift up the nose and let the carriage roll backward until the wing is level and the control bar is in front of the front wheel of the carriage. Engage the parking brake and chock the back of the carriage wheels. Ensure everything in the flight deck is free and clear so the wing can be lifted freely into position. *[Figure 5-30]* Lift the wing into position and lock the carriage mast. This position is unique to each manufacturer as some masts hinge above the flight deck. Refer to the POH for details on a specific aircraft. *[Figure 5-31]* Install the carriage front tube. Secure the control bar to the front tube with a bungee. *[Figure 5-32]* Attach any fairing or seats as required. *[Figure 5-33]*

Figure 5-30. *Wing in position and carriage chocked to lift the wing.*

Figure 5-31. *Lifting the wing up into position.*

Figure 5-32. *Attaching the front tube.*

Figure 5-33. *Installing the seats.*

An alternate method of setting up the wing is to do so on the ground. This is not preferable because the sail is susceptible to getting dirty. However, this method could be used for setting up wings if it is windy or if recommended by a particular manufacturer. The ground method steps are the same as those in the assembly procedure except after the control bar is assembled, the wing is rolled over so the control frame is under the wing. The wing is assembled as if it were standing on its control frame. After the wing is tensioned, the nose is lifted, the control frame pulled forward, and the nose wire secured. This is not a common practice, and the POH should be reviewed for details on this method if it is allowed by the manufacturer.

Taking Down the WSC Aircraft

Find a suitable area to take down the wing, preferably grass, cement, or pavement out of the wind. The best place is in a large hangar so no wind gusts can affect the takedown. If outside, align the wing perpendicular to the wind.

It is important to note that during the take down process, all protective pads must be put in the proper place so that no hardware can rub against the sail or frame during transport. The POH should specify what pads go where. Overall, pad everything along the wing keel plus the kingpost to prevent cosmetic and/or structural damage occurring during transport.

Taking down a WSC aircraft is done in the reverse order of assembly with the following additional steps provided to get the wing neatly packed and organized into the bag. After the wing is detensioned and the battens have been removed from the wing, keep the right and left battens separate for easier sorting during the next assembly.

Carefully bring the wings in towards the keel and pull the sail material out and over the top of the leading edges. Lower the kingpost and pad it top and bottom. This is also the time to pad the area underneath where the control frame is attached to the keel and where the wires are attached to the rear of the keel. *[Figure 5-34]* Bring the leading edges to the keel and keep the sail pulled out over the top of the leading edge, roll it up, and tuck the sail into the leading edge stiffener. Fasten around the leading edge with sail ties. *[Figure 5-35]* It is best to take one sail tie and secure the two leading edges together so it fits into the bag. *[Figure 5-36]* Continue with the reverse order (bag on, flip wing over, and disassemble control frame at downtube and control bar junction). After the control frame is disassembled and laid flat along the wing as shown, the wires are not organized. *[Figure 5-37]* Pull the cables forward towards the nose and organize them so they are straight. Install the protective control frame pads and carefully zip up the bag while tucking everything in so there is no stress on the zipper. *[Figure 5-38]*

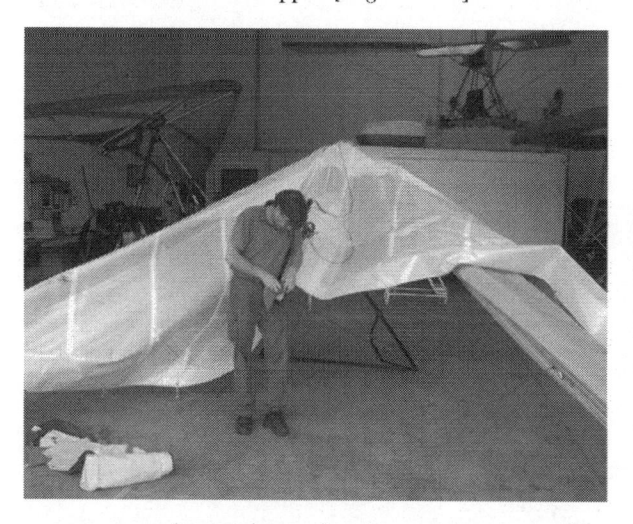

Figure 5-34. *Padding the keel and kingpost with the right hand sail over the top of the leading edge.*

Figure 5-35. *Left hand side rolled up and secured with wing tie. Rolling right hand sail which will also be secured with wing tie.*

Figure 5-36. *Securing both leading edges together so the wing easily fits into the bag.*

Figure 5-37. *Control bar folded down along leading edges but wires not yet organized.*

Figure 5-38. *Carefully zipping bag with minimum stress by tucking in wires and organizing components.*

Wing Tuning

Wings are designed to fly straight with a range of trim speeds determined by the manufacturer. If the wing does not fly straight or trim to the manufacturer's specifications, it must be tuned to fly properly. Any wing adjustment can change the handling and stability characteristics of the wing. Each wing is unique and the tuning procedures are unique for each wing. It is very important to follow the specific tuning procedures in the POH/AFM for the specific wing. The following are general guidelines to understand the tuning process.

Tuning the Wing To Fly Straight

Wings may turn to the right or left (depending on which way the propeller turns) at high power settings because of the turning effect described earlier in the aerodynamics section. If it does not fly straight for cruising flight, visually examine for any asymmetric right and left features on the wing before making any adjustments. Look for symmetry in the twist angle. Inspect the leading edge for any discontinuities, bumps, or an irregular leading edge stiffener. Ensure the pockets are zippered and symmetrical on both sides. Ensure the reflex lines are clear, straight, and routed properly. Check the battens to ensure the right and left match (do not make any adjustments in the battens initially because reflex may have been added at the factory initially for tuning), and ensure the battens match the manufacturer's batten pattern. Check the batten tension on both sides and the leading edge tension to ensure it is symmetrical. If it is a used wing just acquired, research the history of the wing to see what might have happened which would cause it to not fly straight. For new wings, contact the manufacturer for advice.

If these checks do not make the wing fly straight, then adjust the twist in the wing according to the manufacturer's instructions. More twist on one side decreases angle of attack, produces less lift, and will drop the wing, which makes it turn in the direction where more twist was added. For example, with an unwanted left hand turn, either decrease the twist on the left hand wing (increase angle of attack at the tip) or increase the twist on the right hand wing (decrease the angle of attack at the tip).

Batten tension is one way of fixing very mild turns. Increasing the batten tension at the tips especially decreases twist and raises the wing. For normal mild turns, most wings have an adjustment at the tip where you can rotate the wing tip around the leading edge. This is the easiest and most effective wing twist adjustment. *[Figure 5-39]* For some models, reflex at the root can be adjusted on a side to adjust a significant turn. More reflex on a side means wing up, similar to reducing twist in a wing. As emphasized above, the POH for each manufacturer must be used for adjusting twist for wing tuning.

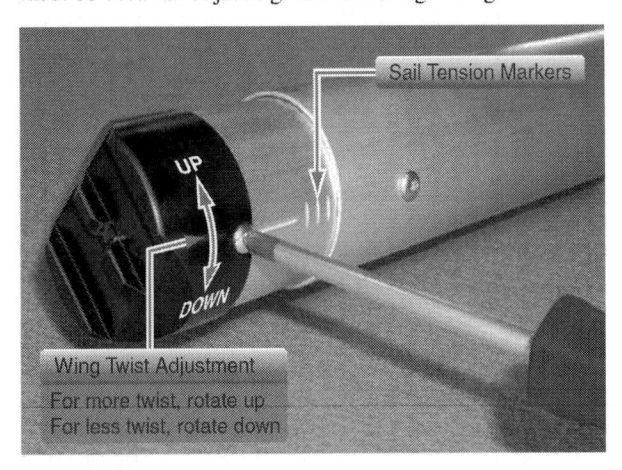

Figure 5-39. *Left hand wing tip twist adjustment shown without sail.*

Adjusting the tension on the leading edge is another method of adjusting the wing twist. However, different wings will react differently when tension is adjusted, so the POH must be followed for a particular wing. Some manufacturers do not suggest adjusting sail tension to adjust twist, but require equal tension with other adjustments to remedy an unwanted turn. For those wings utilizing asymmetrical sail tension to adjust twist, the following information is provided. Adjusting sail tension is most effective on slower wings with lots of twist. Adjusting sail tension affects some high performance wings differently, making it necessary to consult the POH. However, on most wings, increasing sail tension at the tip increases leading edge flex, resulting in more twist.

Tuning the Wing To Fly Slower or Faster

Most wings allow the hang point attachment to move forward to increase trim speed and back to decrease trim speed. If there is a situation where the hang point is at the most forward position and the wing trims below the manufacturer

5-14

recommended speed, or the trim speed is within 10 miles per hour (mph) of the stall speed, an alternate method for increasing the trim speed is needed. For this situation, the twist must be reduced symmetrically to increase the angle of attack on the tips so they provide more lift and lower the nose for proper trim.

This can be done by pulling back more on the crosstube tensioning cables which reduces the twist in the wing. However, this procedure reduces the stability of the wing and decreases the handling ability of the wing because it is stiffer. This is a common adjustment for hang gliding wings for inflight trim, however this adjustment should only be made on WSC wings as specified in the POH for a specific wing.

Raising and lowering the reflex lines affects airfoil reflex and also changes the trim speed of the wing. Lower reflex lines speed the wing up and make it less stable, raising the reflex lines slows the wing and make it more stable. Some manufactures have this as an adjustable setting which can be varied during flight, other manufactures have this adjustment where it can be made on the ground. Other manufactures do not recommend this adjustment because it can lower the certified stability of the wing.

Preflight Inspection

Each aircraft must have a routine preflight inspection before flight. Use a written checklist during preflight and ground operations to maintain an established procedure. *[Figure 5-40]* A written checklist is required so nothing is forgotten. Ground checklists include preflight preparation, preflight inspection, occupant preflight brief, flight deck management, startup, taxi, before takeoff, and aircraft shutdown. Be smart and follow the regulations—use a written checklist. All checklists should be secured so they do not fly out of the flight deck in flight and hit the propeller. Securing with zippered pockets and having lanyards for the checklists is recommended. Manufacturers of Special Light-Sport Aircraft (S-LSA) have checklists that come with the aircraft. Pilots with an experimental aircraft may need to develop their own.

Certificates and Documents

The first step of preflight inspection is to ensure the aircraft is legally airworthy which is determined in part, by the following certificates and documents:

- **A**irworthiness certificate
- **R**egistration certificate
- **O**perating limitations, which may be in the form of an FAA-approved AFM/POH, placards, instrument markings, or any combination thereof
- **W**eight and balance

ARROW is the acronym commonly used to remember these items. The PIC is responsible for making sure the proper documentation is on board the aircraft when operated. *[Figure 5-41]*

Figure 5-41. *Registration and airworthiness certificates are required to be in plain view.*

Aircraft logbooks are not required to be on board when it is operated. However, inspect the aircraft logbooks prior to flight to confirm the WSC aircraft has had all required inspections. The owner/operator must keep maintenance records for the airframe and powerplant. At a minimum, there must be an annual condition inspection within the preceding 12 calendar months. In addition, the WSC aircraft may also need a 100-hour inspection in accordance with 14 CFR part 91 if it is used for hire (e.g., for training operations). *[Figure 5-42]* If a transponder system is used, the transponder must be inspected within each preceding 24 calendar months.

Figure 5-40. *Laminated index cards are handy for checklists, and sized to fit into the flight suit zippered pocket.*

5-15

WSC LSA Maintenance Requirements

S-LSA-certified by FAA accepted ASTM consensus standards
• Annual and 100-hour condition inspection may be performed by:
  - LSA Repairman with Maintenance rating (120-hour course)
  - A&P or FAA certificated repair station
• Maintenance,* repair, and alterations may be performed by:
  - LSA Repairman with Maintenance rating (as authorized by manufacturer)
  - A&P or FAA certificated repair station (as authorized by manufacturer)

E-LSA including:
• Ultralights/trainers transitioned to LSA that meet the criteria of 14 CFR Section 21.191(i)(1)**
• Manufacturer S-LSA kits that meet the criteria of 14 CFR Section 21.191(i)(2) (not amateur built)
• Converted from S-LSA that meet the criteria of 14 CFR Section 21.191(i)(3) (see 14 CFR Section 41.1(b) for servicing)
  - Annual condition inspection may be performed by:
    > LSA Repairman with Maintenance rating (120-hour course)
    > A&P or FAA certificated repair station
    > Owner Repairman with Inspection rating (16-hour course)
  - Owner can be trained in his/her own aircraft and does not need 100-hour inspection.
  - Servicing, repair, and alterations may be performed by anyone.***

Amateur built that meet the definition of LSA and criteria of 14 CFR section 21.191(g)
• Annual condition inspection may be performed by:
  - Original builder gets Repairman certificate for that specific airplane and can perform annual condition inspection:
  - If owner was not original builder, Annual condition inspection may be performed by:
    > A&P or FAA certificated repair station or original builder
    > Original builder
• Owner can be trained in his/her own aircraft; 100-hour inspection not necessary
• Servicing, repair, and alterations may be performed by anyone***

* Simple "preventive maintenance" as specified by manufacturer can be done by the owner and operator of a S-LSA with a Sport Pilot or higher certificate.
** 100-hour inspection if used for training, compensation, or hire (if applicable) before January 31, 2010 (towing no end date) may be performed by LSA Repairman with Maintenance rating, A&P or FAA certificated repair station.
*** Maintenance is a common term, but it is not used here because the FAA uses the word "maintenance" to refer to a specific level of service required to be performed by properly trained mechanics.

Figure 5-42. *Maintenance requirements for WSC LSA.*

The pilot must have in his or her possession a Sport pilot certificate for the aircraft being flown, medical eligibility, and a government issued photo identification. For a Sport Pilot Certificate, medical eligibility can be a valid United States driver's license, which also serves as government issued photo identification.

To fly the aircraft with Private Pilot privileges, the pilot needs a valid FAA minimum third class medical certificate accompanied by a government issued photo identification and Private Pilot certificate for WSC aircraft. See Chapter 1, Introduction to Weight-Shift Control, for details on specific pilot certificates and privileges.

Routine Preflight Inspection

The accomplishment of a safe flight begins with a careful and systematic routine preflight inspection to determine if the aircraft is in a condition for safe flight. The preflight inspection should be performed in accordance with a printed checklist provided by the manufacturer for the specific model of the aircraft. However, the following general areas are applicable to all WSC aircraft.

The preflight inspection begins as soon as a pilot approaches the aircraft. Since the WSC aircraft can be transported by trailer, first and foremost, look for any damage that may have occurred during takedown, loading, transit, unloading, and setup. Make note of the general appearance of the aircraft, looking for obvious discrepancies such as tires with low air pressure, structural distortion, wear points, and dripping fuel or oil leaks. All tie-downs, control locks, and chocks should be removed during the unloading process.

The pilot must be thoroughly familiar with the locations and functions of the aircraft systems, switches, and controls. Use the preflight inspection as an orientation when operating a particular model for the first time.

The actual walk-around routine preflight inspection has been used for years from the smallest general aviation airplane to the largest commercial jet. The walk-around is thorough and systematic, and should be done the same way each time an aircraft is flown. In addition to seeing the aircraft up close, it requires taking the appropriate action whenever a discrepancy is discovered. A WSC aircraft walk-around covers four main tasks:

1. Wing inspection
2. Carriage inspection
3. Powerplant inspection
4. Equipment check

Throughout the inspection, check for proper operation of systems, secure nuts/bolts/attachments/hardware, look for any signs of deterioration or deformation of any components/systems, such as dents, signs of excessive wear, bending, tears, or misalignment of any components and/or cracks.

Each WSC aircraft should have a specific routine preflight inspection checklist, but the following can be used as an example and guideline.

Wing Inspection

Start with the nose. Inspect the nose plates and the attachment to the leading edges and keel. Ensure the nose plates are not cracked and the bolts are fastened securely. Check the wire attachments, top and bottom.

Inspect the control frame, down tubes and control bar for dents and ensure they are straight. Inspect the control frame attachment to the keel. Inspect the control bar to down tube brackets and bolts. *[Figure 5-43]* Inspect fore and aft flying wire condition, attachment to the keel, and the lower control bar corner brackets.

Figure 5-44. *Inspecting the flying wire attachment to the leading edge and crossbar along with all the hardware at this junction.*

Figure 5-43. *Inspecting the control frame brackets and flying wire attachments.*

Figure 5-45. *Examining inside the tip of the wing to inspect all the components.*

Inspect the left side flying wire attachment to the control bar bracket and condition of the flying wire up to the wing attachment. Examine the flying wire attachment to the leading edge and crossbar, as well as all hardware at this crossbar and leading edge junction. *[Figure 5-44]* Inspect the condition of the crossbar and the leading edge from the nose to the tip. Any discrepancies or tears in the leading edge fabric must lead to more detailed investigation of the leading edge spar itself.

Inspect the tip area, including the washout strut and general condition of the tip. If it is a double surface wing, look inside the tip and examine the inside of the wing and its components. *[Figure 5-45]*

From the tip, inspect the surface condition of the fabric. Generally, if the fabric has not been exposed to sunlight for long periods and stored properly, the wing fabric should stay in good shape.

Move along the trailing edge of the wing, inspecting the condition of the trailing edge and the tip batten attachments back to the keel. *[Figure 5-46]* Inspect the sail material, top and bottom, on the wing. Note that the trailing edge is

Figure 5-46. *Inspecting the trailing edge of the wing.*

vulnerable to rocks flying up from the wheels and hitting the propeller. Therefore, it is especially important to inspect the trailing edge in detail before each flight.

At the aft keel area in the middle of wing, inspect the kingpost and all the condition of the wires from the kingpost to ensure they are not wrapped around the trailing edge battens. *[Figure 5-47]* Inspect the wing tensioning hardware where the crossbar tensioning cables attach to the rear of the keel. Repeat this same sequence for the right (or opposite) side of the wing, in the reverse order. Inspect the condition of the wing attachment to the carriage, including the backup cable. *[Figure 5-48]*

Figure 5-47. *Inspecting the kingpost, top wires, and crossbar tension hardware.*

Figure 5-48. *Inspecting the wing attachment to the carriage.*

Carriage Inspection

Inspect the mast from the top to the bottom and the carriage keel from the back to the front. *[Figure 5-49]* Check the front tube attachment and top and bottom security attachments. Check the seat security and seat attachments from the keel to the mast.

Figure 5-49. *Inspecting the front keel and seat attachments to the keel.*

Check the front nose wheel for proper play, tire inflation, and secure axle bolt. Test the ground steering bar and ensure there is smooth steering range of motion. Check the front shocks, if installed, the brakes for rust and corrosion, loose nuts/bolts, alignment, cracks, signs of hydraulic fluid leakage, and hydraulic line security and abrasion, if so equipped. *[Figure 5-50]* Check the foot throttle for smooth operation and assure the parking brake is secured.

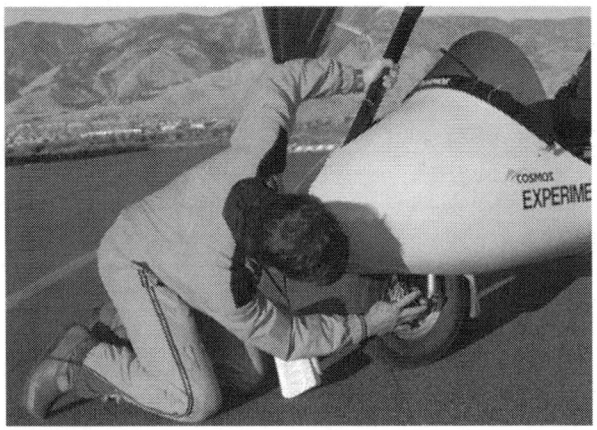

Figure 5-50. *Checking the front wheel, tire, and front fork assembly.*

Inspect the main landing gear drag struts, attachment to the keel, and attachment to the rear wheels. Examine the rear tires for proper inflation and tread plus the wheel attachment nut for security. Check main landing gear strut, landing gear shock absorber strut, and shock absorber operation. *[Figure 5-51]* Inspect all landing gear strut attachments to the airframe. Inspect the other side's rear landing gear by repeating the above procedure in reverse. Check all cowling for secure attachment and cracks. *[Figure 5-52]*

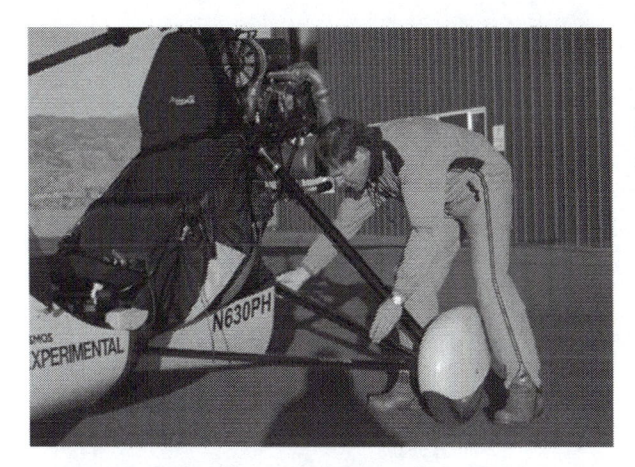

Figure 5-51. *Checking the rear landing gear struts.*

Figure 5-52. *Checking the cowl attachment for security and cracks.*

Powerplant Inspection

Inspect engine attachment to the carriage for security and cracks. In addition to looking at the bolts and mounts, shake the propeller, as shown in *Figure 5-53*, to provide a secure check of the propeller, gearbox, engine, and engine attachment to the carriage.

Fuel System

- Inspect fuel tank attachment and condition.
- Inspect fuel vent system, and ensure the fuel supply line is open (some WSC aircraft have fuel shut off valves outside the fuel tank).

Figure 5-53. *Checking the security of the engine to the airframe.*

- Inspect fuel pickup and fuel line running up to fuel filter. While inspecting all fuel lines, jiggle all fittings and connections to ensure they are secure.
- Inspect fuel filter and continue to follow fuel line up to fuel pump.
- Inspect the security and condition of fuel pump.
- Inspect fuel lines up to carburetors. *[Figure 5-54]*

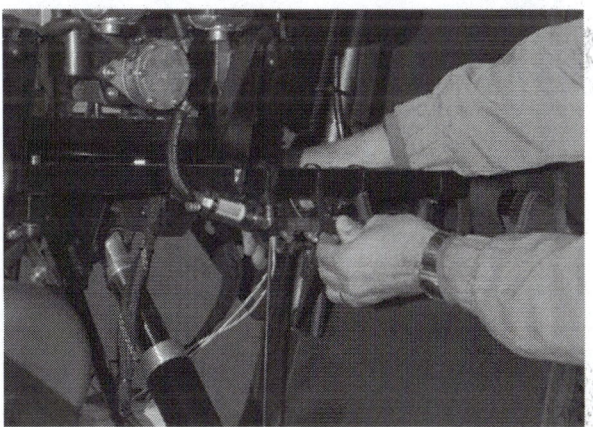

Figure 5-54. *Checking the security and condition of the fuel lines and fuel filter condition.*

Induction System

- Inspect carburetors, including float bowl attachment and rubber bushing from carburetors into engine.
- Inspect fuel lines from float bowls to carburetor inlet.
- Inspect air inlet filter to ensure it is clean and secure. *[Figure 5-55]*

Figure 5-55. *Checking the security of the air inlet filter and the security of the carburetors to the engine.*

Ignition System

- Inspect ignition system wires to spark plugs.
- Inspect spark plug caps and wires to CDI units to ensure they are secure and fastened. *[Figure 5-56]*
- Ensure ignition switches are turned off.

Figure 5-56. *Checking spark plug cap security to the spark plugs.*

Cooling Systems

Ensure there is clear airflow for any cooling system fan or radiator. Ensure no insects or birds created an obstruction to the airflow for the engine cooling system.

Air cooled—rotate the propeller and ensure that the cooling fan rotates also.

Water cooled—check the coolant level to ensure there is cooling fluid in the system.

Four stroke with additional oil coolers—ensure the oil cooler has clear airflow and that nothing is blocking it.

Exhaust Systems

Inspect exhaust attachment to engine, and EGT senders. Slightly jiggle the exhaust system to inspect the springs holding it together. All springs must be secure. Inspect the condition of exhaust system for cracks and attachment security. *[Figure 5-57]*

Figure 5-57. *Inspecting the exhaust system by jiggling the outlet pipe and checking the springs.*

Propeller Gearbox

Rotate the propeller in the proper direction only and inspect blades for cracks or nicks. Listen and feel for smooth operation and engine compression while rotating the propeller. Inspect propeller attachment to the gearbox and the gearbox attachment to the engine.

Throttle System

Check all throttle controls for smooth operation and proper travel and locking. Also check choke and/or primer system for proper operation and travel.

Flight Deck Inspection

The following should be performed for a flight deck inspection:

- Check seat security and proper adjustment for pilot and passenger.
- Check seat belt attachment and seatbelt operation.
- Inspect the gauges for security and readability.
- Switch electrical master on and check gauges for expected readings. *[Figure 5-58]*
- Check ballistic parachute handle for security and proper location.

Fuel

Overall, particular attention should be paid to the fuel quantity, type/grade, and quality. Modern WSC two- and four-stroke engines are designed to use auto gas with various octane ratings as specified by the manufacturer for different models. If auto gas is stored for more than 3 weeks, octane value may fall below the recommended rating. In this situation, it is best to drain the gas and use fresh gas. For engines designed for auto gas, aviation gasoline (AVGAS) 100LL can be mixed and used

Figure 5-58. *Checking the flight deck instruments for readability and security. Turning on the main electrical power to verify proper instrument readings.*

on a limited basis but the lead in this is not good for the engine and additional precautions/procedures should be researched for the particular make/model of engine for primary use.

Always use a higher grade/octane of fuel rather than a lower grade, or detonation will severely damage the engine in a very short period of time. Check the aircraft operation manual and the engine manual for the type of fuel to use.

When attempting to fuel for maximum capacity, remember that many fuel tanks are very sensitive to attitude. Fill the aircraft on a level surface and check to ensure the amount of fuel in the tanks is adequate for the planned flight plus 30 minutes of reserve. Check the level in the fuel tank plus the panel-mounted gauge, if so equipped.

To transport gasoline, clear gas cans are preferable because the fuel is visible through the container and allows a pilot to look at the container for fuel level. *[Figure 5-59]*

An important step in any preflight is to check for water and other sediment contamination. Avgas is more probable to have water in the fuel tanks because auto gas typically has alcohol in it to boost the octane. Alcohol absorbs water, running it harmlessly through the system.

When using 100LL Avgas, water tends to accumulate in fuel tanks from condensation, particularly in partially filled tanks. Because water is heavier than fuel, it tends to collect in the low points of the fuel system. If Avgas is used, drain any water from the low point in the system.

Oil

A four-stroke engine's oil level should be checked during each preflight and rechecked with each refueling. Four-stroke engines can be expected to consume a small amount

Figure 5-59. *Translucent fuel containers with premixed oil (right) and auto gas only (left).*

of oil during normal operation. If consumption grows or suddenly changes, qualified maintenance personnel should investigate.

If the Rotax 912 oil level is low when the oil is checked, rotate the propeller in the correct direction (counterclockwise, facing it) to pump any oil from the engine back into the oil tank for a proper measurement and recheck oil level before adding oil. *[Figure 5-60]*

Figure 5-60. *Four-stroke engine showing the oil reservoir where the dip stick is located to check the oil.*

Check the reservoir level of two-stroke engines with oil injection at each gas fill-up. It is also very important to ensure the oil reservoir has clear air vent holes to allow continuous flow of oil to lubricate the engine. Always use the same type of oil because different types of oil harden and stop the oil injection process, resulting in a seized engine. Additionally, check to see if the oil injection system lines from the tank to the carburetors are clean and secure. Some two-stroke engines have a separate lubrication system for the inlet rotary valve; this system should be checked for proper level and leaks. *[Figure 5-61]* When adding fuel and oil, ensure that the caps has been securely replaced.

Figure 5-61. *Two-stroke engine showing oil injection reservoir and level, rotary inlet valve reservoir and level, and liquid cooled reservoir for checking coolant levels.*

Ready Aircraft To Enter Flight Deck

Either before or after the routine preflight inspection, the aircraft should be unsecured, positioned for starting, and readied to enter the flight deck. A checklist provides the basic steps.

- Untie aircraft, secure tie down ropes in aircraft, or coil neatly if they stay at airport.
- Remove ground chocks and secure in aircraft.
- Locate a suitable area to start engine that is free of dirt and has minimal dust, preferably a paved or grassy area away from people and objects.
- Position aircraft so prop blast is clear; verify that brakes are on, throttle is closed, and propeller area is cleared.
- Position into wind, if possible, for best cooling during warm up.

Occupant Preflight Brief

A preflight briefing is required to ensure the passenger is informed on the proper use of safety equipment and exit information. This can be done before entering the aircraft, and must be accomplished before starting the engine. Manufacturers of S-LSA aircraft typically have printed briefing cards that should be used. The following is a comprehensive checklist that can be used as a guideline for any preflight briefing:

- Seat belt fasten and unfasten procedures. Seat belts must be worn for takeoff and landing (and should always be worn during flight).
- What passengers can hold onto and what not to touch.
- Positive exchange of controls using a three step process : "You take the controls," "I have the controls," "You have the controls."
- Look for other ground and air traffic.
- Flight deck entrance and exit procedures including emergency exit.
- Ballistic parachute operation procedures.
- Engine-out situation and procedures for planned flight with diversions.
- Hand signals in case electric loads must be shut off or internal aircraft communications not functioning.
- Water landings with engine-out situation, if planned flight over water.
- Ensure nothing can fall out of pockets while in flight. This is especially important since the propeller is in back.
- Helmet fastening and unfastening procedure. *[Figure 5-62]*

Figure 5-62. *Pilot briefing the passenger on how to fasten and unfasten helmet.*

- Review the type of aircraft (special or experimental) which is not an FAA certified standard category aircraft.

- Fire extinguisher operation, if so equipped.
- All safety systems, as required.
- Use restroom before entering aircraft.

Flight Deck Management

After entering the flight deck, the pilot should first ensure that all necessary equipment, documents, checklists, and navigation charts appropriate for the flight are on board. *[Figure 5-63]* If a portable intercom, headsets, or a hand-held global positioning system (GPS) is used, the pilot is responsible for ensuring that the routing of wires and cables does not interfere with the motion or the operation of any control.

Figure 5-63. *Pilot fastens helmet and reviews checklist while in flight deck.*

Regardless of what materials are to be used, they should be neatly arranged and organized in a manner that makes them readily available. The flight deck should be checked for articles that might be tossed about if turbulence is encountered, and any loose items properly secured.

When the pilot is comfortably seated, the safety belt and shoulder harness (if installed) should be fastened and adjusted to a comfortably snug fit. The safety belt must be worn at all times the pilot is seated at the controls.

Checklist After Entering Flight Deck

- Seats adjusted for full operation of all controls.
- Seats locked into position.
- Put on seat belts (lap first, then shoulder) and adjust so all controls and systems can be fully operated.
- Check all control systems for proper operation.
- Check all systems operations.
- Demonstrate and practice flight and emergency equipment and procedures.
- Demonstrate and practice what passengers can hold onto, and what not to touch.
- Demonstrate and practice positive exchange of controls.
- Remove safety pin for ballistic chute operation.
- Install helmet (if applicable) and headphones.
- Check intercom and radio communications systems.
- Install eye protection (safety glasses, helmet shields).

It is important that a pilot operates an aircraft safely on the ground. This includes being familiar with standard hand signals that are used universally for ground operations. *[Figure 5-64]*

Engine Start

The specific procedures for engine start vary greatly since there are as many different methods as there are engines, fuel systems, and starting conditions. The engine start checklist procedures in the POH should be followed. The following are some basic steps that apply to most aircraft:

- Key in, ignition on, master power on
- Check gauges for operation and fuel level.
- Fuel pump on (or pump fuel bulb to fill carburetor bowls)
- System switches on. (Some WSC have specific system switches turned on after the engine is started because engine starting may create lower voltage possibly damaging instruments or systems. If in doubt, start engine and than turn on instruments and systems not needed for starting.)
- Both ignition systems switches on
- Choke/enrichener on (or pump primer as appropriate)
- Throttle closed
- Brakes on
- Ensure propeller area is cleared, loudly announce to propeller area "Clear prop," and wait for any response.
- Start engine through pull cord start or electric start (do not try to hand prop under any circumstances)
- Ensure the aircraft does not move, keeping hands on ignition switches for quick shutdown, if necessary.
- Adjust throttle, choke or enrichener to keep engine running smoothly.

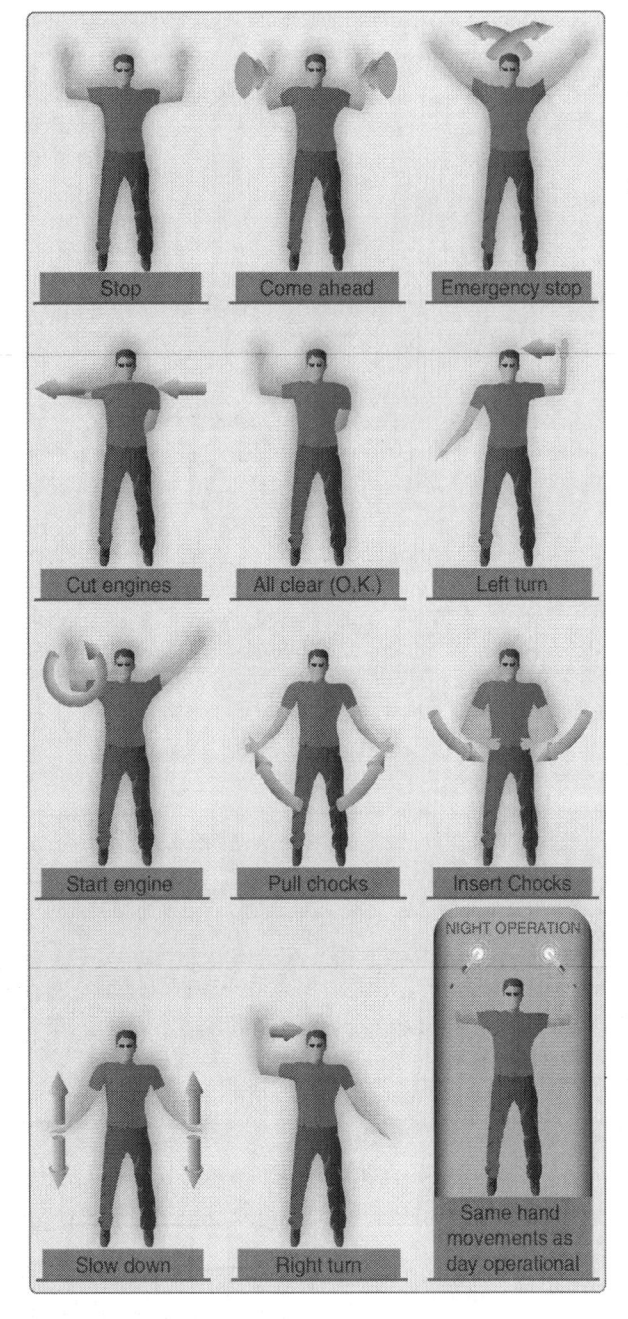

Figure 5-64. *Hand signals for ground operations.*

- Turn on electric instruments if applicable.
- Check gauges for proper ranges (oil pressure, revolutions per minute (rpm), charging voltage, engine temperatures within ranges, etc.)
- Continue to monitor area and shut down engine if any person or animal approaches.

A relatively low rpm setting is recommended immediately following engine start. This is typically a slight increase in the throttle to keep the engine running smoothly. It is not recommended to allow the rpm to race immediately after a start with a cold engine, as there is insufficient lubrication until the oil pressure rises on four-stroke engines, and unequal heating on two-stroke engines. In freezing temperatures, the engine is also exposed to potential mechanical distress until it warms and normal internal operating clearances are reached.

On four-stroke engines, as soon as the engine is started, the oil pressure should be checked. If it does not rise to the manufacturer's specified value, the engine may not be receiving proper lubrication and should be shut down immediately to prevent serious damage.

Taxiing

Since an aircraft is moved under its own power between the startup area and the runway, the pilot must thoroughly understand and be proficient in taxi procedures. When the brakes are first released and the aircraft starts to roll, the brakes should be tested immediately for proper operation. Applying power to start the WSC aircraft moving forward slowly, then retarding the throttle and simultaneously applying pressure smoothly on the brake may be needed to accomplish this. If braking action is unsatisfactory, the engine should be shut down immediately.

When yellow taxiway centerline stripes are provided, they should be followed unless it becomes necessary to deviate to clear aircraft or obstructions. *[Figure 5-65]*

Figure 5-65. *Taxiing on the yellow airport taxi line.*

An awareness of other aircraft that are taking off, landing, or taxiing, and consideration for the right-of-way of others is essential to safety. When taxiing, the pilot's eyes should be looking outside the aircraft, to the sides, as well as the front. The pilot must be aware of the entire area around the aircraft to ensure that it clears all obstructions, people, animals, and other aircraft. If at any time there is doubt about the clearance from an object, the pilot should stop the aircraft and check the clearance. The WSC aircraft does have the advantage of the wing tip capability of being raised and lowered to clear objects.

It is difficult to set any rule for a single, safe taxiing speed. What is reasonable and prudent under some conditions may be hazardous under others. The primary requirements for safe taxiing are positive control, the ability to recognize potential hazards in time to avoid them, and the ability to stop or turn where and when desired without undue reliance on the brakes. Pilots should proceed at a cautious speed on congested or busy ramps. Normally, the speed should be at the rate at which movement of the aircraft is dependent on the throttle. That is, the speed should be low enough that when the throttle is closed, the aircraft can be stopped promptly.

A GPS provides this speed since the airspeed indicator is not effective at these lower speeds. A rule of thumb is 5 mph, brisk walking speed, or 10 mph for long unobstructed areas. When taxiing, it is best to slow down before attempting a turn.

WSC aircraft taxi with the wing typically held in a neutral position, but stronger winds may require positioning of the wing so it cannot be lifted. Position controls properly for wind conditions:

- Strong tailwind—pitch control normal or slight nose up with wings level.
- Strong headwind—pitch control nose down with wings level.
- Strong quartering tail wind—nose normal with upwind wing slightly down so wind cannot catch it, but not to low to cause excess stress on carriage mast.
- Strong quartering head wind—nose down with upwind wing slightly down so wind cannot catch it, but not low enough to cause excess stress on carriage mast.

Checklist for Taxi

Plan taxi path to runway to avoid paths that would put the aircraft behind any propeller or jet blast. Observe other aircraft closely which could start up and taxi in front, if practical.

- Turn on strobe light (if applicable).
- Release brake.
- When first rolling, immediately check brakes, steering, and shut down if either is not functioning properly.
- Observe proper right of way while taxiing.
    - Taxiing aircraft yield to landing aircraft, so landing craft have right of way over taxiing aircraft.
    - Two aircraft approaching head on will turn right (similar to what is done in a car).
    - Two aircraft traveling in same direction, the forward aircraft has right of way because its pilot can not normally see the aircraft in back.
    - With two airplanes converging, the pilot who sees an aircraft on the right must avoid that aircraft. The aircraft on the right has the right of way.
- Runway incursions—observe all taxiway and runway markings.

Runway incursions are a significant risk and must be avoided. This is a most important concept. Taxi slowly and observe the basic airport markings/signs. Clearance to proceed must be obtained prior to taxiing across any runway or entering a runway to takeoff. There could be large aircraft, which may not be able to respond to WSC aircraft quick movements. An important runway marker is the "Hold Short Line." Always stop before reaching this line and get clearance before crossing it. *[Figure 5-66]*

- At a towered airport, this is clearance from the tower. Always read back tower instructions clearance when received from tower before proceeding.
- At a nontowered airport, the clearance procedure is to listen to and monitor all air traffic on the airport radio frequency. Observe all air traffic taxiing and in the pattern. After listening on the radio and observing all possible traffic, announce position and intentions before crossing runway or entering runway. If crossing runway, announce once you have taxied across that you are clear of runway.

Figure 5-66. *Taxi on the airport yellow taxi line, but stop at the "hold short line" to get clearance before taxiing across or onto an active airport runway.*

Before Takeoff Check

The before takeoff check is the systematic procedure for making a check of the engine, controls, systems, instruments, and avionics prior to flight. Normally, it is performed after taxiing to a position near the takeoff end of the runway. Taxiing to that position usually allows sufficient time for the engine to warm up to at least minimum operating temperatures. This ensures adequate lubrication and internal engine clearances before being operated at high power settings. Many engines require that the oil temperature or engine temperature reach a minimum value, as stated in the AFM/POH, before high power is applied.

Some WSC aircraft are ram air cooled, where the cooling air must be rammed into the cooling radiator during flight. On the ground, however, little or no air is forced through the radiator. Prolonged ground operations may cause engine overheating. Some designs place the cooling radiators near the propeller so the propeller produces reasonable airflow to cool the engine.

Air cooled two-stroke engine aircraft may have an integral engine driven cooling fan and can idle indefinitely without overheating. Monitoring engine temperature to be within limits is important for aircraft operations on the ground.

After taxiing to the runway entrance runup area and before beginning the pretakeoff check, the aircraft should be positioned clear of other aircraft. When you taxi out to the run up area, position yourself where other aircraft can easily taxi to a suitable run up area. There should not be anything behind the aircraft that might be damaged by the prop blast. To minimize overheating during engine run-up, it is recommended that the aircraft be headed as nearly as possible into the wind. After an aircraft is properly positioned for the run-up, the nose wheel should be pointed straight.

During the engine run-up, the surface under the WSC aircraft should be firm (a smooth, paved, or turf surface, if possible) and free of debris. Otherwise, the propeller may pick up pebbles, dirt, or other loose objects and hurl them backward or into the sail. *[Figure 5-67]*

While performing the engine run-up, the pilot must divide attention inside to look at the instruments and outside the aircraft to look for other traffic. If the parking brake slips, or if application of the brakes is inadequate for the amount of power applied, the aircraft could move forward unnoticed if attention is fixed only inside the aircraft.

Each aircraft has different features and equipment, and the before takeoff checklist provided by the WSC manufacturer

Figure 5-67. *Positioned in the aircraft run up area before takeoff, the WSC is ready to perform the pretakeoff checklist.*

should be used to perform the run-up. Here is a general checklist.

- Verify the strobe light is on (if applicable).
- Trim is set to proper speed for takeoff.
- Brakes are set.
- Ignition check—always divide attention into and out of the flight deck in case the brakes can not hold the aircraft still at the higher power settings. (Some ignition checks are done at idle; see POH for engine specifics.) If the brakes start to slip and the aircraft starts moving, decrease power immediately and reevaluate how to run up and keep the aircraft stationary during run up. Run up engine to consistent rpm higher than idle. Switch from both ignition systems to one and watch for a slight drop in rpm. Do the same for the other ignition system.
- Verify engine temperatures (EGT, CHT, oil and/or water) and oil pressure are within the acceptable ranges.

At towered airports, obtain clearance from tower when ready for takeoff. At nontowered airports, when all air traffic is clear from observations and radio communications and while holding short before the runway boundary (hold short) line, announce the aircraft is entering the runway. This is a pilot's clearance at a self-announce airport to enter the runway. At all airports, do a visual verification that there are no aircraft landing before entering the runway.

After Landing

During the after-landing roll, the WSC aircraft should be gradually slowed to normal taxi speed before turning off the landing runway. Any significant degree of turn at faster speeds could result in the WSC aircraft tipping over and subsequent damage. *[Figure 5-68]*

Figure 5-68. *After landing, the pilot slows to the appropriate taxi speed before following the yellow taxi lines to exit the runway.*

To give full attention to controlling the WSC aircraft during the landing roll, the after-landing check should be performed only after the aircraft is brought to a complete stop clear of the active runway.

Postflight, Parking, and Securing

A flight is never complete until the engine is shut down and the WSC aircraft is secured. A pilot should consider this an essential part of any flight. Unless parking in a designated, supervised area, the pilot should select a location which prevents propeller or jet blast of other airplanes from striking the WSC aircraft.

The pilot should always use the procedures in the manufacturer's checklist for shutting down the engine and securing the airplane. Some of the important items include:

- Set the parking brakes on.
- Set throttle to idle and let engine cool down to manufactures specifications.
- Turn ignition switch off.
- Turn electrical units and radios off.
- Turn master electrical switch to off.

After engine shutdown and exiting the aircraft, the pilot should accomplish a postflight inspection. When the flight is complete, the aircraft should be hangared or tied down appropriately for the situation.

There are a number of ways to park and secure the WSC aircraft depending on the situation. With normal aircraft tie downs, little to no wind, and a short time frame for unsupervised parking, the WSC aircraft can be secured by tying both leading edge cross bar junctions to the typical airport wing ties. The control bar is secured to the front tube with a bungee chord to stabilize the nose or the control bar can be pulled back and attached to the seat rail to keep the nose down in case of a possible headwind. *[Figure 5-69]*

Figure 5-69. *Typical tie down for light wind. Left hand WSC control bar pulled back to lower nose for possible headwind, right hand control bar fastened to front tube.*

If higher winds are present, the WSC aircraft can be positioned so the wind is blowing from the side and the wing tip is lowered on the windward side so the wind is pushing down on the wing. This can be used to exit the aircraft and tie the wing down in higher winds. *[Figures 5-70 through 5-72]*

Figure 5-70. *Pilot's view of the left hand wing lowered into the wind, allowing the pilot to exit the aircraft in higher winds with the wind pushing down on the wing from the side.*

Figure 5-71. *Wing tied down with tip on ground into wind.*

Figure 5-72. *Group of WSC aircraft tied down with wing tips lowered into prevailing wind.*

For overnight or higher wind tie down, the complete wing can be lowered to the ground with a four point tie down. Each wing at the crossbar/leading edge junction plus the nose and rear of the keel can be tied down for greater resistance to wind. For humid or dusty areas, a cover is recommended for the carriage to cover the engine and flight deck. *[Figure 5-73]*

Figure 5-73. *Wing lowered and four point tie-down with carriage cover to protect flight deck and engine.*

The best way to secure the WSC aircraft for overnight is to put it in a hangar. If it must be stored outside, remove the wing and fold it up so there is no chance of the wing being damaged in an unforeseen gust front.

Chapter Summary

Preflight preparations should include the overall evaluation of the:

- Pilot: experience, sleep, food and water, drugs or medications, stress, illness and overall aeromedical factors, as discussed in Chapter 1, Introduction to Weight-Shift Control.
- Aircraft: proper transport, fuel, weight (does not exceed maximum), ARROW, takeoff and landing requirements, equipment.
- EnVironment: where to fly, weather conditions, forecast for departure and destination airfields, route of flight, and specific airport patterns/runway lengths. Pilot capabilities must be compared to the weather limitations for the decision of whether to go to the airfield.
- External pressures: schedules, available alternatives, purpose of flight.

Preflight procedures include:

- Set up of the wing and mounting the wing on the carriage (if trailered or taken down).
- Tuning the wing to fly straight and at the proper trim speed.
- Preflight inspection with written checklist of wing, carriage, powerplant, systems, and flight deck.
- Readying aircraft to enter by proper positioning and occupant preflight brief.
- Engine start, taxi, and performing before takeoff check.

Postflight procedures include:

- Taxi off runway to appropriate location.
- Park, exit, post flight and documenting any discrepancies.
- Hangar, secure or take down.

Chapter 6
Flight Manuevers

Introduction

Flying a weight-shift control (WSC) aircraft is not like driving an automobile on the highway. It is also different from operating the controls of an airplane. A WSC pilot holds the control bar, which is a structural component of the wing, in his or her hands. This wing is attached to the carriage and freely rotates laterally and longitudinally about the hang point. Therefore, the "feel" of the WSC is completely different from other aircraft because there are no movable control surfaces actuated through push/pull rods or cables connected to a separate control actuator, such as a stick or yoke.

The pilot feels forces on the wing through the control bar, which is part of the wing structure with no mechanical advantage. Simply, the feel of the WSC is different from other aircraft but the basic flight maneuvers are similar.

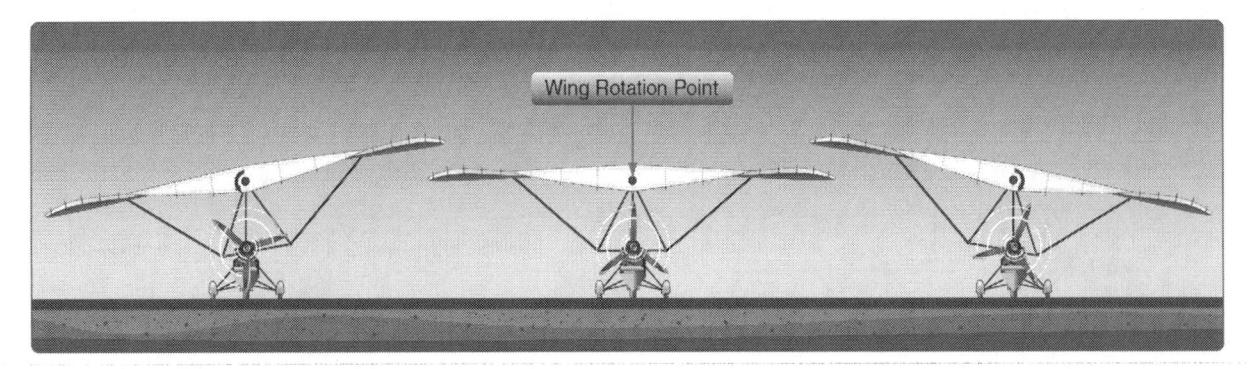

Figure 6-1. *Roll diagram.*

Practicing the basics with precision and understanding the effects on the pilot and the aircraft develop a "feel" for the aircraft in flight so the pilot can concentrate on the flying mission at hand and not on the mechanical movements. The ability to perform any assigned maneuver is only a matter of obtaining a clear visual and mental conception of it so that perfect performance is a habit without conscious effort.

Begin with the flight basics to build a foundation for precision flying. Takeoffs/landings and emergency maneuvers are covered in later chapters. All flying tasks are based on the four fundamental flight maneuvers:

- Straight-and-level flight
- Turns
- Climbs
- Descents

Controlled flight consists of either one or a combination of these basic maneuvers.

Effects and the Use of the Controls

In using the flight controls, the results should be looked at in relation to the pilot. The pilot should always be considered the center of movement of the aircraft or the reference point from which the movements are judged and described. The important concept and a foundation for all flight maneuvers is not to think of the controls in terms of "up" or "down" in respect to the Earth. This is only a relative state to the pilot. Controls need to be thought of in relation to the pilot, so that the control use can be for any flight attitude whether climbing, diving, banking, or a combination of these.

Sideways pressure applied by moving the control bar to the left lowers the right wing in relation to the pilot; moving the control bar to the right lowers the left wing in relation to the pilot. This is roll control as discussed in Chapter 2, Aerodynamics. *[Figure 6-1]*

Pushing and forward pressure applied to the control bar results in the WSC aircraft's nose rising in relation to the pilot slowing down the WSC, while pulling in or back pressure results in the nose lowering in relation to the pilot increasing speed of the WSC. At the same trim speed, increasing the throttle results in the nose remaining at the same level in relation to the pilot but raising pitch with increased throttle and lowering pitch with decreased throttle in relation to the Earth's horizon. Both control bar and throttle effect pitch in relation to the earth's horizon. This is pitch control, as discussed in Chapter 2, Aerodynamics. *[Figure 6-2]*

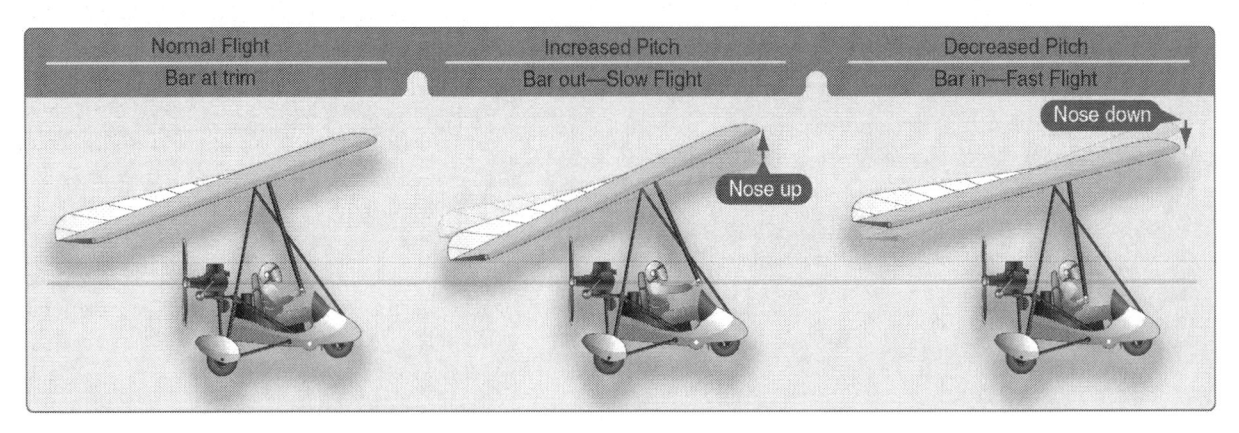

Figure 6-2. *Control bar effect on pitch and airspeed.*

Feel of the Aircraft

All WSC aircraft controls have a natural "live pressure" while in flight and will remain in a neutral position of their own accord if the aircraft is trimmed properly. The pilot should think of exerting a force on the controls against this live pressure or resistance. It is the duration and amount of force exerted on the control bar that affects the controls and maneuvers the WSC aircraft.

The actual amount of the control input is of little importance; but it is important that the pilot maneuver the aircraft by applying sufficient control pressure to obtain a desired result, regardless of how far the control bar is actually moved. The controls should be held lightly, not grabbed and squeezed. A common error for beginning pilots is a tendency to "tightly grip the bar." This tendency should be avoided as it prevents the development of "feel," which is an important part of aircraft control. *[Figure 6-3]*

Figure 6-3. *Hold the control bar with a light touch to feel every movement in the wing.*

However, for WSC aircraft, the controls do need to be gripped during moderate and severe turbulence to make sure the wing does not get ripped out of the pilot's hands. This is why flying a WSC aircraft in turbulence requires strength and endurance. It can be fatiguing if the pilot is not used to or in shape for this type of flying. The initial flight training should be done in calm conditions so the student can use a soft touch on the controls to develop the feel for the WSC aircraft.

The ability to sense a flight condition is often called "feel of the aircraft," but senses in addition to "feel" are also involved. Sounds inherent to flight are an important sense in developing "feel." The air that rushes past an open flight deck can be felt and heard easily within the tolerances of the Practical Test Standards (PTS) of ± 10 knots. When the level of sound increases, it indicates that airspeed is increasing. In addition to the sound of the air, air rushing past is also felt unless an effective wind screen is placed in front of the pilot blocking the wind. *[Figure 6-4]*

Figure 6-4. *Wind shield blocks the wind from hitting the pilot.*

The powerplant emits distinctive sound patterns in different conditions of flight. The sound of the engine in cruise flight sounds different from the sound in a glide or a climb. Overall, there are three sources of actual "feel" that are very important to the pilot.

1. The first source is the pilot's own body as it responds to forces of acceleration. The "G" loads, as discussed in Chapter 2, imposed on the airframe are also felt by the pilot. Centripetal acceleration forces the pilot down into the seat or raises the pilot against the seat belt. Radial accelerations, although minor for WSC aircraft, are caused by minor slips or skids in uncoordinated flight and shift the pilot from side to side in the seat. These forces are all perceptible and useful to the pilot. Flight time plus the pilot's desire to feel the aircraft provides the pilot an excellent "feel" for the aircraft and the ability to detect even the smallest change in flight. A goal for any pilot should be to constantly develop a better feel for their aircraft.

2. The response of the controls to the pilot's touch is another element of "feel," and is one that provides direct information concerning airspeed.

3. Another type of "feel" comes to the pilot through the airframe. It consists mainly of vibration. An example is the aerodynamic buffeting and shaking that precedes a stall. Different airspeeds and power settings can also provide a subtle feel in aircraft vibrations.

Kinesthesia, or the sensing of changes in direction or speed of motion, is one of the most important senses a pilot can develop. When properly developed, kinesthesia can warn the pilot of changes in speed and/or the beginning of a settling or mushing of the aircraft.

The senses that contribute to "feel" of the aircraft are inherent in every person. However, "feel" must be developed. It is a well established fact that the pilot who develops a "feel" for the aircraft early in flight training has little difficulty with advanced flight maneuvers.

Attitude Flying

Flying by attitude means visually establishing the aircraft's attitude with reference to the natural horizon. Attitude is the angular difference measured between an aircraft's axis and the Earth's horizon. As discussed in Chapter 2, Aerodynamics, pitch attitude is the angle formed by the longitudinal axis, and bank attitude is the angle formed by the lateral axis. Rotation about the aircraft's vertical axis (yaw) is termed an attitude relative to the aircraft's flightpath, but not relative to the natural horizon.

In attitude flying, aircraft control is composed of three components:

1. Bank control—control of the aircraft about the longitudinal axis to attain a desired bank angle in relation to the natural horizon. This can be easily seen in a WSC aircraft by looking at the angle the front tube makes with the horizon. *[Figure 6-5]*

2. Pitch control—control of the aircraft about the lateral axis to raise and lower the nose in relation to the natural horizon.

3. Power control—used when the flight situation indicates a need for a change in thrust, which at a constant speed raises and lowers the nose in relationship to the horizon similar to pitch control.

Straight-and-Level Flying

Flying straight and level is the most important flight maneuver to master. It is impossible to emphasize too

Figure 6-5. *Pilot's view of 45° bank angle can be measured with the front tube or the control bar's angle with the horizon.*

strongly the necessity for forming correct habits in flying straight and level. All flight is in essence a deviation from this fundamental flight maneuver. It is not uncommon to find a pilot whose basic flying ability consistently falls just short of minimum expected standards, and upon analyzing the reasons for the shortcomings discover that the cause is the inability to fly straight and level properly.

In learning to control the aircraft in level flight, it is important that the control forces be exerted just enough to produce the desired result. Some wings are more responsive than others. The student should learn to associate the apparent movement of the control bar with the response in pitch and roll. In this way, the student can develop the ability to regulate the change desired in the aircraft's attitude by the amount and direction of forces applied to the controls without the necessity of referring to outside references for each minor correction.

Straight-and-level flight is flight in which a constant heading and altitude are maintained. It is accomplished by making immediate and measured corrections for deviations in direction and altitude from unintentional slight turns, descents, and climbs. Level flight is a matter of consciously fixing the relationship of the position of something on the aircraft, used as a reference point with a point on the horizon. In establishing the reference point on the aircraft, place the aircraft in the desired position and select a reference point. A typical reference point on the WSC aircraft is a point on the front tube.

The WSC aircraft reference point depends on where the pilot is sitting, the pilot's height (whether short or tall), and the pilot's manner of sitting. It is, therefore, important when establishing this relationship, the pilot sit in a normal manner; otherwise the points will not be the same when the normal position is resumed. *[Figures 6-6 and 6-7]*

Straight-and-level flight should first be practiced in calm air where the control movements determine the actual movement through the air and air movement has minimal effect on the aircraft's altitude and direction.

A trim speed needs to be set if the WSC aircraft has an inflight trim system or the trim speed set on the ground is used. The throttle is adjusted so the aircraft is flying level, not climbing or descending. This can be determined by looking at the altimeter or the vertical speed indicator (if so equipped). The throttle setting is the control for maintaining level flight for a specific weight, loading, trim speed, and density altitude.

Level flight is maintained by selecting some portion of the aircraft's nose as a reference point, and then keeping that point in a fixed position relative to the horizon. Using the principles of attitude flying, that position should be cross-checked occasionally against the altimeter to determine whether or not the throttle setting and pitch attitude are correct. If altitude is being gained or lost, the pitch attitude should be readjusted with the throttle in relation to the horizon. Then, recheck the altimeter to determine if altitude is being maintained and adjust the throttle accordingly. The throttle setting for this condition should be noted and all future changes in weight, trim speed, and density altitude referenced to this known throttle setting.

After level flight is mastered in calm air, it can be practiced in air that is moving, minor turbulence or "active air." The throttle settings for similar weight, trim, and density altitude are the same, but more pilot input is required to maintain a constant altitude. The throttle is used to maintain a selected distance above the reference point for local air movement, but the pitch pressure (nose up or nose down) is used to control this attitude for shorter duration air disturbances.

Typically, updrafts or thermals raise the nose of the aircraft and downdrafts at the edge of thermals lower the nose of the aircraft. For minor updrafts the nose is lowered by pitch control input by the pilot slightly increasing the speed of the aircraft to keep the pitch at a constant level. In moderate to severe updrafts, the throttle can be reduced to assist in maintaining a reasonably constant pitch angle with the horizon.

Similarly for minor downdrafts that lower the nose, the nose is raised by pitch control input by the pilot slightly decreasing the speed of the aircraft to keep the pitch at a constant level. An additional caution for raising the nose and decreasing the speed is that raising the nose too high could stall the aircraft. Therefore, caution must be exercised in moderate downdrafts not to reduce the speed too much to approach a stall speed/critical angle of attack. Similar to reducing the throttle in updrafts to reduce pitch angle, increasing the throttle typically increases the pitch angle. *[Figure 6-8]*

WSC aircraft can use the front tube as a reference to align perpendicular with the horizon and the wings leveled. It should be noted that any time the wings are banked even slightly, the aircraft will turn.

The front tube can be used as an indicator to determine turn rate. If the bar is moving side to side to any established reference point, the aircraft is banked and should be corrected to eliminate any turn. The objective of straight-and-level flight is to detect small deviations from level flight as soon as they occur, necessitating only small corrections.

Straight-and-level flight requires almost no application of control pressures if the aircraft is properly trimmed and the

6-5

Figure 6-6. *A reference point on the horizon chosen.*

Figure 6-7. *Pilot's view of a reference point on the front tube chosen for level flight and lined up with the reference point on the horizon for straight-and-level flight.*

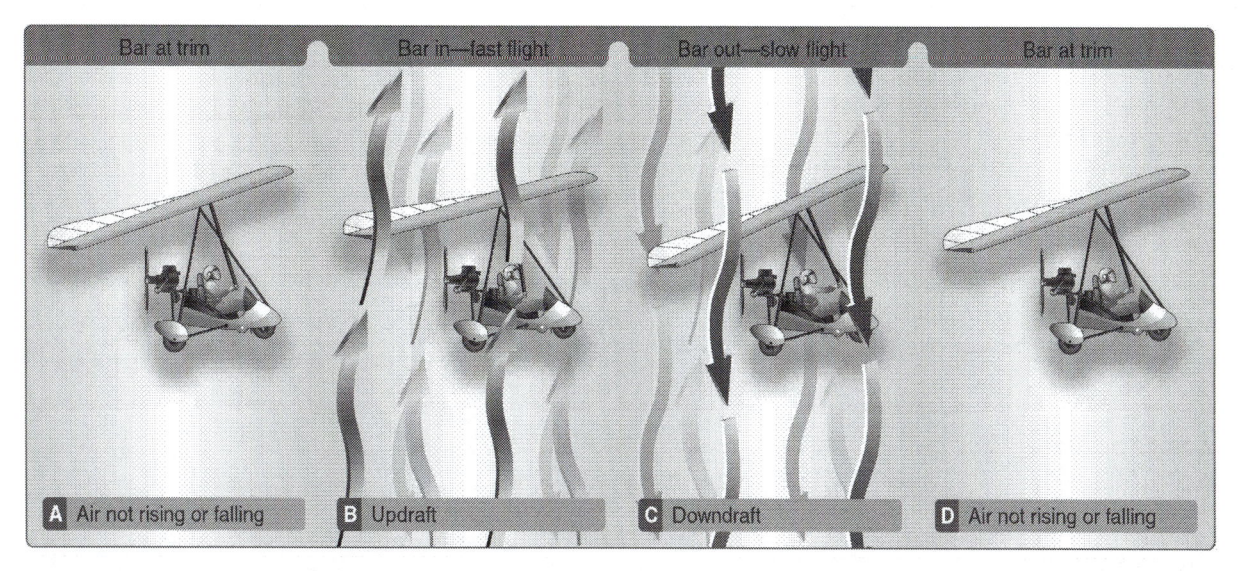

Figure 6-8. *Thermal updraft and downdraft sequence.*

air is smooth. For that reason, pilots must not form the habit of constant, unnecessary control movement. Pilots should learn to recognize when corrections are necessary, and then make a measured response easily and naturally.

Common errors in the performance of straight-and-level flight are:

- Attempting to use improper reference points on the aircraft to establish attitude.
- Forgetting the location of selected reference points.
- Too tight a grip on the flight controls resulting in overcontrol and lack of "feel."
- Improper scanning and/or devoting insufficient time to outside visual reference (head in the flight deck).
- Fixation on the nose (pitch attitude) reference point only.
- Unnecessary or inappropriate control inputs.
- Failure to make timely and measured control inputs when deviations from straight-and-level flight are detected.
- Inadequate attention to sensory inputs in developing feel for the aircraft.

Trim Control

The use of trim systems relieves the pilot of the requirement to exert pressures for the desired flight condition. An improperly trimmed aircraft requires constant control pressures, produces pilot tension and fatigue, distracts the pilot from scanning, and contributes to abrupt and erratic aircraft control.

Most WSC aircraft have a ground adjustable pitch/speed trim system that adjusts the carriage hang point on the wing keel that is set for the desired speed. Some WSC aircraft have additional pitch control systems that can adjust the trim speed in flight as described in Chapter 3, Components and Systems.

There is no yaw trim but the roll trim is usually adjusted on the ground for a wing that has a turn in it. Roll trim is usually adjusted so the wing flies straight in cruise flight. This is a balance between the full power torque of the engine wanting to turn it in one direction and minimum power when the WSC aircraft is in a glide. WSC pilots usually have to exert some pilot roll input for high power engines at full power climb to fly straight because of the engine turning effect.

Level Turns

A turn is made by banking the wings in the direction of the desired turn. A specific angle of bank is selected by the pilot, control pressures are applied to achieve the desired bank angle, and appropriate control pressures are exerted to maintain the desired bank angle once it is established.

Banking is performed with the following steps *[Figure 6-9]*:

Entering a Turn

A. Straight flight

B. Pilot applies sideways pressure to the control bar shifting the weight towards the direction of the desired turn initiating the bank.

C. Turn is established and maintained by moving the control bar back to the center position.

Exiting a Turn

D. Pilot is maintaining stabilized bank and a resultant turn.

E. Pilot shifts weight to opposite side to initiate exit out of the turn.

F. Straight flight is established and maintained by moving the control bar back to the center position.

Coordinating the Controls

Flight controls are used in close coordination when making level turns. Their functions are:

- The WSC is banked with side to side pressure with the control bar and the bank angle established determines the rate of turn at any given airspeed.

- The throttle provides additional thrust used to maintain the WSC in level flight.

- Pitch control moves the nose of the WSC aircraft up or down in relation to the pilot and perpendicular to the wings. Doing this sets the proper pitch attitude and speed in the turn.

Turns are classified to determine the bank angle as follows:

- Shallow turns are those in which the bank is less than approximately 20°.

- Medium turns are those resulting from a degree of bank that is approximately 20° to 45°.

- Steep turns are those resulting from a degree of bank that is 45° or more.

Changing the direction of the wing's lift toward one side or the other causes the aircraft to be pulled in that direction.

When an aircraft is flying straight and level, the total lift is acting perpendicular to the wings and to the Earth. *[Figure 6-10]* As the WSC is banked into a turn, the lift then becomes the resultant of two components. One, the vertical lift component, continues to act perpendicular to the Earth and opposes gravity. Second, the horizontal lift component (centripetal) acts parallel to the Earth's surface

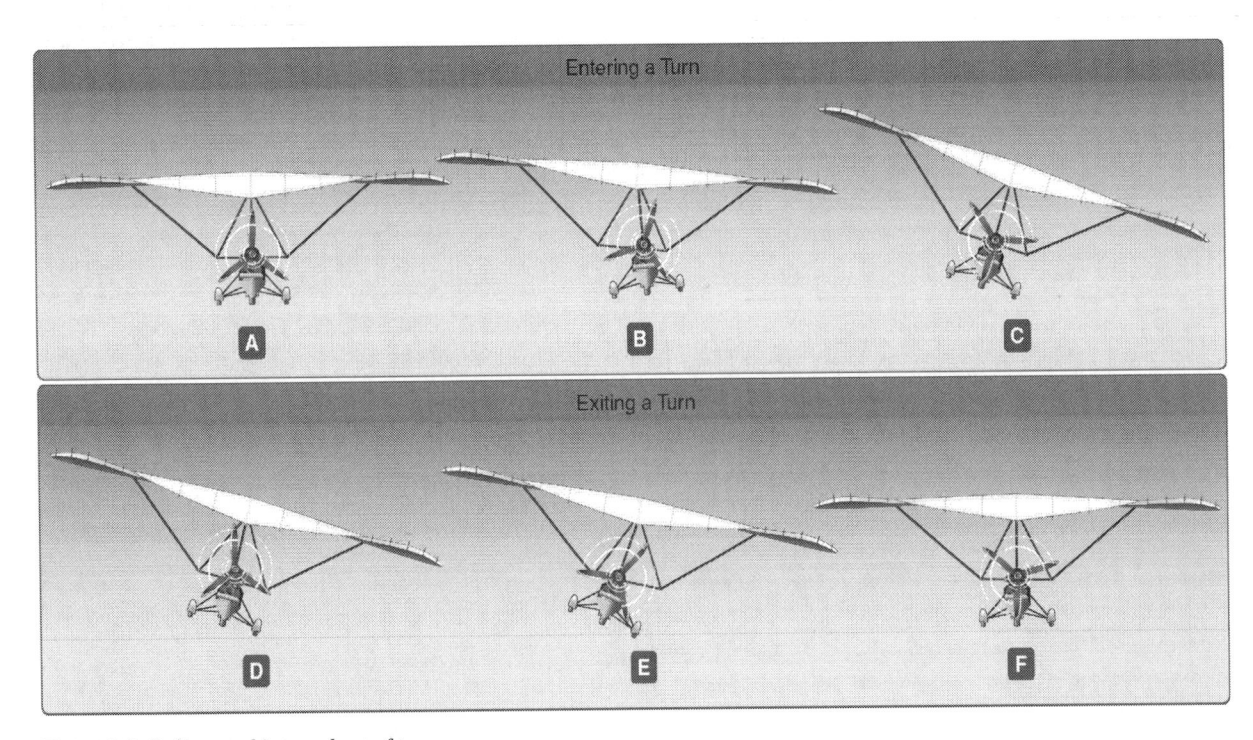

Figure 6-9. *Roll control into and out of turns.*

and opposes inertia (apparent centrifugal force). These two lift components act at right angles to each other causing the resultant total lifting force to act perpendicular to the banked wing of the aircraft. It is the horizontal lift component that actually turns the WSC aircraft. *[Figure 6-10]*

Shallow turns are accomplished by moving the control bar to the side slightly, waiting for the wing to roll the desired amount, and then releasing the side pressure on the control bar back to the center position. The WSC aircraft will stabilize in the turn with no control pressures required. During a shallow turn there is no significant increase in airspeed or G forces that can easily be noticed by the student. *[Figure 6-11]* Once a shallow turn is initiated, it is a good practice to be stabilized at a constant bank and then exit to a predetermined heading. To exit the shallow turn, opposite sideways pressure must be put on the control bar to bring the WSC aircraft back to level flight.

For higher banked turns, the entry speed should be well above 1.3 times the stall speed, which increases significantly in higher banked turns. As an example, at least 1.5 times the stall speed should be the entry speed for a 40 degree banked turn to maintain the 1.3 times the stall speed safety margin. Wings with a trim speed of 1.3 times the stall speed require an increase in speed slightly. In all constant altitude, constant airspeed turns, it is necessary to increase the angle of attack of the wing when rolling into the turn by pushing out on the control bar. This is required because part of the vertical lift has been diverted to horizontal lift. Thus, the total lift must be increased to compensate for this loss. Similarly, the throttle must be increased to maintain the same altitude in steeper banks.

The additional load or G force in a medium banked turn is felt as the pilot is pushed down on the seat with enough force for this effect to be noticed. After the bank has been established in a medium turn, all side-to-side roll pressure applied may be relaxed, but forward pressure to maintain a higher angle of attack is still necessary in a steeper bank. The WSC aircraft remains at the selected bank with no further tendency to roll back to level since all the forces are equalized.

During the turn, roll, pitch, and throttle controls are adjusted to maintain the desired bank angle, speed, and level altitude. Coordinated flight is the coordination of the three controls to achieve a smooth turn to the desired bank angle while maintaining a constant speed and altitude.

The roll-out from a turn is similar to the roll-in, except flight controls are applied in the opposite direction. As the angle of bank decreases, the pitch pressure should be relaxed as necessary to maintain speed and the throttle decreased to maintain altitude.

Since the aircraft continues turning as long as there is any bank, the rollout must be started before reaching the desired heading. The amount of lead required to roll-out of the desired heading depends on the degree of bank used in the turn. Normally, the lead is one-half the degrees of bank. For example, if the bank is 30°, lead the rollout by 15°. As the wings become level, the control pressures should be smoothly relaxed so that the controls are neutralized as the aircraft returns to straight-and-level flight. As the rollout is being completed, attention should be given to outside visual references to determine that the wings are being leveled and the turn stopped.

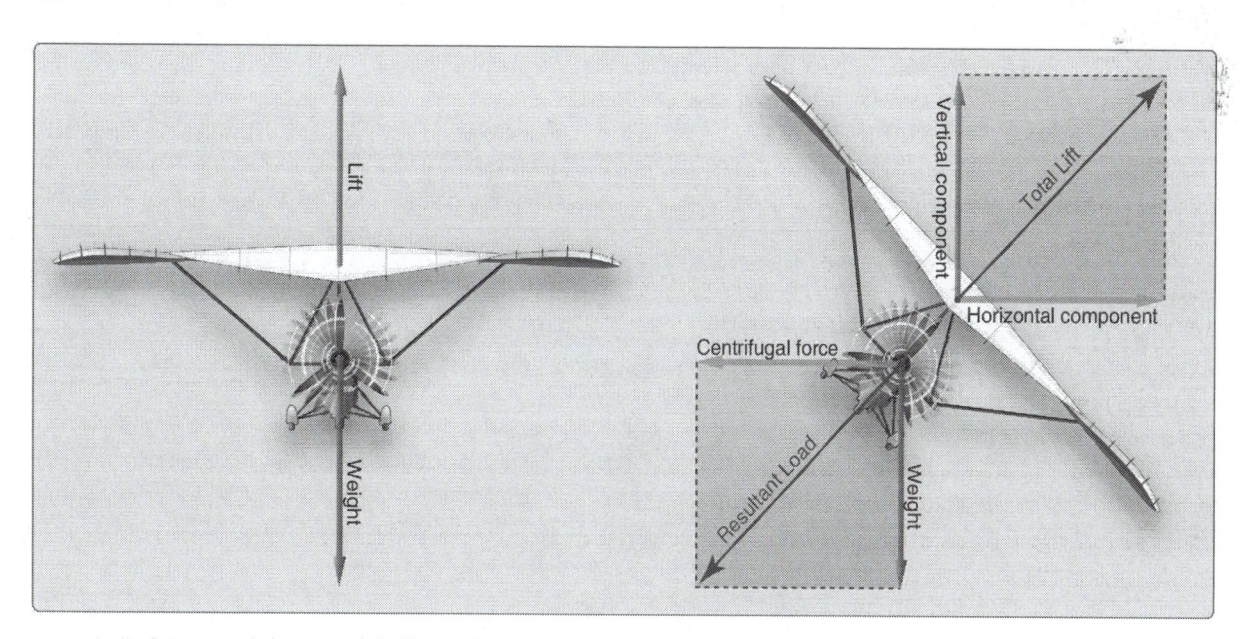

Figure 6-10. *WSC aircraft flying straight (left) and turning with the same lift and weight (right).*

Figure 6-11. *Pilot's view of a shallow turn with a 20° bank.*

To understand the relationship between airspeed, bank, and radius of turn, it should be noted that the rate of turn at any given true airspeed depends on the horizontal lift component. The horizontal lift component varies in proportion to the amount of bank. Therefore, the rate of turn at a given true airspeed increases as the angle of bank is increased. On the other hand, when a turn is made at a higher true airspeed at a given bank angle, the inertia is greater and the horizontal lift component required for the turn is greater causing the turning rate to become slower. Therefore, at a given angle of bank, a higher true airspeed makes the radius of turn larger because the aircraft is turning at a slower rate. *[Figure 6-12]*

When changing from a shallow bank to a medium bank, the airspeed of the wing on the outside of the turn increases in relation to the inside wing as the radius of turn decreases. The additional lift developed because of this increase in speed of the wing balances the inherent lateral stability of the aircraft. At any given airspeed, roll pressure is not required to maintain the bank. If the bank is allowed to increase from a medium to a steep bank, the radius of turn decreases further.

A steep bank is similar to a medium bank but all factors increase. Roll and pitch control pressures must increase, throttle must increase further to maintain altitude, and the G forces increase significantly. Students should build up to steep banked turns gradually after perfecting shallow and medium banked turns. Do not exceed the bank angle limitation in the Pilot's Operating Handbook (POH).

The pilot's posture while seated in the aircraft is very important, particularly during turns. It affects the interpretation of outside visual references. Pilots should not lean away from the turn in an attempt to remain upright in relation to the ground rather than ride with the aircraft. This should be a habit developed early so that the pilot can properly learn to use visual references.

Beginning students should not use large control applications because this produces a rapid roll rate and allows little time for corrections before the desired bank is reached. Slower (small control displacement) roll rates provide more time to make necessary pitch and bank corrections. As soon as the aircraft rolls from the wings-level attitude, the nose should also start to move along the horizon, increasing its rate of travel proportionately as the bank is increased.

The following variations provide excellent guides. If the nose moves up or down when entering a bank, excessive or insufficient pitch control is being applied. During all turns, the controls are used to correct minor variations as they are in straight-and-level flight.

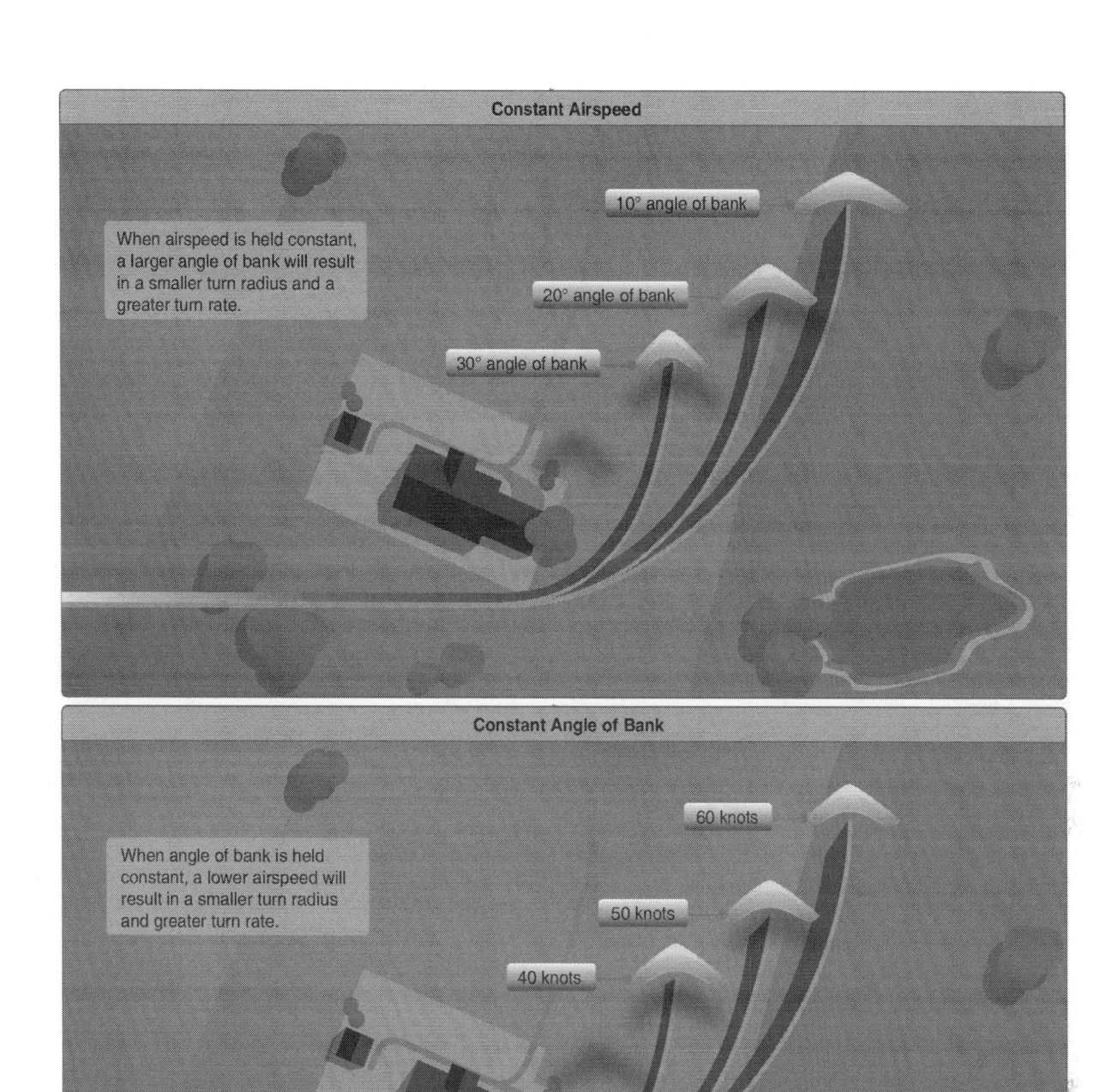

Figure 6-12. *Angle of airspeed and bank regulate rate and radius of turn.*

Instruction in level turns should begin with changing attitude from level to bank, bank to level, and so on with a slight pause at the termination of each phase. This pause allows the WSC to free itself from the effects of any misuse of the controls and ensures a correct start for the next turn. During these exercises, the idea of control forces, rather than movement, should be emphasized by pointing out the resistance of the controls to varying forces applied to them.

Common errors in the performance of level turns are:

- Failure to adequately clear the area before beginning the turn.
- Attempting to sit up straight, in relation to the ground, during a turn, rather than riding with the aircraft.
- Failure to maintain a constant bank angle during the turn.
- Gaining proficiency in turns in only one direction.
- Failure to coordinate the angle of attack to maintain the proper airspeed.
- Failure to coordinate the use of throttle to maintain level flight.
- Altitude gain/loss during the turn.

Climbs and Climbing Turns

When an aircraft enters a climb, it changes its flightpath from level flight to an inclined plane or climb attitude. As discussed in chapter 2, weight in a climb no longer acts in a direction perpendicular to the flightpath. It acts in a rearward direction. This causes an increase in total drag requiring an increase in thrust (power) to balance the forces. An aircraft can only sustain a climb angle when there is sufficient thrust to offset increased drag; therefore, climb is limited by the thrust available. *[Figure 6-13]*

Like other maneuvers, climbs should be performed using outside visual references and flight instruments. It is important that the pilot know the engine power settings and pitch attitudes that produce the following conditions of climb:

- Normal climb—performed at an airspeed recommended by the aircraft manufacturer. Normal climb speed is generally the WSC best rate of climb (V_Y) speed as discussed below. Faster airspeeds should be used for climbing in turbulent air.

- Best rate of climb (V_Y)—the airspeed at which an aircraft will gain the greatest amount of altitude in a given unit of time (maximum rate of climb in feet per minute (fpm)). The V_Y made at full allowable power is a maximum climb. This is the most efficient speed because it has the best lift over drag ratio for the aircraft. This speed is also the best glide ratio speed used for going the greatest distance for the amount of altitude, as discussed later in this chapter. Each aircraft manufacturer is different but a good rule of thumb is that the V_Y is 1.3 times the stall speed. It must be fully understood that attempts to obtain more climb performance than the aircraft is capable of by increasing pitch attitude results in a decrease in the

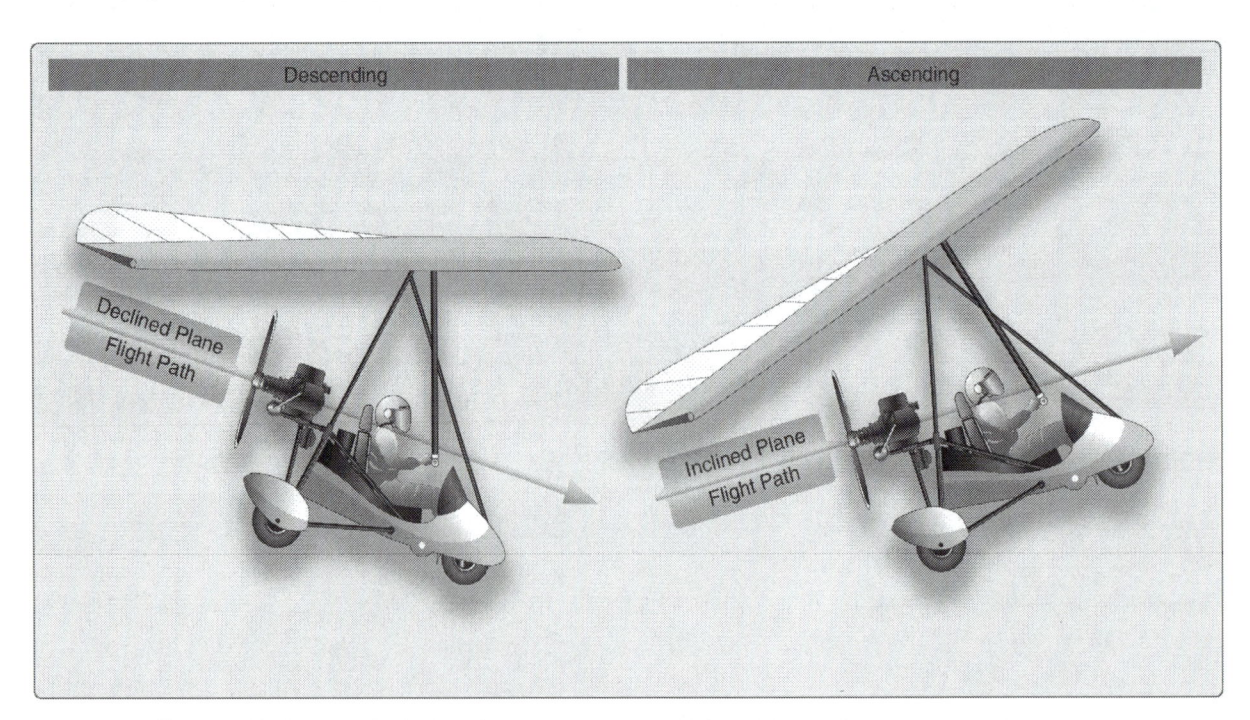

Figure 6-13. *When a WSC aircraft stabilizes in a descent or a climb, the flightpath is a declined or inclined plane.*

rate of altitude gain. Trim is usually set at the V_Y or higher.

- **Best angle of climb (V_X)**—performed at an airspeed that will produce the most altitude gain in a given horizontal distance. Best V_X airspeed is lower than V_Y but higher than minimum controlled airspeed. The V_X results in a steeper climb path, although the aircraft takes longer to reach the same altitude than it would at V_Y. The V_X, therefore, is used in clearing obstacles after takeoff. Since the V_X is closer to the stall speed, caution should be exercised using this speed to climb so as not to stall the WSC aircraft close to the ground with potentially catastrophic consequences. [Figure 6-14]

Climbing flight requires more power than flying level, as described in chapter 2. When performing a climb, the normal climb speed should be established and the power should be advanced to the climb power recommended by the manufacturer. As the aircraft gains altitude during a climb, the engine has a loss in power because the same volume of air entering the engine's induction system gradually decreases in density as altitude increases.

During a climb, a constant heading should be held with the wings level if a straight climb is being performed, or a constant angle of bank and rate of turn if a climbing turn is being performed. To return to straight-and-level flight, when approaching the target altitude, increase the speed to the cruise setting (if different) and decrease throttle for level flight. After the aircraft is established in level flight at a constant altitude and the desired speed, the aircraft should be trimmed (if equipped with an in flight trim system).

In the performance of climbing turns, the following factors should be considered.

- With a constant power setting, the same pitch attitude and airspeed cannot be maintained in a bank as in a straight climb due to the increase in the total lift required.
- The degree of bank should not be too steep. A steep bank significantly decreases the rate of climb. The bank should always remain constant.
- At a constant power setting and turning while climbing, the WSC aircraft climbs at a slightly shallower climb angle because some of the lift is being used to turn.
- Attention should be looking at outside references and scanning for traffic with no more than 25 percent of the time looking at inside flight deck instruments.

There are two ways to establish a climbing turn. Either establish a straight climb and then turn, or enter the climb and turn simultaneously. Climbing turns should be used when climbing to the local practice area. Climbing turns allow better visual scanning, and it is easier for other pilots to see a turning aircraft.

In any turn, the loss of vertical lift and increased induced drag due to increased angle of attack becomes greater as the angle of bank is increased. So, shallow turns should be used to maintain an efficient rate of climb. All the factors that affect the aircraft during level (constant altitude) turns affect it during climbing turns or any other maneuver.

Best angle-of-climb airspeed (V_x) gives the greatest altitude gain in the shortest horizontal distance.

Best rate-of-climb airspeed (V_y) gives the greatest altitude gain in a given unit of time.

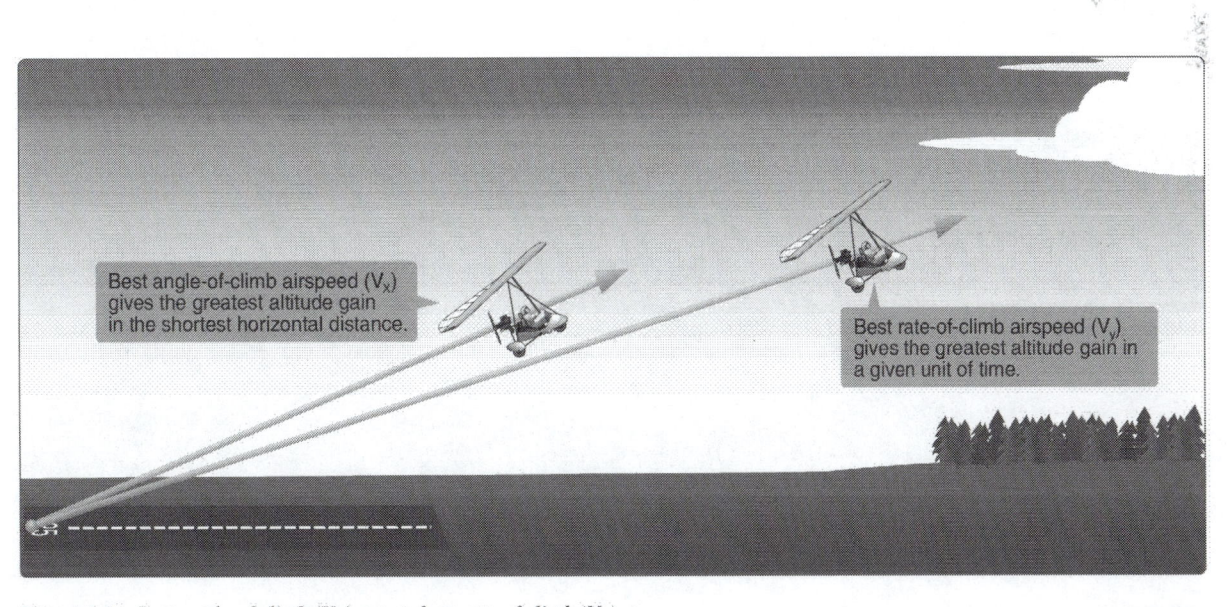

Figure 6-14. *Best angle of climb (V_X) versus best rate of climb (V_Y).*

Common errors in the performance of climbs and climbing turns are:

- A bank angle too high to achieve an efficient climb.
- A speed too high to achieve an efficient climb rate.
- A speed that is too low.
- Attempting to exceed the aircraft's climb capability.
- Inability to keep pitch and bank attitude constant during climbing turns.
- Attempting to establish climb pitch attitude by referencing the airspeed indicator, resulting in "chasing" the airspeed.

Descents and Descending Turns

When an aircraft enters a descent, it changes its flightpath from level to an inclined plane. It is important that the pilot know the power settings and pitch attitudes that produce the following conditions of descent.

- Partial power descent—the normal method of losing altitude is to descend with partial power. This is often termed "cruise" or "en route" descent. The airspeed and power setting recommended by the aircraft manufacturer for prolonged descent should be used. The target descent rate should be 400–500 fpm.
- Steep approach—the normal maneuver used to descend at a steep angle. This is typically used to descend for landing if higher than expected upon approaching the runway. The throttle is set to idle and the airspeed is increased so the excessive drag allows the WSC aircraft to descend at the steepest angle. The control bar is pulled in to achieve this steep approach—the further the bar is pulled in, the steeper the descent rate. Each WSC aircraft is different, but pulling the control bar to the chest may be necessary to achieve the required angle.

- Descent at minimum safe airspeed—a nose-high descent. This should only be used for unusual situations such as clearing high obstacles for a short runway in an emergency situation. The only advantage is a steeper than normal descent angle. This is similar to the best angle of climb speed and should only be used with caution because stalling near the ground could have catastrophic consequences for the pilot, passenger, and people/property on the ground.
- Glide—a basic maneuver in which the aircraft loses altitude in a controlled descent with little or no engine power; forward motion is maintained by gravity pulling the aircraft along an inclined path, and the descent rate is controlled by the pilot balancing the forces of gravity and lift. *[Figure 6-15]*

Although glides are directly related to the practice of power-off accuracy landings, they have a specific operational purpose in normal landing approaches and forced landings after engine failure. Therefore, it is necessary that they be performed more subconsciously than other maneuvers because most of the time during their execution, the pilot gives full attention to details other than the mechanics of performing the maneuver. Since glides are usually performed relatively close to the ground, accuracy of their execution, the formation of proper technique, and habits are of special importance.

The glide ratio of a WSC aircraft is the distance the aircraft, with power off, travels forward in relation to the altitude it loses. For instance, if it travels 5,000 feet forward while descending 1,000 feet, its glide ratio is said to be 5 to 1.

The glide ratio is affected by all four fundamental forces that act on an aircraft (weight, lift, drag, and thrust). If all factors affecting the aircraft are constant, the glide ratio is constant.

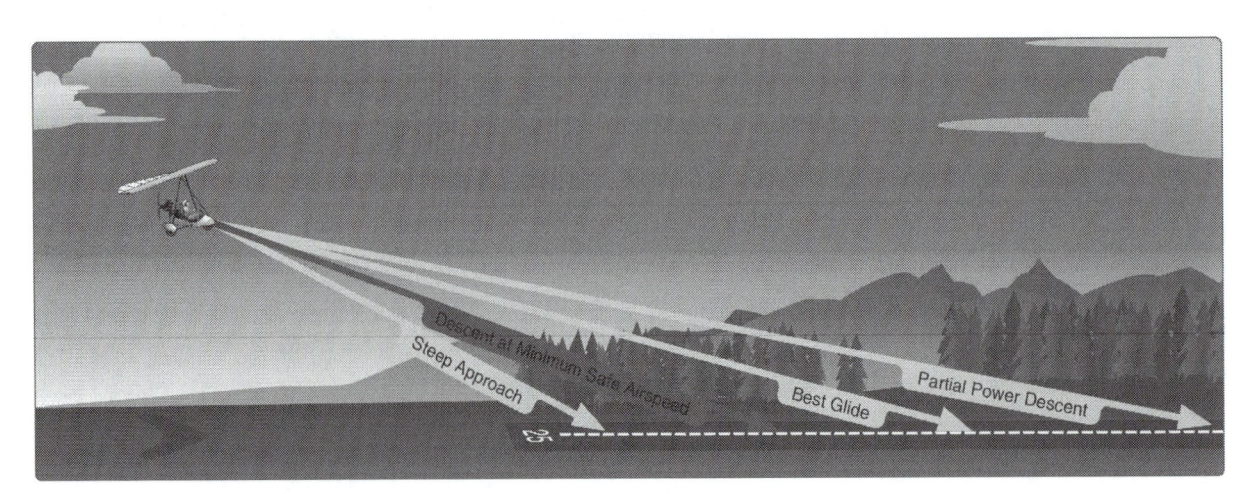

Figure 6-15. *Descent speeds and glide angles.*

Although the effect of wind is not covered in this section, it is a very prominent force acting on the gliding distance of the aircraft in relationship to its movement over the ground. With a tailwind, the aircraft glides farther because of the higher groundspeed. Conversely, with a headwind the aircraft does not glide as far because of the slower groundspeed.

Variations in weight for an aircraft with a rigid wing do not affect the glide angle provided the pilot uses the correct airspeed. Since it is the lift over drag (L_D) ratio that determines the distance the aircraft can glide, weight does not affect the distance. The glide ratio is based only on the relationship of the aerodynamic forces acting on the aircraft. The only effect weight has is to vary the time the aircraft glides. The heavier the aircraft, the higher the airspeed must be to obtain the same glide ratio. For example, if two aircraft having the same L_D ratio but different weights start a glide from the same altitude, the heavier aircraft gliding at a higher airspeed arrives at the same touchdown point in a shorter time. Both aircraft cover the same distance, only the lighter aircraft takes a longer time.

However, the WSC aircraft has different characteristics because it has a flexible airframe. As more weight is added to the WSC wing, it flexes more creating more twist in the wing decreasing aerodynamic efficiency, as discussed in chapter 2. For example, a pilot is accustomed to a glide ratio of 5 to 1 flying solo; a passenger is added, and this glide ratio may decrease to 4 to 1. This decrease in glide ratio for added weight is true for all descent speeds. The amount of decrease in glide ratio varies significantly between manufactures and models because each wing flexes differently. The more flexible the wing is, the greater the decrease in glide ratio. Pilots should become familiar with glide ratios for their aircraft at all speeds and all weights.

Although the propeller thrust of the aircraft is normally dependent on the power output of the engine, the throttle is in the closed position during a glide so the thrust is constant. Since power is not used during a glide or power-off approach, the pitch attitude must be adjusted as necessary to maintain a constant airspeed.

The best speed for the glide is one at which the aircraft travels the greatest forward distance for a given loss of altitude in still air. This best glide speed corresponds to an angle of attack resulting in the least drag on the aircraft and giving the best lift-to-drag ratio (L_{DMAX}). *[Figure 6-16]*

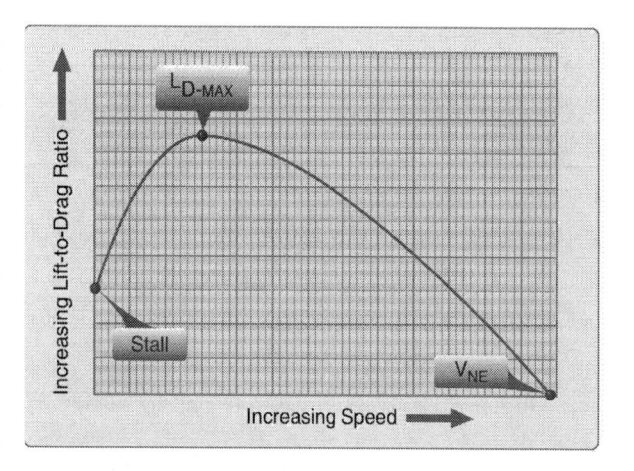

Figure 6-16. L_{DMAX}.

Any change in the gliding airspeed results in a proportionate change in glide ratio. Any speed, other than the best glide speed, results in more drag. Therefore, as the glide airspeed is reduced or increased from the optimum or best glide speed, the glide ratio is also changed. When descending at a speed below the best glide speed, induced drag increases. When descending at a speed above best glide speed, parasite drag increases. In either case, the rate of descent increases and the glide ratio decreases.

This leads to a cardinal rule of aircraft flying that a student pilot must understand and appreciate: the pilot must never attempt to "stretch" a glide by applying nose up pressure and reducing the airspeed below the aircraft's recommended best glide speed. Attempts to stretch a glide invariably result in an increase in the rate and angle of descent and may precipitate an inadvertent stall.

To enter a glide, the pilot should close the throttle and obtain the best glide speed. When the approximate gliding pitch attitude is established, the airspeed indicator should be checked. If the airspeed is higher than the recommended speed, the pitch attitude is too low; if the airspeed is less than recommended, the pitch attitude is too high. Therefore, the pitch attitude should be readjusted accordingly by referencing the horizon. After the adjustment has been made, the aircraft should be retrimmed (if equipped) so that it maintains this attitude without the need to hold pitch pressure on the control bar. The principles of attitude flying require that the proper flight attitude be established using outside visual references first, then using the flight instruments as a secondary check. It is a good practice to always retrim the aircraft after each pitch adjustment.

A stabilized power-off descent at the best glide speed is often referred to as a normal glide. The flight instructor should demonstrate a normal glide, and direct the student pilot to memorize the aircraft's angle and speed by visually checking the:

1. Aircraft's attitude with reference to the horizon.
2. Noting the pitch of the sound made by the air.
3. Pressure on the controls, and the feel of the aircraft.

Due to lack of experience, the beginning student may be unable to recognize slight variations of speed and angle of bank immediately by vision or by the pressure required on the controls. The student pilot must use all three elements consciously until they become habits, and must be alert when attention is diverted from the attitude of the aircraft. A student must be responsive to any warning given by a variation in the feel of the aircraft or controls or by a change in the pitch of the sound.

After a good comprehension of the normal glide is attained, the student pilot should be instructed of the differences in the results of normal and abnormal glides. Abnormal glides are those conducted at speeds other than the normal best glide speed. Pilots who do not acquire an understanding and appreciation of these differences experience difficulties with accuracy landings which are comparatively simple if the fundamentals of the glide are thoroughly understood.

Gliding Turns

Gliding turns have a significant increase in descent rate than straight glides because of the decrease in effective lift due to the direction of the lifting force being at an angle to the pull of gravity. Therefore, it should be clearly understood that the steeper the bank angle, the greater the descent rate.

In gliding turns, the decrease in effective lift due to the direction of the lifting force being at an angle to the pull of gravity make it necessary to use more nose-up pressure than is required for a straight glide. However, as discussed earlier for steeper turns, airspeed must be maintained well above stall speed which increases during turns or the WSC could stall in the turn.

When recovery is being made from a medium or high banked gliding turn, the pitch force which was applied during the turn must be decreased back to trim, which must be coordinated with the roll back to level.

In order to maintain the most efficient or normal glide in a turn, more altitude must be sacrificed than in a straight glide since this is the only way speed can be maintained without power. Attention to the front tube angle with the horizon and the reference point on the front tube provide visual reference of attitudes while gliding. *[Figures 6-17 and 6-18]*

Common errors in the performance of descents and descending turns are:

- Failure to adequately clear the area.
- Inability to sense changes in airspeed through sound and feel.
- Failure to maintain constant bank angle during gliding turns.
- Inadequate nose-up control during glide entry resulting in too steep a glide.
- Attempting to establish/maintain a normal glide solely by reference to flight instruments.
- Attempting to "stretch" the glide by applying nose-up pressure.
- Inadequate pitch control during recovery from straight glides.

Pitch and Power

No discussion of climbs and descents would be complete without touching on the question of what controls altitude and what controls airspeed. The pilot must understand the effects of both power and pitch control, working together, during different conditions of flight.

As a general rule, power is used to determine vertical speed and pitch control is used to determine speed. However, there are many variations and combinations to this general statement. Decreasing pitch and diving do provide a quicker descent but is not typically used as a flight technique for long descents. Changes in pitch through moving the control bar forward and backward are used for maintaining level flight in rising and falling air, and pulling back on the control bar is used for a steep approach technique to lose altitude; however, these techniques are used only for short durations and not the primary altitude control for the WSC.

The throttle is the main control used for determining vertical speed. At normal pitch attitudes recommended by the manufacturer and a constant airspeed, the amount of power used determines whether the aircraft climbs, descends, or remains level at that attitude.

Steep Turn Performance Maneuver

The objective of the steep turn performance maneuver is to develop the smoothness, coordination, orientation, division of attention, and control techniques necessary for the execution of maximum performance turns when the aircraft is near its

Figure 6-17. *Pilot's visual reference of pitch and roll—descending in a shallow bank.*

Figure 6-18. *Pilot's visual reference of pitch and roll—continuing the shallow bank turn but raising the nose slightly with power application. Notice the how the front tube has moved across the horizon and the nose has raised slightly with additional power application to level flight.*

performance limits. Smoothness of control use, coordination, and accuracy of execution are the important features of this maneuver.

The steep turn maneuver consists of a level turn in either direction using a bank angle between 45° to 60°. This causes an overbanking tendency during which maximum turning performance is attained and relatively high load factors are imposed. Because of the high load factors imposed, these turns should be performed at an airspeed that does not exceed the aircraft's design maneuvering speed (V_A). The principles of an ordinary steep turn apply, but as a practice maneuver the steep turns should be continued until 360° or 720° of turn have been completed. *[Figure 6-19]*

An aircraft's maximum turning performance is its fastest rate of turn and its shortest radius of turn, which change with both airspeed and angle of bank. Each aircraft's turning performance is limited by the amount of power its engine is developing, its limit load factor (structural strength), and its aerodynamic characteristics. Do not exceed the maximum bank angle limitation in the POH. For example, a maximum 60° bank angle is a limit used by many manufacturers.

The pilot should realize the tremendous additional load that is imposed on an aircraft as the bank is increased beyond 45°. During a coordinated turn with a 60° bank, a load factor of approximately 2 Gs is placed on the aircraft's structure. Regardless of the airspeed or the type of aircraft involved, a given angle of bank in a turn during which altitude is maintained always produces the same load factor. Pilots must be aware that an additional load factor increases the stalling speed at a significant rate—stalling speed increases with the square root of the load factor. For example, a light aircraft that stalls at 40 knots in level flight stalls at nearly 57 knots in a 60° bank. The pilot's understanding and observance of this fact is an indispensable safety precaution for the performance of all maneuvers requiring turns.

Before starting the steep turn, the pilot should ensure that the area is clear of other air traffic since the rate of turn is quite rapid. After establishing the manufacturer's recommended entry speed or the design maneuvering speed, the aircraft should be smoothly rolled into a selected bank angle between 45° to 60° and the throttle increased to maintain level flight. Always perfect the steep turn at 45° and slowly work up to higher bank angles. As the turn is being established, control bar forward pressure should be smoothly increased to increase the angle of attack. This provides the additional wing lift required to compensate for the increasing load factor.

After the selected bank angle has been reached, the pilot finds that considerable force is required on the control bar and increased throttle is required to hold the aircraft in level flight—to maintain altitude. Because of this increase in the force applied to the control bar, the load factor increases

Figure 6-19. *Steep turns.*

rapidly as the bank is increased. Additional control bar forward pressure increases the angle of attack, which results in an increase in drag. Consequently, power must be added to maintain the entry altitude and airspeed.

During the turn, the pilot should not stare at any one object. Maintaining altitude, as well as orientation, requires an awareness of the relative position of the forward tube and the horizon. The pilot must also be looking for other aircraft mainly towards the direction of the turn while glancing at the instruments to make sure the airspeed and altitude are being maintained. If the altitude begins to increase or decrease a power adjustment may be necessary to maintain the altitude if the bank angle and speed are maintained. All bank angle changes should be done with coordinated use of pitch and throttle control.

The rollout from the turn should be timed so that the wings reach level flight when the aircraft is exactly on the heading from which the maneuver was started. While the recovery is being made, forward bar pressure is gradually released and power reduced, as necessary, to maintain the altitude and airspeed.

Common errors in the performance of steep turns are:
- Failure to adequately clear the area.
- Excessive pitch change during entry or recovery.
- Attempts to start recovery prematurely.
- Failure to stop the turn on a precise heading.
- Inadequate power management resulting in gaining or loosing altitude.
- Inadequate airspeed control.
- Poor roll/pitch/power coordination.
- Failure to maintain constant bank angle.
- Failure to scan for other traffic before and during the maneuver.

Energy Management

The WSC aircraft has very little momentum because of its relative light weight as compared to airplanes. Therefore, it is important that pilots learn to manage the kinetic energy of the WSC. Higher speed and higher power is higher energy. Lower speed and lower power is lower energy. The ability for a pilot to maintain high energy levels in turbulent air and while near the ground is the basis for energy management for WSC.

Energy management should first be practiced at higher altitudes. While maintaining straight-and-level flight, power is increased and decreased, and pitch control must be used. The pilot should start at the trim position and with the appropriate cruise throttle setting. As power is smoothly applied towards full throttle, the WSC aircraft pitch attitude attempts to increase. The pilot should decrease the pitch to maintain level flight. This results in a high energy level.

Once this application is held for a couple seconds, the pilot should then smoothly reduce power to the cruise power setting and increase pitch to maintain level flight. The WSC aircraft is now back to at a lower trim/cruise power in a medium energy level.

Again, increase power and reduce pitch to stay level attaining a high energy level. Now, reduce power to idle and as the nose lowers, increase pitch. The pilot must be aware of the decreasing energy levels occurring during this phase of the maneuver for this is usually a precursor to accidents when approaching the runway. The pilot should recognize this scenario and promptly apply the power as appropriate to prevent the aircraft from descending. Additionally, the pilot must be aware of the slow flight and stall characteristics to prevent a stall and to maintain a specified heading.

Once the student masters this maneuver successfully at higher altitudes, energy management can be practiced with low passes down the runway in calm winds at higher energy levels, then at the lower trim/cruise power medium energy level, and finally higher to medium trim/cruise power energy levels. Low passes over the runway fine tunes the student's skills for energy management and is an excellent exercise to prepare students for landings.

It is important to understand that higher energy levels should be used while maneuvering near the ground especially in turbulent or crosswind conditions. This is discussed in Chapter 7, Takeoff and Departure Climbs, that higher energy is recommended as the WSC aircraft lifts off and initially climbs out from the runway.

Higher energy is also recommended for a power on approach where the airspeed is higher than the normal approach speed; and the power is higher than the normal approach power. There is still a descent rate, but the WSC aircraft has more overall energy to handle turbulence and crosswinds. *[Figure 6-20]*

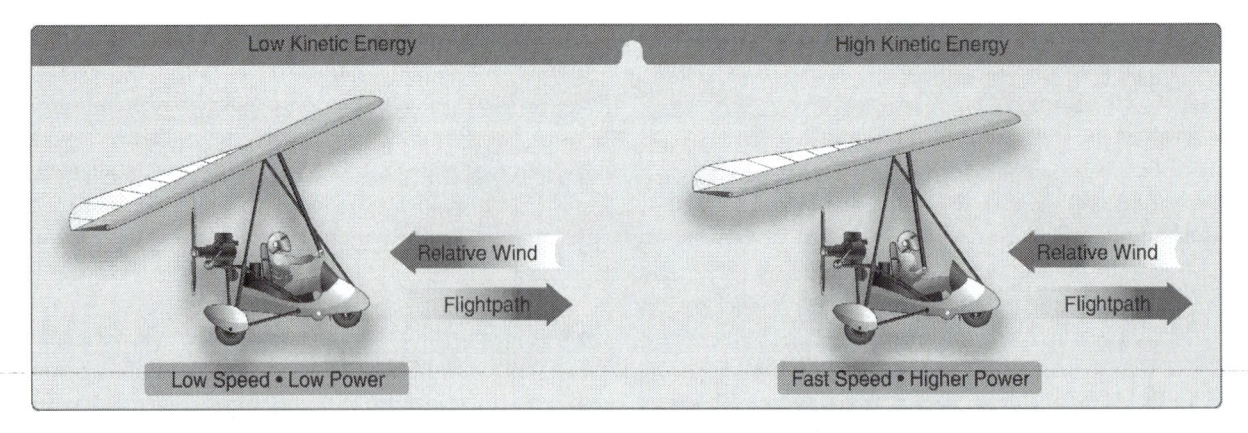

Figure 6-20. *Energy management: low and high kinetic energy for level flight.*

Slow Flight and Stalls

As discussed in chapter 2, the maintenance of lift and control of an aircraft in slow flight requires a certain minimum airspeed and angle of attack. This critical airspeed depends on certain factors, such as gross weight, load factors, and density altitude. The minimum speed below which further controlled flight is impossible is called the stalling speed. An important feature of pilot training is the development of the ability to estimate and "feel" the margin of speed above the stalling speed. Also, the ability to determine the characteristic responses of the aircraft at different airspeeds is of great importance to the pilot. The student pilot, therefore, must develop this awareness in order to safely avoid stalls and to operate an aircraft correctly and safely at slow airspeeds.

As discussed in chapter 2, the nose stalls while the tips keep flying. Therefore, the definition of stall speed of the WSC aircraft is the speed at which the nose starts stalling. The control bar is pushed forward and buffeting is felt on the control bar as the root reaches the critical angle of attack. Separation of the laminar airflow occurs, creating turbulence that can be felt in the control bar. There is a loss of positive roll control as the nose buffets and lowers as it loses lift.

Slow Flight

The objective of maneuvering during slow flight is to develop the pilot's sense of feel and ability to use the controls correctly and to improve proficiency in performing maneuvers that require slow airspeeds.

Slow flight is broken down into two distinct speeds:

1. V_X and the short field descent speed that was discussed earlier, and,
2. Minimum controlled airspeed, the slowest airspeed at which the aircraft is capable of maintaining controlled flight without indications of a stall—usually 2 to 3 knots above stalling speed as discussed below.

The minimum controlled airspeed maneuver demonstrates the flight characteristics and degree of controllability of the aircraft at its minimum flying speed. By definition, the term "flight at minimum controllable airspeed" means a speed at which any further increase in angle of attack or load factor causes an immediate stall. Instruction in flight at minimum controllable airspeed should be introduced at reduced power settings with the airspeed sufficiently above the stall to permit maneuvering, but close enough to the stall to sense the characteristics of flight at very low airspeed—sloppy control, ragged response to control inputs, difficulty maintaining altitude, etc. Maneuvering at minimum controllable airspeed should be performed using both instrument indications and outside visual reference. It is important that pilots form the habit of frequent reference to the flight instruments, especially the airspeed indicator, while flying at very low airspeeds. However, the goal is to develop a "feel" for the aircraft at very low airspeeds to avoid inadvertent stalls and to operate the aircraft with precision.

The objective of performing the minimum controlled airspeed is to fly straight and level and make shallow level turns at minimum controlled airspeed. To begin a minimum controlled airspeed maneuver, the WSC is flown at trim speed straight and level to maintain a constant altitude. The nose is then raised as the throttle is reduced to maintain a constant altitude.

As the speed decreases further, the pilot should note the feel of the flight controls, pitch pressure, and difficulty of maintaining a straight heading with the increased side-to-side pilot input forces required to keep the wings level. At some point the throttle must be increased to remain level after the WSC has slowed below it's maximum L_D speed. The pilot should also note the sound of the airflow as it falls off in tone. There is a large difference by manufacturer and model, but the bar generally should not be touching the forward tube at minimum controlled airspeed. For example, the control bar would be 1 to 3 inches from the front tube at minimum controlled airspeed. *[Figure 6-21]*

6-20

Trim flight	Control bar is moved forward, slowing the WSC		Minimum controlled airspeed
Normal straight-and-level flight	Power is decreased slightly as the nose is raised to slow to minimum controlled airspeed	Power applied for straight-and-level flight at minimum controlled airspeed	Shallow turns are performed in level flight at minimum controlled airspeed

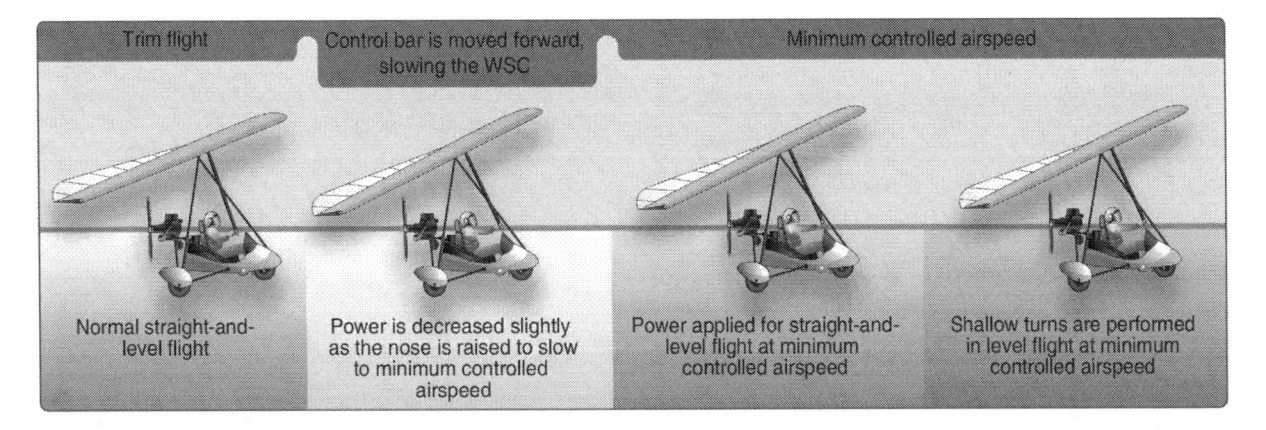

Figure 6-21. *Minimum controlled airspeed maneuver.*

The pilot should understand that when flying below the minimum drag speed (L/D$_{MAX}$), the aircraft exhibits a characteristic known as "speed instability." If the aircraft is disturbed by even the slightest turbulence, the airspeed decreases. As airspeed decreases, the total drag increases resulting in a further loss in airspeed. Unless more power is applied and/or the nose is lowered, the speed continues to decay to a stall. This is an extremely important factor in the performance of slow flight. The pilot must understand that, at speeds less than minimum drag speed, the airspeed is unstable and will continue to decay if allowed to do so.

It should also be noted that the amount of power to remain level at minimum controlled airspeed is greater than that required at the minimum drag speed which is also the best glide ratio speed and the best rate of climb speed.

When the attitude, airspeed, and power have been stabilized in straight-and-level flight, turns should be practiced to determine the aircraft's controllability characteristics at this minimum speed. During the turns, power and pitch attitude may need to be increased to maintain the airspeed and altitude. The objective is to acquaint the pilot with the lack of maneuverability at minimum controlled airspeed, the danger of incipient stalls, and the tendency of the aircraft to stall as the bank is increased. A stall may also occur as a result of turbulence, or abrupt or rough control movements when flying at this critical airspeed.

Once flight at minimum controllable airspeed is set up properly for level flight, a descent or climb at minimum controllable airspeed can be established by adjusting the power as necessary to establish the desired rate of descent or climb.

Common errors in the performance of slow flight are:

- Failure to adequately clear the area.
- Inadequate forward pressure as power is reduced, resulting in altitude loss.
- Excessive forward pressure as power is reduced, resulting in a climb, followed by a rapid reduction in airspeed and "mushing."
- Inadequate compensation for unanticipated roll during turns.
- Fixation on the airspeed indicator.
- Inadequate power management.
- Inability to adequately divide attention between aircraft control and orientation.

Stalls

A stall occurs when the smooth airflow over the aircraft's wing root is disrupted and the lift degenerates rapidly. This is caused when the wing root exceeds its critical angle of attack. This can occur at any airspeed in any attitude with any power setting.

The practice of stall recovery and the development of awareness of stalls are of primary importance in pilot training. The objectives in performing intentional stalls are to familiarize the pilot with the conditions that produce stalls, to assist in recognizing an approaching stall, and to develop the habit of taking prompt preventive or corrective action.

Pilots must recognize the flight conditions that are conducive to stalls and know how to apply the necessary corrective action. They should learn to recognize an approaching stall by sight, sound, and feel. The following cues may be useful in recognizing the approaching stall:

- Positioning the control bar toward the front tube
- Detecting a stall condition by visually noting the attitude of the aircraft for the power setting

- Hearing the wind decrease on the structure and pilot
- Feeling the wind decrease against the pilot
- Sensing changes in direction or speed of motion, or kinesthesia—probably the most important and best indicator to the trained and experienced pilot. If this sensitivity is properly developed, it warns of a decrease in speed or the beginning of a settling or mushing of the aircraft.

During the practice of intentional stalls, the real objective is not to learn how to stall an aircraft, but to learn how to recognize an approaching stall and take prompt corrective action. Though the recovery actions must be taken in a coordinated manner, they are broken down into the following three actions for explanation purposes.

First, at the indication of a stall, the pitch attitude and angle of attack must be decreased positively and immediately. Since the basic cause of a stall is always an excessive angle of attack, the cause must first be eliminated by releasing the control bar forward pressure that was necessary to attain that angle of attack or by moving the control bar backwards. This lowers the nose and returns the wing to an effective angle of attack.

The amount of movement used depends on the design of the wing, the severity of the stall, and the proximity of the ground. In some WSC aircraft, the bar can be left out and as the nose stalls, the wing lowers to an angle of attack and keeps flying since the tips do not stall. However, even though WSC aircraft generally have gentle stall characteristics, higher performance wings may not be as forgiving. Therefore during a stall, the control bar should be moved back to reduce the angle of attack and properly recover from the stall. The object for all WSC aircraft is to reduce the angle of attack but only enough to allow the wing to regain lift as quickly as possible and obtain the appropriate airspeed for the situation with the minimum loss in altitude.

Power application in a stall is different than an airplane. Since power application in a WSC aircraft produces a nose-up moment after a stall has occurred and the pitch has decreased from the control bar movement, power should be applied. The flight instructor should emphasize, however, that power is not essential for a safe stall recovery if sufficient altitude is available. Reducing the angle of attack is the only way of recovering from a stall regardless of the amount of power used. Stall recoveries should be practiced with and without the use of power. Usually, the greater the power applied during the stall recovery, the less the loss of altitude.

Third, straight-and-level flight should be regained with coordinated use of all controls. Practice of power-on stalls should be avoided due to potential danger of whipstalls, tucks, and tumbles, as detailed later in ths chapter.

Power-off (at idle) turning stalls are practiced to show what could happen if the controls are improperly used during a turn from the base leg to the final approach. The power-off straight-ahead stall simulates the attitude and flight characteristics of a particular aircraft during the final approach and landing.

Usually, the first few practices should include only approaches to stalls with recovery initiated as soon as the first buffeting or partial loss of control is noted. Once the pilot becomes comfortable with this power-off procedure, the aircraft should use some power and be slowed in such a manner that it stalls in as near a level pitch attitude as is possible. The student pilot must not be allowed to form the impression that in all circumstances a high pitch attitude is necessary to exceed the critical angle of attack, or that in all circumstances a level or near level pitch attitude is indicative of a low angle of attack. Recovery should be practiced first without the addition of power by merely relieving enough control bar forward pressure that the stall is broken and the aircraft assumes a normal glide attitude. Stall recoveries should then be practiced with the addition of power during the recovery to determine how effective power is in executing a safe recovery and minimizing altitude loss.

Stall accidents usually result from an inadvertent stall at a low altitude in which a recovery was not accomplished prior to contact with the surface. As a preventive measure, stalls should be practiced at a minimum altitude of 1,500 feet AGL or that which allows recovery no lower than 1,000 feet AGL. Recovery with a minimum loss of altitude requires a reduction in the angle of attack (lowering the aircraft's pitch attitude), application of power, and termination of the descent without accelerating to a high airspeed and unnecessary altitude loss.

The factors that affect the stalling characteristics of the aircraft are wing design, trim, bank, pitch attitude, coordination, drag, and power. The pilot should learn the effect of the stall characteristics of the aircraft being flown. It should be reemphasized that a stall can occur at any airspeed, in any attitude, or at any power setting, depending on the total number of factors affecting the particular aircraft.

Whenever practicing turning stalls, a constant pitch and bank attitude should be maintained until the stall occurs. In a banked stall or if the wing rolls as it stalls, side to side control bar movement is required to level the wings as well as pull the bar back to reduce the angle of attack.

Power-Off Stall Manuever

The practice of power-off stalls is usually performed with normal landing approach conditions in simulation of an accidental stall occurring during landing approaches. Aircraft equipped with trim should be trimmed to the approach configuration. Initially, airspeed in excess of the normal approach speed should not be carried into a stall entry since it could result in an abnormally nose-high attitude. Before executing these practice stalls, the pilot must be sure the area is clear of other air traffic.

To start the power-off stall maneuver, reduce the throttle to idle (or normal approach power). Increase airspeed to the normal approach speed and maintain that airspeed. When the approach attitude and airspeed have stabilized, the aircraft's nose should be smoothly raised to an attitude that induces a stall. If the aircraft's attitude is raised too slowly, the WSC aircraft may slow only to minimum controlled airspeed and not be able to reach an angle of attack that is high enough to stall. The position of the control bar at which the WSC stalls can vary greatly for different manufacturers and makes/models. Some can stall abruptly when the control bar is inches from the front tube.

If the aircraft's attitude is raised too quickly, the pitch attitude could rise above the manufacturer's limitation. A good rule of thumb is 3 to 4 seconds from stabilized approach speed to pull the control bar full forward. The wings should be kept level and a constant pitch attitude maintained until the stall occurs. The stall is recognized by clues, such as buffeting, increasing descent rate, and nose down pitching.

Recovering from the stall should be accomplished by reducing the angle of attack by pulling the bar back and accelerating only to the trim speed while simultaneously increasing the throttle to minimize altitude loss if needed. Once the WSC accelerated to trim speed, the control bar can be pushed out to return back to normal trim attitude and speed. If there is any rolling during the stall or the stall recovery the control bar should be moved side to side to maintain a straight heading.

It is not necessary to go into a steep dive in a WSC aircraft to recover from a stall. This only loses more altitude than required and should be discouraged. The nose should be lowered as necessary to regain flying speed and returned to a normal flight attitude as soon as possible. *[Figure 6-22]*

Recovery from power-off stalls should also be practiced from shallow banked turns to simulate an inadvertent stall during a turn from base leg to final approach. During the practice of these stalls, care should be taken that the turn continues at a uniform rate until the complete stall occurs. When stalling in a turn, it does not affect the recovery procedure. The angle of attack is reduced and the wings leveled simultaneously with power applied if needed for altitude control. In the practice of turning stalls, no attempt should be made to stall the aircraft on a predetermined heading. However, to simulate a turn from base to final approach, the stall normally should be made to occur within a heading change of approximately 90°. After the stall occurs, the recovery should be made straight ahead with minimum loss of altitude, and accomplished in accordance with the recovery procedure discussed earlier.

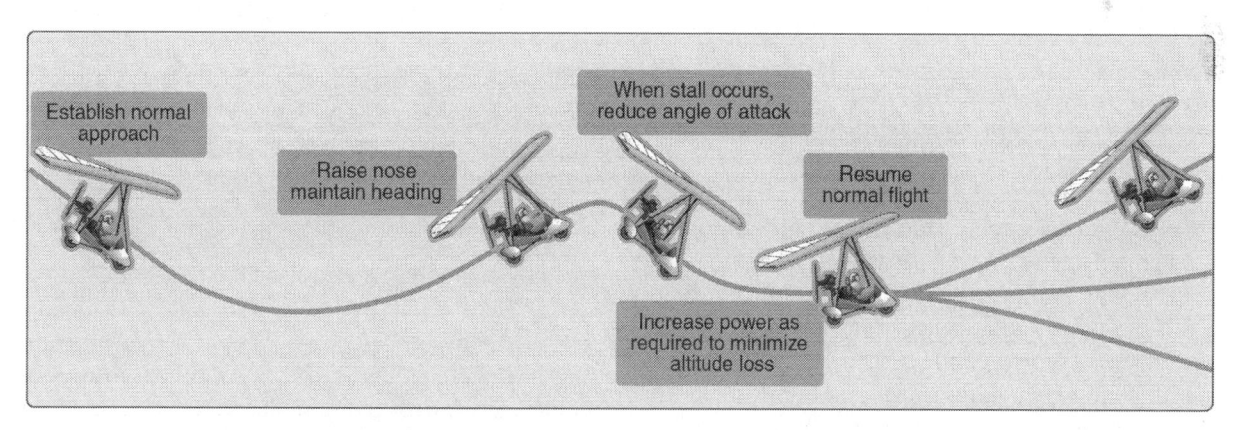

Figure 6-22. *Power-off stall and recovery.*

Whip Stall and Tumble Awareness

As discussed in chapter 2, the WSC aircraft does not have a tail with a vertical stabilizer similar to an airplane, and there is the possibility of the wing tucking and tumbling. If a WSC tumbles, this will most likely result in a structural failure of the WSC and serious injury or death to the pilot and/or passenger. It is most important for the pilot to understand tumble awareness and use all means to avoid such an occurrence. The pilot can avoid a tuck and tumble by:

- Flying within the manufacturer's limitations.
- Flying in conditions that are not conducive to tucks and tumbles.
- Obtaining the proper training in pitch stability for the WSC.

Flying within the manufacturer's pitch and airspeed limitations is simply adhering to the POH/AFM limitations. Depending on the manufacturer, this could mean no full power stalls, not exceeding pitch limits of ± 40 pitch angle, not flying below the safe flying speed in turbulence, etc. Manufacturer's limitations are provided for the specific aircraft to avoid tucks and tumbles.

Preflight preparation is the first step to avoid the possibility of a tuck/tumble to avoid flying in strong weather conditions. This could be strong winds that create wind shear or strong convective thermals that create updrafts and downdrafts. This weather analysis is part of the preflight preparation weather analysis. The second pilot decision regarding appropriate weather while flying is to look at the environment during flight to understand and evaluate the situation. Weather conditions should always be evaluated as the flight progresses with ADM used to determine the best outcome for the situation. This could be turning back or landing depending on the situation.

As a student or pilot progresses, turbulence will be encountered. Use the procedures for flying straight and level as shown in *Figure 6-8*. Use this exercise as a foundation for developing pitch control awareness to keep the wing managed with proper control bar pitch and throttle control.

For high pitch angles, the POH may have specific procedures that should be followed for the particular WSC aircraft, but the following general guidelines are provided. After reviewing the aerodynamic aspects of the tuck/tumble in chapter 2, refer to the following tuck/tumble awareness and avoidance procedures.

As defined in the aerodynamics section, a whip stall is a high pitch angle when the tips stall because they exceed the critical angle of attack. This can be the result of strong turbulence or power-on stall, pilot induced, or any combination of these factors. A pilot must avoid all of these factors to avoid the possibility of a whip stall resulting in a tumble, but the following procedures are provided for tumble avoidance in case a whip stall or a nose rotating down below the manufacturer's limitations is encountered.

The aircraft rotates nose down. *[Figure 6-23, Whip Stall to Phase 1]* Push the control bar out to the front tube and level wings while increasing to full power and keeping control bar full out to reduce overpitching. *[Figure 6-23, Phase 1 to Phase 2]* If rotation is so severe that it progresses to phase 4 and the WSC aircraft is tumbling, the ballistic parachute (if so equipped) should be deployed.

There are other weather situations in which the nose is not at a high pitch attitude, where the back of the wing can get pushed up and enter phase 1 without an unusually high pitch attitude or whip stall. If pitched nose low, increase to full power while pushing the control bar full out to reduce nose-down pitching rotation. Generally, the control bar full out and full throttle create a nose-up moment.

It takes extremely strong weather conditions and/or pilot error to tuck/tumble a WSC aircraft. Experienced pilots fly all day in moderate turbulence, but building experience flying in turbulence should be approached slowly and cautiously to determine the pilot and aircraft capabilities and limitations.

A Scenario

The following is one example of a scenario that could lead to a tuck/tumble. It is based on a viable training program in one location but lack of experience in another location.

A student obtains his or her pilot's license with the minimum number of hours for the pilot certificate. The new pilot trained, soloed, and obtained his or her license only in conditions near the ocean where there was typically an inverted midday sea breeze with little to no convective turbulence (thermals). This developed confidence for flying in winds up to 15 knots but no experience was gained in thermals. In fact, the pilot was not aware that strong thermals could be hazardous.

Now, with a new license, the pilot visits his parents in the middle of the high desert of Colorado. Unfamiliar with the local conditions, the new pilot gets a weather report of winds to 15 knots, something the pilot has experienced before. By the time the pilot arrives at the airport, discusses the situation with the airport officials, and sets up the WSC aircraft, it is 2:00 in the afternoon. The wind is generally calm but increasing to 15 knots occasionally. There are towering cumulus clouds in the sky surrounding the current airport similar to clouds that the pilot had seen far inland from where he or she took instruction and soloed.

The pilot takes off in relatively calm winds, but it is unusually bumpy air. Without any experience in the high desert or with thermal conditions, the pilot has misjudged the conditions and is flying in strong thermal convection. The new pilot climbs out trying to get above the turbulence, which usually works near the beach because of the mechanical turbulence near the ground. However, the turbulence increases.

As the pilot is climbing to a pattern altitude of 1,000 feet AGL at full throttle, the aircraft is pitched nose up while the pilot lets the force of the updraft raise the nose. Never has the pilot felt the nose rise with this type of force before. The pilot is shocked and disoriented at this high pitch attitude, but eventually lets up on the throttle. But now at an unusually high pitch angle, the WSC nose flies into the downdraft of the thermal. At the same time, the updraft is still pushing up on the tips of the wing while the downdraft is pushing down on the nose creating a forward rotation with a weightless sensation. Before the pilot knows it, the wing is rotating pitch down for a vertical dive. *[Phase 1* in *Figure 6-23]* The student remembers from training that "in a nose down rotation into a steep dive the control bar is pushed full forward and full throttle applied" and initiates this corrective action. The pilot reaches the vertical dive, but because of the corrective action the WSC aircraft recovers from the dive and proceeds back to land safely.

What went wrong? What were the errors? How could this near catastrophe have been avoided?

- In a new area and unfamiliar with the conditions, the new pilot should have asked the local instructor or other pilots about the conditions for the day. Local WSC pilots are a great resource for flying the local conditions, but pilots of any category aircraft are knowledgeable of the conditions and could have provided advice for the new pilot. This might have prevented the new pilot from attempting this flight.

- Flying in a new environment and not understanding the power of midday thermals in the high desert should have forced the new pilot to scrap this midday flight. The pilot should have started flying in the morning when there is little thermal convection and gained experience and understanding about the weather in this new area.

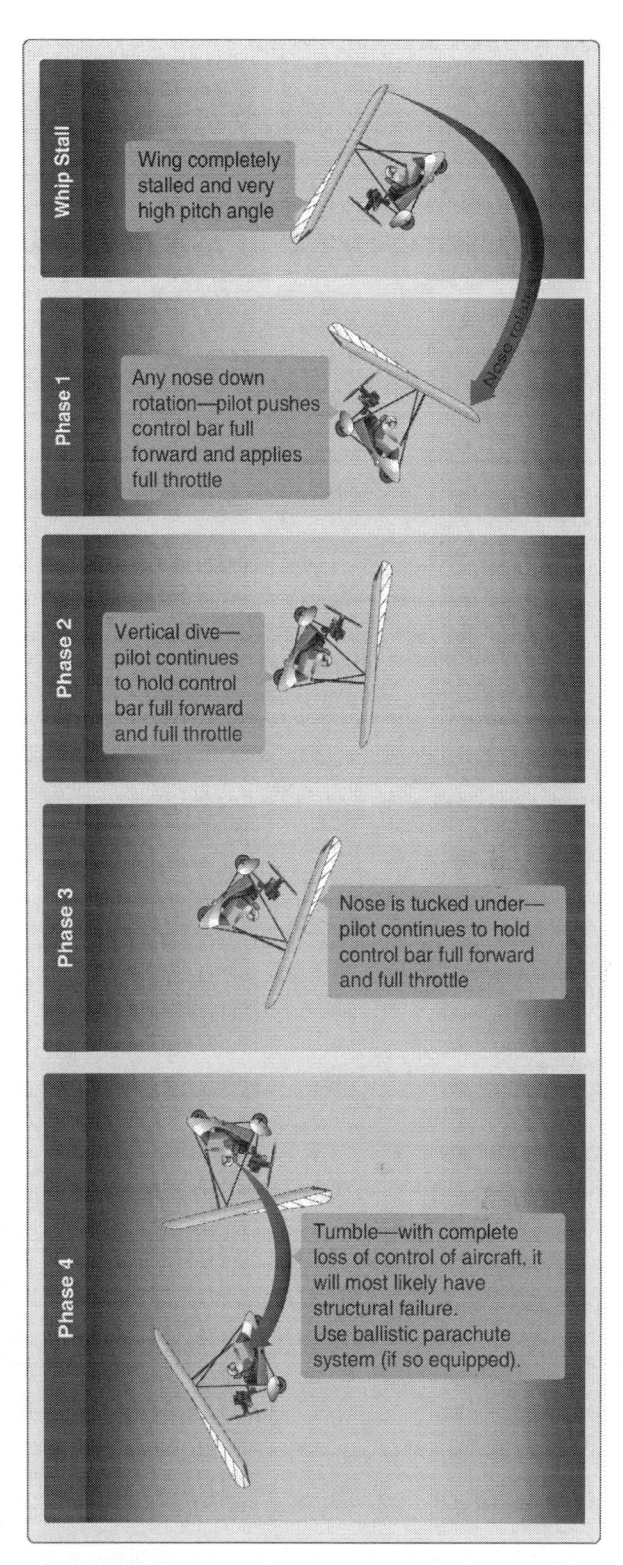

Figure 6-23. *Whip stall/tuck/tumble sequence.*

- Better preflight planning should have been accomplished, especially in a new location. The pilot should have known to obtain convective information and realize it was going to be too bumpy for his or her limited experience. The pilot was accustomed to seeing towering cumulus clouds where he or she trained, but they were way inland and not in the normal flying area. Here clouds were observed all around.

- Site observations indicated strong thermal activity. Observation of winds picking up to 15 knots and then becoming calm normally indicates thermal activity. The pilot was familiar with steady 15 knot winds, but did not understand that calm wind increasing cyclically to 15 knots indicates thermal activity.

- The pilot did not initially react to the updraft and resultant high pitch angle properly because pitch management habits had not been developed. The pilot hit the updraft and allowed the force of the updraft to move the control bar forward, increasing the pitch angle while not letting up on the throttle immediately. Both the control bar forward and full throttle forced the nose too high, creating the high pitch angle and whip stall condition. At the same time, the WSC aircraft flew into the downdraft, starting the nose-down rotation.

- If the pilot had reacted quickly, pulled in the bar while letting up on the throttle and immediately going into the strong thermal, the high pitch angle would not have been achieved and the strong forward rotation would not have happened so abruptly.

After the series of errors occurred, the pilot finally performed the preventive action to avoid a tumble—from the basic training of "If the WSC is at a high pitch angle and the nose starts to rotate down to a low pitch angle, increase to full power while pushing the control bar full out to avoid a tumble."

Chapter Summary

Knowledge of the effects and use of the controls is basic to develop a "feel" of the aircraft and become accustomed to "attitude" flying. This is the basis for all flight maneuvers. The four basic WSC flight maneuvers requiring pilot proficiency are:

- Straight-and-level flight.
- Level turns.
- Climbs and climbing turns.
- Descents and descending turns.

Once the basic maneuvers are mastered, the steep turn allows the pilot to achieve maximum performance from the aircraft. Energy management techniques provide the basis for flying in different atmospheric conditions and introduce the student to precise pitch and power control. Slow flight and stall provide the pilot an awareness of the ability of the WSC to fly at the lower end of the WSC performance.

Whip stalls and tumbles are unique to WSC flight, and pilot awareness and avoidance is an important concept for WSC pilots to understand.

Chapter 7
Takeoff and Departure Climbs

Introduction

This chapter discusses takeoffs and departure climbs in weight-shift control (WSC) aircraft with tricycle landing gear under normal conditions, crosswinds, and under conditions which require maximum performance. A thorough knowledge of takeoff principles, both in theory and practice, is extremely valuable throughout a pilot's career. It often prevents an attempted takeoff that would result in an accident, or during an emergency, makes a takeoff possible under critical conditions in which a pilot with less knowledge and lesser technique would normally fail.

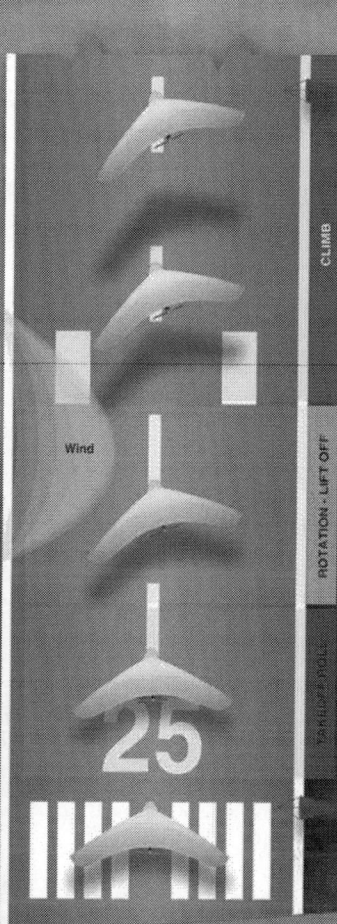

The takeoff, though relatively simple, often presents the most hazards of any part of a flight. The importance of thorough knowledge, faultless technique, and sound judgment cannot be overemphasized.

It must be remembered that the manufacturer's recommended procedures, including configuration and airspeeds, and other information relevant to takeoffs and departure climbs in a specific make and model WSC aircraft are contained in the Airplane Flight Manual/Pilot's Operating Handbook (AFM/POH). If any of the information in this chapter differs from the manufacturer's recommendations as contained in the AFM/POH, the manufacturer's recommendations take precedence.

Terms and Definitions

Although the takeoff and climb is one continuous maneuver, it is divided into three separate steps for purposes of explanation: takeoff roll, lift-off, and initial climb after becoming airborne. [Figure 7-1]

- Takeoff roll (ground roll)—the portion of the takeoff procedure during which the aircraft is accelerated from standstill to an airspeed that provides sufficient lift for it to become airborne.

- Lift-off (rotation)—the act of becoming airborne as a result of the wings lifting the aircraft off the ground or the pilot rotating the nose up, increasing the angle of attack to start a climb.

- Initial climb—begins when the aircraft leaves the ground and an initial pitch attitude has been established to climb away from the takeoff area. Normally, it is considered complete when the aircraft has reached a safe maneuvering altitude, or an en route climb has been established.

Prior to Takeoff

Before taxiing onto the runway or takeoff area, the pilot should ensure that the engine is operating properly and that all controls, including trim (if equipped), are set in accordance with the before takeoff checklist. In addition, the pilot must make certain that the approach and takeoff paths are clear of other aircraft. At uncontrolled airports, pilots should announce their intentions on the common traffic advisory frequency (CTAF) assigned to that airport. When operating from an airport with an operating control tower, pilots must contact the tower operator and receive a takeoff clearance before taxiing onto the active runway.

It is not recommended to take off immediately behind another aircraft, particularly large, heavily loaded transport airplanes because of the wake turbulence that is generated. Even smaller aircraft can generate vortices that can cause the WSC aircraft to lose control during takeoff. Always wait for aircraft vortices to clear before taking off.

While taxiing onto the runway, the pilot can select ground reference points that are aligned with the runway direction as aids to maintaining directional control during the takeoff. These may be runway centerline markings, runway lighting, distant trees, towers, buildings, or mountain peaks.

Normal Takeoff

A normal takeoff is one in which the aircraft is headed into the wind, or the wind is very light. Also, the takeoff surface is firm and of sufficient length to permit the aircraft to gradually accelerate to normal lift-off and climb-out speed, and there are no obstructions along the takeoff path.

Figure 7-1. *Takeoff and climb.*

There are two reasons for making a takeoff as nearly into the wind as possible. First, the aircraft's speed while on the ground is much lower than if the takeoff were made downwind, thus reducing wear and stress on the landing gear. Second, a shorter ground roll and, therefore, much less runway length is required to develop the minimum lift necessary for takeoff and climb. Since the aircraft depends on airspeed in order to fly, a headwind provides some of that airspeed, even with the aircraft motionless, from the wind flowing over the wings.

Takeoff Roll

After taxiing onto the runway, the WSC aircraft should be carefully aligned with the intended takeoff direction and the nosewheel positioned straight down the runway on the centerline. After releasing the brakes, the throttle should be advanced smoothly and continuously to takeoff power. *[Figure 7-2]* This can be done with the foot or the hand cruise throttle.

Figure 7-2. *Lined up in the middle of the runway and ready to apply full power for takeoff.*

The advantage of using the foot throttle is that the takeoff can be aborted quickly if required. The disadvantage is that the foot can slip off or be knocked off during the critical takeoff phase of flight. The advantage of using the hand cruise throttle during takeoff is having a solid and set throttle that the pilot does not have to worry about holding during the takeoff phase of flight. Students have been known to release the foot throttle on takeoff, resulting in catastrophic consequences during the lift-off and initial climb phases of flight. Students may be encouraged to use the hand throttle by the instructor or the instructor must be able to immediately apply the hand or secondary foot throttle if a student lets up on the throttle during this critical takeoff and climb phase.

An abrupt application of power may cause the aircraft to yaw sharply to the left (or right depending on the propeller rotation) because of the torque effects of the engine and propeller. This is most apparent in high horsepower engines. As the aircraft starts to roll forward, the pilot should ensure that both feet are on the front steering fork and not applying the brake.

As speed is gained, the control bar fore and aft pitch tends to assume a neutral trim position. The wing should be maintained level side to side with the control bar. At the same time, directional control should be maintained with smooth, prompt, positive nosewheel steering throughout the takeoff roll. The effects of engine torque at the initial speeds tend to pull the nose to the left (or right depending on the propeller rotation). The pilot must steer the WSC aircraft straight down the middle of the runway with the feet. The positioning of the wing has no effect of steering on the ground. The common saying among WSC pilots is "you steer with your feet, you fly with your hands."

While the speed of the takeoff roll increases, increasingly more pressure is felt on the control bar to the ground roll trim position. Letting the wing pitch pressures determine the fore and aft control bar position provides the least drag for the WSC aircraft to accelerate. The pilot maintains directional control down the center of the runway with the foot steering, keeps the wings level side to side, and allows the wing to determine the pitch angle during the acceleration.

Lift-Off

Since a good takeoff depends on the proper takeoff attitude, it is important to know how this attitude appears and how it is attained. The ideal takeoff attitude requires only minimum pitch adjustments shortly after the airplane lifts off to attain the speed for the best rate of climb (V_Y). *[Figure 7-3]* The pitch attitude necessary for the aircraft to accelerate to V_Y speed should be demonstrated by the instructor and memorized by the student. Initially, the student pilot may have a tendency to hold excessive control bar forward/nose up pressure just after lift-off, resulting in an abrupt pitch-up. The flight instructor should be prepared for this. For a normal takeoff, the WSC aircraft should lift off the ground gradually and smoothly.

Each type of WSC aircraft has a best pitch attitude for normal lift-off; however, varying conditions may make a difference in the required takeoff technique. A rough field, a smooth field, a hard surface runway, or a short or soft, muddy field, calls for a slightly different technique as does smooth air in contrast to a strong, gusty wind. The different techniques for those other-than-normal conditions are discussed later in this chapter.

As the WSC aircraft accelerates and obtains the speed it needs to lift off, a slight push forward on the control bar

Figure 7-3. *Initial roll and takeoff attitude.*

provides the initial attitude to lift-off. This is often referred to as "rotating." At this point, the climb speed should be immediately established for the particular condition. For calm winds, this would be the trim position or the manufacturer recommended takeoff safety airspeed. The wings must be kept level by applying side to side pressure as necessary.

Since some forward pressure was required to rotate, this pressure must be relaxed smoothly so that takeoff attitude is not too high. This requires the control bar being brought back to trim and applying some nose down pressure to avoid popping off as the WSC aircraft leaves the ground. Each make and model is different and the high power WSC aircraft must provide more nose down pressure after rotation to keep the attitude low. A good takeoff is a smooth and gradual liftoff. It is important to hold the correct attitude constant after rotation and liftoff.

As the aircraft leaves the ground, the pilot must continue to be concerned with maintaining the wings in a level attitude, as well as holding the proper pitch attitude. An outside visual scan to attain/maintain proper pitch and bank attitude must be intensified at this critical point.

During takeoffs in a strong, gusty wind, it is advisable that an extra margin of speed be obtained before the WSC aircraft is allowed to leave the ground. A takeoff at the normal takeoff speed may result in a lack of positive control, or a stall, when the WSC aircraft encounters a sudden lull in strong, gusty wind, or other turbulent air currents. In this case, the pilot should allow the aircraft to stay on the ground longer by pulling the control bar towards the chest keeping the nose down to attain more speed; then make a smooth, positive rotation to leave the ground.

Initial Climb

Upon lift-off, the WSC aircraft should be flying at the approximate pitch attitude that allows it to accelerate to at least the manufacturers takeoff safety speed. This is usually close to the best climb rate speed V_Y providing the greatest altitude gain in a period of time. Higher speeds should be used if the air is turbulent to assure the WSC does not stall from a strong wind gust. This speed should be maintained during the initial climb out in case of an engine failure. This is especially important with higher power engines and larger wings to avoid a high pitch attitude during this critical phase of the takeoff. With a lower pitch attitude and a faster speed, the WSC aircraft can recover easier from an engine failure on takeoff. This is discussed in greater detail in the emergency procedures chapter of this handbook. For example, from liftoff to 200 feet it is a good practice to keep a low pitch angle to anticipate an engine failure; above 200 feet, V_Y can be used as a climb speed. *[Figures 7-4 and 7-5]*

After liftoff and throughout the climb, the engine instruments should be checked for proper cooling and oil pressure (if so equipped) since this is the critical time when temperature rises and should stabilize within the manufacturer's specifications.

The manufacturer's recommended takeoff power should be maintained until reaching an altitude of at least 500 feet above the surrounding terrain or obstacles. The combination of V_Y and takeoff power assures the maximum altitude gained in the time during takeoff. This provides the pilot the greatest altitude from which the aircraft can be safely maneuvered in case of an engine failure or other emergency.

Figure 7-4. *Initial takeoff grass strip with control bar pulled in slightly for a higher speed after liftoff in case of engine failure.*

Figure 7-5. *Best climb speed control bar position for this WSC is shown after initial climb where there is sufficient altitude for easy recovery in case of engine failure.*

Since the power on the initial climb is fixed at the takeoff power setting, the airspeed must be controlled by making slight pitch adjustments using the control bar. However, the pilot should not fixate on the airspeed indicator when making these pitch changes, but continue to scan outside to adjust the attitude in relation to the horizon and the feel of the aircraft. The WSC aircraft can be flown by using bar position and the feel of the air to determine proper airspeed; it is not necessary to look at the airspeed indicator to determine exact airspeed. In accordance with the principles of flying a WSC aircraft, the pilot should first make the necessary pitch change with reference to the bar position, and then glance at the airspeed indicator as a check to see if the new speed is correct.

After the recommended climb airspeed has been established and a safe maneuvering altitude has been reached, the power should be adjusted to the recommended climb setting (if different) and the WSC aircraft trimmed (if so equipped) to relieve the control pressures. This makes it easier to hold a constant attitude and airspeed.

During initial climb, it is important that the takeoff path remain aligned with the runway to avoid drifting into obstructions or the path of another aircraft that may be taking off from a parallel runway. Proper scanning techniques are essential to a safe takeoff and climb, not only for maintaining attitude and direction, but also for collision avoidance in the airport area. *[Figure 7-6]*

Figure 7-6. *Pilots view showing WSC centered in the middle of the runway during initial climb.*

When the student pilot nears the solo stage of flight training, it should be explained that the aircraft's takeoff performance is much different when the instructor is out of the aircraft. Due to decreased load, the WSC aircraft becomes airborne sooner and climbs more rapidly. The pitch attitude that the student has learned to associate with initial climb differs significantly due to decreased weight. This can be a dramatic effect since a 250 pound instructor could reduce the total weight of the WSC aircraft by 30 percent. This gives the student the sensation of lying on his or her back during initial takeoff and the reaction is to let off the throttle with serious consequences if the student is using the foot throttle. It must be emphasized by the instructor that the student will seem to be rotated and going straight up, but not to let up on the throttle. The reaction of the student is to pull in the control bar to lower the high pitch attitude. This is where the cruise throttle should be used to eliminate this common problem. The increase in performance is significant when the student first solos in the same aircraft, which must be explained and understood. If the situation is unexpected, it may result in increased tension that may remain throughout the flight. Frequently, the existence of this tension and the uncertainty that develops due to the perception of an "abnormal" takeoff results in poor performance on the subsequent landing.

Common errors in the performance of normal takeoffs and departure climbs are:

- Failure to adequately clear the area prior to taxiing into position on the active runway.
- Abrupt use of the throttle.
- Letting off the foot throttle after takeoff.
- Failure to check engine instruments for signs of malfunction after liftoff and climb.
- Failure to anticipate the aircraft's left turning tendency on initial acceleration and takeoff.
- Overcorrecting for left turning tendency.
- Overcorrecting for roll.
- Relying solely on the airspeed indicator rather than developing a feel for indications of speed and controllability during acceleration and lift-off.
- Failure to attain proper lift-off attitude.
- Overcontrol of pitch during initial lift-off to climbout.
- Failure to attain/maintain best rate of climb airspeed (V_Y).
- Failure to employ the principles of attitude flying during climb-out, resulting in "chasing" the airspeed indicator.

Crosswind Takeoff

While it is usually preferable to take off directly into the wind whenever possible or practical, there are many instances when circumstances or judgment indicate otherwise. Therefore, the pilot must be familiar with the principles and techniques involved in crosswind takeoffs, as well as those for normal takeoffs.

The manufacturers maximum wind and crosswind component in the POH should not be exceeded. The following procedures are for operation within these limitations.

Takeoff Roll

The technique used during the initial takeoff roll in a crosswind is generally the same as used in a normal takeoff, except that the pilot must control the wing's tendency to weathervane into the wind during the takeoff roll. Additionally, the pilot should keep the WSC aircraft on the ground and accelerate to a higher speed before rotation.

As the aircraft is taxied into takeoff position, it is essential that the windsock and other wind direction indicators be checked so that the presence of a crosswind may be recognized and anticipated. During taxi and takeoff, the windward side of the wing needs to be slightly lowered so as to not let the wind get under it and lift it off; but not too low or additional pilot effort is required and unnecessary stress is placed on the carriage.

The crosswind takeoff is performed similar to the normal takeoff except two different techniques are utilized. First, as the WSC aircraft accelerates and the pilot steers the carriage straight down the runway, the wing will want to weathervane into the wind. This creates stress on the wing attachment to the carriage, the carriage mast, and the keel of the carriage. Therefore, the pilot must hold the wing control bar straight to the carriage which requires significant force and muscle. Second, the pilot must accelerate to a higher speed before rotating to account for the crosswind component. This requires the nose to be held down to prevent the WSC from popping off the ground before the higher airspeed is obtained.

Since this technique requires the pilot to muscle the wing rather than using a light touch, it requires a mastery of the normal takeoff before crosswind takeoffs should be attempted. As the WSC aircraft accelerates down the runway, the forces of the wing try to weathervane it into the wind and the nose raises up to trim. The wing should be held straight with the nose down until rotation where the wing is held straight and the nose raised.

Rotation and Lift-Off

When a faster rotation speed than normal takeoff is achieved, a smooth but quicker push out to rotate is desired to get the front and rear wheels into the air quickly, avoiding any tendency to remain on the rear wheels. After lift-off, the WSC automatically rotates into the relative wind since momentum is straight down the runway and the characteristics of the wing point it directly into the relative wind. The WSC sets up the wind correction angle (or crab angle as it is also called) as it lifts off. *[Figure 7-7]*

Initial Climb

After lift-off, the WSC aircraft is pointed toward the wind and the ground track is headed straight down the runway centerline. Maintain this ground track aligned directly down the centerline of the runway "crabbing" into the wind. Crabbing is a term used to adjust flight controls into the crosswind to maintain a straight ground track while the WSC is pointed towards the wind, as seen in *Figure 7-8*. To maintain the ground track it is important to look straight down the runway centerline and steer to stay on that ground track even though the WSC is pointed towards the wind and not directly down the runway. Because the force of a crosswind may vary markedly within a few hundred feet of the ground, frequent checks of actual ground track should be made *[Figure 7-7]* or the WSC could drift to the side if the wind correction angle is not maintained. The remainder of

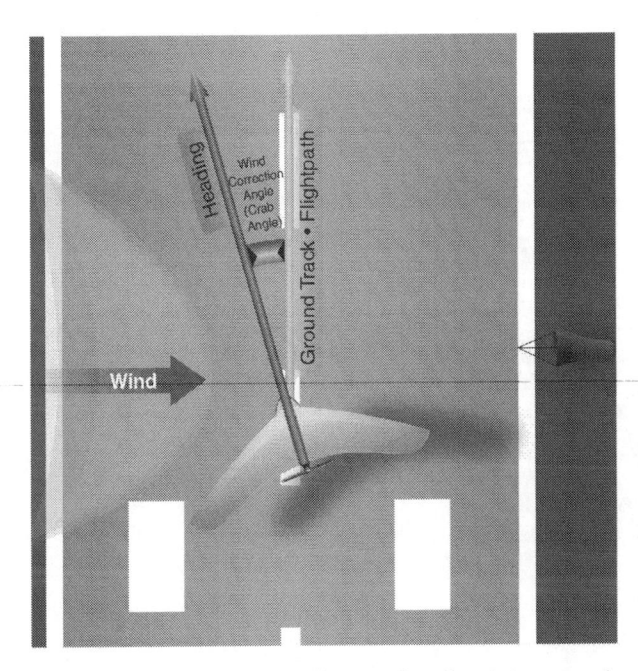

Figure 7-7. *Wing correction angle (or crab angle as is is commonly called).*

the climb technique is the same used for normal takeoffs and climbs maintaining the proper ground track with the proper wing correction angle/crab angle. *[Figure 7-8]*

In addition to normal takeoffs, additional common errors in the performance of crosswind takeoffs are:

- Letting the windward side of the wing get too high.
- Allowing the wing to weathervane into the wind during the takeoff roll.
- Not obtaining additional speed before rotation.
- Too slow of a rotation during lift-off.
- Inadequate drift correction after lift-off.

Ground Effect on Takeoff

Ground effect is a condition of improved performance encountered when the aircraft is operating very close to the ground. Ground effect can be detected and measured up to an altitude of about one wingspan above the surface. *[Figure 7-9]* However, ground effect is most significant when the WSC aircraft is maintaining a constant attitude at low airspeed and low altitude. Examples are during takeoff when the aircraft lifts off and accelerates to climb speed, and also during the landing flare before touchdown. When the wing is under the influence of ground effect, there is a reduction in upwash, downwash, and wingtip vortices.

Since the WSC wing is a high wing aircraft, the effects are not as pronounced as a low wing airplane, but during rotation, the reduction in induced drag is about 25 percent

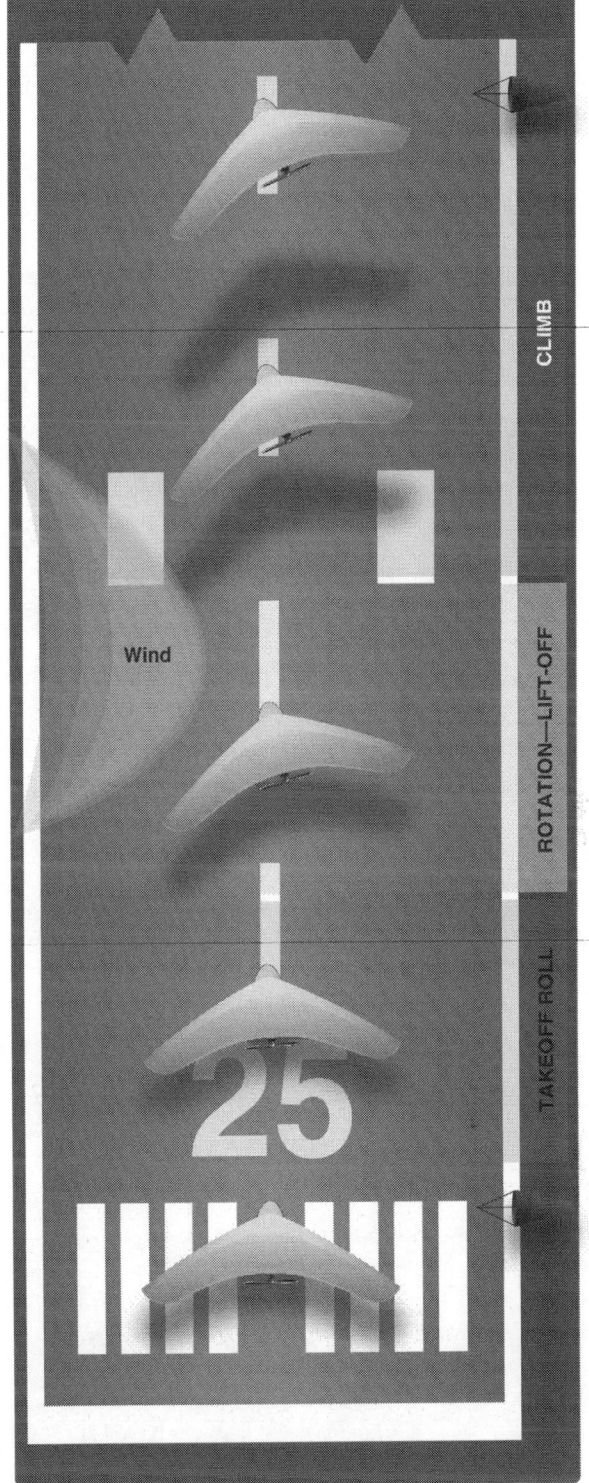

Figure 7-8. *Crosswind takeoff.*

and decreases as the WSC aircraft climbs. At high speeds where parasite drag dominates, induced drag is a small part of the total drag. Consequently, the effects of ground effect are of greater concern during takeoff and landing.

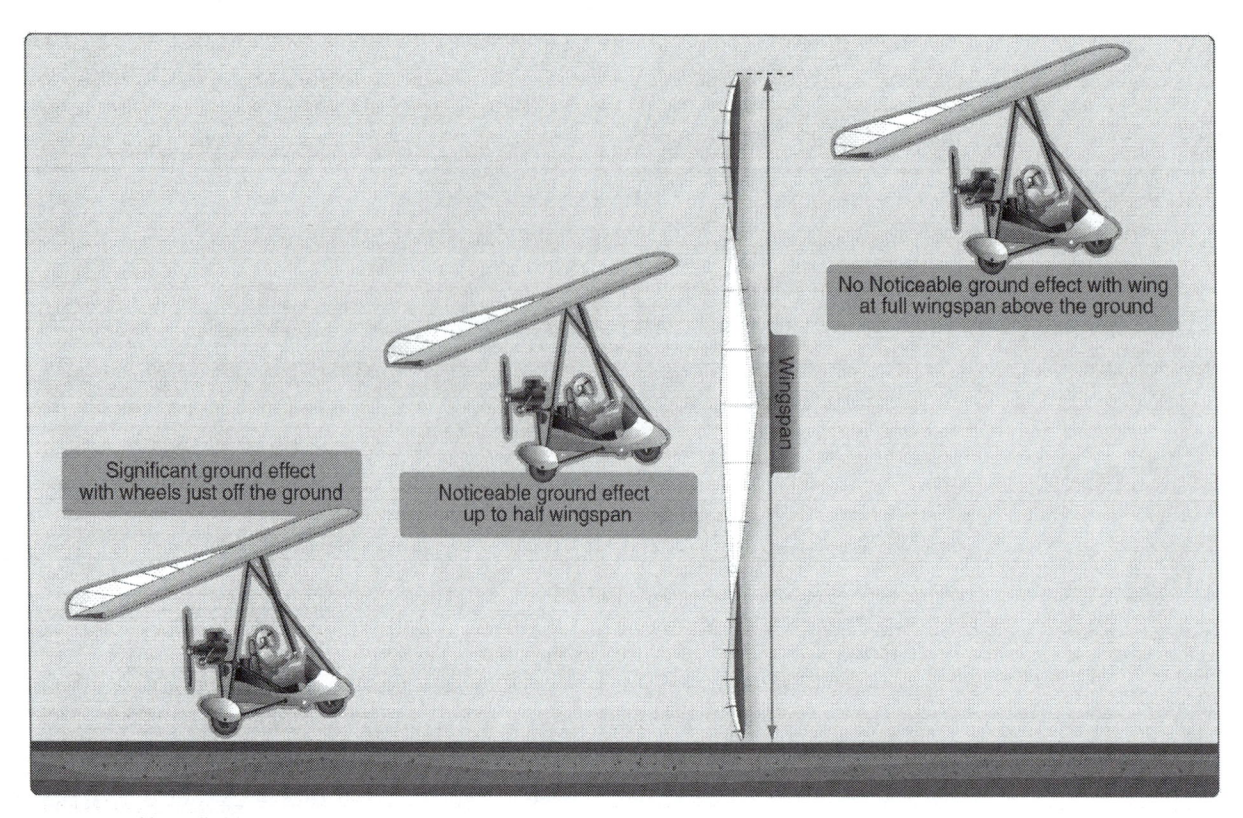

Figure 7-9. *Ground effect area.*

On takeoff, the takeoff roll, lift-off, and the beginning of the initial climb are accomplished in the ground effect area. As the aircraft lifts off and climbs out of the ground effect area the following occurs.

- The WSC aircraft requires an increase in angle of attack to maintain the same lift coefficient.
- The WSC aircraft experiences an increase in induced drag and thrust required.

Due to the reduced drag in ground effect, the aircraft may seem capable of taking off below the recommended airspeed with less thrust. However, as the aircraft rises out of ground effect with an insufficient airspeed, initial climb performance may prove to be marginal due to increased drag. Under conditions of high density altitude, high temperature, and/or maximum gross weight, the aircraft may become airborne at an insufficient airspeed but unable to climb out of ground effect. Consequently, the aircraft may not be able to clear obstructions or may settle back on the runway. The point to remember is that additional power is required to compensate for increases in drag that occur as an aircraft leaves ground effect. But during an initial climb, the engine is already developing maximum power. The only alternative is to lower pitch attitude to gain additional airspeed, which results in inevitable altitude loss. Therefore, under marginal conditions, it is important that the aircraft take off at the recommended speed that provides adequate initial climb performance.

Ground effect is important to normal flight operations. If the runway is long enough, or if no obstacles exist, ground effect can be used to advantage by utilizing the reduced drag to improve initial acceleration. Additionally, the procedure for takeoff from unsatisfactory surfaces is to take as much weight on the wings as possible during the ground run, and to lift off with the aid of ground effect before true flying speed is attained. It is then necessary to reduce the angle of attack to attain normal airspeed before attempting to fly away from the ground effect area.

Short Field Takeoff and Steepest Angle Climb

Takeoffs and climbs from fields in which the takeoff area is short or the available takeoff area is restricted by obstructions require the pilot to operate the WSC aircraft at the limit of its takeoff performance capabilities. To depart from such an area safely, the pilot must exercise positive and precise control of attitude and airspeed so that takeoff and climb performance results in the shortest ground roll and the steepest angle of climb.

The achieved result should be consistent with the performance section of the AFM/POH. In all cases, the power setting, trim setting, airspeed, and procedures prescribed by the manufacturer should be followed.

In order to accomplish a short field takeoff and steepest angle climb safely, the pilot must have adequate knowledge in the use and effectiveness of the best angle-of-climb (V_X) speed and the best rate-of-climb (V_Y) speed for the specific make and model of WSC aircraft being flown.

The speed for V_X is that which results in the greatest gain in altitude for a given distance over the ground. V_X is usually less than V_Y but greater than minimum controlled airspeed. It should be noted that this maneuver is not performed in normal situations. Flying at V_X speed close to the ground in gusty winds can result in a stall with catastrophic consequences.

If clearing an obstacle is questionable, the WSC aircraft should be packed up and trailered away. If a pilot decides to perform a short field takeoff, then a number of factors can be optimized to contribute to a short field takeoff such as leaving your passenger and/or baggage in the area, waiting for favorable winds or lower density altitude, and picking the longest runway path with the shortest obstacle to clear.

However, if a short field takeoff is going to be performed and all possible factors have been optimized, the following procedure is provided. The procedure is similar to the normal takeoff but the following additional procedure is used for this maneuver.

Takeoff Roll

Taking off from a short field requires the takeoff to be started from the very beginning of the takeoff area. The WSC manufacturer's recommended specific trim setting should be set before starting the takeoff roll. This permits the pilot to give full attention to the proper technique and the aircraft's performance throughout the takeoff.

Some authorities prefer to hold the brakes until the maximum obtainable engine revolutions per minute (rpm) is achieved before allowing the WSC aircraft to begin its takeoff run. However, it has not been established that this procedure results in a shorter takeoff run in all WSC aircraft, many of which can not hold the brakes at full throttle. If the brakes are not held with the throttle advanced to full and then released, takeoff power should be applied immediately to full throttle as fast as possible without the engine bogging down to accelerate the aircraft as rapidly as possible. The WSC aircraft should be allowed to roll with the wing finding the trim position for minimum drag during acceleration to the lift-off speed.

Lift-Off and Climb Out

At V_X speed, the WSC aircraft should be smoothly and firmly rotated by applying control bar forward pressure to an attitude that results in the V_X airspeed. After becoming airborne, a wings-level climb should be maintained at V_X until obstacles have been cleared. Thereafter, the pitch attitude may be lowered slightly and the climb continued at V_Y speed until reaching a safe maneuvering altitude.

Remember that an attempt to rotate off the ground prematurely or to climb too steeply may cause the WSC aircraft to settle back to the runway or into the obstacles. Even if the aircraft remains airborne, the initial climb remains flat and climb performance/obstacle clearance ability is seriously degraded until V_X airspeed is achieved. *[Figure 7-10]*

Figure 7-10. *Short field takeoff.*

In addition to normal takeoffs, common errors in the performance of short field takeoffs are:

- Deciding to do a questionable short field takeoff when the WSC aircraft can be packed up and driven away.
- Failure to adequately determine the best path with the longest run and shortest obstacle.
- Failure to utilize all available runway/takeoff area.
- Failure to wait for the best atmospheric conditions of density altitude and wind direction.
- Failure to reduce all possible weight from the WSC aircraft.
- Failure to have the WSC aircraft properly trimmed prior to takeoff.
- Premature lift-off resulting in high drag.
- Holding the WSC aircraft on the ground unnecessarily.
- Inadequate rotation resulting in excessive speed after lift-off.
- Inability to attain/maintain best V_X airspeed.
- Fixation on the airspeed indicator during initial climb.

Soft/Rough Field Takeoff and Climb

Takeoffs and climbs from soft fields require the use of operational techniques for getting the WSC aircraft airborne as quickly as possible to eliminate the drag caused by tall grass, soft sand, mud, and snow, and may or may not require climbing over an obstacle. The technique makes judicious use of ground effect and requires a feel for the WSC aircraft and fine control touch. These same techniques are also useful on a rough field where it is advisable to get the aircraft off the ground as soon as possible to avoid damaging the landing gear.

Soft surfaces or long, wet grass usually reduce the aircraft's acceleration during the takeoff roll so much that adequate takeoff speed might not be attained if normal takeoff techniques were employed.

It should be emphasized that the WSC aircraft is different from most aircraft. The high wing creates a high center of gravity in which the front wheel can bog down in soft fields and flip the WSC aircraft forward. The propeller in the back pushing down on the front wheel also contributes to this unique situation. This is a limitation for WSC aircraft that should not be ignored. WSC aircraft that land in soft fields or sand may not be able to take off. There is a wide variation of manufacturer designs with the least preferable being a skinny, high pressure, highly loaded front tire. WSC aircraft with large wide tires that can be operated at low pressure are designed for operation in soft and rough fields. *[Figures 7-11* through *7-13]*

Correct takeoff procedure for soft fields and rough fields is quite different from that appropriate for short fields with firm, smooth surfaces. To minimize the hazards associated with takeoffs from soft or rough fields, support of the aircraft's weight must be transferred as rapidly as possible from the wheels to the wings as the takeoff roll proceeds. Establishing and maintaining a relatively high angle of attack with a nose-high pitch attitude as early as possible achieves this.

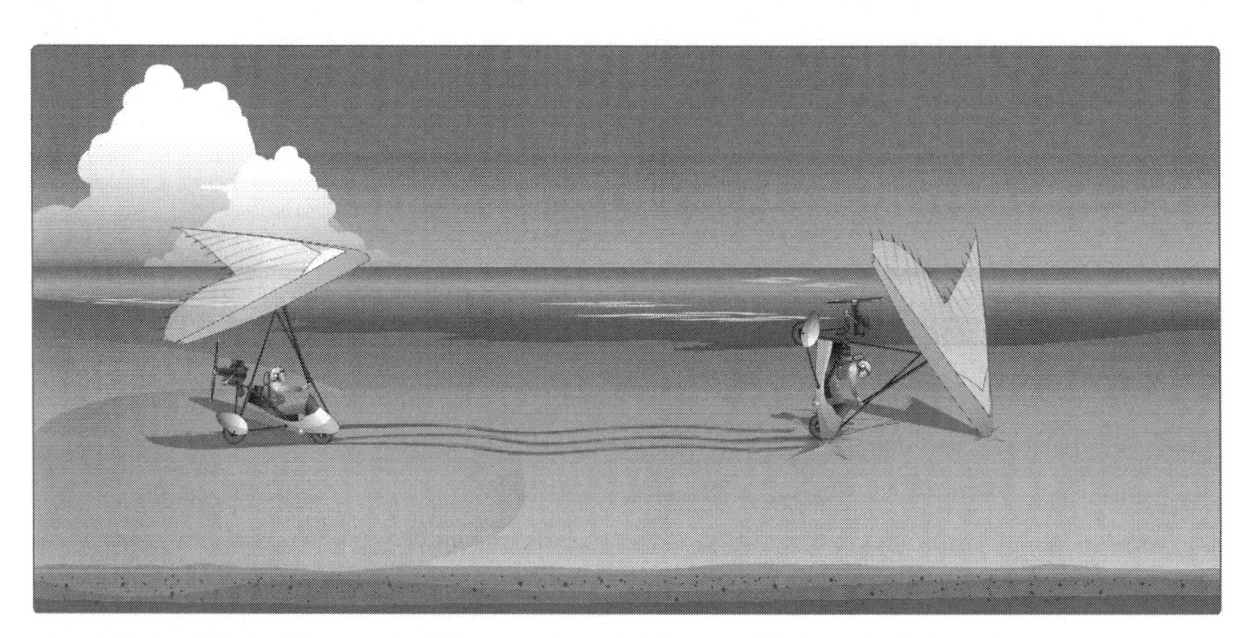

Figure 7-11. *Soft field takeoff limitation for WSC aircraft: front wheel digs in and WSC aircraft rolls forward.*

Figure 7-12. *Example of a WSC aircraft designed with a wide low-pressure front wheel for soft field operation.*

Figure 7-13. *Grass fields are commonly used for WSC operations but require a longer time to accelerate to takeoff speed.*

Stopping on a soft surface, such as mud, snow or sand, might bog the aircraft down; therefore, it should be kept in continuous motion with sufficient power while lining up for the takeoff roll.

Takeoff Roll

As the aircraft is aligned with the takeoff path, takeoff power is applied smoothly and rapidly. As the aircraft accelerates, the control bar is moved full forward to the front tube to establish a positive angle of attack and to reduce the weight supported by the nosewheel because any lift on the wing takes load off of the landing gear.

When the aircraft is held at a nose-high attitude throughout the takeoff run and as speed increases and lift develops, the wings progressively relieve the wheels of more and more of the WSC's weight, thereby minimizing the drag caused by surface irregularities or adhesion. If this attitude is accurately maintained, the aircraft virtually flies itself off the ground, becoming airborne at airspeed slower than a safe climb speed because of ground effect. *[Figure 7-14]*

Lift-Off and Initial Climb

After becoming airborne, the nose should be lowered very gently with the wheels clear but just above the surface to allow the aircraft to utilize ground effect to accelerate to V_Y, or V_X if obstacles must be cleared. Extreme care must be exercised immediately after the aircraft becomes airborne and while it accelerates to avoid settling back onto the surface. An attempt to climb prematurely or too steeply may cause the aircraft to settle back to the surface as a result of losing the benefit of ground effect. An attempt to climb out of ground effect before sufficient climb airspeed is attained may result in aircraft incapacity to continue climbing as the ground effect area is traveled, even with full power for lower powered WSC aircraft. Therefore, it is essential that the aircraft remain in ground effect until at least V_X is reached. This requires a feel for the WSC aircraft and a very fine control touch in order to avoid overcontrolling the pitch control as required control pressures change with aircraft acceleration. Simply getting off the ground as quickly as possible and flying in ground effect is the goal.

In addition to normal takeoffs, additional common errors in the performance of soft/rough field takeoffs are:

- Attempting a takeoff with a WSC that is not equipped with the proper tires.
- Minimum air pressure not used in tires.
- Insufficient control bar forward pressure during initial takeoff roll, resulting in inadequate angle of attack.
- Poor directional control.
- Climbing too steeply after lift-off.
- Abrupt and/or excessive pitch control while attempting to level off and accelerate after lift-off.
- Allowing the aircraft to "mush" or settle resulting in an inadvertent touchdown after lift-off.
- Attempting to climb out of ground effect area before attaining sufficient climb speed.

Rejected Takeoff/Engine Failure

Emergency or abnormal situations can occur during a takeoff that requires a pilot to reject the takeoff while still on the runway. Circumstances such as a malfunctioning powerplant, items dislodging during takeoff, inadequate acceleration, runway incursion, or air traffic conflict may be reasons for a rejected takeoff.

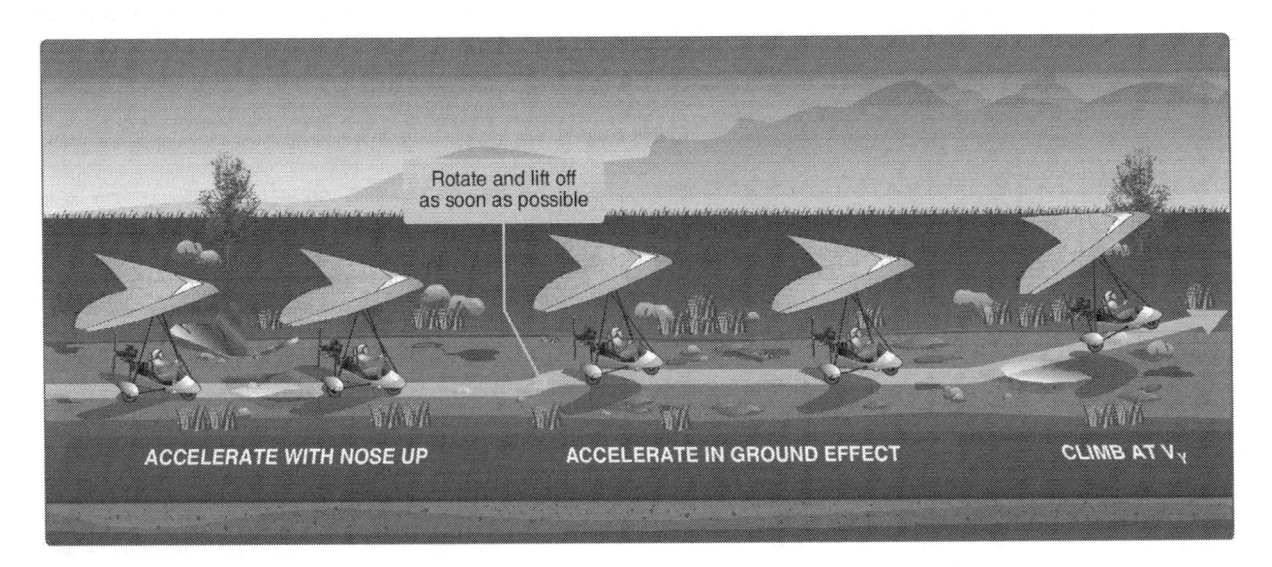

Figure 7-14. *Rough and soft field takeoff.*

Prior to takeoff, the pilot should have in mind a point along the runway at which the aircraft should be airborne. If that point is reached and the WSC aircraft is not airborne, immediate action should be taken to discontinue the takeoff. Properly planned and executed, chances are excellent the aircraft can be stopped on the remaining runway without using extraordinary measures, such as excessive braking that may result in loss of directional control, damage, and/or personal injury.

In the event a takeoff is rejected, the power should be reduced to idle or the engine shut off and maximum braking applied while maintaining directional control. If it is necessary to shut down the engine due to a fire, the fuel supply should be shut off and the magnetos turned off. In all cases, the manufacturer's emergency procedure should be followed.

What characterizes all power loss or engine failure occurrences after lift-off is urgency. In most instances, the pilot has only a few seconds after an engine failure to decide what course of action to take and to execute it. Unless prepared in advance to make the proper decision, there is an excellent chance the pilot will make a poor decision, or make no decision at all and allow events to rule.

In the event of an engine failure on initial climb-out, the pilot's first responsibility is to maintain aircraft control. At a climb pitch attitude without power, the WSC is at or near a stalling angle of attack. It is essential the pilot immediately lower the pitch attitude by pulling the control bar back to the chest immediately to prevent a stall. As discussed earlier in the climb section, a preventative measure is to climb to a safe altitude, 200 feet was used as an example, at least the minimum safe climb speed as recommended by the manufacturer to lower pitch angle as a safety measure for this situation to minimize a high pitch angle close to the ground. The pilot should establish a controlled glide toward a plausible landing area (preferably straight ahead on the remaining runway).

Noise Abatement

Aircraft noise problems have become a major concern at many airports throughout the country. Many local communities have pressured airports into developing specific operational procedures that help limit aircraft noise while operating over nearby areas. For years now, the Federal Aviation Administration (FAA), airport managers, aircraft operators, pilots, and special interest groups have been working together to minimize aircraft noise for nearby sensitive areas. As a result, noise abatement procedures have been developed for many of these airports that include standardized profiles and procedures to achieve these lower noise goals.

Airports that have noise abatement procedures provide information to pilots, operators, air carriers, air traffic facilities, and other special groups that are applicable to their airport. These procedures are available to the aviation community by various means. Most of this information comes from the Airport/Facility Directory (A/FD), local and regional publications, printed handouts, operator bulletin boards, safety briefings, and local air traffic facilities.

At airports that use noise abatement procedures, reminder signs may be installed at the taxiway hold positions for applicable runways. These are to remind pilots to use and comply with noise abatement procedures on departure. Pilots who are not familiar with these procedures should ask the tower or air traffic facility for the recommended procedures. In any case, pilots should be considerate of the surrounding community while operating their aircraft to and from such an airport. This includes operating as quietly, yet safely as possible.

Chapter Summary

Normal Takeoff is straight down runway centerline with rotation at proper airspeed and initial climb at safe airspeed and moderate pitch angle to account for engine failure. Once to safe maneuvering altitude en route climb speed is maintained. Cross wind takeoffs are similar to normal takeoffs except wing must be held straight to ground path during acceleration and greater speed is obtained before rotation. Short field takeoffs are performed by ensuring that sufficient runway is available for takeoff and utilizing best-angle-of-climb speed (V_X) until obstacle is cleared. Rough or soft field takeoffs are performed by keeping the weight off the nosewheel, and lifting off into the ground effect to gain speed as soon as possible.

Precautions should always be taken by climbing at faster airspeeds and lower pitch angles in case of an engine failure/rejected landing.

Chapter 8
The National Airspace System

Airspace Classification

Introduction

The National Airspace System (NAS) is the network of all components regarding airspace in the United States. This comprehensive label includes air navigation facilities, equipment, services, airports or landing areas, sectional charts, information/services, rules, regulations, procedures, technical information, manpower, and material. Many of these system components are shared jointly with the military. To conform to international aviation standards, the United States adopted the primary elements of the classification system developed by the International Civil Aviation Organization (ICAO). This chapter provides a general discussion of airspace classification. Detailed information on the classification of airspace, operating procedures, and restrictions is found in the Aeronautical Information Manual (AIM).

This handbook departs from the conventional norm, in that the airspace discussions are presented in reverse order, in the belief that it is much easier to learn the airspace from least complicated to most complicated; also, the information presented for basic visual flight rules (VFR) weather minimums is only that necessary for weight-shift control (WSC) aircraft operations.

The two categories of airspace are regulatory and nonregulatory. Within these two categories, there are four types: uncontrolled, controlled, special use, and other airspace.

Airspace is charted on sectional charts as shown in the some examples for the specific airspaces on the chapter. The specific airspace symbols are shown on the legend for each sectional chart. *[Figure 8-1]* The WSC aircraft pilot should study and refer to the specifics of the AIM; FAA-H-8083-25, Pilot's Handbook of Aeronautical Knowledge; and Title 14 of the Code of Federal Regulations (14 CFR) part 91 for additional information regarding airspace and operations within that airspace.

Uncontrolled Airspace

Class G Airspace

Class G or uncontrolled airspace is the portion of the airspace that has not been designated as Class A, B, C, D, or E. Class G airspace extends from the surface to the base of controlled airspace (Class B, C, D, and E) above it as shown in *Figures 8-2* and *8-3*.

Most Class G airspace is overlaid with Class E airspace, beginning at either 700 or 1,200 feet above ground level (AGL). In remote areas of the United States, Class G airspace extends above 700 and 1,200 AGL to as high as 14,500 feet before the Class E airspace begins. *[Figure 8-2]* The pilot is advised to consult the appropriate sectional chart to ensure that he or she is aware of the airspace limits prior to flight in an unfamiliar area. *[Figure 8-4]*

There are no communications, entry, equipment, or minimum pilot certificate

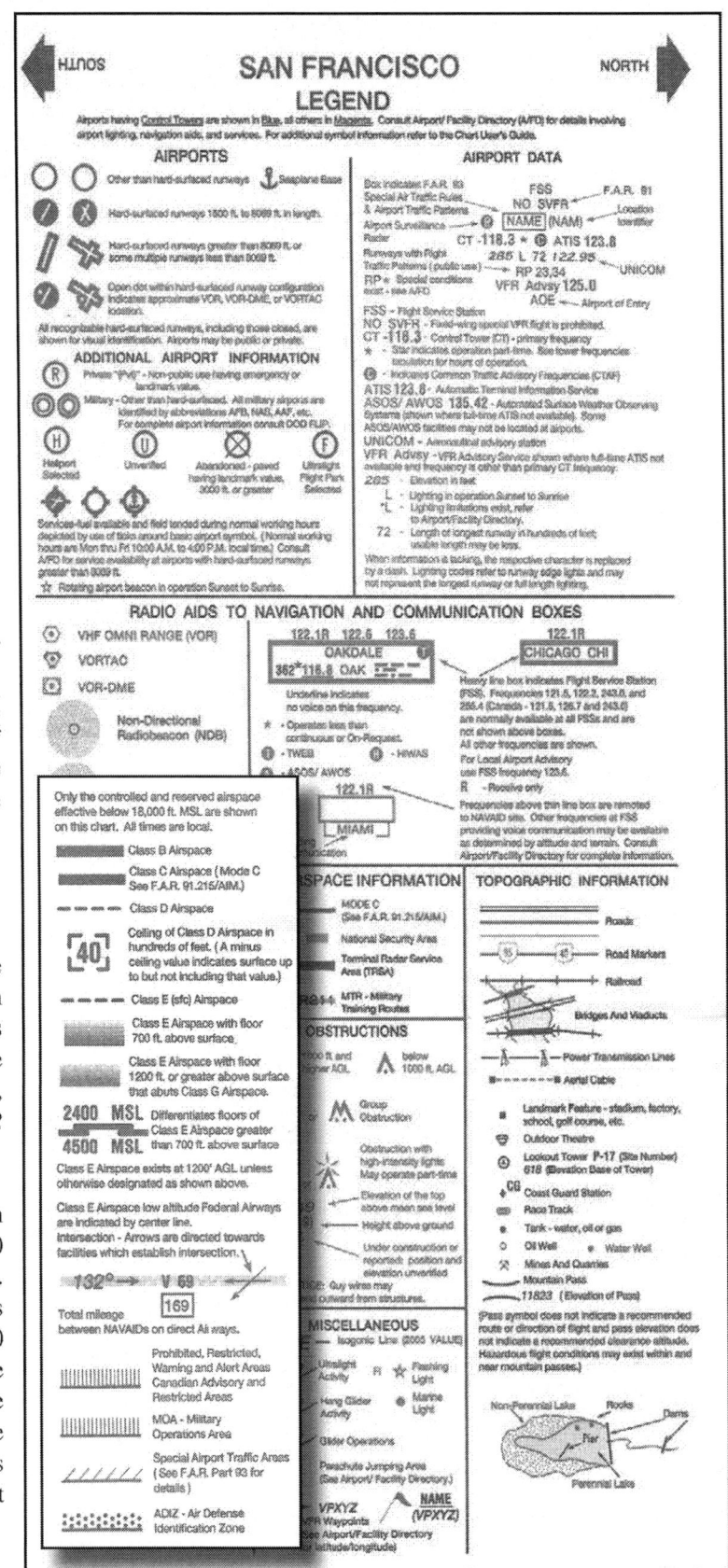

Figure 8-1. *Each student, pilot, and instructor should have a current sectional chart for the flight area.*

8-2

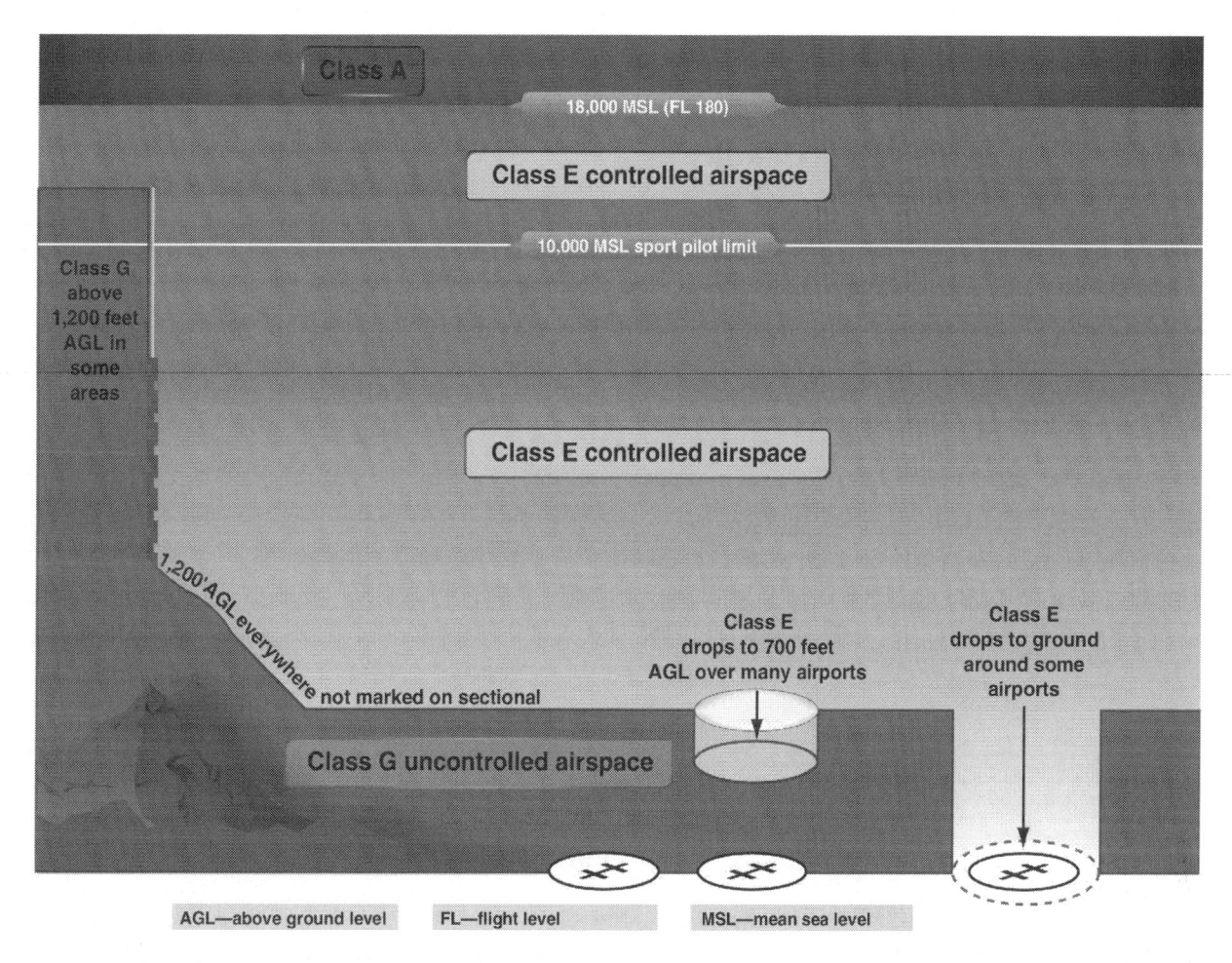

Figure 8-2. *Class G uncontrolled airspace and Class E controlled airspace.*

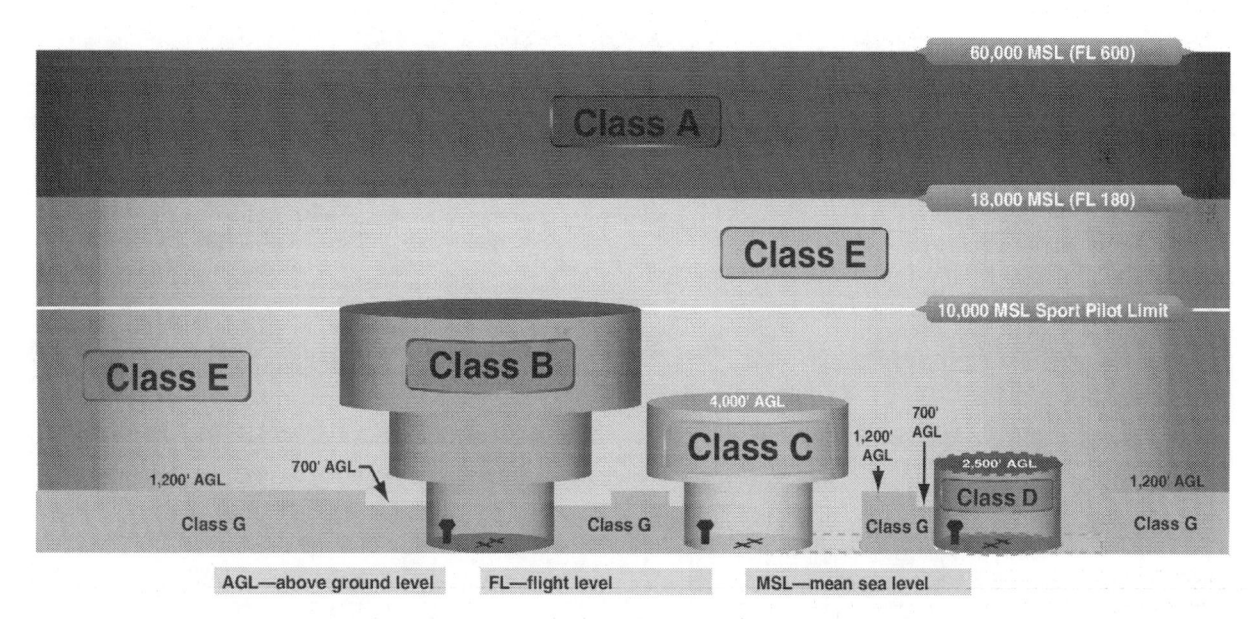

Figure 8-3. *Class G airspace extends from the surface to the base of controlled airspace (Class B, C, D, and E).*

8-3

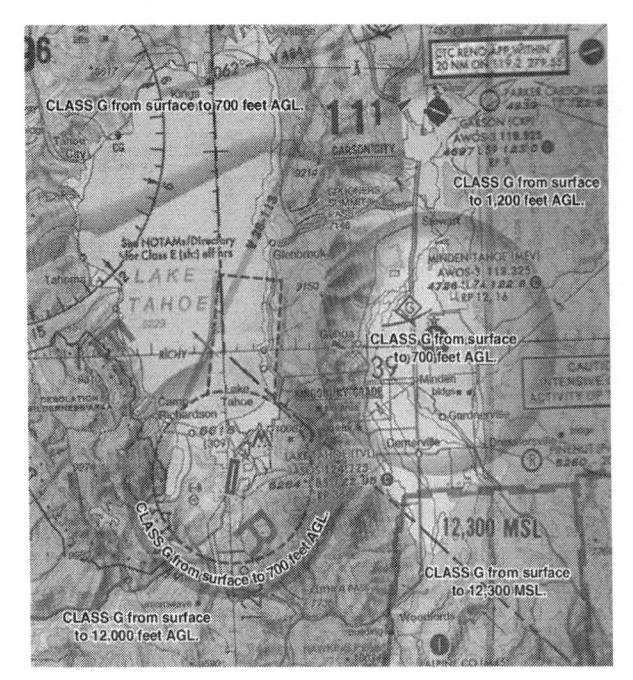

Figure 8-4. *Class G airspace as shown on a sectional chart.*

requirements to fly in uncontrolled Class G airspace unless there is a control tower. *[Figure 8-5]*

If operations are conducted at an altitude of ≤ 1,200 feet AGL, the pilot must remain clear of clouds. If the operations are conducted more than 1,200 feet AGL but less than 10,000 feet mean sea level (MSL), cloud clearances are 1,000 feet above, 500 feet below, and 2,000 feet horizontally from any cloud(s). A popular mnemonic tool used to remember basic cloud clearances is "C152," a popular fixed-wing training aircraft. In this case, the mnemonic recalls, "Clouds 1,000, 500, and 2,000."

Visibility in Class G airspace below 10,000 MSL day flight is one statute mile (SM) for private pilots and three SM for sport pilots. See *Figure 8-6* for specific Class G weather minimums for WSC pilots.

Controlled Airspace

Controlled airspace is a generic term that covers the different classifications of airspace and defined dimensions within which ATC service is provided in accordance with the airspace classification. Controlled airspace consists of:

- Class E
- Class D
- Class C
- Class B
- Class A

Class E Airspace

Generally, if the airspace is not Class A, B, C, or D, and is controlled airspace, then it is Class E airspace. Class E airspace extends upward from either the surface or a designated altitude to the overlying or adjacent controlled

Class Airspace	Entry Requirements	Equipment	Minimum Pilot Certificate
A	ATC Clearance	IFR Equipped	Instrument Rating
B	ATC Clearance	Two-Way Radio, Transponder with Altitude Reporting Capability	Private—Except a student or recreational pilot may operate at other than the primary airport if seeking private pilot certification and if regulatory requirements are met. †
C	Two-Way Radio Communications Prior to Entry	Two-Way Radio, Transponder with Altitude Reporting Capability	†
D	Two-Way Radio Communications Prior to Entry	Two-Way Radio	†
E	None for VFR	No Specific Requirement	No Specific Requirement
G	None	No Specific Requirement	No Specific Requirement

† Sport pilots must have training and a logbook endorsement.

Figure 8-5. *Requirements for airspace operation.*

Basic VFR Weather Minimums			
Airspace*		Flight visibility[†]	Distance from clouds
Class A		Not applicable	Not applicable
Class B		3 statute miles	Clear of clouds
Class C		3 statute miles	500 feet below 1,000 feet above 2,000 feet horizontal
Class D		3 statute miles	500 feet below 1,000 feet above 2,000 feet horizontal
Class E	Less than 10,000 feet MSL	3 statute miles	500 feet below 1,000 feet above 2,000 feet horizontal
	At or above 10,000 feet MSL*	5 statute miles	1,000 feet below 1,000 feet above 1 statute mile horizontal
Class G	1,200 feet or less above the surface (regardless of MSL altitude)		
	Day, except as provided in 14 CFR section 91.155(b).	1 statute mile[†]	clear of clouds
	Night, except as provided in 14 CFR section 91.155(b).	3 statute miles	500 feet below 1,000 feet above 2,000 feet horizontal
	More than 1,200 feet above the surface but less than 10,000 feet MSL		
	Day.	1 statute mile[†]	500 feet below 1,000 feet above 2,000 feet horizontal
	Night[‡]	3 statute miles	500 feet below 1,000 feet above 2,000 feet horizontal
	More than 1,200 feet above the surface and at or above 10,000 feet MSL*		
		5 statute miles	1,000 feet below 1,000 feet above 1 statute mile horizontal

[†] Sport pilots must maintain 3 SM or better visibility in all airspace.
[‡] Sport pilots are not authorized to fly at night.
* Sport pilots are not authorized to fly above 10,000 feet MSL.

Figure 8-6. *Basic weather minimums for WSC operations in the different classes of airspace.*

airspace. *[Figures 8-3* and *8-7]* Also Class E is federal airways beginning at 1,200 feet AGL extending 4 nautical miles (NM) on each side, extending up to 18,000 feet.

Unless designated at a lower altitude, Class E airspace begins at 1,200 AGL over the United States, including that airspace overlying the waters within 12 NM of the coast of the 48 contiguous states and Alaska, and extends up to but not including 18,000 feet.

There are no specific communications requirements associated with Class E airspace *[Figure 8-5];* however, some Class E airspace locations are designed to provide approaches for instrument approaches, and a pilot would be prudent to ensure that appropriate communications are established when operating near those areas.

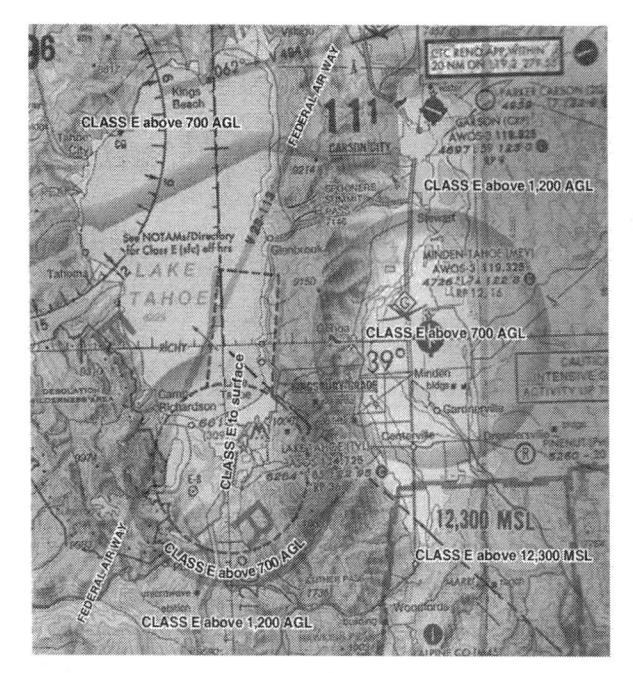

Figure 8-7. *Class E airspace as shown on a sectional chart.*

If WSC aircraft operations are being conducted below 10,000 feet MSL, minimum visibility requirements are three statute miles and basic VFR cloud clearance requirements are 1,000 feet above, 500 feet below, and 2,000 feet horizontal (remember the C152 mnemonic). Operations above 10,000 feet MSL for private pilots of WSC aircraft require minimum visibility of five statute miles and cloud clearances of at least 1,000 feet above, 1,000 feet below, and one statute mile horizontally. *[Figure 8-5]* See *Figure 8-6* for specific VFR visibility requirements.

Towered Airport Operations

All student pilots must have an endorsement to operate within Class B, C, and D airspace and within airspace for airports that have a control tower, per 14 CFR section 61.94 or 14 CFR section 61.95. Only private pilot students can operate within Class B airspace with the proper endorsements per 14 CFR section 61.95. Sport pilots must also have an endorsement per 14 CFR section 61.325 to operate within Class B, C, and D airspace and within airspace for airports with a control tower. *[Figure 8-5]* All students and Sport pilots have further restrictions regarding the specific Class B airports out of which they may operate, per 14 CFR section 91.131.

Class D Airspace

Class D is that airspace from the surface to 2,500 feet AGL (but charted in MSL) surrounding smaller airports with an operational control tower. *[Figures 8-3 and 8-8]* The configuration of each Class D airspace area is individually tailored. When instrument procedures are published, the airspace is normally designed to contain the procedures.

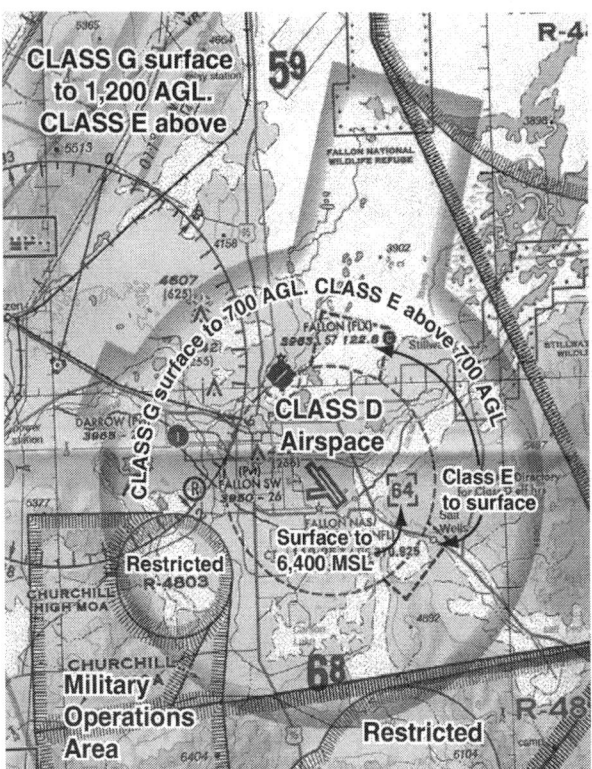

Figure 8-8. *Class D airspace shown on a sectional chart.*

Unless otherwise authorized, each aircraft must establish two-way radio communications with the ATC facility providing air traffic services prior to entering the airspace and thereafter maintain those communications while in the airspace. Radio contact should be initiated far enough from the Class D airspace boundary to preclude entering the Class D airspace before two-way radio communications are established. It is important to understand that if the controller responds to the initial radio call without using the WSC aircraft's call sign, radio communications have not been established, and the WSC aircraft may not enter the Class D airspace.

Many airports associated with Class D airspace do not operate a control tower on a 24-hour-a-day basis. When not in operation, the airspace will normally revert to Class E or G airspace, with no communications requirements. Refer to the AF/D for specific hours of operation airports.

The minimum visibility requirements for Class D airspace are three statute miles; cloud clearances are the 1,000 above, 500 below and 2,000 vertical. *[Figure 8-6]*

Class C Airspace

Class C airspace normally extends from the surface to 4,000 feet above the airport elevation surrounding those airports having an operational control tower, that are serviced by a radar approach control, and with a certain number of IFR and passenger enplanements (larger airline operations). *[Figures 8-3 and 8-9]* This airspace is charted in feet MSL, and is generally of a five NM radius surface area that extends from the surface to 4,000 feet above the airport elevation, and a 10 NM radius area that extends from 1,200 feet to 4,000 feet above the airport elevation. There is also a noncharted outer area with a 20 NM radius, which extends from the surface to 4,000 feet above the primary airport, and this area may include one or more satellite airports. *[Figure 8-9]*

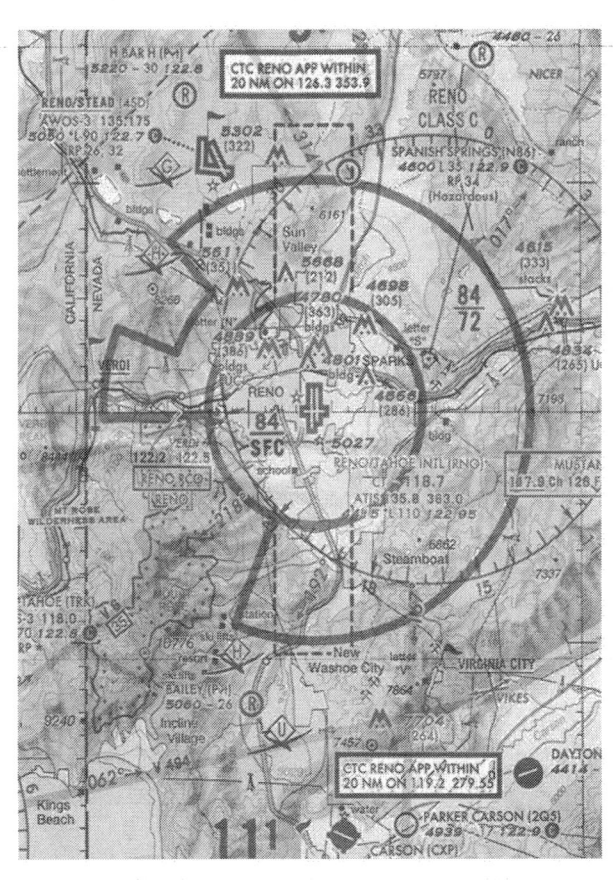

Figure 8-9. *Class C airspace as shown on a sectional chart.*

WSC aircraft can fly into Class C airspace by contacting the control tower first, establishing communications (same as Class D), and having an altitude encoding transponder. Aircraft can enter Class C airspace without a transponder if prior permission from ATC is received 1 hour before entry, per 14 CFR section 91.215(d)(3). Aircraft may fly under the Class C upper tier of airspace without a transponder but not over the top of Class C airspace lateral boundaries.

Cloud clearances in Class C airspace are the same as Class D airspace: minimum visibility of three statute miles, and a minimum distance from clouds of 1,000 feet above, 500 feet below, and 2,000 feet horizontal.

Since Class C has significant air traffic, many with larger airplanes creating stronger vortices, the pilot must be aware that the chance of encountering catastrophic wingtip vortices is greater at airports with larger air traffic.

Class B Airspace

Class B airspace is generally airspace from the surface to 10,000 feet MSL surrounding the nation's busiest airports in terms of IFR operations or passenger enplanements. *[Figures 8-3 and 8-10]* The configuration of each Class B airspace area is individually tailored and consists of a surface area and two or more additional layers (some Class B airspace areas resemble upside-down wedding cakes), and is designed to contain all published instrument procedures once an aircraft enters the airspace.

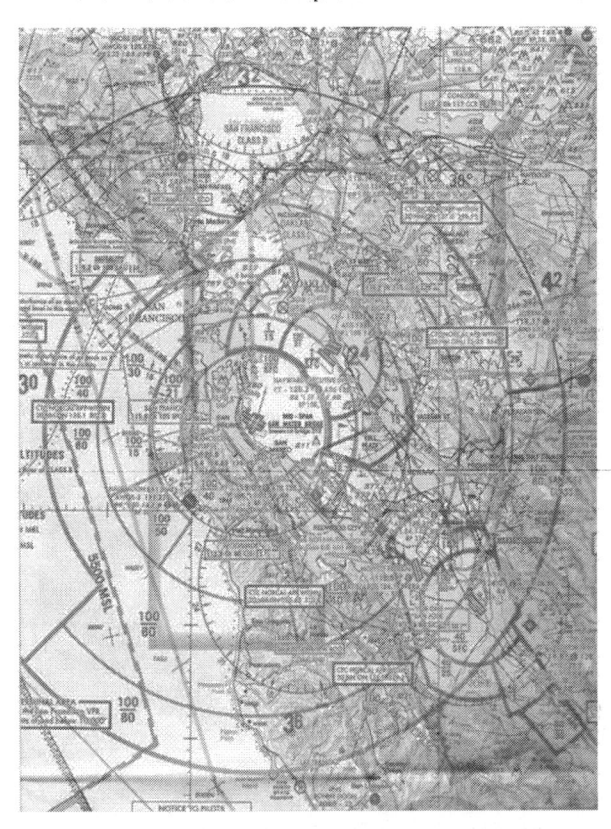

Figure 8-10. *Class B airspace as shown on a sectional chart.*

Equipment requirements are the same as for Class C airspace; however, due to air traffic congestion, the WSC aircraft pilot requesting entry to Class B airspace may be denied entry. Since aircraft operating in Class B airspace have a radar signature and ATC provides aircraft separation, there is a difference in the cloud clearance requirements. Visibility remains three statute miles, but minimum cloud clearance requirement is to remain clear of clouds. *[Figure 8-6]*

Airspace Above 10,000' MSL and Below 18,000'

For WSC aircraft flying above 10,000 feet MSL, the visibility must be greater than 5 SM and cloud clearances increase to 1,000 feet below, 1,000 feet above, and 1 SM horizontal. If the WSC aircraft was not certificated with an electrical system, an altitude encoding transponder is required per 14 CFR section 91.215.

Oxygen is required for the pilot above 12,500 MSL up to and including 14,000 feet MSL if the flight at those levels is more than 30 minutes duration. At altitudes above 14,000 feet MSL, oxygen is required for the pilot during the entire flight time at those altitudes. At altitudes above 15,000 feet MSL, each occupant of the aircraft must be provided with supplemental oxygen.

Class A Airspace

Class A airspace is generally the airspace from 18,000 feet MSL up to and including FL 600, including the airspace overlying the waters within 12 NM of the coast of the 48 contiguous states and Alaska. Unless otherwise authorized, all operations in Class A airspace are conducted under IFR. Class A airspace is not applicable to WSC pilots.

Special Use Airspace

Special use airspace is the designation for airspace in which certain activities must be confined, or where limitations may be imposed on aircraft operations that are not part of those activities.

Special use airspace usually consists of:
- Prohibited areas
- Restricted areas
- Warning areas
- Military operation areas (MOAs)
- Alert areas
- Controlled firing areas
- Parachute jump areas

Except for controlled firing areas, special use airspace areas are depicted on visual sectional charts. *[Figure 8-11]* Controlled firing areas are not charted because their activities are suspended immediately when spotter aircraft, radar, or ground lookout positions indicate an aircraft might be approaching the area. Nonparticipating aircraft are not required to change their flightpaths. Special use airspace areas are shown in their entirety (within the limits of the chart), even when they overlap, adjoin, or when an area is designated within another area. The areas are identified by type and identifying name or number, positioned either within or immediately adjacent to the area. *[Figure 8-11]*

Figure 8-11. *Special use airspace designations as appear on sectional charts.*

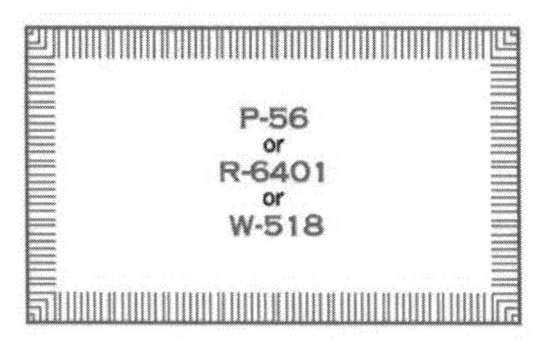

Prohibited, restricted or warning areas; alert areas; and MOAs are further defined with tables on sectional charts for their altitudes, time of use, controlling agency/contact facility and controlling agency contact frequency. *[Figure 8-12]*

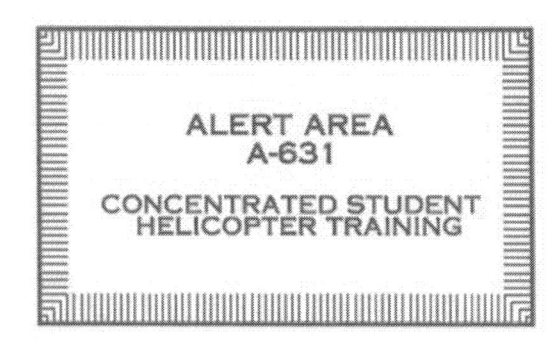

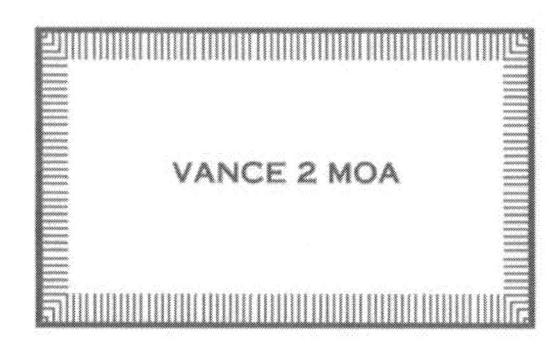

Prohibited Areas

Prohibited areas contain airspace of defined dimensions within which the flight of aircraft is prohibited. Such areas

SPECIAL USE AIRSPACE ON SAN FRANCISCO SECTIONAL CHART

Unless otherwise noted altitudes are MSL and in feet. Time is local.
"TO" on altitude means "To and including."
FL – Flight Level
NO A/G – No air to ground communications.
Contact nearest FSS for information.

† Other times by NOTAM.
NOTAM – Use of this term in Restricted Areas indicates FAA and DoD NOTAM systems. Use of this term in all other Special Use areas indicates the DoD NOTAM system.

U.S. P–PROHIBITED, R–RESTRICTED, A–ALERT, W–WARNING, MOA–MILITARY OPERATIONS AREA

NUMBER	ALTITUDE	TIME OF USE	CONTROLLING AGENCY/ CONTACT FACILITY	FREQUENCIES
R-2513	TO FL 240	CONTINUOUS	OAKLAND CNTR	128.7 307.0
R-2531	TO BUT NOT INCL 4000	1000-2050 MON-FRI OCNL SAT & SUN WHEN ACTIVATED BY NOTAM 24 HRS IN ADVANCE	NORCAL TRACON	123.85 278.3
R-4803	TO BUT NOT INCL FL 180	0715-2330	OAKLAND CNTR	128.8 285.5 (N,E) 125.75 319.8 (S,W)
R-4804 A	TO BUT NOT INCL FL 180	0715-2330	OAKLAND CNTR	125.75 319.8
R-4810	TO 17,000	0715-2330	OAKLAND CNTR	125.75 319.8

Figure 8-12. *Example of the additional information provided on sectional charts for special use airspace.*

are established for security or other reasons associated with the national welfare. These areas are published in the Federal Register and are depicted on sectional charts. The area is charted as a "P" followed by a number (e.g., "P-56 A and B"). *[Figure 8-13]*

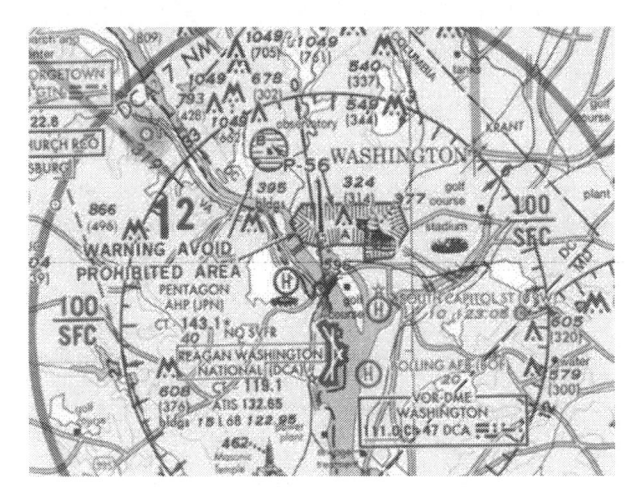

Figure 8-13. *Prohibited area in Washington, D.C., on a sectional chart.*

Restricted Areas

Restricted areas are areas where operations are hazardous to nonparticipating aircraft and contain airspace within which the flight of aircraft, while not wholly prohibited, is subject to restrictions. Activities within these areas must be confined because of their nature, or limitations may be imposed upon aircraft operations that are not a part of those activities, or both. Restricted areas denote the existence of unusual, often invisible, hazards to aircraft (e.g., artillery firing, aerial gunnery, or guided missiles). Penetration of restricted areas is illegal without authorization from the using or controlling agency may be extremely hazardous to the aircraft and its occupants. ATC facilities apply the following procedures:

1. If the restricted area is not active and has been released to the Federal Aviation Administration (FAA), the ATC facility will allow the aircraft to operate in the restricted airspace without issuing specific clearance for it to do so.

2. If the restricted area is active and has not been released to the FAA, the ATC facility will issue a clearance which will ensure the aircraft avoids the restricted airspace.

Restricted areas are charted with an "R" followed by a number (e.g., "R-4803 and R-4810") and are depicted on the sectional charts. *[Figure 8-14]*

Warning Areas

Warning areas consist of airspace which may contain hazards to nonparticipating aircraft in international airspace. The activities may be much the same as those for a restricted area. Warning areas are established beyond the three mile limit and are depicted on sectional charts.

Military Operations Areas (MOAs)

MOAs consist of airspace of defined vertical and lateral limits established for the purpose of separating certain military training activity from IFR traffic. There is no restriction against a pilot operating VFR in these areas; however, a pilot should be alert since training activities may include acrobatic and abrupt maneuvers. MOAs are depicted by name and with defined boundaries on sectional, VFR terminal area, and en route low altitude charts and are not numbered (e.g., "CHURCHILL HIGH MOA," "CHURCHILL LOW

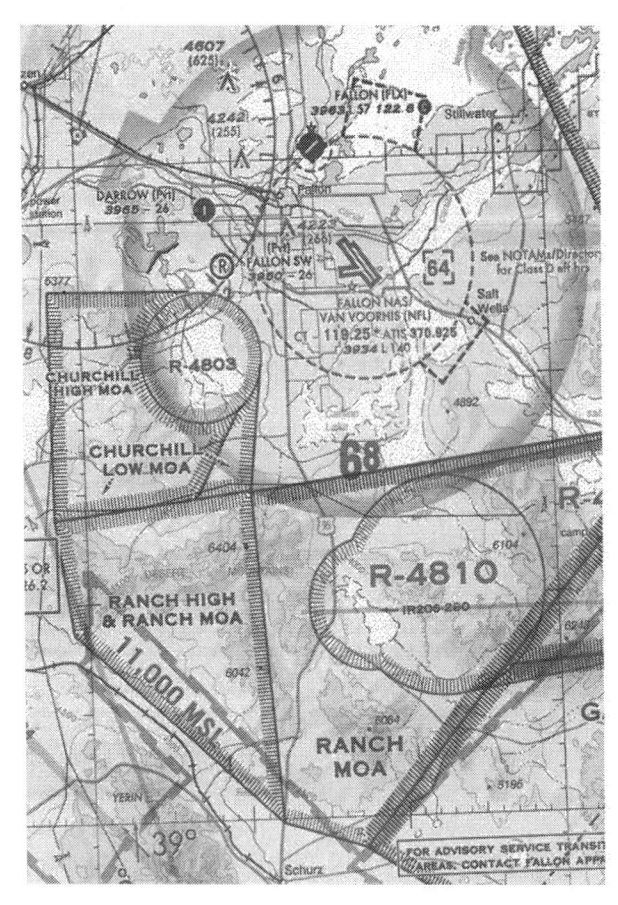

Figure 8-14. *Special use airspace: restricted and MOA examples.*

MOA," "RANCH HIGH & RANCH MOA" and "RANCH MOA"). *[Figure 8-14]* MOA is further defined on sectional charts with times of operation, altitudes affected, and the controlling agency frequency for the MOA to contact for current activity. *[Figure 8-15]*

Alert Areas

Alert areas are depicted on sectional charts with an "A" followed by a number (e.g., "A-211" as in *Figure 8-16*) to inform nonparticipating pilots of areas that may contain a high volume of pilot training or an unusual type of aerial activity. Pilots should be particularly alert when flying in these areas. All activity within an alert area shall be conducted in accordance with regulations, without waiver. Pilots of participating aircraft, as well as pilots transiting the area, shall be equally responsible for collision avoidance.

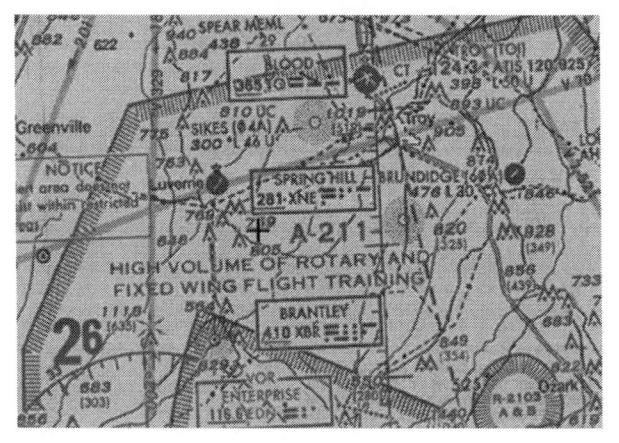

Figure 8-16. *Alert area (A-211).*

Controlled Firing Areas

Controlled firing areas contain military activities, which, if not conducted in a controlled environment, could be hazardous to nonparticipating aircraft. The difference between controlled firing areas and other special use airspace is that activities must be suspended when a spotter aircraft,

MOA NAME	ALTITUDE*	TIME OF USE†	CONTROLLING AGENCY/ CONTACT FACILITY	FREQUENCIES
AUSTIN 1	200 AGL	0800-2100 MON-FRI	OAKLAND CNTR	128.8 285.5
			SALT LAKE CITY CNTR	132.25 338.35
BISHOP	200 AGL	0600-2200 MON-FRI	LOS ANGELES CNTR	
CARSON	500 AGL	0715-2330	OAKLAND CNTR	128.8 285.5
CHINA	3000 AGL	0800-SS	OAKLAND CNTR	132.2 350.3
CHURCHILL HIGH	9000	0715-2245 MON-FRI 0800-1800 SAT	OAKLAND CNTR	
CHURCHILL LOW	500 AGL TO 9000	0715-2245 MON-FRI 0800-1800 SAT	OAKLAND CNTR	
FOOTHILL 1	2000 AGL	INTERMITTENT BY NOTAM	OAKLAND CNTR	123.8 353.8
FOOTHILL 2	2000 AGL	INTERMITTENT BY NOTAM	OAKLAND CNTR	123.8 353.8 (N,W)
GABBS CENTRAL	100 AGL	0715-2330	OAKLAND CNTR	125.75 319.8 (N,S,W)
GABBS NORTH	100 AGL	0715-2330	OAKLAND CNTR	128.8 285.5 (N,W) 125.75 (S)
GABBS SOUTH	100 AGL	0715-2330	OAKLAND CNTR	125.75 319.8 (N,S,W)
HUNTER HIGH	11,000	INTERMITTENT BY NOTAM	OAKLAND CNTR	126.9 343.8
HUNTER LOW A	200 AGL TO BUT NOT INCL 11,000	INTERMITTENT BY NOTAM	OAKLAND CNTR	128.7 307.0
HUNTER LOW D	1500 AGL TO 6000	INTERMITTENT BY NOTAM	OAKLAND CNTR	128.7 307.0
ISABELLA	200 AGL	0600-2200 MON-FRI	JOSHUA APP	133.65

Figure 8-15. *MOA is further defined on sectional charts with times of operation, altitudes affected, and the controlling agency to contact for current activity.*

radar, or ground lookout position indicates an aircraft might be approaching the area.

Parachute Jump Areas

Parachute jump areas are published in the Airport/ Facility Directory (A/FD). Sites that are used frequently are depicted on sectional charts. Each pilot should listen to the appropriate airport radio frequency for parachute operations and be alert for aircraft which might be conducting parachute operations.

Other Airspace Areas

Other airspace areas is a general term referring to the majority of the remaining airspace. It includes:

- Airport advisory areas
- Military training routes (MTRs)
- Temporary flight restrictions (TFRs)
- Terminal Radar Service Areas
- National security areas

Local Airport Advisory

A local airport advisory is an area within 10 statute miles (SM) of an airport where a control tower is not operating, but where a flight service station (FSS) is located. At these locations, the FSS provides advisory service to arriving and departing aircraft. See AIM section 3-5-1 for more information on using the local airport flight station services.

Military Training Routes (MTRs)

National security depends largely on the deterrent effect of our airborne military forces. To be proficient, the military services must train in a wide range of airborne tactics. One phase of this training involves "low level" combat tactics. The required maneuvers and high speeds are such that they may occasionally make the see-and-avoid aspect of VFR flight more difficult without increased vigilance in areas containing such operations. In an effort to ensure the greatest practical level of safety for all flight operations, the Military Training Route (MTR) program was conceived.

These routes are usually established below 10,000 feet MSL for operations at speeds in excess of 250 knots. Some route segments may be defined at higher altitudes for purposes of route continuity. Routes are identified as IFR (IR), and VFR (VR), followed by a number. MTRs with no segment above 1,500 feet AGL are identified by four numeric characters (e.g., IR1206, VR1207). MTRs that include one or more segments above 1,500 feet AGL are identified by three numeric characters (e.g., IR206, VR207). IFR Low Altitude En Route Charts depict all IR routes and all VR routes that accommodate operations above 1,500 feet AGL. IR routes are conducted in accordance with IFR regardless of weather conditions.

MTRs are usually indicated with a gray line on the sectional chart. A WSC aircraft pilot flying in the area of VRs or IRs should question the briefer during the weather brief to find out if any of the routes are in use, and a possible time frame for opening and closing. While it is true that the WSC aircraft pilot has the right of way, the WSC aircraft will generally come out worse in a midair conflict with a fast-moving military aircraft. MTRs, such as the example depicted in *Figure 8-17*, are also further defined on sectional charts.

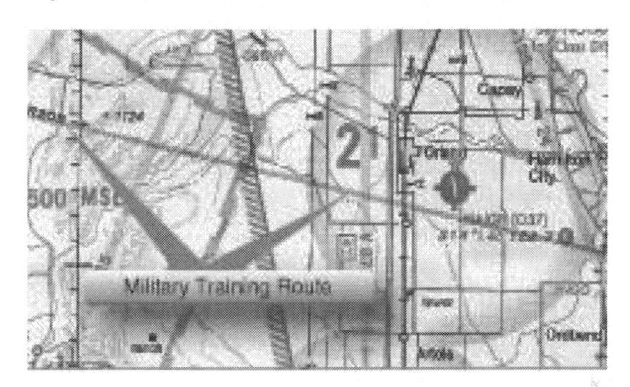

Figure 8-17. *MTR chart symbols.*

Temporary Flight Restrictions (TFRs)

TFRs are put into effect when traffic in the airspace would endanger or hamper air or ground activities in the designated area. For example, a forest fire, chemical accident, flood, or disaster-relief effort could warrant a TFR, which would be issued as a Notice to Airmen (NOTAM). The NOTAM begins with the phrase "FLIGHT RESTRICTIONS" followed by the location, effective time period, area defined in statute miles, and altitudes affected, which aircraft flying in the area must avoid. The NOTAM also contains the FAA coordination facility and telephone number, the reason for the restriction, and any other information deemed appropriate. The pilot should check NOTAMs as part of flight planning.

The reasons for establishing a temporary restriction are to:

- Protect persons and property in the air or on the surface from an existing or imminent hazard;
- Provide a safe environment for the operation of disaster relief aircraft;
- Prevent unsafe congestion of sightseeing aircraft above an incident or event, which may generate a high degree of public interest;
- Protect declared national disasters for humanitarian reasons;

- Protect the President, Vice President, or other public figures; and
- Provide a safe environment for space agency operations.

It is a pilot's responsibility to be aware of TFRs in his or her proposed area of flight. One way to check is to visit the FAA website, www.tfr.faa.gov, and verify that there is not a TFR in the area. Another resource is to ask the flight briefer at 800-WX-BRIEF during the preflight briefing.

Terminal Radar Service Areas (TRSA)

Terminal Radar Service Areas (TRSA) are areas where participating pilots can receive additional radar services. The purpose of the service is to provide separation between all IFR operations and participating VFR aircraft.

The primary airport(s) within the TRSA become(s) Class D airspace. The remaining portion of the TRSA overlies other controlled airspace, which is normally Class E airspace beginning at 700 or 1,200 feet and established to transition to/from the en route terminal environment. TRSAs are depicted on VFR sectional charts and terminal area charts with a solid black line and altitudes for each segment. The Class D portion is charted with a blue segmented line. Participation in TRSA services is voluntary; however, pilots operating under VFR are encouraged to contact the radar approach control and take advantage of TRSA service. Operations inside the TFR area must be conducted under the provisions of a waiver. Should such an operation be contemplated, the WSC aircraft pilot should consult with the local Flight Service District Office (FSDO) well in advance of the event.

National Security Areas (NSAs)

NSAs consist of airspace with defined vertical and lateral dimensions established at locations where there is a requirement for increased security and safety of ground facilities. Flight in NSAs may be temporarily prohibited by regulation under the provisions of 14 CFR part 99, and prohibitions are disseminated via NOTAM.

Published VFR Routes

Published VFR routes are for transitioning around, under, or through some complex airspace. Terms such as VFR flyway, VFR corridor, Class B airspace, VFR transition route, and terminal area VFR route have been applied to such routes. These routes are generally found on VFR terminal area planning charts.

Flight Over Charted U.S. Wildlife Refuges, Parks, and Forest Service Areas

The landing of aircraft is prohibited on lands or waters administered by the National Park Service, U.S. Fish and Wildlife Service, or U.S. Forest Service without authorization from the respective agency. Exceptions include:

1. When forced to land due to an emergency beyond the control of the operator;
2. At officially designated landing sites; or
3. An approved official business of the Federal Government.

Pilots are requested to maintain a minimum altitude of 2,000 feet above the surface of the following: national parks, monuments, seashores, lakeshores, recreation areas, and scenic riverways administered by the National Park Service, National Wildlife Refuges, Big Game Refuges, Game Ranges, and Wildlife Ranges administered by the U.S. Fish and Wildlife Service and wilderness and primitive areas administered by the U.S. Forest Service.

WSC Operations

WSC preflight planning should include a review of the airspace that is flown. A local flight may be close to the field and include only Class G and Class E airspace. Minimum visibility and cloud clearance may be the only requirements to be met. However, a radio to communicate to the airport traffic and an altimeter to fly at the proper airport pattern altitude is recommended.

If flying to control tower airports or through Class B, C, or D airspace, determine if the WSC meets all of the equipment requirements of that airspace. *[Figure 8-5]* Also review qualifications to determine if the minimum pilot requirements of the airspace are met. If the minimum aircraft and/or pilot requirements of the airspace are not met, then the preflight planning should include a course around the airspace. Extra time and fuel is required for the circumnavigation and should be taken into consideration prior to departure.

WSC and Air Traffic Control

In nontowered airspace, airspace separation from other aircraft is the responsibility of the pilot. Separation from higher speed traffic may require flightpaths different than faster traffic. For flight and communicating with a control tower, the WSC pilot may be asked to expedite or deviate from a traditional course. The WSC pilot must work with ATC in advising of the airspeed and surface wind limitations. Safe operation in controlled airspace requires that the controller understand the performance and limits of the WSC aircraft.

Navigating the Airspace

Knowledge of airspace dimensions, requirements to enter the airspace, and geographical location of the airspace is the responsibility of all pilots. The current sectional chart is the primary official tool to determine the airspace flying within or avoiding.

Pilotage is navigation by reference to landmarks to determine location and the location of airspace. Pilotage is the best form of navigation to ensure that you avoid airspace not authorized to enter. Locating your position on the sectional chart and locating/identifying the airspace you want to enter/avoid requires preflight planning on the ground and situational awareness in the air.

For all flights, pilots must be sure to have enough fuel to complete the flight. For longer cross-country flights, this requires the pilot to check winds aloft and calculate the groundspeed for the planned altitude and forecast wind. The resultant time to the destination and the fuel consumption determines the fuel required to make the flight. This preflight planning is especially important for slower WSC aircraft because increased headwind components provide significant time increases to get to fuel stops than faster aircraft. Although 14 CFR section 91.151 requires airplanes to have at least 30 minutes of reserve fuel for an intended fuel stop; this minimum is also recommended for WSC aircraft. The Pilot's Handbook of Aeronautical Knowledge chapter on navigation provides procedures in navigation, plotting a course, determining groundspeed for the predicted wind, headings and the required fuel for intended legs of the flight. For any cross-country flight, a flight log should be used and the planned groundspeed should be compared to the actual GPS groundspeed measured in flight. If the GPS groundspeed is lower than the planned groundspeed, the time en route and the fuel reserves must be evaluated to assure the WSC aircraft does not run out of fuel during the flight.

GPS is a very popular form of navigation used by WSC pilots. The GPS receiver is small, simple to use, and inexpensive compared to other forms of electronic (radio) navigation. Simple modes of operation provide actual groundspeed and time to a waypoint. More sophisticated GPSs have aviation databases and provide the pilot a considerable amount of information about airports and airspace. When using GPS to determine airspace or airport position, boundaries, and/or information, the aviation database in the GPS may not exactly match the information as depicted on the sectional chart. If there is a difference between the sectional chart and GPS information, the sectional chart should be considered correct.

A WSC pilot using GPS should ensure that the batteries are fresh and the aviation database is current. Never rely on the GPS as a primary navigation system. Pilotage using the sectional chart is the primary navigation system when flying beyond visual range of a familiar airport. The GPS is used only as a backup aid for navigation.

With proper preflight planning and constant evaluation of the planned verses actual flight performance, cross-country flight is practical in the NAS for WSC pilots.

Chapter Summary

At first glance, the NAS appears to be a complex arena in which to operate such a simple aircraft. This chapter simplifies the airspace for the reader, and makes it readily apparent that it is possible to operate a WSC aircraft safely, without causing conflict.

Simple courtesy and common sense go a long way in airspace operations. A complete and thorough understanding of the airspace, combined with good decision-making, will allow the pilot to do what he or she wishes, with recognition of the needs of other users of the sky.

Chapter 9
Ground Reference Maneuvers

Introduction

Ground reference maneuvers and their related factors are used in developing a high degree of pilot skill. Although most of these maneuvers are not performed in normal everyday flying, the elements and principles involved are applicable to performance of the customary pilot operations. The maneuvers aid the pilot in analyzing the effect of wind and other forces acting on the aircraft and in developing a fine control touch, coordination, and the division of attention necessary for accurate and safe maneuvering of the aircraft.

The early part of a pilot's training is conducted at relatively high altitudes for the purpose of developing technique, knowledge of maneuvers, coordination, feel, and the handling of the aircraft in general. This training requires that most of the pilot's attention be given to the actual handling of the aircraft, the results of control pressures on the action, and attitude of the aircraft.

As soon as the pilot shows proficiency in the fundamental maneuvers, it is necessary that he or she be introduced to ground reference maneuvers requiring attention beyond practical application and current knowledge base.

It should be stressed that during ground reference maneuvers, it is equally important that previously learned basic flying technique be maintained. The flight instructor should not allow any relaxation of the student's previous standard of technique simply because a new factor is added. This requirement should be maintained throughout the student's progress from maneuver to maneuver. Each new maneuver should embody some advanced knowledge and include principles of the preceding maneuver in order to maintain continuity. Each new skill introduced should build on one already learned so that orderly, consistent progress can be made.

Maneuvering by Reference to Ground Objects

Ground track or ground reference maneuvers are performed at relatively low altitudes while applying wind drift correction as needed to follow a predetermined track or path over the ground. These maneuvers are designed to develop the ability to control the aircraft and to recognize and correct for the effect of wind, while dividing attention among other matters. This requires planning ahead of the aircraft, maintaining orientation in relation to ground objects, flying appropriate headings to follow a desired ground track, and being cognizant of other air traffic in the immediate vicinity.

Ground reference maneuvers should be flown at an altitude of approximately 500 to 1,000 feet above ground level (AGL). The actual altitude will depend on the ability to reach a safe landing area if there is an engine failure during the maneuver and the type of air in which the maneuvers are being flown. If there is significant vertical movement of the air, higher altitudes should be used to avoid the possibility of flying below 400 feet AGL, the minimum altitude recommended in the Practical Test Standards (PTS).

Overall, the following factors should be considered in determining the appropriate altitudes for ground reference maneuvers:

- The speed with relation to the ground should not be so apparent that events happen too rapidly.

- The radius of the turn and the path of the aircraft over the ground should be easily noted and changes planned and effected as circumstances require.

- Drift should be easily discernable but should not overtax the student in making corrections.

- Objects on the ground should appear in their proportion and size.

- The altitude should be low enough to render any gain or loss apparent to the student, but not recommended lower than 400 feet above the highest obstruction and in no case lower than 500 feet above any person, vessel, vehicle, or structure.

During these maneuvers, both the instructor and the student should be alert for available forced-landing fields. The area chosen should be away from communities, livestock, or groups of people to prevent becoming an annoyance or hazard. Due to the altitudes at which these maneuvers are performed, there is little time available to search for a suitable field for landing in the event the need arises.

Drift and Ground Track Control

Whenever an object is free from the ground, it is affected by the medium surrounding it. This means that a free object moves in whatever direction and speed that the medium moves.

For example, if a powerboat were crossing a still river, the boat could head directly to a point on the opposite shore and travel on a straight course to that point without drifting. However, if the river were flowing swiftly, the water current would require consideration. That is, as the boat progresses forward on its own power, it must also move upstream at the same rate the river is moving it downstream. This is accomplished by angling the boat upstream sufficiently to counteract the downstream flow. If this is done, the boat follows the desired track across the river from the departure point directly to the intended destination point. If the boat is not headed sufficiently upstream, it would drift with the current and run aground at some point downstream on the opposite bank. *[Figure 9-1]*

As soon as an aircraft becomes airborne, it is free of ground friction. Its path is then affected by the air mass in which it is flying; therefore, the aircraft (like the boat) does not always track along the ground in the exact direction that it is headed. When flying with the longitudinal axis of the aircraft aligned with a road, it may be noted that the aircraft gets closer to or farther from the road without any turn having been initiated by the pilot. This would indicate that the air mass is moving sideward in relation to the aircraft. Since the aircraft is flying

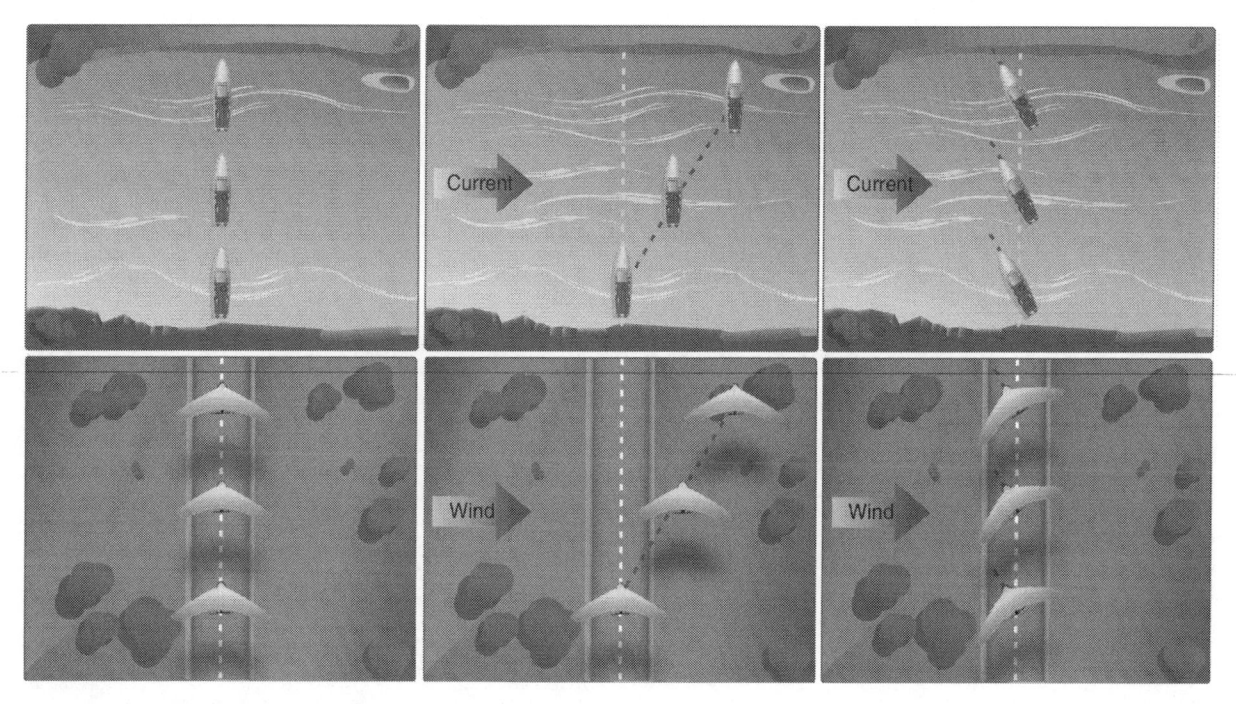

Figure 9-1. *Wind drift and wind correction angle (crab angle).*

within this moving body of air (wind), it moves or drifts with the air in the same direction and speed, just like the boat moved with the river current.

When flying straight and level and following a selected ground track, the preferred method of correcting for wind drift is to head the aircraft (wind correction angle) sufficiently into the wind to cause the aircraft to move forward into the wind at the same rate the wind is moving it sideways. Depending on the wind velocity, this may require a large wind correction angle or one of only a few degrees. This wind correction angle is also commonly known as the crab angle. When the drift has been neutralized, the aircraft follows the desired ground track.

To understand the need for drift correction during flight, consider a flight with a wind velocity of 20 knots from the left and 90° to the direction the aircraft is headed. After 1 hour, the body of air in which the aircraft is flying has moved 20 nautical miles (NM) to the right. Since the aircraft is moving with this body of air, it too has drifted 20 NM to the right. In relation to the air, the aircraft moved forward; but in relation to the ground, it moved forward as well as 20 NM to the right.

There are times when the pilot needs to correct for drift while in a turn. *[Figure 9-2]* Throughout the turn, the wind is acting on the aircraft from constantly changing angles. The relative wind angle and speed govern the time it takes for the aircraft to progress through any part of a turn. This is due to the constantly changing groundspeed. When the aircraft is headed into the wind, the groundspeed is decreased; when headed downwind, the groundspeed is increased. Through the crosswind portion of a turn, the aircraft must be turned sufficiently into the wind to counteract drift.

To follow a desired circular ground track, the wind correction angle must be varied in a timely manner because of the varying groundspeed as the turn progresses. The faster the groundspeed, the faster the wind correction angle must be established; the slower the groundspeed, the slower the wind correction angle may be established. It can be seen then that the steepest bank and fastest rate of turn should be made on the downwind portion of the turn and the shallowest bank and slowest rate of turn on the upwind portion.

The principles and techniques of varying the angle of bank to change the rate of turn and wind correction angle for controlling wind drift during a turn are the same for all ground track maneuvers involving changes in direction of flight.

When there is no wind, it should be simple to fly along a ground track with an arc of exactly 180° and a constant radius because the flightpath and ground track would be identical. This can be demonstrated by approaching a road at a 90° angle and, when directly over the road, rolling into a medium-banked turn. Then, maintaining the same angle of bank throughout the 180° of turn. *[Figure 9-2]*

To complete the turn, the rollout should be started at a point where the wings become level as the aircraft again reaches the road at a 90° angle and is directly over the road just as the

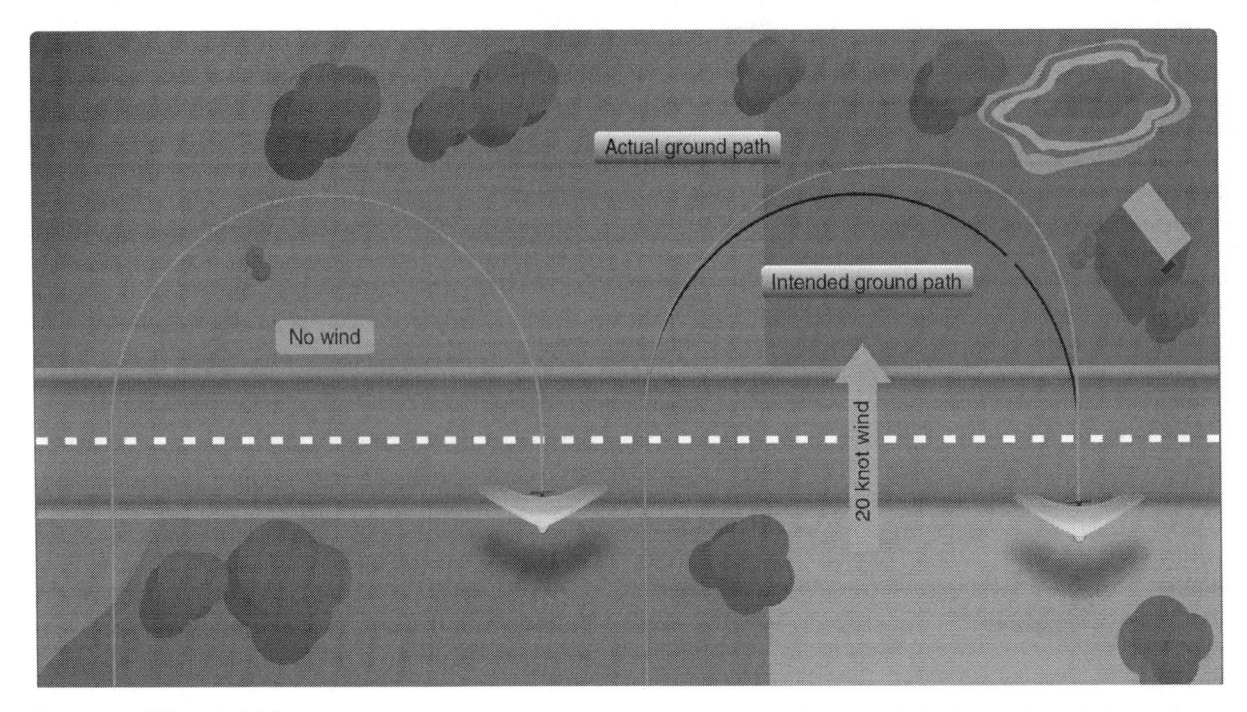

Figure 9-2. *Effect of wind during a turn.*

turn is completed. This would be possible only if there were absolutely no wind and if the angle of bank and the rate of turn remained constant throughout the entire maneuver.

If the turn were made with a constant angle of bank and a wind blowing directly across the road, it would result in a constant radius turn through the air. However, the wind effects would cause the ground track to be distorted from a constant radius turn or semicircular path. The greater the wind velocity, the greater the difference between the desired ground track and the flightpath. To counteract this drift, the flightpath can be controlled by the pilot in such a manner as to neutralize the effect of the wind and cause the ground track to be a constant radius semicircle.

The effects of wind during turns can be demonstrated after selecting a road, railroad, or other ground reference that forms a straight line parallel to the wind. Fly into the wind directly over and along the line and then make a turn with a constant medium angle of bank for 360° of turn. *[Figure 9-3]* The aircraft returns to a point directly over the line but slightly downwind from the starting point, the amount depending on the wind velocity and the time required to complete the turn. The path over the ground is an elongated circle, although in reference to the air it is a perfect circle. Straight flight during the upwind segment after completion of the turn is necessary to bring the aircraft back to the starting position.

A similar 360° turn may be started at a specific point over the reference line, with the aircraft headed directly downwind. In this demonstration, the effect of wind during the constant banked turn drifts the aircraft to a point where the line is re-intercepted, but the 360° turn is completed at a point downwind from the starting point.

Another reference line which lies directly crosswind may be selected and the same procedure repeated. If wind drift is not corrected, the aircraft is headed in the original direction at the completion of the 360° turn, but has drifted away from the line a distance dependent on the amount of wind.

From these demonstrations, it can be seen where and why it is necessary to increase or decrease the angle of bank and the rate of turn to achieve a desired track over the ground. The principles and techniques involved can be practiced and evaluated by the performance of the ground track maneuvers discussed in this chapter.

Rectangular Course

Normally, the first ground reference maneuver introduced to the pilot is the rectangular course. Reference *Figure 9-4* throughout this rectangular course section. The rectangular course is a training maneuver in which the ground track of the aircraft is equidistant from all sides of a selected rectangular area on the ground. The maneuver simulates the conditions encountered in an airport traffic pattern. While performing the maneuver, the altitude and airspeed should be held constant.

The maneuver assists the student pilot in perfecting:

- Practical application of the turn.

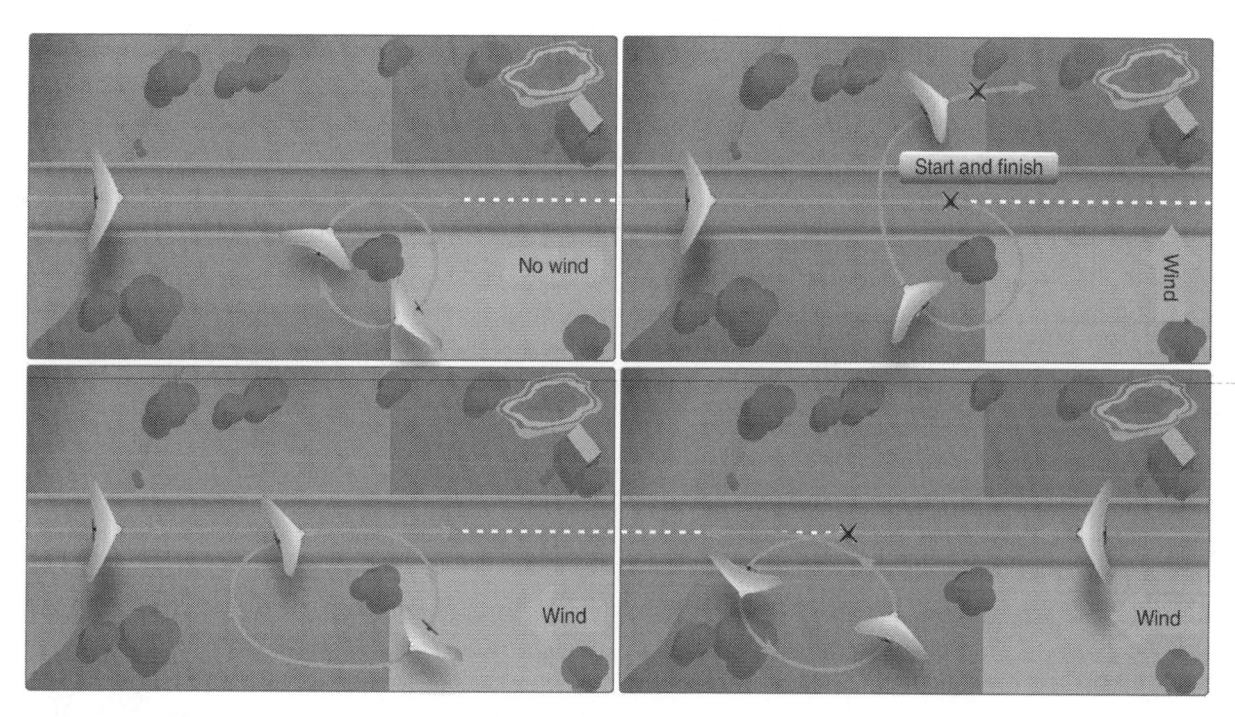

Figure 9-3. *Effect of wind during turns.*

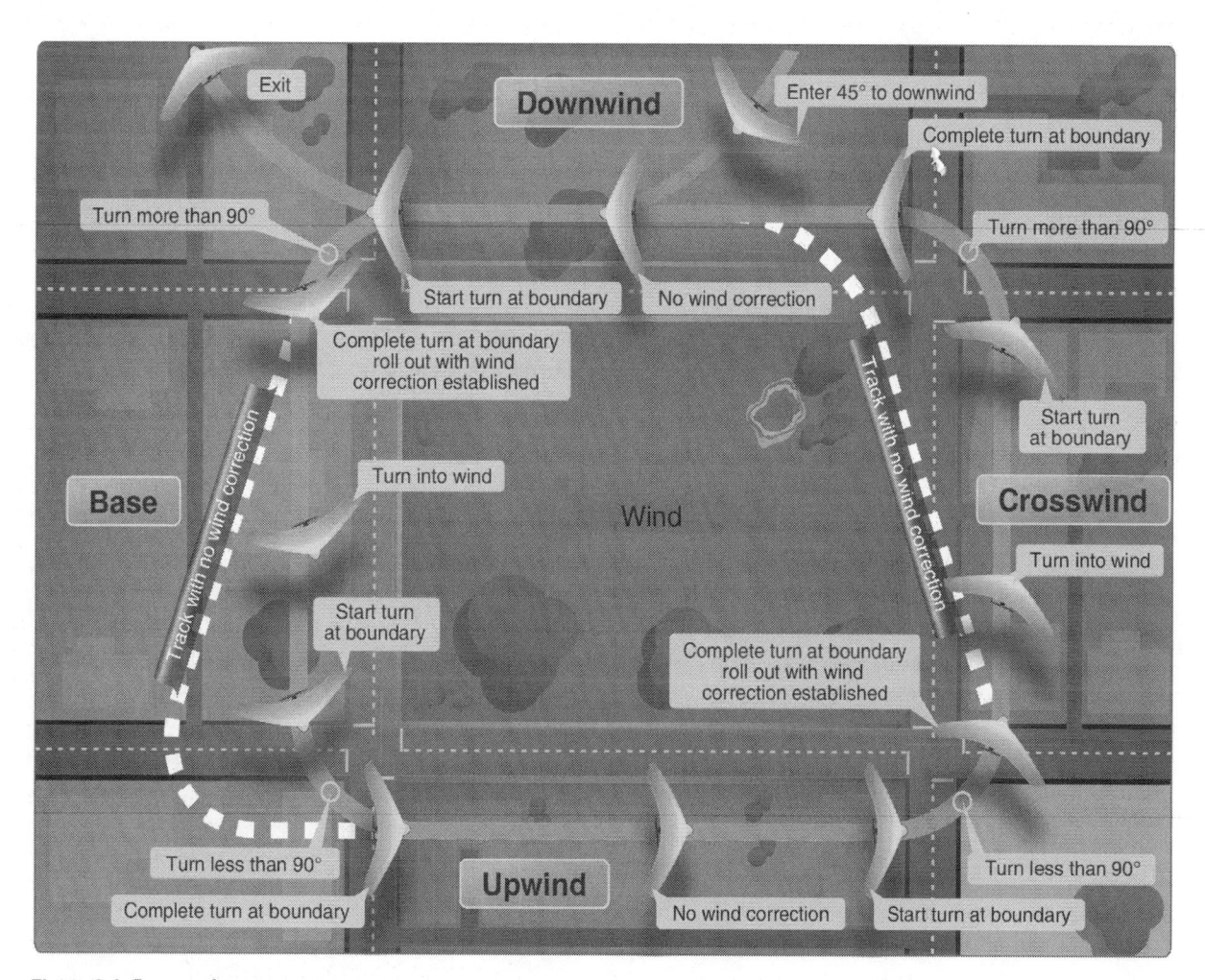

Figure 9-4. *Rectangular course.*

9-5

- Division of attention between the flightpath, ground objects, and the handling of the aircraft.
- Timing of the start of a turn so that the turn is fully established at a definite point over the ground.
- Timing of the recovery from a turn so that a definite ground track is maintained.
- Establishing a ground track and determining the appropriate "crab" angle.

As for other ground track maneuvers, one of the objectives is to develop division of attention between the flightpath and ground references while controlling the aircraft and watching for other aircraft in the vicinity. Another objective is to develop recognition of drift toward or away from a line parallel to the intended ground track. This is helpful in recognizing drift toward or away from an airport runway during the various legs of the airport traffic pattern.

For this maneuver, a square or rectangular field (bound on four sides by section lines or roads that are approximately one-half mile in length) should be selected away from other air traffic. The aircraft should be flown parallel to and at a uniform distance just to the outside of the field boundaries, not quite above the boundaries so that the flightpath may be easily observed from either seat by looking out the side of the aircraft. The closer the track of the aircraft is to the field boundaries, the steeper the bank necessary at the turning points. The distance of the ground track from the edges of the field should be the same regardless of whether the course is flown to the left or right. Turns should be started when the aircraft is abeam the corner of the field boundaries, and the bank normally should not exceed 45°. These should be the determining factors in establishing the distance from the boundaries for performing the maneuver.

Although the rectangular course may be entered from any direction, this discussion assumes entry on a downwind. On the downwind leg, the wind is a tailwind and results in increased groundspeed. Consequently, the turn onto the next leg is entered with a fairly fast rate of roll-in with relatively steep bank. As the turn progresses, the bank angle is reduced gradually because the tailwind component is diminishing, resulting in a decreasing groundspeed.

During and after the turn onto this leg (the equivalent of the base leg in a traffic pattern), the wind tends to drift the aircraft away from the field boundary. To compensate for the drift, the amount of turn is more than 90°.

The rollout from this turn must be such that as the wings become level, the aircraft is turned slightly toward the field and into the wind to correct for drift. The aircraft should again be the same distance from the field boundary and at the same altitude as on other legs. The base leg should be continued until the upwind leg boundary is being approached. Once more, the pilot should anticipate drift and turning radius. Since drift correction was held on the base leg, it is necessary to turn less than 90° to align the aircraft parallel to the upwind leg boundary. This turn should be started with a medium bank angle with a gradual reduction to a shallow bank as the turn progresses. The rollout should be timed to assure paralleling the boundary of the field as the wings become level. *[Figure 9-5]*

While the aircraft is on the upwind leg, the next field boundary should be observed as it is being approached to plan the turn onto the crosswind leg. Since the wind is a headwind on this leg, it reduces the aircraft's groundspeed and tries to drift the aircraft toward the field during the turn onto the crosswind leg. For this reason, the roll-in to the turn must be slow and the bank relatively shallow to counteract this effect. As the turn progresses, the headwind component decreases, allowing the groundspeed to increase. Consequently, the bank angle and rate of turn are increased gradually to assure that upon completion of the turn, the crosswind ground track continues the same distance from the edge of the field. Completion of the turn with the wings level should be accomplished at a point aligned with the upwind corner of the field.

As the wings are rolled level, the proper drift correction is established with the aircraft turned into the wind with a change in heading of less than 90°. If the turn has been made properly, the field boundary will again be the same distance as it was in the previous legs. While on the crosswind leg, the wind correction angle should be adjusted as necessary to maintain a uniform distance from the field boundary.

As the next field boundary is being approached, the pilot should plan the turn onto the downwind leg. Since a wind correction angle is being held into the wind and away from the field while on the crosswind leg, this next turn requires a turn of more than 90°. Since the crosswind becomes a tailwind, causing the groundspeed to increase during this turn, the bank initially should be medium and progressively increased as the turn proceeds. To complete the turn, the rollout must be timed so that the wings become level at a point aligned with the crosswind corner of the field just as the longitudinal axis of the aircraft again becomes parallel to the field boundary. The distance from the field boundary should be the same as from the other sides of the field.

Usually, drift should not be encountered on the upwind or the downwind leg, but it may be difficult to find a situation where the wind is blowing exactly parallel to the field boundaries. This would make it necessary to use a slight wind correction

Figure 9-5. *Pilot's view coming out of a left turn to straighten out for the rectangular leg on the lower left. The next left turn of the rectangular course is shown by the red line for reference.*

angle on all the legs. It is important to anticipate the turns to correct for groundspeed, drift, and turning radius. When the wind is behind the aircraft, the turn must be faster and steeper; when it is ahead of the aircraft, the turn must be slower and shallower. These same techniques apply while flying in airport traffic patterns.

Common errors in the performance of rectangular courses are:

- Failure to adequately clear the area.
- Failure to establish proper altitude prior to entry (typically entering the maneuver while descending).
- Failure to establish appropriate wind correction angle, resulting in drift.
- Gaining or losing altitude.
- Poor coordination (typically gaining or losing airspeed during the turns).
- Abrupt control usage.
- Inability to divide attention adequately between aircraft control and maintaining ground track.
- Improper timing in beginning and recovering from turns.
- Inadequate visual lookout for other aircraft.

S-Turns Across a Road

An S-turn across a road is a practice maneuver in which the aircraft's ground track describes semicircles of equal radii on each side of a selected straight line on the ground. Reference *Figure 9-6* throughout this S-turn across the road section. The straight line may be a road, fence, railroad, or section line that lies perpendicular to the wind and should be of sufficient length for making a series of turns. A constant altitude should be maintained throughout the maneuver.

S-turns across a road present one of the most elementary problems in the practical application of the turn and in the correction for wind drift in turns. While the application of this maneuver is considerably less advanced in some respects than the rectangular course, it is taught after the student has been introduced to that maneuver in order that the student may have a knowledge of the correction for wind drift in straight flight along a reference line before the student attempts to correct for drift by playing a turn.

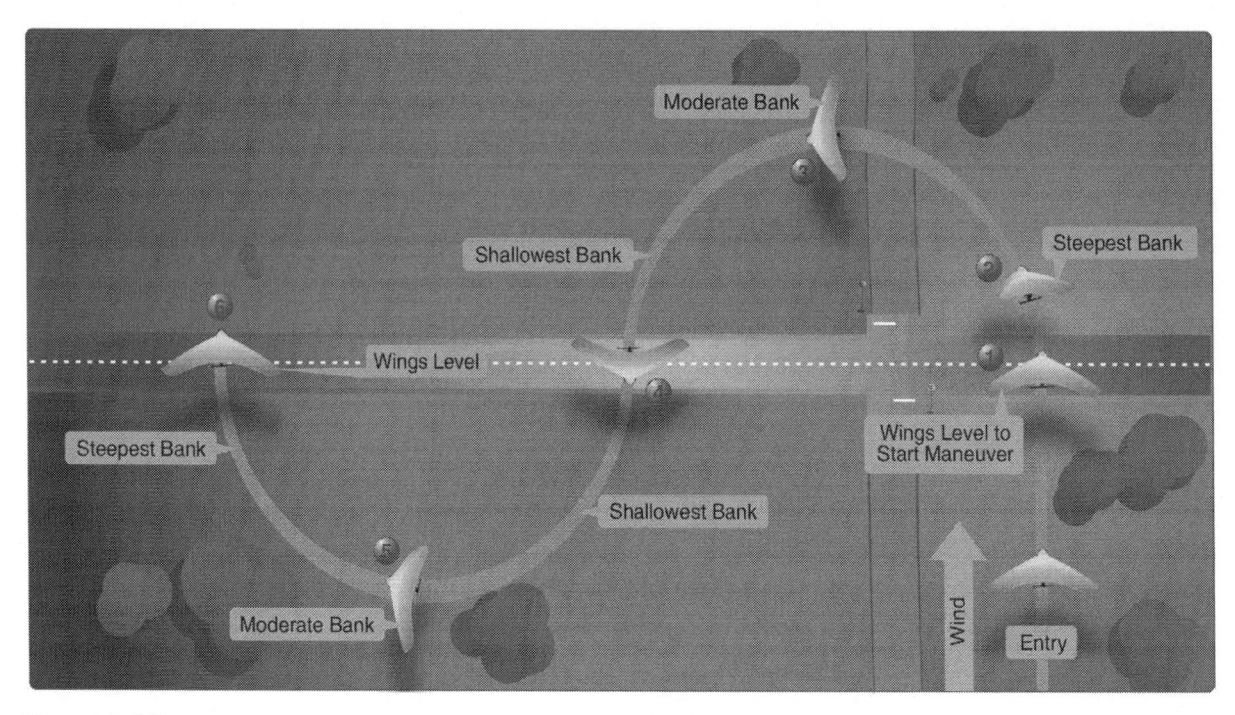

Figure 9-6. *S-Turn.*

The objectives of S-turns across a road are to develop the ability to compensate for drift during turns, orient the flightpath with ground references, follow an assigned ground track, arrive at specified points on assigned headings, and divide the pilot's attention. The maneuver consists of crossing the road at a 90° angle and immediately beginning a series of 180° turns of uniform radius in opposite directions, re-crossing the road at a 90° angle just as each 180° turn is completed. The maneuver can be started with either a left hand turn or a right hand turn to go in either direction. *Figure 9-6* starts the turn in a left hand turn as an example.

Accomplishing a constant radius ground track requires a changing roll rate and angle of bank to establish the wind correction angle. Both increase or decrease as the groundspeed increases or decreases.

The bank must be steepest when beginning the turn on the downwind side of the road and must be shallowed gradually as the turn progresses from a downwind heading to an upwind heading. On the upwind side, the turn should be started with a relatively shallow bank and then gradually steepened as the aircraft turns from an upwind heading to a downwind heading. In this maneuver, the aircraft should be rolled from one bank directly into the opposite just as the 90° reference line on the ground is crossed.

Before starting the maneuver, a straight ground reference line or road that lies 90° to the direction of the wind should be selected, then the area checked to ensure that no obstructions or other aircraft are in the immediate vicinity.

The road should be approached from the upwind side at the selected altitude on a downwind heading. When directly over the road, the first turn should be started immediately. *[Figure 9-6, position 1* and *Figure 9-7]* With the aircraft headed downwind, the groundspeed is greatest and the rate of departure from the road is rapid; the roll into the steep bank must be fairly rapid to attain the proper wind correction angle. *[Figure 9-6, position 2]* This prevents the aircraft from flying too far from the road and from establishing a ground track of excessive radius.

Figure 9-7. *Pilot's view of crossing a reference line (road) at 90° wings level starting the S-turn maneuver.*

During the latter portion of the first 90° turn, when the aircraft's heading is changing from a downwind heading to a crosswind heading, the groundspeed becomes less and the rate of departure from the road decreases.

[Figure 9-6, position 2 to 3, and *Figure 9-8]* The wind correction angle is at the maximum when the aircraft is headed directly crosswind. *[Figure 9-6, position 3]*

Figure 9-8. *Pilot's view in starting semicircle turning left from downwind to crosswind.*

After turning 90°, the aircraft's heading becomes more and more an upwind heading, the groundspeed decreases, and the rate of closure with the road becomes slower. If a constant steep bank were maintained, the aircraft would turn too quickly for the slower rate of closure and would prematurely be headed perpendicular to the road. Because of the decreasing groundspeed and rate of closure while approaching the upwind heading, it is necessary to gradually shallow the bank during the remaining 90° of the semicircle, so that the wind correction angle is removed completely *[Figure 9-9]* and the wings become level as the 180° turn is completed at the moment the road is reached. *[Figure 9-6, position 4]*

Figure 9-9. *Student completing semicircle, preparing to level out to cross perpendicular to the road.*

At the instant the road is being crossed at 90° to it, a turn in the opposite direction should be started. Since the aircraft is still flying into the headwind, the groundspeed is relatively low. Therefore, the turn must be started with a shallow bank to avoid an excessive rate of turn that would establish the maximum wind correction angle too soon. The degree of bank should be that which is necessary to attain the proper wind correction angle so the ground track describes an arc the same size as the one established on the downwind side.

Since the aircraft is turning from an upwind to a downwind heading, the groundspeed increases and after turning 90° the rate of closure with the road increases rapidly. *[Figure 9-6, position 5]* Consequently, the angle of bank and rate of turn must be progressively increased so that the aircraft has turned 180° at the time it reaches the road. Again, the rollout must be timed so the aircraft is in straight-and-level flight directly over and perpendicular to the road. *[Figure 9-6, position 6]*

Throughout the maneuver a constant altitude and airspeed should be maintained, and the bank should be changing constantly to effect a true semicircular ground track.

Common errors in the performance of S-turns across a road are:

- Failure to adequately clear the area.
- Creating too small of a radius/too high of a banked turn during the start of the maneuver.
- Creating banked turns too high to complete the maneuver.
- Poor coordination creating variations in airspeeds.
- Gaining or losing altitude.
- Inability to visualize the half circle ground track.
- Poor timing in beginning and recovering from turns.
- Faulty correction for drift.
- Inadequate visual lookout for other aircraft.
- Inability to judge closure rates to the road and adjust the bank angle so the semi-circle is completed at 90° to the reference road.

Turns Around a Point

Turns around a point, as a training maneuver, is a logical extension of the principles involved in the performance of S-turns across a road. The objectives are to:

- Further perfect turning technique.
- Perfect the ability to control the aircraft subconsciously while dividing attention between the flightpath and ground references.

- Teach the student that the radius of a turn is a distance that is affected by the degree of bank used when turning with relation to a definite object.
- Develop a keen perception of altitude.
- Perfect the ability to correct for wind drift while in turns.

In turns around a point, the aircraft is flown in two or more complete circles of uniform radii or distance from a prominent ground reference point using a maximum bank of approximately 45° while maintaining a constant altitude.

The factors and principles of drift correction that are involved in S-turns are also applicable in this maneuver. As in other ground track maneuvers, a constant radius around a point requires a constantly changing angle of bank and angles of wind correction if any wind exists. The closer the aircraft is to a direct downwind heading where the groundspeed is greatest, the steeper the bank and the faster the rate of turn required to establish the proper wind correction angle. The more nearly it is to a direct upwind heading where the groundspeed is least, the shallower the bank and the slower the rate of turn required to establish the proper wind correction angle. Throughout the maneuver, the bank and rate of turn must be varied gradually in proportion to the groundspeed.

The point selected for turns around a point should be prominent, easily distinguished by the pilot, and yet small enough to present precise reference. *[Figures 9-10* through *9-12]* Isolated trees, crossroads, or other similar small landmarks are usually suitable. Right and left hand turns about a point should be practiced to develop technique in both directions. The example used here is right hand turns.

To enter turns around a point, the aircraft should be flown on a downwind heading to one side of the selected point at a distance equal to the desired radius of turn. When any significant wind exists, it will be necessary to roll into the initial bank at a rapid rate so that the steepest bank is attained abeam of the point when the aircraft is headed directly downwind. By entering the maneuver while heading directly downwind, the steepest bank can be attained immediately. Thus, if a maximum bank of 45° is desired, the initial bank is 45° if the aircraft is at the correct distance from the point. Thereafter, the bank is shallowed gradually until the point is reached at which the aircraft is headed directly upwind. At this point, the bank should be gradually steepened until the steepest bank is again attained when heading downwind at the initial point of entry.

Just as S-turns require that the aircraft be turned into the wind in addition to varying the bank, so do turns around a point. During the downwind half of the circle, the aircraft's nose is progressively turned toward the inside of the circle; during the upwind half, the nose is progressively turned toward the outside. The downwind half of the turn around the point may be compared to the downwind side of the S-turn across a road; the upwind half of the turn around a point may be compared to the upwind side of the S-turn across a road.

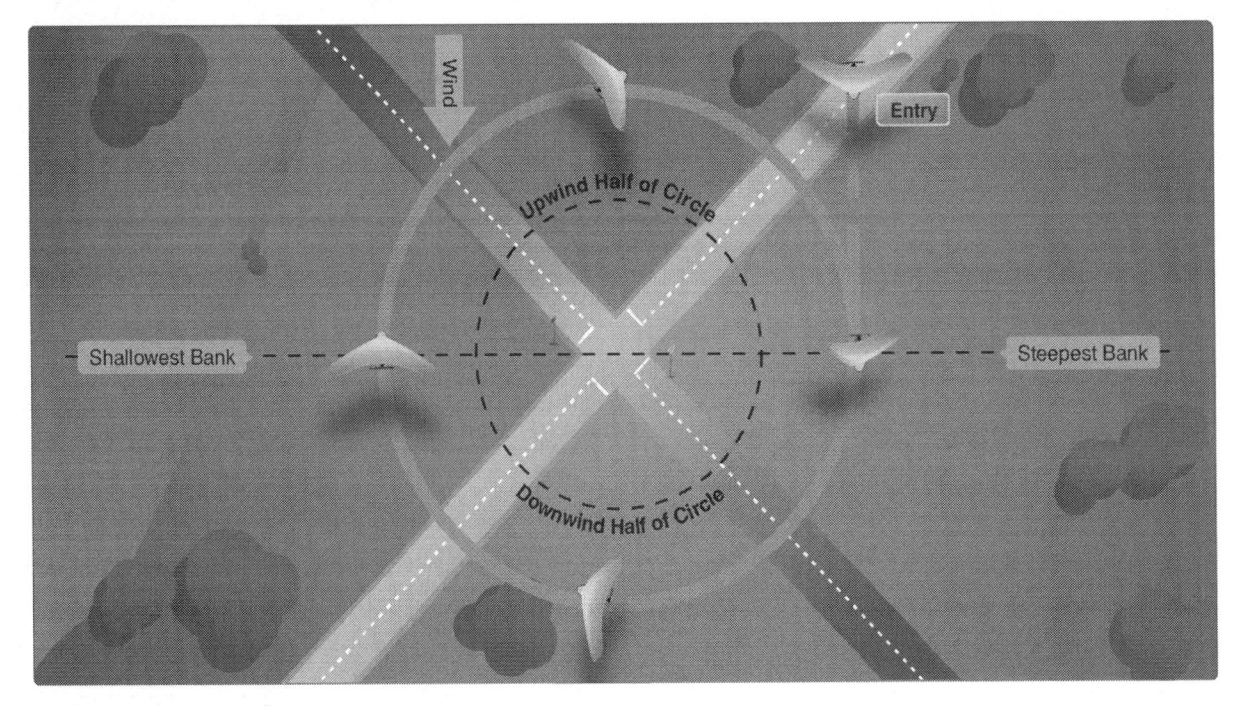

Figure 9-10. *Turns around a point.*

Figure 9-11. *Downwind portion of turn about a point, which is the gazebo jutting out into the lake. Notice the wing is low on the downwind portion where the angle of bank is greatest.*

Figure 9-12. *Upwind portion of the turn about a point. Notice the wing is higher because bank angle is not at as steep during the upwind portion headed into the wind to maintain a constant radius circle.*

As the pilot becomes experienced in performing turns around a point and has a good understanding of the effects of wind drift and varying the bank angle and wind correction angle as required, entry into the maneuver may be from any point. When entering the maneuver at a point other than downwind, however, the radius of the turn should be carefully selected. Be sure to take into account the wind velocity and groundspeed so that an excessive bank is not required later on to maintain the proper ground track. The flight instructor should place particular emphasis on the effect of an incorrect initial bank.

Common errors in the performance of turns around a point are:

- Failure to clear the area adequately.
- Failure to establish appropriate bank on entry.
- Failure to recognize wind drift.
- Inadequate bank angle and/or inadequate wind correction angle on the downwind portion of the circle, resulting in drift away from the reference point.
- Excessive bank and/or inadequate wind correction angle on the upwind side of the circle, resulting in drift towards the reference point.
- Gaining or losing altitude.
- Inability to maintain a constant airspeed.
- Inadequate visual lookout for other aircraft.
- Inability to direct attention outside the aircraft while maintaining precise aircraft control.

Chapter Summary

Ground reference maneuvers and related factors are used in developing a high degree of pilot skill in analyzing the effect of wind and other forces acting on the aircraft for accurate and safe maneuvering of the aircraft. The specific maneuvers are:

- Rectangular course,
- S-turns across a road, and
- Turns about a point.

These are training maneuvers that should be mastered to within the tolerances in the PTS.

Chapter 10
Airport Traffic Patterns

Introduction

Just as roads and streets are needed in order to facilitate automobile traffic, airports are needed to facilitate aircraft traffic. Every flight begins and ends at an airport. An airport, as defined by Title 14 of the Code of Federal Regulations (14 CFR) section 1.1, is an area of land or water that is used or intended to be used for the landing and takeoff of aircraft. For this reason, it is essential pilots learn the traffic rules, procedures, and patterns that may be in use at various airports.

When an automobile is driven on congested city streets, it can be brought to a stop to give way to conflicting traffic; however, an aircraft can only be slowed down. Consequently, specific traffic patterns and traffic control procedures have been established at designated airports. Traffic patterns provide specific routes for takeoffs, departures, arrivals, and landings. The exact nature of each airport traffic pattern is dependent on the runway in use, wind conditions, obstructions, and other factors.

Airport Operations

Airports vary in complexity from small grass or sod strips to major terminals having multiple paved runways and taxiways. Regardless of the type of airport, the pilot must know and abide by the rules and general operating procedures applicable to the airport being used. These rules and procedures are based not only on logic or common sense but also on courtesy, and their objective is to keep air traffic moving with maximum safety and efficiency. The use of any traffic pattern, service, or procedure does not alter the responsibility of pilots to see and avoid other aircraft.

Generally, there are two types of airport operations:

- Uncontrolled airports where there is no control tower
- Controlled airports where there is a control tower with an air traffic controller

Airport operations is a prerequisite for reading and understanding this chapter. The Pilot's Handbook of Aeronautical Knowledge (FAA-H-8083-25) chapter on airport operations is the starting point for this subject. Additionally, the portions of the Aeronautical Information Manual (AIM) covering aeronautical lighting and other airport visual aids, airspace, and air traffic control, should be studied prior to reading this chapter.

The following airport patterns are applicable to both towered and nontowered airport operations; however, in nontowered airports the pilot should use the information presented in this chapter along with the references provided in the summary to coordinate with the other air traffic. When flying at towered airports, the principles must be understood to understand the air traffic controller's instructions. The pilot is always responsible for "see and avoid" and must continually look for other aircraft in towered and nontowered operations.

Standard Airport Traffic Patterns

To assure that air traffic flows into and out of an airport in an orderly manner, an airport traffic pattern is established appropriate to the local conditions, including the direction and placement of the pattern, altitude to be flown, and procedures for entering and leaving the pattern. Unless the airport displays approved visual markings indicating that turns should be made to the right, pilots should make all turns in the pattern to the left.

When operating at an airport with an operating control tower, the pilot receives by radio a clearance to approach or depart, as well as pertinent information about the traffic pattern. If there is not a control tower, it is the pilot's responsibility to determine the direction of the traffic pattern, to comply with the appropriate traffic rules, and to display common courtesy toward other pilots operating in the area.

The pilot is not expected to have extensive knowledge of all traffic patterns at all airports; but if the pilot is familiar with the basic rectangular pattern, it is easy to make proper approaches and departures from most airports, regardless of whether they have control towers. At airports with operating control towers, the tower operator may instruct pilots to enter the traffic pattern at any point or to make a straight-in approach without flying the usual rectangular pattern. Many other deviations are possible if the tower operator and the pilot work together in an effort to keep traffic moving smoothly. Jets or heavy aircraft frequently fly wider and/or higher patterns than lighter aircraft and in many cases make a straight-in approach for landing.

The standard rectangular traffic pattern and terms are illustrated in *Figure 10-1*. The terms of an airport in the pattern after takeoff are described in *Figure 10-1*.

Departure leg—the flightpath which begins after takeoff and continues straight ahead along the extended runway centerline.

Crosswind leg—a flightpath at right angles to the landing runway off its takeoff end.

Downwind leg—a flightpath parallel to the landing runway in the opposite direction of landing.

Base leg—a flightpath at right angles to the landing runway off its approach end and extending from the downwind leg to the intersection of the extended runway centerline (third left hand 90° turn).

Final approach—a flightpath in the direction of landing along the extended runway centerline from the base leg to the runway.

Upwind leg—a flightpath parallel to the landing runway in the direction of landing (not shown in *Figure 10-1*).

The traffic pattern altitude is usually 1,000 feet above the elevation of the airport surface; however, many airports use different pattern altitudes for different types of aircraft. This information can be found in the Airport/Facility Directory (A/FD). The use of a common or known altitude at a given airport is a key factor in minimizing the risk of collisions at airports without operating control towers because aircraft can be expected to be at a certain level making it easier to see.

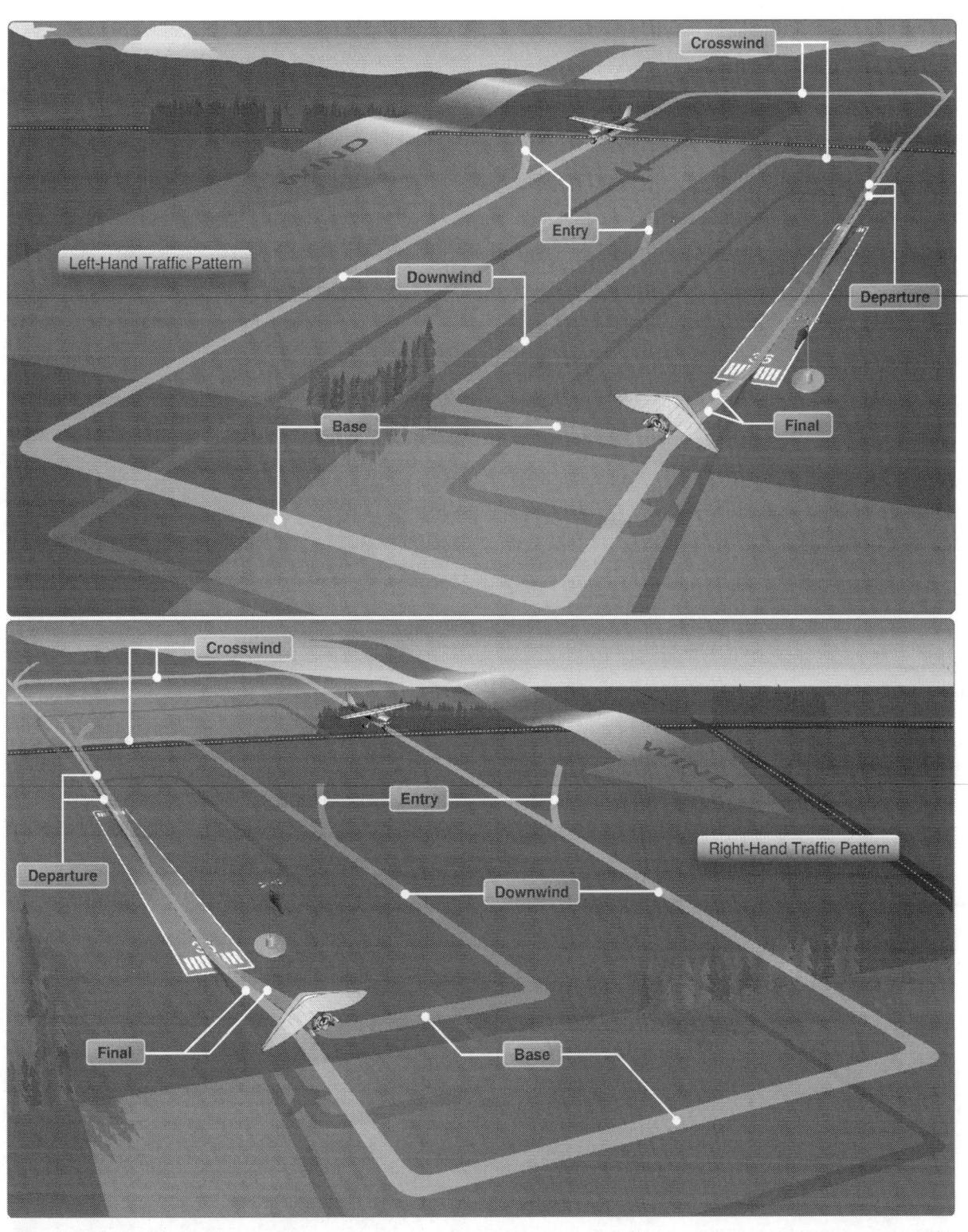

Figure 10-1. *Left and right hand traffic patterns. The WSC pattern altitude shown is the same as the airplane but the slower WSC aircraft uses a smaller "inside pattern" or "tight pattern."*

10-3

Compliance with the basic rectangular traffic pattern reduces the possibility of conflicts at airports without an operating control tower. It is imperative that the pilot form the habit of exercising constant vigilance in the vicinity of airports even though the air traffic appears to be light. The objective is to have both the fast and the slower weight-shift control (WSC) aircraft completing the pattern at the same interval.

The slower the aircraft is, the tighter the pattern is, as shown in *Figure 10-1*. The terminology is a "tight pattern" or "inside pattern" for the slower WSC aircraft in operations with faster aircraft. Using *Figure 10-1* as an example, if the airplane is flying the pattern at 80 knots and the WSC aircraft is flying an inside pattern at 40 knots (that is half the distance), then the WSC aircraft and the airplane will fly around the pattern with the same interval. The WSC pilot must determine the size of the pattern to create the same interval. This is commonplace at nontowered airports where WSC aircraft operate with faster aircraft. Both aircraft are going around the pattern at the same time with the slower WSC aircraft flying a tighter pattern and the faster airplane flying the larger pattern. In *Figure 10-2*, the WSC aircraft is establishing an inside airport pattern turning from crosswind to downwind. In *Figure 10-3*, the aircraft shown is in the middle of the downwind leg flying an inside pattern.

When entering the traffic pattern at an airport without an operating control tower, inbound pilots are expected to listen to the other aircraft on the CTAF (Common Traffic Advisory Frequency), observe other aircraft already in the pattern, and conform to the traffic pattern in use. If other aircraft are not in the pattern, then traffic indicators on the ground and wind indicators must be checked to determine which runway and traffic pattern direction should be used. *[Figure 10-4 and 10-5]* Many airports have L-shaped traffic pattern indicators displayed with a segmented circle adjacent to the runway. The short member of the L shows the direction in which traffic pattern turns should be made when using the runway parallel to the long member. These indicators should be checked while at a distance away from any pattern that might be in use, or while at a safe height above pattern altitudes. When the proper traffic pattern direction has been determined, the pilot should then proceed to a point clear of the pattern before descending to the pattern altitude.

Figure 10-2. *After takeoff and departure, turning from the crosswind to the downwind leg while climbing to pattern altitude.*

Figure 10-3. *Weight-shift control on the downwind leg of an airport inside pattern.*

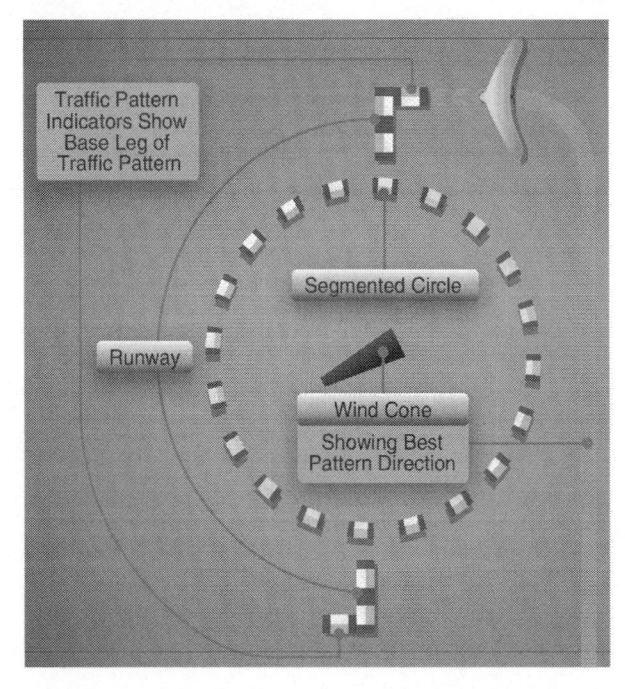

Figure 10-4. *Left hand pattern for runway in both directions.*

10-5

As discussed earlier, all patterns are left hand unless indicated otherwise. Sectional aeronautical charts list a right hand pattern along with the airport information as shown in *Figure 10-6*. The segmented circle of *Figure 10-5* and the airport shown in *Figure 10-6* both clearly show the patterns for this airport.

Figure 10-5. *Left hand pattern for one direction and right hand pattern for other direction.*

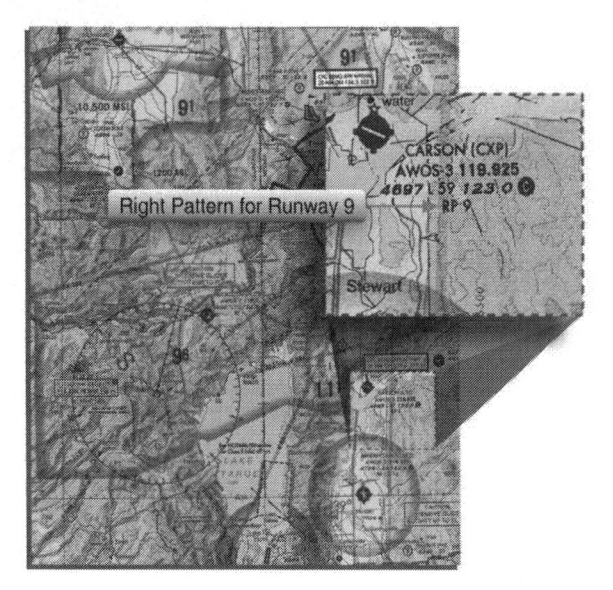

Figure 10-6. *Example of traffic pattern indicator on sectional showing right hand pattern for runway 9. See Figure 10-5 for segmented circle for this airport.*

A segmented circle in *Figure 10-7* provides traffic patterns so there is no air traffic over the lower right hand area, which could be a hazard or populated area.

Inbound to an uncontrolled airport, the CTAF frequency should be monitored to listen for other aircraft in the pattern to find out what is the active runway being used by other air traffic. *[Figure 10-8]*

When approaching an airport for landing, the traffic pattern should be entered at a 45° angle to the downwind leg, headed toward a point abeam of the midpoint of the runway to be used for landing as shown in *Figures 10-1* and *10-7*. Arriving aircraft should be at the proper traffic pattern altitude before entering the pattern and should stay clear of the traffic flow until established on the entry leg. Entries into traffic patterns while descending create specific collision hazards and should always be avoided. During the WSC 45° entry into the pattern, the WSC aircraft must pass through the larger airplane pattern, so it is essential that alert see-and-avoid procedures plus additional radio communications be practiced during this transition.

The entry leg should be of sufficient length to provide a clear view of the entire traffic pattern and to allow the pilot adequate time for planning the intended path in the pattern and the landing approach.

The downwind leg is a course flown parallel to the landing runway but in a direction opposite to the intended landing direction. This leg for the slower WSC aircraft should be approximately ¼ to ½ mile out from the landing runway, and at the specified traffic pattern altitude unless the airport specifically specifies a lower altitude for WSC aircraft. *[Figure 10-9]* The faster airplanes would be ½ to 1 mile out from the landing runway. During this leg, the before landing check should be completed. Pattern altitude should be maintained until abeam the approach end of the landing runway. At this point, power should be reduced and a descent begun. The downwind leg continues past a point abeam the approach end of the runway to a point approximately 45° from the approach end of the runway, and a medium bank turn is made onto the base leg.

The base leg is the transitional part of the traffic pattern between the downwind leg and the final approach leg. Depending on the wind condition, it is established at a sufficient distance from the approach end of the landing runway to permit a gradual descent to the intended touchdown point. The ground track of the aircraft while on the base leg should be perpendicular to the extended centerline of the landing runway, although the longitudinal axis of the aircraft may not be aligned with the ground track when it is necessary to turn into the wind to counteract drift. While on the base leg and before turning onto the final approach, the pilot must ensure that there is no danger of colliding with another aircraft

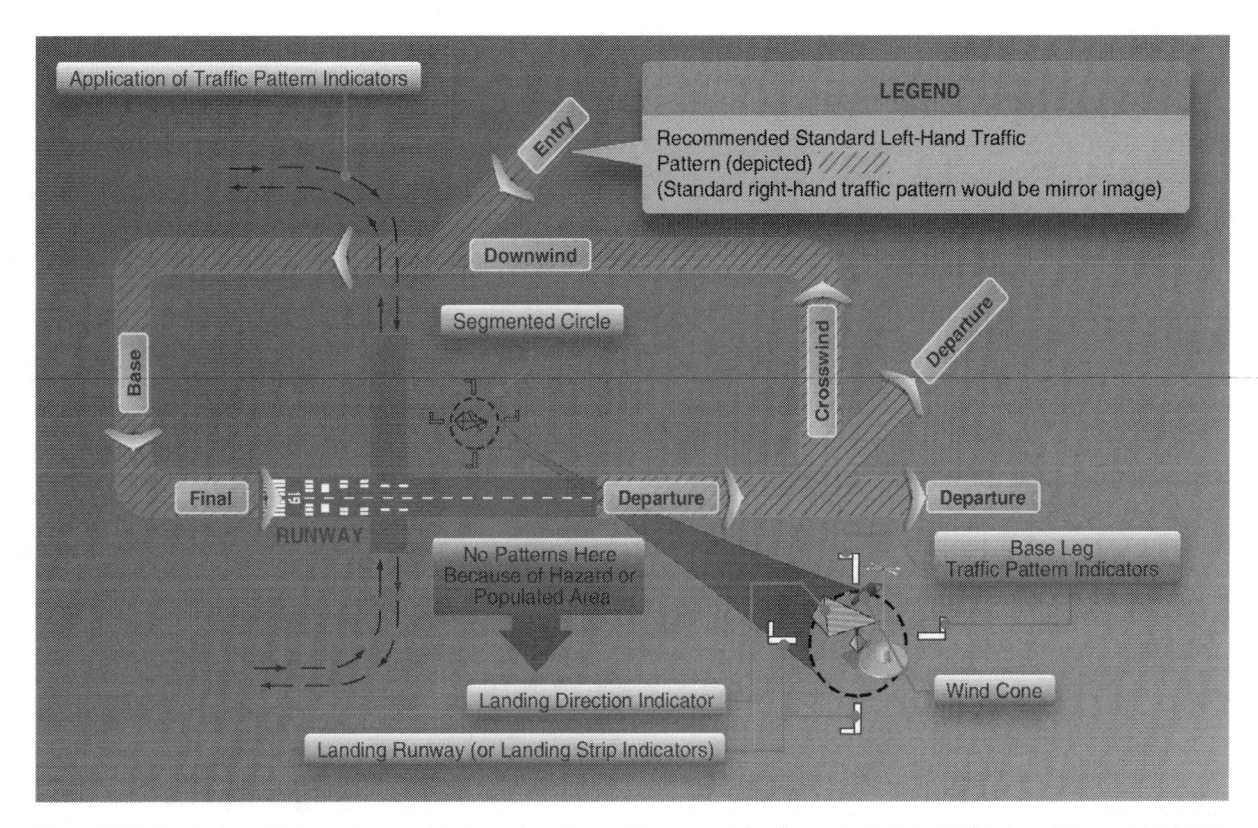

Figure 10-7. *An airport with two runways and a hazard, noise sensitive, or populated area to the lower right where the segmented circle specifies traffic not to fly over this area.*

Figure 10-8. *Approaching a busy airport with multiple runways and listening to the Common Traffic Advisory Frequency (CTAF) for the pattern being used because of the wind conditions.*

Figure 10-9. *After hearing other aircraft using the normal pattern as described in the Airport/Facility Directory (A/FD), pilot descended and entered the downwind leg (landing runway highlighted in red) midfield within gliding distance of the runway in case of an engine failure.*

that may be on the final approach. This is especially important since the WSC aircraft is in a tighter pattern and could be flying onto the final approach of faster airplanes.

The final approach leg is a descending flightpath starting from the completion of the base-to-final turn and extending to the point of touchdown. This is probably the most important leg of the entire pattern because the pilot's judgment and procedures must be the sharpest to control the airspeed and descent angle accurately while approaching the intended touchdown point.

As stipulated in 14 CFR part 91, aircraft while on final approach to land or while landing have the right-of-way over other aircraft in flight or operating on the surface. When two or more aircraft are approaching an airport for the purpose of landing, the aircraft at the lower altitude has the right of way. A pilot should not take advantage of this rule to cut in front of or overtake another aircraft on final approach.

The departure leg of the rectangular pattern is a straight course aligned with, and leading from, the takeoff runway. This leg begins at the point the aircraft leaves the ground and continues until the 90° turn onto the crosswind leg is started. On the departure leg after takeoff, the pilot should continue climbing straight ahead, and, if remaining in the traffic pattern, commence a turn to the crosswind leg beyond the departure end of the runway within 300 feet of pattern altitude. If departing the traffic pattern, continue straight out or exit with a 45° turn (to the left when in a left-hand traffic pattern; to the right when in a right-hand traffic pattern) beyond the departure end of the runway after reaching pattern altitude.

An upwind leg is a course flown parallel to the landing runway, but in the same direction as the intended landing direction. The upwind leg continues past a point abeam the departure end of the runway to where a medium bank 90° turn is made onto the crosswind leg. The upwind leg is also the transitional part of the traffic pattern when on the final approach and a go-around is initiated and climb attitude is established. When a safe altitude is attained, the pilot should commence a shallow bank turn to the right side of the runway. This allows better visibility of the runway for departing aircraft. *[Figure 10-10]*

The crosswind leg is the part of the rectangular pattern that is horizontally perpendicular to the extended centerline of the takeoff runway and is entered by making approximately a 90° turn from the departure or upwind leg. On the crosswind leg, the aircraft proceeds to the downwind leg position.

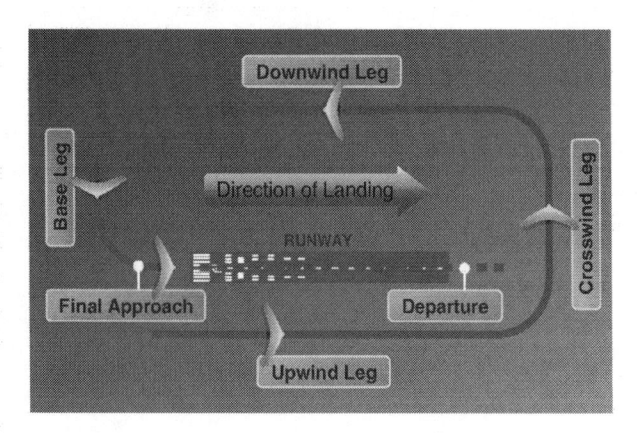

Figure 10-10. *Upwind leg.*

In most cases, the takeoff is made into the wind in which case it is now approximately perpendicular to the aircraft's flightpath. As a result, the aircraft has to be turned or headed slightly into the wind while on the crosswind leg to maintain a ground track that is perpendicular to the runway centerline extension.

Chapter Summary

Airport patterns provide organized air traffic flows into and out of an airport. An airport traffic pattern is established appropriate to the local conditions, including the direction and placement of the pattern, altitude to be flown, and procedures for entering and leaving the pattern.

The legs of an airport pattern from takeoff are:

- Departure—direction of takeoff on the centerline of the runway
- Crosswind—first 90° turn flying perpendicular to the takeoff direction
- Downwind—second 90° turn flying parallel to the takeoff direction opposite the direction of takeoff and landing
- Base—third 90° turn flying perpendicular towards the runway centerline
- Final—forth 90° turn headed down the centerline of the runway to land

Pilots must research and determine from preflight preparation the possible runways and patterns for runways at the intended airports for the flight. The pilot must determine the actual pattern at the airport from observation and talking with other pilots on the CTAF or from the wind direction if no other pilots are in the pattern. Normal airport patterns are always left hand unless indicated otherwise.

Additional information on airport operations can be found in the Pilot's Handbook of Aeronautical Knowledge, the Aeronautical Information Manual (AIM), Chapter 2, Aeronautical Lighting and Other Airport Visual Aids, Chapter 4, Air Traffic Control, and Chapter 5, Air Traffic Procedures; and 14 CFR part 91, Subpart B, Flight Rules, Subpart C, Equipment, Instrument and Certificate Requirements, and Subpart D, Special Flight Operations.

Chapter 11
Approaches and Landings

Introduction

Approaches and landings are critical maneuvers and require the skills built from basic flight maneuvers, ground reference maneuvers, and airport traffic patterns. A proper approach is required for a proper roundout and touchdown. With the large number of environmental variables the pilot must consider, in addition to the skill to judge aircraft speed, descent rate, and distance above the ground, landing is normally the last basic maneuver the student learns before solo.

Approaches and landings will be first discussed with the fundamentals of a normal approach and landing in calm winds on a large hard-surfaced runway. This will provide the basis for specific power-on, crosswind, and steep approach maneuvers, as well as other types of approaches and landings that WSC commonly encounter.

Normal (Calm Wind) Approaches and Landings

A normal or regular approach and landing involves the use of procedures for what is considered a simple situation. It provides the minimum number of variables for the student pilot to learn during the first landings; that is, when engine power is at idle, wind is light, and the final approach is made directly into the wind, the final approach path has no obstacles, and the landing surface is firm and of ample length to bring the aircraft gradually to a stop. This includes normal runways used for WSC that are asphalt, concrete, solid dirt, gravel or short grass. The selected landing point should be beyond the runway's approach threshold but within the first one-third portion of the runway.

The factors involved and the procedures described for the normal approach and landing also have applications to the other-than-normal approaches and landings which are discussed later in this chapter. Therefore, the principles of simple (or normal) operations are explained first and must be understood before proceeding to more complex operations.

To assist the pilot in understanding the factors that influence judgment and procedures, the last part of the approach pattern and the actual landing is divided into five phases:

- Base leg
- Final approach
- Roundout
- Touchdown
- After-landing roll

Remember that the manufacturer's recommended procedures, including aircraft configuration, airspeeds, power, and other information relevant to approaches and landings in a specific make and model aircraft are contained in the Aircraft Flight Manual (AFM) and/or Pilot's Operating Handbook (POH) for that aircraft. If any of the information in this chapter differs from the aircraft manufacturer's recommendations as contained in the AFM/POH, the aircraft manufacturer's recommendations take precedence.

Throttle Use

As discussed in Chapter 2, Aerodynamics, the WSC aircraft has a good glide ratio, and normal landings can easily be done with the power at idle. It is a good practice to master the landings with the throttle at idle so that the glide angle, speeds, and descent rates become habit and part of a normal routine. This is helpful so that, if there is an engine failure, the pilot is accustomed to landing with minimum power and is able to spot land the WSC aircraft for emergency conditions at or beyond a specified point. As a general practice for normal landings in calm conditions or a slight headwind, the throttle should be brought back to idle at the start of the base leg for landings.

Title 14 of the Code of Federal Regulations (14 CFR), section 91.119, Minimum Safe Altitudes: General, is an important safety precaution and states: "Except when necessary for takeoff or landing, no person may operate an aircraft anywhere below... an altitude allowing, if a power unit fails, an emergency landing without undue hazard to persons or property on the surface." This allows long final approaches "with power when necessary," but overall, it is important to be no lower than an altitude from which you can glide to a safe landing area. For the purposes of this approach-and-landing discussion, it is assumed that there are no safe landing areas other than the runway.

It should be noted that the power is above idle for some landing situations, such as:

- Students first learning to land; a slower rate of descent is the result of higher power settings. In this case, the landings would be done with a target farther down the runway so a safe landing could always be made with engine failure.

- Shallower descent angle if directed by air traffic control (ATC), or a longer final approach is required.

- High winds and/or turbulent conditions requiring a higher energy level.

For landings where throttle is required, the foot throttle is typically used so the hands can stay on the control bar while approaching the ground for this critical phase of flight. However, the hand/cruise throttle may be set above idle for specific situations as required by the pilot. Higher power settings for approaches and landings are discussed later in this chapter.

Base Leg

The placement of the base leg is one of the more important judgments made by the pilot in any landing approach. *[Figure 11-1]* The pilot must accurately judge the altitude and distance from which the descent results in landing at the desired point.

The base leg should be started at a point where the power can be brought back to idle and the WSC aircraft can glide to the landing spot at the approach speed recommended by the manufacturer. The intended landing point should not be at the end of the runway on a threshold or numbers, but beyond at the landing lines. *[Figure 11-2]* This provides some margin if the landing is shorter than anticipated. For smaller runways that do not have these markings, establish an appropriate

Figure 11-1. *Base leg and final approach.*

landing point beyond the start of the runway, allowing plenty of room for the after-landing roll. At much larger airports, the landing can be done farther down the runway or at a location where the pilot can taxi off the runway and not delay other air traffic behind the aircraft.

After turning onto the base leg, the pilot should continue the descent with reduced power and approach airspeed as recommended by the manufacturer. As discussed in Chapter 7, Takeoff and Departure, this speed is at least 1.3 times the stall speed. Landing trim should be adjusted according to manufacturer specifications (if equipped).

Drift correction should be established and maintained to follow a ground track perpendicular to the extension of the centerline of the runway on which the landing is to be made. Since the final approach and landing are normally made into the wind, there may be a crosswind during the base leg. The aircraft must be angled sufficiently into the wind to prevent drifting farther away from the intended landing point.

The base leg should be continued to the point where a medium- to shallow-banked turn aligns the aircraft's path directly with the centerline of the landing runway. This descending turn should be completed at a safe altitude that is dependent upon the height of the terrain and any obstructions along the ground track. The turn to the final approach should also be sufficiently above the airport elevation to permit a

Figure 11-2. *Typical landing position on runway.*

final approach long enough for the pilot to accurately estimate the resultant point of touchdown, while maintaining the proper approach airspeed. This requires careful planning for the starting point and radius of the turn. *[Figure 11-3]* Normally, it is recommended that the angle of bank not exceed a medium bank because the steeper the angle of bank, the higher the airspeed at which the aircraft stalls. Since the base-to-final turn is made at a relatively low altitude, it is important that a stall not occur at this point. If an extremely steep bank is needed to prevent overshooting the proper final approach path, it is advisable to discontinue the approach, go around, and plan to start the turn earlier on the next approach rather than risk a hazardous situation.

Figure 11-3. *On base preparing to turn onto final.*

Final Approach

After the base-to-final approach turn is completed, the aircraft should be aligned directly in the extension of the centerline of the runway. The objective of a good final approach is to approach the runway with sufficient energy (manufacturer's recommended airspeed) to land at or beyond some predetermined point. The landing area should provide sufficient runway behind for variations in approach conditions and runway ahead to allow either a full stop or a go-around if needed.

If there is a crosswind of any kind, the aircraft should be pointed into the wind slightly (see the Crosswind Approaches and Landings section). Focus should be to keep the ground track aligned with the centerline of the runway or landing surface, so that drift (if any) is recognized immediately. On a normal approach, with no crosswind drift, the longitudinal axis should be kept aligned with the runway centerline throughout the approach and landing.

After aligning the aircraft with the runway centerline, speed is adjusted as required for the desired rate of descent. Slight increases in power, if lower than expected, may be necessary to maintain the descent angle at the desired approach airspeed.

The descent angle should be controlled throughout the approach so that the aircraft lands in the center of the runway at the aiming point, as discussed earlier. The descent angle is affected by all four fundamental forces that act on an aircraft (lift, drag, thrust, and weight). If all the forces are constant, the descent angle is constant in calm air. The pilot can control these forces by adjusting the airspeed and power. The final approach sequence is shown in *Figures 11-4* through *11-8*.

Figure 11-4. *Turning from base onto final.*

Figure 11-5. *Lining up on the runway centerline and maintaining position.*

In a descent for final approach, if the WSC is slowed with an angle of attack that is too high and without an increase of power, the aircraft settles very rapidly and touches down short of the desired area. For this reason, the pilot should never try to stretch a glide by applying forward control bar pressure alone to reach the desired landing area. Because this brings the speed below the minimum drag speed, the gliding distance decreases if power is not added simultaneously.

Figure 11-6. *Coming to the runway and increasing speed slightly within 50 feet of the ground.*

Figure 11-7. *Maintaining speed and position over the middle of the runway.*

Figure 11-8. *Starting the roundout by increasing angle of attack (AOA) slightly at about 10 to 15 feet above the runway.*

Additionally, this is a lower energy approach and may be slower than the manufacturer's safe approach speed. The proper angle of descent to the runway must be maintained at the minimum speed recommended by the manufacturer, with a flatter descent angle obtained with increases in power as required. Steeper descent angles are obtained with headwinds or the pilot increasing speed/decreasing the angle of attack, both of which are covered later in this chapter.

Estimating Height and Movement

During the final approach, roundout, and touchdown, vision is of prime importance. To provide a wide scope of vision and to foster good judgment of height and movement, the pilot's head should assume a natural, straight-ahead position. The pilot's visual focus should not be fixed on any one side or any one spot ahead of the aircraft. The pilot should maintain a deliberate awareness of the runway centerline (if available) or distance from either side of the runway within his or her peripheral field of vision.

Accurate estimation of distance is, besides being a matter of practice, dependent upon how clearly objects are seen; vision must be focused properly so that important objects stand out as clearly as possible. Speed blurs objects at close range. For example, one can note this effect in an automobile moving at high speed. Nearby objects seem to merge together in a blur, while objects farther away stand out clearly. The driver subconsciously focuses the eyes sufficiently far ahead of the automobile to see objects distinctly.

The distance at which the pilot's vision is focused should be proportionate to the speed at which the aircraft is traveling over the ground. Thus, as speed is reduced during the roundout, the focus distance ahead of the aircraft should be decreased accordingly.

If the pilot attempts to focus on a reference that is too close or looks directly down, the reference is blurred, and the reaction is either too abrupt or too late. In this case, the pilot's tendency is to overcontrol, round out high, and make a stalled, drop-in landing. When the pilot focuses too far ahead, accuracy in judging the closeness of the ground is lost and the consequent reaction is too slow since there is no apparent necessity for action. This results in the aircraft flying into the ground nose first without a proper roundout.

The best way to recognize and become accustomed to heights and speeds for a particular WSC aircraft is to perform low passes over the runway, as discussed earlier, with energy management. Perform a normal approach first, then a high-energy pass at a higher speed, and then medium-energy passes at lower speeds. These exercises are performed first in calm winds at a height, as an example, at which the wheels are 10 feet above the runway, then lowering to just inches above the runway as the pilot's skills build. The objective is to become proficient at flying straight down the runway centerline at a constant altitude. This exercise provides the opportunity to determine height and speed over the runway before any landings are performed. These should generally be performed in mild conditions. Higher energy and greater heights above the runway are required in windier and bumpier conditions.

Roundout (Flare)

The roundout is a slow, smooth transition from a normal approach speed to a landing attitude, gradually rounding out the flightpath to one that is parallel with, and within a very few inches above, the runway. When the aircraft, in a normal descent, approaches within what appears to be 10 to 15 feet above the ground, the roundout or flare should be started and be a continuous process slowing until the aircraft touches down on the ground.

It should be noted that the terms "roundout" and "flare" are defined and used interchangeably throughout the aviation industry for slowing the aircraft during final approach and touching down. The term "roundout" is used in this handbook since it provides a better description for the WSC landing process and WSC students are more successful learning landings using the term roundout instead of flare.

As the aircraft reaches a height where the back wheels are one to two inches above the ground, the roundout is continued by gradually pushing the control bar forward as required to maintain one to two inches above the runway as the WSC aircraft slows. *[Figure 11-9]* This causes the aircraft's nosewheel to gradually rise to the desired landing attitude. The AOA should be increased at a rate that allows the aircraft to continue flying just above the runway as forward speed decreases until the control bar is full forward and the back wheels settle onto the runway.

During the roundout, the airspeed is decreased to touchdown speed while the lift is controlled so the aircraft settles gently onto the landing surface. The roundout should be executed at a rate at which the proper landing attitude and the proper touchdown airspeed are attained simultaneously just as the wheels contact the landing surface.

The rate at which the roundout is executed depends on the aircraft's height above the ground, the rate of descent, and the airspeed. A roundout started excessively high must be executed more slowly than one from a lower height to allow the aircraft to descend to the ground while the proper landing attitude is being established. The rate of rounding out must also be proportionate to the rate of closure with the ground. When the aircraft appears to be descending very slowly, the increase in pitch attitude (slowing of the WSC) must be made at a correspondingly low rate.

Visual cues are important in roundout at the proper altitude and maintaining the wheels a few inches above the runway until eventual touchdown. Roundout cues are dependent primarily on the angle at which the pilot's central vision intersects the ground (or runway) ahead and slightly to the side. Proper depth perception is a factor in a successful roundout, but the visual cues used most are those related to changes in runway or terrain perspective and to changes in the size of familiar objects near the landing area such as fences, bushes, trees, hangars, and even sod or runway texture. The pilot should direct central vision at a shallow downward angle of 10° to 15° toward the runway as the roundout is initiated. *[Figure 11-10]*

Maintaining the same viewing angle causes the point of visual interception with the runway to move progressively rearward toward the pilot as the aircraft loses altitude. This is an important visual cue in assessing the rate of altitude loss.

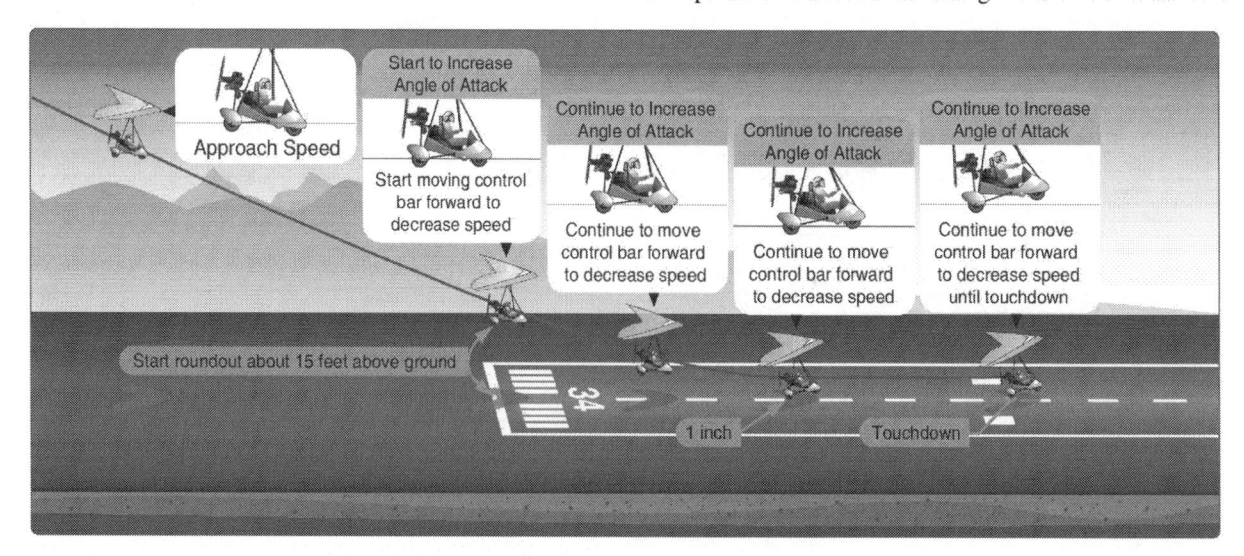

Figure 11-9. *Changing angle of attack during roundout by slowly and continuously pushing forward on the control bar until touchdown.*

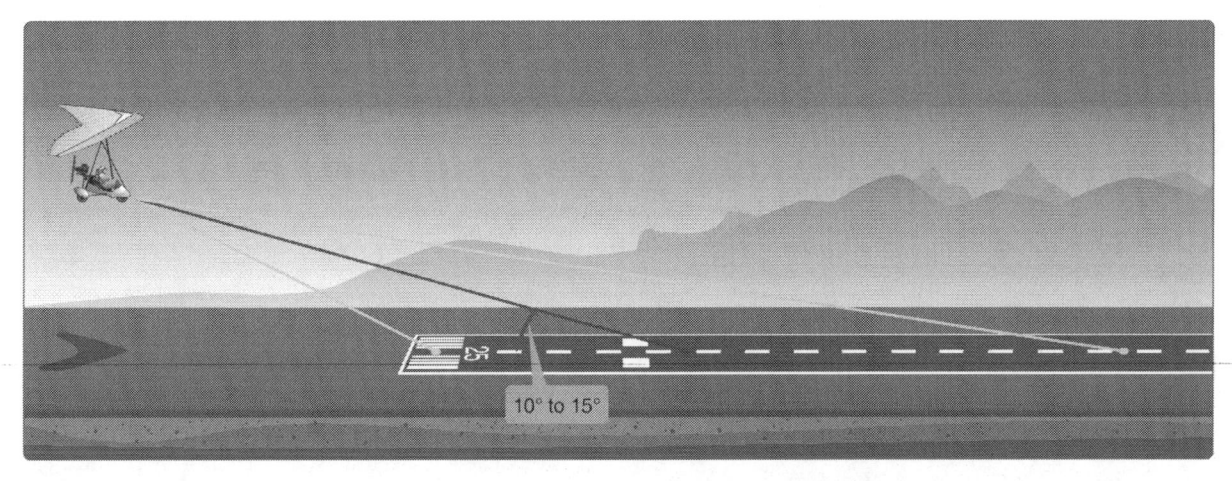

Figure 11-10. *To obtain necessary visual cues, the pilot should look toward the runway at a shallow angle.*

Conversely, forward movement of the visual interception point indicates an increase in altitude and would mean that the pitch angle was increased too rapidly resulting in an over roundout. The following are also used to judge when the wheels are just a few inches above the runway: location of the visual interception point in conjunction with assessment of flow velocity of nearby off-runway terrain, and the similarity in appearance of height above the runway ahead of the aircraft to the way it looked when the aircraft was taxied prior to takeoff.

A common error during the roundout is rounding out too much and too fast. This error can easily be avoided by gradually increasing the AOA with a controlled descent until the wheels are one inch above the surface and never climbing during a roundout with a gradual and controlled roundout.

Figure 11-11. *Maintaining speed from final approach in the center of the runway at about 20 feet above the runway.*

Touchdown

After a controlled roundout, the touchdown is the gentle settling of the aircraft onto the landing surface. For calm air conditions, the roundout can be made with the engine idling, and touchdown can be made at minimum controllable airspeed so that the aircraft touches down on the main gear at the approximate stalling speed. As the aircraft settles, the proper landing attitude is attained by application of whatever control bar forward pressure is necessary. In calm wind conditions, the goal is to round out smoothly and have the control bar touch the front tube as the back wheels touch the ground. *[Figures 11-11* through *11-14]* Once the rear wheel settles to the surface, the nosewheel settles to the ground. The control bar should be pulled all the way back to eliminate the possibility of lifting off the ground because of a wind gust. Pulling the nose down completely can also be used for aerodynamic braking if needed.

After-Landing Roll

The landing process must never be considered complete until the aircraft decelerates to normal taxi speed during the landing roll or has been brought to a complete stop when clear of the landing area. Many accidents have occurred as a result of pilots abandoning their vigilance and positive control after getting the aircraft on the ground.

Figure 11-12. *Starting the roundout at about 10 to 15 feet above the runway surface.*

Figure 11-13. *Continuing the roundout as speed bleeds off and the WSC back wheels are inches above the runway.*

Figure 11-14. *Completing the roundout with the control bar full forward and the back wheels settling to the runway.*

The pilot must make only slight turns to maintain direction until the WSC has slowed to taxiing speed. An abrupt turn at high speed could possibly lift a rear wheel, roll the WSC over, or force the wingtip to the ground. The WSC must slow to taxing speed before before any sharp turn can be made to exit the runway.

The brakes of an aircraft serve the same primary purpose as the brakes of an automobile—to reduce speed on the ground. Maximum brake effectiveness is just short of the skid point. If the brakes are applied so hard that skidding takes place, braking becomes ineffective. Skidding can be stopped by releasing the brake pressure. Also, braking effectiveness is not enhanced by alternately applying and reapplying brake pressure. The brakes should be applied firmly and smoothly as necessary.

WSC aircraft have nosewheel or rear wheel braking systems. For nosewheel systems, if braking is required right away, the nose should be lowered so the nosewheel touches the ground and the brakes can be applied. The nose should be lowered for any aerodynamic braking at the higher speeds.

Lowering the nose also provides greater force on the front wheel for superior braking effectiveness. Any skidding of the front wheel with braking causes the loss of directional control of the WSC aircraft and the skidding must be stopped by letting up on the brake. Skidding can be the greatest problem operating on slick surfaces such as wet grass. Rear wheel braking systems are heavier and more complex, but provide better braking force because there are two wheels instead of one and there is more weight on the rear wheels. Braking effectiveness should be evaluated by the pilot for each type of runway being used. If the available runway permits, the speed of the aircraft should be allowed to dissipate in a normal manner with minimum use of brakes. *[Figure 11-15]*

Figure 11-15. *WSC aircraft follows the taxi line to exit the runway while slowing the aircraft and maintaining control of the wing.*

The control bar serves the same purpose on the ground as in the air—it changes the lift and drag components of the wings. During the after-landing roll, the control bar should be used to keep the wings level in much the same way it is used in flight. If a wing starts to rise, roll control should be applied to lower it. Procedures for crosswind conditions are explained further in the Crosswind Approach and Landing section of this chapter.

Effect of Headwinds During Final Approach

A headwind plays a prominent role in the gliding distance over the ground. Strong headwinds decrease the glide as shown in the comparison in *Figure 11-16A* with no wind normal glide versus *Figure 11-16B* in headwind with steeper glide. To account for a steeper glide in a headwind, the base leg must be positioned closer to the approach end of the runway than would be required with a light wind. Therefore,

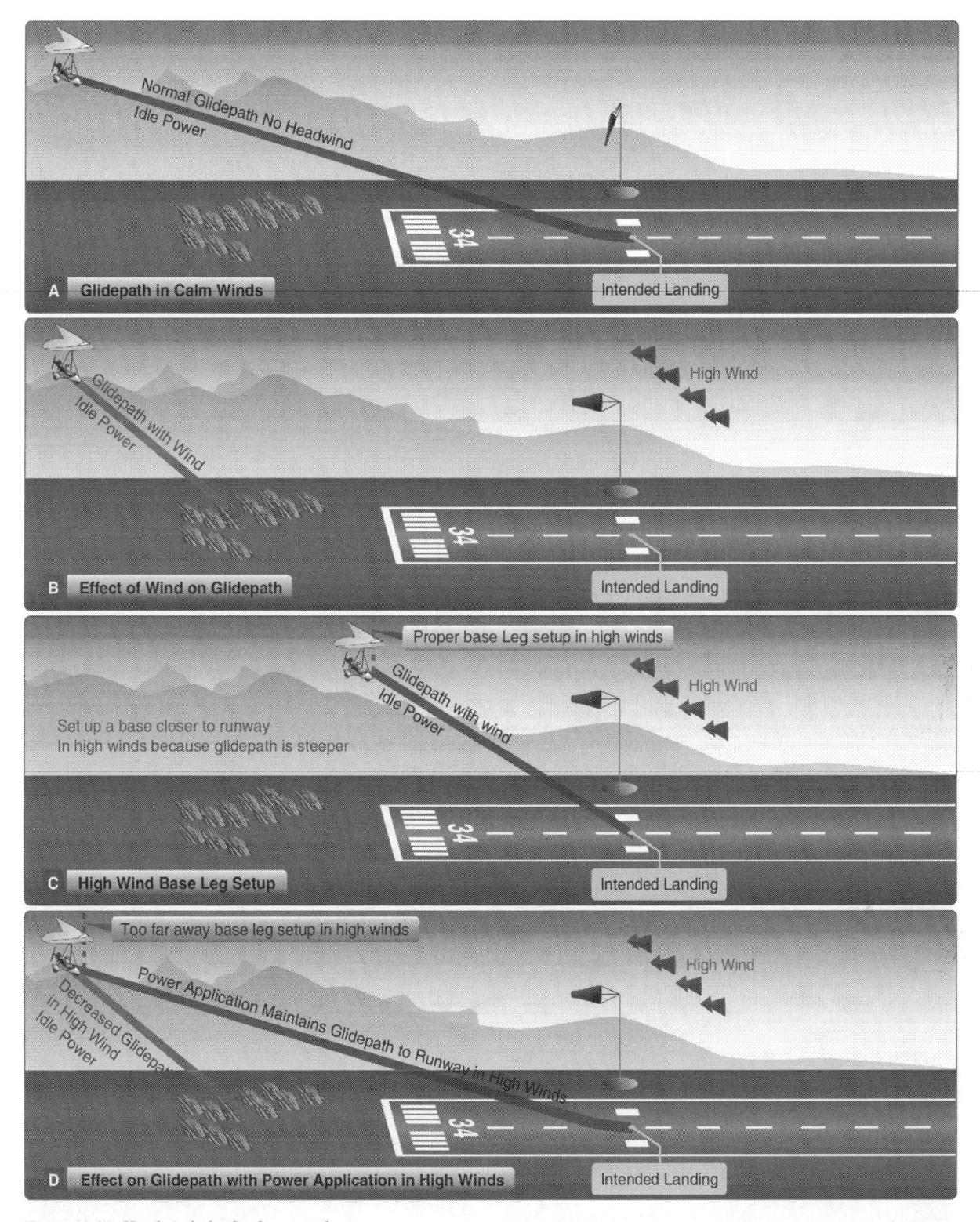

Figure 11-16. *Headwinds for final approach.*

the base leg must be made closer to the runway to land in the intended area in a headwind. *[Figure 11-16 C]* However, if more headwind is experienced during final approach, increased power is required to make the intended landing area. *[Figure 11-16 D]*

Naturally, the pilot does not have control over the wind but may correct for its effect on the aircraft's descent by adjusting the base leg of the pattern. The wind can vary significantly at different attitudes and locations in the pattern. If the pilot does not notice the headwind until the base leg, the base

11-9

leg should be cut short and the pilot should head towards the runway sooner. This would provide the best possibility of making the runway if there is an engine failure in this situation. *[Figure 11-17]*

Additionally, during strong headwinds, more energy (power and airspeed) should be used since the wind gradient (slowing of the wind near the ground because of the friction of the ground) could reduce the airspeed and cause a stall on approach near the ground in higher winds.

Stabilized Approach Concept

A stabilized approach is one in which the pilot establishes and maintains a constant angle glidepath toward a predetermined point on the landing runway. It is based on the pilot's judgment of certain visual clues and depends on the maintenance of a constant final descent airspeed.

An aircraft descending on final approach at a constant rate and airspeed is traveling in a straight line toward a point on the ground ahead. This point is not the point on which the aircraft touches down because some float inevitably occurs during the roundout.

The point toward which the aircraft is progressing is termed the "aiming point." *[Figure 11-18]* It is the point on the ground at which, if the aircraft maintains a constant glidepath and was not rounded out for landing, it would strike the ground. To a pilot moving straight ahead toward an object, it appears to be stationary. This is how the aiming point can be distinguished—it does not move. However, objects in front of and beyond the aiming point do appear to move as the distance is closed, and they appear to move in opposite directions. During instruction in landings, one of the most important skills a student pilot must acquire is the use of visual cues to accurately determine the true aiming point from any distance out on final approach. From this, the pilot is able not only to determine if the glidepath results in an undershoot or overshoot, but also to predict the touchdown point to within a few feet taking into account float during roundout.

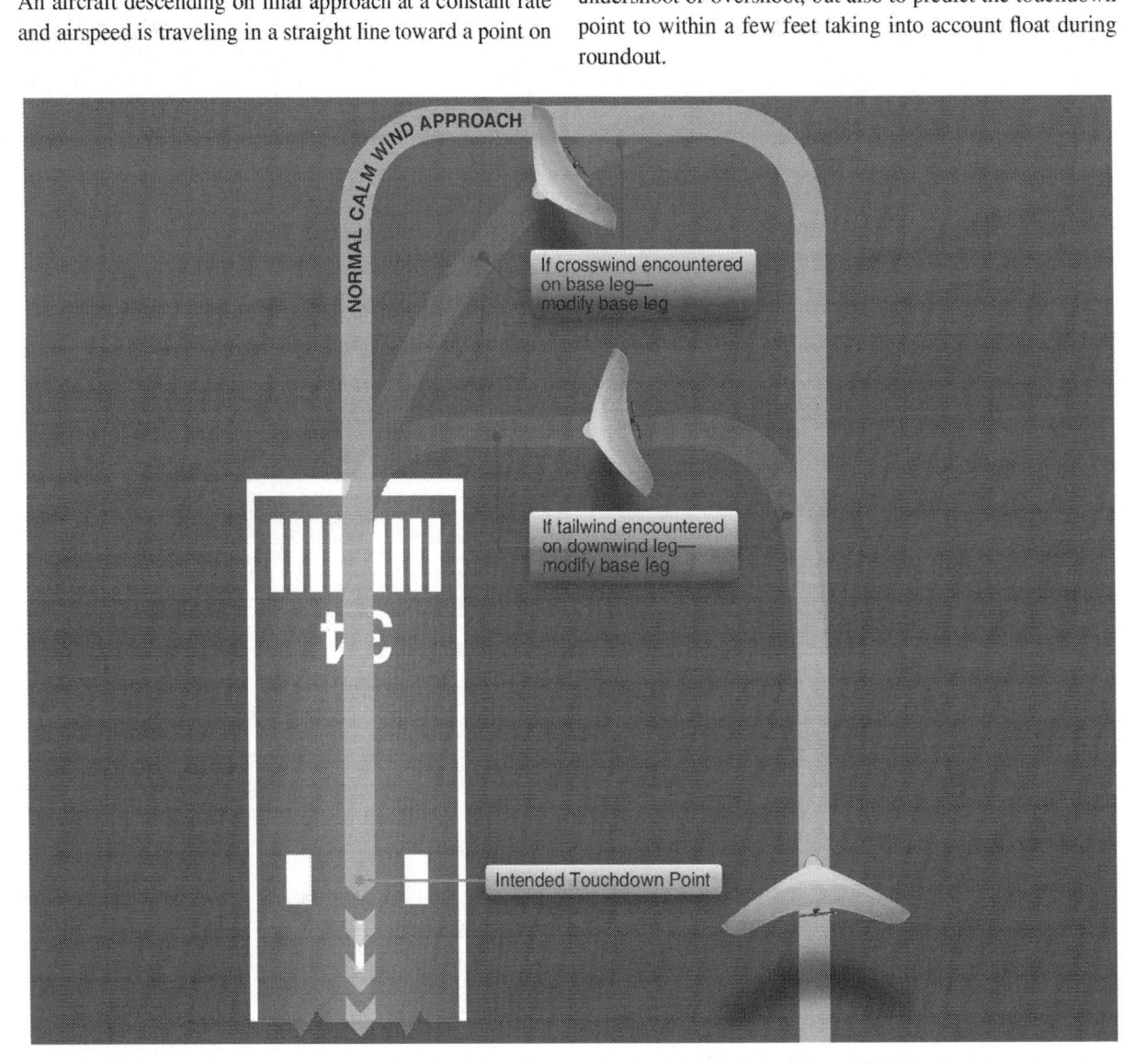

Figure 11-17. *Modified base leg if winds higher than intended are encountered during the base leg of the pattern.*

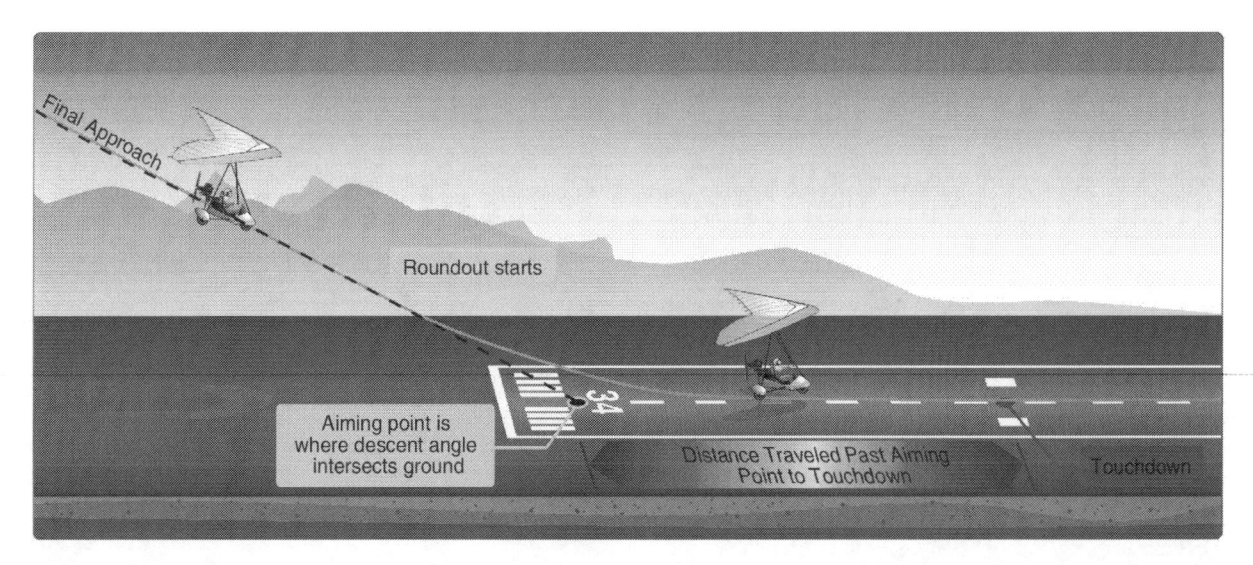

Figure 11-18. *Stabilized approach.*

For a constant angle glidepath, the distance between the horizon and the aiming point remain constant. If a final approach descent has been established but the distance between the perceived aiming point and the horizon appears to increase (aiming point moving down, away from the horizon), then the true aiming point and subsequent touchdown point is farther down the runway. If the distance between the perceived aiming point and the horizon decreases (aiming point moving up toward the horizon), the true aiming point is closer than perceived.

When the aircraft is established on final approach, the shape of the runway image also presents clues regarding what must be done to maintain a stabilized approach to a safe landing. A runway is normally shaped in the form of an elongated rectangle. When viewed from the air during the approach, perspective causes the runway to assume the shape of a trapezoid with the far end appearing narrower than the approach end, and the edge lines converging in the distance. If the aircraft continues down the glidepath at a constant angle (stabilized), the image the pilot sees is still trapezoidal but of proportionately larger dimensions.

During a stabilized approach, the runway shape does not change. *[Figure 11-19]* If the approach becomes shallower, the runway appears to shorten and become wider. Conversely, if the approach is steepened, the runway appears to become longer and narrower. *[Figure 11-20]*

The objective of a stabilized approach is to select an appropriate touchdown point on the runway and adjust the glidepath so that the true aiming point and the desired touchdown point coincide. Immediately after rolling out of base leg and onto final approach, the pilot should adjust the speed so that the aircraft descends directly toward the aiming point. With the approach set up in this manner, the pilot is free to devote full attention to outside references. The pilot should not stare at any one place, but rather scan from one area to another, such as from the aiming point to the horizon, to the trees and bushes along the runway, to an area well short of the runway, and back to the aiming point. In this way, the pilot is more apt to perceive a deviation from the desired glidepath and whether or not the aircraft is proceeding directly toward the aiming point.

If the pilot perceives any indication that the aiming point on the runway is not where desired, an adjustment must be made to the glidepath. This in turn moves the aiming point. For instance, if the pilot perceives that the aiming point is significantly short of the desired touchdown point and results in an undershoot, an increase in power is warranted. The minimum airspeed recommended by the manufacturer must be maintained. This results in a shallowing of the glidepath with the resultant aiming point moving toward the desired touchdown point. Conversely, if the pilot perceives that the aiming point is farther down the runway than the desired touchdown point and results in an overshoot, the glidepath should be steepened by an increase in speed with the throttle at idle. It is essential that deviations from the desired glidepath be detected early, so that only slight and infrequent adjustments to glidepath are required.

If a situation arises in which the required corrections become larger (and possibly more frequent) as the aircraft draws closer to the runway, an unstabilized approach results.

Common errors in the performance of normal approaches and landings include the following:

- Not realizing there is a tailwind during downwind to complete an early base
- Inadequate wind drift correction on the base leg

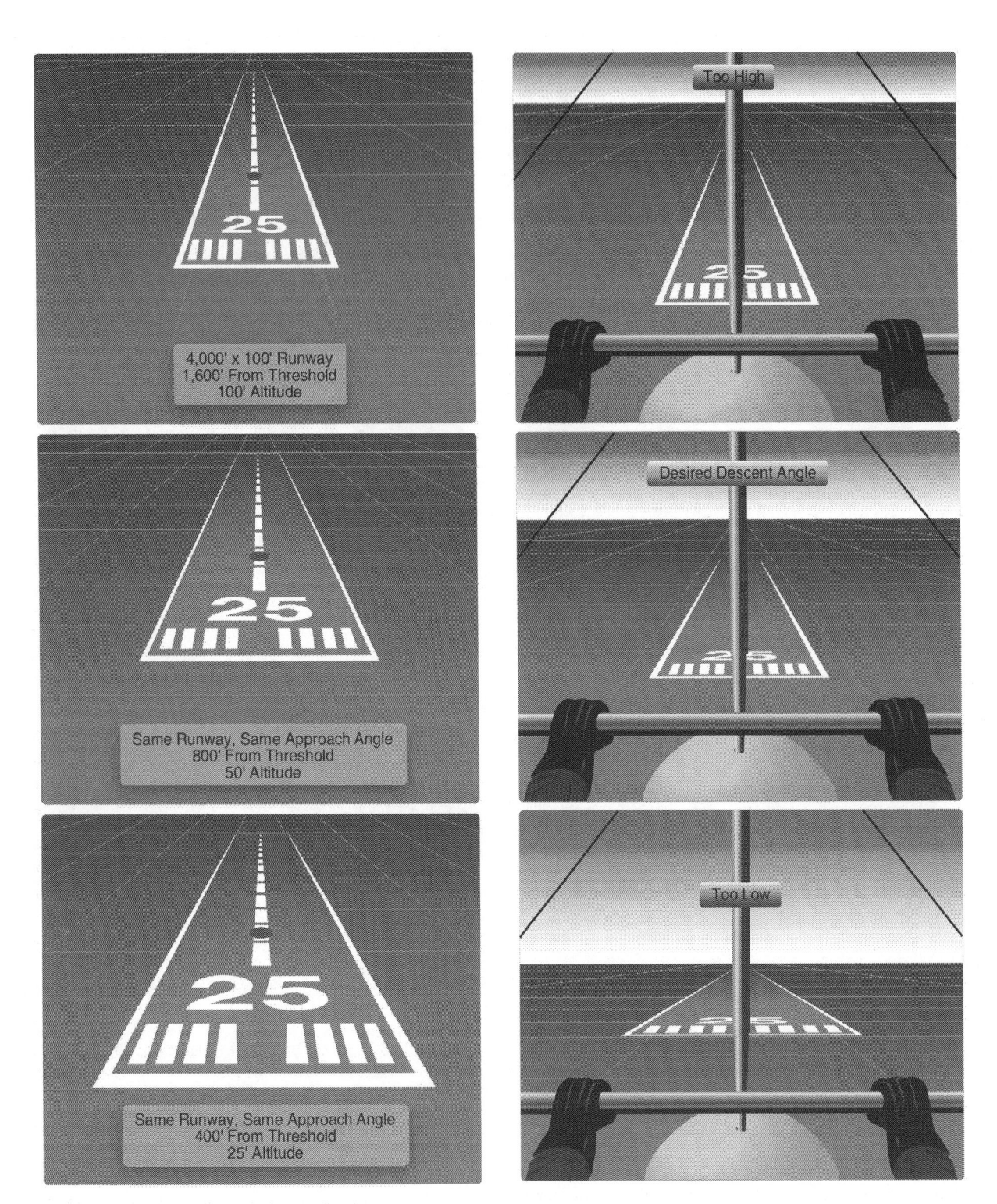

Figure 11-19. *Runway shape during stabilized approach.*

Figure 11-20. *Change in runway shape if approach becomes narrow or steep.*

11-12

- Overshooting or undershooting the turn onto final approach
- Unstabilized approach
- Attempting to maintain altitude or reach the runway by slowing WSC aircraft below the minimum manufacturer's recommended approach airspeed
- Gaining any altitude during the roundout
- Rounding out too fast during landing
- Focusing too close to the aircraft, resulting in an overly high roundout
- Focusing too far from the aircraft, resulting in an overly low roundout
- Touching down prior to attaining proper landing attitude
- Failure to lower the nose after the rear wheels touch down
- Failure to lower the nose after the front wheel touches down
- Excessive braking after touchdown

Go-Around (Rejected Landings)

Whenever landing conditions are not satisfactory, a go-around is warranted. There are many factors that can contribute to unsatisfactory landing conditions. Situations such as ATC requirements, unexpected appearance of hazards on the runway, overtaking another aircraft, wind shear, wake turbulence, mechanical failure and/or an unstabilized approach are all examples of reasons to discontinue a landing approach and make another approach under more favorable conditions. The assumption that an aborted landing is invariably the consequence of a poor approach, which in turn is due to insufficient experience or skill, is a fallacy. The go-around is not strictly an emergency procedure. It is a normal maneuver that may at times be used in an emergency situation. Like any other normal maneuver, the go-around must be practiced and perfected. The flight instructor should emphasize early in the student pilot's training that the go-around maneuver is an alternative to any approach and/or landing.

Although the need to discontinue a landing may arise at any point in the landing process, the most critical go-around is one started when very close to the ground. Therefore, the earlier a condition that warrants a go-around is recognized, the safer the go-around/rejected landing is. The go-around maneuver is not inherently dangerous in itself. It becomes dangerous only when delayed unduly or executed improperly. Delay in initiating the go-around normally stems from one or both of two sources:

1. Landing expectancy or set—the anticipatory belief that conditions are not as threatening as they are and that the approach will surely be terminated with a safe landing, and
2. Pride—the mistaken belief that the act of going around is an admission of failure to execute the approach properly. The improper execution of the go-around maneuver stems from a lack of familiarity with the two cardinal principles of the procedure: power and speed.

Power

Power is the pilot's first concern. The instant the pilot decides to go around, full or maximum allowable takeoff power must be applied smoothly and without hesitation and held until flying speed and controllability are restored. Applying only partial power in a go-around is never appropriate unless the WSC aircraft is at an unusually high pitch angle. The pilot must be aware of the degree of inertia that must be overcome before an aircraft that is settling toward the ground can regain sufficient airspeed to become fully controllable and capable of turning safely or climbing. The application of power should be smooth as well as positive. Abrupt movements of the throttle in some aircrafts causes the engine to falter.

Speed

Speed is always critical when close to the ground. When power is added, a deliberate effort on the part of the pilot is required to keep the nose from pitching up prematurely. The aircraft executing a go-around must be maintained well beyond the stall point before any effort is made to gain altitude or to execute a turn. Raising the nose too early may produce a stall from which the aircraft could not recover if the go-around is performed at a low altitude. The manufacturer's recommended climb speed should be established and maintained during the initial phase of the go around.

A concern for quickly regaining altitude during a go-around produces a natural tendency to push the nose up. The pilot executing a go-around must accept the fact that an aircraft will not climb until it can fly, and it will not fly below stall speed. In some circumstances, it may be desirable to lower the nose briefly to gain airspeed. *[Figure 11-21]*

During the initial part of an extremely low go-around, the aircraft may settle onto the runway and bounce. This situation is not particularly dangerous if the aircraft is kept straight and a constant, safe speed is maintained. The aircraft is rapidly approaching safe flying speed and the advanced power will cushion any secondary touchdown.

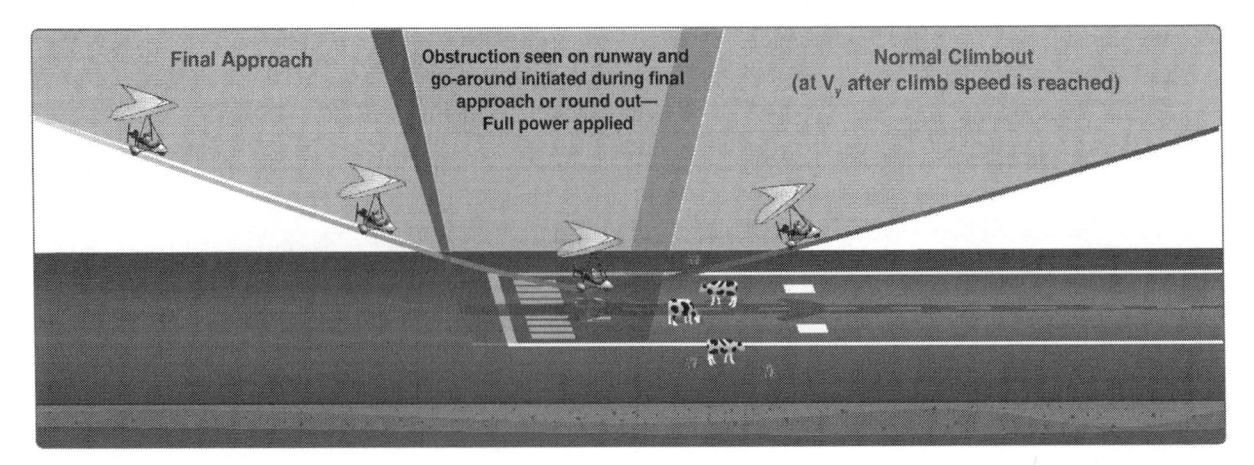

Figure 11-21. *Go-around procedure.*

Common errors in the performance of go-around (rejected landings) are:

- Failure to recognize a condition that warrants a rejected landing,
- Indecision,
- Delay in initiating a go-round,
- Failure to apply maximum allowable power in a timely manner,
- Improper speed,
- Attempting to climb out of ground effect prematurely, and
- Failure to adequately compensate for torque/P-factor.

Short and Soft Field Landing Techniques

Many WSC aircraft land routinely on short and soft fields. The type of WSC and appropriate systems for short and soft field was discussed in the Components and Systems chapter. Here, some techniques for these landing areas are discussed.

Short-Field Approaches and Landings

Short-field approaches and landings require the use of procedures for approaches and landings at fields with a relatively short landing area or where an approach is made over obstacles that limit the available landing area. *[Figure 11-22]* As in short-field takeoffs, it is one of the most critical of the maximum performance operations. It requires that the pilot fly the aircraft at one of its crucial performance capabilities while close to the ground in order to land safely within confined areas.

To land within a short field or confined area, the pilot must have precise, positive control of the rate of descent and airspeed to produce an approach that clears any obstacles, results in little or no floating during the roundout, and permits the aircraft to be stopped in the shortest possible distance. As with the short takeoff maneuver, this should only be done

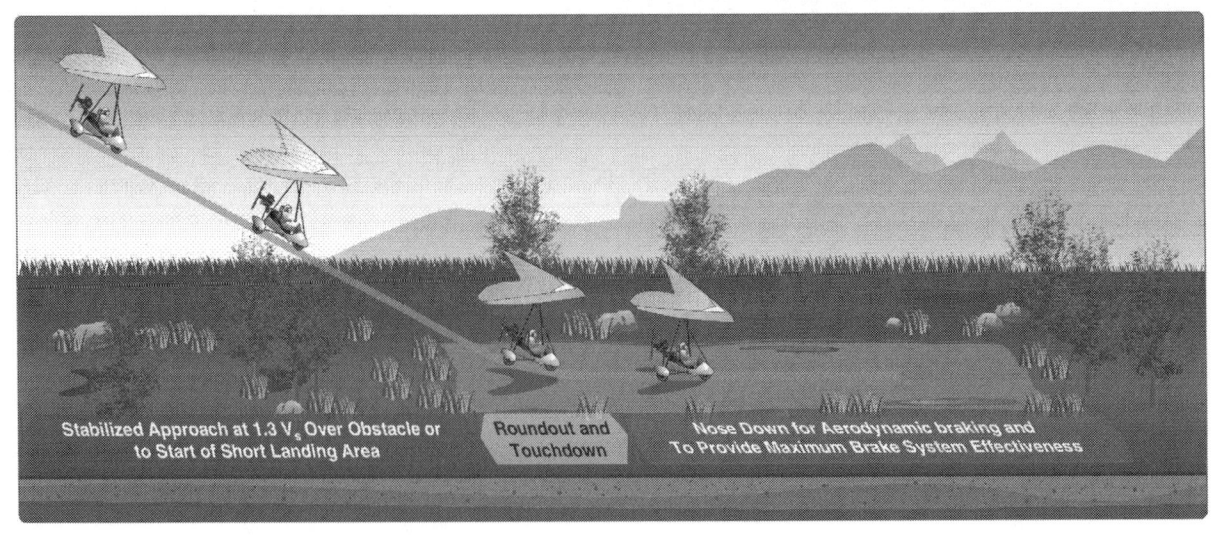

Figure 11-22. *Short field landing.*

for unusual situations or emergency operations and is not recommended. There are numerous airports, fields, and other areas to land, so preflight planning should avoid short-field landings. However, short-field procedures are provided for information.

A stabilized approach is essential. These procedures generally involve the starting to final approach from an altitude of at least 500 feet higher than the touchdown area. In the absence of a manufacturer's recommended approach speed and in calm winds, example approach speeds are 1.3 times the stall speed or 8 knots above the stall speed. For example, in an aircraft that stalls at 30 knots with power off, the approach speed should be 38 to 40 knots. This maneuver should not be performed in gusty air because of the slow speeds and close proximity to the ground. If it is necessary to accomplish in gusty air, no more than one-half the gust factor should be added. An excessive amount of airspeed could result in a touchdown with an after-landing roll that exceeds the available landing area.

For the steepest glide angle to clear obstacles such as trees or buildings, the maneuver should be performed at idle power; if the landing surface does not have obstacles that must be flown over, power on approach may be used to reach the landing surface. The pilot should simultaneously adjust the power and the speed to establish and maintain the proper descent angle. A coordinated combination of both speed and power (if used) adjustments is required to set up a stabilized approach.

The short-field approach and landing is in reality an accuracy approach to a spot landing. The procedures previously outlined in the section on the stabilized approach concept should be used. If it appears that the obstacle clearance is excessive and touchdown will occur well beyond the desired spot leaving insufficient room to stop, lowering the pitch attitude and reducing power (if used) steepen the descent path and increase the rate of descent. If it appears that the descent angle will not ensure safe clearance of obstacles, power should be increased to shallow the descent path and decrease the rate of descent. Care must be taken to avoid an excessively low airspeed. If the speed is allowed to become too low, an increase in pitch and application of full power may result in a further rate of descent. This occurs when the AOA is too great and creating so much drag that the maximum available power is insufficient to overcome it. This is generally referred to as operating in the region of reversed command or operating on the back side of the power curve.

Because the final approach over obstacles is made at a relatively steep approach angle and at the minimum manufacturer's recommended approach speed, the initiation of the roundout must be judged accurately to avoid flying into the ground or stalling prematurely and sinking rapidly. A lack of floating during the roundout with sufficient control to touch down properly is one verification that the approach speed was correct.

Upon touchdown, the nose should be brought down completely for aerodynamic braking and providing maximum pressure on the wheels for using the braking system. Immediately upon touchdown, appropriate braking should be applied to minimize the after-landing roll. The aircraft should be stopped within the shortest possible distance consistent with safety and controllability. If the situation arises and the minimum landing distance is required, the WSC can be landed above the normal speed, the nose brought down for aerodynamic braking while the brakes are applied for the shortest distance possible.

Soft and Rough Field Approaches and Landings
Landing on fields that are rough or have soft surfaces, such as snow, sand, mud, tall grass, or a rocky/bumpy field requires unique procedures. When landing on such surfaces, the objective is to touch down as smoothly as possible and at the lowest possible landing speed. The pilot must control the aircraft so that the wings support the weight of the aircraft as long as is practical to minimize drag and stresses imposed on the landing gear by the rough or soft surface.

Similar to the soft field for takeoff, proper gear—specifically big tires with a large wing and overall low weight—should be utilized for soft or rough field operations. Refer to appropriate gear and warnings in Chapter 7, Takeoff and Departure Climbs, for soft or rough field operation as a prerequisite for this chapter.

The approach for the soft field landing is similar to the normal approach used for operating into long, firm landing areas. The major difference between the two is that, during the soft or rough field landing, the distance on the soft/rough field is minimized and the weight is kept off the wheels by the lift of the wing when on the soft/rough field. Power can be used throughout the level-off and touchdown to ensure touchdown at the lowest possible airspeed, with the WSC aircraft flown onto the ground with the weight fully supported by the wings. The touchdown should be planned for minimal taxi distance to the stopping point so there is the shortest possible distance with weight on the landing gear on the rough/soft surface. *[Figure 11-23]*

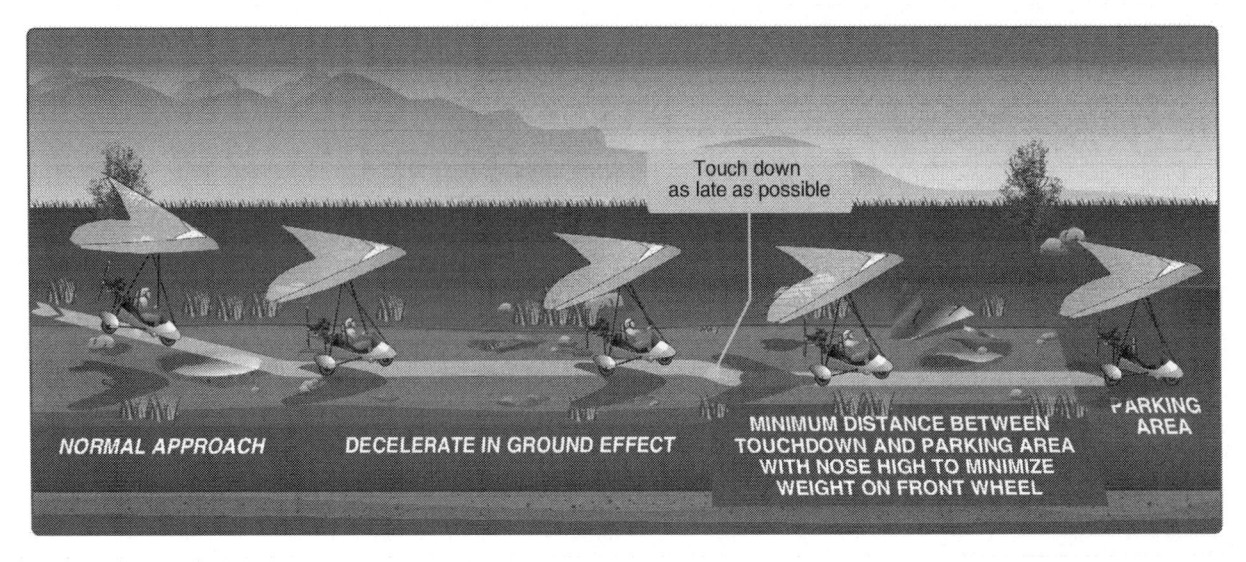

Figure 11-23. *Soft/rough field approach and landing.*

Touchdown on a soft or rough field should be made at the lowest possible airspeed with the aircraft in a nose-high pitch attitude. After the main wheels touch the surface, the pilot should hold bar-forward pressure to keep the nosewheel off the surface. Using forward control bar pressure and engine power, the pilot can control the rate at which the weight of the aircraft is transferred from the wings to the wheels.

Field conditions may warrant that the pilot maintain a flight condition where the main wheels are just touching the surface, but the weight of the aircraft is still being supported by the wings until a suitable taxi surface is reached. At any time during this transition phase, before the weight of the aircraft is being supported by the wheels and before the nosewheel is on the surface, the pilot should be able to apply full power and perform a safe takeoff (obstacle clearance and field length permitting) should the pilot elect to abandon the landing. Once committed to a landing, the pilot should gently lower the nosewheel to the surface. A slight reduction of power usually helps ease the nosewheel down.

The use of brakes on a soft field is not needed and should be avoided as this tends to impose a heavy load on the nose gear due to premature or hard contact with the landing surface causing the nosewheel to dig in. The soft or rough surface itself provides sufficient reduction in the aircraft's forward speed. Often upon landing on a very soft field, the pilot needs to increase power to keep the aircraft moving and from becoming stuck on the soft surface.

Power-on Approach and Landing for Turbulant Air

Power-on approaches at an airspeed above the normal approach speed should be used for landing in turbulent air. This provides for more energy and positive control of the aircraft when strong horizontal wind gusts, wind sheer, or up and down drafts, are experienced. Like other power-on approaches (when the pilot can vary the amount of power), a coordinated combination of both speed and power adjustments is usually required. It is easiest to think of flying the aircraft onto the ground at an airspeed above the stall speed. The additional power provides the pilot the ability to reduce the descent rate to touch the wheels gently to the surface at a higher speed. Landing in turbulent air is where practice and experience in energy management are utilized. This precise coordination of power and speed for higher energy landings should first be practiced in calm air and can be used as the next step in learning landings after the student becomes proficient at low approaches.

To determine the additional approach speed to flying in turbulence, one procedure is to use the normal approach speed plus one-half of the wind gust factors. The wind gust factor is determined by how much the airspeed varies while flying. If the normal approach speed is 50 knots and the wind gusts are at 15 knots, an airspeed of 57 knots is appropriate. Another method is to ensure the aircraft is at least at V_Y speed plus the wind gust factor. In any case, the airspeed that the aircraft manufacturer recommends.

An adequate amount of power should be used to maintain the proper airspeed and descent path throughout the approach and the throttle retarded to idling position only after the main wheels contact the landing surface. Care must be exercised in not closing the throttle before the pilot is ready for touchdown. In this situation, the sudden or premature closing of the throttle may cause a sudden increase in the descent rate that could result in a hard landing.

Landings from power-on approaches in turbulence should be such that the touchdown is made with the aircraft in approximately level flight attitude. The pitch attitude at touchdown should be only enough to prevent the nosewheel from contacting the surface before the main wheels have touched the surface. Most WSC are designed so the front wheel is higher than the back wheels in this situation, but each WSC is different. This must be evaluated for each model. After touchdown, the pilot should reduce the throttle to idle and pull the control bar all the way to the chest to lower the nose and prevent the WSC aircraft from lifting off until it slows below the stall speed. The aircraft should be allowed to decelerate normally with the aerodynamic braking of the wing with the nose lowered, and assisted by the wheel brakes as required.

Crosswind Approaches and Landings

Many runways or landing areas are made such that landings must be made while the wind is blowing across rather than parallel to the landing direction. All pilots should be prepared to cope with these situations when they arise. The same basic principles and factors involved in a normal and power-on approach and landing apply to a crosswind approach and landing; therefore, only the additional procedures required for correcting for wind drift are discussed here.

Crosswind approaches and landings are more challenging than normal landings because of the wind drift in the pattern, crab angles on approach, and generally more mechanical turbulence for the final approach and roundout because of buildings and/or trees along the sides of the runway. Since mechanical turbulence would typically increase as the aircraft descends closer to the ground, power-on approaches and techniques for flying in turbulence should be utilized.

Crosswind Pattern Procedures

Since WSC aircraft typically fly tighter patterns, the pattern should be modified if the crosswind is in a direction pushing the WSC aircraft toward the runway. Refer to *Figure 11-24* for the following discussion. The normal or typical pattern downwind and base for calm winds is shown in blue. This pattern would also be used if there were an opposite crosswind from that shown blowing from the runway toward the base leg. If a strong crosswind (15 knots as an example, which is a limitation for many WSC) is noticed while flying the down wind or the runway wind indicators show this crosswind, at "A" the decision should be made to modify the pattern, making it wider by flying out to location "B." An extended downwind should then be made farther than the typical normal pattern to "C." This provides additional distance from the runway for the base leg, which will be at a much higher groundspeed than normal because the WSC is flying in a strong tailwind from point "C" to "D." The turn must be made at "D" to set up for final approach at "E" where there is a significant crab angle. From the final approach at "E" to touchdown, the pilot has sufficient time to establish the ground track in the center of the runway and evaluate if the landing should be completed, a go-around performed, or a different landing location selected with more favorable wind conditions.

Effects and Hazards of High Crosswinds for Approaches and Landings

Figure 11-24 illustrates a scenario that includes the effects and hazards of high wind, referencing groundspeed, high rates of turn, and power requirements for making downwind turns in close proximity to the ground.

During the downwind leg of the pattern, the pilot does not notice the strong wind blowing the WSC aircraft into the runway. From points A to W, the pilot reduces power as normal but does not crab into the wind and drifts with the wind toward the runway between points A and W. This leads the pilot to be closer to the runway when he or she turns onto base. The pilot turns onto base and is traveling at high groundspeed and the strong tailwind leads to the pilot passing the runway centerline normal final approach at point X. From points X to Y, the pilot starts the turn for final approach late because of the high groundspeed. The WSC aircraft past the runway centerline leads the pilot to increase the bank to make it back to the centerline. The previous errors lead the pilot into a high bank angle at low altitude pointed down in a rapid descent. This leads the pilot to apply full power at Y, which drives the WSC aircraft into ground at point Z.

The error chain that led to this accident could have been avoided at two primary points. First, the pilot should have noticed flying in a crosswind or indications of a strong crosswind on the runway from airport wind indicators at A. He or she should have then widened the pattern into the crosswind from A to B and performed the recommended crosswind procedure described earlier.

Second, if the pilot did not realize the high wind blowing to the runway until point X was reached, the wings should have been leveled and a go-around performed without trying to "make it" back to the runway as shown in the yellow "go-around" path shown on *Figure 11-24*.

For strong crosswinds beyond the capabilities of the pilot or limitations of the WSC aircraft, an alternate landing strip should be found. This could be another airport or landing strip that faces into the wind. An option at uncontrolled airports is to choose an alternate runway or even a taxiway that faces into the wind. Some of the larger airports with wide runways make it possible to land at an angle if needed; some are wide enough to land across the main runway. At towered airports, the air traffic controller can assist the pilot and provide an alternate landing area if requested.

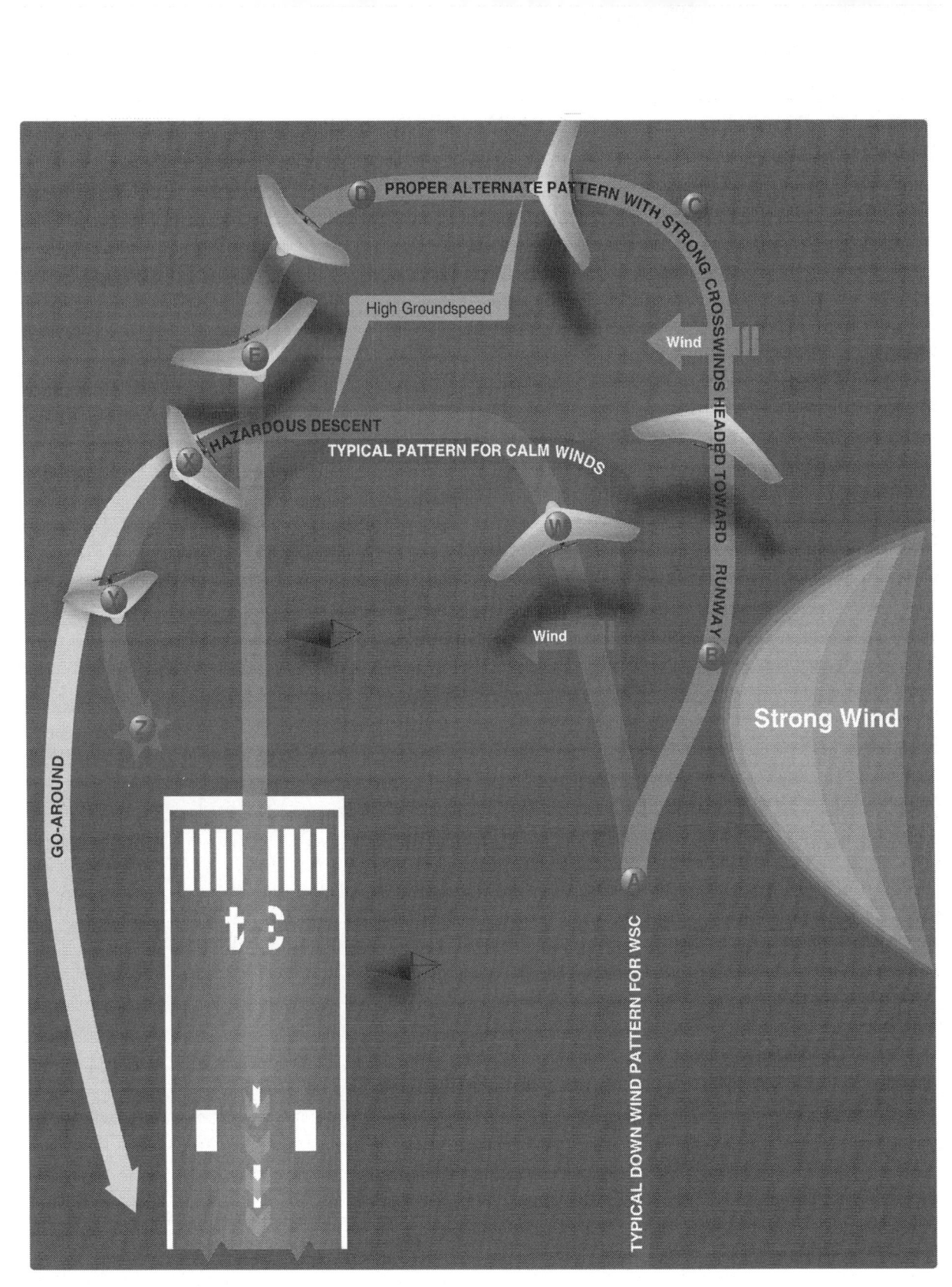

Figure 11-24. *Crosswind procedures and effects/hazards of high crosswinds.*

11-18

Crosswind Landings

When in final approach, the wind correction angle (crab angle) is established by heading toward the wind with the wings level so that the aircraft's ground track remains aligned with the centerline of the runway. *[Figure 11-25]* This crab angle is maintained all the way to touchdown, when the rear wheels hit first and rotate the carriage and wing around so the front wheel touches the ground with the carriage going straight. However, if in turbulent air or pitched forward during the touchdown, with the front wheel touching the ground first, the pilot should lightly control the steering of the front wheel to be headed in the direction the carriage is going. WSC carriage front landing gear typically has camber that tends to steer the front wheel naturally in the direction of travel, so a light touch on the front wheel as it touches the ground allows it to find its own direction of travel. Once the front wheel is on the ground, lower the nose to keep the WSC on the ground and steer as required down the center of the runway.

The procedure for the wing during the roundout is the same as that for normal and turbulent roundout and touchdowns. The exception is that after touchdown the windward wing should be lowered slightly so the wind cannot get under it to flip the WSC aircraft during later landing roll and taxi.

Maximum Crosswind Velocities

Takeoffs and landings in certain crosswind conditions are inadvisable and even dangerous. *[Figure 11-26]* If the crosswind is great enough, a hazardous landing condition may result. Therefore, takeoff and landing capabilities with respect to the reported surface wind conditions and available landing directions must be considered.

WSC crosswind limitations have been tested and are included in the POH. The headwind and crosswind components for a given situation can be determined by reference to a crosswind component chart. *[Figure 11-27]* It is imperative that pilots determine the maximum crosswind component of each aircraft flown and avoid operations in wind conditions that exceed the capability of the aircraft. The automatic weather observation system (AWOS) or automatic surface observation system (ASOS) at airports is useful in determining the measured velocity for this evaluation.

Common errors in the performance of crosswind approaches and landings include:

- Failure to recognize a strong crosswind blowing at the runway during the downwind leg;

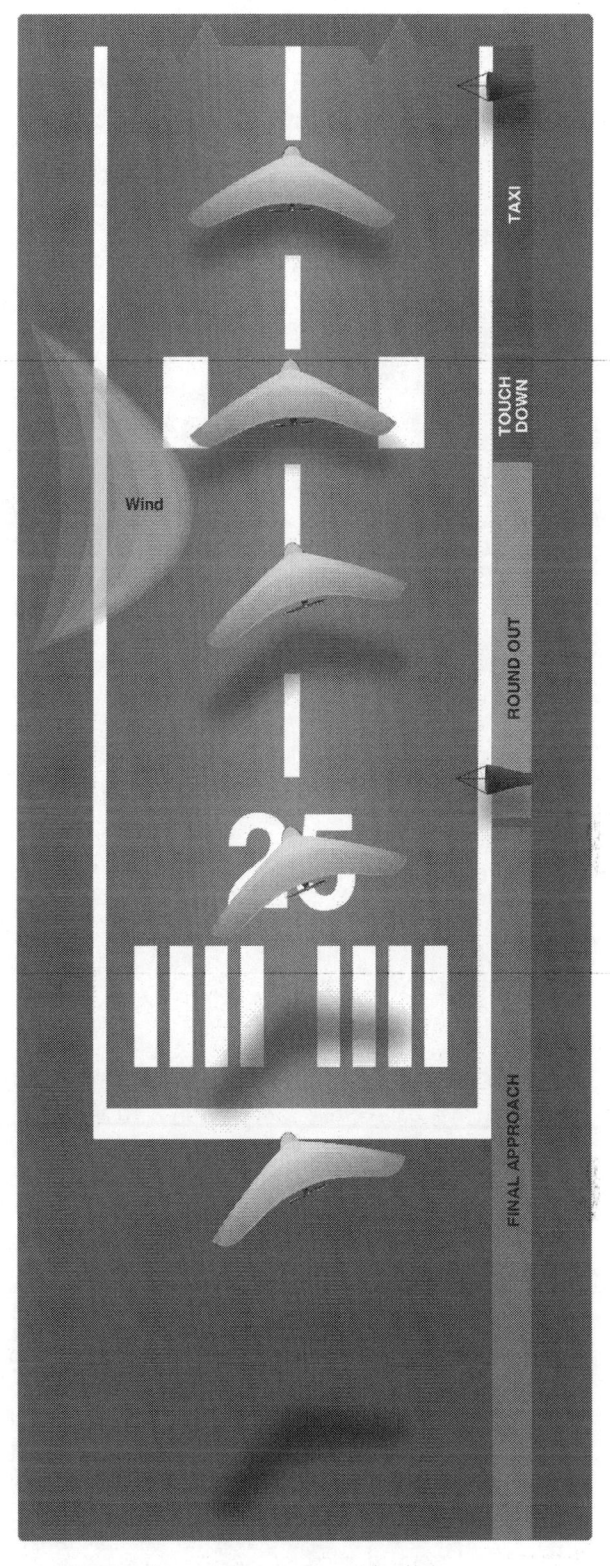

Figure 11-25. *Crosswind approach and landing.*

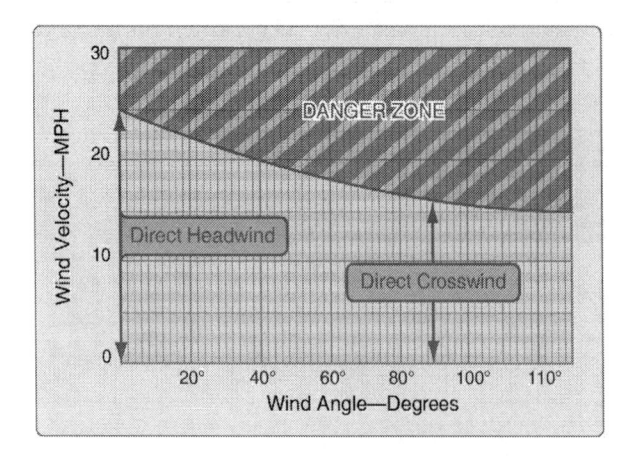

Figure 11-26. *Example of a crosswind limitations chart.*

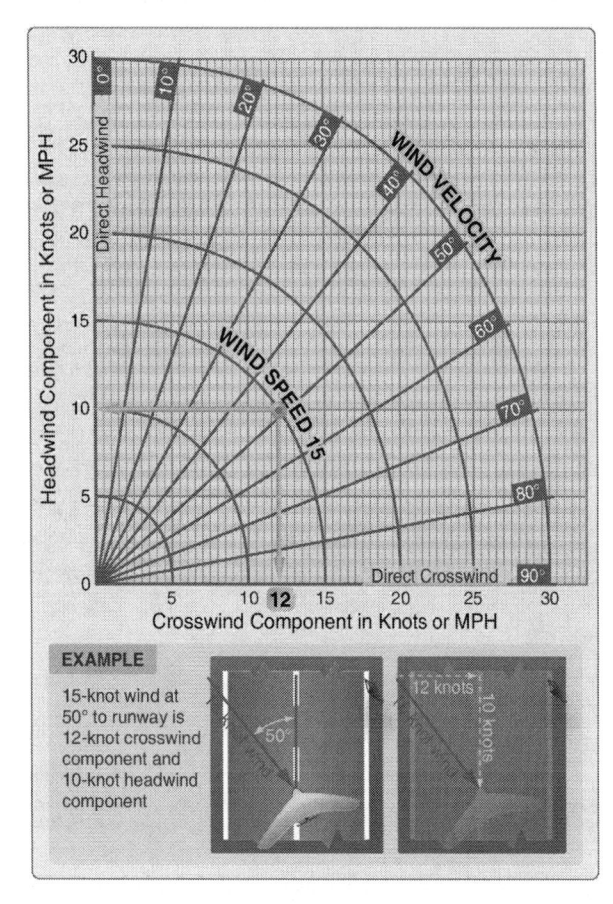

Figure 11-27. *Example of a crosswind component chart.*

- Failure to modify the pattern for strong crosswind conditions;
- Failure to do a go-around when the final approach to the runway is downwind of the runway centerline;
- Attempting to land in crosswinds that exceed the pilot's capabilities;
- Attempting to land in crosswinds that exceed the aircraft's maximum demonstrated crosswind component;
- Inadequate compensation for wind drift on the turn from base leg to final approach, resulting in undershooting or overshooting;
- Inadequate compensation for wind drift on final approach;
- Unstabilized approach;
- Touchdown while drifting;
- Excessive pressure on the nosewheel steering during touchdown;
- Excessive airspeed on touchdown;
- Failure to apply appropriate flight control inputs during rollout;
- Failure to maintain direction control on rollout; and
- Excessive braking.

Steep Approaches

A steep approach is a valuable maneuver for WSC aircraft. *[Figure 11-28]* It is better to be too high for an approach rather than too low for an approach in case the engine fails. A steep approach can be used to reach the landing point easily; if too low, the aircraft lands short. Steep approaches are used routinely by many pilots to help ensure making the landing point if the engine fails.

Figure 11-28. *Pilot view of runway where a steep approach would be required.*

The two types of procedures (or a combination thereof) used are based on the angle of descent required. To perform a steep approach, evaluation of the situation considers the angle of descent required to land at or within 400 feet of a specified point in which the steep angle or alternating turns are utilized. For all steep approaches, the throttle is brought to idle.

Steep Angle

For situations in which an increase in the descent angle is needed for the intended landing spot, the normal procedure is to increase speed above the best L_D speed in order to descend. The greater the speed is, the greater the parasitic drag and descent angle.

Each design has different descent rates based on the parasitic drag of the wing and carriage. For example, a single surface with an exposed crossbar wing and a stick carriage (no streamlined cowling) increases the descent angle quickly because of the dramatic increases in drag with increased speed. A double surface wing with a streamlined carriage does not develop parasitic drag as fast with increased speed and is less able to achieve a steep angle with increased speed. The pilot should understand that this characteristic is unique to the make/model being flown. This steep angle technique is the optimum steep approach procedure because the aircraft is lined up on the runway and the pilot can easily judge the glideslope using the stabilized approach method covered earlier. *[Figure 11-29]*

Increase speed as required to obtain the descent angle for the intended touchdown point. Use the stabilized approach technique to obtain the increased angle for the aiming point. At the higher speeds and greater descent, slow to the normal approach speed, intersect the normal final approach path, and perform the landing required for that particular situation (calm air/crosswinds/turbulent air). As the student gains proficiency at steep approach techniques, the altitude to transition from the high speed steep angle to the normal approach speed can be lowered and eventually combined into one continuous roundout for landing started at a higher altitude than the normal approach and roundout. For this situation, note that with the increased speed the roundout covers additional distance that should be accounted for as the speed is decreased.

Alternating Turns

If at a height at which a steep approach is necessary, but the aircraft is too high to obtain an angle steep enough to make the intended landing area, alternating turns can be made to decrease altitude to a point at which the steep angle technique could be applied for the remainder of the descent. These alternating turns should be performed no lower than 400 feet above ground level (AGL). The turns should be an equal distance from the runway centerline extension to keep track and maintain the relative position on the runway centerline. The bank and direction of turns across the runway centerline should be determined by how much altitude must be lost to position the WSC aircraft for utilization of the steep angle technique for the remainder of the steep approach, if required. *[Figure 11-30]*

Power-Off Accuracy Approaches

Power-off accuracy approaches are made by gliding with the engine idling through a specific pattern to a touchdown beyond and within 200 feet of a designated line or mark on the runway. The objective is to instill in the pilot the judgment and knowledge of procedures necessary for accurate flight, without power, to a safe landing. This simulates procedures for an emergency engine-out situation. The ability to estimate the distance an aircraft glides to a landing is the real basis of all power-off accuracy approaches and landings. This largely determines the amount of maneuvering that may be done from a given altitude. In addition to the ability to estimate distance, the ability to maintain the proper glide while maneuvering the aircraft is required.

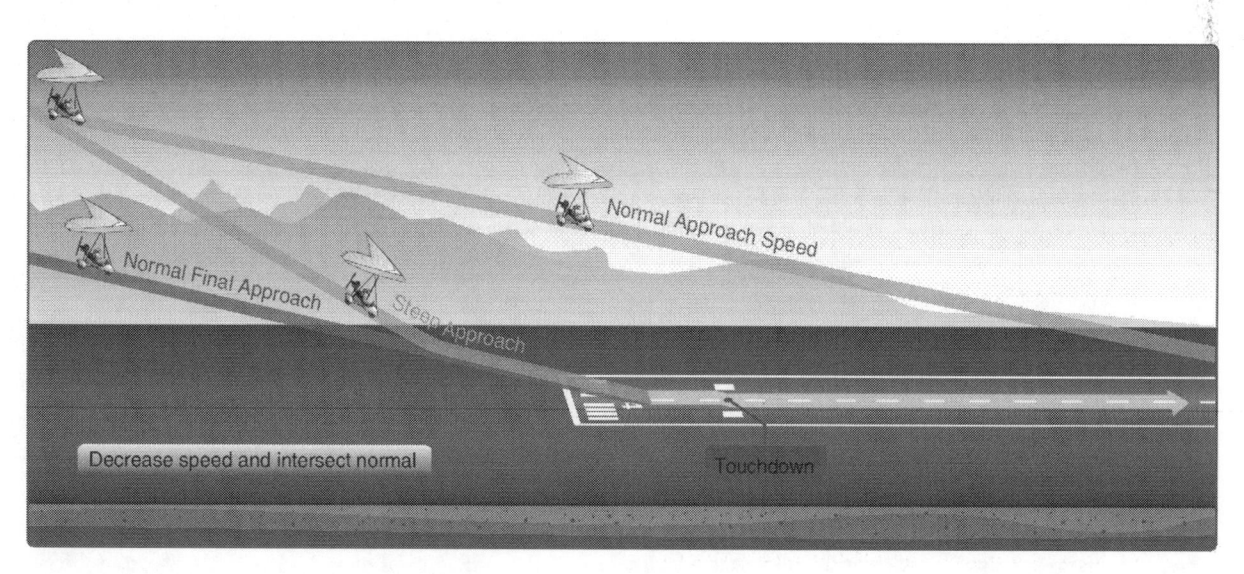

Figure 11-29. *Steep approach—steep angle technique.*

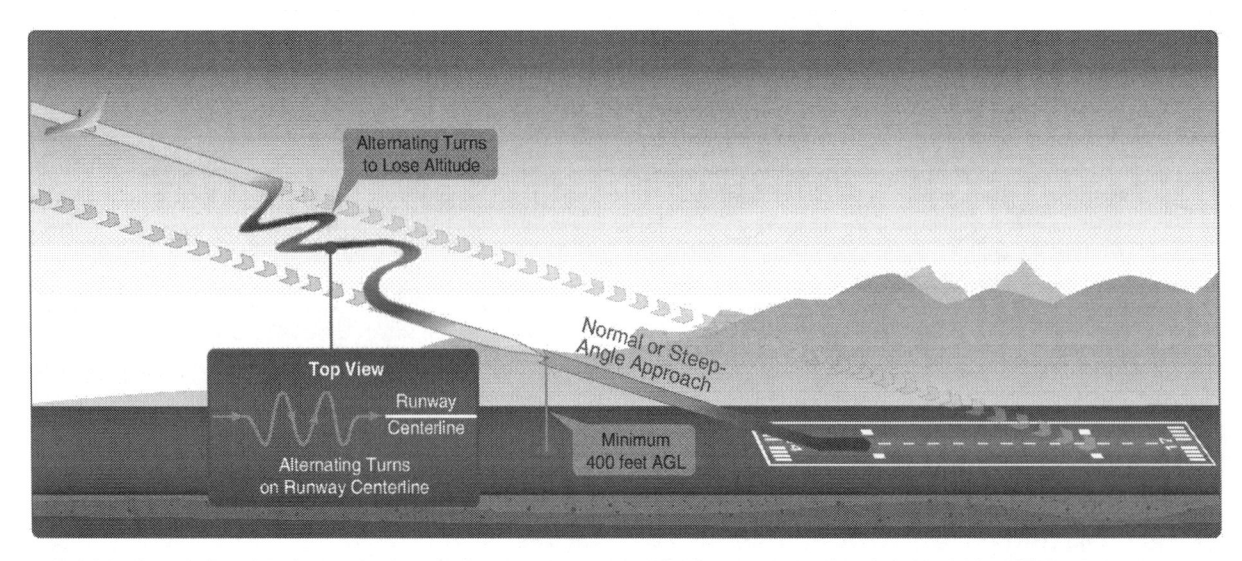

Figure 11-30. *Alternating turns used if too high to lose enough altitude to position for a normal or steep-angle approach.*

With experience and practice, altitudes up to approximately 1,000 feet can be estimated with fair accuracy, while above this level the accuracy in judgment of height above the ground decreases since features tend to merge. The best aid in perfecting the ability to judge height above this altitude is altimeter indications and associating them with the general appearance of the Earth.

The judgment of altitude in feet, hundreds of feet, or thousands of feet is not as important as the ability to estimate gliding angle and its resultant distance. The pilot who knows the normal glide angle of the aircraft can estimate with reasonable accuracy the approximate spot along a given ground path at which the aircraft lands, regardless of altitude. The pilot who also has the ability to estimate altitude accurately can judge how much maneuvering is possible during the glide, which is important to the choice of landing areas in an actual emergency.

Unlike a normal approach in which power is available when needed, for a power-off approach the power is fixed at the idle setting. Pitch attitude is adjusted to control the airspeed, which also changes the glide or descent angle. As discussed in the basic flight maneuvers descents and the steep approach maneuver, lowering the nose to a speed above the best glide angle causes the descent angle to steepen. If the airspeed is too high, raise the nose, and when the airspeed is too low, lower the nose. If the pitch attitude is raised too high, the aircraft settles rapidly due to low airspeed and insufficient lift. For this reason, never try to stretch a glide to reach the desired landing spot.

Uniform approach patterns such as the 90°, 180°, or 360° power-off approaches are described further in this chapter. Practice in these approaches provides the pilot with a basis on which to develop judgment in gliding distance and in planning an approach. The 180° power-off approach from pattern altitude should be the normal landing procedure in calm winds. This should become routine and develop the ability to accurately judge the landing for an engine-out situation. Remember, the steep approach technique can always be used if the aircraft is a little high, but do not stretch a glide by lowering the speed if too low.

The basic procedure in these approaches involves closing the throttle at a given altitude and gliding to a key position. This position, like the pattern itself, must not be allowed to become the primary objective; it is merely a convenient point in the air from which the pilot can judge whether the glide safely terminates at the desired spot. The selected key position should be one that is appropriate for the available altitude and the wind condition. From the key position, the pilot must constantly evaluate the situation. It must be emphasized that, although accurate spot touchdowns are important, safe and properly executed approaches and landings are vital. The pilot must never sacrifice a good approach or landing just to land on the desired spot.

All power-off approaches must be practiced to avoid interfering with normal traffic flow at busy airports, so the place and timing must be evaluated by the instructor to prevent airport traffic conflicts. This is especially important for the 360° power-off approach.

90° Power-Off Approach

The 90° power-off approach is made from a base leg and requires only a 90° turn onto the final approach. The approach path may be varied by positioning the base leg closer to or farther away from the approach end of the runway according to wind conditions. *[Figure 11-31]* The glide from the key

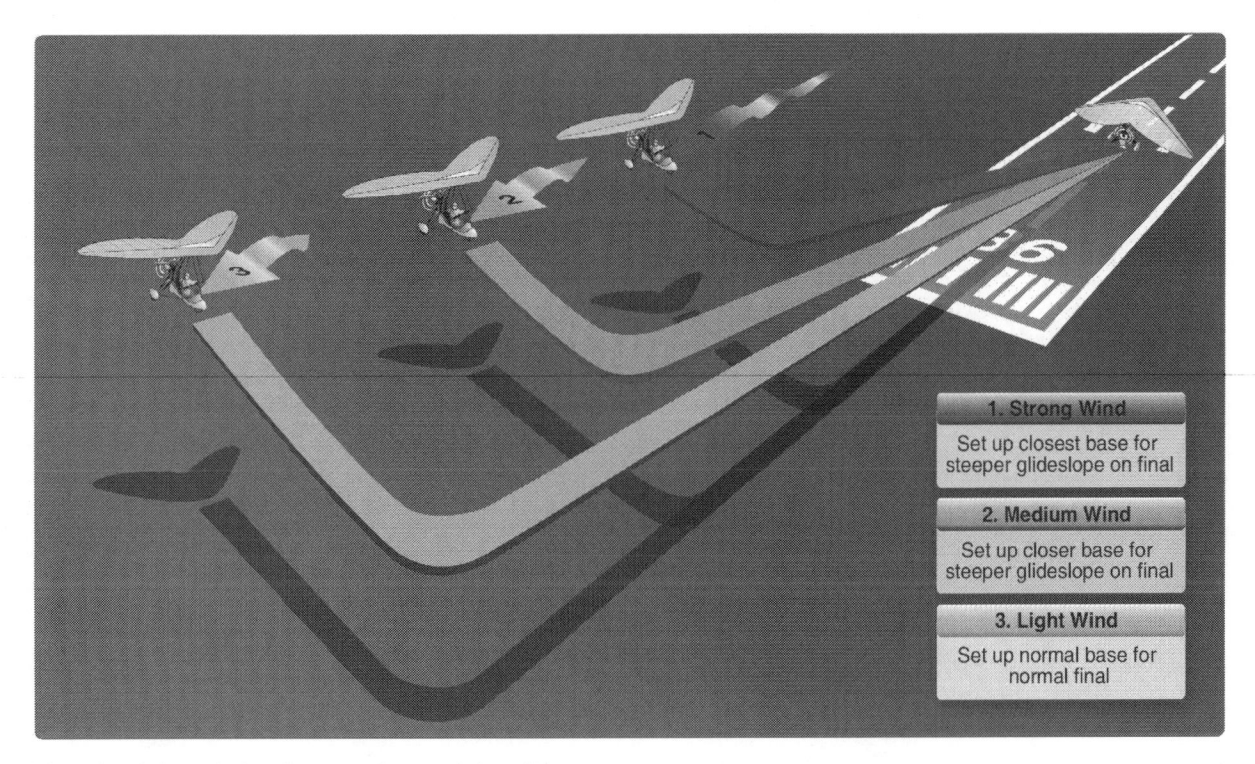

Figure 11-31. *Plan the base leg according to wind conditions.*

position on the base leg through the 90° turn to the final approach is the final part of all accuracy landing maneuvers. Steep approach procedures may be used during the final approach if needed.

The 90° power-off approach usually begins from a rectangular pattern below normal pattern altitude as long as this point is above 500 feet AGL. The before-landing checklist should be completed on the downwind leg.

After a medium-banked turn onto the base leg is completed and key position obtained, the throttle should be completely reduced to idle and the airspeed set to approach speed. *[Figure 11-32]* At this position, the intended landing spot appears to be on a 45° angle from the aircraft's nose.

The pilot can determine the strength and direction of the wind from the amount of crab necessary to hold the desired ground track on the base leg. This helps in planning the turn onto the final approach. The base-to-final turn should be planned and accomplished so that upon rolling out of the turn the aircraft is aligned with the runway centerline. Slight adjustments in pitch attitude may be necessary to control the glide angle and airspeed. However, never try to stretch the glide to reach the desired landing spot. After the final approach glide has been established, full attention is given to making a good, safe landing rather than concentrating on the selected landing spot. In any event, it is better to execute a good landing 200 feet from the spot than to make a poor landing precisely on the spot.

180° Power-Off Approach

The 180° power-off approach is executed by gliding with the power off from a given point on a downwind leg to a preselected landing spot. *[Figure 11-33]* It is an extension of the principles involved in the 90° power-off approach just described. Its objective is to further develop judgment in estimating distances and glide ratios, in that the aircraft is flown without power from a higher altitude and through a 90° turn to reach the base-leg position at a proper altitude for executing the 90° approach.

The 180° power-off approach requires more planning and judgment than the 90° power-off approach. In the execution of 180° power-off approaches, the aircraft is flown on a downwind heading parallel to the landing runway. The altitude from which this type of approach should be started in the downwind leg is at a normal pattern altitude. This power-off approach should be the normal procedure except for normal light wind landings, the throttle can be brought back to idle between the downwind leg key position and the turn onto the base leg depending on the height and distance from the runway. When abreast of or opposite the desired landing spot or a location closer to the turn onto base if the WSC is further from the runway, the throttle should be closed and the WSC aircraft set to the best glide speed. The point at which the throttle is closed is the downwind key position.

11-23

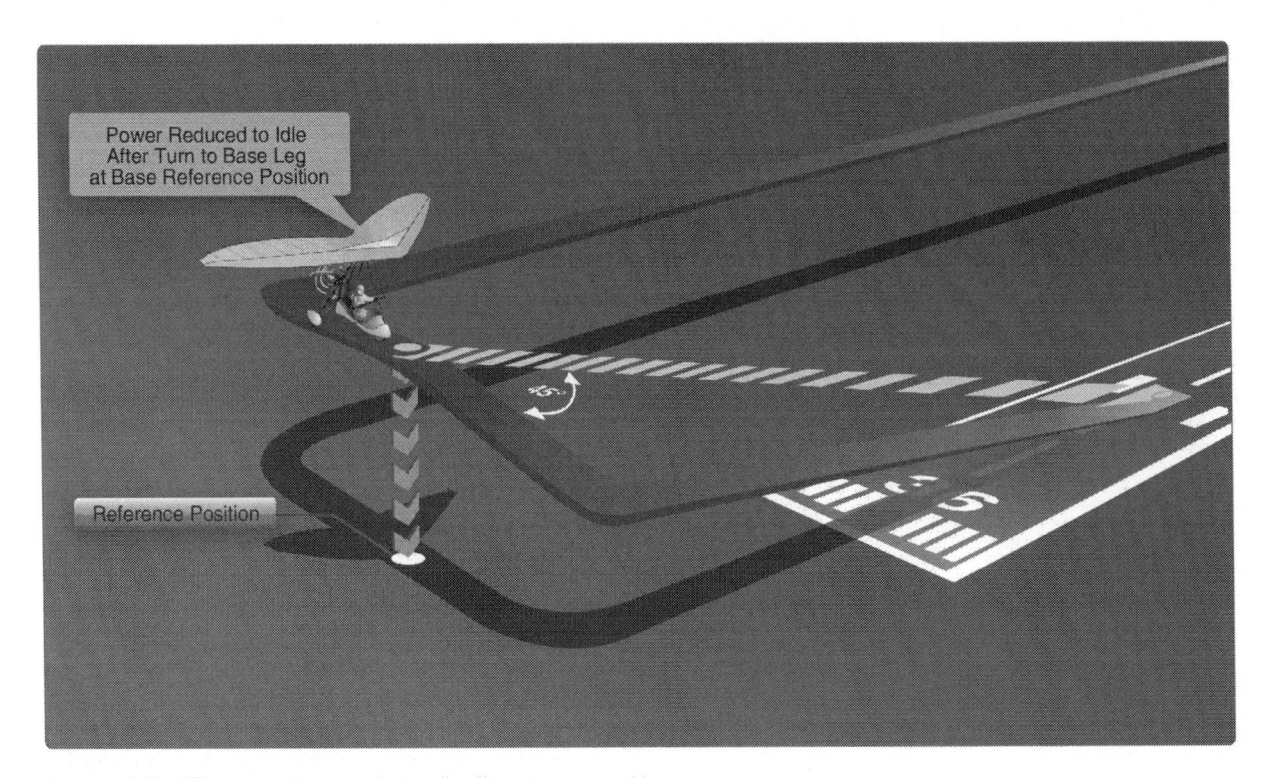

Figure 11-32. *90° power-off approach showing 45° reference position.*

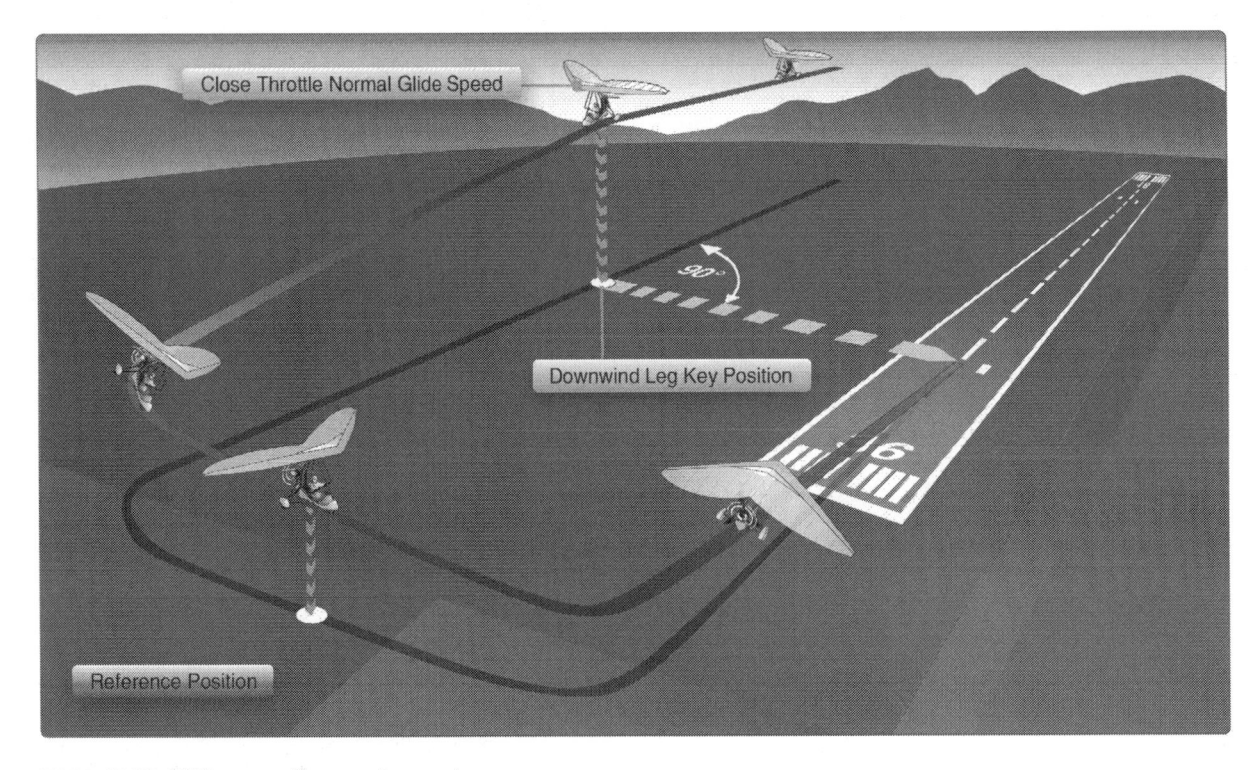

Figure 11-33. *180° power-off approach example.*

The turn from the downwind leg to the base leg should be a uniform turn with a medium or slightly steeper bank. The degree of bank and amount of this initial turn depends upon the glide angle of the aircraft and the velocity of the wind. Again, the base leg should be positioned as needed for the altitude or wind condition. Position the base leg to conserve or dissipate altitude to reach the desired landing spot. The turn onto the base leg should be made at an altitude high enough and close enough to permit the aircraft to glide to what would normally be the base key position in a 90° power-off approach.

Although the key position is important, it must not be overemphasized or considered as a fixed point on the ground. Many inexperienced pilots have the false understanding of it as a particular landmark, such as a tree, crossroad, or other visual reference to be reached at a certain altitude. This leaves the pilot at a total loss any time such objects are not present. Both altitude and geographical location should be varied as much as practical to eliminate any such conception. After reaching the base key position, the approach and landing are the same as in the 90° power-off approach.

360° Power-Off Approach

The 360° power-off approach is one in which the aircraft glides through a 360° change of direction to the preselected landing spot. The entire pattern is designed to be circular but the turn may be shallowed, steepened, or discontinued at any point to adjust the accuracy of the flightpath. The 360° approach is started from a position over the approach end of the landing runway or slightly to the side of it, with the aircraft headed in the proposed landing direction. *[Figure 11-34]* It is usually initiated from approximately 2,000 feet or more above the ground—where the wind may vary significantly from that at lower altitudes. This must be taken into account when maneuvering the aircraft to a point from which a 90° or 180° power-off approach can be completed.

After the throttle is closed over the intended point of landing, the proper glide speed should immediately be established and a medium-banked turn made in the desired direction to arrive at the downwind reference position opposite the intended landing spot. The altitude at the downwind reference position should be approximately 1,000 feet above the ground. After reaching that point, the turn should be continued to arrive at a base-leg key position.

The angle of bank can be varied as needed throughout the pattern to correct for wind conditions and to align the aircraft with the final approach. The turn to final should be completed at a minimum altitude of 300 feet above the terrain.

Common errors in the performance of power-off accuracy approaches include:

- Downwind leg too far from the runway/landing area;

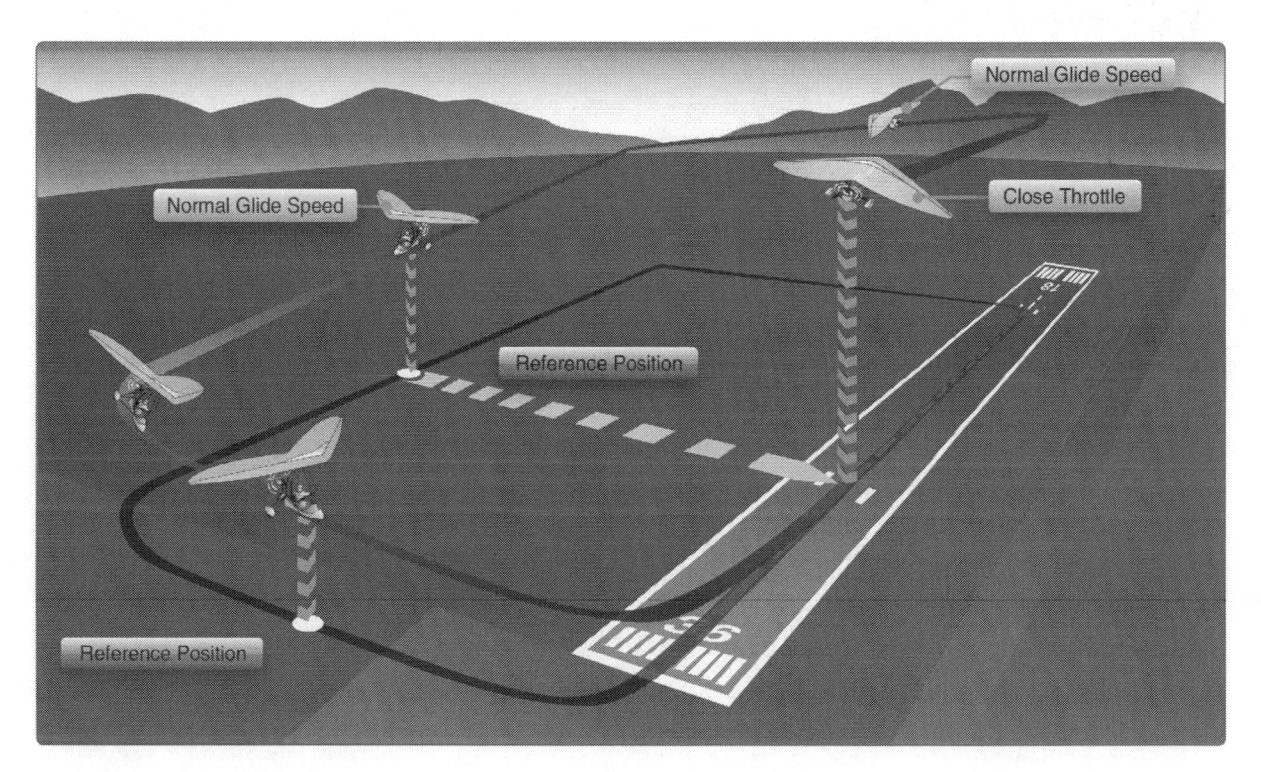

Figure 11-34. *360° power-off approach.*

11-25

- Overextension of downwind leg resulting from tailwind;
- Inadequate compensation for wind drift on base leg;
- Attempting to "stretch" the glide during undershoot;
- Forcing the aircraft onto the runway in order to avoid overshooting the designated landing spot.

Emergency Approaches and Landings (Simulated Engine Out)

From time to time on dual flights, the instructor should give surprise simulated emergency landings by retarding the throttle and calling "simulated emergency landing." The objective of these simulated emergency landings is to develop pilot accuracy, judgment, planning, procedures, and confidence.

When the instructor calls "simulated emergency landing," the pilot should immediately establish the best glide speed and the aircraft trimmed (if so equipped) to maintain that speed.

A constant gliding speed should initially be maintained because variations of gliding speed nullify all attempts at accuracy in judgment of gliding distance and the landing spot. The many variables, such as altitude, obstruction, wind direction, landing direction, landing surface and gradient, and landing distance requirements of the aircraft determine the pattern and approach procedures to use.

Utilizing any combination of normal gliding maneuvers, from wings level to steep turns, the pilot should eventually arrive at the normal reference position at a normal traffic pattern altitude for the selected landing area. From this point on, the approach is as nearly as possible a normal power-off approach as described previously in the Power-off Accuracy Approaches section. Steep approach techniques may be used for final approach if required.

If the student is high above the desired emergency landing area, large low-banked circles above the area should be made and widened or narrowed as required to provide downwind and final reference points for the landing. *[Figure 11-35]*

Despite the greater choice of fields afforded by higher altitudes, the inexperienced pilot may be inclined to delay making a decision and, despite considerable altitude in which to maneuver, errors in maneuvering and estimation of glide distance may develop.

All pilots should learn to determine the wind direction and estimate its speed from any means available. This could be a feel of the wind drift on the WSC, GPS ground speed versus true airspeed, and visual indicators such as the windsock at

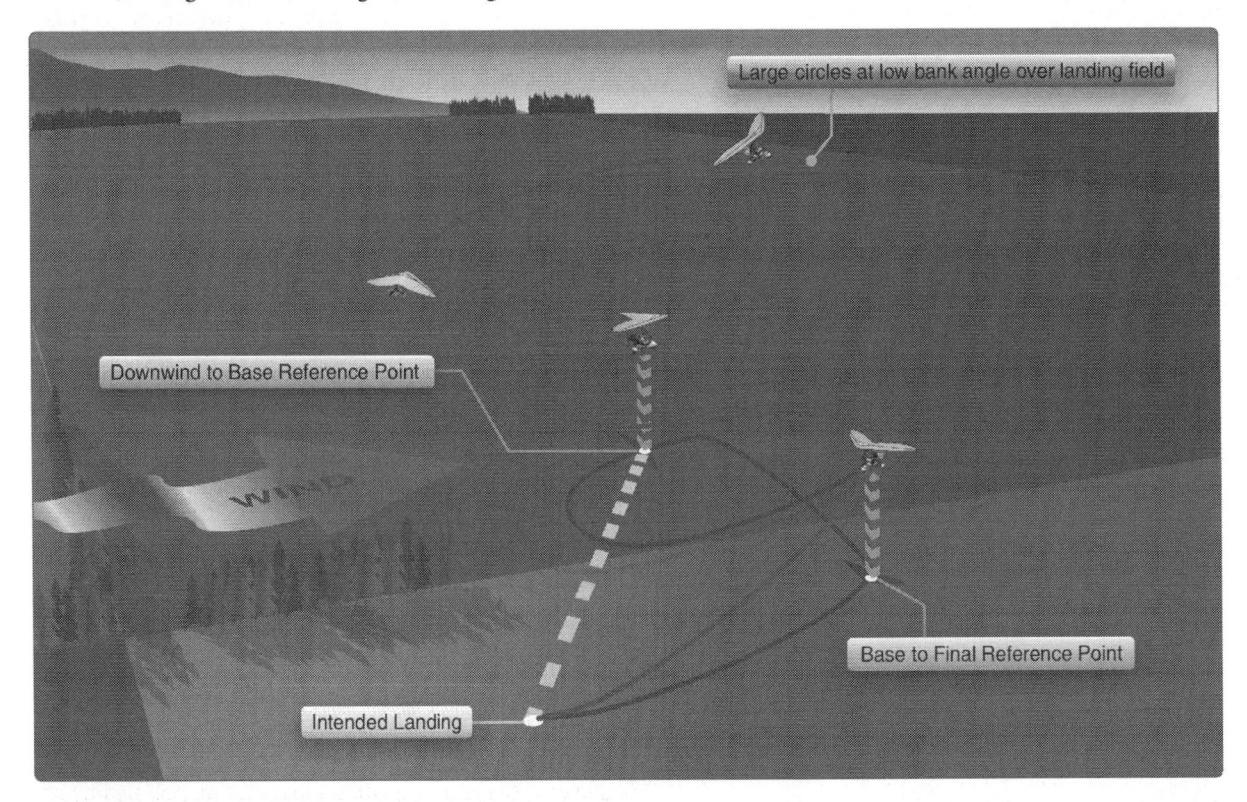

Figure 11-35. *If high enough over the intended landing area, remain over intended landing area with large low-banked circles to establish reference points for landing.*

the airport, smoke from factories or houses, dust, fires, flags, ripples on water surfaces, and windmills.

Once a field has been selected, the student pilot should always be required to indicate it to the instructor. Normally, the student should be required to plan and fly a pattern for landing on the field first elected until the instructor terminates the simulated emergency landing. This gives the instructor an opportunity to explain and correct any errors; it also gives the student an opportunity to see the results of the errors. However, if the student realizes during the approach that a poor field has been selected—one that would obviously result in disaster if a landing were to be made—and there is a more advantageous field within gliding distance, a change to the better field should be permitted. The hazards involved in these last-minute decisions, such as excessive maneuvering at very low altitudes, should be thoroughly explained by the instructor. Steep approaches, varying the position of the base leg, and varying the turn onto final approach should be stressed as ways of correcting for misjudgment of altitude and glide angle.

Eagerness to get down is one of the most common faults of inexperienced pilots during simulated emergency landings. In giving way to this, they forget about speed and arrive at the edge of the field with too much speed to permit a safe landing. Too much speed may be just as dangerous as too little; it results in excessive floating and overshooting the desired landing spot. It should be impressed on the students that they cannot dive at a field and expect to land on it if it is short.

During all simulated emergency landings, the engine should be kept warm and cleared. During a simulated emergency landing, the student should have control of the foot throttle and the instructor should have control of a second throttle. The instructor should tell the student to increase the throttle when needed, but the instructor should be ready with the second throttle in case the student does not apply it as required.

Every simulated emergency landing approach should be terminated as soon as it can be determined whether a safe landing could have been made. In no case should it be continued to a point where it creates an undue hazard or an annoyance to persons or property on the ground.

In addition to flying the aircraft from the point of simulated engine failure to where a reasonable safe landing could be made, the student should also be taught certain emergency flight deck procedures. The habit of performing these flight deck procedures should be developed to such an extent that, when an engine failure actually occurs, the student checks the critical items that would be necessary to get the engine operating again while selecting a field and planning an approach. Combining the two operations—accomplishing emergency procedures and planning and flying the approach—is difficult for the student during early training in emergency landings.

There are definite steps and procedures to be followed in a simulated emergency landing. Although they may differ somewhat from the procedures used in an actual emergency, they should be learned thoroughly by the student and each step called out to the instructor. The use of a checklist is strongly recommended. Most aircraft manufacturers provide a checklist of the appropriate items.

Critical items to be checked should include the quantity of fuel and the position of the magneto switch. Many actual emergency landings could have been prevented if the pilots had developed the habit of checking these critical items during flight training to the extent that it carried over into later flying.

Faulty Approaches and Landings

Low Final Approach
When the base leg is too low, insufficient power is used, or the velocity of the wind is misjudged, sufficient altitude may be lost, which causes the aircraft to be well below the proper final approach path. In such a situation, the pilot would need to apply considerable power to maintain or gain altitude as required to fly the aircraft (at an excessively low altitude) up to the runway threshold. When the proper approach path has been intercepted, the correct approach attitude should be reestablished, the power reduced, and a stabilized approach maintained. *[Figure 11-36]* Do not increase the pitch attitude without increasing the power since the aircraft decelerates rapidly and may approach the critical AOA and stall. If there is any doubt about the approach being safely completed, it is advisable to execute an immediate go-around.

High Final Approach
When the final approach is too high, perform a steep approach as required for the height above the landing spot. Refer to the steep approach section earlier in this chapter.

Slow Final Approach
When the aircraft is flown at slower-than-normal airspeed on the final approach, pilot determination of the rate of sink (descent) and the height of roundout is difficult. During an excessively slow approach, the wing is operating near the critical AOA and, depending on the pitch attitude changes and control usage, the aircraft may stall or sink rapidly and contact the ground with a hard impact.

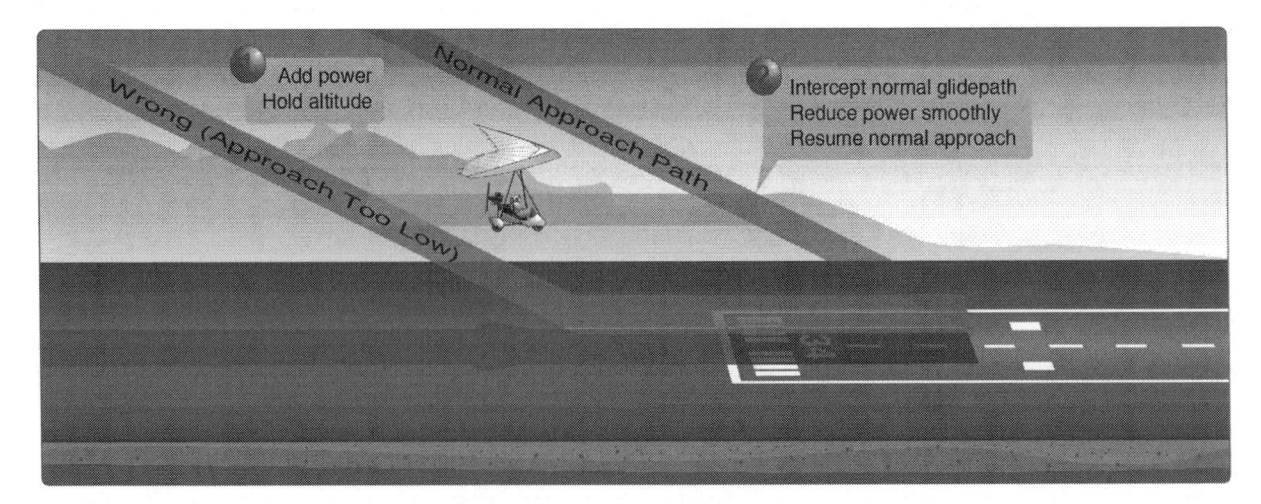

Figure 11-36. *Right and wrong methods of correction for low final approach.*

Whenever a low-speed approach is noted, the pilot should apply power and accelerate the aircraft to reduce the sink rate to prevent a stall. This should be done while still at a high enough altitude to reestablish the correct approach airspeed and attitude. If too slow and too low, it is best to execute a go-around.

Use of Power

Power can be used if required during the approach and roundout to compensate for errors in judgment. The pilot should be ready to use the foot throttle while managing the energy throughout the landing, utilizing energy management procedures for the current landing conditions. Power can be added to reduce the descent rate if needed; thus, the descent can be slowed to an acceptable rate. After the aircraft has touched down, it is necessary to close the throttle to remove additional thrust and lift allowing the aircraft to stay on the ground.

High Roundout

Sometimes when the aircraft appears to stop moving downward temporarily, the roundout has been made too rapidly and the aircraft is flying level, too high and too slow above the runway. Continuing the roundout would further reduce the airspeed, resulting in an increase in AOA to the critical angle. This would result in the aircraft stalling and dropping hard onto the runway. To prevent the hard drop, pitch attitude should be reduced slightly to increase speed to approach speed while throttle is added to maintain altitude. After speed has been increased and altitude maintained, the throttle and speed can both be reduced smoothly and gradually for a gradual descent with a normal roundout and touchdown.

Although speed is needed after the high roundout is noticed in order to be corrected, the power application must be enough to remain level and not initially descend as the speed is increased. Energy management proficiency is critical. If too little throttle is added, the momentary decrease in lift that would result from lowering the nose and decreasing the AOA may be so great that the aircraft might contact the ground with the nosewheel first, which could then collapse. As for all landing maneuvers that are questionable and the outcome is uncertain, it is recommended that a go-around be executed.

Late or Rapid Roundout

Starting the roundout too late or pushing the control forward too rapidly to prevent the aircraft from touching down prematurely balloons the aircraft up above the runway. Suddenly increasing the AOA and stalling the aircraft during a roundout is a dangerous situation since it may cause the aircraft to land extremely hard on the main landing gear and then bounce back into the air.

Recovery from this situation requires prompt and positive application of power and a lowering of the nose to increase speed prior to occurrence of the stall. This may be followed by a normal landing, if sufficient runway is available, similar to the high roundout discussed above—otherwise the pilot should immediately execute a go-around.

Floating During Roundout

If the airspeed on final approach is excessive, it usually results in the aircraft floating in ground effect. This is not a problem if there is plenty of runway and if the pilot floats with the wheels just inches above the surface. Simply maintain this position inches above the runway, slowly rounding out as required until the speed bleeds off for a normal touchdown. If conditions are turbulent, the nose can be lowered gradually and the aircraft flown onto the ground, as discussed earlier in the landing in turbulence procedures.

If the aircraft is well past the desired landing point and the available runway is insufficient, perform a go-around immediately.

Ballooning During Roundout

If the pilot misjudges the rate of sink during a landing and thinks the aircraft is descending faster than it should, there is a tendency to increase the pitch attitude and AOA too rapidly. This not only stops the descent, but actually starts the aircraft climbing. This climbing during the roundout is known as ballooning. Ballooning can be dangerous because the height above the ground is increasing and the aircraft may be rapidly approaching a stall. The altitude gained in each instance depends on the airspeed or the speed with which the pitch attitude is increased.

When ballooning is slight, the nose should be lowered to increase speed and return to a gradual descent. Recovery procedures are similar to those for rounding out too high: lowering the nose slightly and increasing the throttle to remain level. Then, the pilot gradually reduces throttle and speed for a controlled descent rate with the throttle at idle during touchdown.

When ballooning is excessive, it is best to execute a go-around immediately; do not attempt to salvage the landing. Full power must be applied and the nose lowered before the aircraft enters a stalled condition.

The pilot must be extremely cautious of ballooning when there is a crosswind present because the crosswind correction may be inadvertently released or it may become inadequate. Because of the lower airspeed after ballooning, the crosswind affects the aircraft more. Consequently, crabbing has to be increased to compensate for the increased drift. It is imperative that the pilot makes certain that directional control is maintained. If there is any doubt, or the aircraft starts to drift, execute a go-around.

Bouncing During Touchdown

When the aircraft contacts the ground with a sharp impact as the result of an improper attitude or an excessive rate of sink, it can bounce back into the air. The severity of the bounce depends on the airspeed at the moment of contact and the rebound attitude the WSC aircraft. It can increase the AOA and, in addition to bouncing, be lifted. It can rebound in a yawed condition and/or nose up or down. Design and situational factors create their own unique scenarios.

The corrective action for a bounce is the same as for ballooning and similarly depends on its severity. When the bounce is very slight and there is not an extreme change in the aircraft's pitch attitude, a follow-up landing may be executed by applying sufficient power to cushion the subsequent touchdown and smoothly adjusting the pitch to the proper touchdown attitude.

Extreme caution and attention must be exercised any time a bounce occurs, but particularly when there is a crosswind. During the bounce, the wind causes the aircraft to roll with the wind, thus exposing even more surface to the crosswind and drifting the aircraft more rapidly.

When a bounce is severe, the safest procedure is to execute a go-around immediately. No attempt to salvage the landing should be made. Full power should be applied while simultaneously maintaining directional control and lowering the nose to a safe climb attitude. The go-around procedure should be continued even though the aircraft may descend and another bounce may be encountered. It would be extremely foolish to attempt a landing from a bad bounce since airspeed diminishes very rapidly in the nose-high attitude, and a stall may occur before a subsequent touchdown could be made.

Porpoising

In a bounced landing that is improperly recovered, the aircraft comes in nose first, setting off a series of motions that imitate the jumps and dives of a porpoise—hence the name. The problem is improper aircraft attitude at touchdown, sometimes caused by inattention, not knowing where the ground is, or forcing the aircraft onto the runway at an exceedingly high descent rate.

Porpoising can also be caused by improper airspeed control. Usually, if an approach is too fast, the aircraft floats and the pilot tries to force it on the runway when the aircraft still tends to fly. A gust of wind, a bump in the runway, or even a slight push on the control bar sends the aircraft aloft again.

The corrective action for a porpoise is the same as for a bounce, and similarly depends on its severity. When it is very slight with no extreme change in the aircraft's pitch attitude, a follow-up landing may be executed by applying sufficient power to cushion the subsequent touchdown, and smoothly adjusting the pitch to the proper touchdown attitude.

When a porpoise is severe, the safest procedure is to execute an immediate go-around. In a severe porpoise, the aircraft's pitch oscillations can become progressively worse until the aircraft strikes the runway nose first with sufficient force to collapse the nose gear. Pilot attempts to correct a severe porpoise with flight control and power inputs will most likely be untimely and out of sequence with the oscillations, only making the situation worse. No attempt to salvage the landing should be made. Full power should be applied while simultaneously maintaining directional control and lowering the nose to a safe climb attitude.

Wing Rising After Touchdown

In all the proper landing techniques except the soft field, the nose is lowered after the front wheel touches to put a negative AOA on the wing and keep the WSC aircraft on the ground. However, there may be instances when landing in a crosswind that a wing wants to rise during the after-landing roll. This may occur whether or not there is a loss of directional control depending on the amount of crosswind and the degree of corrective action.

Any time an aircraft is rolling on the ground in a crosswind condition, the upwind wing is receiving a greater force from the wind than the downwind wing. This causes a lift differential. Also, as the upwind wing rises, there is an increase in the AOA which increases lift on the upwind wing rolling the aircraft downwind.

When the effects of these two factors are great enough, the upwind wing may rise even though directional control is maintained. If no correction is applied, it is possible that the upwind wing rises sufficiently to cause the downwind wing to strike the ground.

In a crosswind, the windward wing should be lowered slightly as a preventive measure to avoid it from lifting. But in the event a wing starts to rise during the landing roll, the pilot should immediately lower the nose while lowering the wing. The wing should be lowered as soon as possible. The further a wing is allowed to rise before taking corrective action, the more wing surface is exposed to the force of the crosswind.

Hard Landing

When the aircraft contacts the ground during landings, its vertical speed is instantly reduced to zero. Unless provisions are made to slow this vertical speed and cushion the impact of touchdown, the force of contact with the ground may be so great it could cause structural damage to the aircraft.

The purpose of pneumatic tires, shock-absorbing landing gears, and other devices is to cushion the impact and to increase the time in which the aircraft's vertical descent is stopped. The importance of this cushion may be understood from the computation that a 6-inch free fall on landing is roughly equal to a descent of 340 feet per minute. Within a fraction of a second, the aircraft must be slowed from this rate of vertical descent to zero without damage.

During this time, the landing gear together with some aid from the lift of the wings must supply whatever force is needed to counteract the force of the aircraft's inertia and weight. The lift decreases rapidly as the aircraft's forward speed is decreased and the force on the landing gear increases by the impact of touchdown. When the descent stops, the lift is almost zero leaving only the landing gear to carry both aircraft weight and inertia force. The load imposed at the instant of touchdown may easily be three or four times the actual weight of the aircraft, depending on the severity of contact. After a hard landing, the WSC carriage and wing should be inspected by qualified personnel for airworthiness.

Chapter Summary

All landings should consist of evaluating the wind and conditions so a proper base and final are planned to land at or beyond the intended point. After the final approach to the runway, the roundout is started about 10 to 15 feet high and is a gradual descent until the rear wheels are inches above the surface. The rotation is continued as the speed bleeds off to maintain the wheels one to two inches above the runway until minimum controlled airspeed at which the WSC aircraft settles to the ground. A roundout that is too fast, or ballooning where altitude is gained during the landing, is a common mistake and should be avoided.

The best landing technique for light wind conditions is with power brought to idle during the downwind leg of the pattern before the turn to base. Proficiency in power-off accuracy landings with 90° turns, 180° turns, 360° turns, and circling from above are all important safety procedures.

Crosswinds or landing in turbulence requires more energy, including power-on approaches with higher airspeeds. In these conditions, the WSC aircraft can be flown into the ground above the stall speed. Go-arounds are normal procedures and should be performed if there is any question as to the successful outcome of any landing.

Chapter 12
Night Operations

Introduction

It must be understood that flying at night presents a number of new challenges for the pilot and additional equipment for the aircraft. Flying at night in a weight-shift control (WSC) aircraft should be done only with some visual reference to the ground such as city lights or a full moon. Flying with no consistent visual reference to the surface results in disorientation, a likely loss of control, and an accident. New WSC aircraft can be fitted with instruments similar to those in airplanes in order to fly at night without visual reference to the horizon, but this is not recommended. However, flying with instruments is covered in this chapter.

Pilot Requirements

Flying at night requires additional pilot skills and a private pilot certificate. It is possible to have a private pilot certificate with a "Night Flight Prohibited" limitation if the pilot did not complete night flight training and is restricted from night flight, similar to that for Sport Pilots. This is an option for pilots who want a private pilot certificate but do not plan to fly at night. If the pilot first obtains the private certificate with the night limitation, the limitation can be removed after completing the private pilot WSC night training. The training that must be accomplished at night for WSC private pilot night flying privileges is:

1. One cross-country flight over 75 nautical miles (NM) total distance, and
2. Ten takeoffs and landings (each landing involving a flight in the traffic pattern) at an airport.

Sport pilots or private pilots with the night limitation are not allowed to fly at night; however, they can fly after sunset during civil twilight until night if the aircraft is properly equipped with position lights. Civil twilight is when the sun is less than 6° below the horizon, about 30 minutes before sunrise or after sunset, and varies by latitude throughout the year. It is the time when there is enough light outdoors for activities to be conducted without additional lighting. *[Figure 12-1]* If it is overcast and visibility is inadequate, good pilot judgment would dictate not to fly after sunset.

Equipment and Lighting

Title 14 of the Code of Federal Regulations (14 CFR) part 91 specifies the minimum aircraft equipment required for flight during civil twilight and night flight. This equipment includes only position lights. Normal standard category aircraft are required to have this additional equipment as would also be recommended for WSC night flight, including anti-collision light, landing lights, adequate electrical source for lights, and spare fuses. The standard instruments required for instrument flight under 14 CFR part 91 are a valuable asset for aircraft control at night but are not required.

Aircraft position lights are required on all aircraft from sunset to sunrise in an arrangement similar to those on boats and ships. A red light is positioned on the left wing tip, a green light on the right wing tip, and a white light on the tail. *[Figures 12-2 and 12-3]* This arrangement allows the pilot to determine the general direction of movement of other aircraft in flight. If both position lights of another aircraft are observed, a red light on the right and a green light on the left, the aircraft is flying toward the pilot and could be on a collision course. Similarly, a green light on the right and a red light on the left indicate the aircraft is flying in the same direction as the pilot observing the lights. Landing lights are not only useful for taxi, takeoffs, and landings, but also provide an additional means by which aircraft can be seen at night by other pilots. *[Figure 12-4]*

The Federal Aviation Administration (FAA) has initiated a voluntary pilot safety program called "Operation Lights On." The "lights on" idea is to enhance the "see and be seen" concept of averting collisions in the air and on the ground and to reduce the potential for bird strikes. Pilots are encouraged to turn on their landing lights when operating within 10 miles of an airport. This is for both day and night or in conditions of reduced visibility. This should also be done in areas where flocks of birds may be expected.

Although turning on aircraft lights supports the "see and be seen" concept, pilots should not become complacent about keeping a sharp lookout for other aircraft. Most aircraft lights blend in with stars or city lights at night and go unnoticed

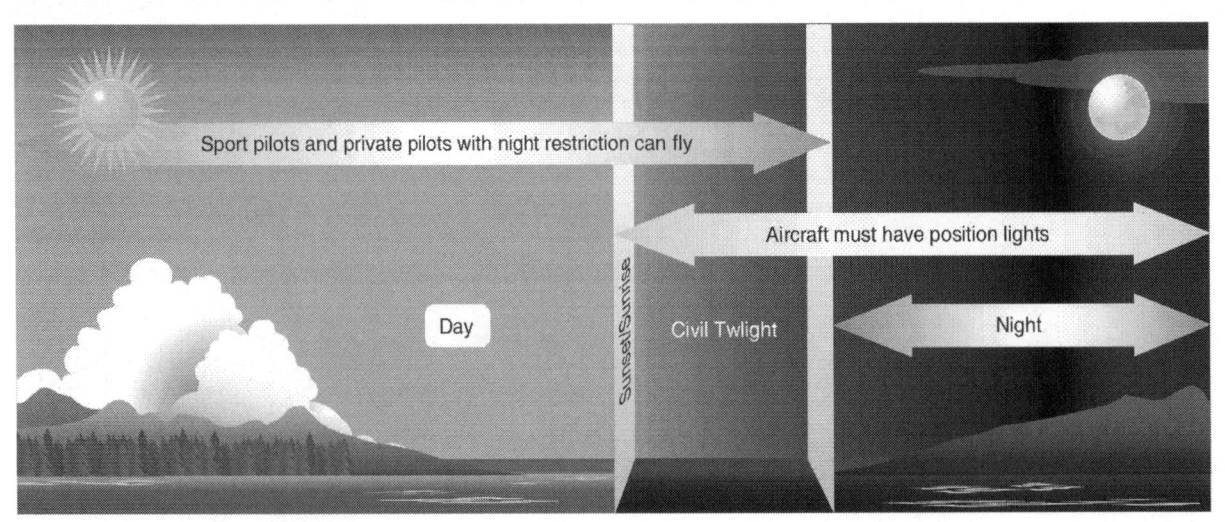

Figure 12-1. *Day, twilight, and night time.*

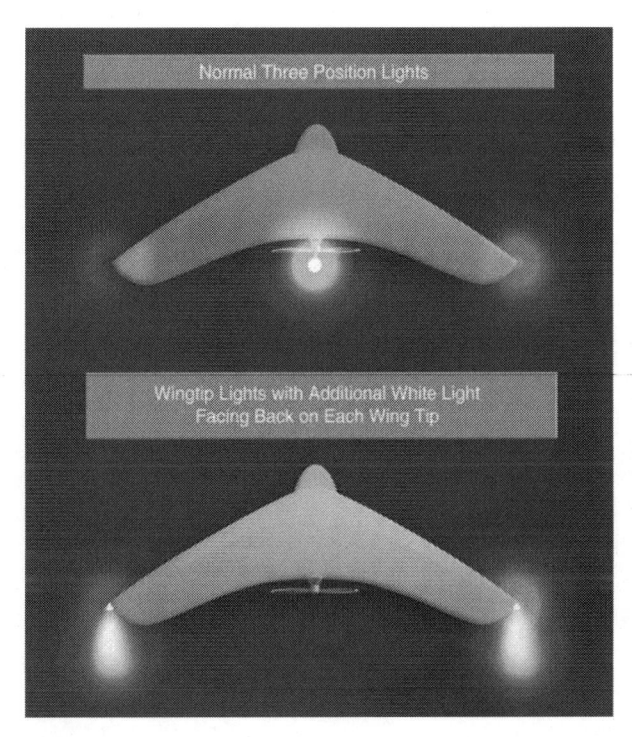

Figure 12-2. *Position lights.*

unless a conscious effort is made to distinguish them from other lights.

Pilot Equipment

Before beginning a night flight, carefully consider personal equipment that should be readily available during the flight.

Figure 12-3. *Modern LED position lights on carriage wheel pants simplify the installation with no wires running from the carriage to the wing tips.*

At least one reliable flashlight is recommended as standard equipment on all night flights. Remember to place a spare set of batteries in the flight kit. A spare flashlight is the better choice, eliminating the need to change batteries during flight.

Figure 12-4. *Landing light on WSC aircraft taxiing at night.*

12-3

A D-cell size flashlight with a bulb switching mechanism that can be used for white or red light is preferable. The white light is used while performing the preflight visual inspection on the ground, and the red light is used when performing flight deck operations. Since the red light is nonglaring, it does not impair night vision. Some pilots prefer two flashlights, one with a white light for preflight and the other a penlight with a red light. The latter can be suspended by a string around the neck to ensure the light is always readily available. Be aware that if a red light is used for reading an aeronautical chart, the red features of the chart will not show up.

Aeronautical charts are essential for night cross-country flight and, if the intended course is near the edge of the chart, the adjacent chart should also be available. The lights of cities and towns can be seen at surprising distances at night, and if this adjacent chart is not available to identify those landmarks, confusion could result. Regardless of the equipment used, organization of the flight deck eases the burden on the pilot and enhances safety. *[Figure 12-5]*

Airport and Navigation Lighting Aids

The lighting systems used for airports, runways, obstructions, and other visual aids at night are other important aspects of night flying.

Lighted airports located away from congested areas can be identified readily at night by the lights outlining the runways. Airports located near or within large cities are often difficult to identify in the maze of lights. It is important to know the exact location of an airport relative to the city, and also be able to identify these airports by the characteristics of their lighting pattern.

Aeronautical lights are designed and installed in a variety of colors and configurations, each having its own purpose. Although some lights are used only during low ceiling and visibility conditions, this discussion includes only the lights that are fundamental to visual flight rules (VFR) night operation.

It is recommended that prior to a night flight, and particularly a cross-country night flight, the pilot check the availability and status of lighting systems at the destination airport. This information can be found on aeronautical charts and in the Airport/Facility Directory (A/FD). The status of each facility can be determined by reviewing pertinent Notices to Airmen (NOTAMs).

A rotating beacon is used to indicate the location of most airports. The beacon rotates at a constant speed, thus

Figure 12-5. *WSC aircraft equipped for night cross-country flight with flashlight and aeronautical charts on kneeboards.*

producing what appears to be a series of light flashes at regular intervals. These flashes may be one or two different colors that are used to identify various types of landing areas. For example:

- Lighted civilian land airports—alternating white and green
- Lighted civilian water airports—alternating white and yellow
- Lighted military airports—alternating white and green, but are differentiated from civil airports by dual peaked (two quick) white flashes, then green

Beacons producing red flashes indicate obstructions or areas considered hazardous to aerial navigation. Steady burning red lights are used to mark obstructions on or near airports and sometimes to supplement flashing lights on en route obstructions. High intensity flashing white lights are used to mark some supporting structures of overhead transmission lines that stretch across rivers, chasms, and gorges. These high intensity lights are also used to identify tall structures, such as chimneys and towers.

As a result of technological advancements in aviation, runway lighting systems have become quite sophisticated to accommodate takeoffs and landings in various weather conditions. However, the pilot whose flying is limited to VFR needs to be concerned only with the following basic lighting of runways and taxiways.

The basic runway lighting system consists of two straight parallel lines of runway-edge lights defining the lateral limits of the runway. These lights are aviation white, although aviation yellow may be substituted for a distance of 2,000 feet from the far end of the runway to indicate a caution zone. At some airports, the intensity of the runway-edge lights can be adjusted to satisfy the individual needs of the pilot. The length limits of the runway are defined by straight lines of lights across the runway ends. At some airports, the runway threshold lights are aviation green, and the runway end lights are aviation red.

At many airports, the taxiways are also lighted. A taxiway-edge lighting system consists of blue lights that outline the usable limits of taxi paths. See the Pilot's Handbook of Aeronautical Knowledge for additional information on airport lighting.

Night Vision

Generally, most pilots are poorly informed about night vision. Human eyes never function as effectively at night as the eyes of nocturnal animals, but if humans learn how to use their eyes correctly and know their limitations, night vision can be improved significantly. The human eye is constructed so that day vision is different from night vision. Therefore, it is important to understand the eye's construction and how the eye is affected by darkness.

Innumerable light-sensitive nerves called cones and rods are located at the back of the eye or retina, a layer upon which all images are focused. These nerves connect to the cells of the optic nerve, which transmits messages directly to the brain. The cones are located in the center of the retina, and the rods are concentrated in a ring around the cones. [Figure 12-6]

The function of the cones is to detect color, details, and faraway objects. The rods function when something is seen out of the corner of the eye or peripheral vision. They detect objects, particularly those that are moving, but do not give detail or color—only shades of gray. Both the cones and the rods are used for vision during daylight.

Although there is not a clear-cut division of function, the rods make night vision possible. The rods and cones function in daylight and in moonlight; in the absence of normal light, the process of night vision is almost entirely a function of the rods.

The fact that the rods are distributed in a band around the cones and do not lie directly behind the pupils makes off-center viewing (looking to one side of an object) important during night flight. During daylight, an object can be seen best by looking directly at it, but at night a scanning procedure to permit off-center viewing of the object is more effective. Therefore, the pilot should consciously practice this scanning procedure to improve night vision.

The eye's adaptation to darkness is another important aspect of night vision. When a dark room is entered, it is difficult to see anything until the eyes become adjusted to the darkness. In the adaptation process, the pupils of the eyes first enlarge to receive as much of the available light as possible. After approximately 5 to 10 minutes, the cones become adjusted to the dim light and the eyes become 100 times more sensitive to light than they were before the dark room was entered. About 30 minutes is needed for the rods to become adjusted to darkness; when they do adjust, they are about 100,000 times more sensitive to light than in the lighted area. After the adaptation process is complete, much more can be seen, especially if the eyes are used correctly.

The **rods** and **cones** (film) of the **retina** are the receptors which record the image and transmit it through the **optic nerve** to the brain for interpretation.

Rod concentration

Lens

Iris

Optic nerve

Retina

Pupil
The **pupil** (aperture) is the opening at the center of the **iris**. The size of the pupil is adjusted to control the amount of light entering the eye.

Cornea
Light passes through the **cornea** (the transparent window on the front of the eye) and then through the **lens** to focus on the retina.

Area of best day vision

Cones active

Area of best night vision

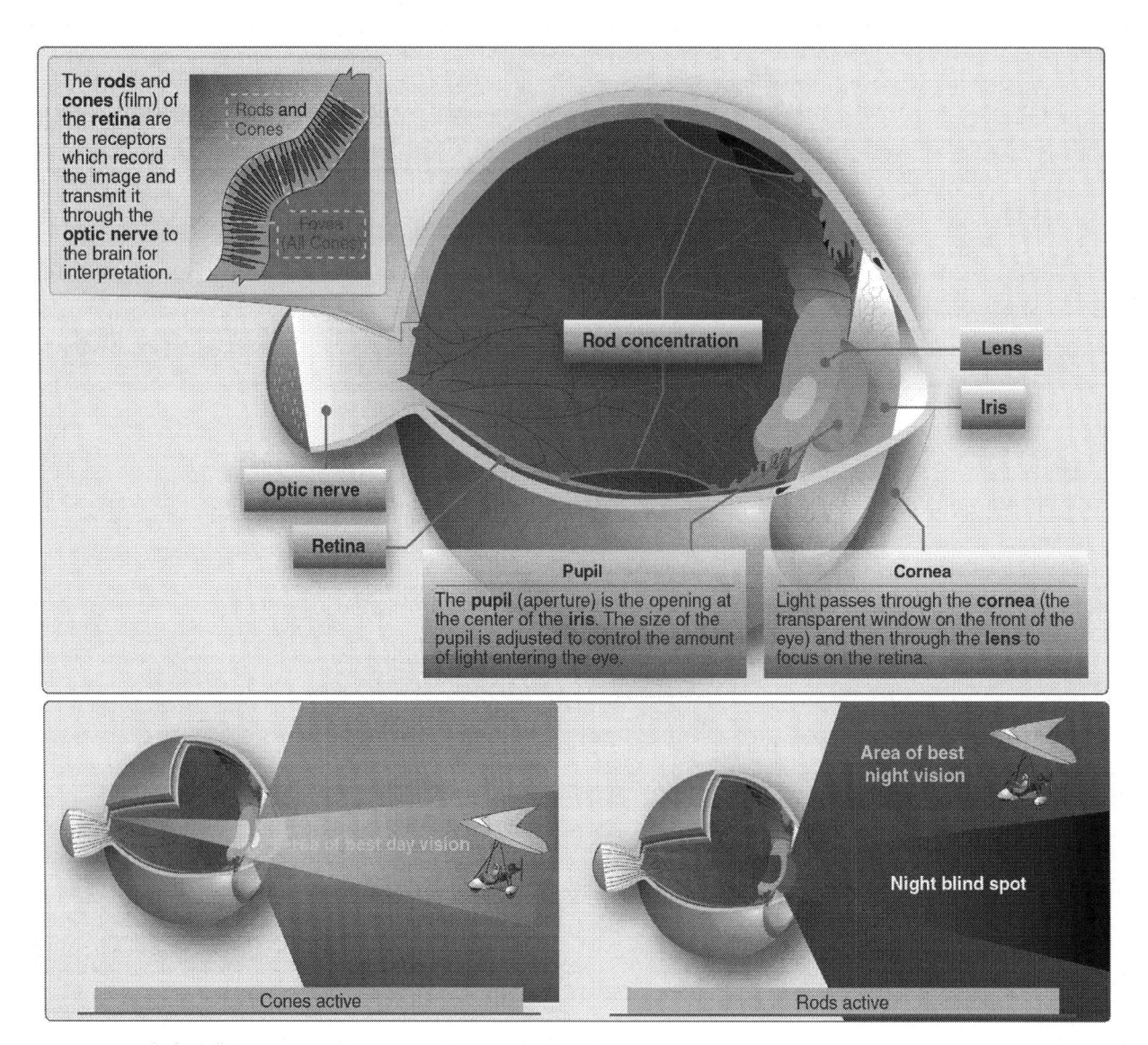

Night blind spot

Rods active

Figure 12-6. *Rods and cones.*

After the eyes have adapted to the dark, the entire process is reversed when entering a lighted room. The eyes are first dazzled by the brightness, but become completely adjusted in a few seconds, thereby losing their adaptation to the dark. Now, if the dark room is reentered, the eyes again go through the long process of adapting to the darkness.

Before and during night flight, the pilot must consider the adaptation process of the eyes. First, the eyes should be allowed to adapt to the low level of light. Then, the pilot should avoid exposing them to any bright white light that would cause temporary blindness and possibly result in serious consequences.

Temporary blindness, caused by an unusually bright light, may result in illusions or afterimages until the eyes recover from the brightness. The brain creates these illusions reported by the eyes. This results in misjudging or incorrectly identifying objects, such as mistaking slanted clouds for the horizon or a populated area for a landing field. Vertigo is experienced as a feeling of dizziness and imbalance that can create or increase illusions. The illusions seem very real and pilots at every level of experience and skill can be affected. Recognizing that the brain and eyes can play tricks in this manner is the best protection for flying at night.

Good eyesight depends upon physical condition. Fatigue, colds, vitamin deficiency, alcohol, stimulants, smoking, or medication can seriously impair vision. Keeping these facts in mind and taking appropriate precautions should help safeguard night vision.

In addition to the principles previously discussed, the following actions aid in increasing night vision effectiveness:

- Adapt the eyes to darkness prior to flight, and keep them adapted. About 30 minutes is needed to adjust the eyes to maximum efficiency after exposure to a bright light.
- Use oxygen during night flying, if available. Keep in mind that a significant deterioration in night vision can occur at altitudes as low as 5,000 feet.
- Close one eye when exposed to bright light to help avoid the blinding effect.
- Avoid wearing sunglasses after sunset.
- Move the eyes more slowly than in daylight.
- Blink the eyes if vision becomes blurred.
- Concentrate on seeing objects.
- Force the eyes to view off center.
- Maintain good physical condition.
- Avoid smoking, drinking, and using drugs that may be harmful.

Unique WSC Flight Characteristics

If the WSC aircraft is trimmed properly and the pilot is proficient in the basic flight maneuvers of climbs, cruise, and descent procedures, the WSC aircraft speed is easily determined with control bar pressure and position for normal flight conditions. A pilot can also determine basic climbs and descents through the feel of the aircraft with the airspeed and throttle positions. Therefore, basic pitch control can be done by a proficient pilot with his or her eyes closed.

As discussed in Chapter 2, Aerodynamics, WSC aircraft are generally not designed to be roll stable, and any engine turning effect or movement of the air can put the WSC aircraft into a roll, which it maintains unless corrected by the pilot. In other words, releasing the control bar in a WSC aircraft will not level a bank back to straight flight. The pilot must continually provide input to fly a constant heading even if this control is small corrections. In other words, the pilot cannot level the wings or fly a straight heading for very long with his or her eyes closed.

To maintain a constant heading or ground track, one of three instruments can be used: magnetic compass, global positioning system (GPS), and aircraft heading indicator. Without a visual reference, these can be used to fly straight. An attitude indicator can be used on WSC aircraft providing additional instrument reference. These instruments and others are discussed later in this chapter.

Night Illusions

In addition to night vision limitations, pilots should be aware that night illusions could cause confusion and concerns during night flying. The following discussion covers some of the common situations that cause illusions associated with night flying.

A false horizon can occur when the natural horizon is obscured or not readily apparent. It can be generated by confusing bright stars and city lights. It can also occur while flying toward the shore of an ocean or a large lake. Because of the relative darkness of the water, the lights along the shoreline can be mistaken for stars in the sky. *[Figure 12-7]*

Figure 12-7. *At night, the horizon may be hard to discern due to dark terrain and misleading light patterns on the ground.*

On a clear night, distant stationary lights can be mistaken for stars or other aircraft. Even the northern lights can confuse a pilot and indicate a false horizon. Certain geometrical patterns of ground lights, such as a freeway, runway, approach, or even lights on a moving train can cause confusion. Dark nights tend to eliminate reference to a visual horizon. As a result, pilots need to rely less on outside references at night and more on flight and navigation instruments.

Visual autokinesis can occur when a pilot stares at a single light source for several seconds on a dark night. The result is that the light appears to be moving. The autokinesis effect does not occur if the pilot expands the visual field. It is a good procedure to vary visual focus and not become fixed on one source of light.

Distractions and problems can result from a flickering light in the flight deck, such as anticollision lights, strobe lights, or other aircraft lights which can cause flicker vertigo. If continuous, the possible physical reactions can be nausea, dizziness, grogginess, confusion, headaches, or unconsciousness. The pilot should try to eliminate any light source causing blinking or flickering problems in the flight deck.

A black-hole approach occurs when the landing is made from over water or unlighted terrain on which runway lights are the only sources of light. Without peripheral visual cues to help, pilots have trouble orienting themselves relative to Earth. The runway can seem out of position (downsloping or upsloping) and, in the worst case, result in landing short of the runway. If an electronic glideslope or visual approach slope indicator (VASI) is available, it should be used. If navigation aids (NAVAIDs) are unavailable, careful attention should be given to using the flight instruments to assist in maintaining orientation and a normal approach. If at any time the pilot is unsure of his or her position or attitude, a go-around should be executed.

Bright runway and approach lighting systems, especially where few lights illuminate the surrounding terrain, may create the illusion of less distance to the runway. In this situation, the tendency is to fly a higher approach. Also, when flying over terrain with only a few lights, it makes the runway recede or appear farther away. With this situation, the tendency is common to fly a lower-than-normal approach. If the runway has a city in the distance on higher terrain, the tendency is to fly a lower-than-normal approach. A good review of the airfield layout and boundaries before initiating any approach helps the pilot maintain a safe approach angle.

Illusions created by runway lights result in a variety of problems. Bright lights or bold colors advance the runway, making it appear closer. Night landings are further complicated by the difficulty of judging distance and the possibility of confusing approach and runway lights. For example, when a double row of approach lights joins the boundary lights of the runway, there can be confusion where the approach lights terminate and runway lights begin. Under certain conditions, approach lights can make the aircraft seem higher in a turn to final than when its wings are level.

Preparation and Preflight

Night flying requires that pilots be aware of and operate within their abilities and limitations. Although careful planning of any flight is essential, night flying demands more attention to the details of preflight preparation and planning.

Preparation for a night flight should include a thorough review of the available weather reports and forecasts with particular attention given to temperature-dew point spread. A narrow temperature-dew point spread may indicate the possibility of ground fog. Emphasis should also be placed on wind direction and speed, since wind effects on the aircraft cannot be as easily detected at night as during the day.

On night cross-country flights, appropriate aeronautical charts should be selected, including the appropriate adjacent charts. Course lines should be drawn in black to be more distinguishable.

Prominently lighted checkpoints along the prepared course should be noted. Rotating beacons at airports, lighted obstructions, lights of cities or towns, and lights from major highway traffic all provide excellent visual checkpoints. The use of a GPS with a lighted screen adds significantly to the safety and efficiency of night flying.

All personal equipment should be checked prior to flight to ensure proper functioning. It is very disconcerting to find at the time of need that a flashlight does not work.

All aircraft lights should be turned on momentarily and checked for operation. Position lights can be checked for loose connections by tapping the light fixture. If the lights blink while being tapped, further investigation to determine the cause should be made prior to flight.

The parking ramp should be examined prior to entering the aircraft. During the day, it is quite easy to see stepladders, chuckholes, wheel chocks, and other obstructions, but at night it is more difficult. A check of the area can prevent taxiing mishaps.

Starting, Taxiing, and Runup

After the pilot is seated in the flight deck and prior to starting the engine, all items and materials to be used on the flight should be arranged in such a manner that they will be readily available and convenient to use.

Extra caution should be taken at night to assure the propeller area is clear. Turning the rotating beacon on or flashing the aircraft position lights serves to alert persons nearby to remain clear of the propeller. To avoid excessive drain of electrical current from the battery, it is recommended that unnecessary electrical equipment be turned off until after the engine has been started.

After starting and before taxiing, the taxi or landing light should be turned on. Continuous use of the landing light with revolutions per minute (rpm) power settings normally used for taxiing may place an excessive drain on the aircraft's electrical system. Also, overheating of the landing light could become a problem because of inadequate airflow to carry the heat away. Landing lights should be used as necessary while taxiing. When using landing lights, consideration should be given to not blinding other pilots. Taxi slowly, particularly in congested areas. If taxi lines are painted on the ramp or taxiway, these lines should be followed to ensure a proper path along the route.

The before takeoff and runup should be performed using the checklist. During the day, forward movement of the aircraft can be detected easily. At night, the aircraft could creep forward without being noticed unless the pilot is alert for this possibility. Hold or lock the brakes during the runup and be alert for any forward movement. *[Figure 12-8]*

Figure 12-8. *Reviewing before-takeoff checklist, which is included for the flight with the sectional charts on the kneeboard.*

Takeoff and Climb

Night flying is very different from day flying and demands more attention of the pilot. The most noticeable difference is the limited availability of outside visual references. Therefore, flight instruments should be used as a reference in controlling the aircraft. This is particularly true on night takeoffs and climbs. The flight deck lights should be adjusted to a minimum brightness that allows the pilot to read the instruments and switches but not hinder the pilot's outside vision. This also eliminates light reflections on the windshield and instruments.

After ensuring that the final approach and runway are clear of other air traffic, or when cleared for takeoff by the tower, the landing lights and taxi lights should be turned on and the WSC aircraft lined up with the centerline of the runway. If the runway does not have centerline lighting, use the painted centerline and the runway edge lights. After the aircraft is aligned, the heading indicator should be noted or set to correspond to the known runway direction. The magnetic compass should read the exact direction of the runway. The GPS does not provide meaningful information while stopped or turning because it measures ground track and needs to be moving to register enough points to provide accurate data.

To begin the takeoff, the brakes should be released and the throttle smoothly advanced to maximum allowable power. As the aircraft accelerates, it should be kept moving straight ahead between and parallel to the runway-edge lights.

The procedure for night takeoffs is the same as for normal daytime takeoffs except that many of the runway visual cues are not available. Therefore, the airspeed flight instrument can be checked during the takeoff roll to ensure the proper airspeed in being obtained. As the airspeed reaches the normal lift-off speed, the pitch attitude should be adjusted to that which establishes a normal climb. This should be accomplished by using the normal control bar position for the desired climb speed. After liftoff, instruments can be checked for proper heading, and airspeed. *[Figures 12-9 and 12-10]*

The darkness of night often makes it difficult to note whether the airborne aircraft is getting closer to or farther from the surface. To ensure the aircraft continues in a positive climb, be sure a climb is indicated on the attitude indicator (if equipped), vertical speed indicator (VSI), and altimeter. It is also important to ensure the airspeed is at best climb speed.

Necessary pitch and bank adjustments should be made by referencing the attitude, heading, or ground track indicators. Heading indicators include both the aircraft heading indicators and the magnetic compass. Once the aircraft starts moving and establishing a ground track straight down the runway, the GPS has data points to establish a ground track and becomes useful once in flight. It is recommended that turns not be made until reaching a safe maneuvering altitude.

Although the use of the landing lights provides help during the takeoff, they become ineffective soon after liftoff when

Figure 12-9. *Classic instrument gauges for WSC aircraft.*

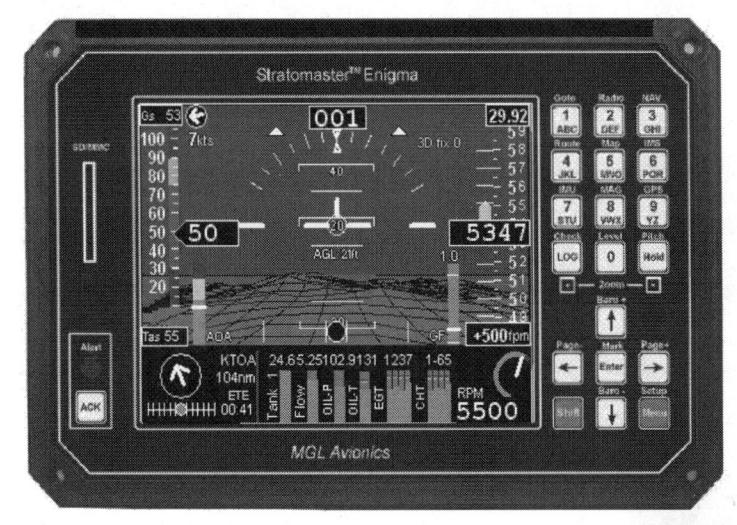

Figure 12-10. *Digital panel instrument gauges for WSC aircraft.*

pilot flying under VFR must exercise caution to avoid flying into clouds or a layer of fog. Usually, the first indication of flying into restricted visibility conditions is the gradual disappearance of lights on the ground. If the lights begin to take on an appearance of being surrounded by a halo or glow, the pilot should use caution in attempting further flight in that same direction. Such a halo or glow around lights on the ground is indicative of ground fog. Remember that if a descent to land must be made through fog, smoke, or haze, the horizontal visibility is considerably less. Under no circumstances should a night flight be made during poor or marginal weather conditions.

The pilot should practice and acquire competency in straight-and-level flight, climbs and descents, level turns, climbing and descending turns, and steep turns. The pilot should also practice these maneuvers with all the flight deck lights turned off. This blackout training is necessary if the pilot experiences an electrical or instrument light failure. Training should also include using the navigation equipment and local NAVAIDs.

In spite of fewer references or checkpoints, night cross-country flights do not present particular problems if preplanning is adequate, and the pilot continues to monitor position, time estimates, and fuel consumption. The GPS is the most valuable instrument for day and night cross-country flying. For night cross-country flying, spare batteries or a GPS hooked to the aircraft electric system with a battery backup is recommended. NAVAIDs, the aircraft has climbed to an altitude at which the light beam no longer extends to the surface. The light can cause distortion when it is reflected by haze, smoke, or fog that might exist in the climb. Therefore, when the landing light is used for the takeoff, it may be turned off after the climb is well established provided other traffic in the area does not require its use for collision avoidance.

A properly lit instrument panel and visual reference to the ground with city lights are recommended for night flying. *[Figure 12-11]*

Orientation and Navigation

At night, it is usually difficult to see clouds and restrictions to visibility, particularly on dark nights or under overcast. The

Figure 12-11. *A properly lit instrument panel and city lights provide recommended conditions for night flying.*

if available, should also be used to assist in monitoring en route progress.

Crossing large bodies of water at night in single-engine aircraft is hazardous and not recommended by day or night. This is from the standpoint of landing (ditching) in the water, but especially at night because with little or no lighting the horizon blends with the water making depth perception and orientation difficult. During poor visibility conditions over water, the horizon becomes obscure and may result in a loss of orientation. Even on clear nights, the stars may be reflected on the water surface which could appear as a continuous array of lights making the horizon difficult to identify.

Lighted runways, buildings, or other objects may cause illusions when seen from different altitudes. At an altitude of 2,000 feet, a group of lights on an object may be seen individually; while at 5,000 feet or higher, the same lights could appear to be one solid light mass. These illusions may become quite acute with altitude changes and, if not overcome, could present problems in respect to approaches to lighted runways.

Approaches and Landings

When approaching the airport to enter the traffic pattern and land, it is important that the runway lights and other airport lighting be identified as early as possible. If the airport layout is unfamiliar to the pilot, sighting of the runway may be difficult until very close-in due to the maze of lights observed in the area. *[Figure 12-12]* The pilot should fly toward the rotating beacon until the lights outlining the runway are distinguishable. To fly a traffic pattern of proper size and direction, the runway threshold and runway-edge lights must be positively identified. Once the airport lights are seen, these lights should be kept in sight throughout the approach.

Distance may be deceptive at night due to limited lighting conditions. A lack of intervening references on the ground and the inability of the pilot to compare the size and location of different ground objects cause this. This also applies to the estimation of altitude and speed. Consequently, more dependence must be placed on flight instruments, particularly the altimeter and the airspeed indicator.

When entering the traffic pattern, allow for plenty of time to complete the before landing checklist. If the heading indicator contains a heading bug, setting it to the runway heading is an excellent reference for the pattern legs.

Every effort should be made to maintain the recommended airspeeds and execute the approach and landing in the same manner as during the day. A low, shallow approach is definitely inappropriate during a night operation. The

Figure 12-12. *Use light patterns for orientation.*

altimeter and VSI should be constantly cross-checked against the aircraft's position along the base leg and final approach. A visual approach slope indicator (VASI) is an indispensable aid in alerting a pilot of too low of a glidepath. The typical VASI is set to 3° for the recommended aircraft approach. This 19 to 1 glide ratio is too low for a WSC aircraft. A normal glide ratio for WSC aircraft is 5 to 1, which is 11°, much higher than the normal 3° to 4° used by aircraft. Therefore, for WSC VASI final approaches both white lights should be visible. If a pilot sees red over white, or especially both reds, the approach is too low and altitude should be gained, or at least maintained to get above the normal VASI 3° to 4° approach at night. This steeper approach allows the WSC aircraft to glide to the runway and land safely in the event of engine failure. *[Figure 12-13]*

After turning onto the final approach and aligning the aircraft midway between the two rows of runway-edge lights, the pilot should note and correct for any wind drift. Throughout the final approach, pitch and power should be used to maintain a stabilized approach. Usually, halfway through the final approach, the landing light should be turned on. Earlier use of the landing light may be necessary because of "Operation Lights On" or for local traffic considerations. The landing light is sometimes ineffective since the light beam usually does not reach the ground from higher altitudes. The light may even be reflected back into the pilot's eyes by any existing haze, smoke, or fog. This disadvantage is overshadowed by the safety considerations provided by using the "Operation Lights On" procedure around other traffic.

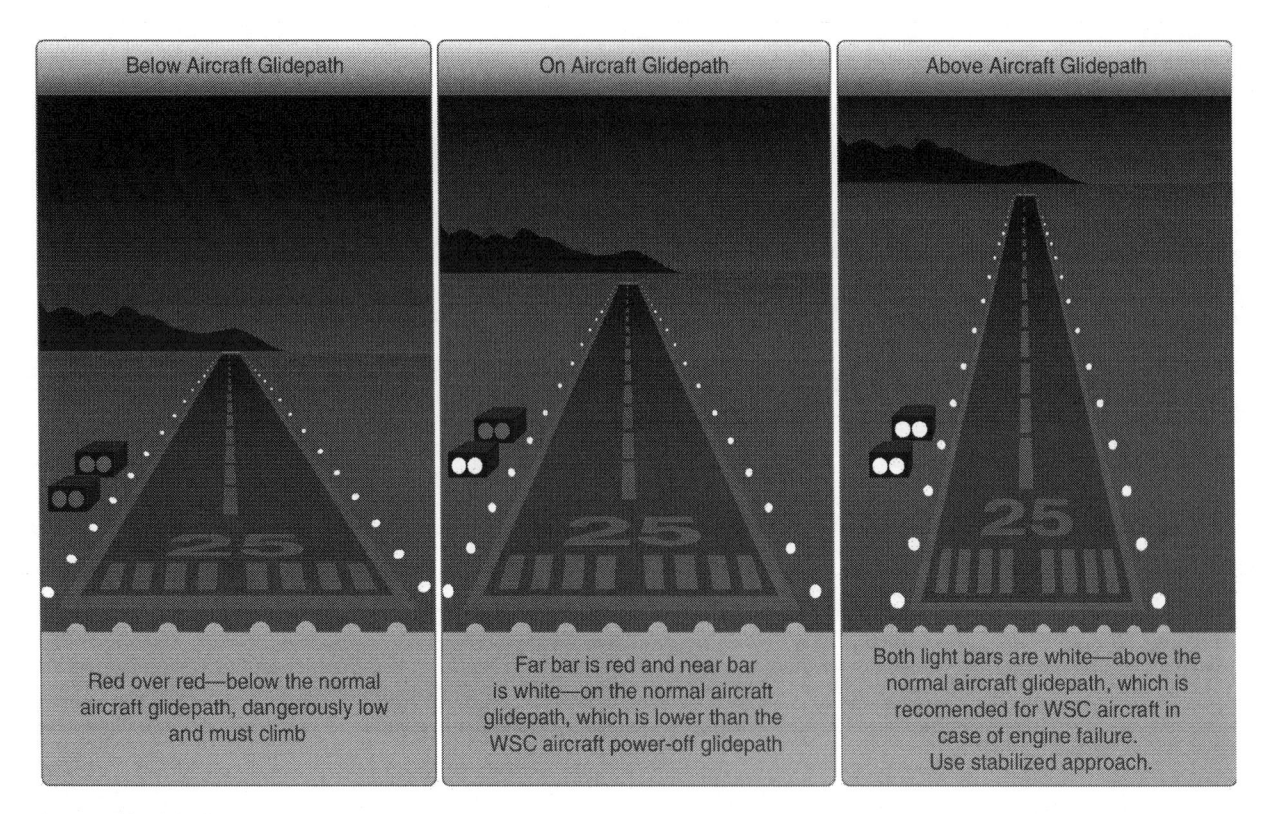

Below Aircraft Glidepath	On Aircraft Glidepath	Above Aircraft Glidepath
Red over red—below the normal aircraft glidepath, dangerously low and must climb	Far bar is red and near bar is white—on the normal aircraft glidepath, which is lower than the WSC aircraft power-off glidepath	Both light bars are white—above the normal aircraft glidepath, which is recomended for WSC aircraft in case of engine failure. Use stabilized approach.

Figure 12-13. *VASI.*

The approach and landings should be made in the same manner as in day landings as discussed in Chapter 11, Approaches and Landings. At night, the judgment of height, speed, and sink rate is impaired by the scarcity of observable objects in the landing area. The inexperienced pilot may have a tendency to round out too high until attaining familiarity with the proper height for the correct roundout. To aid in night landings, approach with power on to reduce the descent rate providing more time for the pilot to see the runway and start the roundout once the runway is visible. To aid in determining the proper roundout point, continue a constant approach descent until the landing lights reflect on the runway and tire marks on the runway can be clearly seen. At this point, the roundout should be started smoothly and the throttle gradually reduced to idle as the aircraft is touching down. *[Figure 12-14]* During landings without the use of landing lights, the roundout may be started when the runway lights at the far end of the runway first appear to be rising higher than the nose of the aircraft. This demands a smooth and very timely roundout, and requires that the pilot feel for the runway surface using power and pitch changes, as necessary, for the aircraft to settle slowly to the runway. Blackout landings should always be included in night pilot training as an emergency procedure.

Night Emergencies

Perhaps the pilot's greatest concern about flying a single-engine aircraft at night is the possibility of a complete engine failure and the subsequent emergency landing. This is a legitimate concern, even though continuing flight into adverse weather and poor pilot judgment account for most serious accidents.

If the engine fails at night, several important procedures and considerations to keep in mind are:

- Maintain positive control of the aircraft and establish the best glide configuration and airspeed. Turn the aircraft toward an airport or away from congested areas.

- Check to determine the cause of the engine malfunction, such as the position of fuel shutoff, magneto switch, or primer. If possible, the cause of the malfunction should be corrected immediately and the engine restarted.

- Announce the emergency situation to Air Traffic Control (ATC) or UNICOM. If already in radio contact with a facility, do not change frequencies unless instructed to change.

- Consider an emergency landing area close to public access if possible. This may facilitate rescue or help, if needed.

- Maintain orientation with the wind to avoid a downwind landing.

- Complete the before landing checklist, and check the landing lights for operation at altitude and turn on in sufficient time to illuminate the terrain or obstacles along the flightpath. The landing should be completed in the normal landing attitude at the slowest possible airspeed. If the landing lights are unusable and outside visual references are not available, the aircraft should be held minimum controlled airspeed until the ground is contacted.

- After landing, turn off all switches and evacuate the aircraft as quickly as possible.

Chapter Summary

Night flight requires additional training, a private pilot certificate, and should be performed only when there is adequate reference with the Earth, such as city lights or a full moon. Night flight should never be performed over open water.

Night illusions require reference to flight instruments. WSC pilots can determine pitch control by feel but cannot determine roll and heading by feel so instrumentation such as a heading indicator, magnetic compass, or GPS is needed for directional reference.

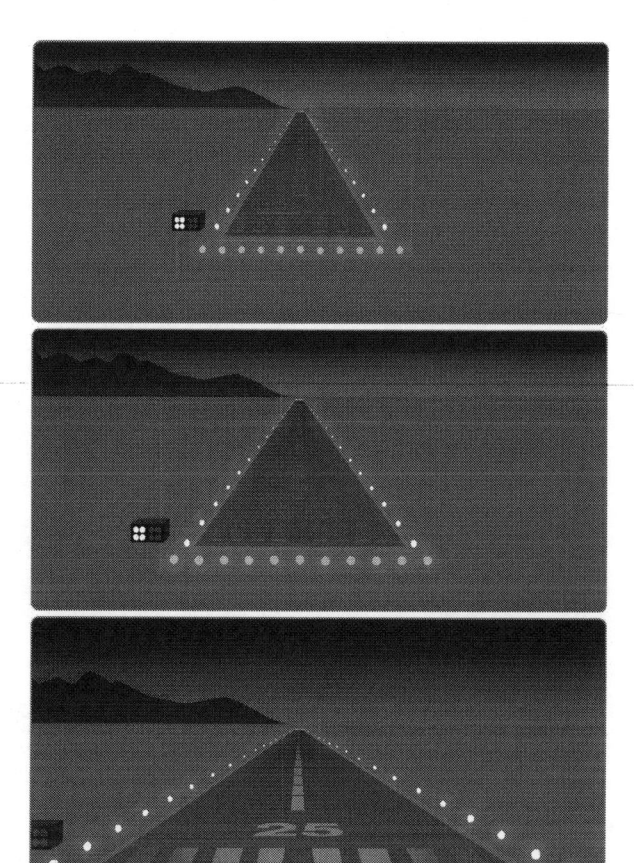

Figure 12-14. *Roundout when tire marks are visible.*

12-13

Chapter 13
Abnormal and Emergency Procedures

Introduction
This chapter contains information on dealing with abnormal and emergency situations that may occur in flight. Aeronautical decision-making (ADM), a systematic approach to determine the best course of action in response to a given set of circumstances, should always be used rather than making a quick decision without determining the best outcome. Most emergencies can be prevented by making the proper decisions. This may be the first go/no-go decision of whether to fly, when to fly, or where to fly. All safe flights start with proper preflight planning.

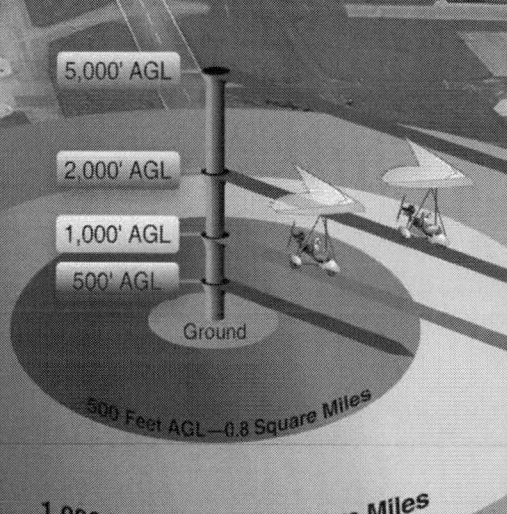

Throughout this chapter, all abnormal and emergency decisions should be based on ADM. Some situations allow more time than others to evaluate the outcome. ADM should be applied to any unplanned or unexpected situation presented.

In addition to ADM, the key to any emergency situation, and/or preventing a abnormal situation from progressing to a true emergency is a thorough familiarity with, and adherence to, the procedures developed by the manufacturer and contained in the Aircraft Flight Manual and/or Pilot's Operating Handbook (AFM/POH). The following guidelines are generic and not meant to replace the manufacturer's recommended procedures. Rather, they are meant to enhance the pilot's general knowledge in the area of abnormal and emergency operations. If any of the guidance in this chapter conflicts with the manufacturer's recommended procedures for a particular make and model weight-shift control (WSC) aircraft, the manufacturer's recommended procedures take precedence.

Ballistic Parachute System (BPS)

The ballistic parachute system (BPS) provides an additional safety margin to flying WSC aircraft. However, if utilized when other alternatives would produce a better outcome or if not deployed with the proper procedures, BPS system use could create a worse situation than not using a BPS. The BPS should be used only as a last alternative and only after other options have been evaluated through ADM. *[Figure 13-1]*

Figure 13-1. *WSC aircraft coming down under a ballistic parachute system.*

The choice of adding a BPS as an additional system for emergencies is up to the pilot. This decision should be made by evaluating the disadvantages of an additional system, its advantages, and the situations in which the system would be utilized.

Advantages of a BPS:

- BPS can be used if there is a total loss of control of the WSC. The term "loss of control" is key to when the BPS should be deployed. Always fly the aircraft first, but if the pilot cannot control or regain control of the aircraft (loss of control), this is when the BPS should be used. Loss of control might result from midair collisions or wake tip vortices with other aircraft. A loss of control could also result from structural failure due to inadequate preflight or lack of proper maintenance.

- BPS can be used if the engine quits and there are no suitable landing areas. Although pilots try to have a suitable landing area within gliding distance, there are times when a parachute could be used with an engine failure, such as over high trees.

- Pilot incapacitation is a situation where the BPS could be used. This could be a pilot-in-command (PIC) illness, such as a heart attack, or an external factor, such as a bird strike in the face temporally blinding the pilot. For example, if the pilot is incapacitated by a bird strike, the pilot could feel for the handle and pull it. Other designs allow the pilot and passenger to be able to reach and actuate the BPS, while other designs have two separate handles for the pilot and a passenger. Many passengers feel safer if they know they can actuate the BPS if the pilot is unable to fly the aircraft.

- Pilot disorientation with loss of control of the aircraft is a situation where the BPS could be used. In the unusual situation of severe vertigo or spatial disorientation preventing the pilot from differentiating up from down, such as severe turbulence, night flying, or flying into bad weather, a BPS could be used. Attempts should always be made to regain composure; if attempts fail, then the BPS is an option.

Disadvantages of having BPS:

- It provides a false sense of security. A pilot might believe that the BPS can save him or her from hazardous situations, which could cause the pilot to develop hazardous attitudes, exceed limitations, and make bad decisions.

- The pilot could deploy the parachute when it is not needed. A BPS should be utilized only as a last alternative to normal emergency procedures. It should not be used when ADM produces a better alternative for the situation at hand.
- BPS systems installed on a WSC aircraft have greater initial cost, maintenance, and weight.
- A BPS can be deployed accidentally. This can happen when the actuation handle is not properly placed, or when deployed by occupants not following appropriate procedures.
- BPS systems may not fire or could tangle during the deployment. Like any system, it can fail or not be operated properly, so there is no guarantee it will fire or deploy properly. However, if it is mounted, maintained, and operated properly, the chances of a successful deployment are good.

The BPS should not be used in abnormal or emergency situations, such as engine failure when suitable landing areas are within gliding distance. Other situations in which to avoid using a BPS are during strong winds/convection/turbulence, or if lost. Alternatives and greater detail is presented for these situations where a BPS is not used later in this chapter.

Procedures for Using a BPS

In an emergency situation where ADM is used and the best outcome for the given situation is the use of a BPS, the following general procedure for properly operating the BPS is:

- Select the proper location if still in control of the aircraft. Consider wind drift and a descent rate of 900 to 1,800 feet per minute (fpm). A minimum 500 feet above ground level (AGL) is recommended for complete deployment that is low enough to provide accurate targeting at intended area. (If below 500 feet AGL, consider this a low deployment and skip this step.)
- Shut off the engine (this is especially important for pusher WSC).
- Slow down and lift the wing on the side where the chute will deploy (if a side deployment and above 500 feet AGL).
- Pull the BPS deployment handle hard and as far as it will go. This can be more than 12 inches in some situations.
- Hold the control bar firmly with bent arms until parachute inflates.
- Steer the descending WSC aircraft toward best landing spot, if possible (some installations that hang from the top at the hang point center of gravity (CG) may allow some directional control).
- Before impact, put hands in front of face and keep arms and legs in and tight to body.
- After impact, exit aircraft immediately.

Emergency Landings

This section contains information on emergency landing techniques in WSC aircraft. The guidelines that are presented apply to the more adverse terrain conditions for which no practical training is possible. The objective is to instill in the pilot the knowledge that almost any terrain can be considered suitable for a survivable crash landing if the pilot knows how to slow and secure the WSC aircraft while using the WSC structure for protection of the pilot and passenger.

Types of Emergency Landings

The different types of emergency landings are:

- Forced landing—an immediate landing, on or off an airport, necessitated by the inability to continue further flight. A typical example is an aircraft forced down by engine failure.
- Precautionary landing—a premeditated landing, on or off an airport, when further flight is possible but inadvisable. Examples of conditions that may call for a precautionary landing include deteriorating weather, being lost, fuel shortage, and gradually developing engine trouble.
- Ditching—a forced landing on water.

A precautionary landing is less hazardous than a forced landing because the pilot has more time for terrain selection and approach planning. In addition, the pilot can use power to compensate for errors in judgment or technique. The pilot should be aware that too many situations calling for a precautionary landing are allowed to develop into immediate forced landings when the pilot uses wishful thinking instead of reason, especially when dealing with a self-inflicted predicament. Trapped by weather or facing fuel exhaustion, the pilot who does not give any thought to the feasibility of a precautionary landing accepts an extremely hazardous alternative.

Psychological Hazards

There are several factors that may interfere with a pilot's ability to act promptly and properly when faced with an emergency. These factors include reluctance to accept the emergency situation, the desire to save the aircraft, and undue concern about getting hurt.

A pilot who allows the mind to become paralyzed at the thought that the aircraft will be on the ground in a very short time, regardless of the pilot's actions or hopes, is severely handicapped. An unconscious desire to delay the dreaded moment may lead to such errors as a delay in the selection of the most suitable landing area within reach and indecision in general. Desperate attempts to correct whatever went wrong at the expense of aircraft control fall into the same category.

The pilot who has been conditioned during training to expect to find a relatively safe landing area whenever the flight instructor closes the throttle for a simulated forced landing may ignore all basic rules of airmanship to avoid a touchdown in terrain where aircraft damage is unavoidable. Typical consequences are making a 180° turn back to the runway when available altitude is insufficient, stretching the glide without regard for minimum control speed in order to reach a more appealing field, or accepting an approach and touchdown situation that leaves no margin for error. The desire to save the aircraft, regardless of the risks involved, may be influenced by two other factors: the pilot's financial stake in the aircraft and the certainty that an undamaged aircraft implies no bodily harm. There are times, however, when a pilot should be more interested in sacrificing the aircraft so that the occupants can safely walk away from it.

Fear is a vital part of the self-preservation mechanism. However, when fear leads to panic, we invite that which we want most to avoid. The survival records favor pilots who maintain their composure and know how to apply the general concepts and procedures that have been developed through the years. The success of an emergency landing is as much a matter of the mind as of skills.

Basic Safety Concepts
A pilot who is faced with an emergency landing in terrain that makes extensive aircraft damage inevitable should keep in mind that the avoidance of crash injuries is largely a matter of:

1. Keeping vital structure (flight deck where the pilot and passenger are seated) relatively intact by using dispensable structure, such as wings, landing gear, and carriage bottom to absorb the violence of the stopping process before it affects the occupants.

2. Avoiding forward wing movement relative to the carriage, allowing the mast to rotate into the flight deck occupants, or the front tube to compress and break, providing structure to impale/stab the occupants.

The advantage of sacrificing dispensable structure is demonstrated daily on the highways. A head-on car impact against a tree at 20 miles per hour (mph) is less hazardous for a properly restrained driver than a similar impact against the driver's door. Statistics indicate that the extent of crushable structure between the occupants and the principal point of impact on the aircraft has a direct bearing on the severity of the transmitted crash forces and, therefore, on survivability. Compared to an airplane, the WSC aircraft has less structure to absorb the impact and is moving slower, but the same principles apply.

Avoiding forcible contact with the front tube, cowling, dashboard, or outside structure is a matter of seat and body security with the use of seatbelts. Unless the occupant decelerates at the same rate as the surrounding structure, no benefit is realized from its relative intactness. The occupant is brought to a stop violently in the form of a secondary collision.

Dispensable aircraft structure is not the only available energy-absorbing medium in an emergency situation. Vegetation, trees, and even manmade structures may be used for this purpose. Cultivated fields with dense crops, such as mature corn and grain, are almost as effective in bringing an aircraft to a stop with repairable damage as an emergency arresting device on a runway. *[Figure 13-2]* Brush and small trees provide considerable cushioning and braking effect without destroying the aircraft. When dealing with natural and manmade obstacles with greater strength than the dispensable aircraft structure, the pilot must plan the touchdown in such a manner that only nonessential structure is "used up" in the principal slowing down process.

Figure 13-2. *Using vegetation to absorb energy.*

It should be noted that examples presented here are not to

be practiced because these situations are hazardous and can damage the WSC and injure occupants. These examples are shown for informational purposes, in case similar situations arise in the future.

The overall severity of a deceleration process is governed by speed (groundspeed) and stopping distance. The most critical of these is speed; doubling the groundspeed quadruples the total destructive energy and vice versa. Even a small change in groundspeed at touchdown, resulting from wind or pilot technique, affects the outcome of a controlled crash. It is important that the actual touchdown during an emergency landing be made at the lowest possible controllable airspeed using all available means.

Most pilots instinctively—and correctly—look for the largest available flat and open field for an emergency landing. Actually, very little stopping distance is required if the speed can be dissipated uniformly; that is, if the deceleration forces can be spread evenly over the available distance. This concept is designed into the arresting gear on aircraft carriers, and provides a nearly constant stopping force from the moment of hookup.

For example, assuming a uniform 2 G deceleration while landing into a headwind with a 25 mph groundspeed, the stopping distance is about 10.5 feet; in a downwind landing at 50 mph groundspeed, the required stopping distance is 42 feet—about four times as great. *[Figure 13-3]* Although these figures are based on an ideal deceleration process, it is interesting to note what can be accomplished in an effectively used short stopping distance. Additionally, landing uphill reduces the stopping distance and landing downhill increases the stopping distance. Understanding the need for a firm but uniform deceleration process in very poor terrain enables the pilot to select touchdown conditions that spread the breakup of dispensable structure over a short distance, thereby reducing the peak deceleration of the flight deck area. A careful consideration must be made considering wind, slope, and terrain.

Attitude and Sink Rate Control

The most critical and often the most inexcusable error that can be made in the planning and execution of an emergency landing, even in ideal terrain, is the loss of initiative over the aircraft's attitude and sink rate at touchdown. When the touchdown is made on flat, open terrain, an excessive nose-low pitch attitude brings the risk of "sticking" the nose in the ground. Steep bank angles just before touchdown should also be avoided, as they increase the stalling speed and the likelihood of a wingtip strike.

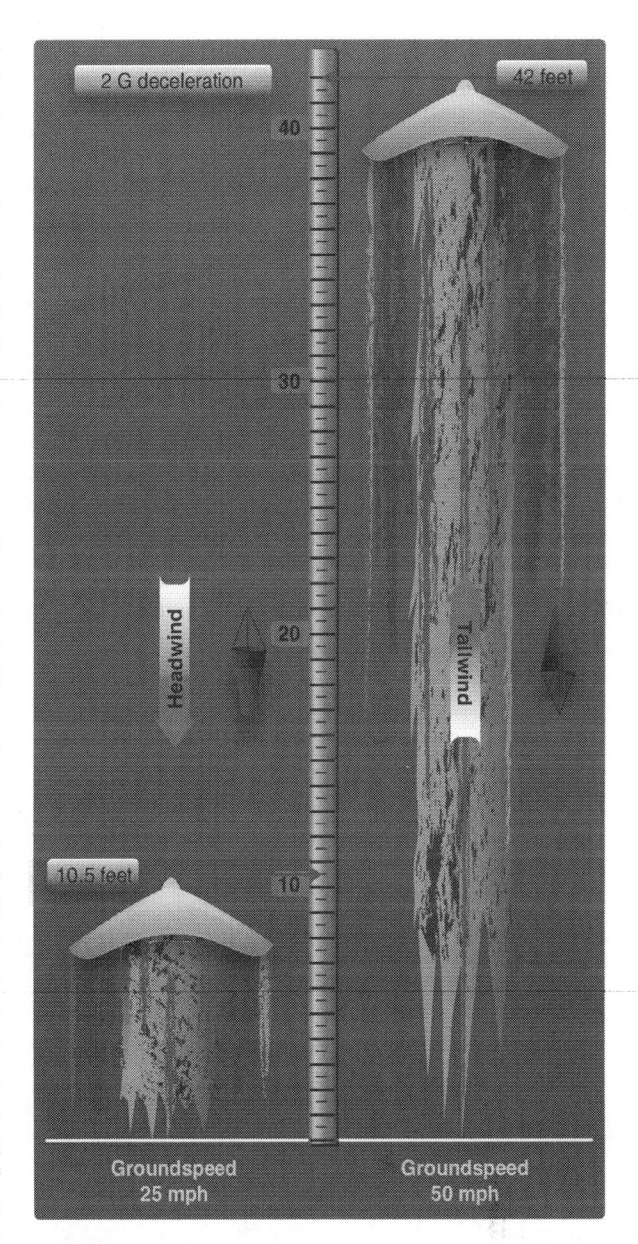

Figure 13-3. *Stopping distance vs. groundspeed.*

Since the aircraft's vertical component of velocity is immediately reduced to zero upon ground contact, it must be kept well under control. A flat touchdown at a high sink rate (well in excess of 500 feet per minute (fpm)) on a hard surface can be injurious without destroying the flight deck structure depending on the design of the airframe and the shock absorbing system. On soft terrain, an excessive sink rate may cause digging in of the nose wheel with the wing and/or WSC aircraft rotating forward into the ground, stopping with severe forward deceleration or tumbling with higher speeds.

Terrain Selection

A pilot's choice of emergency landing sites is governed by the:

- Route selected during preflight planning and
- Height above the ground when the emergency occurs.

The only time the pilot has a very limited choice is during low and slow flying or during takeoff if the landing approach is always within gliding distance of the runway.

It should be understood that the amount of area for available landing sites increases at a rapid rate with increased altitude. *[Figure 13-4]* As an example, a WSC aircraft with a 5 to 1 glide ratio flying at 500 feet AGL has 500 feet multiplied by five feet horizontal (or 2,500 feet) radius on the ground to select a suitable landing area. For example, use a ½ mile radius. The area of available landing spots is $\pi \times r^2$, approximately 0.8 square miles. At 1,000 feet AGL, this area would be 3.1 square miles; at 2,000 feet AGL, this is about 12.5 square miles; and at 5,000 AGL, this is almost 80 square miles.

Additionally, flying in a downwind direction provides more area to be covered while flying upwind reduces the amount of area that can be covered while looking for a suitable landing area.

If beyond gliding distance of a suitable open area, the pilot should judge the available terrain for its energy absorbing capability. If the emergency starts at a considerable height above the ground, the pilot should be more concerned about first selecting the desired general area than a specific spot. Terrain appearances from altitude can be very misleading and considerable altitude may be lost before the best spot can be pinpointed. For this reason, the pilot should not hesitate to discard the original plan for one that is clearly better. However, as a general rule, the pilot should not change his or her mind more than once.

Approach

When the pilot has time to maneuver, the planning of the approach should be governed by three factors:

1. Wind direction and velocity
2. Dimensions and slope of the chosen field
3. Obstacles in the final approach path and the field itself

These three factors are seldom compatible. When compromises must be made, the pilot should aim for a wind/obstacle/terrain combination that permits a final approach with some margin for error in judgment or technique. A pilot who overestimates the gliding range may be tempted to stretch the glide

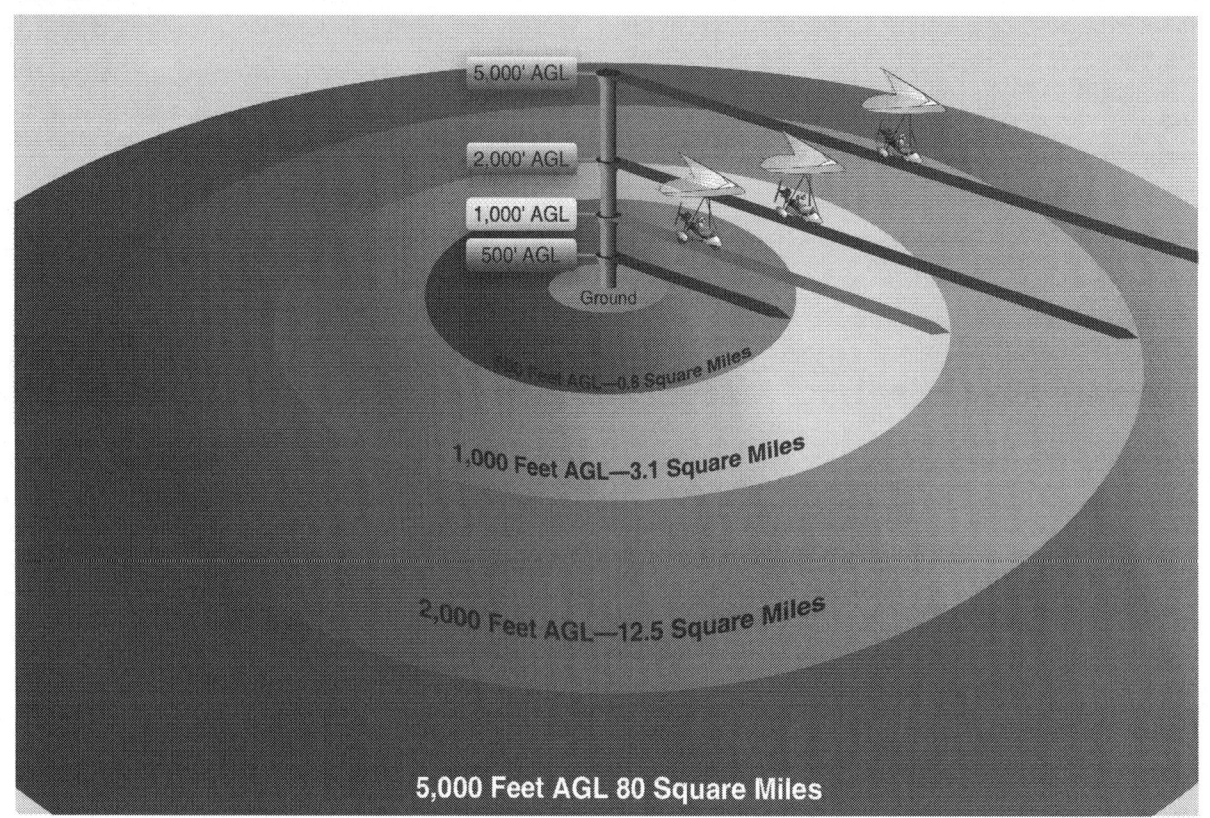

Figure 13-4. *Increased altitude provides increased landing options.*

across obstacles in the approach path. For this reason, it is sometimes better to plan the approach over an unobstructed area regardless of wind direction. Experience shows that a collision with obstacles at the end of a ground roll, or slide, is much less hazardous than striking an obstacle at flying speed before the touchdown point is reached.

Terrain Types
Since an emergency landing on suitable terrain resembles a situation with which the pilot should be familiar through training, only the more unusual situation is discussed.

Confined Areas
The natural preference to set the aircraft down on the ground should not lead to the selection of an open spot between trees or obstacles where the ground cannot be reached. Once the intended touchdown point is reached, and the remaining open and unobstructed space is very limited, it may be better to force the aircraft down on the ground than to delay touchdown until it stalls (settles). An aircraft decelerates faster after it is on the ground than while airborne.

A river or creek can be an inviting alternative in otherwise rugged terrain. The pilot should ensure that the water or creek bed can be reached without snagging the wings. The same concept applies to road landings with one additional reason for caution: manmade obstacles on either side of a road may not be visible until the final portion of the approach.

When planning the approach across a road, it should be remembered that most highways and even rural dirt roads are paralleled by power or telephone lines. Only a sharp lookout for the supporting structures or poles may provide timely warning.

If the only possible landing alternative is a small clearing and it is not possible to land the WSC aircraft, the BPS should be deployed, if equipped, as discussed earlier.

Trees
Although a tree landing is not an attractive prospect, the following general guidelines help to make the experience survivable.

For example, if the trees are taller than 15 feet and not dense enough to assure the wing could be set on top of them, use the BPS if so equipped. This provides two possible chances of hanging up in the trees and a slower descent rate if the WSC aircraft does not become lodged in the trees and continues a descent to the ground.

If the trees are estimated to be shorter than 15 feet or a BPS is not installed on the WSC aircraft, landing in the trees should be performed as follows:

- Keep the groundspeed low by heading into the wind.

- Make contact at minimum indicated airspeed, but not below stall speed, and "hang" the wing in the tree branches in a nose-high landing attitude. Involving the underside of the fuselage and both wings in the initial tree contact provides a more even and positive cushioning effect. Hold the control bar with both hands more than shoulder width apart and bend elbows to lessen the impact of the control bar against the chest. *[Figure 13-5]*

Figure 13-5. *Using treetops to "hang" the wing during an emergency landing.*

- Avoid direct contact of the fuselage with heavy tree trunks.

- Try to land in low, closely spaced trees with wide, dense crowns (branches) close to the ground, which are much better than tall trees with thin tops; the latter allow too much free fall height. (A free fall from 75 feet results in an impact speed of about 40 knots or about 4,000 fpm.)

- Ideally, initial tree contact should be symmetrical; that is, both wings should meet equal resistance in the tree branches. This distribution of the load helps to maintain proper aircraft attitude. It may also preclude the loss of one wing, which invariably leads to a more rapid and less predictable descent to the ground.

- If heavy tree trunk contact is unavoidable once the aircraft is on the ground, it is best to involve both wings simultaneously by directing the aircraft between two properly spaced trees. However, do not attempt this maneuver while still airborne.

Water Landings (Ditching)

Preflight planning for any flight where a water landing is possible should include personal flotation devices for the pilot and occupants. A hook knife should also be accessible for the pilot and passenger. A beach or landing spot where an emergency landing can be made on land, is preferred to landing in water. If a water landing must be made, the aircraft should be positioned close to land in shallow water, if possible, preferably four to five feet deep to use as a cushion but still deep enough to stand in with the head above water.

With any altitude above the water, preparations should be made to get rid of any items that would make it more difficult to exit the WSC aircraft and swim once it enters the water. This would include removing boots for swimming, discarding any camera lanyards, headphones, or other unnecessary items that could hinder the exit from the WSC aircraft once underwater.

There are not many actual accounts of WSC aircraft ditching in water, but all accounts at stalling above the water or flying it in at minimum controlled airspeed stops the WSC aircraft abruptly and puts the occupants under water immediately. Depending on the speed, the WSC could tumble over the water before stopping. Another account of a BPS deployment provided a successful entry into the water. In any event, the pilot and passenger would most likely be under water immediately and disorientated. There are two alternate techniques that have been successfully used for ditching in the water:

- Flying to the water and stalling just above the surface
- Using the BPS

Stalling Just Above the Water's Surface

With a stronger wind, flying to the water and stalling just above the surface is a viable alternative to landing in the water. It has been done a number of times successfully. The WSC aircraft should be flown directly into the wind to slow down the groundspeed as much as practical. Once the wheels are close to the water surface just above minimum controlled airspeed, abruptly push the control bar out to enter the water at the slowest speed possible. Take a deep breath and hold it before hitting the water.

Using the BPS

An alternate water landing technique is to use the BPS. This should not be used in calm winds because the parachute would come down over the WSC aircraft and the lines could entangle the occupants during the escape. A slight breeze or greater wind (some ripples on the water) is needed for this technique so the parachute does not come down directly onto the WSC aircraft. Use the BPS deployment technique discussed earlier. Take a deep breath and hold it before hitting the water.

Once Under Water in the WSC Aircraft

Once in the water, immediately release the seat belt, free yourself and passenger of any restrictions, and swim to the surface. If disoriented, swim toward light or follow bubbles upward to the surface. The WSC will be sinking, so escape must be made quickly. The control bar must be pushed forward at all costs to release the pilot to exit the aircraft and swim to the surface. The forces of the water could push the control bar back and pin the front seat/pilot into the seat. If the landing is in shallow water, the pressure pinning the pilot into the seat may stop when the WSC aircraft sinks to the bottom.

Emergency Equipment and Survival Gear

For any flight away from the airport, basic supplies should be carried in case there is engine failure. At a minimum, supplies should include a mobile phone/radio for retrieval, clothes appropriate for the environment, ropes to tie down the WSC aircraft, cash/valid credit cards, and food/water.

In the case of flying cross-country or over remote areas, emergency equipment should be carried for a possible extended period of being stranded. In addition to the basics listed above, suplies for the appropriate time in the elements should be carried. Survival gear for protection from the elements should include clothing for hot and cold climates, as applicable. Without proper clothing, someone can die within hours from hypothermia or heat exhaustion. Water is also very important for survival. Food is important, but a person can survive over a week without it. Additional items to include are a knife, signal mirror, extra portable radio and batteries, emergency smoke/flares, and a large space blanket doubling as tarp.

Other items specific to unique terrain and climate zone should also be considered. For mountain terrain, a saw, shovel, water purifier, and 100-foot rope would be appropriate. For large bodies of water, flotation devices, extra water, and a water purifier would be added to the basic survival gear. If in desert conditions, bring a lot of water and hats for shade. In situations of extreme temperature changes, add both sun shading and layered clothing to the gear as appropriate.

Engine Failure After Takeoff

As discussed earlier in Chapter 7, Takeoff and Departure Climbs, proper takeoff technique provides lower pitch angles during the initial climb to provide the slowest possible descent rate for an engine failure after takeoff. The pitch angle and altitude available for engine failure at takeoff are the controlling factors in the successful accomplishment of an emergency landing. If an actual engine failure should occur immediately after takeoff and before a safe maneuvering altitude is attained, it is usually inadvisable to attempt to turn back to the takeoff field. Instead, it is safer to establish the proper glide attitude immediately, and select a field directly ahead or slightly to either side of the takeoff path.

The decision to continue straight ahead is often difficult to make unless the problems involved in attempting to turn back are seriously considered. First, the takeoff was probably made into the wind. To return to the takeoff field, a downwind turn must be made. This increases the groundspeed and rushes the pilot even more in the performance of procedures and in planning the landing approach. Second, the aircraft loses considerable altitude during the turn and might still be in a bank when the ground is contacted, resulting in cartwheeling (a catastrophe for the occupants, as well as the aircraft). After turning downwind, the apparent increase in groundspeed could mislead the pilot into a premature attempt to slow the aircraft to a stall. Finally, it is more than one 180° turn. For example, it is first a 225° turn in one direction, then another 45° turn in the other direction, totaling 310° of turn. *[Figure 13-6]*

On the other hand, continuing straight ahead or making a slight turn allows the pilot more time to establish a safe landing attitude. The landing can be made as slowly as desired, but more importantly, the aircraft can be landed while under control.

At airports where the runways are much longer than needed, there is typically ample runway to make a straight ahead landing. If a tight pattern is being used and the crosswind leg is started at the end of the runway, turning back the additional 90° to the runway could be the best option, depending on the suitability of landing areas straight ahead.

Depending on the specific design of the WSC aircraft considering weight, wing, and carriage, this maneuver can

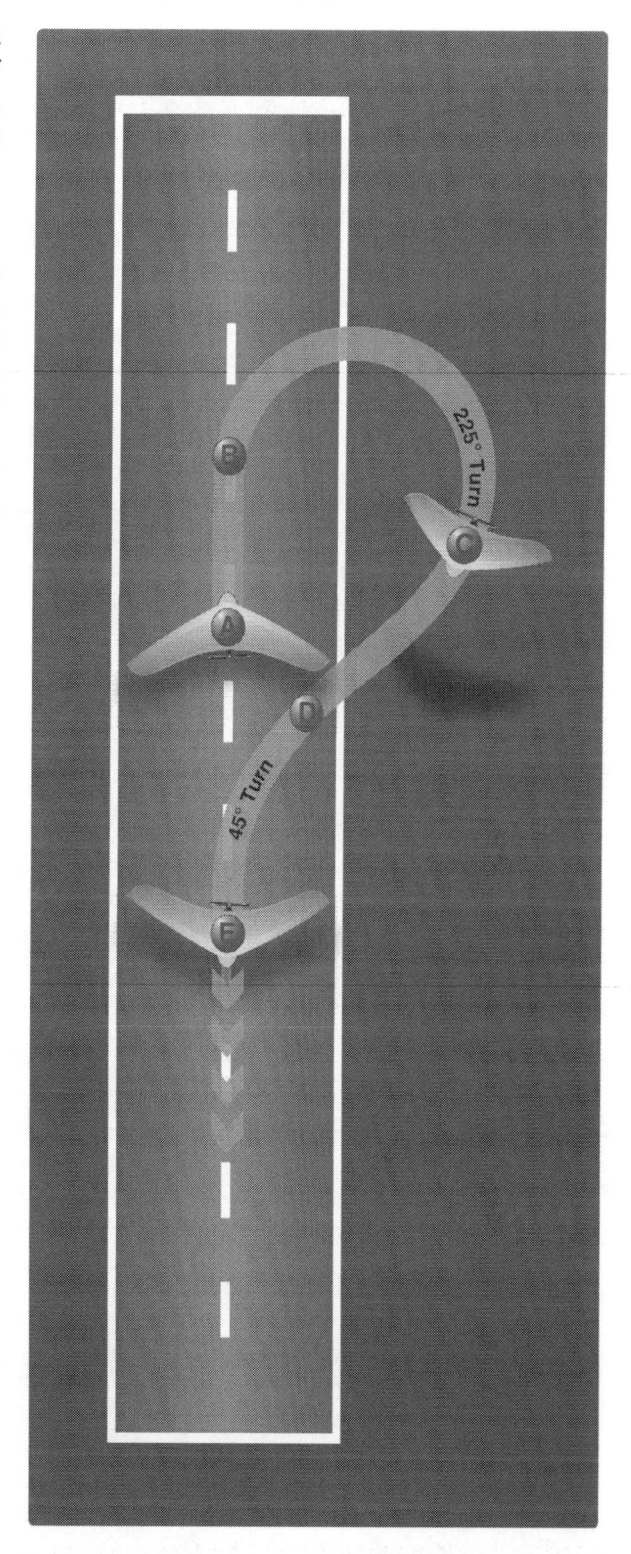

Figure 13-6. *Amount of turn required to land back on the takeoff runway.*

be performed with no reaction time and as low as 250 to 500 feet AGL. However, the pilot should determine the minimum altitude that such a maneuver would require of a particular aircraft. Experimentation at a much higher, safe altitude, 700 feet AGL as an example, should give the pilot an approximation of height lost in a descending 225° and 45° turn at idle power. Starting high above the ground at low bank angles and monitoring the altitude loss while doing the required turns to line back up on the runway provides a good reference. Finding the best bank angle to perform the required turns for this maneuver with minimum altitude loss is key to optimizing this maneuver and developing a habit if this maneuver is needed in a real emergency.

By adding a safety factor of about 30 percent to account for reaction time and no thrust from the propeller, the pilot should arrive at a practical decision height. The ability to make these turns does not necessarily mean that the departure runway can be reached in a power-off glide; this depends on the wind, the distance traveled during the climb, the height reached, and the glide distance of the aircraft without power.

This is a highly advanced maneuver with turns close to the ground. This should be practiced well into the training program with the instructor. For example, consider an aircraft which has taken off and climbed to an altitude of 350 feet AGL when the engine fails. After a typical 4-second reaction time, the pilot pulls down the nose, maintains control of the aircraft, and elects to turn back to the runway, losing 50 feet. *[Figure 13-6, A to B]* The pilot performs the 225° turn and loses 300 feet. *[Figure 13-6, B to C]* The pilot must glide back to the runway, losing another 50 feet. *[Figure 13-6, C to D]* The pilot must turn another 45° to head the aircraft toward the runway, losing another 50 feet. *[Figure 13-6, D to E]* By this time the total change in direction is 310°, the aircraft will have descended 450 feet, placing it 100 feet below the runway.

Emergency Descents

An emergency descent is a maneuver for descending as rapidly as possible to a lower altitude or to the ground for an emergency landing. The need for this maneuver may result from an uncontrollable fire, avoidance of other aircraft, weather, or any other situation demanding an immediate and rapid descent. The objective is to descend the aircraft as quickly as possible within the structural limitations of the aircraft. Simulated emergency descents should be made in a turn to check for other air traffic below and to look around for a possible emergency landing area. A radio call announcing descent intentions may be appropriate to alert other aircraft in the area. When initiating the descent, a bank angle of approximately 45° to 60° should be established to maintain positive load factors ("G" forces) on the aircraft.

Generally, the steeper the bank angle is, the quicker the descent is. But caution should be exercised with steep bank angles for extended periods because the high G forces and rotation can cause disorientation or motion sickness, which might make matters worse. The manufacturer's bank and speed limitations should not be exceeded.

Emergency descent training should be performed as recommended by the manufacturer, including the configuration and airspeeds. The power should be reduced to idle. The pilot should never allow the aircraft's airspeed to surpass the never-exceed speed (V_{NE}) or go above the maximum maneuvering (V_A) speed, as applicable. In the case of an engine fire, a high airspeed descent could extinguish the fire. The descent should be made at the maximum allowable bank angle and airspeed consistent with the procedure used. This provides increased loads and drag and therefore the loss of altitude as quickly as possible. The recovery from an emergency descent should be initiated at an altitude high enough to ensure a safe recovery back to level flight or a precautionary landing.

When the descent procedure is established and stabilized during training and practice, the descent should be terminated. For longer descents, alternating turn directions should be used so the pilot does not become disorientated. Prolonged practice of emergency descents should be avoided to prevent excessive cooling of the engine cylinders. *[Figure 13-7]*

Inflight Fire

A fire in flight demands immediate and decisive action. The pilot must be familiar with the procedures to meet this emergency as contained in the AFM/POH for the particular aircraft. For the purposes of this handbook, inflight fires are classified as: engine fires and electrical fires. If a fire extinguisher is installed on the WSC aircraft, the passenger should be briefed on its use and the pin should be connected to the extinguisher by a lanyard so it cannot be dropped into the propeller, creating a worse situation.

Engine Fire

An inflight engine fire is usually caused by a failure that allows a flammable substance such as fuel, oil, or hydraulic fluid to come in contact with a hot surface. This may be caused by a mechanical failure of the engine itself, an engine-driven accessory, a defective induction or exhaust system, or a broken line. Engine fires may also result from maintenance errors, such as improperly installed/fastened lines and/or fittings, resulting in leaks.

Engine fires can be indicated by smoke and/or flames coming from the engine area. They can also be indicated by discoloration, bubbling, and/or melting of the engine cowling

Figure 13-7. *Emergency descent showing alternate right and left hand steep descending turns.*

skin in cases where flames and/or smoke are not visible to the pilot. By the time a pilot becomes aware of an inflight engine fire, it usually is well developed. Unless the aircraft manufacturer directs otherwise in the AFM/POH, the first step after discovering a fire is to shut off the fuel supply to the engine (if so equipped). The ignition switch should be left on in order to use up the fuel that remains in the fuel lines and components between the fuel selector/shutoff valve and the engine (if equipped with an electric fuel pump). This procedure may starve the fire of fuel and cause the fire to die naturally. If the flames are snuffed out, no attempt should be made to restart the engine.

If the engine fire is oil-fed, the smoke is thick and black, as opposed to a fuel-fed fire which produces bright flames with less smoke.

Some light aircraft emergency checklists direct the pilot to shut off the electrical master switch. However, the pilot should consider that unless the fire is electrical in nature, or a crash landing is imminent, deactivating the electrical system prevents the use of radios for transmitting distress messages and also causes air traffic control (ATC) to lose transponder returns.

The pilot must be familiar with the aircraft's emergency descent procedures and remember that:

- An engine fire on a WSC aircraft means the flames are going to the rear of the aircraft where minimum components are exposed. If the BPS is used, it would change the direction of the flames, possibly setting the wing and/or fuselage on fire. The flames could also burn the parachute line, creating worse problems.
- The aircraft may be structurally damaged to the point that its controllability could be lost at any moment.
- The aircraft may still be on fire and susceptible to explosion.
- The aircraft is expendable—the only thing that matters is the safety of those on board.

Electrical Fires

The initial indication of an electrical fire is usually a slight amount of smoke and the distinct odor of burning insulation, which may not be noticeable in a WSC open flight deck. Once an electrical fire is detected, the pilot should attempt to identify the faulty circuit by checking circuit breakers, instruments, avionics, and lights. If the faulty circuit cannot be readily detected and isolated, and flight conditions permit, the battery master switch should be turned off to remove the possible source of the fire. However, any materials that have been ignited may continue to burn.

If electrical power is absolutely essential for the flight, an attempt may be made to identify and isolate the faulty circuit by:

1. Turning the electrical master switch off.
2. Turning all individual electrical switches off.
3. Turning the master switch back on.
4. Selecting electrical switches that were on before the fire indication one at a time, permitting a short time lapse after each switch is turned on to check for signs of odor, smoke, or sparks.

This procedure, however, has the effect of recreating the original problem. The most prudent course of action is to land as soon as possible.

The electrical fire could expand into a larger fire in the carriage. A fire in the cabin presents the pilot with two immediate demands: attacking the fire and getting the aircraft safely on the ground as quickly as possible.

System Malfunctions
Electrical System

The loss of electrical power can deprive the pilot of communications and navigation systems, but for day/VFR conditions this is not a life threatening situation because most engines ignition systems are on a separate electrical system and not dependent on the battery for keeping the engine running. However, losing communications does present some challenges especially if operating at a controlled tower airport in which procedures in the Airman's Information Manual (AIM) would be followed.

Pitot-Static System

The source of the pressure for operating the airspeed indicator, the vertical speed indicator, and the altimeter is the pitot-static system. Most WSC aircraft have pressure for the airspeed indicator. If this becomes plugged, the airspeed indicator may not read properly. If it is suspected that the airspeed indicator is not reading properly, use the feel of the aircraft and the trim position to determine speed. It is perfectly safe to fly a WSC aircraft without an airspeed indicator if the pilot has developed a feel of the aircraft since the trim position speed is known and all other speeds can be determined based on the feel of the air and the pressure on the control bar.

Altitude and vertical speed utilize static pressure. Because there is typically no static line connecting these, they operate independently. Therefore, if one fails or becomes plugged, the other can act as a reference. For example, if the altimeter fails for any reason, the vertical speed indicator would provide the pilot with information on whether the aircraft was climbing, level, or descending. The global positioning system (GPS) (if equipped) could also provide altitude readings. If the vertical speed indicator failed, the altimeter could provide information on whether the aircraft was climbing, level, or descending by looking at the altitude reading over time.

Landing Gear Malfunction

If there is any landing gear malfunction before or during takeoff, the flight or takeoff should be aborted and the malfunction fixed before attempting another takeoff. However, if a malfunction takes place during or after takeoff in which the landing gear is not completely functional for landing, the situation should be evaluated using aeronautical decision-making (ADM) to make the best choice based on the outcome of the situation.

If a tire falls off, a known flat of the tire is evident, or a landing gear strut has shaken loose or become damaged, precautionary measures must be taken to minimize the results from landing with a defective landing gear.

Fly to a smooth runway where the WSC aircraft can skid and not stop abruptly and tumble. Inform the local ATC, UNICOM, or multicom frequency that there is a MAYDAY in order to obtain immediate help for a crash landing.

There is no hurry to land, so use ADM to survey the situation and make the best decision on where and how to land. Find a location that has medical support, a smooth runway that minimizes abrupt stops/tumbling, and land into the wind for the best outcome. Attempt to make a normal approach into the wind with the lowest possible speed to touchdown.

Inadvertant Propeller Strike

A propeller strike in a pusher WSC aircraft is more dangerous than in any other aircraft. If an object or the propeller is flung up into the wing trailing edge, a structural failure could occur. This situation should not be underestimated or ignored.

Procedures should be implemented and followed to avoid propeller strikes from articles flying out of the flight deck. Passengers sitting in the back are the greatest risk to propeller strikes. A comprehensive preflight brief with proper flight deck management procedures should reveal any open pockets or items that could dislodge and fly into the propeller. The passenger in the back should be instructed not to take off gloves, helmet, or glasses, or pull out a camera/mobile phone without a lanyard. However, the passenger in the rear seat cannot be monitored completely; it is possible that items could fly out of the flight deck and go through the propeller, presenting a serious situation.

If a bird strike occurs or anything else hits the propeller, reduce throttle immediately and evaluate the situation. The severity of the vibration is the key element to determining what to do. If the vibration is severe, shut off the engine and make an emergency landing. Minor vibration can be tolerated, but the risk of flying with a damaged propeller, which could dislodge and hit the sail, should be minimized. It is best to shut down the engine and perform an emergency landing.

Stuck or Runaway Throttle

Throttles can stick above idle or unexpectedly increase, which is called a runaway throttle. If on the ground, a runaway throttle can be disastrous if not anticipated and mitigated. A pilot (and instructor, if teaching) should always have access to the ignition system in order to shut it off immediately in the event of a throttle stuck above idle or a runaway throttle. A runaway throttle can be caused by the pilot or student pushing on the throttle pedal during taxi or startup, thinking it is the right brake, as in an airplane. Setting the cruise throttle to full open rather than full closed during startup also causes a runaway throttle. On startup, the checklists must be followed, including cruise throttle closed, foot off of foot throttle, brake on, propeller cleared, etc. The PIC must have control of the ignition to shut it off immediately during startup and taxi.

A runaway or stuck throttle during flight can be handled by climbing or flying to a suitable location where the engine can be shut off and a safe engine-off landing can be made.

Abnormal Engine Instrument Indications

The AFM/POH for the specific aircraft contains information that should be followed in the event of any abnormal engine instrument indications. The table in *Figure 13-8* offers generic information on some of the more commonly experienced inflight abnormal engine instrument indications, their possible causes, and corrective actions. It is important to know that when an engine temperature probe fails, it usually reads an unusually low value, zero, or does not register. This should be taken into account when evaluating the situation with engine instruments.

MALFUNCTION	PROBABLE CAUSE	CORRECTIVE ACTION
For all engines			
Slow loss of RPM during cruise flight	Carburetor or induction icing or air filter clogging	Apply carburetor heat. If dirty filter is suspected, divert to closest airport.
High cylinder head temperature (CHT)	Insufficient airspeed for cooling (for ram air cooling systems)	Reduce throttle. Increase airspeed.
	Improper mixture adjustment	Reduce throttle. Land as soon as possible.
	Detonation or preignition	Reduce power, increase cooling airflow. Land as soon as practical.
Very high cylinder head temperatures (CHT) and climbing	Cooling system failure	Reduce throttle and land as soon as practical. Shut off engine if readings climb well above manufacturer's limits to avoid engine damage.
Low cylinder head temperature (CHT)	Excessively rich mixture	Reduce altitude.
	Extended glides without clearing engine	Clear engine long enough to keep temperatures at minimum range.
High exhaust gas temperature (EGT)	Lean mixture from improper jetting (can result from jetting set for higher altitude airport and flying to lower altitude airport)	Reduce throttle. Land as soon as practical.
	Lean mixture from additional air leaking into induction system	Reduce throttle. Land as soon as possible.
Low exhaust gas temperature (EGT)	Rich mixture from improper jetting	Land as soon as practical.
Ammeter indicating discharge	Magneto/generator failure	Shed unnecessary electrical load. Land as soon as practicable.
Rough running engine	Improper mixture	Land as soon as practical.
	Carburetors out of adjustment or out of synchronization (more evident at lower rpm)	Idle at higher rpm. Land as soon as practical.
	Detonation or preignition	Reduce power. Land as soon as practical.
	Induction air leak	Reduce power. Land as soon as practical.
	Plugged fuel nozzle (for fuel injection)	Reduce power. Land as soon as practical.
For four-stroke engines only			
High oil temperature	Oil congealed in cooler	Reduce power. Land. Preheat engine.
	Inadequate engine cooling	Reduce power. Increase airspeed.
	Detonation or preignition	Observe cylinder head temperatures for high reading. Descend to enrich mixture.
	Forthcoming internal engine failure	Land as soon as possible.
	Defective thermostatic oil cooler control	Land as soon as possible.
Low oil temperature	Engine not warmed up to operating temperature	Warm engine in prescribed manner.
High oil pressure	Cold oil	Warm engine in prescribed manner.
	Possible internal plugging	Reduce power. Land as soon as possible.
Low oil pressure	Broken pressure relief valve	Land as soon as possible.
	Insufficient oil	Land as soon as possible.
	Burned out bearings	Land as soon as possible.
Fluctuating oil pressure	Low oil supply, loose oil lines, defective pressure relief valve	Land as soon as possible.

Figure 13-8. *Common inflight abnormal engine instrument indications, causes, and corrective inflight actions.*

Weather Related Emergencies

High Winds and Strong Turbulence

Preflight planning for intended airports and winds aloft over the planned route and possible diversions can provide the pilot a means of anticipating the winds that would exceed aircraft or pilot capabilities. However, unanticipated high winds can create an emergency for any aircraft. High winds during cruise flight are not a danger unless they create extreme/severe turbulence, or the pilot is flying with questionable fuel reserves into a headwind that is stronger than expected.

High Winds and Turbulence During Cruise Flight

If the winds at cruise altitude provide an unanticipated slower groundspeed than planned, and the fuel reserves are questionable, the flight should be diverted to an alternate airport so there is no chance of running out of fuel for the intended flight. Stronger headwinds and crosswinds slow the groundspeed; tailwinds increase the groundspeed, resulting in the ability to reach airports that are farther away. The GPS is an accurate tool for measuring an aircraft's groundspeed during flight.

In high winds, it is generally advisable to cruise with enough ground clearance to assure that turbulence or sinking air does not reduce altitude to an unsafe level. For example, maintain at least 1,000 feet AGL when flying in strong winds to be far enough away from the ground to account for any turbulence, wind shear, or downdrafts.

If a pilot is flying and sees high wind or a gust front approaching with blowing dust or other indicators, a decision must be made to land and secure the WSC aircraft before the gust front hits, or turn and fly away from the area as fast as possible. Never fly into a gust front. If it looks like strong winds, it probably is and avoiding it is wise.

Strong turbulence can be created from high winds, wind shear, rising/falling unstable air, or any combination of these. As described in the basic flight maneuvers chapter, the pilot should keep the wings and pitch angle within the manufacturer's limitations through power and control bar flying techniques. Generally, if the turbulence continues to increase, fly back to where the turbulence was less severe instead of continuing where the turbulence might become more severe. However, if the pitch becomes too high and a whip stall occurs, as the nose drops into a dive, the pilot should push the control bar full forward and apply full power for the best chance of recovering to normal flight and not progressing into a tumble. The best whip stall/tumble avoidance is to avoid severe turbulence and keeping the nose within the manufacturer's limitations.

High Winds and Turbulence During Takeoffs and Landings

Takeoffs in high winds can simply be avoided by deciding not to fly. However, if a pilot takes off and encounters high winds or turbulence, high energy should be maintained throughout the climb and departure.

If it is determined that the winds are too high for landing at the intended location, divert to another location or wait until the strong winds subside to land. This is where the Automated Weather Observation Station (AWOS), Automated Surface Observing System (ASOS), or radio contact with other airports can assist the pilot in finding an airport with wind conditions within the pilot's capabilities and aircraft limitations.

If the headwind is within the pilot's capabilities and aircraft limitations but the crosswinds are above any limitations, the pilot may need to land on a taxiway or sideways on a runway that is wide enough, thus reducing the crosswind component to acceptable levels. Strong winds produce strong mechanical turbulence on the lee side of objects which should be considered and avoided during any takeoff or landing in strong winds.

High Winds During Taxi

For strong head winds during taxi, the nose must be lowered to keep the WSC aircraft on the ground. Raising the nose could allow the WSC aircraft to lift off. In any case, the nose should be lowered completely to keep the WSC aircraft on the ground. In strong tail winds, the nose must be raised so that the wind does not get underneath the wing and lift it up from the back and possibly tumble it forward. If the wing starts to lift from the back, release the brake and push the control bar forward to keep the wing from lifting and possibly tumbling forward.

Strong crosswinds during taxi must be managed by keeping the wing level or slightly down into the wind so the wind does not catch it, lift up, and topple the WSC aircraft to the side, causing significant damage. If the wind pushes down on the wing, it could pin it to the ground which is the better option. If the wing does become pinned from the wind, the pilot can give some throttle and steer into the wind, rotating around the tip and freeing the wing from the pinned state. This may cause damage to the tip from scraping on the ground. If the windward side gets too high and wind gets under the wing lifting it from the side, all efforts should be made to hold it down while the front wheel is turned downwind and the nose raised to turn with the wind and avoid tumbling sideways.

Taxiing to a location that is on the leeward side of a structure into the wind shadow provides the best option for exiting the WSC aircraft in high winds. When available, seek assistance to exit and/or secure the WSC. If no wind shadow is available, the pilot can turn the WSC aircraft into crosswind and pin the wing to exit.

Inadvertent Flight into Instrument Meteorological Conditions (IMC)

Proper flight planning using available weather resources should allow a pilot to avoid flying when the probability of low visibility is high. It is expected that WSC pilots exercise good judgment and not attempt to fly when the visibility is questionable. However, this section is included as background for this emergency procedure for inadvertent flight into instrument meteorological conditions (IMC), flight without visual reference to the horizon.

Although it is possible to get an attitude indicator installed in a WSC aircraft, there are no training requirements for flying by instruments for sport or private pilot WSC ratings. Samples of these instruments are shown in *Figures 13-9* and *13-10*.

Sport pilots are not allowed to fly unless there is visual reference to the surface and three miles visibility. This is different for private pilots for whom there is not a requirement for visual reference to the ground and the minimum flight visibility is only one statute mile (SM).

Accident statistics show that the average airplane pilot who has not been trained in attitude instrument flying, or one whose instrument skills have eroded, will lose control of the aircraft in about 10 minutes once forced to rely solely on instrument reference. WSC pilots without any instrument training attempting to use instruments in IMC conditions would lose control much sooner. No WSC pilot should attempt flight into IMC conditions.

The purpose of this section is to provide guidance on practical emergency measures to maintain aircraft control in the event a VFR pilot encounters IMC conditions. The main goal is not instrument flying; it is to help the VFR pilot keep the aircraft under adequate control until suitable visual references are regained.

The first steps necessary for surviving an encounter with IMC by a VFR pilot are:

- Recognition and acceptance of the gravity of the situation and the need for immediate remedial action.

Figure 13-9. *Optional analog gauges for instrument flying: attitude indicator (top middle) and direction indicator (lower left) not typically installed on WSC aircraft.*

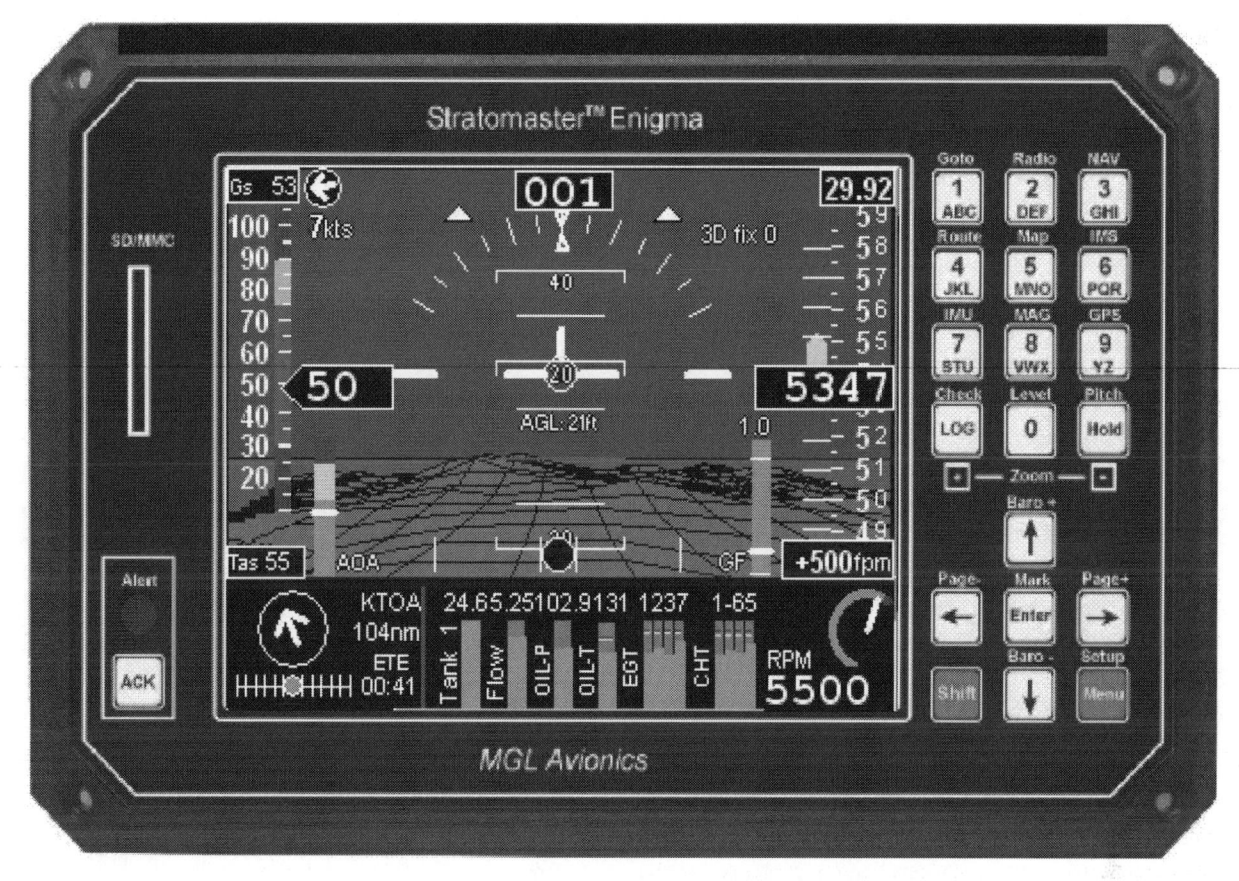

Figure 13-10. *Digital panel with attitude indicator and direction indicator used on some WSC aircraft.*

- Maintaining control of the aircraft.
- Obtaining the appropriate assistance in getting the aircraft out of IMC conditions.

Recognition

A VFR pilot is in IMC conditions anytime he or she is unable to maintain aircraft attitude control by visual reference to the natural horizon, regardless of the circumstances or the prevailing weather conditions. Additionally, the VFR pilot is in IMC any time he or she is inadvertently or intentionally and for an indeterminate period of time unable to navigate or establish geographical position by visual reference to landmarks on the surface. These situations must be accepted by the pilot involved as a genuine emergency requiring immediate action.

As discussed earlier, when entering conditions in which visibility is decreasing or IMC, the pilot should turn around, climb, or descend immediately and return to where ground visibility is known. Do not continue assuming that conditions will clear and visibility will be regained.

Maintaining Aircraft Control

Once the pilot recognizes and accepts the situation, he or she must understand that the only way to control the aircraft safely is by using and trusting the flight instruments. Attempts to control the aircraft partially by reference to flight instruments while searching outside the flight deck for visual confirmation of the information provided by those instruments results in inadequate aircraft control. This may be followed by spatial disorientation and complete loss of control.

The most important point to be stressed is that the pilot must not panic. Recognize the situation and take immediate action. The task at hand may seem overwhelming, and the situation may be compounded by extreme apprehension. The pilot must make a conscious effort to relax and understand that the only concern at this point is to fly toward known visibility. If climbing into a cloud, reduce throttle and descend. If descending into a cloud, increase throttle and climb out of the cloud. If visibility is suddenly lost (e.g. flying into a cloud), turn 180° and fly toward known visibility.

The pilot should remember that a person cannot feel control pressures with a tight grip on the controls. Relaxing and learning to control with the eyes and the brain instead of muscles usually takes considerable conscious effort.

The pilot must believe that the flight instruments show the aircraft's pitch attitude and direction regardless of what the natural senses tell. The vestibular sense (motion sensing by the inner ear) can confuse the pilot. Because of inertia, the sensory areas of the inner ear cannot detect slight changes in aircraft attitude nor can they accurately sense attitude changes which occur at a uniform rate over a period of time. On the other hand, false sensations are often generated, leading the pilot to believe the pitch attitude or direction attitude of the aircraft has changed when, in fact, it has not. These false sensations result in the pilot experiencing spatial disorientation.

Attitude Control

Attitude is defined as "The position of an aircraft as determined by the relationship of its axes and a reference, usually the earth's horizon." For WSC, the pitch and the roll are the relevant attitudes.

Most aircraft are generally, by design, inherently stable platforms and, except in turbulent air, maintain approximately straight-and-level flight if properly trimmed and left alone. They are designed to maintain a state of equilibrium in pitch, roll, and yaw. The pilot must be aware, however, that a change about one axis affects the other axes. The WSC aircraft is stable in the yaw and pitch axes, but less stable in the roll axis. The yaw and pitch axes of the WSC are easy to control, but the roll axis is the challenge for WSC aircraft control in IMC. The key to emergency aircraft attitude and directional control, therefore, is to:

- Fly at the normal trim speed. To climb, increase throttle; to descend, decrease throttle. To fly level, fly at the throttle setting that provides level flight. The vertical speed indicator or altimeter provides information regarding pitch attitude.

- Resist the tendency to overcontrol the aircraft. Fly with fingertip control. No attitude changes should be made unless the flight instruments indicate a definite need for a change.

- Make all attitude changes smooth and small, yet with positive pressure.

The primary instrument for roll control is the attitude indicator if so equipped. *[Figures 13-9 and 13-10]*

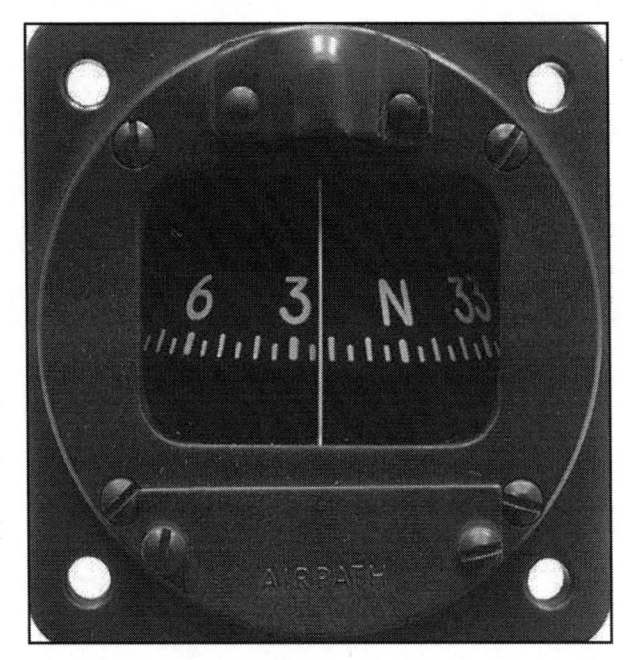

Figure 13-11. *Analog magnetic compass.*

For aircraft not equipped with an attitude indicator, a magnetic compass *[Figure 13-11]* or a GPS *[Figure 13-12]* are the instruments that can be used for roll control. The compass stays stationary and the WSC aircraft rotates around the compass dial. A pilot is flying wings level if the compass heading is not changing. If the compass is changing direction, the aircraft is banked into a turn. Similarly, the GPS provides ground track. If flying wings level, the GPS ground track is steady. If the GPS ground track is changing, the aircraft is in a bank and turning.

Turns

Turns are perhaps the most potentially dangerous maneuver for the untrained instrument pilot for two reasons:

- The normal tendency of the pilot to overcontrol, leading to steep banks.

- The inability of the pilot to cope with the instability resulting from the turn.

As an example, a 180° turn would be the most likely turn to exit a cloud and return to where there is visibility with the surface. The direction the turn started should be noted in order to determine the direction needed to exit the IMC conditions. For example, if heading North when flying into the cloud, turn 180° and head South to exit the cloud.

13-18

When a turn must be made, the pilot should anticipate and cope with the relative instability of the roll axis. The smallest practical bank angle should be used—in any case no more than 10° bank angle. *[Figure 13-13]* A shallow bank takes very little vertical lift from the wings, resulting in little if any deviation in altitude, and the WSC aircraft can continue to be flown at trim speed. It may be helpful to turn 90° and then reduce the bank and return to level flight. This process may relieve the progressive overbanking that often results from prolonged turns. Repeat the process twice until heading in the opposite direction of entry in order to exit. Once on the proper heading to exit the IMC conditions, maintain this heading until obtaining visual reference with the surface.

Turns with a magnetic compass or a GPS would be similar but the only indication of bank angle is the rate at which the compass or GPS is rotating. The rotation should be slow and steady and not increase in speed. Any increase in compass or GPS rotation should be slowed by decreasing the bank back to level flight to avoid increasing the bank. Practicing gentle turns and observing the rotational speed of the compass and GPS under VFR conditions will help a pilot recognize an acceptable rotational speed flying at trim speed should need ever arise.

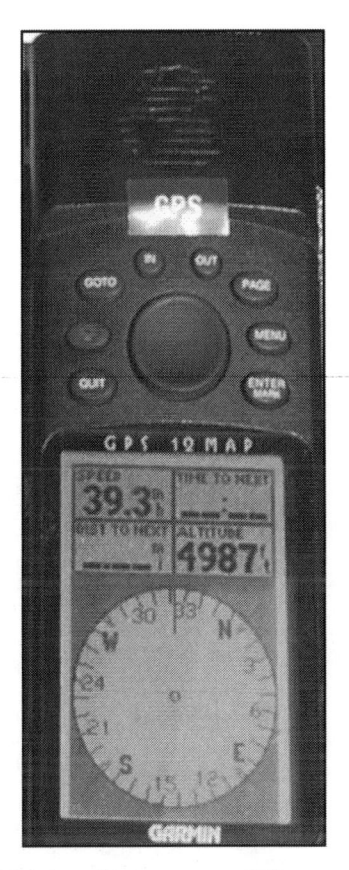

Figure 13-12. *Global positioning system (GPS).*

Figure 13-13. *Level turn.*

13-19

Chapter Summary

Most emergency situations can be avoided through proper maintenance and preflight planning. The following summarizes emergency procedures when they are warranted.

- Emergency landings require careful thought to evaluate wind and terrain for a successful outcome.

- Emergency descents may be required because of weather, avoiding other aircraft, or aircraft fire.

- Corrective action for system malfunction depends on the specific aircraft procedures.

- High winds and turbulence are less of a threat when the WSC aircraft is a significant distance above the ground. It is takeoff and especially landing where high winds and turbulence become the biggest problem. Do not takeoff, fly, or land when the winds and turbulence exceed aircraft limitations or pilot capabilities.

- If the VFR pilot flies into IMC conditions, the pilot should return to an area of known VFR conditions.

- The BPS should be used as a last option and only if total loss of control with no chance of recovery, pilot incapacitation, or engine failure over hostile terrain.

Glossary

100-hour inspection. An inspection required by 14 CFR section 91.409 for FAA-certificated aircraft that are operated for hire, or are used for flight instruction for hire. A 100-hour inspection is similar in content to an annual inspection, but it can be conducted by an aircraft mechanic who holds an Airframe and Powerplant rating, but does not have an Inspection Authorization. A list of the items that must be included in an annual or 100-hour inspection is included in 14 CFR part 43, Appendix D.

14 CFR. See Title 14 of the Code of Federal Regulations.

14 CFR Part 1. Federal Aviation Regulation from 14 CFR, pertaining to definitions and abbreviations of terms.

14 CFR Part 61. Federal Aviation Regulation from 14 CFR, pertaining to the issuance of pilot and instructor certificates and ratings.

14 CFR Part 67. Federal Aviation Regulation from 14 CFR, pertaining to medical standards and certification for pilots.

14 CFR Part 91. Federal Aviation Regulation from 14 CFR, pertaining to general operating and flight rules.

800-WX-BRIEF. Phone number for reaching an FAA Automated Flight Service Station 24 hours a day almost anywhere in the United States.

Aborted takeoff. To terminate a planned takeoff when it is determined that some condition exists which makes takeoff or further flight dangerous.

Above ground level (AGL). The actual height above ground level (AGL) at which the aircraft is flying.

Acceleration. Force involved in overcoming inertia, and which may be defined as a change in velocity per unit of time.

AD. See Airworthiness Directive.

ADM. See aeronautical decision-making.

Adverse yaw. A flight condition at the beginning of a turn in which the nose of the aircraft starts to move in the direction opposite the direction the turn is being made, caused by the induced drag produced by the downward-deflected tip holding back the wing as it begins to rise.

Aerodynamics. The science of the action of air on an object, and with the motion of air on other gases. Aerodynamics deals with the production of lift by the aircraft, the relative wind, and the atmosphere.

Aeronautical chart. A map used in air navigation containing all or part of the following: topographic features, hazards and obstructions, navigation aids, navigation routes, designated airspace, and airports. See also Sectional Chart.

Aeronautical decision-making (ADM). A systematic approach to the mental process used by pilots to consistently determine the best course of action in response to a given set of circumstances.

A/FD. See airport/facility directory.

AFM. See aircraft flight manual.

AFSS. See automated flight service station.

Aircraft. A device that is used or intended to be used for flight in the air.

Aircraft accident. An occurrence associated with the operation of an aircraft that takes place between the time any person boards the aircraft with the intention of flight and all such persons have disembarked, and in which any person suffers death or serious injury or in which the aircraft receives substantial damage. (NTSB 830.2)

Aircraft categories. (1) As used with respect to the certification, ratings, privileges, and limitations of airmen, means a broad classification of aircraft. Examples include: powered parachute, airplane, rotorcraft, glider, lighter-than-air, and weight-shift control. (2) As used with respect to the certification of aircraft, means a grouping of aircraft based upon intended use or operating limitations. Examples include: transport, normal, utility, acrobatic, limited, restricted, and provisional.

Aircraft flight manual (AFM). Also called the Pilot's Operating Handbook (POH), a document developed by the aircraft manufacturer and approved by the FAA. It is specific to a particular make and model aircraft by a serial number, and contains operating procedures and limitations.

Aircraft operating instructions (AOI). An alternative to the approved term, Pilot's Operating Handbook.

Airfoil. Any surface, such as a wing or propeller, which provides aerodynamic force when it interacts with a moving stream of air.

Airmanship. A sound acquaintance with the principles of flight, the ability to operate an airplane with competence and precision both on the ground and in the air, and the exercise of sound judgment that results in optimal operational safety and efficiency.

Airmanship skills. The skills of coordination, timing, control touch, and speed sense in addition to the motor skills required to fly an aircraft.

Airport. An area of land or water that is used or intended to be used for the landing and takeoff of aircraft, including its buildings and facilities, if any.

Airport/facility directory (A/FD). A publication of the Federal Aviation Administration containing information on all airports, seaplane bases, and heliports open to the public. The A/FD contains communication data, navigational facilities, and certain special notices and procedures.

Airspace. The space above a certain geographical area.

Airworthiness. A state in which an aircraft or component meets the conditions of its type design and is in a condition for safe operation.

Airworthiness Certificate. A certificate issued by the FAA to aircraft that have been proven to meet the minimum standards set down by the Code of Federal Regulations.

Airworthiness Directive (AD). A regulatory notice sent out by the FAA to the registered owner of an aircraft informing the owner of a condition that prevents the aircraft from continuing to meet its conditions for airworthiness. Compliance with AD notes must be within the required time limit, and the fact of compliance, the date of compliance, and the method of compliance must be recorded in the aircraft's maintenance records.

Altimeter. A flight instrument that indicates altitude by sensing pressure changes.

AME. See Aviation Medical Examiner.

Ammeter. An instrument installed in series with an electrical load used to measure the amount of current flowing through the load.

Angle of attack (AOA). The acute angle between the chord line of the airfoil and the direction of the relative wind.

Angle of incidence. The angle formed by the chord line of the wing at the keel of a WSC and a line parallel to the longitudinal axis of the WSC carriage. The angle of incidence changes in the WSC controlled by the pilot.

Anhedral. A downward slant from root to tip of an aircraft's wing opposite from dihedral.

Annual inspection. A complete inspection of an aircraft and engine, required by the Code of Federal Regulations, to be accomplished every 12 calendar months on all certificated aircraft. Only an A&P technician holding an Inspection Authorization can conduct an annual inspection.

AOA. See angle of attack.

AOI. See aircraft operating instructions.

Arm. The horizontal distance in inches from the reference datum line to the center of gravity of an item. Used in weight and loading calculations.

AROW. Certificates and documents required to be onboard an aircraft to determine airworthiness: Airworthiness certificate, Registration certificate, Operating limitations, Weight and balance data.

ASOS. See Automated Surface Observing System.

Aspect ratio. Span of a wing divided by its average chord.

Asymmetrical airfoil. An airfoil section that is not the same on both sides of the chord line.

ATC. Air traffic control.

ATIS. See Automatic Terminal Information Service.

Attitude. The position of an aircraft as determined by the relationship of its axes and a reference, usually the earth's horizon.

Attitude of pilot. A personal motivational predisposition to respond to persons, situations, or events in a given manner that can, nevertheless, be changed or modified through training as sort of a mental shortcut to decision-making.

Attitude management of pilot. The ability to recognize hazardous attitudes in oneself and the willingness to modify them as necessary through the application of an appropriate antidote thought.

Automated flight service station. An FAA air traffic facility that provides pilot briefings, en route radio communications, and VFR search-and-rescue services.

Automated Surface Observing System (ASOS). Weather reporting system which provides surface observations every minute via digitized voice broadcasts and printed reports.

Automated Weather Observing System (AWOS). Automated weather reporting system consisting of various sensors, a processor, a computer-generated voice subsystem, and a transmitter to broadcast weather data.

Automatic Terminal Information Service (ATIS). The continuous broadcast (by radio or telephone) of recorded noncontrol, essential but routine information in selected terminal areas.

Aviation Medical Examiner (AME). A medical doctor authorized to perform aviation medical exams for aviators.

Axes of an aircraft. Three imaginary lines that pass through an aircraft's center of gravity. The axes can be considered as imaginary axes around which the aircraft turns. The three axes pass through the center of gravity at 90° angles to each other. The axis from nose to tail is the longitudinal axis, the axis that passes side to side along the wingspan is the lateral axis and the axis that passes vertically through the center of gravity is the vertical axis.

Ballistic parachute system (BPS). An optional parachute system activated by the pilot where the parachute is extracted for the WSC by a rocket.

Balloon. The result of a roundout (flare) that is too aggressive during landing, causing the aircraft to climb.

Bank attitude. The angle of the lateral axis relative to the horizon.

Base leg. A flight path at right angles to the landing runway off its approach end. The base leg normally extends from the downwind leg to the intersection of the extended runway centerline.

Battens. The airfoil ribs of a WSC that are removed to fold up the wing.

Best-angle-of-climb speed (V_X). The speed at which the aircraft produces the most gain in altitude in a given distance.

Best glide. The airspeed at which the aircraft glides the furthest for the least altitude lost when in non-powered flight.

Best-rate-of-climb speed (V_Y). The speed at which the aircraft produces the most gain in altitude in a given amount of time.

BPS. See ballistic parachute system.

Calibrated airspeed (CAS). Indicated airspeed corrected for installation error and instrument error. Although manufacturers attempt to keep airspeed errors to a minimum, it is not possible to eliminate all errors throughout the airspeed operating range. This error is generally greatest at low airspeeds. In the cruising and higher airspeed ranges, indicated airspeed and calibrated airspeed are approximately the same. Refer to the airspeed calibration chart to correct for possible airspeed errors.

Camber. The curvature of a wing when looking at a cross section. A wing has upper camber on its top surface and lower camber on its bottom surface.

Carburetor. (1) Pressure: A hydromechanical device employing a closed feed system from the fuel pump to the discharge nozzle. It meters fuel through fixed jets according to the mass airflow through the throttle body and discharges it under a positive pressure. Pressure carburetors are distinctly different from float-type carburetors, as they do not incorporate a vented float chamber or suction pickup from a discharge nozzle located in the venturi tube. (2) Float-type: Consists essentially of a main air passage through which the engine draws its supply of air, a mechanism to control the quantity of fuel discharged in relation to the flow of air, and a means of regulating the quantity of fuel/air mixture delivered to the engine cylinders.

Carburetor ice. Ice that forms inside the carburetor due to the temperature drop caused by the vaporization of the fuel. Induction system icing is an operational hazard because it can cut off the flow of the fuel/air charge or vary the fuel/air ratio.

Carriage. The engine and seats, attached by a structure to wheels; sometimes referred to as the fuselage, cockpit, chaise, or airframe.

Carriage keel. The lower center tube in the carriage that runs fore and aft which connects the mast to the front tube.

CAS. See calibrated airspeed.

Cavitation. A condition that exists in a fluid pump when there is not enough pressure in the reservoir to force fluid to the inlet of the pump. The pump picks up air instead of fluid.

Center of gravity (CG). The point at which an aircraft would balance if it were possible to suspend it at that point. It is the mass center of the aircraft, or the theoretical point at which the entire weight of the WSC is assumed to be concentrated. It may be expressed in inches from the reference datum, or in percent of mean aerodynamic chord (MAC). The location depends on the distribution of weight in the aircraft.

Center of lift. The location along the chord line of an airfoil at which all the lift forces produced by the airfoil are considered to be concentrated.

Center of pressure (CP). The point along the wing chord line where lift is considered to be concentrated.

Centrifugal force. The apparent force occurring in curvilinear motion acting to deflect objects outward from the axis of rotation. For instance, when pulling out of a dive, it is the force pushing you down in your seat.

Centripetal force. The force in curvilinear motion acting toward the axis of rotation. For instance, when pulling out of a dive, it is the force that the seat exerts on the pilot to offset the centrifugal force.

Certificated Flight Instructor (CFI). A flight instructor authorized by the FAA to provide flight instruction in designated category of aircraft.

Certified Flight Instructor with a Sport Pilot Rating (CFIS). A flight instructor authorized by the FAA to provide flight instruction in designated category of aircraft for sport pilots only.

CFI. See Certified Flight Instructor.

CFIS. See Certified Flight Instructor with a Sport Pilot Rating.

CFR. See Code of Federal Regulations.

CG. See center of gravity.

Checklist. A list of procedures that provides a logical and standardized method to operate a particular make and model aircraft.

Checkride. A practical test administered by an FAA examiner or designated examiner for the purpose of issuing an FAA certificate or rating.

Chord line. An imaginary straight line drawn through an airfoil from the leading edge to the trailing edge.

Circuit breaker. A circuit-protecting device that opens the circuit in case of excess current flow. A circuit breaker differs from a fuse in that it can be reset without having to be replaced.

C_L. See coefficient of lift.

Class A Airspace. Airspace from 18,000 feet MSL up to and including FL 600, including the airspace overlying the waters within 12 NM of the coast of the 48 contiguous states and Alaska; and designated international airspace beyond 12 NM of the coast of the 48 contiguous states and Alaska within areas of domestic radio navigational signal or ATC radar coverage, and within which domestic procedures are applied.

Class B Airspace. Airspace from the surface to 10,000 feet MSL surrounding the nation's busiest airports in terms of IFR operations or passenger numbers. The configuration of each Class B airspace is individually tailored and consists of a surface area and two or more layers, and is designed to contain all published instrument procedures once an aircraft enters the airspace. For all aircraft, an ATC clearance is required to operate in the area, and aircraft so cleared receive separation services within the airspace.

Class C Airspace. Airspace from the surface to 4,000 feet above the airport elevation (charted in MSL) surrounding those airports having an operational control tower, serviced by radar approach control, and having a certain number of IFR operations or passenger numbers. Although the configuration of each Class C airspace area is individually tailored, the airspace usually consists of a 5 NM radius core surface area that extends from the surface up to 4,000 feet above the airport elevation, and a 10 NM radius shelf area that extends from 1,200 feet to 4,000 feet above the airport elevation.

Class D Airspace. Airspace from the surface to 2,500 feet above the airport elevation (charted in MSL) surrounding those airports that have an operational control tower. The configuration of each Class D airspace area is individually tailored, and when instrument procedures are published, the airspace will normally be designed to contain the procedures.

Class E Airspace. Airspace that is not Class A, Class B, Class C, or Class D, and is controlled airspace.

Class G Airspace. Airspace that is uncontrolled, except when associated with a temporary control tower, and has not been designated as Class A, Class B, Class C, Class D, or Class E airspace.

Clear air turbulence. Turbulence not associated with any visible moisture.

Clearance. ATC permission for an aircraft to proceed under specified traffic conditions within controlled airspace, for the purpose of providing separation between known aircraft.

Code of Federal Regulations (CFR). Regulations issued by the U.S. Federal Government as published in the Federal Register.

Coefficient of lift (C_L). The ratio between lift pressure and dynamic pressure.

Cold front. The boundary between two air masses where cold air is replacing warm air.

Combustion. Process of burning the fuel/air mixture in the engine in a controlled and predictable manner.

Combustion chamber. The section of the engine into which fuel is injected and burned.

Common Traffic Advisory Frequency (CTAF). A frequency designed for the purpose of carrying out airport advisory practices while operating to or from an airport without an operating control tower. The CTAF may be a UNICOM, Multicom, automated flight service station, or tower frequency and is identified in appropriate aeronautical publications.

Controlled airspace. An airspace of defined dimensions within which air traffic control service is provided to IFR flights and to VFR flights in accordance with the airspace classification. Note: "controlled airspace" is a generic term that encompasses Class A, Class B, Class C, Class D, and Class E airspace.

Control bar. The structural part of the wing that connects the flying wires the the wing and keel. This is also used for the pilot to control the WSC pitch and roll in flight.

Control frame. The wing structural triangle which connects the control bar to the wing keel and provides the structure for the lower flying wire attachments.

Control pressure. The amount of physical exertion on the control column necessary to achieve the desired attitude.

Control tower. A terminal facility that uses air/ground communications, visual signaling, and other devices to provide ATC services to aircraft operating in the vicinity of an airport or on the movement area. Authorizes aircraft to land or takeoff at the airport controlled by the tower or to transit the Class D airspace area regardless of the flight plan or weather conditions. May also provide approach control services (radar or nonradar).

Controllability. A measure of the response of an aircraft relative to the pilot's flight control inputs.

Course. The intended direction of flight in the horizontal plane measured in degrees from north.

Coordinated turn. Turn made by an aircraft where the horizontal component of lift is equal to the centrifugal force of the turn.

Crab angle. The angle formed between the direction an aircraft is pointed and the direction it is tracking over the ground, resulting from a crosswind component. Also called the wind correction angle.

Crewmember. A person assigned to perform duty in an aircraft during flight time.

Crew resource management (CRM). The application of team management concepts in the flight deck environment, including single pilots of general aviation aircraft. Pilots of small aircraft, as well as crews of larger aircraft, must make effective use of all available resources: human resources, hardware, and information. Human resource groups include but are not limited to pilots, dispatchers, cabin crewmembers, maintenance personnel, and air traffic controllers.

Critical angle of attack. The angle of attack at which a wing stalls regardless of airspeed, flight attitude, or weight.

CRM. See crew resource management.

Crossbar. The structural component of the WSC wing that holds the leading edges in place.

Crosswind. Wind blowing across rather than parallel to the direction of flight. In a traffic pattern, the crosswind leg is a flight path at right angles to the landing runway off its upwind end.

Crosswind component. The wind component, measured in knots, at 90° to the longitudinal axis of the runway.

Crosswind correction. Correction applied in order to maintain a straight ground track during flight when a crosswind is present.

Crosswind landing. Landing made with a wind that is blowing across rather than parallel to the landing direction.

Crosswind takeoffs. Takeoffs made during crosswind conditions.

CTAF. See Common Traffic Advisory Frequency.

Datum. An imaginary vertical plane or line from which all measurements of moment arm are taken. The datum is established by the manufacturer.

DECIDE Model. Model developed to help pilots remember the six-step decision-making process: Detect, Estimate, Choose, Identify, Do, Evaluate.

Density altitude. Pressure altitude corrected for variations from standard temperature. When conditions are standard, pressure altitude and density altitude are the same. If the temperature is above standard, the density altitude is higher than pressure altitude. If the temperature is below standard, the density altitude is lower than pressure altitude. This is an important altitude because it is directly related to the PPC's performance.

Departure leg. The leg of the rectangular traffic pattern that is a straight course aligned with, and leading from, the takeoff runway.

Designated pilot examiner (DPE). An individual designated by the FAA to administer practical tests to pilot applicants.

Detonation. The sudden release of heat energy from fuel in an aircraft engine caused by the fuel-air mixture reaching its critical pressure and temperature. Detonation occurs as a violent explosion rather than a smooth burning process.

Dew. Moisture that has condensed from water vapor. Usually found on cooler objects near the ground, such as grass, as the near-surface layer of air cools faster than the layers of air above it.

Dewpoint. The temperature at which air reaches a state of water saturation.

Dihedral. The positive acute angle between the lateral axis of an airplane and a line through the center of a wing or horizontal stabilizer. Dihedral contributes to the lateral stability of an aircraft.

Directional stability. Stability about the vertical axis of an aircraft, whereby an aircraft tends to return, on its own, to flight aligned with the relative wind when disturbed from that equilibrium state. The wing design is the primary contributor to directional stability, causing a WSC in flight to align with the relative wind.

Ditching. Emergency landing in water.

Double-surface wing. Two pieces of fabric for most of the WSC wing which enclose the crossbar; typically used for higher speed wings.

Downwind leg. Leg of the traffic pattern flown parallel to the landing runway, but in a direction opposite to the intended landing direction.

DPE. See designated pilot examiner.

Drag. An aerodynamic force on a body acting parallel and opposite to the relative wind. The resistance of the atmosphere to the relative motion of an aircraft. Drag opposes thrust and limits the speed of the aircraft.

Drag coefficient (C_D). A dimensionless number used to define the amount of total drag produced by an aircraft.

Drift angle. Angle between heading and track.

Drift correction. Correction that is applied to counter the affects of wind on an aircraft's flight and ground track.

Dual flight. Flight time that is received and logged as training time. Dual flight time must be endorsed by a Certificated Flight Instructor.

Dynamic hydroplaning. A condition that exists when landing on a surface with standing water deeper than the tread depth of the tires. When the brakes are applied, there is a possibility that the brake will lock up and the tire will ride on the surface of the water, much like a water ski. When tires are hydroplaning, directional control and braking action are virtually impossible. An effective anti-skid system can minimize the effects of hydroplaning.

Dynamic pressure. The pressure a moving fluid would have if it were stopped. Reference 14 CFR section 61.51(h).

Dynamic stability. The property of an aircraft that causes it, when disturbed from straight-and level flight, to develop forces or moments that restore the original condition of straight and level.

EFAS. See En Route Flight Advisory Service.

EGT. See exhaust gas temperature.

E-LSA (Experimental Light-Sport Aircraft). An aircraft issued an experimental certificate under 14 CFR part 21.

ELT. See emergency locator transmitter.

Emergency frequency. Frequency that is used by aircraft in distress to gain ATC assistance. 121.5 MHz is an international emergency frequency guarded by Flight Service Stations and some military and civil aircraft. Reference AIM paragraph 6-3-1.

Emergency locator transmitter (ELT). A small, self-contained radio transmitter that will automatically, upon the impact of a crash, transmit an emergency signal on 121.5, 243.0, or 406.0 MHz.

Energy management. The ability for a pilot to maintain high kinetic energy levels in turbulent air and while near the ground is energy management for WSC. Higher speed and higher power is higher energy. Lower speed and lower power is lower energy.

En Route Flight Advisory Service (EFAS). An en route weather-only AFSS service.

Encoding altimeter. A special type of pressure altimeter used to send a signal to the air traffic controller on the ground, showing the pressure altitude the aircraft is flying.

Error chain. A series of mistakes that may lead to an accident or incident. Two basic principles generally associated with the creation of an error chain are: (1) one bad decision often leads to another; and (2) as a string of bad decisions grows, it reduces the number of subsequent alternatives for continued safe flight. Aeronautical decision making is intended to break the error chain before it can cause an accident or incident.

Evaporation. The transformation of a liquid to a gaseous state, such as the change of water to water vapor.

Exhaust. The rear opening of a turbine engine exhaust duct. The nozzle acts as an orifice, the size of which determines the density and velocity of the gases as they emerge from the engine.

Exhaust gas temperature (EGT). The temperature of the exhaust gases as they leave the cylinders of a reciprocating engine.

Exhaust manifold. The part of the engine that collects exhaust gases leaving the cylinders.

FAA. See Federal Aviation Administration.

FAA inspector. FAA personnel who can administer practical and proficiency tests and can issue pilot certificates.

FAA knowledge exam. Written exam administered by the FAA as a prerequisite for pilot certification. Passing the knowledge and practical exams is required for pilot applicants to be issued FAA certificates or ratings.

Federal airways. Class E airspace areas that extend upward from 1,200 feet to, but not including, 18,000 feet MSL, unless otherwise specified.

Federal Aviation Administration (FAA). The federal agency within the Department of Transportation that has the responsibility of promoting safety in the air, by both regulation and education.

Federal Aviation Regulations (FARs). The former name of the part of 14 CFR comprised of rules prescribed by the FAA governing all aviation activities in the United States.

Field elevation. The highest point of an airport's usable runways measured in feet from mean sea level.

Final. Leg of the traffic pattern that is a descending flightpath starting from the completion of the base-to-final turn and extending to the point of touchdown.

Fixed-pitch propellers. Propellers with fixed blade angles. Fixed-pitch propellers are designed as climb propellers, cruise propellers, or standard propellers.

Fixed-wing aircraft. An aircraft whose wing is rigidly attached to the structure. The term fixed-wing is used to distinguish these aircraft from rotary-wing aircraft, such as helicopters and autogiros.

Flare. See roundout.

Flight plan. Specified information relating to the intended flight of an aircraft that is filed orally or in writing with an FSS or an ATC facility.

Flightpath. The line, course, or track along which an aircraft is flying or is intended to be flown.

Fog. Cloud consisting of numerous minute water droplets and based at the surface; droplets are small enough to be suspended in the earth's atmosphere indefinitely. (Unlike drizzle, it does not fall to the surface. Fog differs from a cloud only in that a cloud is not based at the surface, and is distinguished from haze by its wetness and gray color.)

Force (F). The energy applied to an object that attempts to cause the object to change its direction, speed, or motion. In aerodynamics, it is expressed as F, T (thrust), L (lift), W (weight), or D (drag), usually in pounds.

Four forces. The four fundamental forces of flight: lift, weight, drag and thrust.

Four-stroke engine. The principle of operation for some reciprocating engines involving the conversion of fuel energy into mechanical energy. The strokes are called intake, compression, power, and exhaust.

Front. The boundary between two different air masses.

Front tube. The structural member of the carriage that attaches to the top of the carriage mast to the front of the fuselage. It acts as a control stop for the control bar to avoid high angles of attack.

Fuel efficiency. Defined as the amount of fuel used to produce a specific thrust or horsepower divided by the total potential power contained in the same amount of fuel.

Fuel injection. A fuel metering system used on some aircraft reciprocating engines in which a constant flow of fuel is fed to injection nozzles in the heads of all cylinders just outside of the intake valve. It differs from sequential fuel injection in which a timed charge of high-pressure fuel is sprayed directly into the combustion chamber of the cylinder.

Fuel system. The system that delivers fuel to the carburetors or the fuel injection system composed of a fuel tank, fuel pickup, fuel filter, and fuel pump.

Fuselage. The section of the WSC carriage that consists of the cockpit, containing seats for the occupants and attachments for the landing gear and wing.

G loads. Load imposed on an airframe due to inertia (centrifugal force). 1G of load factor represents the weight of the actual aircraft. 2G represents effectively twice the aircraft's actual weight.

Glidepath. The path of an aircraft relative to the ground while approaching a landing.

Glide ratio. The ratio of the forward distance traveled to the vertical distance an aircraft descends when it is operating without power. For example, an aircraft with a glide ratio of 10:1 will descend about 1,000 feet for every 2 miles (10,560 feet) it moves forward.

Global positioning system (GPS). A satellite based radio positioning, navigation, and time transfer system used for as a reference for navigation and measures ground speed.

Go-around. The termination of a landing approach. Reference the AIM Pilot/Controller Glossary.

Go/No-go decision. Decision of whether or not to make a flight based on environmental, personal or mechanical factors. A focus area for human factors study.

GPS. See global positioning system.

Gross weight. The total weight of a fully loaded aircraft including the fuel, oil, crew, passengers, and cargo.

Ground-adjustable propeller. A type of aircraft propeller whose blade pitch angle can be adjusted when the engine is not running. The adjustment requires loosening the blades in the hub.

Ground effect. A condition of improved performance encountered when an airfoil is operating very close to the ground. When an airfoil is under the influence of ground effect, there is a reduction in upwash, downwash, and wingtip vortices. As a result of the reduced wingtip vortices, induced drag is reduced.

Ground track. The aircraft's path over the ground when in flight.

Ground wires. The wires on top of the wing attached to the king post which hold up the wings on the ground and during negative loads during flight. The fore to aft ground wires which hold the king post in place fore to aft.

Groundspeed (GS). The actual speed of an aircraft over the ground. It is true airspeed adjusted for wind. Groundspeed decreases with a headwind, and increases with a tailwind. A GPS measures ground speed.

Hazardous Inflight Weather Advisory Service (HIWAS). Recorded weather forecasts broadcast to airborne pilots over selected VORs.

Heading. The direction in which the nose of the aircraft is pointing during flight.

Headwind. A wind which blows from the direction the aircraft is flying. The ground speed of an aircraft (the speed the aircraft is moving over the ground) is less than the speed through the air by the velocity of the headwind.

Headwind component. The component of atmospheric winds that acts opposite to the aircraft's flightpath.

HIWAS. See Hazardous Inflight Weather Advisory Service.

Horsepower. The term, originated by inventor James Watt, means the amount of work a horse could do in one second. One horsepower equals 550 foot-pounds per second, or 33,000 foot-pounds per minute.

Hour meter. An instrument installed in many aircraft to show the actual number of hours the engine has operated.

Hydroplaning. A condition that exists when landing on a surface with standing water deeper than the tread depth of the tires. When the brakes are applied, there is a possibility that the brake will lock up and the tire will ride on the surface of the water, much like a water ski. When the tires are hydroplaning, directional control and braking action are virtually impossible. An effective anti-skid system can minimize the effects of hydroplaning.

Hyperventilation. Occurs when an individual is experiencing emotional stress, fright, or pain, and the breathing rate and depth increase, although the carbon dioxide level in the blood is already at a reduced level. The result is an excessive loss of carbon dioxide from the body, which can lead to unconsciousness due to the respiratory system's overriding mechanism to regain control of breathing.

Hypoxia. State of oxygen deficiency in the body sufficient to impair functions of the brain and other organs.

ICAO. See International Civil Aviation Organization.

Ident. Air Traffic Control request for a pilot to push the button on the transponder to identify return on the controller's scope.

IFR. See instrument flight rules.

ILS. See instrument landing system.

IMC. See instrument meteorological conditions.

Indicated airspeed (IAS). The direct instrument reading obtained from the airspeed indicator, uncorrected for variations in atmospheric density, installation error, or instrument error. Manufacturers use this airspeed as the basis for determining airplane performance. Takeoff, landing, and stall speeds listed in the AFM or POH are indicated airspeeds and do not normally vary with altitude or temperature.

Indicated altitude. The altitude read directly from the altimeter (uncorrected) when it is set to the current altimeter setting.

Incident. An occurrence other than an accident, associated with the operation of an aircraft, which affects or could affect the safety of operations.

Induced drag. That part of total drag which is created by the production of lift. Induced drag increases with a decrease in airspeed.

Instrument flight rules (IFR). Rules governing the procedures for conducting instrument flight. Also a term used by pilots and controllers to indicate type of flight plan.

Instrument landing system (ILS). An electronic system that provides both horizontal and vertical guidance to a specific runway, used to execute a precision instrument approach procedure. Instrument meteorological conditions (IMC).

Meteorological conditions expressed in terms of visibility, distance from clouds, and ceiling less than the minimums specified for visual meteorological conditions. Flight without visual reference to the horizon.

Interference drag. Type of drag produced by placing two objects adjacent to one another. Combines the effects of form drag and skin friction.

International Civil Aviation Organization (ICAO). The United Nations agency for developing the principles and techniques of international air navigation, and fostering planning and development of international civil air transport.

International standard atmosphere (IAS). A model of standard variation of pressure and temperature.

Inversion. An increase in temperature with altitude.

Isobars. Lines which connect points of equal barometric pressure.

Jet stream. A high-velocity narrow stream of winds, usually found near the upper limit of the troposphere, which flows generally from west to east.

Keel. See wing keel and carriage keel.

Judgment. The mental process of recognizing and analyzing all pertinent information in a particular situation, a rational evaluation of alternative actions in response to it, and a timely decision on which action to take.

KIAS. Knots indicated airspeed.

Kinesthesia. The sensing of movements by feel.

King post. The post on top of the wing which is attached to the keel that holds used for the ground wires which hold up the wings on the ground and during negative loads during flight.

Knowledge exam. See FAA Knowledge Exam.

Lateral axis. An imaginary line passing through the center of gravity of a WSC and extending across the WSC from one side of the aircraft to the other side.

Leading edge. The part of an airfoil that meets the airflow first. This as a structural tube on the WSC airfoil.

Lift. One of the four main forces acting on an aircraft. On a WSC, an upward force created by the effect of airflow as it passes over and under the wing.

Lift coefficient. A coefficient representing the lift of a given airfoil. Lift coefficient is obtained by dividing the lift by the free-stream dynamic pressure and the representative area under consideration.

Lift/drag ratio. The efficiency of an airfoil section. It is the ratio of the coefficient of lift to the coefficient of drag for any given angle of attack.

Lift-off. The act of becoming airborne as a result of the wings lifting the airplane off the ground, or the pilot rotating the nose up, increasing the angle of attack to start a climb.

Light-Sport Aircraft (LSA). An aircraft that meets the requirements defined in 14 CFR section 1.1, regardless of airworthiness certification.

Limit load factor. Amount of stress, or load factor, that an aircraft can withstand before structural damage or failure occurs.

Load factor. The ratio of a specified load to the total weight of the aircraft. The specified load is expressed in terms of any of the following: aerodynamic forces, inertial forces, or ground or water reactions. Also referred to as G-loading.

Logbook. A record of activities: flight, instruction, inspection and maintenance. Reference 14 CFR part 43, 14 CFR section 61.51, and 14 CFR section 91.417.

Longitude. Measurement east or west of the Prime Meridian in degrees, minutes, and seconds. The Prime Meridian is 0° longitude and runs through Greenwich, England. Lines of longitude are also referred to as meridians.

Longitudinal axis. An imaginary line through an aircraft from nose to tail, passing through its center of gravity about which the aircraft rolls in flight. The longitudinal axis is also called the roll axis of the aircraft.

Longitudinal stability (pitching). Stability about the lateral axis. A desirable characteristic of an airplane whereby it tends to return to its trimmed angle of attack after displacement.

LSA. See Light-Sport Aircraft.

MAC. See mean aerodynamic chord.

Magnetic compass. A device for determining direction measured from magnetic north.

Magneto. A self-contained engine-driven unit that supplies electrical current to the spark plugs, completely independent of the airplane's electrical system. Normally there are two magnetos per engine.

Make/model. Refers to the manufacturer and model of a specific aircraft.

Maneuvering altitude. An altitude above the ground that allows a sufficient margin of height to permit safe maneuvering.

Maneuvering speed (V_A). The maximum speed at which full, abrupt control movement can be used without overstressing the airframe.

Maneuverability. Ability of an aircraft to change directions along a flightpath and withstand the stresses imposed upon it.

Mast. The carriage structural component that is attached to the rear of the carriage keel and the top of the front tube. The top is the carriage attachment the wing.

Maximum gross weight. The maximum authorized weight of the aircraft and all of its equipment as specified in the POH/AFM/AOI for the aircraft.

Maximum structure cruising speed (V_{NO}). The speed not to exceed except in smooth air; the upper limit of the green arc.

Mean aerodynamic chord (MAC). The average distance from the leading edge to the trailing edge of the wing.

Mean sea level (MSL). The average height of the surface of the sea for all stages of tide. A number preceding MSL indicates altitude in feet above mean sea level.

Mechanical Turbulence. Type of turbulence caused by obstructions on the ground interfering with smooth flow of the wind. Trees, buildings and terrain can all cause mechanical turbulence.

Medical certificate. Acceptable evidence of physical fitness on a form prescribed by the Administrator.

Medium-banked turn. Turn resulting from a degree of bank (approximately 20 to 45 degrees) at which the WSC remains at a constant bank.

METAR. See Aviation Routine Weather Report.

Microbursts. A strong downdraft which normally occurs over horizontal distances of 1 NM or less and vertical distances of less than 1,000 feet. In spite of its small horizontal scale, an intense microburst could induce windspeeds greater than 100 knots and downdrafts as strong as 6,000 feet per minute.

Military Operations Area (MOA). Airspace of defined vertical and lateral limits established for the purpose of separating certain military training activity from IFR traffic.

Military Training Routes (MTR). Special routes developed to allow the military to conduct low-altitude, high-speed training.

Minimum controllable airspeed. An airspeed at which any further increase in angle of attack, increase in load factor, or reduction in power, would result in an immediate stall.

Minimum drag speed (L/D_{MAX}). The point on the total drag curve where the lift-to-drag ratio is the greatest. At this speed, total drag is minimized.

Mindset. A factor in aeronautical decision making where decision making is influenced by preconceived ideas about the outcome of events. For example, an expectation of improving weather conditions can lead to increased risk during a flight.

Mixture. The ratio of fuel to air entering the engine's cylinders.

MOA. See Military operations Area.

Mode C transponder. A receiver/transmitter which will generate a radar reply signal upon proper interrogation; the interrogation and reply being on different frequencies. Mode C means the reply signal includes altitude information.

Moment. A force that causes or tries to cause an object to rotate. The product of the weight of an item multiplied by its arm. Moments are expressed in pound-inches (lb-in). Total moment is the weight of the PPC multiplied by the distance between the datum and the CG.

Moment arm. The distance from a datum to the applied force.

MSL. See mean sea level.

National Airspace System (NAS). The common network of United States airspace. air navigation facilities, equipment and services, airports or landing areas; sectional charts, information and services; rules, regulations and procedures, technical information; and manpower and material.

National Security Area (NSA). Area consisting of airspace of defined vertical and lateral dimensions established at locations where there is a requirement for increased security and safety of ground facilities. Pilots are requested to voluntarily avoid flying through the depicted NSA. When it is necessary to provide a greater level of security and safety, flight in NSAs may be temporarily prohibited. Regulatory prohibitions are disseminated via NOTAMs.

National Transportation Safety Board (NTSB). A United States Government independent organization responsible for investigations of accidents involving aviation, highways, waterways, pipelines, and railroads in the United States. NTSB is charged by congress to investigate every civil aviation accident in the United States.

NAVAID. Naviagtional aid.

NAV/COM. Navigation and communication radio.

Newton's Third Law of Motion. Whenever one body exerts a force on another, the second body always exerts on the first, a force that is equal in magnitude but opposite in direction.

Nontowered Airport. An airport that does not have an operating control tower. Two-way radio communications are not required at uncontrolled airports, although it is good operating practice for pilots to transmit their intentions on the specified frequency.

NOTAM. See Notice to Airmen.

Notice to Airmen. A notice containing information concerning facilities, services, or procedures, the timely knowledge of which is essential to personnel concerned with flight operations.

Notice To Airman (NOTAM). Notice to Airman that is regulatory in nature.

Octane. The rating system of gasoline with regard to its antidetonating qualities.

Operating limitations. Limitations published by aircraft manufacturers to define limitations on maneuvers, flight load factors, speeds and other limits. Presented in the aircraft in the form of placards and printed in the limitations section of the aircraft flight manual.

Overcontrolling. Using more movement in the control column than is necessary to achieve the desired pitch-and-bank condition.

Overshooting. The act of over flying an intended spot for landing or flying through a course intended for intercept.

Overspeed. A condition in which an engine has produced more rpm than the manufacturer recommends, or a condition in which the actual engine speed is higher than the desired engine speed as set on the propeller control.

Overtemp. A condition in which a device has reached a temperature above that approved by the manufacturer or any exhaust temperature that exceeds the maximum allowable for a given operating condition or time limit. Can cause internal damage to an engine.

Parallel runways. Two or more runways at the same airport whose centerlines are parallel. In addition to runway number, parallel runways are designated as L(left) and R(right) or if three parallel runways exist, L(left), C (center) and R(right).

Parasite drag. That part of total drag created by the design or shape of PPC parts. Parasite drag increases with an increase in airspeed.

Pattern altitude. The common altitude used for aircraft maneuvering in the traffic pattern. Usually 1,000 above the airport surface.

Personality tendencies. Personal traits and characteristics of an individual that are set at a very early age and extremely resistant to change.

P-factor. A tendency for an aircraft to yaw to the left due to the descending propeller blade on the right producing more thrust than the ascending blade on the left. This occurs when the aircraft's longitudinal axis is in a climbing attitude in relation to the relative wind. The P-factor would be to the right if the aircraft had a counterclockwise rotating propeller.

PIC. See pilot in command.

Pilotage. Navigational technique based on flight by reference to ground landmarks.

Pilot in command. The pilot responsible for the operation and safety of an aircraft.

Pilot's Operating Handbook (POH). A document developed by the aircraft manufacturer and contains the Aircraft Flight Manual (AFM) information or Aircraft Operating Instructions (AOI) information.

Pitch. The rotation of a WSC about its lateral axis.

Pitch angle. The angle between the wing and the horizontal plane of the earth.

Pitch attitude. The angle of the longitudinal axis relative to the horizon. Pitch attitude serves as a visual reference for the pilot to maintain or change airspeed.

Placards. Small statements or pictorial signs permanently fixed in the cockpit and visible to the pilot. Placards are used for operating limitations (e.g., weight or speeds) or to indicate the position of an operating lever (e.g., landing gear retracted or down and locked).

Planform. The shape or form of a wing as viewed from above. It may be long and tapered, short and rectangular, or various other shapes.

POH. See Pilot's Operating Handbook.

Positive Dynamic Stability. The tendency over time for an aircraft to return to a predisturbed state.

Position lights. Lights on an aircraft consisting of a red light on the left wing, a green light on the right wing, and a white light on the tail. The Code of Federal Regulations requires that these lights be displayed in flight from sunset to sunrise.

Positive static stability. The initial tendency to return to a state of equilibrium when disturbed from that state.

Porpoising. Oscillating around the lateral axis of the aircraft during landing.

Powered parachute (PPC). A powered aircraft comprised of a flexible or semi-rigid wing connected to a fuselage (cart) so that the wing is not in position for flight until the aircraft is in motion. The fuselage of a powered parachute contains the aircraft engine, a seat for each occupant and is attached to the aircraft's landing gear.

Power-off descent. Aircraft configuration where a descent occurs with power at idle.

Powerplant. A complete engine and propeller combination with accessories.

PPC. See powered parachute.

PPCL. Powered parachute land.

PPCS. Powered parachute sea.

Practical test. Flight test administered by an FAA examiner or designated examiner as a prerequisite for pilot certification. Successful completion of the practical test is required to earn a pilot certificate or rating. Commonly known as a checkride.

Practical Test Standards (PTS). An FAA published document of standards that must be met for the issuance of a particular pilot certificate or rating. FAA inspectors and designated pilot examiners use these standards when conducting pilot practical tests, and flight instructors use the PTS while preparing applicants for practical tests.

Preflight inspection. Aircraft inspection conducted to determine if an aircraft is mechanically and legally airworthy.

Preignition. Ignition occurring in the cylinder before the time of normal ignition. Preignition is often caused by a local hot spot in the combustion chamber igniting the fuel/air mixture.

Pressure altitude. The altitude indicated when the altimeter setting window (barometric scale) is adjusted to 29.92. This is the altitude above the standard datum plane, which is a theoretical plane where air pressure (corrected to 15 °C) equals 29.92 "Hg. Pressure altitude is used to compute density altitude, true altitude, true airspeed, and other performance data.

Private airport. Airport that is privately owned and not available to the public without prior permission. They are depicted on sectional charts for emergency and landmark purposes.

Private Pilot Certificate. An FAA-issued pilot certificate permitting carriage of passengers on a not-for-hire basis. Reference 14 CFR part 61.

Prohibited area. Designated airspace within which flight of aircraft is prohibited.

Propeller. A device for propelling an aircraft that, when rotated, produces by its action on the air, a thrust approximately perpendicular to its plane of rotation. It includes the control components normally supplied by its manufacturer.

Propeller blade angle. The angle between the propeller chord and the propeller plane of rotation.

Propeller blast. The volume of air accelerated behind a propeller producing thrust.

Propeller slipstream. The volume of air accelerated behind a propeller producing thrust.

PTS. See Practical Test Standards.

Public airport. Airport that is available to the aviation public.

Pusher configuration. Propeller configuration where the propeller shaft faces the rear of the aircraft. Thrust produced by the propeller pushes the aircraft, rather than pulling it.

Reciprocating engine. An engine that converts the heat energy from burning fuel into the reciprocating movement of the pistons. This movement is converted into a rotary motion by the connecting rods and crankshaft.

Reduction gear. The gear arrangement in an aircraft engine that allows the engine to turn at a faster speed than the propeller.

Reflex. The opposite curvature of the airfoil at the trailing edge which produces a positive pitching moment of the WSC airfoil.

Reflex lines. Wires attached to the top of the king post and the trailing edge of the airfoil to maintain the reflex of the airfoil, used on some wings for trim by raising and lowering the trailing edge of the wing.

Region of reverse command. Flight regime in which flight at a higher airspeed requires a lower power setting and a lower airspeed requires a higher power setting in order to maintain altitude.

Registration certificate. A federal certificate that documents aircraft ownership.

Relative humidity. The ratio of the existing amount of water vapor in the air at a given temperature to the maximum amount that could exist at that temperature; usually expressed in percent.

Relative wind. The direction the wind strikes an airfoil. If a wing moves forward horizontally, the relative wind moves backward horizontally. Relative wind is parallel to and opposite the flightpath of the airplane.

Restricted area. Airspace designated under 14 CFR part 73 within which the flight of aircraft, while not wholly prohibited, is subject to restriction.

Ribs. The parts of an aircraft wing structure that give the wing its aerodynamic cross section. WSC has battens that are inserted in to the sail that act as ribs.

Risk. The future impact of a hazard that is not eliminated or controlled.

Risk elements. The four fundamental areas of exposure to risk: the pilot, the aircraft, the environment, and the type of operation that comprise any given aviation situation.

Risk management. The part of the decision making process which relies on situational awareness, problem recognition, and good judgment to reduce risks associated with each flight.

Roll. The rotation of an aircraft about its longitudinal axis. It is controlled by moving the control bar side to side.

Roundout (flare). The slow, smooth transition from a normal approach attitude to a landing attitude. This maneuver is accomplished in a WSC by easing forward on the control bar from approach speed as the WSC gets near the ground for landing to reduce the descent rate to zero as the back whels are inches above the ground, continuing to move the control bar forward reducing speed as the back wheels are inches above the landing surface, and continuing to push the control bar full forward until the back wheels settle to the surface for touchdown.

RPM. Revolutions per minute for the engine crankshaft. A measure of rotational speed. One rpm is one revolution made in one minute.

Runway. A defined rectangular area on a land airport prepared for the landing and takeoff run of aircraft along its length. Runways are normally numbered in relation to their magnetic direction rounded off to the nearest 10 degrees (e.g., Runway 1, Runway 25).

Runway incursion. Any occurrence at an airport involving an aircraft, vehicle, person, or object on the ground that creates a collision hazard or results in loss of separation with an aircraft taking off, intending to takeoff, landing, or intending to land.

Runway threshold markings. Runway threshold markings come in two configurations. They either consist of eight longitudinal stripes of uniform dimensions disposed symmetrically about the runway centerline, or the number of stripes is related to the runway width. A threshold marking helps identify the beginning of the runway that is available for landing. In some instances, the landing threshold may be displaced.

Safety directive. A manufacturer issued change to a S-LSA that must be complied with. This is similar to an airworthiness directive which is a regulatory notice sent out by the FAA to the registered owner of an aircraft informing the owner of a condition that prevents the aircraft from continuing to meet its conditions for airworthiness. Airworthiness Directives (AD notes) must be complied with within the required time limit, and the fact of compliance, the date of compliance, and the method of compliance must be recorded in the aircraft's maintenance records.

SAR. See search and rescue.

Scan. A procedure used by the pilot to visually identify all resources of information in flight.

Scanning. Systematic means of searching for other aircraft. Scanning is most effective when successive areas of the sky are brought into focus using a series of short, regularly spaced eye movements.

Scenario-based training. The instructor provides pilot, aircraft, environment, and operational risk elements to train the student to utilize ADM in making the best decision for the given set of circumstances.

SD. See safety directave.

Sea level. A reference height used to determine standard atmospheric conditions and altitude measurements.

Search and rescue (SAR). A lifesaving service provided through the combined efforts of the federal agencies signatory to the National SAR plan along with state agencies.

Sectional charts. Designed for visual navigation of slow or medium speed aircraft. Topographic information on these charts features the portrayal of relief, and a judicious selection of visual check points for VFR flight. Aeronautical information includes visual and radio aids to navigation, airports, controlled airspace, restricted areas, obstructions and related data.

See and avoid. When weather conditions permit, pilots operating IFR or VFR are required to observe and maneuver to avoid other aircraft. Right-of-way rules are contained in 14 CFR part 91.

Segmented circle. A visual indicator around a windsock or tetrahedron designed to show the traffic pattern for each runway.

Shallow-banked turn. Turns in which the bank is less than approximately 20 degrees.

Single Pilot Resource Management (SRM). Area of human factors study that addresses application of management skills in the cockpit. Single pilots of small aircraft must make effective use of all available resources; human resources, hardware, and information.

Single surface wing. one piece of fabric for most of the airfoil on a WSC with the cross bar exposed to the airflow. Typically used for slower wings.

Situational awareness. The accurate perception and understanding of all the factors and conditions within the four fundamental risk elements that affect safety before, during, and after the flight.

Skills and procedures. The procedural, psychomotor, and perceptual skills used to control a specific aircraft or its systems. They are the airmanship abilities that are gained through conventional training, are perfected, and become almost automatic through experience.

Skin. The outside covering of an aircraft airframe.

Skin friction drag. The type of parasite drag resulting from a rough surface which deflects the streamlines of air on the surface, causing resistance to smooth airflow.

S-LSA (Special Light-Sport Aircraft). An aircraft issued a special airworthiness certificate in accordance with 14 CFR section 21.290 in the light-sport category. These aircraft meet the ASTM industry-developed consensus standards.

Solo flight. Flight that is conducted and logged when a pilot is the sole occupant of an aircraft.

Spatial disorientation. Specifically refers to the lack of orientation with regard to the position, attitude, or movement of the WSC in space.

Special flight permit. A flight permit issued to an aircraft that does not meet airworthiness requirements but is capable of safe flight. A special flight permit can be issued to move an aircraft for the purposes of maintenance or repair, buyer delivery, manufacturer flight tests, evacuation from danger, or customer demonstration. Also referred to as a ferry permit.

Special Use Airspace (SUA). Airspace that exists where activities must be confined because of their nature. Consists of prohibited, restricted, warning, military operations, and alert areas.

Speed. The distance traveled in a given time.

Sport Pilot Certificate. An FAA-issued pilot certificate, allowing the holder to operate a light-sport aircraft in the category, class, make and model for which they are endorsed to do so.

SRM. See Single Pilot Resource Management.

Stabilized Approach. A landing approach in which the pilot establishes and maintains a constant angle glidepath towards a predetermined point on the landing runway. It is based on the pilot's judgment of certain visual cues, and depends on the maintenance of a constant final descent airspeed and configuration.

Stall. A rapid decrease in lift caused by the separation of airflow from the wing's surface brought on by exceeding the critical angle of attack. A stall can occur at any pitch attitude or airspeed.

Stalling speed. For WSC, the power-off stall speed at the maximum takeoff weight (the lower limit of the green arc).

Standard airport traffic pattern. The left-hand turn traffic flow that is prescribed for aircraft landing at, taxiing on, or taking off from an airport. Reference 14 CFR section 91.126 (a)(1) and AIM chapter 4, section 3.

Standard Atmosphere. Consisting of those atmospheric conditions at sea level that include a barometric pressure of 29.92 inches of mercury ("Hg) or 1013.2 millibars, and a temperature of 15 °C (59 °F). Pressure and temperature normally decrease as altitude increases. The standard lapse rate in the lower atmosphere for each 1,000 feet of altitude is approximately 1 "Hg and 2 °C (3.5 °F). For example, the standard pressure and temperature at 3,000 feet mean sea level (MSL) is 26.92 "Hg (29.92 – 3) and 9 °C (15 – 6).

Static pressure. The pressure of air that is still, or not moving, measured perpendicular to the surface exposed to the air.

Static stability. The initial tendency an aircraft displays when disturbed from a state of equilibrium.

Stationary front. A front that is moving at a speed of less than 5 knots.

Steep turn. Turn resulting from a degree of bank of 45 degrees or more.

Straight-in approach. Entry into the traffic pattern by interception of the extended runway centerline (final approach course) without executing any other portion of the traffic pattern.

Stress management. The personal analysis of the kinds of stress experienced while flying, the application of appropriate stress assessment tools, and other coping mechanisms.

Strobe. A high-intensity white flashing light. Strobe lights are located on aircraft wingtips to increase aircraft visibility in low light conditions.

Strut. Wing structural member used to hold the wings in place instead of the flying and ground wires for some designs. The "strutted wing" does not use a kingpost.

Student Pilot Certificate. An FAA issued certificate that permits student pilots to exercise solo pilot privileges with limitations. This can be a student's FAA third class medical or a student pilot certificate issued for flying an LSA using a driver's license as medical eligibility.

SUA. See special use airspace.

Surface analysis chart. A report that depicts an analysis of the current surface weather. Shows the areas of high and low pressure, fronts, temperatures, dewpoints, wind directions and speeds, local weather, and visual obstructions.

Tailwind. Wind blowing in the same direction the aircraft is moving. When an aircraft is flying with a tailwind, its speed over the ground is equal to its speed through the air, plus the speed the air is moving over the ground.

Takeoff clearance. ATC authorization for an aircraft to depart a runway. It is predicated on known traffic and known physical airport conditions.

Taxi. The movement of an aircraft under its own power while on the ground.

Taxiway. Airport area designated for aircraft surface movement.

Temporary flight restriction (TFR). Designated airspace of specified dimension where flight is temporarily restricted or prohibited. NOTAMs are issued to advise airmen of local TFR restrictions.

Terminal aerodrome forecast (TAF). A report established for the 5 statute mile radius around an airport. Utilizes the same descriptors and abbreviations as the METAR report.

Terminal Radar Service Area (TRSA). Area where participating pilots can receive additional radar services, the purpose of which is to provide separation between all IFR operations and participating VFR aircraft.

TFR. See temporary flight restriction.

Thermal. A buoyant plume or bubble of rising air.

Throttle. The control in an aircraft that regulates the power or thrust the pilot wants the engine to develop from the valve in a carburetor or fuel control unit that determines the amount of fuel-air mixture that is fed to the engine.

Thrust. The force which imparts a change in the velocity of a mass. A forward force which propels the WSC through the air.

Thrust line. An imaginary line passing through the center of the propeller hub, perpendicular to the plane of the propeller rotation.

Title 14 of the Code of Federal Regulations (14 CFR). That portion of the code formerly called the Federal Aviation Regulations (FAR) governing the operation of aircraft, airways, and airmen.

Torque. (1) A resistance to turning or twisting. (2) Forces that produce a twisting or rotating motion. (3) In a WSC, the tendency of the aircraft to turn (roll) in the opposite direction of rotation of the engine and propeller.

Total drag. The sum of the parasite and induced drag.

Touch and go. An operation by an aircraft that lands and takes off without stopping.

Touchdown point. The point or intended point at which an aircraft first makes contact with the landing surface.

Touchdown zone. The portion of a runway, beyond the threshold, where it is intended landing aircraft first contact the runway.

Towered airport. An airport that has an operating control tower.

Track. The actual path made over the ground in flight.

Traffic pattern. The traffic flow that is prescribed for aircraft landing at or taking off from an airport.

Traffic pattern indicators. Ground based visual indicators that identify traffic pattern direction at certain airports.

Trailing edge. The aft edge of the airfoil. In normal flight, it is the portion of the airfoil where airflow over the upper surface rejoins the lower surface airflow.

Training bars. An attachment to the control frame which allows the instructor in the rear seat to move the control bar and control the pitch and bank with a solid attachment.

Transponder. The airborne portion of the secondary surveillance radar system. The transponder emits a reply when queried by a radar facility.

Tricycle gear configuration. Landing gear configuration employing a third wheel located on the nose of the aircraft.

True airspeed. Actual airspeed, determined by applying a correction for pressure altitude and temperature to the CAS. Because air density decreases with an increase in altitude, an airplane has to be flown faster at higher altitudes to cause the same pressure difference between pitot impact pressure and static pressure. Therefore, for a given calibrated airspeed, true airspeed increases as altitude increases; or for a given true airspeed, calibrated airspeed decreases as altitude increases.

True altitude. The vertical distance of the airplane above sea level. the actual altitude. It is often expressed as feet above mean sea level (MSL). Airport, terrain, and obstacle elevations on sectional charts are true altitudes.

TRSA. See Terminal Radar Service Area.

Tuck. A nose down situation in a WSC where the pitch angle is over 90 degrees down resulting from a whip stall or severe turbulence.

Tumble. The WSC rotating uncontrollably around its lateral axis from a whip stall or severe turbulence. Results of a tumble would probably cause a structural failure with catastrophic consequences.

Turbulence. An occurrence in which a flow of fluid is unsteady.

Twist. The design of the WSC wing in which a wing is twisted so its angle of attack is less at the tip than at the root.

This decreases the lift the wing produces at the tip to improve the stall characteristics of the wing. Also called washout.

Two-stroke engine. A simple form of reciprocating engine that completes its operating cycle in two strokes of its piston, one down and one up. Two-stroke-cycle engines are inefficient in their use of fuel, but their simplicity makes them popular for powering light-sport aircraft and ultralight vehicles where light weight and low cost are paramount.

Ultralight. A single person only vehicle as defined by 14 CFR section 103.1.

Uncontrolled airspace. Class G airspace that has not been designated as Class A, B, C, D, or E. It is airspace in which air traffic control has no authority or responsibility to control air traffic; however, pilots should remember there are VFR minimums which apply to this airspace.

Unicom. A nongovernment air/ground radio communication station which may provide airport information at public use airports where there is no tower or automated flight service station.

Unusable fuel. Fuel that cannot be consumed by the engine. This fuel is considered part of the empty weight of the aircraft.

Useful load. The weight of the pilot, copilot, passengers, baggage, usable fuel, and drainable oil. It is the basic empty weight subtracted from the maximum allowable gross weight. This term applies to general aviation aircraft only.

Unstabilized approach. The final approach of an aircraft that has not achieved a stable rate of descent or controlled flight track by a predetermined altitude, usually 500 feet AGL.

Unusual attitude. An unintentional, unanticipated, or extreme aircraft attitude.

Useful load. The weight of the pilot, copilot, passengers, baggage, usable fuel, and drainable oil. It is the basic empty weight subtracted from the maximum allowable gross weight. This term applies to general aviation aircraft only.

User-defined waypoints. Waypoint location and other data which may be input by the user, this is the only GPS database information that may be altered (edited) by the user.

Upwind Leg. A flight path parallel to the landing runway in the direction of landing.

Vapor lock. A problem that mostly affects gasoline-fuelled internal combustion engines. It occurs when the liquid fuel changes state from liquid to gas while still in the fuel delivery system. This disrupts the operation of the fuel pump, causing loss of feed pressure to the carburetor or fuel injection system, resulting in transient loss of power or complete stalling. Restarting the engine from this state may be difficult. The fuel can vaporise due to being heated by the engine, by the local climate, or due to a lower boiling point at high altitude.

VASI. See visual approach slope indicator.

Vehicle. Manmade means of transportation; an ultralight aircraft (not a light-sport aircraft).

Venturi. A specially shaped restriction in a tube designed to speed up the flow of fluid passing through in accordance with Bernoulli's principle. Venturis are used in carburetors and in many types of fluid control devices to produce a pressure drop proportional to the speed of the fluid passing through them.

Venturi Effect. The effect of Bernoulli's principle, which states that the pressure of a fluid decreases as it is speeded up without losing or gaining any energy from the outside.

Verified. Confirmation of information or configuration status.

Vertical axis (yaw). An imaginary line passing vertically through the center of gravity of an aircraft. The vertical axis is called the z-axis or the yaw axis.

Vertical speed indicator (VSI). An instrument that uses static pressure to display a rate of climb or descent in feet per minute. The VSI can also sometimes be called a vertical velocity indicator (VVI).

Vertigo. A type of spatial disorientation caused by the physical senses sending conflicting signals to the brain. Vertigo is especially hazardous when flying under conditions of poor visibility and may cause pilot incapacitation, but may be minimized by confidence in the indication of the flight instruments.

VFR. See visual flight rules.

VFR Terminal Area Charts. Charts designated to depict Class B airspace in greater detail and greater scale than sectional charts.

Vg diagram. A chart that relates velocity to load factor. It is valid only for a specific weight, configuration and altitude and shows the maximum amount of positive or negative lift the airplane is capable of generating at a given speed. Also shows the safe load factor limits and the load factor that the aircraft can sustain at various speeds.

V_{NE}. See never-exceed speed.

V_{NO}. See maximum structural cruising speed.

V_S. See stalling speed.

V_X. See best angle-of-climb speed.

V_Y. See best rate-of-climb speed.

Victor airways. Airways based on a centerline that extends from one VOR or VORTAC navigation aid or intersection, to another navigation aid (or through several navigation aids or intersections); used to establish a known route for en route procedures between terminal areas.

Visual approach slope indicator (VASI). A visual aid of lights arranged to provide descent guidance information during the approach to the runway. A pilot on the correct glideslope will see red lights over white lights.

Visual flight rules (VFR). Rules in the Code of Federal Regulations that govern the procedures for conducting flight under visual conditions.

Visual meteorological conditions (VMC). Meteorological conditions expressed in terms of visibility, distance from cloud, and ceiling meeting or exceeding the minimums specified for VFR.

VSI. See vertical speed indicator.

Wake turbulence. Wingtip vortices that are created when an aircraft generates lift. When an aircraft generates lift, air spills over the wingtips from the high pressure areas below the wings to the low pressure areas above them. This flow causes rapidly rotating whirlpools of air called wingtip vortices or wake turbulence.

Warm front. The boundary area formed when a warm air mass contacts and flows over a colder air mass. Warm fronts cause low ceilings and rain.

Warning area. An area containing hazards to any aircraft not participating in the activities being conducted in the area. Warning areas may contain intensive military training, gunnery exercises, or special weapons testing.

Waypoint. A designated geographical location used for route definition or progress-reporting purposes and is defined in terms of latitude/longitude coordinates.

Washout. The design of the WSC wing in which a wing is twisted so its angle of attack is less at the tip than at the root. Washout decreases the lift the wing produces at the tip to improve the stall characteristics of the wing. Also called twist.

Washout strut. The structural member attached to the leading edges which holds the tip twist for the wing at low or negative angles of attack.

WCA. See wind correction angle.

Weather briefing. Means for pilots to gather information vital to the nature of the flight from a flight service station specialist.

Weathervane. The tendency to point into the wind.

Weight. A measure of the heaviness of an object. One of the four main forces acting on an aircraft. The force by which a body is attracted downward toward the center of the Earth (or another celestial body) by gravity. Weight is equal to the mass of the body times the local value of gravitational acceleration.

Weight-Shift Control Aircraft. Powered aircraft with a framed pivoting wing and a fuselage controllable only in pitch and roll by the pilot's ability to change the aircraft's center of gravity with respect to the wing. Flight control of the aircraft depends on the wing's ability to flexibly deform rather than the use of control surfaces.

Whip stall. A pitch attitude that is too high for a WSC, at which the tips would stall from flying outside the WSC limitations or flying in extreme/severe turbulence.

Wind correction angle. Correction applied to the course to establish a heading so that track will coincide with course. Also called the Crab angle.

Wind direction indicators. Indicators that include a wind sock, wind tee, or tetrahedron. Visual reference will determine wind direction and runway in use.

Wind drift correction. Correction applied to the heading of the aircraft necessary to keep the aircraft tracking over a desired track. Also called the wind correction angle or crab angle.

Wind shear. A sudden, drastic shift in wind speed, direction, or both that may occur in the horizontal or vertical plane.

Wing. A fabric skin with an aluminum frame that produces the lift necessary to support the WSC in flight; including the flight wires/control frame below and the ground wires/king post above.

Wing keel. The WSC structural component in the longitudinal center of the wing that connects the two leading edges together at the nose and connects the carriage to the wing.

Wing loading. The amount of weight that a wing must support to provide lift.

Wingspan. The maximum distance from wingtip to wingtip.

Wing twist. A design feature of the WSC that reduces the angle of attack from the root to the tip.

Wingtip vortices. The rapidly rotating air that spills over an aircraft's wings during flight. The intensity of the turbulence depends on the aircraft's weight, speed, and configuration. It is also referred to as wake turbulence. Vortices from heavy aircraft may be extremely hazardous to small aircraft.

World Aeronautical Charts (WAC). A standard series of aeronautical charts covering land areas of the world at a size and scale convenient for navigation (1:1,000,000) by moderate speed aircraft. Topographic information includes cities and towns, principal roads, railroads, distinctive landmarks, drainage, and relief. Aeronautical information includes visual and radio aids to navigation, airports, airways, restricted areas, obstructions and other pertinent data.

WSC. See weight-shift control.

Weight-Shift Control—Land (WSCL). WSC that takes off and lands on land. This can be wheels or ski equipped.

Weight-Shift Control—Sea (WSCS). WSC that takes of the water. This can be pontoons or a boat configuration.

Yaw. Rotation about the vertical axis of an aircraft.

Zulu time. A term used in aviation for Coordinated Universal Time (UTC) which places the entire world on one time standard.

Index

A

abnormal engine instrument indications 13-13
aeronautical decision-making 1-10, 13-1
after landing 5-26
after landing roll 11-7
airfoil 2-1
airport and navigation lighting aids 12-4
airport operations 10-2
airspace 8-2
    Class A Airspace 8-8
    Class B Airspace 8-7
    Class C Airspace 8-6
    Class D Airspace 8-6
    Class E Airspace 8-4
    Class G Airspace 8-2
alert areas 8-10
alternating turns 11-21
angle of attack 2-4
approach 13-6
approaches and landings 12-11
AROW 5-15
aspect ratio 2-5
attitude and sink rate control 13-5
attitude control 13-18
attitude flying 6-4
avoiding pilot errors 1-11
axes of rotation 2-12

B

ballistic parachute system 3-15, 13-2
ballooning during roundout 11-29
bank control 6-4
base leg 10-2, 11-2
basic pilot eligibility 1-9
basic propeller principles 2-20
basic safety concepts 13-4
battens and leading edge stiffener 3-7
before takeoff check 5-26
best angle of climb speed 6-13
best rate of climb speed 6-12

black-hole approach 12-8
bouncing during touchdown 11-29

C

cables and hardware 3-7
camber 2-1
carriage 3-10
carriage inspection 5-18
carriage moments 2-16, 2-17
center of gravity 2-11
certificates and documents 5-15
checklist after entering flight deck 5-23
checklist for taxi 5-25
climbs and climbing turns 6-12
collision avoidance 1-9
communications 3-19
confined areas 13-7
control frame 3-4
controlled airports 10-2
controlled airspace 8-4
controlled firing areas 8-10
cooling systems 5-20
coordinating the controls 6-8
crosswind approaches and landings 11-17
    landings 11-19
    leg 10-2
    takeoff 7-6
crosswind pattern procedures 11-17

D

dashboards and instrument panels 3-16
deck angle 2-4
departure leg 10-2
descents and descending turns 6-14
descent at minimum safe airspeed 6-14
ditching 13-8
downwind leg 10-2
drag 2-7, 2-8
drift and ground track control 9-2
dynamic pressure 2-7

I-1

E

effects and hazards of high crosswinds for
approaches and landings 11-17
effects and the use of the controls 6-2
effect of headwinds during final approach 11-8
electrical fires 13-12
electrical system 3-15, 13-12
emergency approaches and landings 11-26
    descents 13-10
        equipment and survival gear 13-8
        landings 13-3
energy management 6-19
engine and gearbox 3-20
engine failure after takeoff 13-9
engine fire 13-10
engine instruments 3-17
engine start 5-23
entering a turn 6-8
equipment and lighting 12-2
estimating height and movement 11-5
exiting a turn 6-8

F

fatigue 1-13
faulty approaches and landings 11-27
feel of the aircraft 6-3
final approach 10-2, 11-4
flare 11-6
flex wing 2-6
flight deck 3-16
    inspection 5-20
    flight deck management 5-23
flight instruments 3-17
flight operations and pilot certificates 1-8
flight over charted u.s. wildlife refuges, parks, and
forest service areas 8-12
floating during roundout 11-28
forced landing 13-3
forces in flight 2-7
fuel 5-20
fuel system components 3-20

G

glide 6-14
    flight 2-6
    turns 6-16
go-around 11-13
ground adjustable trim systems 3-9
ground effect 2-11
    on takeoff 7-7
ground roll 7-2

H

hang glider 1-4
hard landing 11-30
high angles of attack 2-13
high final approach 11-27
high roundout 11-28
high winds and strong turbulence 13-15
    during cruise flight 13-15
    during takeoffs and landings 13-15
high winds during taxi 13-15
hypothermia 1-13

I

inadvertant propeller strike 13-13
inadvertent flight into instrument meteorological
conditions 13-16
induced drag 2-8
inflight adjustable trim systems 3-10
inflight fire 13-10
initial climb 7-2, 7-4, 7-6
instrument panel arrangements 3-17

K

keel 3-3
kinesthesia 6-4
king post with wires-on-top wing design 3-5

L

landing gear 3-11
    for water and snow 3-14
    malfunction 13-13
lateral axis 2-12
    pitch 2-12
late or rapid roundout 11-28
leading edges 3-2
level turns 6-7
lift 2-7
lift-off 7-2, 7-3
    and climb out 7-9
    and initial climb 7-12
light sport aircraft 1-6
Lilienthal, Otto 1-2
local airport advisory 8-11
local conditions 5-3
longitudinal axis 2-3, 2-13
low angles of attack 2-14
low final approach 11-27

M

maintaining aircraft control 13-17

maneuvering by reference to ground objects 9-2
maximum crosswind velocities 11-19
medical factors 1-13
medium turns 6-8
military operations areas 8-9
military training routes 8-11
motorized hang gliders 1-4

N

national security areas 8-12
navigating the airspace 8-13
navigation instruments 3-17
night flying 12-9
    emergencies 12-12
    illusions 12-7
    takeoff 12-9
    vision 12-5
noise abatement 7-13
normal (calm wind) approaches and landings 11-2
normal climb 6-12
normal takeoff 7-2

O

occupant preflight brief 5-22
oil 5-21
orientation and navigation 12-10
other airspace areas 8-11

P

parachute jump areas 8-11
parasite drag 2-8
partial power descent 6-14
PAVE 5-1
pilot equipment 12-3
pilot requirements 12-2
pitch 2-12
    and power 6-16
    angle 2-4
    control 6-4
    control system 3-8
    moments summary 2-16
    pressures 2-14
pitot-static system 13-12
planform 2-5
pockets and hardware 3-7
porpoising 11-29
positive transfer of controls 1-10
postflight, parking, and securing 5-27
power 11-13

power-off accuracy approaches 11-21
    180° 11-23
    360° 11-25
    90° 11-22
power-off stall manuever 6-23
powerplant inspection 5-19
powerplant system 3-19
power control 6-4
precautionary landing 13-3
preflight actions 5-3
preflight inspection 5-15
preparation and preflight 12-8
prohibited areas 8-8
psychological hazards 13-3
published VFR routes 8-12

R

ready aircraft to enter flight deck 5-22
recognition 13-17
rectangular course 9-4
reflex systems 3-8
regional weather 5-3
rejected landings 11-13
rejected takeoff/engine failure 7-12
resource management 1-12
restricted areas 8-9
Rogallo, Francis 1-2
roll 2-13
    control system 3-9
    stability and moments 2-16
rotation 7-2
rotation and lift-off 7-6
roundout 11-6
routine preflight inspection 5-16
runaway throttle 13-13
runup 12-8
runway incursion avoidance 1-10

S

s-turns across a road 9-7
sail components 3-6
    attachment to wing frame 3-7
    material and panels 3-7
scenario-based training 1-12
setting up the WSC aircraft 5-8
shallow turns 6-8
short-field approaches and landings 11-14
short field takeoff and steepest angle climb 7-8
simulated engine out 11-26

slow final approach 11-27
slow flight 6-20
   and stalls 6-20
soft and rough field takeoff and climb 7-10
   approaches and landings....................................11-15
special use airspace 8-8
speed 11-13
stability and moments 2-13
stabilized approach concept 11-10
stalls 6-21
   exceeding the critical AOA 2-18
standard airport traffic patterns 10-2
starting..12-8
steep angle...11-21
steep approach.. 6-14, 11-20
steep turns 6-8
   performance maneuver 6-16
straight-and-level flying 6-4
structure...3-11
stuck throttle..13-13
system malfunctions...13-12

T

takeoff and climb 12-9
takeoff roll............................... 7-2, 7-3, 7-6, 7-9, 7-12
taking down the wsc aircraft 5-12
taxiing 5-24, 12-8
temporary flight restrictions.......................................8-11
terminal radar service areas 8-12
terrain selection..13-6
terrain types..13-7
the propeller 3-20
throttle use..11-2
thrust 2-7, 2-10
thrust moments...2-18
thrust required for increases in speed.........................2-11
topless wings with struts 3-5
touchdown..11-7
towered airport operations 8-6
transporting 5-7
trim—normal stabilized flight......................................2-13
   control..6-7
   systems 3-9
tuning the wing to fly slower or faster 5-14
tuning the wing to fly straight 5-14
turbulent air approaches and landings......................11-16
turns..13-18
   around a point..9-9

U

uncontrolled airports 10-2
uncontrolled airspace 8-2
unique airfoil and wing design...................................2-13
unique WSC flight characteristics...............................12-7
upwind leg..10-2
use of checklists 1-12
use of power..11-28

V

vertical axis 2-13

W

warning areas 8-9
water landings 13-8
weather..5-3
weather related emergencies 13-15
weight... 2-7, 2-10
weight and loading...5-5
weight, load, and speed 2-20
weight-shift control aircraft 1-7
weight-shift control LSA requirements 1-8
whip stall–tuck–tumble..2-19
   awareness 6-24
wing...3-2
   chord..2-2
   flexibility 2-6
   frame components 3-2
   inspection 5-17
   loading 2-6
   rising after touchdown......................................11-30
   systems 3-8
   tuning..5-14
   twist 2-3
Wright Flyer..1-2
WSC and air traffic control 8-12
WSC operations 8-12

Y

yaw...2-13
   stability and moments...2-17
   stability summary 2-18

Made in the USA
Columbia, SC
20 August 2023